MICROECONOMICS

2001 UPDATE

MICROECONOMICS

PRINCIPLES AND POLICY

EIGHTH EDITION

2001 UPDATE

WILLIAM J. BAUMOL
C.V. Starr Center for Applied Economics
New York University

ALAN S. BLINDER
Princeton University

HARCOURT COLLEGE PUBLISHERS

FORT WORTH   PHILADELPHIA   SAN DIEGO   NEW YORK   AUSTIN   ORLANDO   SAN ANTONIO
TORONTO   MONTREAL   LONDON   SYDNEY   TOKYO

Publisher
Mike Roche

Acquisitions Editor
Thomas Gay

Consulting Developmental Editor
Trish Taylor

Developmental Editor
Laurie Runion

Market Strategist
Janet Hennies

Project Editor
Rebecca Dodson

Art Director
Linda Beaupré

Production Manager
Holly Lewerenz

Cover image copyright © 1999 Bryan Kuntz Photography Inc.

ISBN: 0-03-026856-7   (*Wall Street Journal* edition 0-03-033241-9)

Library of Congress Catalog Card Number: 00-110815

Some material in this work previously appeared in MICROECONOMICS: PRINCIPLES AND POLICY, Eighth Edition, copyright © 2000 by Harcourt, Inc. All rights reserved.

Copyright acknowledgments continue on page 505, which constitutes a continuation of this page.

Address for Domestic Orders
Harcourt, Inc., 6277 Sea Harbor Drive, Orlando, FL 32887-6777
800-782-4479

Address for International Orders
International Customer Service
Harcourt, Inc., 6277 Sea Harbor Drive, Orlando, FL 32887-6777
407-345-3800
(fax) 407-345-4060
(e-mail) hbintl@harcourtbrace.com

Address for Editorial Correspondence
Harcourt College Publishers, 301 Commerce Street, Suite 3700, Fort Worth, TX 76102

Web Site Address
http://www.harcourtcollege.com

Harcourt College Publishers may provide complimentary instructional aids and supplements or supplement packages to those adopters qualified under our adoption policy. Please contact your sales representative for more information. If as an adopter or potential user you receive supplements you do not need, please return them to your sales representative or send them to:

Attention: Returns Department, Troy Warehouse, 465 South Lincoln Drive, Troy, MO 63379

Printed in the United States of America

0 1 2 3 4 5 6 7 8 9   048   10 9 8 7 6 5 4 3 2 1

Harcourt College Publishers

To my four children, Ellen, Daniel, and now Sabrina and Jim.

W.J.B.

To Scott and William, both now well beyond the final exam.

A.S.B.

THE HARCOURT SERIES IN ECONOMICS

Baldani, Bradfield, and Turner
Mathematical Economics

Baumol and Blinder
Economics: Principles and Policy
Eighth Edition
(also available in Micro and Macro paperbacks)

Baumol, Panzar, and Willig
Contestable Markets and the Theory of Industry Structure
Revised Edition

Breit and Elzinga
The Antitrust Casebook: Milestones in Economic Regulation
Third Edition

Brue
The Evolution of Economic Thought
Sixth Edition

Callan and Thomas
Environmental Economic and Management: Theory, Policy, and Applications
Second Edition

Edgmand, Moomaw, and Olson
Economics and Contemporary Issues
Fifth Edition

Gardner
Comparative Economic Systems
Second Edition

Gwartney, Stroup and Sobel
Economics: Private and Public Choice
Ninth Edition
(also available in Micro and Macro paperbacks)

Gwartney and Stroup
Introduction to Economics: The Wealth and Poverty of Nations

Hess and Ross
Economic Development: Theories, Evidence, and Policies

Hirschey
Fundamentals of Managerial Economics: Theories, Evidence, and Policies
Sixth Edition

Hirschey
Managerial Economics
Revised Edition

Hyman
Public Finance: A Contemporary Application of Theory to Policy
Sixth Edition

Kahn
The Economic Approach to Environmental and Natural Resources
Second Edition

Kaserman and Mayo
Government and Business: The Economics of Antitrust and Regulation

Kaufman and Hatchkiss
The Economics of Labor Markets
Fifth Edition

Kennett and Lieberman
The Road to Capitalism: The Economic Transformation of Eastern Europe and the Former Soviet Union

Kreinin
International Economics: A Policy Approach
Eighth Edition

Mankiw
Principles of Economics
Second Edition
(also available in Micro, Macro, Brief Macro, and Essentials paperbacks)

Nicholson
Intermediate Microeconomics and Its Application
Eighth Edition

Nicholson
Microeconomic Theory: Basic Principles and Extensions
Seventh Edition

Ramanathan
Introductory Econometrics with Applications
Fourth Edition

Rukstad
Corporate Decision Making in the World Economy: Company Case Studies

Rukstad
Macroeconomic Decision Making in the World Economy: Text and Cases
Third Edition

Salvatore
Managerial Economics: In a Global Economy
Fourth Edition

Samuelson and Marks
Managerial Economics
Third Edition

Santerre and Neun
Health Economics: Theories, Insights, and Industry Studies
Revised Edition

Scarth
Macroeconomics: An Introduction to Advanced Methods
Third Edition

Sexton
Exploring Economics: Pathways to Problem Solving
(also available in Micro and Macro paperbacks)

Stockman
Introduction to Economics
Second Edition
(also available in Micro and Macro paperbacks)

Walton and Rockoff
History of the American Economy
Eighth Edition

Welch and Welch
Economics: Theory and Practice
Sixth Edition

Yarbrough and Yarbrough
The World Economy: Trade and Finance
Fifth Edition

ABOUT THE AUTHORS

William J. Baumol

William Baumol was born February 26, 1922, in an area of New York City that has since come to be known as Fort Apache. He received his BSS at the College of the City of New York in 1942 and his Ph.D. at the University of London in 1949.

He is Professor of Economics and Director of the C.V. Starr Center for Applied Economics at New York University and Professor Emeritus at Princeton University. He is a frequent consultant to the management of major firms in a wide variety of industries in the United States and other countries, as well as to a number of governmental agencies. In several fields, including the telecommunications and electric utility industries, current regulatory policy is based on his explicit recommendations. Among his many contributions to economics are research on the theory of the firm, the contestability of markets, the economics of the arts and other services—the "cost disease of the services" is often referred to as "Baumol's disease"—and productivity convergence among nations. In addition to economics, he taught a course in wood sculpture at Princeton for about 20 years.

He has been president of the American Economic Association, and three other professional societies. He is an elected member of the National Academy of Sciences, created by the U.S. Congress, and of the American Philosophical Society, founded by Benjamin Franklin. He is also on the board of trustees of the National Council on Economic Education, and of the Theater Development Fund. He is the recipient of nine honorary degrees.

Baumol is the author of 30 books and hundreds of journal and newspaper articles, and his writings have been translated into more than a dozen languages.

Alan S. Blinder

Alan S. Blinder was born in New York City and attended Princeton University, where one of his teachers was William Baumol. After earning a master's degree at the London School of Economics and a Ph.D. at MIT, Blinder returned to Princeton, where he has taught since 1971. He is currently the Gordon S. Rentschler Memorial Professor of Economics and co-director of Princeton's Center for Economic Policy Studies, which he founded.

In January 1993, Blinder went to Washington as part of President Clinton's first Council of Economic Advisers. Then, from June 1994 through January 1996, he served as vice chairman of the Federal Reserve Board. He thus played a role in formulating both the fiscal and monetary policies of the 1990s, topics discussed extensively in this book.

For more than 10 years, Blinder wrote newspaper and magazine columns on economic policy, and his op-ed pieces still appear regularly in various newspapers.

Blinder has been vice president of the American Economic Association and is a member of both the American Philosophical Society and the American Academy of Arts and Sciences. He has two grown sons, and lives in Princeton with his wife, where he plays tennis as often as he can.

■ PREFACE

The economy changes all the time, but certain principles endure. Steadfastly, we refuse to give up the principles that have guided us through seven previous editions of this book. We still follow our original precept that practical issues and developments in the real economy should influence the content of an introductory economics course and determine how its materials are presented. So we begin most chapters with a real problem and use it as a launching pad for our analysis, rather than the reverse. We still refuse to be lured into the claim that everything contained in this volume is of extreme importance for the reader's future. Therefore, throughout the book we single out those materials that we believe to have enduring value for the student. We believe that readers who do not make some effort to understand and remember these matters after the course is ended will have shortchanged themselves.

It has been said that economics is no laughing matter, and that an economist is a person who, having observed something that works in reality, wonders whether it works in theory! This book contains its share of theoretical material. But the theory is not merely an exercise in making students miserable; it is driven by issues that are real and current. As used by physicists, biologists, and economists—indeed by all in the fields of research in colleges and universities—the word *theory* simply means a thorough and rigorous explanation. For example, economists believe that foreign trade can harm some workers but make most members of the community better off. We need theory to explain why. Or another example: Average incomes of people who live in market economies have grown far faster than those of others in countries where the economy is directed by government planners. Again, theory can explain why.

These observations also suggest two major areas in which this book has been changed since the previous edition. Although coverage of trade among nations and economic growth have always played a substantial part in this text, these subjects are now emphasized even more and are raised wherever they are appropriate. We were induced to turn in this direction by recent developments in the United States and in other industrial economies. More and more of what is produced in the typical country is sold abroad rather than to domestic consumers. Correspondingly, ever more of what consumers buy comes from other lands. At the same time, the continuing appearance of new and improved technology enables workers in all countries to produce more than they did before. Yet, despite the resulting prosperity in the United States during most of the last two decades, the earnings of less-educated workers have fallen behind those of workers with more education and higher skills.

To keep up the prosperity, to offer a better future to those who are now less educated, and to deal with the enormous economic problems of the poorer nations of the world, we need to understand the effects of international trade and of improvements in technology. Do they make most of us better off by making products cheaper, so that our incomes go further? Or do they threaten our incomes by making us more vulnerable to foreign competition and labor-saving technology? These crucial issues are addressed at several points in this book. We have provided an entirely new chapter (Chapter 15) analyzing how competition involving improved products and production techniques drives the growth in free-market economies. This chapter offers material that has not been published previously and seems to have no counterpart in other principles texts.

In addition to this new chapter, many parts of the book have been extensively rewritten and reorganized for easier comprehension. Many of these changes follow suggestions of users of the book and others whose opinions we solicited in an extensive survey. In particular, the four core microeconomics chapters were substantially modified with improved readability in mind. In each of these chapters we were careful to retain the features that readers reported as being helpful in earlier editions. We have also added a brief treatment of the principle of comparative advantage to Chapter 4.

NOTE TO THE STUDENT

We would like to offer one suggestion for success in your economics course. Unlike some of the other courses you may be taking, economics is cumulative: Each week's lesson builds upon what you have learned before. You will save yourself a lot of frustration and a lot of work by keeping up on a week-to-week basis. To assist you in doing so, we provide a chapter summary, a list of important terms and concepts, and a selection of questions to help you review the contents of each chapter. Making use of these learning aids will increase your chances of success in your economics course. For additional assistance, we have developed student supplements to help reinforce the concepts in this book and provide opportunity for practice and feedback. See the following list of ancillaries for learning tools that apply specifically to students.

ANCILLARIES

As economic education incorporates new technologies, we have expanded and improved our extensive learning package to accommodate student and instructor needs.

STUDY GUIDE   Craig Swan of the University of Minnesota has revised the student Study Guide to make it an even more valuable tool for understanding the text's main concepts. The Study Guide, which is available in main, micro, and macro split versions, includes:

- Learning objectives

- Lists of important terms and concepts for every chapter

- Quizzes that help students test their understanding and comprehension of concepts

- Multiple-choice tests for self-understanding

- Lists of supplementary readings and study questions for every chapter

- "Economics in Action" sections that use current news articles to illustrate economic concepts

- "Economics Online" exercises that outline useful Internet and Web sources for economic data and information. Periodic updates of these sources will be provided on the Dryden/Harcourt Web page at www.harcourtcollege.com.

INSTRUCTOR'S MANUAL   David O'Hara of Metropolitan State University has extensively revised the Instructor's Manual. Every chapter includes detailed chapter outlines, teaching tips and suggestions, answers to end-of-chapter questions in the main text, and questions for classroom discussion.

MICROECONOMICS TEST BANK   The updated and revised Microeconomics Test Bank by Doug Kinnear of Colorado State University consists of more than 200 questions per chapter and covers Chapters 1–22 and 35 in the text. Every question has been checked to ensure the accuracy and clarity of the answers and painstakingly revised to address the main text revisions. The Test Bank includes true/false, multiple-choice, and short-answer questions that assess students' critical-thinking skills. Easy, medium, and difficult questions outline the process that students must use to arrive at their answers: recall, application, and integration. Questions are organized by text section to help instructors pick and choose their selections with ease.

COMPUTERIZED TEST BANKS   The computerized Test Banks, available in our easy-to-use EXAMaster program, have been enhanced significantly for this edition. EXAMaster allows instructors to add and edit their own questions, create and edit graphics, print scrambled versions of tests, and convert multiple-choice questions to open-ended questions. EXAMaster 99 now includes a more intuitive graphic interface, increased test sizes of up to 500 questions, the capacity to create up to 99 versions of any one test, online testing and grade bookkeeping, and many more features. The new software is now available on CD-ROM in Windows and Macintosh formats.

THE WALL STREET JOURNAL EDITION   Instructors can help students relate the economic concepts in the text to everyday life by ordering the *Wall Street Journal* edition of the textbook. This special edition supplements the standard edition with a discounted 10-week *Wall Street Journal* subscription for students. Professors get a free 1-year subscription when 10 or more of their students order the *Wall Street Journal*. The *Wall Street Journal* provides an effective tie-in to the text because new examples of economic principles appear in each day's paper. Students can activate their subscriptions by simply completing and mailing the business reply card located in the back of the book. This option is available for both the main version of the book and the paperback splits. Instructors interested in finding out more about this program can contact their sales representative or simply call 800-782-4479.

TRANSPARENCY ACETATES   Full color transparency acetates for all important figures and tables in the eighth edition are available for use on an overhead projector. They are available to adopters upon request in microeconomic and macroeconomic sets.

POWERPOINT PRESENTATION SOFTWARE   Steven Shulman of Colorado State University has prepared a comprehensive and user-friendly PowerPoint presentation for use in classroom lectures. The presentation consists of speaking points and chapter outlines that are accompanied by graphs and tables from the main text. *PowerPoint Viewer* is provided in the package.

ECONACTIVE STUDENT CD-ROM   A new HTML-based EconActive student CD-ROM supplement is now available and very easy to use. The look and feel is similar to that of a Web site. The CD-ROM contains chapter-review sections, automatically graded multiple choice and true/false quizzes, "cyberproblems" that launch to the World Wide Web for real-world economic analysis, and more. It also includes interactive graphs and graphing problems that require students to graph solutions.

INSTRUCTOR'S CD-ROM   Beginning with the eighth edition, accompanying instructor's supplements are available on one CD-ROM. Included on the CD-ROM are the PowerPoint slides, Instructor's Manual, and Test Banks.

PRINCIPLES OF ECONOMICS VIDEOTAPE   *Principles of Economics* is a 40-minute videotape that offers students an insightful overview of ten common economic principles: Tradeoffs, Opportunity Cost, Marginal Thinking, Incentives, Trade, Markets, Government's Role, Productivity, Inflation, and The Phillips Curve.

Principles of Economics shows viewers how to apply economic principles to their daily lives. This video is filled with interviews from some of the country's leading economists, and includes profiles of real students facing economic choices, as well as showing the economy's impact on U.S. and foreign companies.

This video can be used at the beginning of a term to give students a general overview of economics, or used one section at a time prior to teaching of one of these principles in your course.

WEB SITE   Valuable resources for both instructors and students can be found on the Internet at www.dryden.com/econ/baumol. For instructors, the PowerPoint presentations and Instructor's Manual are available on the instructors' resources section of the site. Students will find links to economics-related Internet sites, automatically graded practice quizzes, PowerPoint slides for their review, sample chapters from the study guide and *EconActive CD-ROM*, and other resources. Also, career listings for students, leading economic indicator information, and an economic URL database can be found at www.dryden.com.

WEBCT COURSE MANAGEMENT SOFTWARE Harcourt now offers HTML-based software for instructors who are interested in building Web-based learning sites for their students. This software can be utilized by nontechnical users to create entire online courses or simply to post office hours or supplementary course materials for students. Instructors can design Web sites that provide a full array of educational tools, including communications links with their students, Web testing, student grade tracking with access control, database collaboration and searching, and more. It is free of charge to adopters. For more information, call the Harcourt customer service line at 800-237-2665, or visit our home page at www.harcourtcollege.com. You can also visit www.webct.com for a "virtual" tour.

ACTIVITIES MANUAL An activities manual provides instructors with classroom games, activities, and demonstrations designed to illustrate and enliven important economic concepts. These activities have been tremendously popular with instructors and are very useful for classroom learning.

Harcourt College Publishers may provide complimentary instructional aids and supplements or supplement packages to those adopters qualified under its adoption policy. Please contact your sales representative for more information. If, as an adopter or potential user you receive supplements you do not need, please return them to your sales representative or send them to: Returns Department, Troy Warehouse, 465 South Lincoln Drive, Troy, MO 63379.

NOTE TO THE INSTRUCTOR

In trying to improve the book from one edition to the next, we rely heavily on our experiences as teachers. But our experience using the book is minuscule compared with that of the hundreds of instructors who use it nationwide. If you encounter problems or have suggestions for improving the book, we urge you to let us know by writing to us in care of Harcourt College Publishers, 301 Commerce Street, Suite 3700, Fort Worth, TX 76102. Such letters are invaluable, and we are glad to receive both praise and suggestions for improvement. Many such suggestions that were accumulated after publication of the seventh edition have found their way into this new book. Suggested course outlines for both one-semester and one-quarter courses follow.

OUTLINE FOR A ONE-SEMESTER COURSE IN MICROECONOMICS

CHAPTER	TITLE
1	What Is Economics?
2	The Use and Misuse of Graphs
3	The Economy: Myth and Reality
4	Scarcity and Choice: *The* Economic Problem
5	Supply and Demand: An Initial Look
6	Consumer Choice: Individual and Market Demand
7	Demand and Elasticity
8	Production, Inputs, and Cost: Building Blocks for Supply Analysis
9	Output, Price, and Profit: The Importance of Marginal Analysis
10	The Firm and the Industry Under Perfect Competition
11	The Price System and the Case for the Free Market
12	Monopoly
13	Between Competition and Monopoly
14	The Market Mechanism: Shortcomings and Remedies
15	The Microeconomics of Innovation: Prime Engine of Growth
16	Real Firms and their Financing: Stocks and Bonds
17	Pricing the Factors of Production
18	Labor: The Human Input
20	Limiting Market Power: Regulation and Antitrust
21	Taxation and Resource Allocation

Plus any two of the following:

OUTLINE FOR A ONE-QUARTER COURSE IN MICROECONOMICS

WITH THANKS

Finally, and with great pleasure, we turn to the customary acknowledgments of indebtedness. Ours have been accumulating now through eight editions. In these days of specialization, even a pair of authors cannot master every subject that an introductory textbook must cover. Our friends and colleagues Albert Ando, Charles Berry, Rebecca Blank, William Branson, the late Lester Chandler, Gregory Chow, Avinash Dixit, Robert Eisner, Susan Feiner, the late Stephen Goldfeld, Claudia Goldin, Ronald Grieson, Daniel Hamermesh, Yuzo Honda, Peter Kenen, Melvin Krauss, Herbert Levine, the late Arthur Lewis, Burton Malkiel, Edwin Mills, Janusz Ordover, Uwe Reinhardt, Harvey Rosen, Laura Tyson, and Martin Weitzman have all given generously of their knowledge in particular areas over the course of eight editions. We have learned much from them, and only wish we had learned more.

Many economists and students at other colleges and universities offered useful suggestions for improvements, many of which we have incorporated into this eighth edition. We wish to thank Ray Cohn, Illinois State University; George Hoffer, Virginia Commonwealth University; Kirk Kim, University of Wisconsin at Whitewater; Sang Lee, University of Florida; Robby Rosenman, Washington State University; Edward Stuart, Northeastern Illinois University; John Tiemstra, Calvin College; Hendrick Van den Berg, University of Nebraska at Lincoln; Doug Walker, Lousiana State University; and Stephan Weiler, Colorado State University, for their insightful reviews. We especially want to thank Doug Kinnear of Colorado State University for his careful review of the microeconomic split of this new edition.

We also wish to thank the many economists who responded to our survey; their responses were invaluable in planning this revision: Mustafa Acar, Purdue University; Terence J. Alexander, Iowa State University; Samuel Kojo Andon, Southern Connecticut State University; B. W. Balch, Middle Tennessee State University; Donald N. Baum, University of Nebraska at Omaha; David C. Black, The University of Toledo; Morgan K. Bridge, Mesa State College; Jozell Brister, Abilene Christian University; Ted Burczak, Denison University; Anthony Chan, Santa Monica College; John E. Charalambakis, Asbury College; Jonathan Conning, Williams College; Barbara Connolly, Westchester Community College; Carrie Cornwell, Sierra College; Pati Shaw Crabb, Indiana University Southeast; Stephen Cullenberg, University of California, Riverside; Dan Dabney, St. Edward's University; Na Li Dawson, University of Connecticut; Peter C. Dawson, University of Connecticut; Justino De La

Cruz, University of Texas, San Antonio; Bruce Dixon, University of Arkansas, Fayetteville; Heriberto Dixon, Milano Graduate School of Management; Michael Dowd, University of Toledo; Luoana Dulgheru, University of Connecticut; Elizabeth Elmore, The Richard Stockton College of New Jersey; Mona El Shazly, Columbia College; William C. Freund, Pace University, New York City; John B. Gabor, Lake Tahoe Community College; Yilma Gebremariam, Southern Connecticut State University; Robert Godby, University of Wyoming; Eugene W. Gotwalt, George Mason University; Richard R. Hawkins, University of West Florida; Ali Hekmat, College of Eastern Utah; Whitney Hicks, University of Missouri; Farrokh Hormozi, Pace University; John Houchens, University of Wisconsin-Marathan County; Mahmood Hussain, University of Colorado at Boulder; Young-Iob Chung, Eastern Michigan University; John Isbister, University of California at Santa Cruz; Oded Izraeli, Oakland University; Don C. Jackson, Abilene Christian University; Ameeta Jaiswal-Dale, University of St. Thomas; Derek C. Jones, Hamilton College; Brad Kamp, University of South Florida-Tampa; Ashok K. Kapoor, Augsburg College; Mariam Khawar, Elmira College; Mohammed Khayum, University of Southern Indiana; Kamau Kinuthia, South Puget Sound Community College; Robert A. Kleinhenz, California State University-Fullerton; Aric W. Krause, Clarion University of Pennsylvania; Jeffrey A. Krautkraemer, Washington State University; Dr. Samuel M. Laposata, Muhlenberg College; Soyon Lee, Benedictine University; Martin Lefsky, Ocean Township High School; Cynthia S. McCarty, Jacksonville State University; Zagros Madjd-Sadjadi, Golden Gate University; Paul A. Mantegani, Kent School; Margaret Malixi, California State University-Bakersfield; Carrie A. Meyer, George Mason University; Hadley T. Mitchell, Taylor University; Masoud Moghaddam, St. Cloud State University; Kahn A. Mohabbat, Northern Illinois University; W. Douglas Morgan, University of California-Santa Barbara; Francis Mummery, California State University-Fullerton; Michael A. Nelson, Washington State University; Anthony O'Brien, Lehigh University; John F. O'Connell, College of the Holy Cross; David O'Hara, Metropolitan State University; Charles C. Okeke, College of Southern Nevada-Las Vegas; Theodore Paliros, Louisiana State University; Paul Pecorino, University of Alabama; Mark G. Pelletier, Winslow Senior High School, Winslow, Maine; Elida Petrella, Wheeling Jesuit University & Indian Creek High School; Arthur L. Porter, Southern Utah University; Robert C. Rogers, Wright College; Bernard Rose, Rocky Mountain College; Richard E. Rosenberg, University of Wisconsin-Parkside; Robert A. Rosenthal, Stonehill College; Steven Rundle, Biola University; Larry D. Schelhorse, San Diego State University; Stanley W. Samarasinghe, Tulane University; James A. Schloss, The Anthenian School; Calvin Siebert, University of Iowa; Kathleen C. Simmons, Gainesville College; Stefani Smith, Tulane University; Peter J. Snedecor, Northfield Mount Hermon School; Jeffrey Stewart, Miami University; Joseph F. Talarico, Rider University; Robert W. Taylor, Purdue University; Mark O. Tengesdal, Southeastern Oklahoma State University; James Thorson, Southern Connecticut State University; Robert M. Toepper, Concordia University; Robert Tokle, Idaho State University; Karen M. Travis, Pacific Lutheran University; Karen Vorst, University of Missouri-Kansas City; Lawrence A. Waldman, University of New Mexico; Pamela Whalley, Western Washington University; James A. Wilde, University of North Carolina-Chapel Hill; Art Woolf, University of Vermont; William J. Zeis, Bucks County Community College.

Obviously, the book you hold in your hands was not produced by us alone. An essential role was played by the staff at Harcourt College Publishers, including Gary Nelson, Acquisitions Editor for Economics; Thomas Gay, Executive Editor for Economics (2001 Update); Trish Taylor, Consulting Senior Developmental Editor; Tim Hewitt, Developmental Editor; Laurie Runion, Developmental Editor (2001 Update); Charles J. Dierker, Project Editor; Rebecca Dodson, Project Editor (2001 Update); Linda Beaupré, Art Director; Darryl King, Production Manager; Holly Lewerenz, Production Manager (2001 Update); Lindel Blundell, Art and Literary Rights Editor; Annette Coolidge, Photo and Literary Rights Researcher; Debbie K. Anderson, Marketing Strategist; and Janet Hennies, Marketing Strategist (2001 Update).

We also thank our intelligent and delightful secretaries and research coworkers at Princeton University and New York University, Phyllis Durepos and Janeece Roderick, who struggled successfully with the myriad tasks involved in completing the manuscript. Above all, Professor Baumol owes an unrepayable debt to his long-standing partner in crime, Sue Anne Batey Blackman, who updated much of the materials and contributed draft paragraphs, illustrative items, and far more with her usual insight and diligence. By now, Sue Anne undoubtedly knows more about the book than the authors do.

And, finally, there are our wives, Hilda Baumol and Madeline Blinder. They have now participated and helped with this project for nearly a quarter of a century. During that period, this book has quite literally become part of our families. And both their contributions and our affection have grown.

William J. Baumol
Alan S. Blinder

■ TABLE OF CONTENTS

MICROECONOMICS

2001 UPDATE

I
GETTING ACQUAINTED WITH ECONOMICS

Welcome to economics! Some of your fellow students may have warned you that "Econ is boring." Don't believe them—or at least, don't believe them too much. It is true that studying economics may not be as much fun as, say, studying literature or film. But a first course in economics can be an eye-opening experience. There is a vast and important world out there—the economic world—and this book is designed to help you understand it better.

Have you ever wondered whether jobs will be plentiful or scarce when you graduate? Or why a college education becomes more and more expensive?

Was the government right to sue Microsoft? Why can't pollution be eliminated? How did the U.S. economy manage to grow so rapidly in the 1990s while Japan's stagnated? If any of these questions have piqued your curiosity, read on. You may find economics to be more interesting than you had thought!

The five chapters of Part I introduce you to both the subject matter of economics and to some of the methods that economists use to study their subject.

Why does public discussion of economic policy so often show the abysmal ignorance of the participants? Why do I so often want to cry at what public figures, the press, and television commentators say about economic affairs?

Robert M. Solow

WHAT IS ECONOMICS?

Economics is a broad-ranging discipline, both in the questions it asks and the methods it uses to seek answers. Rather than try to define the discipline in a single sentence or paragraph, we will instead introduce you to economics by letting the subject matter speak for itself.

Many of the world's most pressing problems are economic in nature. The first part of the chapter is intended to give you some idea of the sorts of issues that economic analysis helps to clarify and the kinds of solutions that economic principles suggest. The second part briefly introduces the tools that economists use—tools you are likely to find useful in your career, personal life, and role as an informed citizen, long after the course is over.

■ IDEAS FOR BEYOND THE FINAL EXAM

As college professors, we realize it is inevitable that you will forget much of what you learn in this course—perhaps with a sense of relief—soon after the final exam. There is not much point bemoaning this fact; elephants may never forget, but people do.

Nevertheless, some economic ideas are so important that you will want to remember them after the course is over. To help you pick out a few of the most crucial concepts, we have selected nine from among the many contained in this book. Some offer key insights into the workings of the economy. Others bear on important policy issues that appear in newspapers. Others point out common misunderstandings that occur among even the most thoughtful lay observers. As the opening quote of this chapter suggests, many learned judges, politicians, and university administrators who have failed to understand or misused these economic principles could have made wiser decisions than they did.

Each of the *Ideas for Beyond the Final Exam* will be discussed in depth as it occurs in the course of the book and called to your attention at the time by yellow sticky notes in the margin denoting the relevant idea. In addition, we will help you see how these ideas work throughout the book by noting how each chapter topic relates to the relevant ideas in the summary for each chapter. So you should not expect to master them now, but notice how often the same ideas arise as we address economic topics throughout the book. Nonetheless, it is useful to sketch them briefly here both to introduce you to economics and to provide a preview of what is to come.

Ideas for Beyond the Final Exam

IDEA 1: HOW MUCH DOES IT REALLY COST?

Despite dramatic improvements in standards of living since the Industrial Revolution, human society has not come anywhere near a state of unlimited abundance. So people must constantly make choices. If you purchase a new computer, you may have to give up that trip you had planned with friends. If a business decides to retool its factories, it may have to postpone plans for new executive offices. If a government expands its defense program, it may be forced to reduce its outlays on roads or school buildings.

Economists say that the true costs of such decisions are not the number of dollars spent on the computer, the new equipment, or the military establishment, but rather *the value of what must be given up in order to acquire the item*—the vacation trip, the new executive offices, the improved roads, and the new schools. These are called **opportunity costs** because they represent the *opportunities* the individual, firm, or government must forgo to make the desired expenditure. Economists maintain that rational decision making must be based on opportunity costs (Chapters 4, 9, 10, and 14).

The **opportunity cost** of some decision is the value of the next best alternative that must be given up because of that decision (for example, working instead of going to school).

The cost of a college education provides a vivid example that is probably close to your heart. How much do you think it costs to go to college? Most likely you would answer this question by adding together your expenditures on tuition, room and board, books, and the like, and then deducting any scholarship funds you may receive. Suppose that comes to $15,000.

Economists would keep score differently. They would first want to know how much you would be earning if you were not attending college. Suppose that is $16,000 a year. This may sound like an irrelevant piece of information. But because you give up these earnings by attending college, they must be added to your tuition bill as a cost of your education. Nor would economists accept the university's bill for room and board as a measure of your living costs. They would want to know how much more it costs you to live at school rather than at home. Economists would count only this extra cost as an expense. On balance, your college education is probably costing you much more than you think.

IDEA 2: ATTEMPTS TO REPEAL THE LAWS OF SUPPLY AND DEMAND—THE MARKET STRIKES BACK

When a commodity is in short supply, its price naturally tends to rise. Sometimes disgruntled consumers badger politicians into "solving" this problem by imposing a legal ceiling on the price. Similarly, when supplies are abundant—say, when fine weather produces extraordinarily abundant crops—prices tend to fall. Falling prices naturally dismay producers, who often succeed in getting legislation to impose price floors.

But such attempts to repeal the laws of supply and demand usually backfire and sometimes produce results virtually the opposite of those that were intended. Where rent controls are adopted to protect tenants, housing grows scarce because the law makes it unprofitable to build and maintain apartments. When price floors are placed under agricultural products, surpluses pile up.

As we will see in Chapter 5 and elsewhere in this book, such consequences of interfering with the price mechanism are no accident. They follow inevitably from the way free markets work.

IDEA 3: THE SURPRISING PRINCIPLE OF COMPARATIVE ADVANTAGE

Japan produces many products that Americans buy in huge quantities—including cars, TV sets, cameras, and electronic equipment. American manufacturers often complain about Japanese competition and demand protection from the flood of imports that, in their view, threatens American standards of living. Is this view justified?

Economists think not. They maintain that both sides must gain from international trade. But what if the Japanese were able to produce *everything* more cheaply than we can? Wouldn't Americans be thrown out of work and our nation be impoverished?

A remarkable result, called the law of *comparative advantage*, shows that, even in this extreme case, the two nations can still benefit by trading and that each can gain as a result! We will explain this principle first in Chapter 4 and then more fully in Chapter 23, where we will also note some potentially valid arguments in favor of providing special incentives for particular domestic industries. But for now a simple parable will make the reason clear.

Suppose Sally grows up on a farm and is a whiz at plowing. But she is also a successful country singer who earns $4,000 a performance. Should Sally turn down singing engagements to leave time for working the fields? Of course not. Instead she should hire Alfie, a much less efficient farmer, to do the plowing for her. Sally may be better at plowing. But she earns so much more by singing that it makes sense for her to specialize in that and leave the farming to Alfie. Though Alfie is a less skilled farmer than Sally, he is an even worse singer.

So Alfie earns his living in the job at which he at least has a *comparative* advantage (his farming is not as bad as his singing), and both Alfie and Sally gain. The same is true of two countries. Even if one of them is more efficient at everything, both countries can gain by producing the things they do best *comparatively*.

IDEA 4: TRADE IS A WIN-WIN SITUATION

One of the most fundamental ideas of economics is that *both* parties must expect to gain something in a *voluntary* exchange. Otherwise why would they both agree to trade? This principle seems self-evident. Yet it is amazing how often it is ignored in practice.

For example, it was widely believed for centuries that in international trade one country's gain from an exchange must be the other country's loss (Chapter 23). Analogously, some people feel instinctively that if Ms. A profits handsomely from a deal with Mr. B, then Mr. B must have been exploited. Laws sometimes prohibit mutually beneficial exchanges between buyers and sellers—as when a willing worker is condemned to remain unemployed because the wage she is offered is "too low" (Chapter 18), or when the resale of tickets to sporting events ("ticket scalping") is outlawed even though the buyer is happy to get the ticket that he would not obtain at a lower price (Chapter 5).

In every one of these cases, and many more, well-intentioned but misguided reasoning blocks the mutual gains that arise from voluntary exchange—and thereby interferes with one of the most basic functions of an economic system (see Chapter 4).

IDEA 5: THE IMPORTANCE OF THINKING AT THE MARGIN

We will devote many pages of this book to explaining and extolling a type of decision-making process called *marginal analysis* (see especially Chapters 6, 8, 9, and 11), which we can best illustrate by an example.

Suppose an airline is told by its accountants that the full cost of transporting one passenger from Los Angeles to New York is $300. Can the airline profit by offering a reduced fare of $200 to students who fly on a standby basis? The surprising answer is, probably yes. The reason is that most of the costs will be paid whether the plane carries 20 passengers or 120 passengers.

Marginal analysis points out that costs such as maintenance, landing rights, and ground crews are irrelevant to the decision of whether to carry standby passengers for reduced rates. The only costs that *are* relevant are the *extra* costs of writing and processing additional tickets, the food and beverages these passengers consume, the additional fuel required, and so on. These costs are called *marginal costs* and are probably quite small in this example. Any passenger who pays the airline more than its marginal cost will add something to the company's profit. So it probably is more profitable to let the students ride at low fares than to let the plane fly with empty seats.

In many real cases, a failure to understand marginal analysis has led decision makers to reject advantageous possibilities like the reduced fare in our example. These people were misled by calculating in terms of *average* rather than *marginal* cost figures—an error that can be quite costly.

IDEA 6: EXTERNALITIES: A SHORTCOMING OF THE MARKET CURED BY MARKET METHODS

Markets are very adept at producing the goods that consumers want and in just the quantities they desire. They do so by rewarding those who respond to what consumers want and who produce these products economically. Similarly, the market mechanism ferrets out waste and inefficiency by seeing to it that inefficient producers lose money.

This all works out well as long as each exchange involves only the buyer and the seller—and no one else. But some transactions affect third parties who were not involved in the decision. Examples abound. Electric utilities that generate power for Midwestern states also produce pollution—which kills freshwater fish in New York state. A farmer sprays crops with toxic pesticides, but the poison seeps into the ground water and affects the health of neighboring communities.

Such social costs are called *externalities* because they affect parties *external* to the economic transactions that cause them. Externalities escape the control of the market mechanism because no financial incentive motivates polluters to minimize the damage they do—as we will learn in Chapters 14 and 22. So business firms make their products as cheaply as possible, disregarding any environmental harm they may cause.

Yet Chapters 14 and 22 point out a way for the government to use the market mechanism to control undesirable externalities. If the electric utility and the farmer are charged for the damage they do to the air and water, just as they are charged for any coal and fertilizer they use, then they will have a financial incentive to reduce the amount of pollution they generate. Thus, in this case, economists believe that market methods are often the best way to cure one of the market's most important shortcomings.

IDEA 7: WHY THE COSTS OF EDUCATION AND MEDICAL CARE KEEP GROWING

A distressing phenomenon is occurring throughout the industrialized world: The costs of providing many services have risen consistently faster than the rate of inflation. Perhaps the most publicized examples are medical care and education. For example, over a recent 50-year period the daily cost of a hospital stay outstripped the rate of inflation by over 800 percent.

But the phenomenon is not limited to education and health. Many public services have been deteriorating even as they grow more expensive to provide. There are fewer postal deliveries and garbage pickups and larger classes in public schools. Often the problem is blamed on greed, inefficiency, and political corruption. But this cannot be the whole story, because the scenario has been repeated in virtually every other industrialized country, despite great differences in the way public services are provided.

As we shall learn in Chapter 14, the root cause of the problem is economic. It stems, ironically, from the dazzling growth in efficiency of private manufacturing industries. Because technological improvements make workers more productive in manufacturing, wages rise. But wages must rise not only for manufacturing workers, but also for hospital workers, teachers, and other service workers, because otherwise people would leave their low-paying service jobs and compete for high-paying manufacturing jobs.

Unlike manufacturing, however, the technology of labor-intensive personal services is not easily changed. It still takes one person to drive a postal truck, one teacher to teach a class, and four musicians to play a string quartet—just as it always has. So, with wages rising, the costs of these services are forced up. This phenomenon has been called the "cost disease" of the personal services, a malady that affects services as diverse as college teaching, restaurant cooking, and automobile repair.

The cost disease is important to understand not because it excuses the financial record of our governments, but because it suggests what we should expect the future to bring and, perhaps, indicates what policies we should advocate to deal with it.

IDEA 8: THE TRADE-OFF BETWEEN EFFICIENCY AND EQUALITY

In the United States, wages and incomes grew more unequal from the late 1970s through the early 1990s. Highly skilled workers pulled away from low-skilled workers. The rich grew much richer while the poor became (relatively) poorer. Yet U. S. unemployment has been low, and jobs are easy to get. In much of the European Union, things are just the reverse. Unemployment has been persistently high for years—much higher than in the United States. Yet the inequalities of wages and incomes in these countries are smaller and have not grown more extreme.

Many economists feel that these phenomena are two sides of the same coin. Europe and the United States have made different choices of how best to balance the conflicting claims of greater economic efficiency (more output and jobs) versus greater equality.

Roughly speaking, the American solution is to let markets work to promote efficiency—something they are very good at doing—with only minimal government interferences to reduce economic inequalities. (Some of these interferences are studied in Chapter 19.) If very low wages are needed to keep people employed, so be it. That is better than putting them on the dole.

Much of continental Europe takes a different view. They find it scandalous that many Americans work for less than $6 an hour, with virtually no fringe benefits and no job security. European laws prevent this: They mandate not only relatively high minimum wages but also substantial fringe benefits and employment protections. European social welfare programs to protect the poor are also more extensive and generous than the corresponding American programs. And, of course, European taxes must be much higher to pay for all this.

As economists see it, each system's virtue is also its vice. There is an agonizing *trade-off* between the *size* of a nation's output and the degree of *equality* with which that output is distributed. European-style policies designed to divide the proverbial economic pie more equally inadvertently can cause the size of the pie to shrink. American-style arrangements that promote maximal efficiency and output may permit or even breed huge inequalities. Which system is better? There is no clear answer, but we will examine the issue in detail in Chapter 19.

IDEA 9: PRODUCTIVITY GROWTH IS (ALMOST) EVERYTHING IN THE LONG RUN

In Geneva today, a worker in a watch factory turns out more than 100 times as many mechanical watches per year as her ancestors did three centuries earlier. The *productivity* of labor (output per hour of work) in cotton production has probably gone up more than 1,000-fold in 200 years. It is estimated that rising labor productivity has increased the standard of living of a typical American worker more than seven-fold in the past century. This means that Americans now enjoy about seven times as much clothing, housewares, and luxury goods as did a typical inhabitant of the United States 100 years ago. (See Chapters 15 and 18.)

Economic issues such as monopoly and inequality are important to us all and will receive much attention in this book. But in the long run nothing has as great an effect on our material well-being and the amounts society can afford to spend on hospitals, schools, and social amenities as the rate of growth of productivity.

EPILOGUE

These, then, are some of the more fundamental concepts you will find in this book—ideas that we hope you will retain beyond the final exam. There is no need to master them right now, for you will hear much more about each as you progress through the book. Instead, keep them in mind as you read—we will point them out to you as they occur—and look back over this list at the end of the course. You may be amazed to see how natural, or even obvious, they will seem then.

INSIDE THE ECONOMIST'S TOOL KIT

Now that you have some idea of the kinds of issues economists deal with, you should know something about the way they grapple with these problems.

ECONOMICS AS A DISCIPLINE

Economics has something of a split personality. Although clearly the most rigorous of the social sciences, it nevertheless looks decidedly more "social" than "scientific" when compared with, say, physics. An economist must be a jack of several trades, borrowing modes of investigation from numerous fields.

Mathematical reasoning is used extensively in economics, but so is historical study. And neither looks quite the same as when practiced by a mathematician or a historian. Statistical inference plays a major role in modern economic inquiry; but economists have had to modify standard statistical procedures to fit the kinds of data they analyze.

An introductory course in economics will not make you an economist; but it should help you approach social problems dispassionately. You will not find solutions to all society's economic problems in this book. But you should learn how to pose questions in ways that will help produce answers that are both useful and illuminating.

THE NEED FOR ABSTRACTION

Some students find economics unduly abstract and "unrealistic." The stylized world envisioned by economic theory seems only a distant cousin to the world they know. There is an old joke about three people—a chemist, a physicist, and an economist—stranded on an island with an ample supply of canned food but no tools to open the cans. The chemist thinks that lighting a fire under the cans would expand their

"I'm a social scientist, Michael. That means I can't explain electricity or anything like that, but if you ever want to know about people I'm your man."

contents and cause the cans to burst. The physicist advocates building a catapult with which they could smash the cans against some nearby boulders. The economist's suggestion? "Assume we have a can opener."

Economic theory *does* make unrealistic assumptions; you will encounter many of them in the pages that follow. But this propensity to abstract from reality results from the incredible complexity of the economic world, not from any fondness economists have for sounding absurd.

Compare the chemist's simple task of explaining the interactions of compounds in a chemical reaction with the economist's complex task of explaining the interactions of people in an economy. Are molecules motivated by greed or altruism, by envy or ambition? Do they ever emulate other molecules? Do forecasts about them influence their behavior? People, of course, do all these things, and many, many more. It is therefore vastly more difficult to predict human behavior than to predict chemical reactions. If economists tried to keep track of every aspect of human behavior, they would never get anywhere. Thus:

Abstraction from unimportant details is necessary to understand the functioning of anything as complex as the economy.

To appreciate why economists **abstract** from details, imagine the following hypothetical situation. You have just arrived, for the first time in your life, in Los Angeles. You are now at the Los Angeles Civic Center. This is the point marked *A* in Maps 1 and 2, which are alternative maps of part of Los Angeles. You want to drive to the Los Angeles County Museum of Art, point *B* on each map. Which map would you find more useful? You will notice that Map 1 has complete details of the Los Angeles road system. If you are like most people, you will find it hard to read and not very useful for determining how to get from the Civic Center (point *A*) to the Los Angeles County Museum of Art. For this purpose, Map 1 is far too detailed, though for some other purposes (for example, locating some small street in Hollywood) it may be the best map available.

In contrast, Map 2 shows a different perspective of Los Angeles, because it omits many minor roads—we might say they are assumed away—so that the freeways and major arteries stand out more clearly. As a result of this simplification, several routes from the Civic Center to the Los Angeles County Museum of Art emerge. For example, we can take the Hollywood Freeway west to Alvarado Boulevard, go south

Abstraction means ignoring many details in order to focus on the most important elements of a problem.

| MAP 1 | Detailed Road Map of Los Angeles |

SOURCE: © MCMLXXV by North American Maps, P.O. Box 5850, San Francisco, CA 94101.

to Wilshire Boulevard, and then head west again. The museum is on the right. Although we *might* find a shorter route by poring over the details in Map 1, most strangers to the city would prefer Map 2. With its guidance, they are likely to find the museum in a reasonable amount of time. Map 2 seems to *abstract* successfully from a lot of confusing details while retaining the essential aspects of the city's geography. Economic theories strive to do the same thing.

Map 3, which shows little more than the major interstate routes that pass through the greater Los Angeles area, illustrates a danger of which all theorists must beware. Armed only with the information provided on this map, you might never find your way to the art museum. Instead of a useful idealization of the Los Angeles road network, the map makers have produced a map that is oversimplified for our purpose. Too much has been assumed away. Of course, this map was never intended to be used as a detailed tourist guide, which brings us to an important point:

> There is no such thing as one "right" degree of abstraction for all analytic purposes. The proper degree of abstraction depends on the objective of the analysis. A model that is a gross oversimplification for one purpose may be needlessly complicated for another.

Economists are constantly treading the thin line between the concept illustrated in Map 2 and Map 3, between useful generalization about complex issues and gross distortions of the pertinent facts. How can they tell when they have abstracted from reality just enough? There is no objective answer to this question, which is why applied economics is as much art as science. One of the things distinguishing good economics from bad economics is the degree to which analysts are able to find the factors that constitute the equivalent of Map 2 (rather than Maps 1 or 3) for the problem at hand. It is not always easy to do.

For example, suppose you want to learn why different people have different incomes, why some are fabulously rich while others are abjectly poor. People differ in many ways, too many to enumerate, much less to study. The economist must ignore most of these details in order to focus on the important ones. The color of a person's hair or eyes is probably not important to the problem at hand, but the color of his or her skin certainly is. Height and weight may not matter, but education probably does. Proceeding in this way, we pare Map 1 down to the manageable dimensions of Map 2. But there is a danger of going too far, stripping away some of the crucial factors, and winding up with Map 3.

THE ROLE OF ECONOMIC THEORY

A person "can stare stupidly at phenomena; but in the absence of imagination they will not connect themselves together in any rational way." These words of the renowned American philosopher-scientist C. S. Peirce succinctly express the crucial role of theory in scientific inquiry. What do we mean by a theory?

To an economist or natural scientist, the word **theory** means something different from what it means in common parlance. In scientific usage, a theory is *not* an untested assertion of alleged fact. The statement that aspirin provides protection against heart attacks is not a theory; it is a *hypothesis*, which will prove to be true or false once the right sorts of experiments have been completed. Instead, a theory is a deliberate simplification (abstraction) of factual relationships that attempts to explain how those relationships work. It is an *explanation* of the mechanism behind observed phenomena. Thus, gravity forms the basis of theories that describe and explain the paths of the planets.

People who have never studied economics often draw a false distinction between *theory* and *practical policy*. Politicians and business people, in particular, often reject abstract economic theory as something that is best ignored by "practical" people. The irony of these statements is that:

> It is precisely the concern for policy that makes economic theory so necessary and important.

A **theory** is a deliberate simplification of relationships used to explain how those relationships work.

Major Los Angeles Arteries and Freeways | MAP 2 |

| MAP 3 | **Greater Los Angeles Freeways**

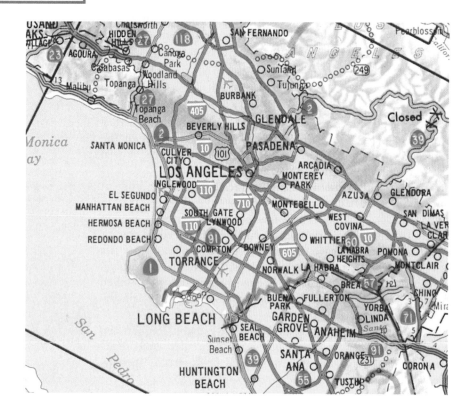

If we could not change the economy through public policy, economics could be a historical and descriptive discipline, asking, for example, how is it that industrial pollution got to be so serious in the 20th century. But deep concern about public policy forces economists to go beyond historical questions. To analyze policy options, they are forced to deal with *possibilities that have not actually occurred.*

For example, to determine what environmental programs will be most effective, they must understand how and why a market economy produces pollution and what might happen if government placed taxes on industrial waste discharges and automobile emissions. Such questions require some *theorizing,* not just examination of the facts, because we need to consider possibilities that never occurred.

Two variables are said to be **correlated** if they tend to go up or down together. But correlation need not imply causation.

The facts, moreover, can sometimes be highly misleading. Data often indicate that two variables move up and down together. But this statistical **correlation** does not prove that either variable *causes* the other. For example, when it rains people drive their cars more slowly, and there are also more traffic accidents. But this correlation does not mean that slow driving causes accidents. Rather, we understand that both phenomena are caused by a common underlying factor—more rain. How do we know this? Not just by looking at the correlation (the degree of similarity) between data on accidents and driving speeds. Data alone tell us little about cause and effect. We must use some simple *theory* as part of our analysis.

Similarly, most economic issues hinge on some question of cause and effect. So simply observing correlations in data is not enough. Only a combination of theoretical reasoning and data analysis can hope to provide useful answers. We must first proceed deductively from assumptions to conclusions and then test the conclusions against data. In that way, we may hope to understand *how,* if at all, different government policies will lead to a lower unemployment rate or *how* a tax on emissions will reduce pollution.

Statistical correlation need not imply causation. Some theory is usually needed to interpret data.

WHAT IS AN ECONOMIC MODEL?

An **economic model** is a representation of a theory or a part of a theory, often used to gain insight into cause and effect. The notion of a "model" is familiar enough to children; and economists—like other scientists—use the term in much the same way that children do.

A child's model automobile or airplane looks and operates much like the real thing, but it is much smaller and much simpler, and so it is easier to manipulate and understand. Engineers for General Motors and Boeing also build models of cars and planes. Although their models are far bigger and much more elaborate than a child's toy, they use them for much the same purposes: to observe the workings of these vehicles "up close," to experiment with them in order to see how they might behave under different circumstances. ("What happens if I do this?") From these experiments, they make educated guesses as to how the real-life version will perform.

Economists use models for similar purposes. The late A. W. Phillips, the famous engineer-turned-economist, was talented enough to construct a working model of the determination of national income in a simple economy by using colored water flowing through pipes. For years this contraption has graced the basement of the London School of Economics. While we will explain theories with words and diagrams later in the book, Phillips's engineering background enabled him to depict the theory with tubes, valves, and pumps. Most economists lack Phillips's manual dexterity, so economic models are generally built with paper and pencil (or a laptop) rather than with wrenches and screwdrivers.

Because many of the models used in this book are depicted in diagrams, we explain the construction and use of various types of graphs in the following chapter. But sometimes economic models are expressed only in words. The statement "Business firms produce the level of output that maximizes their profits" is the basis for a behavioral model whose consequences we explore in some detail in Parts II through V. Don't be put off by seemingly abstract models. Think of them as useful road maps. And remember how hard it would be to find your way around Los Angeles without one.

An **economic model** is a simplified, small-scale version of some aspect of the economy. Economic models are often expressed in equations, by graphs, or in words.

REASONS FOR DISAGREEMENTS: IMPERFECT INFORMATION AND VALUE JUDGMENTS

"If all the earth's economists were laid end to end, they could not reach an agreement," or so the saying goes. Politicians and reporters are fond of pointing out that economists can be found on both sides of many public policy issues. If economics is a science, why do economists quarrel so much? After all, astronomers do not debate whether the earth revolves around the sun or vice versa.

The question reflects a misunderstanding of the nature of science. Disputes are normal at the frontier of any science. For example, astronomers once did argue, and quite vociferously, over whether the earth revolves around the sun. Nowadays, they argue about black holes, gamma-ray bursts, young red supergiants, and other esoterica. These arguments go mostly unnoticed by the public because few of us understand what they are talking about. But economics is a *social* science, so its disputes are aired in public. All sorts of people are eager to join economic debates about inflation, pollution, poverty, and the like.

Furthermore, the fact is that economists agree on much more than is commonly supposed. Virtually all economists, regardless of their politics, agree that taxing polluters is one of the best ways to protect the environment (see Chapters 14 and 22), that rent controls can ruin a city (Chapter 5), and that free trade among nations is preferable to the erection of barriers through tariffs and quotas (see Chapter 23). The list could go on and on. It is probably true that the issues about which economists agree *far* exceed the subjects on which they disagree.

Finally, many disputes among economists are not scientific disputes at all. Sometimes the pertinent facts are simply unknown. For example, you will learn in Chapter 22 that the proper tax to levy on industrial emissions depends on quantitative estimates of the harm done by the pollutant. But, very often, good estimates of this damage are not yet available. For example, while there is reasonable scientific agreement that the earth is slowly warming, there are huge disagreements over how costly global warming may be and over whether human activities are the primary cause of the warming. Such disputes make it difficult to agree on a concrete policy proposal.

Another important source of disagreements is that economists, like other people, come in all political stripes: conservative, middle-of-the-road, liberal, radical. Each may have different values and different views of what constitutes a good society. So each may hold a different view of the "right" solution to a public policy problem, even if they agree on the underlying analysis. Here is an example:

In designing an income tax, society must decide how much of the burden to put on upper income taxpayers. Some people believe the rich should pay a disproportionate share of the taxes. Others disagree, arguing that it is fairer to levy the same income tax rate on everyone.

Economists cannot answer questions like these any more than nuclear physicists could have determined whether dropping the atomic bomb on Hiroshima was a good idea. The decisions rest on moral judgments about the importance of income inequality—judgments that can be made only by the citizenry through its elected officials.

> Although economic science can contribute the best theoretical and factual knowledge there is on a particular issue, the final decision on policy questions often rests either on information that is not currently available or on social values and ethical opinions about which people differ, or on both.

COMMON SENSE: USEFUL BUT DANGEROUS

Many people think sound economic decisions are just a matter of "common sense." If that were so—if untrained but intelligent observers could reach the right decisions using only their instincts and intuition—there would be little reason to study economics. Unfortunately, while common sense is invaluable, it is not always a reliable guide in economics.

True, there are many cases where it is not misleading. Most people undoubtedly realize, for example, that a surge in demand for a product is likely to raise its price, at least for a while. They also understand that increases in the prices of American goods will reduce the quantity we can export to foreign countries. Such simple precepts illustrate why much of economics is just systematized common sense.

But other economic relationships are counterintuitive. Try your intuition on this one. You own a widget manufacturing company that rents a warehouse. Your landlord raises your rent by $10,000 per year. Should you raise the price of your widgets to try to recoup some of your higher costs? Or should you lower your price to try to sell more and "spread your overhead?" We shall see in Chapter 8 that both answers are probably wrong!

We will explain many more counterintuitive economic relationships in this book. By the end, you will have a better sense of when common sense works and when it fails. And you will be able to recognize common fallacies that are all too often offered as pearls of wisdom by public figures, the press, and television commentators.

SUMMARY

1. To help you get the most out of your first course in economics, we have devised a list of nine important ideas that you will want to remember *Beyond the Final Exam*. Briefly, they are as follows:

   a. Opportunity cost is the correct measure of cost.

   b. Attempts to fight market forces often backfire.

   c. Nations can gain from trade by exploiting their comparative advantages.

   d. Both parties gain in a voluntary exchange.

   e. Good decisions typically require marginal analysis that weighs incremental costs against incremental benefits.

f. Externalities may cause the market mechanism to malfunction, but this defect can be repaired by market methods.

g. Personal services are subject to a cost disease that drives their prices inexorably higher.

h. There is a trade-off between efficiency and equality. Many policies that promote one damage the other.

i. In the long run, productivity is almost the only thing that matters for a society's material well-being.

2. Economics is a broad-ranging discipline that uses a variety of techniques and approaches to address important social questions.

3. Because of the great complexity of human behavior, economists are forced to *abstract* from many details, to make generalizations that they know are not quite true, and to organize what knowledge they have in terms of some theoretical structure called a "model."

4. *Correlation* need not imply causation.

5. Economists use simplified models to understand the real world and predict its behavior, much as a child uses a model railroad to learn how trains work.

6. Although these models, if skillfully constructed, can illuminate important economic problems, they rarely can answer the questions that confront policymakers. Value judgments are needed for this purpose, and the economist is no better equipped than anyone else to make them.

7. Common sense is often an unreliable guide to the right economic decision.

KEY TERMS

Opportunity cost   4

Comparative advantage   5

Voluntary exchange   5

Marginal analysis   6

Marginal costs   6

Externalities   6

Productivity   8

Abstraction and generalization   9

Theory   11

Correlation versus causation   12

Economic model   13

QUESTIONS FOR REVIEW

1. Think about how you would construct a *model* of how your college is governed. Which officers and administrators would you include and exclude from your model if the objective were one of the following:

    a. To explain how decisions on financial aid are made?

    b. To explain the quality of the faculty?

    Relate this to the map example in the chapter.

2. Relate the process of *abstraction* to the way you take notes in a lecture. Why do you not try to transcribe every word the lecturer utters? Why do you not just write down the title of the lecture and stop there? How do you decide, roughly speaking, on the correct amount of detail?

3. Explain why a government policymaker cannot afford to ignore economic theory.

**Everything should be made as simple as possible,
but not more so.**

Albert Einstein

THE USE AND MISUSE OF GRAPHS[1]

In Chapter 1, we noted that economists often explain and analyze their models with the help of graphs. This book is full of them. But that is not the only reason for you to study how they work. Most of you will deal with graphs in the future, perhaps frequently. You will see them in newspapers. If you become a doctor you will use graphs to keep track of patients' progress. If you take a job in government, you may use them to keep track of the amount of money that the United States owes to foreign countries. If you join a business firm, you will use them to check profit and sales performance at a glance. If you work in a nonprofit enterprise concerned with social issues, you may use them to examine trends in ethnic composition of cities or to relate the occurrence of felonies to family income.

This chapter will introduce you to some of the techniques of graphic analysis—tools you will use throughout the book and, more important, very likely throughout your working career. Then, in the second part of the chapter, we examine some pitfalls in graphic analysis—common ways in which graphs can be misleading if not drawn and interpreted with care.

---

[1] Students who have a nodding acquaintance with geometry and feel quite comfortable with graphs can safely skip the first part of this chapter and proceed directly to the second part, which begins on page 23.

■ GRAPHS USED IN ECONOMIC ANALYSIS

Economic graphs are invaluable because they can display a large quantity of data quickly and because they facilitate data interpretation and analysis. They enable the eye to take in at a glance important statistical relationships that would be far less apparent from written descriptions or long lists of numbers. But badly constructed graphs can confuse and mislead.[2]

Puzzle: What's Wrong with This Graph?

This figure, which will be explained fully later in this chapter, appears to show that the U.S. economy suffered a catastrophe between 1990 and 1992. From the looks of the graph, in those two years unemployment literally exploded. It suggests that between the beginning and end of the period portrayed, the percent of American workers who were jobless rose about fivefold. We will see later that actual

developments in the labor force were not nearly so serious. The impression that the economy was collapsing is only the result of the

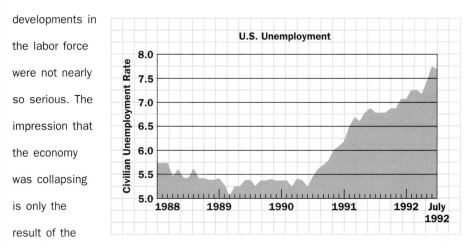

sloppy way the graph was drawn in the publication in which it appeared. This is important because it is not an isolated misuse of graphics. In fact, *most* newspapers and magazines frequently distort statistics in just this way.

TWO-VARIABLE DIAGRAMS

Much of the economic analysis found in this and other books requires that we keep track of two **variables** simultaneously. For example, in studying how markets operate, we will want to keep one eye on the *price* of a commodity and the other on the *quantity* of that commodity that is bought and sold.

For this reason, economists frequently find it useful to display real or imaginary figures in a *two-dimensional graph*, which simultaneously represents the behavior of two economic variables. The numerical value of one variable is measured along the horizontal line at the bottom of the graph (called the *horizontal axis*), starting from the **origin** (the point labeled "0"), and the numerical value of the other is measured up the vertical line on the left side of the graph (called the *vertical* axis), also starting from the origin.

Figures 2–1(a) and 2–1(b) are typical graphs of economic analysis. They depict an imaginary *demand curve*, represented by the red dots in Figure 2–1(a) and the

A **variable** is something measured by a number; it is used to analyze what happens to other things when the size of that number changes (varies).

The "0" point in the lower left-hand corner of a graph where the axes meet is called the **origin.** Both variables are equal to zero at the origin.

---

[2] An interesting and informative book on the subject is called *How to Lie with Statistics* by Darrell Huff and Irving Geis (New York: Norton, 1954).

A Hypothetical Demand Curve for Natural Gas in St. Louis   FIGURE 2-1

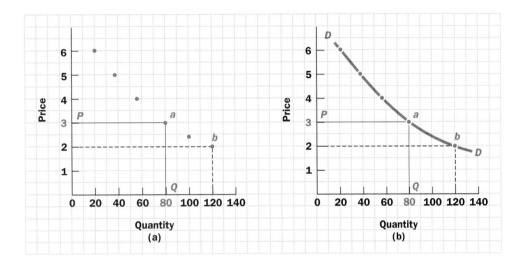

NOTE: Price is dollars per thousand cubic feet; quantity is in billions of cubic feet per year.

heavy red line in Figure 2–1(b). The graphs show the price of natural gas on their vertical axes and the quantity of gas people want to buy at each price on the horizontal axes. The dots in Figure 2–1(a) are connected by the continuous red curve labeled *DD* in Figure 2–1(b).

Economic diagrams are generally read just as one would read latitudes and longitudes on a map. On the demand curve in Figure 2–1, the point marked *a* represents a hypothetical combination of price and quantity of natural gas demanded by customers in St. Louis. By drawing a horizontal line leftward from that point to the vertical axis, we learn that the average price for gas in St. Louis is $3 per thousand cubic feet. By dropping a line straight down to the horizontal axis, we find that consumers want 80 billion cubic feet per year at this price, just as the statistics in Table 2–1 show. The other points on the graph give similar information. For example, point *b* indicates that if natural gas in St. Louis costs only $2 per thousand cubic feet, quantity demanded would be higher—it would reach 120 billion cubic feet per year.

Quantities of Natural Gas Demanded at Various Prices   TABLE 2-1

Price (per thousand cubic feet)	$2	$3	$4	$5	$6
Quantity demanded (billions of cubic feet per year)	120	80	56	38	20

Notice that information about price and quantity is *all* we can learn from the diagram. The demand curve will not tell us what kinds of people live in St. Louis, the size of their homes, or the condition of their furnaces. It tells us about the quantity demanded at each possible price—no more, no less. Specifically, it tells us that when price declines, consumers increase the amount of natural gas that they are willing and able to buy.

A diagram abstracts from many details, some of which may be quite interesting, in order to focus on the two variables of primary interest—in this case, the price of natural gas and the amount of gas that is demanded at each price. All the diagrams used in this book share this basic feature. They cannot tell the reader the "whole story," any more than a map's latitude and longitude figures for a particular city can make someone an authority on that city.

THE DEFINITION AND MEASUREMENT OF SLOPE

One of the most important features of economic diagrams is the rate at which the line or curve being sketched runs uphill or downhill as we move to the right. The demand curve in Figure 2–1 clearly slopes downhill (the price falls) as we follow it to the right (that is, as consumers demand more gas). In such instances we say that *the curve has a negative slope, or is negatively sloped, because one variable falls as the other one rises.*

> The *slope of a straight line* is the ratio of the vertical change to the corresponding horizontal change as we move to the right along the line or, as it is often said, the ratio of the "rise" over the "run."

The four panels of Figure 2–2 show all the possible slopes for a straight-line relationship between two unnamed variables called Y (measured along the vertical axis) and X (measured along the horizontal axis). Figure 2–2(a) shows a negative slope, much like our demand curve. Figure 2–2(b) shows a positive slope, because variable Y rises (we go uphill) as variable X rises (as we move to the right). Figure 2–2(c) shows a *zero* slope, where the value of Y is the same irrespective of the value of X. Figure 2–2(d) shows an *infinite* slope, meaning that the value of X is the same irrespective of the value of Y.

| FIGURE 2-2 | **Different Types of Slope of a Straight-Line Graph** |

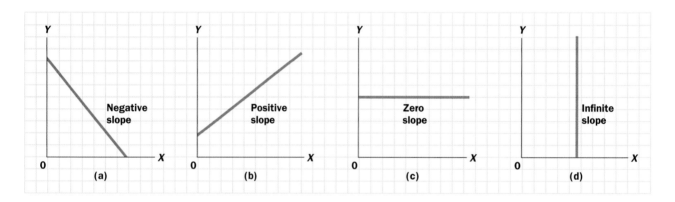

Slope is a numerical concept, not just a qualitative one. The two panels of Figure 2–3 show two positively sloped straight lines with different slopes. The line in Figure 2–3(b) is clearly steeper. But by how much? The labels should help you compute

| FIGURE 2-3 | **How to Measure Slope** |

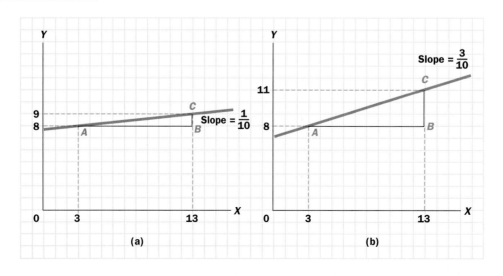

the answer. In Figure 2–3(a) a horizontal movement, *AB*, of 10 units (13 − 3) corresponds to a vertical movement, *BC*, of 1 unit (9 − 8). So the slope is *BC/AB* = 1/10. In Figure 2–3(b), the same horizontal movement of 10 units corresponds to a vertical movement of 3 units (11 − 8). So the slope is 3/10, which is larger—the rise divided by the run is greater than in Figure 2–3 (b)

By definition, the slope of any particular straight line remains the same, no matter where on that line we choose to measure it. That is why we can pick any horizontal distance, *AB*, and the corresponding slope triangle, *ABC*, to measure slope. But this is not true of curved lines.

Curved lines also have slopes, but the numerical value of the slope differs at every point along the curve as we move from left to right.

The four panels of Figure 2–4 provide some examples of *slopes of curved lines*. The curve in Figure 2–4(a) has a negative slope everywhere, while the curve in Figure 2–4(b) has a positive slope everywhere. But these are not the only possibilities. In Figure 2–4(c) we encounter a curve that has a positive slope at first but a negative slope later on. Figure 2–4(d) shows the opposite case: a negative slope followed by a positive slope.

The **tangent** to a curve at some point, *Z*, on that curve is a straight line that touches point *Z* but does not cross the curve at that point.

Behavior of Slopes in Curved Graphs

FIGURE 2–4

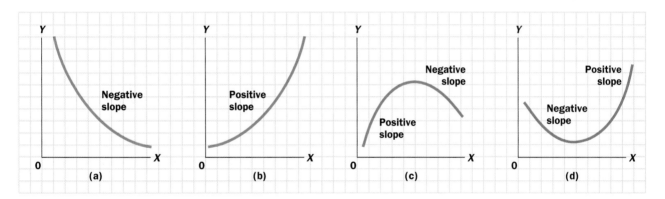

We can measure the slope of a smooth curved line numerically *at any particular point* by drawing a *straight* line that *touches*, but does not *cut*, the curve at the point in question. Such a line is called a **tangent** to the curve.

The slope of a curved line at a particular point is defined as the slope of the straight line that is tangent to the curve at that point.

FIGURE 2–5

How to Measure Slope at a Point on a Curved Graph

Figure 2–5 shows tangents to the red curve at two points. Line *tt* is tangent at point *T*, and line *rr* is tangent at point *R*. We can measure the slope of the curve at these two points by applying the definition. The calculation for point *T*, then, is the following:

$$\text{Slope at point } T = \text{Slope of line } tt = \frac{(\text{Distance } BC)}{(\text{Distance } BA)}$$

$$= \frac{(1 - 5)}{(3 - 1)} = \frac{-4}{2} = -2.$$

A similar calculation yields the slope of the curve at point *R*, which, as we can see from Figure 2–5, must be smaller numerically; that is, the tangent line *rr* is less steep than line *tt*:

$$\text{Slope at point } R = \text{Slope of line } rr$$

$$= \frac{(5 - 7)}{(8 - 6)} = \frac{-2}{2} = -1.$$

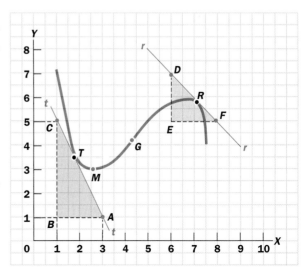

EXERCISE Show that the slope of the curve at point G is about 1.

What would happen if we tried to apply this graphical technique to the high point in Figure 2–4(c) or to the low point in Figure 2–4(d)? Take a ruler and try it. The tangents that you construct should be horizontal, meaning that they should have a slope exactly equal to zero. It is always true that where the slope of a smooth curve changes from positive to negative, or vice versa, there will be at least one point whose slope is zero.

> Curves shaped like hills, such as Figure 2–4(c), have a zero slope at their *highest* point. Curves shaped like valleys, such as Figure 2–4(d), have a zero slope at their *lowest* point.

RAYS THROUGH THE ORIGIN AND 45° LINES

The point at which a straight line cuts the vertical (Y) axis is called the *Y-intercept*. For example, the *Y*-intercept of the line in Figure 2–3(a) is a bit less than 8.

> Lines whose *Y*-intercept is zero have so many special uses in economics and other disciplines that they have been given a special name: a **ray through the origin**, or **a ray**.

Figure 2–6 shows three rays through the origin, and the slope of each is indicated in the diagram. The ray in the center (whose slope is 1) is particularly useful in many economic applications because it marks points where X and Y are equal (as long as X and Y are measured in the same units). For example, at point A we have $X = 3$ and $Y = 3$; at point B, $X = 4$ and $Y = 4$. A similar relation holds at any other point on that ray.

How do we know that this is always true for a ray whose slope is 1? If we start from the origin (where both X and Y are zero) and the slope of the ray is 1, we know from the definition of slope that:

$$\text{Slope} = \frac{\text{Vertical change}}{\text{Horizontal change}} = 1$$

This implies that the vertical change and the horizontal change are always equal, so the two variables must always remain equal. Any point along that ray (for example, point A) is exactly equal in distance from the horizontal and vertical axes (length DA = length CA)—the number on the X-axis (the abscissa) will be the same as the number on the Y-axis (the ordinate).

> Rays through the origin with a slope of 1 are called **45° lines** because they form an angle of 45° with the horizontal axis. A 45° line marks off points where the variables measured on each axis have equal values.[3]

If a point representing some data is above the 45° line, we know that the value of Y exceeds the value of X. Conversely, whenever we find a point below the 45° line, we know that X is larger than Y.

SQUEEZING THREE DIMENSIONS INTO TWO: CONTOUR MAPS

Sometimes problems involve more than two variables, so two dimensions just are not enough. This is unfortunate, because the surface of a sheet of paper is only two-dimensional. When we study a business firm's decision-making process, for example, we may want to keep track simultaneously of three variables: how much labor it employs, how much raw material it imports from foreign countries, and how much output it creates.

FIGURE 2–6

Rays through the Origin

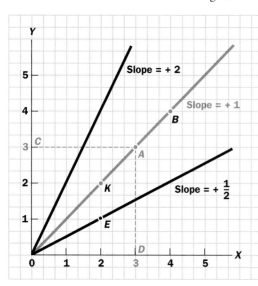

A **45° line** is a **ray through the origin** with a slope of +1. It marks off points where the variables measured on each axis have equal values (assuming both variables are measured in the same units).

A **production indifference map** is a graph whose axes show the quantities of two inputs that are used to produce some output. A curve in the graph corresponds to some given quantity of that output, and the different points on that curve show the different quantities of the two inputs that are enough to produce the given output.

---

[3] The definition assumes that both variables are measured in the same units.

Luckily, economists can use a well-known device for collapsing three dimensions into two, namely a *contour map*. Figure 2–7 is a contour map of the summit of Mt. Everest on the border of Nepal and Tibet. On some of the irregularly shaped "rings" on this map, we find numbers (like 8500) indicating the height (in meters) above sea level at that particular spot on the mountain. Thus, unlike the more usual sort of map, which gives only latitudes and longitudes, this contour map (also called a topographical map) exhibits *three* pieces of information about each point: latitude, longitude, and altitude.

A Geographic Contour Map

FIGURE 2-7

SOURCE: Mount Everest. Alpenvereinskarte. Vienna: Kartographische Anstalt Freytag-Berndt und Artaria, 1957, 1988.

Figure 2–8 looks more like the contour maps encountered in economics. It shows how some third variable, called *Z* (think of it as a firm's output, for example), varies as we change either variable *X* (think of it as a firm's employment) or variable *Y* (think of it as the use of imported raw material). Just like the map of Mt. Owen, any point on the diagram conveys three pieces of data. At point *A*, we can read off the values of *X* and *Y* in the conventional way (*X* is 30 and *Y* is 40), and we can also note the value of *Z* by checking to see on which contour line point *A* falls. (It is on the *Z* = 20 contour.) So point *A* is able to tell us that 30 hours of labor and 40 yards of cloth produce 20 units of output per day. The contour line that indicates 20 units of output shows the various combinations of labor and cloth a manufacturer can use to produce 20 units of output. Economists call such maps **production indifference maps.**

FIGURE 2-8

An Economic Contour Map

Although most of the analyses presented in this book rely on the simpler two-variable diagrams, contour maps will find their applications, especially in the appendixes to Chapters 6 and 8.

PERILS IN THE INTERPRETATION OF GRAPHS

The preceding materials contain just about all you will need in order to understand the simple graphics used in our economic models. We turn now to the second objective of this chapter: to show how statistical data are portrayed on graphs and some of the pitfalls to watch for.

THE INTERPRETATION OF GROWTH TRENDS

Probably the most common form of graph in empirical economics is a year-by-year (or perhaps a month-by-month) depiction of the behavior of some economic variable—the profits of a particular corporation, its annual sales to foreign customers, the number of persons unemployed in the U.S. economy, or some measure of consumer prices. They are called **time-series graphs** and you will find them in newspapers and magazines as well as in this book.

By summarizing an immense amount of data in compact and easily understandable form, time-series graphs can be invaluable, offering an instant visual grasp of trends. But if misused, they can be dangerous. Consider Figure 2–9 as an example. It shows gross domestic product (GDP) in the United States since 1959 and seems to show that the country has grown richer at an enormous rate, increasing to about 18 times its 1959 level in four decades.

A **time-series graph** is a type of two-variable diagram in which time is the variable measured along the horizontal axis. It shows how some variable changed as time passed.

| FIGURE 2-9 | **The GDP of the United States, 1959–1999** |

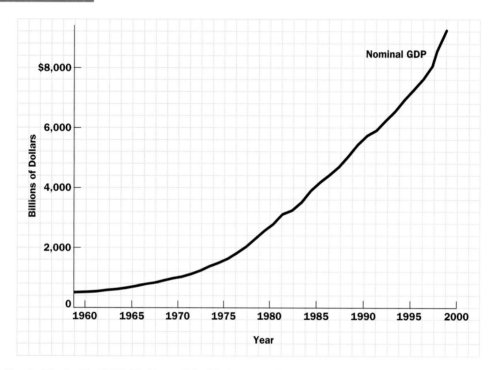

SOURCE: *Economic Report of the President* 2000 (Washington, D.C.: U.S. Government Printing Office, 2000).

However, this graph can easily mislead persons who are not experienced in dealing with such graphs. Perhaps even more dangerous are the lies perpetrated accidentally and unintentionally by people who draw graphs without sufficient care and who may innocently mislead themselves as well as their readers. Most of the spectacular GDP growth over this period is attributable to two mundane influences: inflation and population growth. First, the price of almost everything rose substantially since 1959 because of **inflation.** On average, prices in 1999 were almost five times as large as in 1959. Since each dollar in 1999 bought about one-fifth what it did in 1959, the dollar makes a rather poor measuring stick for comparison of production in the two years. Most of the apparent growth in "output" suggested in Figure 2–9 is really the result of higher prices, not greater production.

Inflation refers to a sustained increase in the average level of prices.

Economists correct for inflation by a process called *deflating by a price index*. Proper deflation changes our original black GDP line to the lower blue line in Figure 2–10, which shows the real growth of *GDP in dollars of constant purchasing power.* Economists call this **real GDP.** By this more informative measure, we find that output in 1999 was nearly *four* times as high as in 1959, not 18 times as high.

Real GDP is the value of all the goods and services produced by an economy in a year, evaluated in dollars of constant purchasing power. Hence, inflation does not raise real GDP.

Nominal GDP, Real GDP, and Real GDP per Capita Since 1959

FIGURE 2-10

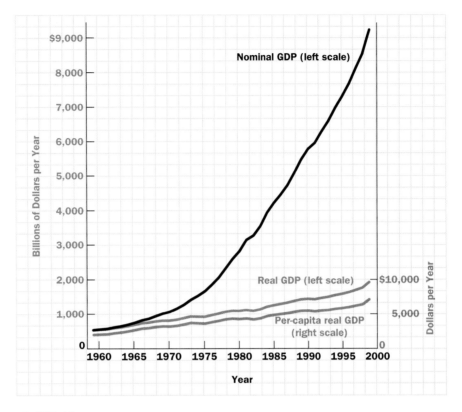

NOTE: Real GDP figures are in 1959 dollars.

SOURCE: *Economic Report of the President* 2000 (Washington, D.C.: U.S. Government Printing Office, 2000).

Second, there were many more Americans alive in 1999 than in 1959—54 percent more, to be exact. So GDP *per person* (economists usually refer to it as "per capita") rose by considerably less than even the blue line in Figure 2–10 indicates. The red line corrects *both* for inflation *and* for population growth by charting the time-series behavior of *GDP per capita* in dollars of constant purchasing power. Americans were indeed richer in 1999 than in 1959, but not nearly by as much as a naive look at Figure 2–9 may suggest. In fact, the American standard of living increased about two and a half times over this period; it did *not* rise eighteenfold, or even fourfold. This shows how misleading it can be simply to "look at the facts." The general conclusion is:

> The facts, as portrayed in a time-series graph almost never "speak for themselves." Because almost everything grows in a growing economy, one must use good judgment and make corrections before drawing conclusions about growth trends. It is often necessary to correct for rising prices or population growth or for other distorting and misleading influences.

DISTORTING TRENDS BY CHOICE OF THE TIME PERIOD

In addition to possible misinterpretations of growth trends, users of statistical data must guard against distortions of trends caused by unskillfully chosen (or unscrupulously chosen) first and last time periods (in other words, starting and end points) for the graph. This is best explained by an example.

Figure 2–11 shows the behavior of average stock market prices from January 1966 to June 1982. The figures have been corrected

"Dow Jonesy enough for you?"

FIGURE 2-11	**Stock Prices, January 1966 to June 1982**

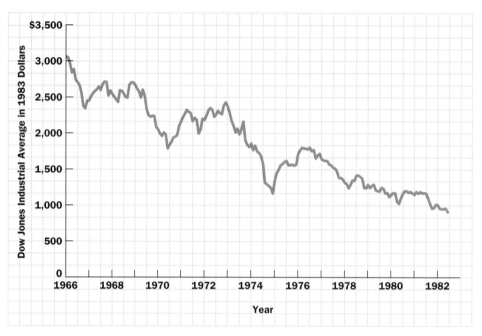

SOURCE: *Economic Report of the President* (Washington, D.C.: U.S. Government Printing Office, various years).

FIGURE 2-12

Stock Prices, January 1993 to January 1998

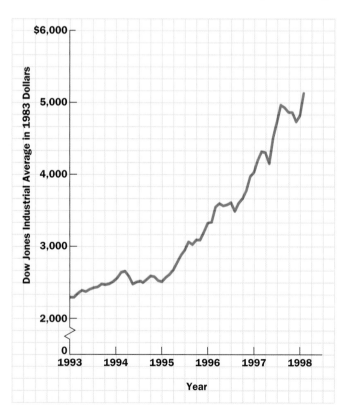

SOURCE: *Economic Report of the President* (Washington, D.C.: U.S. Government Printing Office, various years).

for inflation; that is, they are expressed in dollars of unchanging purchasing power. The graph displays a clear downhill movement that would suggest to anyone who does not have other information that stocks are a terrible investment.

However, an unscrupulous seller of stocks could use the same set of stock market statistics to tell exactly the opposite story by carefully selecting another group of years. Figure 2–12 shows the behavior of average stock prices from January 1993 to January 1998. The size of the increase is quite dramatic. Stocks now look like a rather good investment.

However, a much longer and less-biased choice of period (1925–1999) gives a less distorted picture (Figure 2–13). It indicates that investments in stocks are sometimes profitable and other times unprofitable.

Careful readers of economic data must constantly watch for deliberate or inadvertent distortion resulting from an unfortunate or unscrupulous choice of time period for a graph.

No rules can give absolute protection from this difficulty, but several precautions can be helpful:

- Make sure the first date shown on the graph is not an exceptionally high or low point. In comparison with 1966, a year of unusually high stock market prices, the years immediately following are bound to give the impression of a downward trend.

- For the same reason, make sure the graph does not end in a year that is extraordinarily high or low (although this may be unavoidable if the graph simply ends with figures that are as up-to-date as possible).

- Make sure that (in the absence of some special justification) the graph does not depict only a very brief period, which can easily be atypical.

Full History of Stock Prices, Corrected for Inflation, 1925–1999

FIGURE 2-13

SOURCES: *The Dow Jones Averages, 1885–1985* (centennial edition), ed. Phyllis S. Pierce (Homewood, Ill.: Dow Jones-Irwin, 1986); *Citibase*; U.S. Department of Commerce, Census Bureau, *Historical Statistics of the United States* (Washington, D.C: U.S. Government Printing Office, 1975); and *Economic Report of the President* (Washington, D.C.: U.S. Government Printing Office, various years).

Dangers of Omitting the Origin: The Puzzle Solved

Frequently, the value of an economic variable described by a graph does not fall anywhere near zero during the time period under consideration. For example, between 1988 and 1992 the civilian unemployment rate never fell below 5 percent. This means that a time-series graph showing unemployment over time would have a lot of wasted space between the horizontal axis (where the unemployment rate is zero) and the level of the graph representing 5 percent. There would simply be no data points to plot in that range. It is therefore tempting to *eliminate* this wasted space by beginning the graph at 5 percent, as the magazine *The International Economy* did when it published Figure 2–14 in 1992. This is the graph with which the chapter began, the one that suggests that between 1990 and 1992 unemployment in the United States exploded, increasing more than 700 percent. We will see that the actual rise was much smaller than that. It will be recalled that our puzzle question was: What is wrong with the drawing? The answer is: Nothing—so long as you read it carefully. But a *hasty* glance vastly exaggerates the rise in unemployment. Figure 2–14 makes it look like the United States experienced an economic catastrophe from 1990 to 1992. A less misleading graph, which includes the origin as well as all the "wasted space" in between, appears as Figure 2–15. Note how this alternative presentation gives a dramatically different visual impression. Although the rise in unemployment was distressingly large, it was not nearly so enormous as the previous graph suggested. It rose less than 50 percent, certainly not nearly the 700 percent that the previous figure suggests.

FIGURE 2-14

A Graph Distorted by Omission of the Origin

SOURCE: *The International Economy*, September/October 1992, p. 10.

Why does the actual percentage change appear to be so much smaller in Figure 2–15 than in the previous graph? The answer is that the level of unemployment at the starting point of the graph (1988) was not nearly as low as it appears to have been in Figure 2–14. Omission of the "wasted space" in the graph creates the illusion that the starting point was very low and therefore exaggerates any change in the graph. In Figure 2–15, with the zero point restored, the changes look much less dramatic. (It's like comparing a two-inch spurt of growth in an infant with a two-inch growth spurt in a tall teenager—the baby's starting point is very low, so two inches is a big change, but the teenager's starting point is much higher so the two-inch change is less dramatic.)

Omitting the origin in a graph is dangerous because it exaggerates the magnitudes of the percentage changes that have taken place.

Of course, sometimes it's true that the inclusion of the origin would waste so much space that it is undesirable to include it. In that case, a good practice is to put a clear warning on the graph to remind the reader that this has been done. Figure 2–16 shows one way to do so.

UNRELIABILITY OF STEEPNESS AND CHOICE OF UNITS

The last problem we will consider has consequences similar to the one we have just discussed. We can never trust the impression we get from the steepness of an economic graph. A graph of stock market prices that moves uphill sharply (has a large

FIGURE 2-15

The Same Graph as Figure 2–14 with Origin Point Included

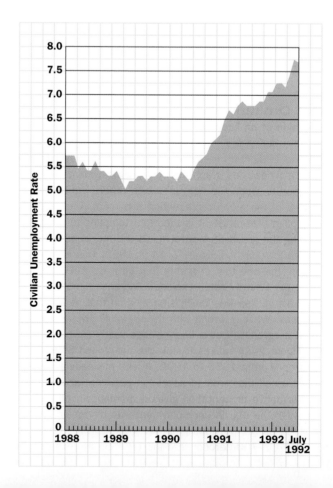

positive slope) appears to suggest that prices are rising rapidly, whereas another graph in which the rate of climb is much slower seems to imply that prices are going up sluggishly. Yet, depending on how one draws the graph, exactly the same statistics can produce a graph that is rising very quickly or very slowly.

This possibility arises because there is no universal, fixed unit of measurement in economics. Hamburger sales can be measured in number of burgers or in pounds of beef. Coal production can be measured in hundredweight (hundreds of pounds) or in tons. Prices can be measured in cents or in dollars or in millions of dollars. Time can be measured in days or in months or in years. Any of these choices is perfectly legitimate, but that choice makes all the difference in the world to the *speed* at which a graph using the resulting figures rises or falls.

An example will bring out the point. Suppose that we have the following (imaginary) data on sales of hamburgers by Daniel's Hamburger House, measuring sales by the number of quarter-pounders purchased and by the amount of beef bought:

The Same Graph as Figure 2–14 with a Warning Break

Month	Hamburgers Purchased	Pounds of Beef Purchased
January	1,000	250
February	1,100	275

Look at Figures 2–17(a) and 2–17(b), one graph showing the data in number of hamburgers and the other showing the data counted in pounds of beef. The line in Figure 2–17(a) seems to suggest that business is rising quite sharply. But in Figure 2–17(b), because a sales increase of 100 quarter-pound hamburgers is the same as a sales increase of 25 pounds of beef, the rise in sales looks much more modest, even though both graphs really give the same information.

Unfortunately, we cannot solve the problem by agreeing always to stick to the same measurement units. Pounds may be the right unit for measuring demand for beef, but they will not do in measuring demand for cloth or for coal. A penny may be the right monetary unit for postage stamps, but it is not a very convenient unit for the cost of airplanes or automobiles.

Slope Depends on Units of Measurement

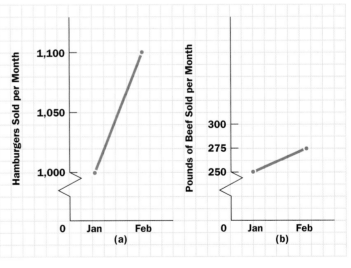

A change in units of measurement stretches or compresses the axis on which the information is represented, which automatically changes the slope of a graph. Therefore, we must never place much faith in the apparent implications of the slope of an ordinary graph in economics.

Later, in Chapter 7 on demand analysis, we will encounter a useful approach economists have adopted to deal with this problem. Instead of calculating changes in "absolute" terms—like pounds of beef or billions of dollars—economists use *percentage* increases as their common units. By using percentages rather than absolute figures, the problem can be avoided. The reason is simple. If we look at our hypothetical hamburger sales figures again, we see that no matter whether we measure the increase in output from January to February in hamburgers (from 1,000 to 1,100) or in pounds of beef (from 250 to 275), the *percentage* increase is the same. 100 is 10 percent of 1,000, and 25 is 10 percent of 250. Since a change in units affects both the numbers *proportionately*, the result is a washout—it does nothing to the percentage calculation and thus does not distort the figure.

1. Because graphs are used so often to portray economic models, it is important for students to acquire some understanding of their construction and use. Fortunately, the graphics used in economics are usually not very complex.

2. Most economic models are depicted in *two-variable diagrams*. We read data from these diagrams just as we read the latitude and longitude on a map: each point represents the values of two *variables* at the same time.

3. In some instances, three variables must be shown at once. In these cases, economists use contour maps, which, as the name suggests, show "latitude," "longitude," and "altitude" all at the same time.

4. Often, the most important property of a line or curve drawn on a diagram will be its slope, which is defined as the ratio of the "rise" over the "run," or the vertical change divided by the horizontal change. Curves that go uphill as we move to the right have *positive slopes*; curves that go downhill have *negative slopes*.

5. By definition, a *straight line* has the same *slope* wherever we choose to measure it. The *slope of a curved line* changes, but the

slope at any point on the curve can be calculated by measuring the slope of a straight line *tangent to the curve* at that point.

6. A *time-series graph* is a particular type of two-variable diagram that is useful in depicting statistical data. Time is measured along the horizontal axis, and some variable of interest is measured along the vertical axis.

7. Although time-series graphs are invaluable in helping us condense a great deal of information in a single picture, they can be quite misleading if they are not drawn and interpreted with care. For example, growth trends can be exaggerated by an inappropriate choice of units of measurement or by a failure to correct for some obvious source of growth (such as rising population). Omitting the origin can make the ups and downs in a time series appear much more extreme than they actually are. Or, by a clever choice of the starting and ending points for the graphs, the same data can be made to tell very different stories. Readers of such graphs—and this includes anyone who ever reads a newspaper—must be on guard for problems like these or they may find themselves misled by "the facts."

Variable   18

Two-variable diagram   18

Horizontal and vertical axes   18

Origin (of a graph)   18

Slope of a straight (or curved) line   20

Negative, positive, zero, and infinite slope   20

Tangent to a curve   21

Y-intercept   22

Ray through the origin, or ray   22

45° line   22

Contour map   23

Production indifference map   23

Time-series graph   24

Inflation   24

Deflating by a price index   24

Real GDP   24

1. Look for a graph in your local newspaper, on the financial page or elsewhere. What does the graph try to show? Is someone trying to convince you of something with this graph? Check to see if the graph is distorted in any of the ways mentioned in this chapter.

2. Portray the following hypothetical data on a two-variable diagram:

Academic Year	Total Enrollment	Enrollment in Economics Courses
1994–1995	3,000	300
1995–1996	3,100	325
1996–1997	3,200	350
1997–1998	3,300	375
1998–1999	3,400	400

Measure the slope of the resulting line, and explain what this number means.

3. From Figure 2–5, calculate the slope of the curve at point *M*.

4. Colin believes that the number of job offers he will get depends on the number of courses in which his grade is B+

or better. He concludes from observation that the following figures are typical:

Number of grades of B+ or better	0	1	2	3	4
Number of job offers	1	3	4	5	6

Put these numbers into a graph like Figure 2–1a. Measure and interpret the slopes between adjacent dots.

5. In Figure 2–6, determine the values of *X* and *Y* at point *K* and at point *E*. What do you conclude?

6. In Figure 2–8, interpret the economic meaning of points *A* and *B*. What do the two points have in common? What is the difference in their economic interpretation?

7. Suppose that between 1998 and 1999 expenditures on dog food rose from $35 million to $70 million and the price of dog food doubled. What do these facts imply about the popularity of dog food?

8. Suppose that between 1990 and 1999 the U.S. population went up 10 percent and that the number of silk neckties imported from Thailand rose from 3,000,000 to 3,100,000. What do these facts imply about the growth in popularity of Thai ties?

E pluribus unum (Out of many, one)

Motto on U.S. currency

THE ECONOMY: MYTH AND REALITY

This chapter introduces you to the U.S. economy and its role in the world. It may seem that no such introduction is necessary, for you have probably lived your entire life in the United States. Every time you work at a summer or part-time job, pay your college bills, or buy a slice of pizza, you not only participate in the American economy; you also observe something about it.

But the casual impressions we acquire in our everyday lives, though sometimes correct, are often misleading. Experience shows that most Americans—not just students—either are unaware of or harbor grave misconceptions about some of the most basic economic facts. One popular myth holds that the United States is inundated with imported goods, mostly from Japan. Another is that business profits account for something like a third of the price we pay for a typical good or service. Also, "everyone knows" that federal government jobs have grown rapidly over the past few decades. In fact, none of these things is true.

So, before we begin to study elaborate theories about how the economy works, it is useful to get a more *accurate* picture of our economy as it really is.

■ THE AMERICAN ECONOMY: A THUMBNAIL SKETCH

The U.S. economy is the biggest national economy on earth, for two very different reasons. First, there are a lot of us. The population of the United States is more than 275 million—making it the third most populous nation on earth after China (1.2 billion) and India (969 million). That vast total includes children, retirees, full-time students, institutionalized people, and the unemployed, none of whom produce much output. But the *working population* of the United States numbers about 134 million. As long as they are reasonably productive, that many people are bound to produce vast amounts of goods and services. And they do.

But population is not the main reason why the U.S. economy is by far the world's biggest. After all, India has about three and one-half times the population of the United States, but its economy is considerably smaller than that of the state of Texas. The second reason why the U.S. economy is so large is that we are a very rich country. Because American workers are among the most productive in the world, our economy produces over $30,000 worth of goods and services for every living American. If each of the 50 states was a separate country, California would be the eighth largest national economy on earth!

Inputs or **factors of production** are the labor, machinery, buildings, and natural resources used to make outputs.

Outputs are the goods and services that consumers want to acquire.

Why are some countries (like the United States) so rich and others (like India) so poor? That is a central question facing economists. It is useful to think of an economic system as a machine that takes **inputs,** such as labor and other things we call **factors of production,** and transforms them into **outputs,** or the things people want to consume. The American economic machine performs this task with extraordinary efficiency, whereas the Indian machine runs quite inefficiently. Learning why is one of the chief reasons to study economics.

Thus, what makes the American economy the center of world attention is our unique combination of prosperity and population. There are other rich countries in the world, like Germany and Switzerland, and there are other countries with huge populations, like China and India. But no nation combines a huge population with high per-capita income the way the United States does. Japan, with an economy less than half the size of ours, is the only nation that comes close.

Although the United States is a rich and populous country, the 50 states certainly were not created equal. Population density varies enormously—from a high of nearly 1,100 people per square mile in crowded New Jersey to a low of just one person per square mile in Alaska. Income variations are much less pronounced. But, still, the average income in Mississippi is only about half that in Connecticut.

A PRIVATE-ENTERPRISE ECONOMY

Part of the secret of America's economic success is that free markets and private enterprise have flourished here. These days more than ever, private enterprise and capitalism are the rule, not the exception, around the globe. But the United States has taken the idea of the free market further than almost any other country. It remains "the land of opportunity."

Every country has a mixture of public and private ownership of property. Even in the darkest days of communism, Russians owned their own personal possessions. In our country, the post office and the electricity-producing Tennessee Valley Authority are enterprises of the federal government, and many cities and states own and operate mass transit facilities and sports stadiums. But the United States stands out among the world's nations as one of the most "privatized." Few industrial assets are publicly owned in the United States. Even many city bus companies, and almost all utilities (such as electricity, gas, and telephones), are run as private companies in the United States; in Europe, they are more often government enterprises, though there is a substantial move toward transfer of government firms to private ownership.

Gross domestic product (GDP) is a measure of the size of the economy or, rather, of the total amount it produces. It is, roughly speaking, the money value of all the goods and services produced in a year.

The United States also has one of the most "marketized" economies on earth. The standard measure of the total output of an economy is called **gross domestic product (or GDP),** a term which appears frequently in the news. The share of GDP

● **THE U.S. SHARE OF WORLD GDP—IT'S NICE TO BE RICH**

The 6 billion people of the world produced approximately $31 trillion worth of goods and services in 1997. The United States, with only 4.6 percent of that population, turned out nearly 27 percent of total output, or almost six times the average share. As the accompanying graph shows, the United States is still the leader in goods and services, with over $30,000 worth of GDP produced per person, or per capita. Just seven major industrial economies (the United States, Japan, Germany, France, Italy, the United Kingdom, and Canada—which account for 12 percent of global population) generated 44 percent of world output and exported 48 percent of total exports.

SOURCE: International Monetary Fund, *World Economic Outlook, May 1998* (Washington, D.C., 1998).

"And may we continue to be worthy of consuming a disproportionate share of this planet's resources."

1998 GDP per Capita in 10 Industrial Countries

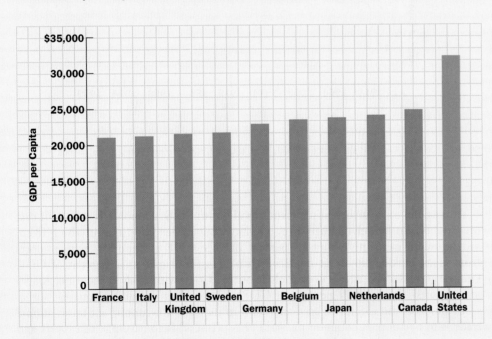

NOTE: GDP is in U.S. dollars, using purchasing-power parities.
SOURCE: Organization for Economic Cooperation and Development, www.oecd.org, accessed June 2000.

that passes through markets in the United States is enormous. Although government purchases of goods and services amount to about 18 percent of GDP, much of that is purchased from private businesses. Direct government *production* of goods is extremely rare in our society, and government services amount to only about 11 percent of GDP.

A RELATIVELY "CLOSED" ECONOMY

All nations trade with one another, and the United States is no exception. Our annual exports exceed $900 billion and our annual imports exceed $1,000 billion. That's a lot of money. But America's international trade often gets more attention than it deserves. The fact is that we produce most of what we consume and consume most of what we produce, though the share of imports and exports has been growing, as Figure 3–1 shows. In 1959 the average of exports and imports was only 4 percent of GDP, a tiny fraction of the total. It has since gone up to about 12 percent. This is no longer negligible, but it still means that over 85 percent of what Americans acquire from the economy every year is made in the U.S.A.

| FIGURE 3–1 | **Share of U.S. GDP Exported and Imported, 1959–1999** |

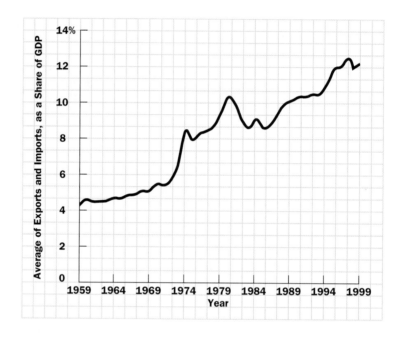

SOURCE: *Economic Report of the President* (Washington, D.C.: U.S. Government Printing Office, various years).

Among the most severe misconceptions about the U.S. economy is the myth that this country no longer manufactures anything, but rather imports everything from, say, Japan. In fact, only about 13 percent of U.S. GDP is imported, with imports from Japan making up about one-seventh of this—or less than 2 percent of GDP. Contrary to a second myth, if we include *services* along with *goods* in the total, America's exports—at about 11 percent of GDP—almost (but not quite) equal imports.

Economists use the terms *open* and *closed* to indicate how important international trade is to a nation. A common measure of "openness" is the average of exports and imports, expressed as a share of GDP. Thus, the Netherlands is considered an extremely **open economy** because it imports and exports about 56 percent of its GDP. (See Table 3–1.) By this criterion, the United States stands out as among the most **closed economies** of the advanced, industrial nations. We export and import a smaller share of GDP than almost all of the countries listed in the table.

An economy is called relatively **open** if its exports and imports constitute a large share of its GDP.

An economy is considered relatively **closed** if they constitute a small share.

A GROWING ECONOMY . . . BUT WITH INFLATION

The next salient fact about the U.S. economy is its growth; it gets bigger almost every year. Gross domestic product in 1999 was around $9.3 trillion, over 18 times

Openness of Various National Economies, 1998

TABLE 3-1

	Openness
Netherlands	56%
Canada	31
Germany	28
United Kingdom	22
Mexico	16
Japan	12
United States	12
Russia	11

NOTE: Dollar amounts are in billions.

SOURCE: For United States, *Economic Report of the President, 1999,* (Washington, D.C.: U.S. Government Printing Office, Feb. 1999). For other countries, *CIA Factbook 1998,* www.odci.gov/cia/publications/factbook.

as much as in 1959. In Figure 3–2 the upper black curve shows that extraordinary upward march. But, as we learned in Chapter 2, a large part of this apparent growth in GDP is due to price inflation—because of higher prices, the *purchasing power* of each 1999 dollar was actually only about one-fifth of each 1959 dollar. Corrected for inflation, we see that *real GDP* (the blue curve in the figure) was only about four times greater in 1999 than in 1959. Another reason for the rise in GDP is the growth in U.S. population. But if a nation's GDP grows no faster than its population, we cannot say that it has become richer, because each person ends up with no more purchasing power. To see how much richer the United States has actually become, we must divide real GDP by the size of the population to obtain *real per-capita* GDP (the red curve in Figure 3–2). It turns out that real income per person in 1999 was only about two and a half times as much as in 1959. That is, still, not a bad performance.

Nominal GDP, Real GDP, and Real GDP per Capita Since 1959

FIGURE 3-2

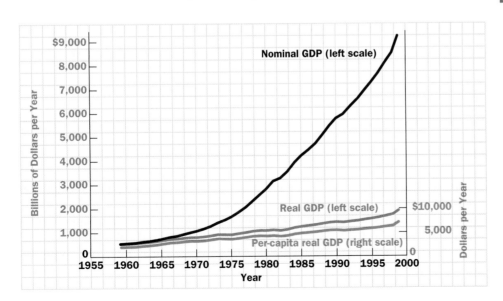

NOTE: Real GDP figures are in 1959 dollars.

SOURCE: *Economic Report of the President* (Washington, D.C.: U.S. Government Printing Office, various years).

BUMPS ALONG THE GROWTH PATH: RECESSIONS

The bird's-eye view that Figure 3–2 offers conceals one more important fact: America's economic growth has been quite irregular. We have experienced alternating periods of good and bad times, which are called *economic fluctuations* or sometimes just *business cycles*. In some years—five since 1959, to be exact—GDP actually declined. Such periods of *declining* economic activity are called **recessions.**

A **recession** is a period of time during which the total output of the economy falls.

The bumps along the American economy's historic growth path are visible upon closer inspection of Figure 3–2 but stand out more clearly in Figure 3–3, which displays the same data in a different way. Here we plot not the *level* of real GDP each year, but rather its *growth rate*—the percentage change from one year to the next. Now the booms and busts that delight and distress people—and swing elections—stand out clearly. From 1983 to 1984, for example, real GDP grew by close to 7 percent, which helped ensure Ronald Reagan's landslide reelection. But from 1990 to 1991, real GDP actually fell by 1 percent, which helped Bill Clinton defeat George Bush.

| FIGURE 3-3 | **The Growth Rate of Real GDP in the United States Since 1959** |

NOTE: Growth rates are for 1959–1960, 1960–1961, and so on.
SOURCE: *Economic Report of the President* (Washington, D.C.: U.S. Government Printing Office, various years).

One important consequence of these ups and downs in economic growth is that *unemployment* varies considerably from one year to the next. (See Figure 3–4) During the Great Depression of the 1930s, unemployment ran as high as 25 percent of the workforce. But it fell to barely over 1 percent during World War II. Within the past few years, the national unemployment rate has been as high as 7.7 percent (in June 1992) and as low as 3.9 percent (in April 2000). In human terms, that 3.8 percentage point difference represents nearly 5 million fewer jobless workers. Understanding why joblessness varies so dramatically, and what we can do about it, is another major reason for studying economics.

● **UNEMPLOYMENT RATES IN EUROPE**

During most of the period after the Second World War, unemployment rates in the industrialized countries of Europe were significantly lower than those in the United States. In the mid-1970s, rates of joblessness in Europe leaped, with double digits becoming common. In September 2000, *The Economist* reported the following unemployment rates:

Switzerland	1.8 %	Australia	6.4 %
Netherlands	2.6	Canada	7.1
Austria	3.2	Germany	9.5
United States	4.1	France	9.7
Japan	4.7	Italy	10.7
Sweden	5.1	Belgium	11.9
United Kingdom	5.3	Spain	14.2
Denmark	5.4		

These days, the U.S. economy is the envy of Europe, and its low unemployment rate is among the main reasons.

SOURCE: *The Economist*, September 16, 2000, p. 114.

The Unemployment Rate in the United States, 1929–1999

FIGURE 3-4

SOURCE: *Economic Report of the President* (Washington, D.C.: U.S. Government Printing Office, various years); and Bureau of the Census, *Historical Statistics of the United States, Colonial Times to 1970* (Washington, D.C.: U.S. Government Printing Office, 1975).

■ THE INPUTS: LABOR AND CAPITAL

Let's now return to the analogy of an economy as a machine turning inputs into outputs. The most important input is human labor: the men and women who run the machines, work behind the desks, and serve you in stores.

FIGURE 3-5

The Composition of Employment by Sex, 1950 and 1999

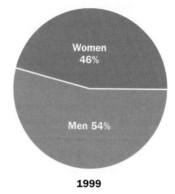

SOURCE: *Economic Report of the President* (Washington, D.C.: U.S. Government Printing Office, various years).

FIGURE 3-6

Working Women as a Percentage of the Labor Force, 1960 versus 1996

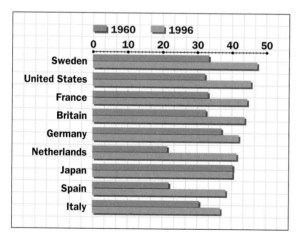

SOURCE: "A Survey of Women and Work," *The Economist*, July 18, 1998, p. 4.

THE AMERICAN WORKFORCE: WHO IS IN IT?

We have already mentioned that about 134 million Americans hold jobs—more than two and a half times as many as the apparently ambitious goal for the country that optimists were proposing during World War II, when Henry Wallace, Franklin Delano Roosevelt's vice president during his third term, sought a goal of employing 60 million workers within the United States. Roughly 54 percent of these 134 million workers are men; 46 percent are women. This ratio represents a drastic change from a generation or two ago, when most women worked only at home (see Figure 3–5). Indeed, the massive entrance of women into the paid labor force has been one of the major social transformations of American life during the second half of the 20th century. In 1950, just 29 percent of women worked in the marketplace; now about 60 percent do. As Figure 3–6 shows, the share of women in the labor forces of other industrial countries has also been growing. The expanding role of women in the labor market has raised many controversial questions—whether they are discriminated against (the evidence suggests that they are), whether the government should compel employers to provide maternity leave, and so on.

In contrast to women, the percentage of teenagers in the workforce has dropped significantly since the mid-1970s (See Figure 3–7.) Young men and women aged 16 to 19 accounted for 8.6 percent of employment in 1974 but only 5.4 percent in 1999. As the baby boom gave way to the baby bust, people under 20 became scarce resources! Still, more than 7 million teenagers hold jobs in the U.S. economy today, and their numbers have increased in the past few years. Most fill low-wage jobs at fast-food restaurants, amusement parks, and the like. Relatively few teenagers can be found in the nation's factories.

THE AMERICAN WORKFORCE: WHAT DOES IT DO?

What do these 134 million working Americans do? The only real answer is: almost anything you can imagine. In 1998, America had 73,000 architects, 4,000 watchmakers, 574,000 computer programmers (who fixed all those Y2K problems!), more than 762,000 carpenters, almost 3 million truck drivers, 429,000 lawyers, 17,000 aircraft assemblers, 156,000 kindergarten teachers, 7,000 bookbinders, close to 500,000 physicians and surgeons, 26,000 oil field roustabouts, 6,400 ship engineers, 226,000 firefighters, and 55,000 economists![1] Figure 3–8 shows the breakdown by economic sector. It holds some surprises for most people. The majority of American workers—like workers in all developed countries—produce services, not goods. In 1998, about 101 million people were employed by service industries in the United States, including 22 million in retail trade, whereas only 25 million produced goods. The popular image of the typical American worker as a blue collar worker—Homer Simpson, if you will— is really quite misleading. Manufacturing companies employ only about 18 million people, and almost a third of those work in offices rather than in the factory. Federal, state, and local governments employ about 20 million people. Contrary to another popular misconception, few of these civil servants work for the *federal* government. Federal *civilian* employment is about 2.7 million—and has fallen every year since 1990.

---

[1] Source: U.S. Bureau of Labor Statistics, *Occupational Employment Statistics Survey 1998*, http://stats.bls.gov., accessed May 25, 2000.

Teenage Employment as a Percentage of Total Employment, 1950–1999

FIGURE 3-7

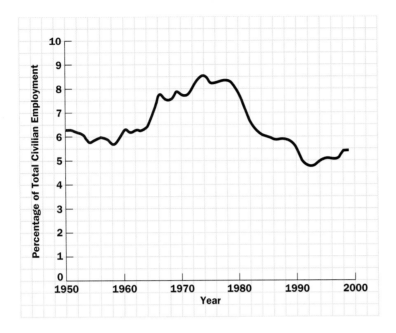

SOURCE: *Economic Report of the President* (Washington, D.C.: U.S. Government Printing Office, various years).

Civilian Employment by Sector, 1998

FIGURE 3-8

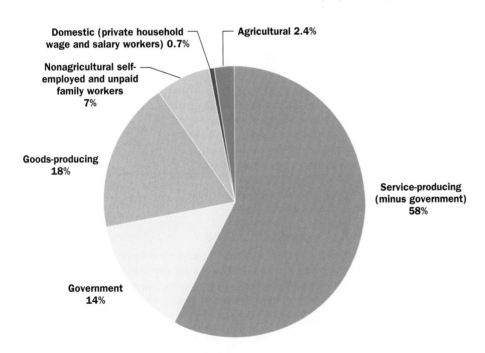

SOURCE: *Economic Report of the President, 1999;* and U.S. Bureau of Labor Statistics, www.stats.bls.gov, accessed February 1999.

At the same time, state and local governments provide about 17 million jobs. Finally, approximately 3.4 million Americans work on farms, and the armed forces employ about 1.5 million workers.

As Figure 3–9 shows, *all* industrialized countries have become "service economies." That is, to a considerable degree, a result of increased demand for labor by the service sector and reduced demand in manufacturing. Activities related to computers, to research, to the transmission of information by teaching and publication, and other information-related activities have provided many new jobs. This means that workers who moved into the service sector of the economy have not gone predominantly into dishwashing or housecleaning or other such low-skill jobs. Many have found employment in service areas where education and experience provide a great advantage. At the same time, technological change has made it possible to produce a given set of manufactured products using fewer and fewer workers. Such labor-saving innovation in manufacturing has moved a considerable share of the labor force out of goods-producing jobs and into the services.

FIGURE 3-9

The Growing Share of Service Sector Jobs, 1967–1996

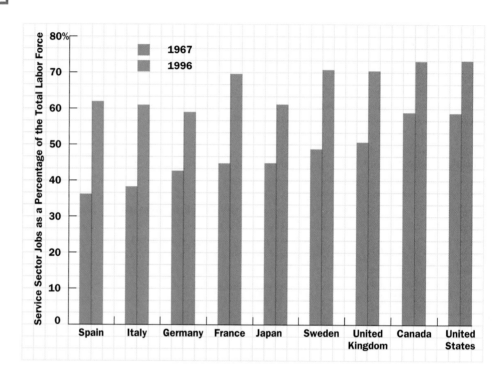

SOURCE: Organization for Economic Cooperation and Development, *Quarterly Labour Force Statistics,* various issues; and www.oecd.org, accessed February 1999.

THE AMERICAN WORKFORCE: WHAT IT EARNS

Altogether, these workers' wages account for nearly three-quarters of the income that the production process generates. That figures up to an average hourly wage of about $13—plus fringe benefits like health insurance and pensions, which can contribute an additional 30 to 40 percent for people holding what are often called "good jobs." Because the average work week is about 35 hours long, a typical weekly pay check is about $455 before taxes. That is hardly a princely sum, and most college graduates can expect to earn more.[2] But it is typical of average wage rates in a rich country like the United States.

Wages in Japan and throughout northern Europe are similar. Indeed, workers in a number of other industrial countries receive higher compensation than American

---

[2] These days, male college graduates typically earn about 85 percent more than men with only high school diplomas, and female college grads earn more than twice what high-school-educated women earn. Source: U.S. Census Bureau, *Measuring 50 Years of Economic Change, 1947–1997* (Washington, D.C.: U.S. Government Printing Office, September 1998.)

workers do, for the first time in many decades. According to the U.S. Bureau of Labor Statistics, in 1997 workers in U.S. manufacturing sectors made less than those in Germany, Belgium, the Netherlands, and Canada (see Figure 3–10). However, U.S. compensation levels still remain well ahead of those in Japan, France, the United Kingdom, and many other countries.

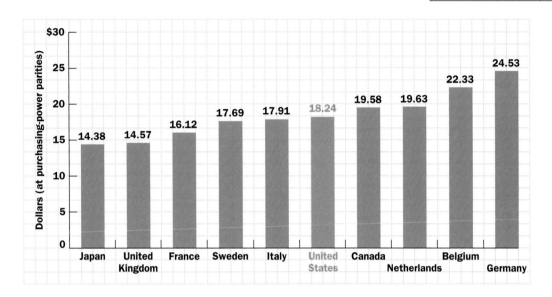

Average Hourly Compensation Rates in Manufacturing, 1997 | FIGURE 3-10

SOURCE: U.S. Bureau of Labor Statistics, http://stats.bls.gov, accessed September 1998; and Organization for Economic Cooperation and Development, www.oecd.org, accessed October 1998.

CAPITAL AND ITS EARNINGS

The rest of national income (after deducting for the tiny sliver of income that goes to land and natural resources) mainly accrues to the owners of *capital*—the machines and buildings that make up the nation's industrial plant.

The total market value of these business assets—a tough number to estimate— is believed to be greater than $25 *trillion*. Because that capital earns an average rate of return of about 10 percent before taxes, total earnings of capital come to about $2,500 billion. Of this, profits are less than half; the rest is mainly interest.

Public opinion polls routinely show that Americans have a distorted view of the level of business profits in our society. The man and woman on the street believe that profits account for about 30 percent of the price of a typical product (see the accompanying box, "Public Opinion on Profits"). In fact, when you spend a dollar in our economy, 65 cents is for labor costs, 11 cents goes to cover the wear and tear on the capital stock,[3] 8 cents is for taxes, 5 cents is for interest, and 2 cents goes to rental income. That leaves about 10 cents for after-tax profits.

■ **THE OUTPUTS: WHAT DOES AMERICA PRODUCE?**

What does all this labor and capital produce? Consumer spending accounts for almost 70 percent of GDP. And what an amazing variety of goods and services it buys! American households spend roughly 60 percent of their budgets on services,

---

[3] Economists and accountants call this *depreciation*. It is a well-known cost of doing business.

● PUBLIC OPINION ON PROFITS

Most Americans think corporate profits are much higher than they actually are. One public opinion poll, for example, found that the average citizen thought that corporate profits *after taxes* amounted to 32 percent of sales for the typical manufacturing company. The actual profit rate at the time was closer to 4 percent!* Interestingly, when a previous poll asked how much profit was "reasonable," the response was 26 cents on every dollar of sales—more than six times as large as profits actually were.

*This poll was conducted in 1986. Corporate profit rates increased considerably in the 1990s.

SOURCE: "Public Attitudes toward Corporate Profits," *Public Opinion Index* (Princeton, N.J.: Opinion Research Corporation, June 1986).

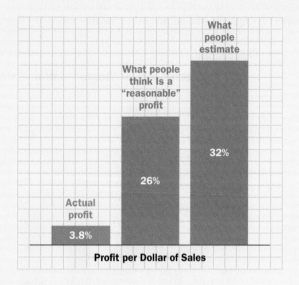

with housing commanding the largest share. They also spend $86 billion annually on their telephone bills, $27 billion on airline tickets, and $47 billion on dentists. The other 40 percent of American budgets goes for goods—ranging from $85 billion per year on new cars to $36 billion on shoes.

This leaves close to a third of GDP for all *nonconsumption* uses. Government services take up about 17 percent, buying such things as airplanes, guns, and the services of soldiers, teachers, and bureaucrats. The rest is mainly business purchases of machinery and industrial structures (about 12 percent of GDP) and consumer purchases of new houses (about 4 percent).

■ THE CENTRAL ROLE OF BUSINESS FIRMS

Calvin Coolidge once said that "the business of America is business." He was largely right. When we peer inside the economic machine that turns inputs into outputs, we see mainly private companies. Astonishingly, the United States has more than *22 million* business firms—about one for every 12 people!

The owners and managers of these businesses hire people, acquire or rent capital goods, and arrange to produce things consumers want to buy. Sound simple? It isn't. About 80,000 businesses fail every year. A few succeed spectacularly. Some do both. Fortunately for the U.S. economy, however, the lure of riches induces hundreds of thousands of people to start new businesses every year—against the odds.

A number of the biggest firms do business all over the world, just as foreign-based *multinational corporations* do business here. Indeed, some people claim that it is now impossible to determine the true "nationality" of a multinational corporation—which may have factories in ten or more countries, sell its wares all over the world, and have stockholders in dozens of nations. (See the accompanying box, "Is That an American Company?") Most of General Motors' profits are generated abroad, for example, and the Honda you drive was probably made in Ohio.

Firms compete with other companies in their *industry*. Most economists believe that this *competition* is the key to industrial efficiency. A sole supplier of a commodity will find it easy to make money, and may therefore fail to innovate or control costs. Its management is liable to become relaxed and sloppy. But a company

---

● IS THAT AN AMERICAN COMPANY?

Robert Reich, a former secretary of labor in the Clinton administration, has argued that it is almost impossible to define the nationality of a multinational company these days. Although many scholars think Reich exaggerates the point, no one doubts that he has one. Here are some examples:

What's the difference between an "American" corporation that makes or buys abroad much of what it sells around the world and a "foreign" corporation that makes or buys in the United States much of what it sells? . . . The mind struggles to keep the players straight. In 1990, Canada's Northern Telecom was selling to its American customers telecommunications equipment made by Japan's NTT at NTT's factory in North Carolina.

If you found that one too easy, try this: Beginning in 1991, Japan's Mazda would be producing Ford Probes at Mazda's plant in Flat Rock, Michigan. Some of these cars would be exported to Japan and sold there under Ford's trademark.

A Mazda-designed compact utility vehicle would be built at a Ford plant in Louisville, Kentucky, and then sold at Mazda dealerships in the United States. Nissan, meanwhile, was designing a new light truck at its San Diego, California, design center. The trucks would be assembled at Ford's Ohio truck plant, using panel parts fabricated by Nissan at its Tennessee factory, and then marketed by both Ford and Nissan in the United States and in Japan. Who is Ford? Nissan? Mazda?

SOURCE: Robert B. Reich, *The Work of Nations* (New York: Knopf, 1991), pp. 124, 131.

---

besieged by dozens of competitors eager to take its business away must constantly seek ways to innovate, cut costs, and build a better mousetrap. The rewards for business success can be magnificent. But the punishment for failure is severe.

■ MEASURING ECONOMIC PROGRESS

One of the American free-market economy's most noteworthy accomplishments is the abundance of growth it has fostered. Never in human history has the real income available to the average inhabitant of a country reached such heights. Studies estimate that in the 14 centuries before the American Revolution, the growth in per-capita income was, on average, approximately *zero*. In contrast, during the 20th century the real income of an average American grew by a factor of nearly 10.[4] Looked at another way, an average American family living around the last turn of the century could afford only *one-tenth* the food, clothing, housing and other amenities that constitute the standard of living today. The change is so enormous that it is difficult to grasp. Just try to imagine how your family's life would be changed if it lost nine out of ten dollars from its consumption expenditure.

The U.S. economy has achieved this remarkable progress through increased American labor *productivity*. Labor productivity is the amount of product that an average worker turns out in a given amount of time, say, per hour of labor. In the United States, over this century, labor productivity in manufacturing has grown by a factor of more than 13: that is, today, a worker turns out 13 times as much in a single hour

---

[4] Angus Maddison, *The Nature and Functioning of European Capitalism: A Historical and Comparative Perspective* (Groningen, Netherlands: University of Groningen, 1997), p. 34.

as her counterpart did around the turn of the century. That, fundamentally, is why we have so much more available to consume than our ancestors did 100 years ago.

We can look at this enormous economic progress another way: by examining what has happened to the costs of the things we purchase. This cannot be done very effectively using dollar prices, because this century has experienced a good deal of inflation, which distorts both prices and wages. Instead, we can measure what really happened to the cost of commodities by asking how many minutes an American must work in order to earn enough to purchase particular items. For example, statistics show that in 1919, in order to buy a pound of chicken an average U.S. worker had to work nearly an hour. Today, at current wages and poultry prices, less than five

FIGURE 3-11

Work Time Needed to Buy Snack Foods, Earlier Dates versus 1997

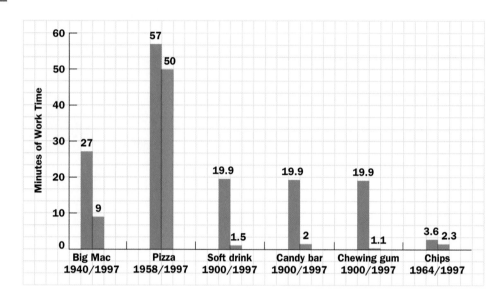

SOURCE: Federal Reserve Bank of Dallas, "Time Well Spent: The Declining *Real* Cost of Living in America," *1997 Annual Report*, 1997.

FIGURE 3-12

Work Time Needed to Buy Various Items for the Home, Earlier Dates versus 1997

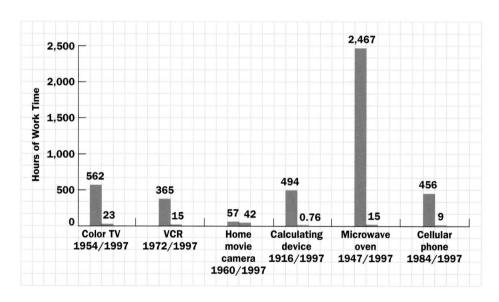

SOURCE: Federal Reserve Bank of Dallas, "Time Well Spent: The Declining *Real* Cost of Living in America," *1997 Annual Report*, 1997.

minutes of labor are required for the purpose! But it is not only chicken or only food that has become much less costly in terms of the labor time needed to pay for it. Figure 3–11 shows how much cheaper a variety of snack foods have become.

Figure 3–12 shows the great cost reductions of various types of electronic equipment—a cut of 98 percent in the cost of a color TV between 1954 and 1997, 96 percent in the cost of a VCR between 1972 and 1997, and 99 percent in the cost of a microwave oven between 1947 and 1997.

But, of course, the most sensational decrease of all is in the cost of computers. Computer capability is standardized in terms of the number of MIPS (million instructions per second) that the computer is capable of handling. To buy a computer today, it costs about 27 minutes of labor per MIPS capacity. In 1984, it cost the wages of 52 *hours* of labor; in 1970, the cost was 1.24 *lifetimes* of labor; and in 1944, the price was a barely believable 733,000 *lifetimes* of labor.

However, the magic of productivity growth has not yet succeeded in invading every sector of the U.S. economy. In particular, the process of college teaching seems to have been able to escape the cost-reducing ability of productivity growth. Figure 3–13 shows the consequences. Between 1965 and 1995, the cost of a college education has risen 33 percent at public universities, whereas at private universities it has gone up by more than 150 percent, from 500 to 1,300 hours.

FIGURE 3–13

Work Time Needed to Buy a College Education, 1965 versus 1997

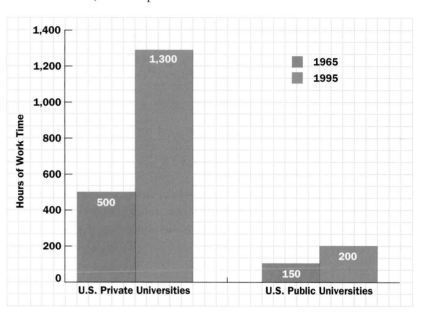

SOURCE: Federal Reserve Bank of Dallas, "Time Well Spent: The Declining *Real* Cost of Living in America," *1997 Annual Report*, 1997.

WHAT'S MISSING FROM THE PICTURE? GOVERNMENT

Thus far we have the following capsule summary of how the U.S. economy works: About 22 million private businesses, energized by the profit motive, employ about 132 million workers and about $25 trillion of capital. These firms bring their enormously diverse wares to market, where they try to sell them to nearly 270 million consumers.

Households and businesses are linked in a tight circle, depicted in Figure 3–14. Firms use their receipts from sales to pay employee wages and interest and profits to people who provide capital. These income flows, in turn, enable consumers to purchase the goods and services that companies produce. This circular flow of money and goods lies at the center of the analysis of how the national economy works. All these activities are linked by a series of interconnected markets, some of which are highly competitive and others of which are less so.

All very well and good. But the story leaves out something important: the role of *government*, which is pervasive even in our decidedly free-market economy. Just what does government do in the U.S. economy—and why?

FIGURE 3–14

The Circular Flow of Goods and Money

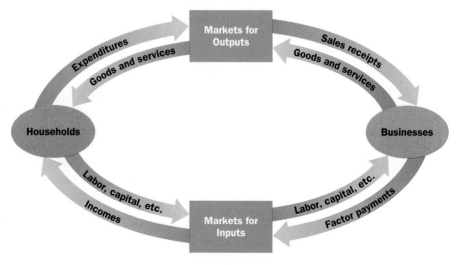

Although an increasing number of tasks seem to get assigned to the state each year, the traditional role of government in a market economy revolves around five jobs:

- Providing certain goods and services such as national defense
- Levying taxes to pay for these goods and services
- Redistributing income
- Regulating business
- Making and enforcing the laws

Every one of these tasks is steeped in controversy and surrounded by intense political debate. We conclude this chapter with a brief look at the role of government.

THE GOVERNMENT AS REFEREE

For the most part, power is diffused in our economy, and people "play by the rules." But, in the scramble for competitive advantage, disputes are bound to arise. Did Company A live up to its contract? Who owns that disputed piece of property? In addition, some unscrupulous businesses are liable to step over the line now and then—via misleading advertising, attempts to monopolize markets, employment of child labor, and the like.

Enter the government as rule maker, referee, and arbitrator. Congress and state and local legislatures pass the laws that define the rules of the economic game. The executive branches of all three governmental levels share the responsibility for enforcing them. And the courts interpret the laws and adjudicate disputes.

THE GOVERNMENT AS BUSINESS REGULATOR

Nothing is pure in this world of ours. Even in "free-market" economies, governments interfere with the workings of free markets in many ways and for myriad reasons. Some government activities seek to make markets work better. For example, America's *antitrust laws* are used to protect competition against possible encroachment by monopoly. Some regulations seek to promote social objectives that unfettered markets do not foster—environmental regulations are a particularly clear case. But some economic regulations have no sensible economic rationale at all!

We mentioned earlier that the American belief in free enterprise runs deep. For this reason, the regulatory role of government is more contentious here than in most other countries. After all, Thomas Jefferson said that government is best which governs least. Two hundred years later, Presidents Reagan, Bush, and Clinton pledged to dismantle regulations—and sometimes did.

GOVERNMENT EXPENDITURES

The most contentious political issues often involve taxing and spending because those are the government's most prominent roles. In 1995 and 1996, President Clinton and the Republican-led Congress battled fiercely over the federal budget. Differences over tax policies and spending cuts even led to some temporary shutdowns of the government. Since then, the federal government has achieved a surplus. For the first time in 30 years, its spending is less than its revenues, and the surplus is expected to continue for many years.

During fiscal year 1998, the federal government spent more than $1.6 *trillion*—a sum that is literally beyond comprehension. Figure 3–15 shows where the money went. Over one-third went for *pensions and income security* programs, which include both social insurance programs (like Social Security and unemployment compensation) and programs designed to assist the poor. About 16 percent went for *national defense*. Another 20 percent was absorbed by *health-care* expenditures, mainly on Medicare and Medicaid. Adding in *interest on the national debt*, these four functions alone accounted for about 88 percent of federal spending. The rest went for a miscellany of other purposes including education, transportation, agriculture, housing, and foreign aid.

Government spending at the state and local levels was about $1.2 trillion in 1996. Education claimed the biggest share of state and local government budgets (33 percent), with health and public welfare programs in second place (17 percent).

Despite this vast outpouring of public funds, many observers believe that serious social needs remain unmet. Critics claim that our public infrastructure (such as bridges and roads) is inadequate, that our educational system is lacking, that we do not do enough for the poor and homeless, and so on. Many people echoed these claims during the 1999 budget debate. The argument was over what should be done with the funds made available by the budget surplus. President Clinton proposed to spend part of it on financing Social Security and education. His Republican opponents argued that government already tries to do too much, and instead advocated a tax reduction.

Although government activity in the United States is substantial, it is quite moderate when we compare it to other leading economies. Figure 3–16 is a bar graph showing government expenditure as share of GDP for 10 countries. We see that the share of government in the U.S. economy is the lowest in this group of countries.

FIGURE 3–15

The Allocation of Government Expenditures

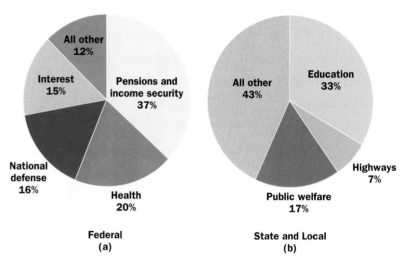

Federal
(a)

State and Local
(b)

SOURCE: *Economic Report of the President, 1999* (Washington, D.C.: U.S. Government Printing Office, February 1999).

Government Spending as a Percentage of GDP, 1997

FIGURE 3–16

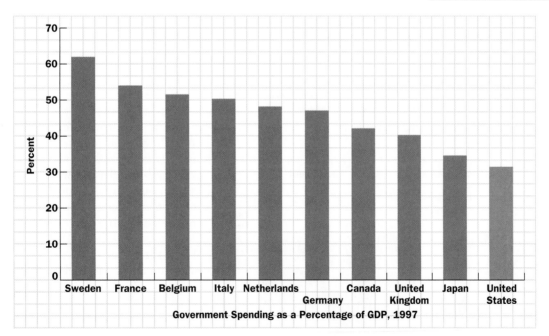

SOURCE: Organization for Economic Cooperation and Development, *Analytical Databank,* www.oecd.org, accessed January 1999.

TAXES IN AMERICA

Taxes finance this array of goods and services, and sometimes it seems that the tax collector is everywhere. We have income and payroll taxes withheld from our paychecks, sales taxes added to our purchases, property taxes levied on our homes; we pay gasoline taxes, liquor taxes, and telephone taxes.

Americans have always felt that taxes are both too many and too high. In the 1980s and 1990s, antitax sentiment became a dominant feature of the U.S. political scene. The old slogan "no taxation without representation" gave way to the new slogan "no new taxes." Yet by international standards, Americans are among the most lightly taxed people in the world. Figure 3–17 compares the fraction of income paid in taxes in the United States with those paid by residents of other wealthy nations.

| FIGURE 3-17 | **The Tax Burden in Selected Countries, 1996** |

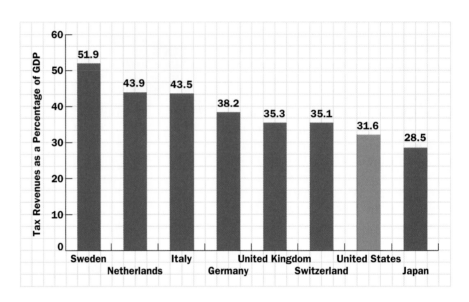

SOURCE: Organization for Economic Cooperation and Development, *Main Economic Indicators*, October 1998, www.oecd.org, accessed January 1999.

| FIGURE 3-18 |

Sources of Government Revenue

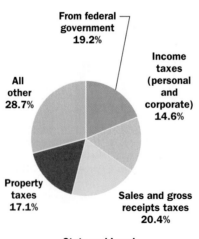

Federal
(a)

State and Local
(b)

SOURCE: *Economic Report of the President, 2000* (Washington, D.C.: U.S. Government Printing Office, February 2000).

How is this money raised? The *personal income tax* is the federal government's biggest revenue source, though the *payroll tax*—a flat-rate tax on wages and salaries up to a certain limit—is not far behind. The rest of federal revenue comes mainly from the *corporate income tax*. Most states and many large cities levy broad-based *sales taxes* on retail purchases, with certain specific exemptions (such as food and rent). Local governments generally raise revenue by levying *property taxes* on homes and business properties. Figure 3–18 shows the breakdown of revenue sources at both the federal and state and local levels.

THE GOVERNMENT AS REDISTRIBUTOR

In a market economy, people earn incomes according to what they have to sell. Unfortunately, many people have nothing to sell but unskilled labor, which commands a paltry price. Others lack even that. Such people fare poorly in unfettered markets. In extreme cases, they are homeless, hungry, and ill. Robin Hood transferred money from the rich to the poor. Some think the government should do the same; others disagree.

If poverty amidst riches offends your moral sensibilities—a personal judgment that each of us must make—two basic remedial approaches are possible. The socialist idea is to force the distribution of income to be more equal by overriding the decisions of the market. "From each according to his ability, to each according to his needs" was Marx's ideal. In practice, things were not quite so noble under socialism. But there is little doubt that incomes in the old Soviet Union were more equally distributed than those in the United States.

The liberal idea is to let free markets determine the distribution of *before-tax* incomes, but then to use the tax system and **transfer payments** to reduce inequality—just as Robin Hood did. This is the rationale for, among other things, **progressive taxation** and the antipoverty programs colloquially known as "welfare." Americans who support redistribution line up solidly behind the liberal approach. But which ways are the best, and how much is enough? No simple answers emerge from debate on these highly contentious questions.

> **Transfer payments** are sums of money that certain individuals receive as outright grants from the government rather than as payments for services rendered.

> A tax is **progressive** if the ratio of taxes to income rises as income rises.

■ CONCLUSION: THE MIXED ECONOMY

Ideology notwithstanding, all nations at all times blend public and private ownership of property in some proportions. All rely on markets for some purposes, but all also assign some role to government. Hence, people speak of the ubiquity of **mixed economies.** But mixing is not homogenization; different countries can and do blend the state and market sectors in different ways. Even today, the Russian economy is a far cry from the Italian economy, which is vastly different from that of Hong Kong.

> A **mixed economy** is one with some public influence over the workings of free markets. There may also be some public ownership mixed in with private property.

While most of you were in elementary school, a stunning historical event occurred: Communism collapsed all over Europe. Now the formerly socialist economies are in the midst of a painful transition from a system in which private property, free enterprise, and markets played subsidiary roles to one in which they are central. These nations are changing the mix, if you will—and dramatically so. To understand why this transformation is at once so difficult and so important, we need to explore the main theme of this book: *What does the market do well, and what does it do poorly?* This task begins in the next chapter.

SUMMARY

1. The U.S. economy is the biggest national economy on earth, both because Americans are rich by world standards and because we are a populous nation. Relative to most other advanced countries, our economy is also exceptionally "privatized" and *closed.*

2. The U.S. economy has grown dramatically over the years. But this growth is exaggerated by looking only at dollar figures, which are distorted by both *inflation* and population growth. To get a better understanding of the growth of living standards, we must look at *real GDP per capita.*

3. The growth path of the U.S. economy has been interrupted by periodic *recessions*, during which unemployment rises.

4. The United States has a big, diverse workforce whose composition by age and sex has been changing substantially. Relatively few workers these days work in factories or on farms; most work in service industries.

5. Employees take home most of the nation's income. Most of the rest goes, in the forms of interest and profits, to those who provide the capital.

6. Productivity and per-capita incomes in the United States and other industrialized countries have grown at rates and reached levels never before achieved in human history.

7. Governments at the federal, state, and local levels employ one-seventh of the American workforce. They finance their expenditures by taxes, which account for about 32 percent of GDP. This percentage is one of the lowest in the industrialized world.

8. In addition to raising taxes and making expenditures, the government in a market economy serves as referee and enforcer of the rules, regulates business in a variety of ways, and redistributes income through taxes and *transfer payments.* For all these reasons, we say that we have a *mixed economy*, which blends private and public elements.

KEY TERMS

Factors of Production 32	Open economy 34	Productivity 43
Inputs 32	Closed economy 34	Transfer payments 49
Outputs 32	Real GDP per capita 35	Progressive tax 49
Gross domestic product (GDP) 32	Recession 36	Mixed economy 49

QUESTIONS FOR REVIEW

1. Which are the two biggest national economies on earth? Why are they so much bigger than the others?

2. What is meant by a "factor of production?" Have you ever sold any on a market?

3. Why do you think per-capita income in Connecticut is nearly double that in Mississippi?

4. Roughly speaking, what fraction of U.S. labor works in factories? In service businesses? In government?

5. It sounds paradoxical to say that most American businesses are small, but most of the output is produced by large businesses. How can this be true?

6. If your purchasing power were reduced by 90 percent, to a 1900 level, what purchases would you give up?

7. What is the role of government in a mixed economy?

Our necessities are few but our wants are endless.

Fortune cookie inscription

SCARCITY AND CHOICE:
THE ECONOMIC PROBLEM

U nderstanding what the market system does well and what it does badly is this book's central task. But to address this complex question, we must first answer a simpler one: What do economists expect the market to accomplish?

The most common answer is that the market resolves what is often called *the* fundamental economic problem: All decisions are constrained by the scarcity of available resources. A dreamer may envision a world free of want, in which everyone drives a BMW and eats caviar, but the earth lacks the resources needed to make that dream come true.

Because resources are scarce, all economic decisions involve *trade-offs*. Should you use that $5 bill to buy a hoagie or some new diskettes for your computer files? Should General Motors invest more money in assembly lines or in research? A well-functioning market system facilitates and guides such decisions, assigning each hour of labor and each kilowatt-hour of electricity to the task where, it is hoped, the input will best serve the public.

This chapter shows how economists analyze choices like these. The same basic principles, based on the concept of *opportunity cost*, apply to the decisions of business firms, governments, and society as a whole. Many of the most basic ideas of economics, such as *efficiency*, *division of labor*, *comparative advantage*, *exchange*, and *the role of markets* appear here for the first time.

Issue: What to Do with the Budget Surplus?

For years, the United States government struggled to cope with a large budget deficit that illustrated all too vividly how scarce public funds really were. Existing programs had to be cut back, and new programs were extremely difficult to finance. Presidents Reagan, Bush, and Clinton all struggled with Congress over tax and spending priorities. Then, between 1997 and 1999, the deficit melted away like the spring snow and the prospect of vast surpluses appeared. With all that new-found money, you might have thought that budget battles would become a thing of the past.

Not so. In fact, the major issue of the 2000 presidential campaign was how best to use the mammoth budget surpluses—which are currently projected to exceed $4 trillion (yes, that's trillion!) over the next decade. Mr. Bush called for a large tax cut plus an expensive plan to partially privatize Social Security. Mr. Gore labeled both of those ideas "risky" and favored instead smaller tax cuts, more debt reduction, and more spending on health, education, and the environment. Yes, $4 trillion is a tidy sum. But it was not enough to meet the priorities of both major candidates. The necessity of making hard choices did not disappear just because the budget showed a surplus.

Even when resources are quite generous, they are never unlimited. So everyone must still make tough choices. An *optimal* decision is one that chooses the most desirable alternative *among the possibilities permitted by the available resources,* which are always scarce in this sense.

■ SCARCITY, CHOICE, AND OPPORTUNITY COST

Resources are the instruments provided by nature or by people that are used to create goods and services. Natural resources include minerals, the soil, water, and air. Labor is a scarce resource, partly because of time limitations (the day has only 24 hours) and partly because the number of skilled workers is limited. Factories and machines are resources made by people. These three types of resources are often referred to as *land, labor,* and *capital.* They are also called *inputs* or *factors of production.*

One of the basic themes of economics is scarcity: the fact that **resources** are always limited. Even Philip II, of Spanish Armada fame and ruler of one of the greatest empires in history, had to cope with frequent rebellions when he could not meet the payroll or even provide basic provisions. In more recent years, the U.S. government has been agonizing over difficult budget decisions even though it spends more than 1.7 trillion dollars annually! That's $1,700,000,000,000.

But the scarcity of *physical resources* is more fundamental than the scarcity of funds. Fuel supplies, for example, are not limitless, and some environmentalists claim that we should now be making some hard choices—such as keeping our homes cooler in winter and warmer in summer and living closer to our jobs. Although energy may be the most widely discussed scarcity, the general principle applies to all the earth's resources—iron, copper, uranium, and so on. Even goods produced by human effort are in limited supply because they require fuel, labor, and other scarce resources as inputs. We can manufacture more cars, but the increased use of labor, steel, and fuel in auto production will mean that we must cut back on something else, perhaps the production of refrigerators. This all adds up to the following fundamental principle of economics, one we will encounter again and again in this text.

Virtually all resources are *scarce,* meaning that humanity has less of them than we would like. Therefore, choices must be made among a *limited* set of possibilities, in full recognition of the inescapable fact that a decision to have more of one thing means that we will have less of something else.

In fact, one popular definition of economics is the study of how best to use *limited* means to pursue *unlimited* ends. Although this definition, like any short statement, cannot possibly cover the sweep of the entire discipline, it does convey the flavor of the economist's stock in trade.

To illustrate the true cost of an item, consider the decision to produce additional cars, and therefore fewer refrigerators. Although the production of a car may cost $15,000 per vehicle, or some other money amount, *its real cost to society is the refrigerators that society must forgo to get an additional car.* If the labor, steel, and energy needed to manufacture a car are sufficient to make 30 refrigerators, the **opportunity cost** of a car is 30 refrigerators. The principle of opportunity cost is so important that we will spend most of this chapter elaborating on it in various ways.

The **opportunity cost** of any decision is the value of the next best alternative that the decision forces the decision maker to forgo.

THE PRINCIPLE OF OPPORTUNITY COST Economics examines the options available to households, businesses, governments, and entire societies, given the limited resources at their command. It studies the logic of how people can make **rational decisions** from among competing alternatives. One overriding principle governs this logic—a principle we introduced in Chapter 1 as one of the *Ideas for Beyond the Final Exam:*

With limited resources, a decision to have *more* of one thing is simultaneously a decision to have *less* of something else. Hence, the relevant *cost* of any decision is its *opportunity cost*—the value of the next best alternative that is given up. Rational decision making must be based on opportunity-cost calculations.

How Much Does It Really Cost?

OPPORTUNITY COST AND MONEY COST

Because we live in a market economy where (almost) everything has its price, students often wonder about the connection or difference between an item's *opportunity cost* and its *market price*. What we just said seems to divorce the two concepts: The true *opportunity cost* of a car is not its market price but the value of the other things (like refrigerators) that could have been made or purchased instead.

But isn't the opportunity cost of a car related to its money cost? The normal answer is yes. The two concepts of cost are usually closely tied because of the way a market economy sets prices. Steel, for example, is used to manufacture both automobiles and refrigerators. If consumers value items that can be made with steel (such as refrigerators) highly, then economists would say that the *opportunity cost* of making a car is high. But, under these circumstances, a well-functioning price system will assign a high price to steel, which will therefore make the *money cost* of manufacturing a car high as well. In summary:

If the market functions well, goods that have high opportunity costs will also have high money costs, and goods whose opportunity costs are low will also have low money costs.

A **rational decision** is one that best serves the objectives of the decision maker, whatever those objectives may be. Such objectives may include a firm's desire to maximize its profits, a government's desire to maximize the welfare of its citizens, or another government's desire to maximize its military might. The term *rational* connotes neither approval nor disapproval of the objective itself.

Yet it would be a mistake to treat opportunity costs and explicit monetary costs as identical. For one thing, sometimes the market does not function well, and hence assigns prices that do not accurately reflect opportunity costs.

Moreover, some valuable items may not bear explicit price tags at all. We encountered one such example in Chapter 1, where we noted that the opportunity cost of a college education may differ sharply from its explicit money cost. Why? Because one important item is typically omitted from the money-cost calculation: the *market value of your time*, that is, the wages you could earn by working instead of attending college. Because you give up these potential wages, which might amount to $15,000 a year or more, in order to acquire an education, they must be counted as a major part of the opportunity cost of going to college.

Other common examples where money costs and opportunity costs diverge are goods and services that are given away "free." For example, some early settlers of the American West destroyed natural amenities such as forests and buffalo herds, which had no market price, leaving later generations to pay the opportunity costs in terms of lost resources. Similarly, you incur no explicit monetary cost to acquire an item that is given away free. But if crowds turn up to demand the "free" commodity, you incur an opportunity cost equal to the value of the next best use of your time.

SCARCITY AND CHOICE FOR A SINGLE FIRM

The nature of opportunity cost is perhaps clearest in the case of a single business firm that produces two outputs from a fixed supply of inputs. Given current technology and the limited resources at its disposal, the more of one good the firm produces, the less of the other it will be able to make. Unless managers explicitly weigh the desirability of each against the other, they are unlikely to make rational production decisions.

Consider the example of Farmer Jones, whose available supplies of land, machinery, labor, and fertilizer are capable of producing the various combinations of soybeans and wheat listed in Table 4–1. Obviously, devoting more resources to soybean production means that Farmer Jones will produce less wheat.

Table 4–1 indicates, for example, that if Jones grows only soybeans, the harvest will be 40,000 bushels. But, if he reduces soybean production to 30,000 bushels, he can also grow 38,000 bushels of wheat. Thus, *the opportunity cost of obtaining 38,000 bushels of wheat is 10,000 fewer bushels of soybeans.* Put another way, the opportunity cost of 10,000 more bushels of soybeans is 38,000 bushels of wheat. The other numbers in Table 4–1 have similar interpretations.

TABLE 4–1		

Production Possibilities Open to a Farmer

Bushels of Soybeans	Bushels of Wheat	Label in Figure 4–1
40,000	0	A
30,000	38,000	B
20,000	52,000	C
10,000	60,000	D
0	65,000	E

FIGURE 4–1	

Production Possibilities Frontier for Production by a Single Firm

THE PRODUCTION POSSIBILITIES FRONTIER

Figure 4–1 presents this same information graphically. Point *A* corresponds to the first line of Table 4–1, point *B* to the second line, and so on. Curves similar to *AE* appear frequently in this book; they are called **production possibilities frontiers.** Any point *on or inside* the production possibilities frontier is attainable. Points *outside* the frontier cannot be achieved with the available resources and technology.

Because resources are limited, the production possibilities frontier always slopes downward to the right. The farmer can *increase* wheat production (move to the right in Figure 4–1) only by devoting more land and labor to growing wheat. But this simultaneously *reduces* soybean production (moves downward) because less land and labor remain available for growing soybeans.

Notice that, in addition to having a negative slope, our production possibilities frontier *AE* has another characteristic; it is "bowed outward." What does this curvature mean?

Suppose Farmer Jones initially produces only soybeans, using even land that is best suited for wheat cultivation (point *A*). Now he decides to switch some

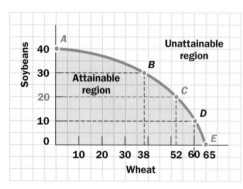

NOTE: Quantities are in thousands of bushels per year.

land from soybean production into wheat production. Which part of the land will he switch? If Jones is sensible, he will use the part best suited to growing wheat. As he shifts to point *B*, soybean production falls from 40,000 bushels to 30,000 bushels as wheat production rises from zero to 38,000 bushels. A sacrifice of only 10,000 bushels of soybeans "buys" 38,000 bushels of wheat.

Imagine now that the farmer wants to produce still more wheat. Figure 4–1 tells us that the sacrifice of an additional 10,000 bushels of soybeans (from 30,000 down to 20,000) will yield only 14,000 more bushels of wheat (see point *C*). Why? The main reason is *that inputs tend to be specialized.* As we noted, at point *A*, the farmer was using resources for soybean production that were actually more suitable for growing wheat. Consequently, their productivity in soybean production was low. When these resources are switched to wheat production, the yield is high.

But this cannot continue forever. As more wheat is produced, the farmer must utilize land and machinery that are better suited to producing soybeans and less well-suited to producing wheat. This is why the first 10,000 bushels of soybeans forgone "buys" the farmer 38,000 bushels of wheat, whereas the second 10,000 bushels of soybeans "buys" only 14,000 bushels of wheat. Figure 4–1 and Table 4–1 show that these returns continue to decline as wheat production expands: The next 10,000-bushel reduction in soybean production yields only 8,000 bushels of additional wheat, and so on.

We can now see that the *slope* of the production possibilities frontier graphically represents the concept of *opportunity cost.* Between points *C* and *B*, for example, the opportunity cost of acquiring 10,000 additional bushels of soybeans is 14,000 bushels of forgone wheat; between points *B* and *A*, the opportunity cost of 10,000 bushels of soybeans is 38,000 bushels of forgone wheat. In general, as we move upward to the left along the production possibilities frontier (toward more soybeans and less wheat), the opportunity cost of soybeans in terms of wheat increases. Putting the same thing differently, as we move downward to the right, the opportunity cost of acquiring wheat by giving up soybeans increases.

THE PRINCIPLE OF INCREASING COSTS

We have just described a very general phenomenon with applications well beyond farming. The **principle of increasing costs** states that as the production of one good expands, the opportunity cost of producing another unit of this good generally increases.

This principle is not a universal fact—exceptions do arise. But it does seem to be a technological regularity that applies to a wide range of economic activities. As our farming example suggests, the principle of increasing costs is based on the fact that resources tend to be at least somewhat specialized. So we lose some of their productivity when they are transferred from doing what they are relatively *good* at to what they are relatively *bad* at. In terms of diagrams such as Figure 4–1, the principle simply asserts that the production possibilities frontier is bowed outward.

Perhaps the best way to understand this idea is to contrast it with a case in which no resources are specialized. Figure 4–2 depicts a production possibilities frontier for producing black shoes and brown shoes. Because the labor and capital used to produce black shoes are just as good at producing brown shoes, the frontier is a straight line. If the firm cuts back its production of black shoes by 10,000 pairs, it gets 10,000 additional pairs of brown shoes. It loses no productivity in the switch because resources are not specialized.

More typically, however, as a firm concentrates more and more of its productive capacity on one commodity, it is forced to employ inputs that are better suited to making another commodity. The firm is forced to vary the *proportions* in which it

A **production possibilities frontier** shows the different combinations of various goods that a producer can turn out, given the available resources and existing technology.

The **principle of increasing costs** states that as the production of a good expands, the opportunity cost of producing another unit generally increases.

FIGURE 4–2

Production Possibilities Frontier with No Specialized Resources

NOTE: Quantities are in thousands of pairs per week.

uses inputs because of the limited quantities of some of the inputs it uses. This fact also explains the typical curvature of the firm's production possibilities frontier.

■ SCARCITY AND CHOICE FOR THE ENTIRE SOCIETY

Like an individual firm, the entire economy is also constrained by its limited resources and technology. If society wants more aircraft and tanks, it will have to give up some boats and automobiles. If it wants to build more factories and stores, it will have to build fewer homes and sports arenas. In general:

The position and shape of the production possibilities frontier that constrains society's choices are determined by the economy's physical resources, its skills and technology, its willingness to work, and how much it has devoted in the past to the construction of factories, research, and innovation.

Because so many nations have debated whether to reduce or augment military strength for so long, let us illustrate the nature of society's choices by the example of choosing between military might (represented by missiles) and civilian consumption (represented by automobiles). Just like a single firm, the economy as a whole faces a production possibilities frontier for missiles and autos, determined by its technology and the available resources of land, labor, capital, and raw materials. This production possibilities frontier may look like curve *BC* in Figure 4–3. If most workers are employed in auto plants, car production will be large, but the output of missiles will be small. If society transfers resources out of auto manufacturing, it can alter the output mix toward more missiles (the move from *D* to *E*). However, something is likely to be lost in the process because physical resources are specialized. The fabric used to make car seats will not help much in missile production. The principle of increasing costs strongly suggests that the production possibilities frontier curves downward toward the axes.

We may even reach a point where the only resources left are not very useful outside of auto manufacturing. In that case, even a large sacrifice of automobiles will get the economy few additional missiles. That is the meaning of the steep segment, *FC*, on the frontier. At point *C* there is little additional output of missiles as compared to point *F*, even though at *C* automobile production has been given up entirely.

The downward slope of society's production possibilities frontier implies that hard choices must be made. Civilian consumption (automobiles) can be increased only by decreasing military expenditure, not by rhetoric nor by wishing it so. The curvature of the production possibilities frontier implies that, as defense spending increases, it becomes progressively more expensive to "buy" additional military strength ("missiles") by sacrificing civilian consumption.

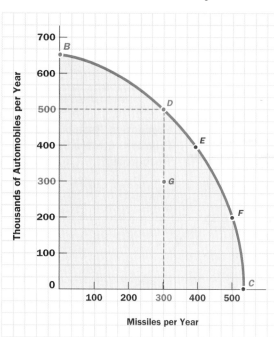

FIGURE 4–3

Production Possibilities Frontier for the Entire Economy

SCARCITY AND CHOICE ELSEWHERE IN THE ECONOMY

We have emphasized that limited resources force hard choices on business managers and society as a whole. But the same type of choices arise elsewhere—in households, universities, and other nonprofit organizations, as well as the government.

The nature of opportunity cost is perhaps most obvious for a household that must decide how to divide its income among the goods and services that compete for the family's attention. If the Simpson family buys an expensive new car, it may be forced to cut back sharply on some other purchases. This fact does not make it unwise to buy the car. But it does make it unwise to buy the car until the family considers the

---

● **THE MILITARY-CIVILIAN OUTPUT TRADE-OFF IN REALITY**

The arms race may have ground to a halt, but space-age technology that helped keep the peace for 50 years is now being channeled in new directions. Literally hundreds of companies have had to face the new reality: Find other applications for current products, or perish.

The innovations have been spectacular. A rocket parts plant in Colorado developed a racing bike frame made from thermoplastic and reinforced carbon fiber. Composite materials, including boron filaments, graphites, and carbon fibers, have long been principal components in jet aircraft. Today, they are as likely to be found in golf club shafts, tennis rackets, ski poles, and even hockey sticks. Racecar companies are trying to take advantage of strong, lightweight materials in car designs.

Spillover benefits haven't been limited to the sports industry. E-Systems, which still does big defense business, demonstrated an innovative touch by adapting spy satellite technology to improve tumor-detection capabilities in mammograms. New uses have even been found for shuttered military bases. San Francisco's Treasure Island Naval Station, for example, is now being used as a movie studio.

SOURCES: Tim Smart, "Beating Swords into Golf Clubs?" *Business Week,* April 18, 1994, p. 85; "Uncle Sam's Fire Sales," *U.S. News & World Report,* January 9, 1995; "Aerospace and Defense," *Forbes,* January 3, 1994, p. 106.

---

full implications for its overall budget. If the Simpsons are to utilize their limited resources most effectively, they must explicitly acknowledge that the opportunity costs of the car are the things they will forgo as a result—perhaps a vacation and an expensive new TV set.

Issue Revisited: Allocating the Budget Surplus

Even a rich and powerful nation like the United States must cope with the limitations implied by scarce resources. The necessity for choice imposed on governments by their limited budgets is similar in character to the problems faced by business firms and households. For the goods and services that it buys from others, a government must prepare a budget similar to that of a very large household. For the items it produces itself—education, police protection, libraries, and so on—it faces a production possibilities frontier much like a business firm does. Even though the U.S. government will spend over $1.7 trillion in 1999, some of the most acrimonious debates between President Clinton and the Congress arise from disagreements about how the government's limited resources should be allocated among competing uses. Even if unstated, the concept of opportunity cost has been central to these debates.

APPLICATION: ECONOMIC GROWTH IN THE UNITED STATES AND THE ASIAN "TIGERS"

Any nation must make one extremely important decision that illustrates the concept of opportunity cost particularly well. This choice is embodied in the question "How fast should the economy grow?" At first, the question may seem ridiculous. Because

Economic growth occurs when an economy is able to produce more goods and services for each consumer.

economic growth means, roughly speaking, that the average citizen gets more and more goods and services, is it not self-evident that faster growth is always better?

Again, the fundamental problem of scarcity looms large. Economies do not grow by magic. Resources must be devoted to the growth process, and all resources are scarce. Cement and steel that might have been used to make swimming pools must be diverted to building factories. Wood that could have been used to make skis must be used for ladders instead. By deciding how much of its resources to devote to *future* needs rather than to *current* consumption, society in effect *chooses* (within limits) how fast it will grow.

In diagrammatic terms, economic growth means that the economy's production possibilities frontier shifts outward over time—like the move from *FF* to *GG* in Figure 4–4(a). Why? Because an outward shift means that the economy can produce more of both outputs. Thus, after growth has occurred, it is possible to produce the combination of products represented by points like *N*, which were impossible before growth. Point *N*, lying outside the economy's original production possibilities frontier, was beyond its means.

How does growth occur? That is, what shifts an economy's production frontier outward? There are many answers. For example, workers may acquire skills and training that enable them to produce more output in an hour. Or the economy may build more factories and machinery, giving up some consumption goods to free up the necessary resources. Finally, inventions like the steam engine, AC electricity, and computers can and *do* increase the economy's productive capacity, thereby shifting its production possibilities frontier outward. However, to improve its technology, the economy must devote more resources to research and development.

Figure 4–4 illustrates the nature of the choice for two different countries by depicting production possibilities frontiers for **consumption goods,** which people consume today (like food and electricity), versus **capital goods,** which can produce larger outputs for future consumption (like reapers and electricity-generating plants). Figure 4–4(a) depicts a society like the United States, which devotes a relatively small quantity of resources to growth, preferring current consumption instead. It chooses a point such as *A* on this year's production possibilities frontier, *FF*. At *A*, consumption is relatively high and production of capital is relatively low, so the production possibilities frontier shifts only to *GG* next year.

A **consumption good** is an item that is available for immediate use by households, one that satisfies people's wants without contributing directly to the economy's future production.

A **capital good** is an item used to produce other goods and services in the future, rather than being consumed today. Factories and machines are examples.

| FIGURE 4–4 | **Growth in Two Economies** |

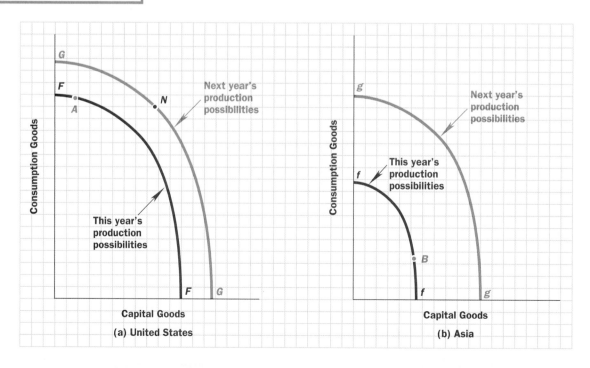

(a) United States

(b) Asia

Figure 4–4(b) depicts a society, such as one of the Asian Tiger economies (Korea, Singapore, Hong Kong, and Taiwan are good examples), that is much more enamored of growth. It selects a point like *B* on its production possibilities frontier, *ff*. At *B*, consumption is much lower and production of capital goods is much higher, so its production possibilities frontier moves all the way to *gg* by next year. Asia grows faster than the United States. But the more rapid growth has a price—an *opportunity cost:* Asian citizens must give up some of the current consumption that Americans enjoy.[1]

An economy grows by giving up some current consumption and producing capital goods for the future instead. The more capital it produces, the faster its production possibilities frontier will shift outward over time.

■ THE CONCEPT OF EFFICIENCY

So far our discussion of scarcity and choice has assumed that either the firm or the economy always operates on its production possibilities frontier rather than *below* it. In other words, we have tacitly assumed that, whatever the firm or economy decides to do, it does so *efficiently*.

Economists define *efficiency* as the absence of waste. An efficient economy utilizes all of its available resources and produces the maximum amount of output that its technology permits.

To see why any point on the economy's production possibilities frontier in Figure 4–3 represents an efficient decision, suppose for a moment that society has decided to produce 300 missiles. The production possibilities frontier tells us that if 300 missiles are to be produced, then the maximum number of automobiles that can be made is 500,000 (point *D* in Figure 4–3). The economy is therefore operating efficiently if it actually produces 500,000 automobiles rather than some smaller amount such as 300,000 (as at point *G*).

Point *D* is efficient, but point *G* is not, because the economy is capable of moving from *G* up to *D*, thereby producing 200,000 more automobiles without giving up any missiles (or anything else). Clearly, failure to take advantage of the option of choosing point *D* rather than point *G* constitutes a wasted opportunity—an inefficiency.

Note that the concept of efficiency does not tell us which point on the production possibilities frontier is *best*. It tells us only that any point that is *below* the frontier cannot be best, because any such point represents wasted resources. For example, should society ever find itself at a point like *G*, the necessity of making hard choices would (temporarily) disappear. It would be possible to increase production of *both* missiles *and* automobiles by moving to a point such as *E*.

Why, then, would a society ever find itself at a point below its production possibilities frontier? Why are resources wasted in real life? The most important reason in today's economy is *unemployment*. When many workers are unemployed, the economy finds itself at a point like *G*, below the frontier, because by putting the unemployed to work in both industries, the economy could produce both more missiles *and* more automobiles. The economy would then move from point *G* to the right (more missiles) and upward (more automobiles) toward a point such as *E* on the production possibilities frontier. Only when no resources are wasted is the economy on the frontier.

Inefficiency occurs in other ways, as well. One prime example is assigning inputs to the wrong task—as when wheat is grown on land best suited to soybean cultivation. Another important type of inefficiency occurs when large firms produce goods that smaller enterprises could make better because they can pay closer attention to

---

[1] A number of economists have argued that the Asian Tigers took this process too far, devoting *too many* resources to growth and not enough to current consumption.

detail, or when small firms produce outputs best suited to large-scale production. Some other examples are the outright waste that occurs because of favoritism (for example, promotion of an incompetent brother-in-law) or restrictive labor practices (for example, requiring a railroad to keep a fireman on a diesel-electric locomotive where there is nothing for him to do).

A particularly unfortunate form of waste is caused by discrimination against African-American, Hispanic, or female workers. When a job is given to a white male in preference to a more qualified African-American woman, society sacrifices potential output and the entire community is apt to be affected adversely. Every one of these inefficiencies means that the community obtains less output than it could have, given the available inputs.

THE THREE COORDINATION TASKS OF ANY ECONOMY

Allocation of resources refers to the society's decisions on how to divide up its scarce input resources among the different outputs produced in the economy and among the different firms or other organizations that produce those outputs.

In deciding how to **allocate its scarce resources,** every society must somehow make three sorts of decisions:

- First, as we have emphasized, it must figure out *how to utilize its resources efficiently;* that is, it must find a way to reach its production possibilities frontier.
- Second, it must decide *what combination of goods to produce*—how many missiles, automobiles, and so on; that is, it must select one specific point on the production possibilities frontier.
- Third, it must decide *how much of each good to distribute to each person,* doing so in a sensible way that does not assign meat to vegetarians and wine to teetotalers.

Societies can and do make each of these decisions—which economists often refer to as *how, what,* and *to whom?*—in many ways. For example, a central planner might tell people how to produce, what to produce, and what to consume, as the authorities used to do, at least to some extent, in the former Soviet Union. But in a market economy, no one group or individual makes such resource allocation decisions explicitly. Rather, consumer demands and production costs allocate resources *automatically* and *anonymously* through a system of prices and markets. As the formerly socialist countries learned, markets do an impressively effective job in carrying out these tasks. To see how markets can do all this, let's consider each task in turn.

SPECIALIZATION FOSTERS EFFICIENT RESOURCE ALLOCATION

Production efficiency is one of the economy's three basic tasks, and societies pursue it in many ways. But one source of efficiency is so fundamental that we must single it out for special attention: the tremendous productivity gains that stem from *specialization.*

THE WONDERS OF THE DIVISION OF LABOR

Division of labor means breaking up a task into a number of smaller, more *specialized* tasks so that each worker can become more adept at a particular job.

Adam Smith, the founder of modern economics, first marveled at how **division of labor** raises efficiency and productivity when he visited a pin factory. In a famous passage near the beginning of his monumental book, *The Wealth of Nations* (1776), he described what he saw:

> One man draws out the wire, another straightens it, a third cuts it, a fourth points it, a fifth grinds it at the top for receiving the head. To make the head requires two or three distinct operations; to put it on is a peculiar business, to whiten the pins is another; it is even a trade by itself to put them into the paper.[2]

---

[2] Adam Smith, *The Wealth of Nations* (New York: Random House, 1937), p. 4.

Smith observed that by dividing the work to be done in this way, each worker became quite skilled in a particular specialty, and the productivity of the group of workers as a whole was greatly enhanced. As Smith related it:

> I have seen a small manufactory of this kind where ten men only were employed. . . . Those ten persons . . . could make among them upwards of forty-eight thousand pins in a day. . . . But if they had all wrought separately and independently . . . they certainly could not each of them have made twenty, *perhaps not one pin in a day.*[3]

In other words, through the miracle of division of labor and specialization, ten workers accomplished what might otherwise have required thousands. This was one of the secrets of the Industrial Revolution, which helped lift humanity out of the abject poverty that had been its lot for centuries.

THE AMAZING PRINCIPLE OF COMPARATIVE ADVANTAGE

But specialization in production fosters efficiency in an even more profound sense. Adam Smith noticed that *how* goods are produced can make a huge difference to productivity. But so can *which* goods are produced. The reason is that people (and businesses, and nations) have different abilities. Some can repair automobiles, whereas others are wizards with numbers. Some are handy with computers, and others can cook. An economy will be most efficient if people specialize in doing what they do best and then trade with one another, so the accountant gets her car repaired and the computer programmer gets to eat tasty and nutritious meals.

This much is obvious. What is less obvious—and is one of the great ideas of economics—is that two people (or two businesses, or two countries) can generally gain from trade *even if one of them is more efficient than the other in producing everything.* A simple parable will help explain why.

Some lawyers can type better than their administrative assistants. Should such a lawyer fire her assistant and do her own typing? Not likely. Even though the lawyer may type better than the assistant, good judgment tells her to concentrate on practicing law and leave the typing to a lower-paid assistant. Why? Because the *opportunity cost* of an hour devoted to typing is an hour less time spent with clients, which is a far more lucrative activity.

This example illustrates the principle of **comparative advantage** at work. The lawyer specializes in arguing cases despite her advantage as a typist because she has a *still greater* advantage as an attorney. She suffers some direct loss by leaving the typing to a less-efficient employee. But she more than makes up for that loss by the income she earns selling her legal services to clients.

Precisely the same principle applies to nations. As we shall learn in greater detail in the chapter on international trade, comparative advantage underlies the economic analysis of international trade patterns. A country that is particularly adept at producing certain items—such as aircraft manufacturing in the United States, coffee growing in Brazil, and oil extraction in Saudi Arabia—should specialize in those activities, producing more than it wants for its own use. The country can then take the money it earns from its exports and purchase from other nations items that it does not make for itself.

The underlying logic is precisely the same as in our lawyer-typist example. The United States might, for example, be better than Japan at manufacturing both computers and television sets. But if the United States is vastly more efficient at producing computers, but only slightly more efficient at making TV sets, it pays for the United States to specialize in computer manufacture, for Japan to specialize in TV production, and for the two countries to trade.[4]

One country is said to have a **comparative advantage** over another in the production of a particular good relative to other goods if it produces that good less inefficiently as compared with the other country.

---

[3] Ibid., p. 5.

[4] This particular example is considered in detail in the chapter that examines international trade.

This principle, called the *law of comparative advantage*, was discovered by David Ricardo, one of the giants in the history of economic analysis, almost 200 years ago. It is one of the *Ideas for Beyond the Final Exam* introduced in Chapter 1.

THE LAW OF COMPARATIVE ADVANTAGE   Even if one country (or one worker) is worse than another country (or another worker) in the production of *every* good, it is said to have a *comparative advantage* in making the good at which it is *least inefficient*—compared to the other country. Ricardo discovered that two countries can gain by trading even if one country is more efficient than another in the production of *every* commodity. Precisely the same logic applies to individual workers or to businesses.

In determining the most efficient patterns of production and trade, it is comparative advantage that matters. Thus, a country can gain by importing a good from abroad even if that good can be produced more efficiently at home. Such imports make sense if they enable the country to specialize in producing goods at which it is *even more efficient*.

The Surprising Principle of Comparative Advantage

SPECIALIZATION LEADS TO EXCHANGE

The gains from specialization are welcome, but they create a problem: With specialization, people no longer produce only what they want to consume themselves. The workers in Adam Smith's pin factory had no use for the thousands of pins they produced each day; they wanted to trade them for things like food, clothing, and shelter. Similarly, the administrative assistant has no personal use for the legal briefs she types. Thus, specialization requires some mechanism by which workers producing pins can *exchange* their wares with workers producing such things as cloth and potatoes, and office workers can turn their typing skills into things they want to consume.

Without a system of exchange, the productivity miracle achieved by comparative advantage and the division of labor would do society little good. With it, standards of living have risen enormously. As we observed in Chapter 1, such exchange benefits *all* participants.

Trade Is a Win-Win Situation

MUTUAL GAINS FROM VOLUNTARY EXCHANGE   Unless someone is deceived or misunderstands the facts, a *voluntary* exchange between two parties must make both parties better off—or else why would each party agree? Trading increases production by permitting specialization, as we have just seen. But even if no additional goods are produced as a result of the act of trading, the welfare of society is increased because each individual acquires goods that are more suited to his or her needs and tastes. This simple but fundamental precept of economics is another of our *Ideas for Beyond the Final Exam*.

Although people can and do trade goods for other goods, a system of exchange works better when everyone agrees to use some common item (such as pieces of paper with unique markings printed on them) for buying and selling things. Enter *money*. Then workers in pin factories, for example, can be paid in money rather than in pins, and they can use this money to purchase cloth and potatoes. Textile workers and farmers can do the same.

These two phenomena—specialization and exchange (assisted by money)—working in tandem led to vast improvements in humanity's well-being. But what forces induce workers to join together so that society can enjoy the fruits of the division of labor? And what forces establish a smoothly functioning system of exchange so that people can first exploit their comparative advantages and then acquire what they want to consume? One alternative is to have a central authority telling people what to do. But Adam Smith explained and extolled another way of organizing and coordinating economic activity—markets and prices can coordinate those activities.

■ MARKETS, PRICES, AND THE THREE COORDINATION TASKS

Smith noted that people are adept at pursuing their own self-interests, and that a **market system** harnesses this self-interest remarkably well. As he put it—with pretty clear religious overtones—in doing what is best for themselves, people are "led by an invisible hand" to promote the economic well-being of society as a whole.

Those of us who live in a well-functioning market economy like the United States tend to take the achievements of the market for granted, much like the daily rising and setting of the sun. Few bother to think about, say, what makes Florida oranges show up daily in South Dakota supermarkets. Although the process by which the market guides the economy in such an orderly fashion is subtle and complex, the general principles are well known.

The market deals with efficiency in production through the profit motive, which discourages firms from using inputs wastefully. Valuable resources (such as energy) command high prices, giving producers strong incentives to use them efficiently. The market mechanism also guides firms' output decisions, matching quantities produced to consumer preferences. A rise in the price of wheat because of increased demand for bread, for example, will persuade farmers to produce more wheat and devote less of their land to soybeans.

Finally, a price system distributes goods among consumers in accord with their tastes and preferences, using voluntary exchange to determine who gets what. Consumers spend their incomes on the things they like best (among those they can afford). But the ability to buy goods is hardly divided equally. Workers with valuable skills and owners of scarce resources can sell what they have at attractive prices. With the incomes they earn, they can purchase generous amounts of goods and services. Those who are less successful in selling what they own receive lower incomes and so can afford to buy less. In extreme cases, they may suffer severe deprivation.

This, in broad terms, is how a market economy solves the three basic problems facing any society: how to produce any given combination of goods efficiently, how to select an appropriate combination of goods to produce, and how to distribute these goods sensibly among people. As we proceed through the following chapters, you will learn much more about these issues. You will see that they constitute the central theme that permeates not only this text, but the work of economists in general. As you progress through the book, keep in mind two questions:

- ■ What does the market do well?
- ■ What does it do poorly?

There are numerous answers to both questions, as you will learn in subsequent chapters.

> Society has many important goals. Some of them, such as producing goods and services with maximum efficiency (minimum waste), can be achieved extraordinarily well by letting markets operate more or less freely.
>
> Free markets will not, however, achieve all of society's goals. For example, they often have trouble keeping unemployment low. In fact, the unfettered operations of markets may even run counter to some goals—such as protection of the environment. Many observers also believe that markets do not necessarily distribute income in accord with ethical or moral norms.
>
> But even in cases where markets do not perform at all well, there may be ways of harnessing the power of the market mechanism to remedy its own deficiencies, as you will learn in later chapters.

A **market system** is a form of economic organization in which resource allocation decisions are left to individual producers and consumers acting in their own best interests without central direction.

■ LAST WORD: DON'T CONFUSE ENDS WITH MEANS

Economic debates often have political and ideological overtones. So we think it important to close this chapter by emphasizing that the central theme that we have just outlined is neither a *defense of* nor an *attack on* the capitalist system. Nor is it a "conservative" position. One does not have to be a conservative to recognize that the market mechanism can be an extraordinarily helpful instrument for the pursuit of economic goals. Most of the formerly socialist countries of Europe have been working hard to "marketize" their economies, and even the communist People's Republic of China has taken huge strides in that direction.

The point is not to confuse ends with means in deciding how much to rely on market forces. Liberals and conservatives surely have different goals. But the means chosen to pursue these goals should, for the most part, be chosen on the basis of how effective they are, not on some ideological prejudgments.

Even Karl Marx emphasized that the market is remarkably efficient at producing an abundance of goods and services that had never been seen in precapitalist history. Such wealth can be used to promote conservative goals, such as reducing tax rates, or to facilitate goals favored by liberals, such as providing more generous public aid for the poor.

Certainly, the market cannot deal with every economic problem. Indeed, we have just noted that the market is the *source* of a number of significant problems. But the evidence accumulated over centuries leads economists to believe that most economic problems are best handled by market techniques. The analysis in this book is intended to help you identify both the objectives the market mechanism can reliably achieve and those that it will fail to promote, or at least not promote very effectively. We urge you to forget the slogans you have heard—whether from the left or from the right—and make up your own mind after learning the material in this book.

SUMMARY

1. Supplies of all *resources* are limited. Because resources are scarce, a *rational decision* is one that chooses the best alternative among the options that are possible with the available resources.

2. With limited resources, a decision to obtain more of one item is also a decision to give up some of another. What we give up is called the *opportunity cost* of what we get. The opportunity cost is the true cost of any decision. This is one of the *Ideas for Beyond the Final Exam.*

3. When markets function effectively, firms are led to use resources efficiently and to produce the things that consumers want most. In such cases, opportunity costs and money costs (prices) correspond closely. When the market performs poorly, or when important costly items do not get price tags, opportunity costs and money costs can diverge.

4. A firm's *production possibilities frontier* shows the combinations of goods it can produce, given the current technology and the resources at its disposal. The frontier is usually bowed outward because resources tend to be specialized.

5. The *principle of increasing costs* states that as the production of one good expands, the opportunity cost of producing another unit of that good generally increases.

6. Like a firm, the economy as a whole has a production possibilities frontier whose position is determined by its technology and by the available resources of land, labor, capital, and raw materials.

7. A firm or an economy that ends up at a point below its production possibilities frontier is using its resources inefficiently or wastefully. This is what happens, for example, when there is unemployment.

8. *Economic growth* means there is an outward shift in the economy's production possibilities frontier. The faster the growth, the faster this shift occurs. But growth requires a sacrifice of current consumption—which is its opportunity cost.

9. Economists define *efficiency* as the absence of waste. It is achieved primarily by the gains in productivity brought about through *specialization* that exploits *division of labor* and *comparative advantage* and by a *system of exchange.*

10. Two countries (or two people) can gain by specializing in the activity in which each has a comparative advantage and then trading with one another. These gains from trade remain available even if one country is inferior at producing everything. This so-called *principle of comparative advantage* is one of our *Ideas for Beyond the Final Exam.*

11. If an exchange is voluntary, both parties must benefit, even if no additional goods are produced. This is another of the *Ideas for Beyond the Final Exam.*

12. Every economic system must find a way to answer three basic questions: How can goods be produced most efficiently? How much of each good should be produced? How should goods be distributed?

13. The *market system* works very well in solving some of society's basic problems, but it fails to remedy others and may, indeed, create some of its own. Where and how it succeeds and fails constitute the central theme of this book and characterize the work of economists in general.

KEY TERMS

Resources   52

Scarcity   52

Choice   52

Opportunity cost   53

Rational decision   53

Outputs   54

Inputs (means of production)   54

Production possibilities frontier   54

Principle of increasing costs   55

Economic growth   58

Consumption good   58

Capital good   58

Efficiency   59

Allocation of resources   60

Three coordination tasks   60

Specialization   60

Division of labor   60

Comparative advantage   61

Exchange   62

Market system   63

QUESTIONS FOR REVIEW

1. Discuss the resource limitations that affect:

   a. the poorest person on earth

   b. Bill Gates, the richest person on earth

   c. a farmer in Kansas

   d. the government of Indonesia

2. If you were president of your college, what would you change if your budget were cut by 10 percent? By 25 percent? By 50 percent?

3. If you were to leave college, what things would change in your life? What, then, is the opportunity cost of your education?

4. A person rents a house for which she pays the landlord $12,000 a year. The house can be purchased for $100,000, and the tenant has this much money in a bank account that pays 4 percent interest per year. Is buying the house a good deal for the tenant? Where does opportunity cost enter the picture?

5. Construct graphically the production possibilities frontier for the nation of Stromboli, using the data given in the following table. Does the principle of increasing cost hold in Stromboli?

6. Consider two alternatives for Stromboli in the year 2000. In case (a), its inhabitants eat 60 million pizzas and build only 6,000 pizza ovens. In case (b), the population eats only 15 million pizzas but builds 18,000 ovens. Which case will lead to a more generous production possibilities frontier for Stromboli in 2001?

7. Sarah's Snack Shop sells two brands of potato chips. Brand X costs Sarah 60 cents per bag, and Brand Y costs Sarah $1. Draw Sarah's production possibilities frontier if she has $60 budgeted to spend on potato chips. Why is it not "bowed out"?

8. Raising chickens requires several types of feed, such as corn and soy meal. Consider a farm in the former Soviet Union. Try to describe how decisions on the number of chickens to be raised, and the amount of each feed to use in raising them, were made under the old communist regime. If the farm is now privately owned, how does the market guide the decisions that used to be made by the central planning agency?

9. The United States is one of the world's wealthiest countries. Think of a recent case in which the decisions of the U.S. government were severely constrained by scarcity. Describe the trade-offs that were involved. What were the opportunity costs of the decisions that were actually made?

Stromboli's 2000 Production Possibilities

Pizzas per year	Pizza Ovens per year
75,000,000	0
60,000,000	6,000
45,000,000	11,000
30,000,000	15,000
15,000,000	18,000
0	20,000

The free enterprise system is absolutely too important to be left to the voluntary action of the marketplace.

Florida Congressman Richard Kelly, 1979

SUPPLY AND DEMAND: AN INITIAL LOOK

Scarcity, choice, and coordination constitute the basic problem of economics, as we saw in Chapter 4. In this chapter we study the most basic tool for investigation of these subjects: supply and demand. Whether your course concentrates on macroeconomics or microeconomics, you will find that it uses the so-called law of supply and demand as the fundamental tool of economic analysis. Economists use supply and demand analysis to study issues as diverse as inflation and unemployment, the international value of the dollar, government regulation of business, and environmental protection. So careful study of this chapter will pay rich dividends, both in this course and in any other economics courses you may take. Supply and demand curves—graphs that relate price to quantity supplied and quantity demanded, respectively—show how prices and quantities are determined in a free market.

One major theme of the chapter is that governments around the world and throughout recorded history have tampered with the price mechanism. We will see that these bouts with Adam Smith's invisible hand often have produced undesirable side effects that surprised and dismayed the authorities. The invisible hand fights back!

This chapter uses graphs such as those described in Chapter 2 extensively. If you have difficulties with these graphs, we suggest that you review the first part of that chapter before proceeding.

Application: What in the World Happened to Those Asian Currencies?

A worldwide financial crisis began in the last half of 1997, when the currencies of several Asian economies, including Thailand, Indonesia, Malaysia, and South Korea,

plummeted in value. The most spectacular example was the fall of the Indonesian rupiah. In July 1997, it took about 2,500 rupiah to buy one U.S. dollar. By winter, it took about 10,000. This means that, relative to the dollar, the rupiah lost a stunning 75 percent of its value in just a few months.

What could have caused such a calamitous drop in the value of the rupiah? The answer is complicated, and not entirely rational. We shall have much more to say about the Asian economic crisis later in the book. But the essence of the rupiah's problem, as we shall see in this chapter, involved nothing more complex than the rudimentary law of supply and demand.

■ THE INVISIBLE HAND

The invisible hand is a phrase used by Adam Smith to describe how, by pursuing their own self-interests, people in a market system are "led by an invisible hand" to promote societal well-being.

Adam Smith greatly admired the price system. He marveled at its accomplishments—both as an efficient producer of goods and as a guarantor that consumers' preferences are obeyed. Many people since Smith's time have shared his enthusiasm for the concept of the **invisible hand,** but many have not. His contemporaries in the American colonies, for example, were often unhappy with the prices produced by free markets and thought they could do better by legislative decree. They could not,

● PRICE CONTROLS AT VALLEY FORGE

George Washington, the history books tell us, was beset by many enemies during the winter of 1777–1778, including the British, their Hessian mercenaries, and the merciless winter weather. But he had another enemy that the history books ignore, an enemy that meant well but almost destroyed his army at Valley Forge. As the following excerpt explains, that enemy was the Pennsylvania legislature.

> In Pennsylvania, where the main force of Washington's army was quartered . . . the legislature . . . decided to try a period of price control limited to those commodities needed for use by the army. . . . The result might have been anticipated by those with some knowledge of the trials and tribulations of other states. The prices of uncontrolled goods, mostly imported, rose to record heights. Most farmers kept back their produce, refusing to sell at what they regarded as an unfair price. Some who had large families to take care of even secretly sold their food to the British who paid in gold.
>
> After the disastrous winter at Valley Forge when Washington's army nearly starved to death (thanks largely to these well-intentioned but misdirected laws), the ill-fated experiment in price controls was finally ended. The Continental Congress on June 4, 1778, adopted the following resolution:
>
> "Whereas . . . it hath been found by experience that limitations upon the prices of commodities are not only ineffectual for the purposes proposed, but likewise productive of very evil consequences . . . resolved, that it be recommended to the several states to repeal or suspend all laws or resolutions within the said states respectively limiting, regulating or restraining the Price of any Article, Manufacture or Commodity."

SOURCE: Robert L. Schuettinger and Eamonn F. Butler, *Forty Centuries of Wage and Price Controls* (Washington, D.C.: Heritage Foundation, 1979), p. 41. Reprinted by permission.

Valley Forge.

as explained in the accompanying box, "Price Controls at Valley Forge." In countless other instances, the public was outraged by the prices charged on the open market, particularly in the case of housing rents, interest rates, and insurance rates.

Attempts to control interest rates (which are the price of borrowing money) go back hundreds of years before the birth of Christ, at least to the code of laws compiled under the Babylonian king Hammurabi in about 1800 B.C. Our historical legacy also includes a rather long list of price ceilings on foods and other products imposed in the reign of Diocletian, emperor of the declining Roman Empire. More recently, Americans have been offered the "protection" of a variety of price controls.

Laws have placed ceilings on some prices (such as rents) to protect buyers, whereas legislation has placed floors under other prices (such as farm products) to protect sellers. Yet, somehow, everything such regulation touches seems to end up in even greater disarray than it was before. Despite rent controls, rents in New York City have soared. Despite laws against "scalping," tickets for popular shows and sports events sell at tremendous premiums—tickets to the Super Bowl, for example, often fetch thousands of dollars on the "gray" market. Taxis cost much more in New York City (where they are tightly regulated) than in Washington, D.C. (where they are not).

To understand what goes wrong when markets are tampered with, we must first learn how they operate unfettered. This chapter takes a first step in that direction by studying the machinery of supply and demand. Then, at the end of the chapter, we return to the issue of price controls.

Every market has both buyers and sellers. We begin our analysis on the consumers' side of the market.

■ DEMAND AND QUANTITY DEMANDED

People commonly think of consumer demands as fixed amounts. For example, when product designers propose a new computer model, management asks: "What is its market potential?" Similarly, government bureaus conduct studies to determine how many engineers the workforce will require (demand) in subsequent years.

Economists respond that such questions are not well posed—that there is no single answer to such a question. Rather, they say, the "market potential" for computers or the number of engineers that will be "required" depends on a great number of influences, including the price charged for each.

> The **quantity demanded** of any product normally depends on its price. Quantity demanded also depends on a number of other determinants, including population size, consumer incomes, tastes, and the prices of other products.

The **quantity demanded** is the number of units of a good that consumers want to buy over a specified period of time.

Because prices play a central role in a market economy, we begin our study of demand by focusing on how quantity demanded depends on price. A little later, we will bring the other determinants of quantity demanded back into the picture. For now, we consider all influences other than price as fixed; this assumption, often stated as "other things being equal," holds for virtually any static economic analysis. Consider, as an example, the quantity of milk demanded. Almost everyone purchases at least some milk. However, if the price of milk is very high, its "market potential" may be very small. People will find ways to get along with less milk, perhaps by switching to fruit juice or soda. If the price of milk declines, people will tend to drink more milk. They may give their children larger portions or switch away from juices and sodas. Thus:

> There is no one demand figure for milk, for computers, or for engineers. Rather, there is a different quantity demanded at each possible price, all other influences being held constant.

A **demand schedule** is a table showing how the quantity demanded of some product during a specified period of time changes as the price of that product changes, holding all other determinants of quantity demanded constant.

A **demand curve** is a graphical depiction of a demand schedule. It shows how the quantity demanded of some product during a specified period of time will change as the price of that product changes, holding all other determinants of quantity demanded constant.

THE DEMAND SCHEDULE

Table 5–1 displays this hypothetical information for milk in what we call a **demand schedule**. It indicates how much milk consumers in a particular area are willing and able to buy at different possible prices during a specified period of time, other things held equal. Specifically, the table shows the quantity of milk that will be demanded in a year at each possible price ranging from $1.50 to 90 cents per quart. We see, for example, that at a relatively low price, like $1 per quart, customers wish to purchase 70 billion quarts per year. But if the price were to rise to, say, $1.40 per quart, quantity demanded would fall to 50 billion quarts.

A **shift in a demand curve** occurs when any variable other than price changes. If consumers want to buy *more* at any given price than they wanted previously, the demand curve shifts to the right (or outward). If they desire *less* at any given price, the demand curve shifts to the left (or inward).

Common sense tells us why this happens.[1] First, as prices rise, some customers will reduce the quantity of milk they consume. Second, higher prices will induce

TABLE 5–1	**Demand Schedule for Milk**

Demand Schedule for Milk

Price per Quart	Quantity Demanded	Label in Figure 5–1
$1.50	45	A
1.40	50	B
1.30	55	C
1.20	60	E
1.10	65	F
1.00	70	G
0.90	75	H

NOTE: Quantity is in billions of quarts per year.

---

[1] This common-sense answer is examined more fully in later chapters.

some customers to drop out of the market entirely—for example, by switching to soda or juice. On both counts, quantity demanded will decline as the price rises.

As the price of an item rises, the quantity demanded normally falls. As the price falls, the quantity demanded normally rises, all other things held constant.

THE DEMAND CURVE

The information contained in Table 5–1 can be summarized in a graph like Figure 5–1, which is called a **demand curve.** Each point in the graph corresponds to a line in the table. This curve shows the relationship between price and quantity demanded. For example, to sell 70 billion quarts per year, the price must be one dollar. This is

shown at point *G* in Figure 5–1. If, instead, the price is $1.40, consumers will demand only 50 billion quarts (point *B*). Because the quantity demanded declines as the price increases, the demand curve has a negative slope.[2]

Notice the last phrase in the definitions of the demand schedule and the demand curve: "holding all other determinants of quantity demanded constant." What are some of these "other things," and how do they affect the demand curve?

FIGURE 5-1

Demand Curve for Milk

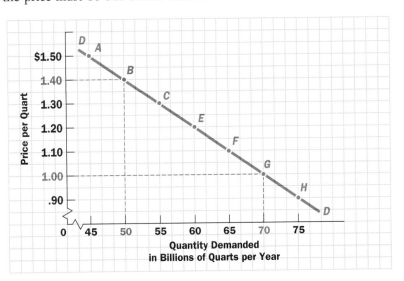

SHIFTS OF THE DEMAND CURVE

The quantity of milk demanded is subject to a variety of influences other than the price of milk. Changes in population size and characteristics, consumer incomes and tastes, and the prices of alternative beverages such as soda and orange juice presumably change the quantity of milk demanded, even if the price of milk does not change.

Because the demand curve for milk depicts only the relationship between the quantity of milk demanded and the price of milk, holding all other factors constant, a change in any of these *other* factors produces a **shift of the entire demand curve.** More generally:

A change in the price of a good produces a movement *along* a fixed demand curve. By contrast, a change in any other variable that influences quantity demanded produces a shift of the *entire* demand curve.

FIGURE 5-2

Movements along versus Shifts of a Demand Curve

If consumers want to buy more milk at every given price than they wanted previously, the demand curve shifts to the right (or outward). If they desire less at every given price, the demand curve shifts to the left (or inward toward the origin).

Figure 5–2 shows this distinction graphically. If the price of milk falls from $1.30 per quart to $1.10, and quantity demanded rises accordingly, we move along demand curve D_0D_0 from point *C* to point *F*, as shown by the blue arrow. If, on the other hand, consumers suddenly decide that they like milk better than they did formerly, or if more

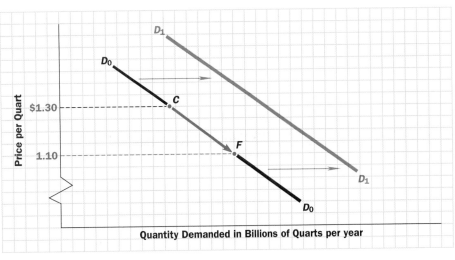

Quantity Demanded in Billions of Quarts per year

sumers suddenly decide that they like milk better than they did formerly, or if more

---

[2] If you need to review the concept of slope, refer back to Chapter 2.

children are born who need more milk, the entire demand curve shifts outward from D_0D_0 to D_1D_1, as indicated by the red arrows. To make this general idea more concrete, and to show some of its many applications, let us consider some specific examples of those "other things" that can shift demand curves.

CONSUMER INCOMES   If average incomes rise, consumers will purchase more of most goods, including milk, even if the prices of those goods remain the same. That is, increases in income normally shift demand curves outward to the right, as depicted in Figure 5–3(a), where the demand curve shifts outward from D_0D_0 to D_1D_1, establishing a new equilibrium price and quantity.

FIGURE 5–3	**Shifts of the Demand Curve**

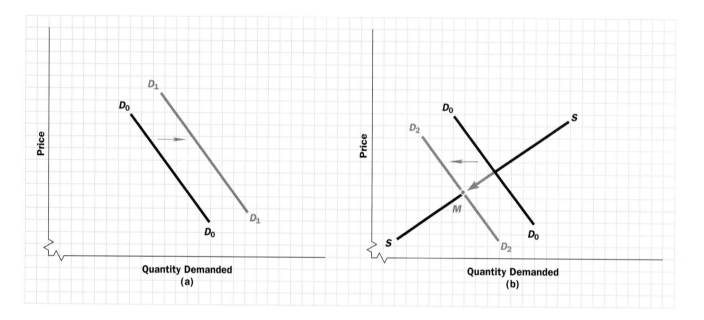

POPULATION   Population growth affects quantity demanded in more or less the same way as increases in average incomes. For instance, a larger population will presumably want to consume more milk, even if the price of milk and average incomes do not change, thus shifting the entire demand curve to the right, as in Figure 5–3(a). The equilibrium price and quantity both rise. And increases in particular population segments can elicit shifts in demand—for example, the United States in recent years has been experiencing a miniature population boom of people in their mid- to late-20s. Dubbed "Generation X," this fast-growing group has sparked higher demand for big-ticket items such as sport-utility vehicles and contemporary furniture.

In Figure 5–3(b) we see that a decrease in population should shift the demand curve for milk to the left from D_0D_0 to D_2D_2.

CONSUMER PREFERENCES   If the dairy industry mounts a successful advertising campaign extolling the benefits of drinking milk, families may decide to buy more at any given price. If so, the entire demand curve for milk would shift to the right, as in Figure 5–3(a). Alternatively, a medical report on the dangers of kidney stones may persuade consumers to drink less milk, thereby shifting the demand curve to the left, as in Figure 5–3(b). Again, these are general phenomena:

If consumer preferences shift in favor of a particular item, its demand curve will shift outward to the right, as in Figure 5–3(a).

An interesting example of this phenomenon was the mushrooming demand for Beanie Babies. Collectors snapped up these toy animals so quickly that retailers couldn't keep them in their stores.

PRICES AND AVAILABILITY OF RELATED GOODS   Because soda, orange juice, and coffee are popular drinks that compete with milk, a change in the price of any of these other beverages can be expected to shift the demand curve for milk. If any of these alternative drinks becomes cheaper, some consumers will switch away from milk. Thus, the demand curve for milk will shift to the left, as in Figure 5–3(b). Other price changes shift the demand curve for milk in the opposite direction. For example, suppose that cookies, which are often consumed with milk, become less expensive. This may induce some consumers to drink more milk and thus shift the demand curve for milk to the right, as in Figure 5–3(a). In general:

> Increases in the prices of goods that are substitutes for the good in question (as soda is for milk) move the demand curve to the right. Increases in the prices of goods that are normally used together with the good in question (such as cookies and milk) shift the demand curve to the left.

This is just what happened when a frost wiped out almost half of Brazil's coffee bean harvest in 1995. The three biggest U.S. coffee producers raised their prices by 45 percent, and, as a result, the demand curve for alternative beverages like tea shifted to the right. Then in 1998, coffee prices dropped about 34 percent, and this influenced the demand curve for tea to shift toward the left (or toward the origin), all other things being equal.

Although the preceding list does not exhaust the possible influences on quantity demanded, we have said enough to suggest the principles followed by demand and shifts of demand. Let us therefore turn to the supply side of the market.

■ SUPPLY AND QUANTITY SUPPLIED

Like quantity demanded, the quantity of milk that is supplied by business firms such as dairy farms is not a fixed number; it also depends on many things. Obviously, we expect more milk will be supplied if there are more dairy farms, or more cows per farm. Cows may give less milk if bad weather deprives them of their feed. As before, however, let's turn our attention first to the relationship between the *price* and *quantity* of milk supplied.

Economists generally suppose that a higher price calls forth a greater **quantity supplied**. Why? Remember our analysis of the principle of increasing cost in Chapter 4 (page 55). According to that principle, as more of any farmer's (or the nation's) resources are devoted to milk production, the opportunity cost of obtaining another quart of milk increases. Farmers will therefore find it profitable to increase milk production only if they can sell the milk at a higher price—high enough to cover the additional costs incurred to expand production.

> The **quantity supplied** is the number of units that sellers want to sell over a specified period of time.

In other words, it normally will take higher prices to persuade farmers to raise milk production. This idea is quite general and applies to the supply of most goods and services.[3] As long as suppliers want to make profits and the principle of increasing costs holds:

> As the price of any commodity rises, the quantity supplied normally rises. As the price falls, the quantity supplied normally falls.

THE SUPPLY SCHEDULE AND THE SUPPLY CURVE

Table 5–2 shows the relationship between the price of milk and its quantity supplied. Tables such as this are called **supply schedules;** they show how much sellers are willing to provide during a specified period at alternative possible prices. This particular supply schedule shows that a low price like $1 per quart will induce suppliers to provide only 40 billion quarts, whereas a higher price like $1.30 will induce them to provide much more—70 billion quarts.

> A **supply schedule** is a table showing how the quantity supplied of some product during a specified period of time changes as the price of that product changes, holding all other determinants of quantity supplied constant.

---

[3] This analysis is carried out in much greater detail in later chapters.

● A 20,000 PERCENT BOUNCE: NOW THAT'S VOLATILITY

This 1998 newspaper story shows the dramatic effect on prices that can sometimes result from a shift in a demand curve.

Because no one can stockpile electricity . . . prices have proved to be extremely volatile at times of high demand like this summer's heat waves. Here is the *Cinergy-Power Markets Week* daily index, in dollars per megawatt hour. When heat waves blistered much of the country in June and July, utility customers like Juana Esparza of Dallas ran fans and air conditioners nonstop, and power demand soared.

SOURCE: *The New York Times,* Business Section, August 23, 1998, p. 4.

Source:
Enron
Corporation

NOTE: Price is in dollars per megawatt hour.

Supply Schedule for Milk

TABLE 5-2

Price per Quart	Quantity Supplied	Label in Figure 5–4
$1.50	90	a
1.40	80	b
1.30	70	c
1.20	60	e
1.10	50	f
1.00	40	g
0.90	30	h

NOTE: Quantity is in billions of quarts per year.

A **supply curve** is a graphical depiction of a supply schedule. It shows how the quantity supplied of some product during a specified period of time will change as the price of that product changes, holding all other determinants of quantity supplied constant.

FIGURE 5-4

Supply Curve for Milk

As you might have guessed, when information like this is plotted on a graph, it is called a **supply curve**. Figure 5–4 is the supply curve corresponding to the supply schedule in Table 5–2, showing the relationship between the price of milk and the quantity supplied. It slopes upward because quantity supplied is higher when price is higher. Notice again the same phrase in the definition: "holding all other determinants of quantity supplied constant." What are these "other determinants"?

SHIFTS OF THE SUPPLY CURVE

Like quantity demanded, the quantity supplied in a market typically responds to many influences other than price. The weather, the cost of feed, the number and size of dairy farms, and a variety of other factors all influence how much milk will be brought to market. Because the supply curve depicts only the relationship between the price of milk and the quantity of milk supplied, holding all other influences constant, a change in any of these other determinants of quantity supplied will cause the entire supply curve to shift. That is:

> A change in the price of the good causes a movement *along* a fixed supply curve. But price is not the only influence on quantity supplied. If any of these other influences change, the *entire* supply curve shifts.

Figure 5–5 depicts the distinction graphically. A rise in price from $1.10 to $1.30 will raise quantity supplied by moving along supply curve S_0S_0 from point *f* to point *c*. But any rise in quantity supplied attributable to an influence other than price will shift the *entire* supply curve outward to the right from S_0S_0 to S_1S_1, as shown by the red arrows. Let us consider what some of these other influences are and how they shift the supply curve.

FIGURE 5-5

Movements along versus Shifts of a Supply Curve

SIZE OF THE INDUSTRY We begin with the most obvious influence. If more farmers enter the milk industry, the quantity supplied at any given price will increase. For example, if each farm provides 600,000 quarts of milk per year at a price of $1.10 per quart, then 100,000 farmers provide 60 billion quarts, but 130,000 farmers provide 78 billion. Thus, when more farms are in the industry, the quantity of milk supplied will be greater at any given price—and hence the supply curve will move farther to the right.

Figure 5–6(a) illustrates the effect of an expansion of the industry from 100,000 farms to 130,000 farms—a rightward shift of the supply curve from S_0S_0 to S_1S_1. Figure 5–6(b) illustrates the opposite case: a contraction of the industry from 100,000 farms to 62,500 farms. The supply curve shifts inward to the left from S_0S_0 to S_2S_2. Even if no farmers enter or leave the industry, results like those depicted in Figure 5–6 can be produced by expansion or contraction of the *existing* farms.

| FIGURE 5–6 | **Shifts of the Supply Curve** |

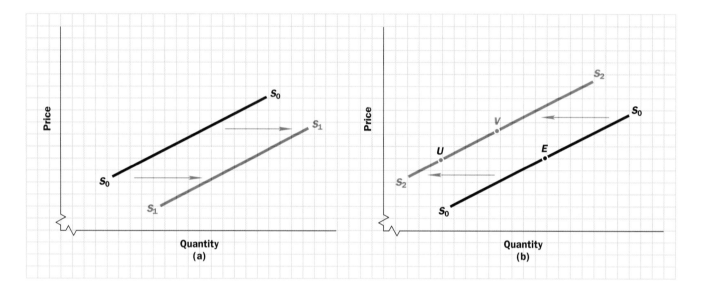

Quantity
(a)

Quantity
(b)

TECHNOLOGICAL PROGRESS   Another influence that shifts supply curves is tech-nological change. Suppose some enterprising farmer discovers that cows produce more milk if they listen to Mozart during milking time. Thereafter, at any given price, farms will be able to produce more milk; that is, the supply curve will shift outward to the right, as in Figure 5–6(a). This, again, illustrates a general influence that applies to most industries:

> Technological progress that reduces costs will shift the supply curve outward to the right.

Automakers, for example, have been able to reduce production costs since indus-trial technology invented robots that can be programmed to work on several differ-ent car models. This technological advance has shifted the supply curve outward.

PRICES OF INPUTS   Changes in input prices also shift supply curves. Suppose a drought raises the price of animal feed. Farmers will have to pay more to keep their cows alive and healthy and consequently will no longer be able to provide the same quantity of milk at each possible price. This example illustrates that:

> Increases in the prices of inputs that suppliers must buy will shift the supply curve inward to the left.

PRICES OF RELATED OUTPUTS   Dairy farms sell products other than milk. If cheese prices rise sharply, farmers may decide to use some raw milk to make cheese, thereby reducing the quantity of milk supplied. On a supply-demand diagram, the supply curve would then shift inward, as in Figure 5–6(b).

Similar phenomena occur in other industries, and sometimes the effect goes the other way. For example, suppose that the price of beef goes up, which increases the quantity of meat supplied. That, in turn, will raise the number of cowhides supplied even if the price of leather does not change. Thus, a rise in the price of beef will lead to a rightward shift in the supply curve of leather. In general:

A change in the price of one good produced by a multiproduct industry may be expected to shift the supply curves of other goods produced by that industry.

A **supply-demand diagram** graphs the supply and demand curves together. It depicts the equilibrium price and quantity.

A **shortage** is an excess of quantity demanded over quantity supplied. When there is a shortage, buyers cannot purchase the quantities they desire.

■ SUPPLY AND DEMAND EQUILIBRIUM

To analyze how the free market determines price, we must compare the desires of consumers (demand) with the desires of producers (supply) to see whether the two plans are consistent. Table 5–3 and Figure 5–7 help us do this.

Table 5–3 brings together the demand schedule from Table 5–1 and the supply schedule from Table 5–2. Similarly, Figure 5–7 puts the demand curve from Figure 5–1 and the supply curve from Figure 5–4 on a single graph. Such graphs are called **supply-demand diagrams,** and you will encounter many of them in this book. Notice that, for reasons already discussed, the demand curve has a negative slope and the supply curve has a positive slope. That is generally true of supply-demand diagrams.

In a free market, price and quantity are determined by the intersection of the supply and demand curves. At only one point in Figure 5–7, point *E*, do the supply curve and the demand curve intersect. At the price corresponding to point *E*, which is $1.20 per quart, the quantity supplied and the quantity demanded are both 60 billion quarts per year. This means that, at a price of $1.20 per quart, consumers are willing to buy exactly what producers are willing to sell.

At any lower price, such as $1, only 40 billion quarts of milk will be supplied (point *g*) whereas 70 billion quarts will be demanded (point *G*). Thus, quantity demanded will exceed quantity supplied. There will be a **shortage** equal to 70 minus 40, or 30 billion quarts. Price will thus be driven up by unsatisfied demand. Alternatively, at a higher price like $1.50, quantity supplied will be 90 billion quarts (point *a*) while quantity demanded will be only 45 billion (point *A*). Quantity supplied will exceed quantity demanded—constituting a **surplus** equal to 90 minus 45, or 45 billion quarts.

FIGURE 5-7

Supply-Demand Equilibrium

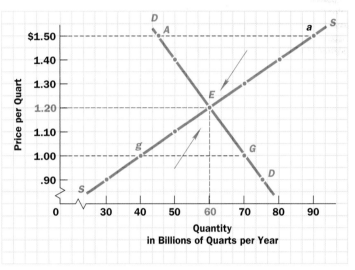

A **surplus** is an excess of quantity supplied over quantity demanded. When there is a surplus, sellers cannot sell the quantities they desire to supply.

Determination of the Equilibrium Price and Quantity of Milk

TABLE 5-3

Price per Quart	Quantity Demanded	Quantity Supplied	Surplus or Shortage?	Price Direction
$1.50	45	90	Surplus	Fall
1.40	50	80	Surplus	Fall
1.30	55	70	Surplus	Fall
1.20	60	60	Neither	Unchanged
1.10	65	50	Shortage	Rise
1.00	70	40	Shortage	Rise
0.90	75	30	Shortage	Rise

NOTE: Quantity is in billions of quarts per year.

Non Sequitur Survival Guide for the Nineties © The Washington Post

An **equilibrium** is a situation in which there are no inherent forces that produce change. Changes away from an equilibrium position will occur only as a result of "outside events" that disturb the status quo.

Because $1.20 is the price at which quantity supplied and quantity demanded are equal, we say that $1.20 per quart is the equilibrium price in this market. Similarly, 60 billion quarts per year is the equilibrium quantity of milk. The term **equilibrium** merits a little explanation, because it arises so frequently in economic analysis.

An equilibrium is a situation in which there are no inherent forces that produce change. Think, for example, of a pendulum resting at its center point. If no outside force (such as a person's hand) comes to push it, the pendulum will remain exactly where it is; it is therefore in equilibrium.

But if you give the pendulum a shove, its equilibrium will be disturbed and it will start to move upward. When it reaches the top of its arc, the pendulum will, for an instant, be at rest again. But this is not an equilibrium position, for the force of gravity will pull the pendulum downward. Thereafter, gravity and friction will govern its motion from side to side. Eventually, we know, the pendulum will return to its original position. The fact that the pendulum tends to return to it original position is described by saying that this position is a stable equilibrium. And that position is the only equilibrium position of the pendulum. At any other point, inherent forces will cause the pendulum to move.

The concept of equilibrium in economics is similar and can be illustrated by our supply-and-demand example. Why is no price other than $1.20 an equilibrium price in Table 5–3 or Figure 5–7? What forces will change any other price?

Consider first a low price like $1, at which quantity demanded (70 billion quarts) exceeds quantity supplied (40 billion). If the price were this low, many frustrated customers would be unable to purchase the quantities they desired. In their scramble for the available supply of milk, some would offer to pay more. As customers sought to outbid one another, the market price would be forced up. Thus, a price below the equilibrium price cannot persist in a free market because a shortage sets in motion powerful economic forces that push price upward.

Similar forces operate if the market price is above the equilibrium price. If, for example, the price should somehow get to be $1.50, Table 5–3 tells us that quantity supplied (90 billion quarts) would far exceed quantity demanded (45 billion). Producers would be unable to sell their desired quantities of milk at the prevailing price, and some would undercut their competitors by reducing price. Such competitive price cutting would continue as long as the surplus remained, that is, as long as quantity supplied exceeded quantity demanded. Thus, a price above the equilibrium price cannot persist indefinitely.

We are left with a clear conclusion. The price $1.20 per quart and the quantity 60 billion quarts per year is the only price-quantity combination that does not sow the seeds of its own destruction. It is thus the only equilibrium for this market. Any lower price must rise, and any higher price must fall. It is as if natural economic forces place a magnet at point E that attracts the market, just as gravity attracts a pendulum.

The pendulum analogy is worth pursuing further. Most pendulums are more frequently in motion than at rest. However, unless they are repeatedly buffeted by outside forces (which, of course, is exactly what happens to pendulums used in clocks), pendulums gradually return to their resting points. The same is true of price and quantity in a free market. They are moved about by shifts in the supply and demand curves that we have already described. So markets are not always in equilibrium. But, if nothing interferes with them, experience shows that they normally move toward equilibrium.

THE LAW OF SUPPLY AND DEMAND

In a free market, the forces of supply and demand generally push the price toward its equilibrium level, the price at which quantity supplied and quantity demanded are equal. Like most economic "laws," some markets will occasionally disobey the law of supply and demand. Markets sometimes display shortages or surpluses for long periods of time. Prices sometimes fail to move toward equilibrium. But the "law" is a fair generalization that is right far more often than it is wrong.

The **law of supply and demand** states that, in a free market, the forces of supply and demand generally push the price toward the level at which quantity supplied and quantity demanded are equal.

EFFECTS OF DEMAND SHIFTS ON SUPPLY-DEMAND EQUILIBRIUM

Figure 5–3 showed how developments other than changes in price—such as increases in consumer income—can shift the demand curve. We saw that a rise in income, for example, will shift the demand curve to the right, meaning that at any given price, consumers—with their increased purchasing power—will buy more of the good than before. This, in turn, will move the equilibrium point, changing both market price and quantity sold.

This market adjustment, shown in Figure 5–8(a) adds a supply curve to Figure 5–3(a) so that we can see what happens to the supply-demand equilibrium. In the example in the graph, the quantity demanded at the old equilibrium price of $1.20 increases from 60 billion quarts per year (point E on the demand curve D_0D_0) to 75 billion (point R on the demand curve D_1D_1). We know that $1.20 is no longer the equilibrium price, because at this price quantity demanded (75 billion quarts) exceeds quantity supplied (60 billion). To restore equilibrium, the price must rise. The diagram shows that the new equilibrium occurs at point T, where the price is $1.30 per

The Effects of Shifts of the Demand Curve | **FIGURE 5-8**

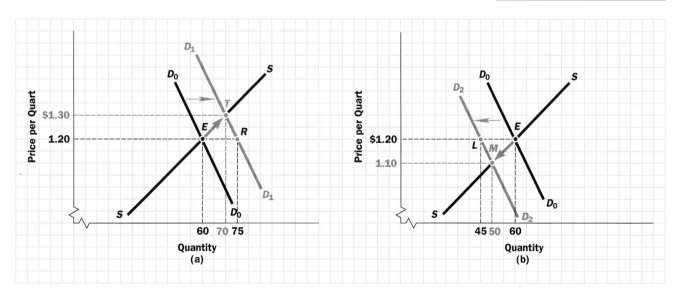

(a)   **(b)**

NOTE: Quantity is in billions of quarts per year.

quart and both quantities demanded and supplied are 70 billion quarts per year. This illustrates a general result:

> Any influence that makes the demand curve shift outward to the right, and does not affect the supply curve, will raise the equilibrium price and the equilibrium quantity.[4]

Everything works in reverse if consumer incomes fall. Figure 5–8(b) depicts a leftward (inward) shift of the demand curve that results from a decline in consumer incomes. For example, the quantity demanded at the previous equilibrium price ($1.20) falls from 60 billion quarts (point E) to 45 billion (point L on the demand curve D_2D_2). The initial price is now too high and must fall. The new equilibrium will eventually be established at point M, where the price is $1.10 and both quantity demanded and quantity supplied are 50 billion quarts. In general:

> Any influence that shifts the demand curve inward to the left, and that does not affect the supply curve, will lower both the equilibrium price and the equilibrium quantity.

Application Revisited: The Fall of the Rupiah

As we observed early in the chapter, sharp drops in the values of a number of Asian currencies, especially the Indonesian rupiah, stunned the world in 1997. What happened?

The basic problem was that people lost confidence in the rupiah—which translated into a sharp leftward shift in the demand curve, like that depicted in Figure 5–3(b). Specifically, foreigners became worried about the stability of the rupiah and decided to hold less of it. Similarly, Indonesians became concerned about the large losses they would suffer if the rupiah fell, and therefore they did the same.

As we know, when the demand curve in a market shifts inward, the price normally falls. In this case, the relevant price was the exchange rate—the price of a rupiah in terms of U.S. dollars—and it dropped precipitously as the market equilibrium moved from point E to point M.

SUPPLY SHIFTS AND SUPPLY-DEMAND EQUILIBRIUM

A story precisely analogous to that of the effects of a demand shift on equilibrium price and quantity applies to supply shifts. Figure 5–6 described the effects on the supply curve of milk if the number of farms increase. Figure 5–9(a) now adds a demand curve to the supply curves of Figure 5–6 so that we can see the supply-demand equilibrium. Notice that at the initial price of $1.20, the quantity supplied after the shift is 78 billion quarts (point I on the supply curve S_1S_1), which is 30 percent more than the original quantity demanded of 60 billion (point E on the supply curve S_0S_0). We can see from the graph that the price of $1.20 is too high to be the equilibrium price; the price must fall. The diagram shows that the new equilibrium point is J, where the price is $1.10 per quart and the quantity is 65 billion quarts per year. In general:

> Any change that shifts the supply curve outward to the right, and does not affect the demand curve, will lower the equilibrium price and raise the equilibrium quantity.

This must always be true if the industry's demand curve has a negative slope, because the greater quantity supplied can be sold only if price is decreased to induce

---

[4] For example, when incomes rise rapidly in many developing countries, the demand curves for a variety of consumer goods shift rapidly outward to the right. In Japan, for example, the demand for used Levi's jeans and Nike running shoes from America skyrocketed in the early 1990s as status-conscious Japanese consumers searched for outlets for their rising incomes.

Effects of Shifts of the Supply Curve   FIGURE 5-9

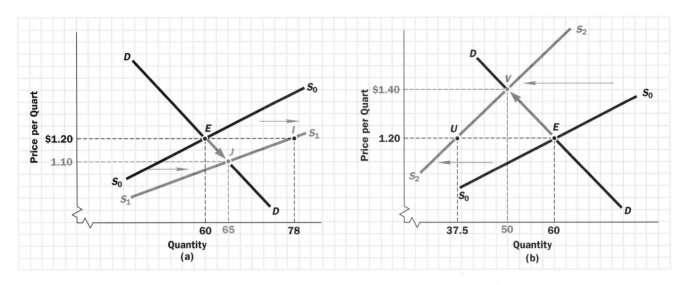

NOTE: Quantity is in billions of quarts per year.

customers to buy more.[5] The cellular phone industry is a case in point. As more providers have entered the industry, the cost of cellular service has plummeted. Some cellular carriers have even given away telephones as sign-up bonuses.

Figure 5–9(b) illustrates the opposite case: a contraction of the industry. The supply curve shifts inward to the left and equilibrium moves from point E to point V, where the price is $1.40 and quantity is 50 billion quarts per year. In general:

> Any factor that shifts the supply curve to the left, and does not affect the demand curve, will raise the equilibrium price and reduce the equilibrium quantity.

Many outside forces can disturb equilibrium in a market by shifting the demand curve or the supply curve, either temporarily or permanently. In 1998, gasoline prices dropped because recession in Asia reduced demand, and a reduction in use of petroleum resulted from a mild winter. In the summer of 1998, severely hot weather and lack of rain damaged the cotton crop in the United States. Often these outside influences change the equilibrium price and quantity by shifting either the supply curve or the demand curve. If you look again at Figures 5–8 and 5–9, you can see clearly that any event that causes either the demand curve or the supply curve to shift will also change the equilibrium price and quantity.

APPLICATION: WHO REALLY PAYS THAT TAX?

Supply and demand analysis offers insights that may not be readily apparent. Here is an example. Suppose your state legislature raises the gasoline tax by 10 cents per gallon. Service station operators will then have to collect 10 additional cents in taxes on every gallon they pump. They will consider this higher tax as an addition to their costs and will shift it to you and other consumers by raising the price of gas by 10 cents a gallon. Right? No, it's wrong—or rather, partly wrong.

The gas station owners would certainly *like* to shift the entire tax to buyers, but the market mechanism will allow them to shift only *part* of it—perhaps 6 cents per gallon. They will then be stuck with the remainder—4 cents in our example. Figure 5–10, which is just another supply-demand graph, shows why.

The demand curve is the blue curve *DD*. The supply curve before the tax is the black curve $S_0 S_0$. Before the new tax, the equilibrium point is E_0 and the price is $1.04. We can interpret the supply curve as telling us at what price sellers are will-

---

[5] Graphically, whenever a positively sloped curve shifts to the right, its intersection point with a negatively sloping curve must always move lower. Just try drawing it yourself.

FIGURE 5-10

Who Pays for a New Tax on Products?

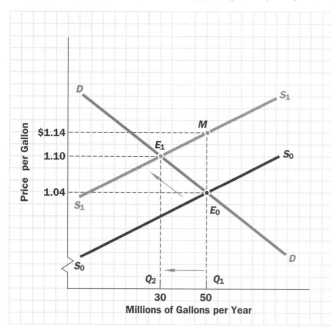

ing to provide any given quantity. For example, they are willing to supply quantity $Q_1 = 50$ million gallons per year if the price is $1.04 per gallon.

So what happens as a result of the new tax? Because they must now turn 10 cents per gallon over to the government, gas station owners will be willing to supply any given quantity only if they get 10 cents more per gallon than they did before. Therefore, to get them to supply quantity $Q_1 = 50$ million gallons, a price of $1.04 per gallon will no longer suffice. Only a price of $1.14 per gallon will now induce them to supply 50 million gallons. Thus, at quantity $Q_1 = 50$, the point on the supply curve will move up by 10 cents, from point E_0 to point M. Because firms will insist on the same 10-cent price increase for any other quantity they supply, the *entire* supply curve will shift up by the 10-cent tax—from the black curve $S_0 S_0$ to the new red supply curve $S_1 S_1$. And, as a result, the supply-demand equilibrium point will move from E_0 to E_1 and the price will increase from $1.04 to $1.10.

The supply curve shift may give the impression that gas station owners have succeeded in passing the entire 10-cent increase on to consumers—the distance from E_0 to M—but look again. The *equilibrium* price has only gone up from $1.04 to $1.10. That is, the price has risen by only 6 cents, not by the full 10-cent amount of the tax. The gas station will have to absorb the remaining 4 cents of the tax.

Now this really *looks* as though we have pulled a fast one on you—a magician's sleight of hand. After all, the supply curve has shifted upward by the full amount of the tax, and yet the resulting price increase has covered only part of the tax rise. However, a second look shows that, like most apparent acts of magic, this one has a simple explanation. The explanation arises from the *demand* side of the supply-demand mechanism. The negative slope of the demand curve means that when prices rise, at least some consumers will reduce the quantity of gasoline they demand. That will force sellers to give up part of the price increase. In other words, firms must absorb part of the tax—4 cents—that consumers are unwilling to pay. But note also that the equilibrium quantity Q_1 has fallen from 50 million gallons to $Q_2=30$ million gallons—so both consumers and suppliers lose out in some sense.

This example is not an oddball case. It is almost always true. The cost of any increase in a tax on any commodity will usually be paid partly by the consumer, partly by the seller. This is true regardless of whether the legislature says that it is imposing the tax on the sellers or on the buyers. Whichever way it is phrased, the economics are the same: The supply-demand mechanism ensures that the tax will be shared by both parties.

FIGHTING THE INVISIBLE HAND: THE MARKET FIGHTS BACK

Attempts to Repeal the Laws of Supply and Demand— The Market Strikes Back

As we have noted in our *Ideas for Beyond the Final Exam*, lawmakers and rulers have often been dissatisfied with the outcomes of free markets. From Rome to South Dakota and from biblical times to the space age, they have battled the invisible hand. Sometimes, rather than trying to make adjustments in the workings of the market, governments have tried to raise or lower the prices of specific commodities by decree. In many such cases, the authorities felt that market prices were, in some sense, immorally low or immorally high. Penalties were therefore imposed on anyone offering the commodities in question at prices above or below those established by the authorities. Such legally imposed constraints on prices are called "price ceilings" and "price floors." To see their result, we will focus on the use of price ceilings.

RESTRAINING THE MARKET MECHANISM: PRICE CEILINGS

A **price ceiling** is a legal maximum on the price that may be charged for a commodity.

The market has proven itself a formidable foe that strongly resists attempts to get around its decisions. In case after case where legal price ceilings are imposed, virtually the same series of consequences ensues:

1. *A persistent shortage develops because quantity demanded exceeds quantity supplied.* Queuing (people waiting in lines), direct rationing, or any of a variety of other devices, usually inefficient and unpleasant, must substitute for the distribution process provided by the price mechanism. Example: Rampant shortages in Eastern Europe and the former Soviet Union helped precipitate the revolts that ended communism.

2. *An illegal, or "black," market often arises to supply the commodity.* Usually some individuals are willing to take the risks involved in meeting unsatisfied demands illegally. Example: Although most states ban the practice, ticket "scalping" occurs at most popular sporting events and rock concerts.

3. *The prices charged on illegal markets are almost certainly higher than those that would prevail in free markets.* After all, lawbreakers expect some compensation for the risk of being caught and punished. Example: Illegal drugs are normally quite expensive. (See the accompanying Policy Debate box, "Economic Aspects of the War on Drugs.")

4. *A substantial portion of the price falls into the hands of the illicit supplier instead of going to those who produce the good or who perform the service.* Example: A constant complaint during the public hearings that marked the history of theater ticket price controls in New York City was that the "ice" (the illegal excess charge) fell into the hands of ticket scalpers rather than going to those who invested in, produced, or acted in the play.

5. *Investment in the industry generally dries up. Because price ceilings reduce the monetary returns that investors can legally earn, less capital will be invested in industries that are subject to price controls.* Even fear of impending price controls can have this effect. Example: Price controls on farm products in Zambia have prompted peasant farmers and large agricultural conglomerates alike to cut back production rather than grow crops at a loss. The result has been thousands of lost jobs and widespread food shortages.

CASE STUDY: RENT CONTROLS IN NEW YORK CITY

These points and others are best illustrated by considering a concrete example of price ceilings. New York is the only major city in the United States that has legislated rent controls continuously since World War II. Rent controls, of course, are intended to protect the consumer from high rents. But most economists believe that rent control does not help the cities or their residents and that, in the long run, it makes almost everyone worse off. Elementary supply-demand analysis shows us why.

Figure 5–11 is a supply-demand diagram for rental units in New York. Curve DD is the demand curve and the curve SS is the supply curve. Without controls, equilibrium would be at point *E*, where rents average $2,000 per month and three million units are occupied. If rent controls are effective, they must set a ceiling price below the equilibrium price of $2,000. But with a low rent ceiling, such as $1,200, the quantity of housing demanded will be 3.5 million units (point *B*) while the quantity supplied will be only 2.5 million units (point *C*).

The diagram shows a shortage of one million apartments. This theoretical concept of a "shortage" manifests itself in New York City as an abnormally low vacancy rate—typically about half of the national urban average.

FIGURE 5-11

Supply-Demand Diagram for Rental Housing

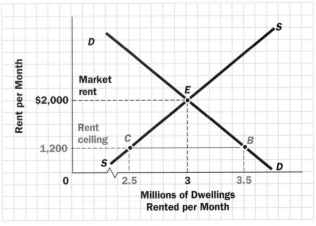

● **POLICY DEBATE** | ECONOMIC ASPECTS OF THE WAR ON DRUGS

For years now, the U.S. government has engaged in a highly publicized "war on drugs." Billions of dollars have been spent on trying to stop illegal drugs at the border. In some sense, interdiction has succeeded: Federal agents have seized literally tons of cocaine and other drugs. Yet these efforts have made barely a dent in the flow of drugs to America's city streets. Simple economic reasoning explains why.

When drug interdiction works, it shifts the supply curve of drugs to the left, thereby driving up street prices. But that, in turn, raises the rewards for potential smugglers and attracts more criminals into the "industry," which shifts the supply curve back to the right. The net result is that increased shipments of drugs to our shores replace much of what the authorities confiscate. This is why many economists believe that any successful antidrug program must concentrate on reducing demand, which would lower the street price of drugs, not on reducing supply, which can only raise it.

Some people suggest that the government should go even further and legalize many drugs. Although this remains a highly controversial position that few are ready to endorse, the reasoning behind it is straightforward. A stunningly high fraction of all the violent crimes committed in America—especially robberies and murders—are drug-related. One major reason is that street prices of drugs are so high that addicts must steal to get the money, and drug traffickers are all too willing to kill to protect their highly profitable "businesses."

How would things differ if drugs were legal? Because South American farmers earn pennies for drugs that sell for hundreds of dollars on the streets of Los Angeles and New York, we may safely assume that legalized drugs would be vastly cheaper. In fact, according to one estimate, a dose of cocaine would cost less than 50 cents. That, proponents point out, would reduce

drug-related crimes dramatically. When, for example, was the last time you heard of a gang killing connected with the distribution of cigarettes or alcoholic beverages?

The argument against legalization of drugs is largely moral: Should the state sanction potentially lethal substances? But there is also an economic aspect. The vastly lower street prices of drugs that would surely follow legalization would increase drug use. Thus, while legalization would almost certainly reduce crime, it would also produce more addicts. The key question here is: How many more addicts? (Nobody has a good answer.) If you think the increase in quantity demanded would be large, you are unlikely to find legalization an attractive option.

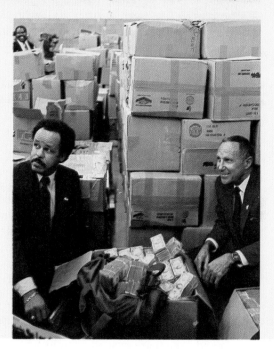

Naturally, rent controls have spawned a lively black market in New York. The black market raises the effective price of rent-controlled apartments in many ways, including bribes, so-called key money paid to move up on a waiting list, and requirements that force prospective tenants to purchase worthless furniture at inflated prices.

According to the diagram, rent controls reduce the quantity supplied from 3 million to 2.5 million apartments. How does this show up in New York? First, some property owners, discouraged by the low rents, have converted apartment buildings into office space or other uses. Second, some apartments have been inadequately maintained. After all, rent controls create a shortage, which makes even dilapidated apartments easy to rent. Third, some landlords have actually abandoned their buildings rather than pay rising tax and fuel bills. These abandoned buildings rapidly become eyesores and eventually pose threats to public health and safety.

With all of these problems, why do rent controls persist in New York City? And why do other cities sometimes move in the same direction?

Part of the explanation is that most people simply do not understand the problems that rent controls create. Another part is that landlords are unpopular politically. But a third, and important, part of the explanation is that not everyone is hurt by rent controls—and those who benefit from controls fight hard to preserve them. In New York, for example, many tenants pay rents that are only a fraction of what their apartments would fetch on the open market. They are, naturally enough, quite happy with this situation. This last point illustrates another very general phenomenon:

> Virtually every price ceiling or floor creates a class of people that benefits from the regulations. These people use their political influence to protect their gains by preserving that status quo, which is one reason why it is so hard to eliminate price ceilings or floors.

RESTRAINING THE MARKET MECHANISM: PRICE FLOORS

Interferences with the market mechanism are not always designed to keep prices low. Agricultural price supports and minimum wages provide two notable examples in which the law keeps prices *above* free-market levels. **Price floors** are typically accompanied by a standard series of symptoms:

A **price floor** is a legal minimum on the price that may be charged for a commodity.

1. *A surplus develops as sellers cannot find enough buyers.* Example: Surpluses of various agricultural products have been a persistent—and costly—problem for the U.S. government. The problem is even worse in the European Union (EU), where the common agricultural policy holds prices even higher. One source estimates that this policy accounts for half of all EU spending.[6]

2. *Where goods, rather than services, are involved, the surplus creates a problem of disposal.* Something must be done about the excess of quantity supplied over quantity demanded. Example: The U.S. government has often been forced to purchase, store, and then dispose of large amounts of surplus agricultural commodities.

3. *To get around the regulations, sellers may offer discounts in disguised—and often unwanted—forms.* Example: When airline fares were regulated by the government, airlines offered more and better food and stylish uniforms for flight attendants instead of lowering fares. Today, the food is worse, but tickets cost much less.

4. *Regulations that keep prices artificially high encourage overinvestment in the industry.* Even inefficient businesses whose high operating costs would doom them in an unrestricted market can survive beneath the shelter of a generous price floor. Example: This is why the airline and trucking industries both went through painful "shakeouts" of the weaker companies in the 1980s, when they were deregulated and allowed to charge market-determined prices.

Once again, a specific example is useful.

CASE STUDY: SUGAR PRICE SUPPORTS

America's extensive program of farm price supports began in 1933 as a "temporary method of dealing with an emergency"—farmers were going broke in droves. These price supports are still with us today, even though farmers in the United States make up less than 3 percent of the workforce.[7] One of the more controversial farm price supports involves the sugar industry. Sugar producers receive low-interest loans from the federal government and a guarantee that the price of sugar will not fall below a certain level.

But in a market economy like ours, Congress cannot simply set prices by decree; it must take some action to enforce the price floor. In the case of sugar, that "something" is limiting both domestic production and foreign imports, thereby shifting

---

[6] *The Economist*, Feb. 20, 1999.

[7] Under major legislation passed in 1996, many agricultural price supports were supposed to be phased out over a seven-year period. However, in actuality, many support programs have changed little, especially for sugar.

FIGURE 5-12

**Supporting the Price
of Sugar**

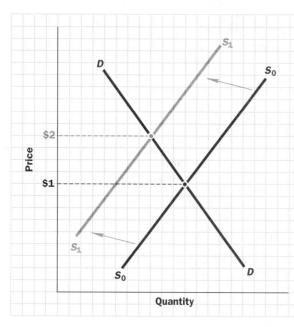

the supply curve inward to the left. Figure 5–12 displays the mechanics. Government policies shift the supply curve inward from S_0S_0 to S_1S_1 and drive the U.S. price up from \$1 to \$2 per pound. The more the supply curve shifts inward, the higher the price.

The sugar industry obviously benefits from the price-control program. But consumers pay for it in the form of higher prices for sugar and sugar-filled products such as soft drinks, candy bars, and cookies. Estimates vary, but the federal sugar price support program costs consumers somewhere around \$1.5 billion a year.

If all of this sounds a bit abstract to you, take a look at the ingredients in a U.S.-made soft drink. Instead of sugar, you will likely find "high-fructose corn syrup" listed as a sweetener. Foreign producers generally use sugar. But in the United States, sugar is simply too expensive to be used for this purpose.

A CAN OF WORMS

Our two case studies—rent controls and sugar price supports—illustrate some of the major side effects of price floors and ceilings, but barely hint at others. Difficulties arise that we have not even mentioned, for the market mechanism is a tough bird that imposes suitable retribution on those who seek to evade it by government decree. Here is a partial list of other problems that may arise when prices are controlled.

FAVORITISM AND CORRUPTION   When price ceilings or floors create shortages or surpluses, someone must decide who gets to buy or sell the limited quantity that is available. This can lead to discrimination along racial or religious lines, political favoritism, or corruption in government. For example, many prices were held at artificially low levels in the former Soviet Union, making queuing for certain goods quite common. But, somehow, Communist party officials and other favored groups were able to purchase the scarce commodities that others could not get.

UNENFORCEABILITY   Attempts to limit prices are almost certain to fail in industries with numerous suppliers, simply because the regulating agency must monitor the behavior of so many sellers. People will usually find ways to evade or violate the law, and something like the free-market price will generally reappear. But there is an important difference: Because the evasion process, whatever its form, will have some operating costs, those costs must be borne by someone. Normally, that someone is the consumer.

AUXILIARY RESTRICTIONS   Fears that a system of price controls will break down invariably lead to regulations designed to shore up the shaky edifice. Consumers may be told when and from whom they are permitted to buy. The powers of the police and the courts may be used to prevent the entry of new suppliers. Occasionally, an intricate system of market subdivision is imposed, giving each class of firms a protected sphere in which others are not permitted to operate. For example, in New York City there are laws banning conversion of rent-controlled apartments to condominiums.

LIMITATION OF VOLUME OF TRANSACTIONS   To the extent that controls succeed in affecting prices, they can be expected to reduce the volume of transactions. Curiously, this is true regardless of whether the regulated price is above or below the free-market equilibrium price. If it is set above the equilibrium price, quantity demanded will be below the equilibrium quantity. On the other hand, if the imposed price is set below the free-market level, quantity supplied will be cut down. Because sales volume cannot exceed either the quantity supplied or the quantity demanded, a reduction in the volume of transactions is the result.[8]

---

[8] See Review Question 9 at the end of the chapter.

MISALLOCATION OF RESOURCES   Departures from free-market prices are likely to result in misuse of the economy's resources because the connection between production costs and prices is broken. For example, Russian farmers used to feed their farm animals bread instead of unprocessed grains because price ceilings kept the price of bread ludicrously low. In addition, just as more complex locks lead to more sophisticated burglary tools, more complex regulations lead to the use of yet more resources for their avoidance.

Economists put it this way. Free markets are capable of dealing efficiently with the three basic coordination tasks outlined in Chapter 4: deciding what to produce, how to produce it, and to whom the goods should be distributed. Price controls throw a monkey wrench into the market mechanism. Though the market is surely not flawless, and government interferences often have praiseworthy goals, good intentions are not enough. Any government that sets out to repair what it sees as a defect in the market mechanism runs the risk of causing even more serious damage elsewhere. As a prominent economist once quipped, societies that are too willing to interfere with the operation of free markets soon find that the invisible hand is nowhere to be seen.

A SIMPLE BUT POWERFUL LESSON

Astonishing as it may seem, many people in authority do not understand the law of supply and demand, or act as if it were not there. For example, a few years ago *The New York Times* carried a dramatic front page picture of the president of Kenya setting fire to a large pile of elephant tusks that had been confiscated from poachers. The accompanying story explained that the burning was intended as a symbolic act to persuade the world to halt the ivory trade.[9] One may well doubt whether the burning really touched the hearts of criminal poachers. However, one economic effect was clear. By reducing the supply of ivory on the world market, the burning of tusks forced up the price of ivory, which raised the illicit rewards reaped by those who slaughter elephants. That could only encourage more poaching—precisely the opposite of what the Kenyan government sought to accomplish.

SUMMARY

1. An attempt by government regulations to force prices above or below their equilibrium levels is likely to lead to shortages or surpluses, to black markets in which goods are sold at illegal prices, and to a variety of other problems. The market always strikes back at attempts to repeal the law of supply and demand.

2. The quantity of a product that is demanded is not a fixed number. Rather, quantity demanded depends on such factors as the price of the product, consumer incomes, and the prices of other products.

3. The relationship between quantity demanded and price, holding all other things constant, can be displayed graphically on a demand curve.

4. For most products, the higher the price, the lower the quantity demanded. So the demand curve usually has a negative slope.

5. The quantity of a product that is supplied also depends on its price and many other influences. A supply curve is a graphical representation of the relationship between quantity supplied and price, holding all other influences constant.

6. For most products, the supply curves have positive slopes, meaning that higher prices lead to supply of greater quantities.

7. A change in quantity demanded that is caused by a change in the price of the good is represented by a movement *along* a fixed demand curve. A change in quantity demanded that is caused by a change in any other determinant of quantity demanded is represented by a *shift* of the demand curve.

8. This same distinction applies to the supply curve: Changes in price lead to movements along a fixed supply curve; changes in other determinants of quantity supplied lead to shifts of the whole supply curve.

9. A market is said to be in equilibrium when quantity supplied is equal to quantity demanded. The equilibrium price and quantity are shown by the point on a graph where the supply and demand curves intersect. The law of supply and demand states that price and quantity tend to gravitate to this point in a free market.

10. Changes in consumer incomes, tastes, technology, prices of competing products, and many other influences cause shifts

[9] *The New York Times*, July 19, 1989.

in either the demand curve or the supply curve and produce changes in price and quantity that can be determined from supply-demand diagrams.

11. A tax on a good generally leads to a rise in the price at which the taxed product is sold. However, the rise in price is generally less than the tax, so consumers usually pay less than the entire tax.

12. Consumers generally pay only part of a tax because the resulting rise in price leads them to buy less and the cut in the quantity they demand helps to keep price down.

KEY TERMS

Quantity demanded   70

Demand schedule   70

Demand curve   71

Shift of the demand curve   71

Quantity supplied   73

Supply schedule   73

Supply curve   75

Supply-demand diagram   77

Shortage   77

Surplus   77

Equilibrium price and quantity   78

Equilibrium   78

Law of supply and demand   79

Shifts in versus movements along supply and demand curves   80

Price ceiling   83

Price floor   85

QUESTIONS FOR REVIEW

1. How often do you rent videos? Would you do so more often if a rental cost half as much? Distinguish between your demand curve for home videos and your "quantity demanded" at the current price.

2. What shapes would you expect for demand curves for the following:

   a. A medicine that means life or death for a patient?

   b. French fries in a food court with kiosks offering many types of food?

3. The following are the assumed supply and demand schedules for hamburgers in Collegetown:

Demand Schedule

Price	Quantity Demanded per Year
$2.25	6,000
2.00	8,000
1.75	10,000
1.50	12,000
1.25	14,000
1.00	16,000

Supply Schedule

Price	Quantity Supplied per Year
$2.25	15,000
2.00	14,000
1.75	13,000
1.50	12,000
1.25	11,000
1.00	10,000

   a. Plot the supply and demand curves and indicate the equilibrium price and quantity.

   b. What effect would a decrease in the price of beef (a hamburger input) have on the equilibrium price and quantity of hamburgers, assuming all other things were to remain constant? Explain your answer with the help of a diagram.

   c. What effect would an increase in the price of pizza (a substitute commodity) have on the equilibrium price and quantity of hamburgers, assuming again that all other things were held constant? Use a diagram in your answer.

4. Suppose the supply and demand schedules for bicycles are as follows:

Price	Quantity Demanded per Year	Quantity Supplied per Year
$160	20,000,000	12,000,000
200	18,000,000	14,000,000
240	16,000,000	16,000,000
280	14,000,000	18,000,000
320	12,000,000	20,000,000
360	10,000,000	22,000,000

   a. Graph these curves and show the equilibrium price and quantity.

   b. Now suppose that it becomes unfashionable to ride a bicycle, so the quantity demanded at each price falls by 4 million bikes per year. What is the new equilibrium price and quantity? Show this solution graphically. Explain why the quantity falls by less than 4 million bikes per year.

   c. Suppose instead that several major bicycle producers go out of business, thereby reducing the quantity supplied by 4 million bikes at every price. Find the new equilibrium price and quantity, and show it graphically. Explain again why quantity falls by less than 4 million.

   d. What are the equilibrium price and quantity if the shifts described in Review Questions 4(b) and 4(c) happen at the same time?

5. The following table summarizes information about the market for principles of economics textbooks:

Price	Quantity Demanded per Year	Quantity Supplied per Year
$40	2,100	100
50	1,100	300
60	600	600
70	350	1,000
80	225	1,500

a. What is the market equilibrium price and quantity of textbooks?

b. In order to quell outrage over tuition increases, the college places a $50 limit on the price of textbooks. How many textbooks will be sold now?

c. While the price limit is still in effect, automated publishing increases the efficiency of textbook production. Show graphically the likely effect of this innovation on the market price and quantity.

6. Show how the following demand curves are likely to shift in response to the indicated changes:

a. The effect of a drought on the demand curve for umbrellas.

b. The effect of higher popcorn prices on the demand curve for movie tickets.

c. The effect on the demand curve for coffee of a decline in the price of Coca-Cola.

7. Discuss the likely effects of the following:

a. Rent ceilings on the market for apartments.

b. Floors under wheat prices on the market for wheat.

Use supply-demand diagrams to show what may happen in each case.

8. U.S. government price supports for milk led to a chronic surplus of milk. In an effort to reduce the surplus about a decade ago, Congress offered to pay dairy farmers to slaughter cows. Use two diagrams, one for the milk market and one for the meat market, to illustrate how this policy should have affected the price of meat. (Assume that meat is sold in an unregulated market.)

9. It is claimed in this chapter that either price floors or price ceilings reduce the actual quantity exchanged in a market. Use a diagram or diagrams to test this conclusion, and explain the common sense behind it.

10. The same rightward shift of the demand curve may produce a very small or a very large increase in quantity, depending on the slope of the supply curve. Explain with diagrams.

11. In 1981, when regulations were holding the price of natural gas below its free-market level, then-Congressman Jack Kemp of New York said the following in an interview with *The New York Times*: "We need to decontrol natural gas, and get production of natural gas up to a higher level so we can bring down the price."[10] Evaluate the congressman's statement.

12. From 1990 to 1997 in the United States, the number of working men grew by 6.7 percent; the number of working women grew 11 percent. During this time, average wages for men grew by 20 percent, while average wages for women grew 25 percent. Which of the following two explanations seems more consistent with the data?

a. Women decided to work more, raising their relative supply (relative to men).

b. Discrimination against women declined, raising the relative (to men) demand for female workers.

13. The two accompanying diagrams show supply and demand curves for two substitute commodities: tapes and compact discs (CDs).

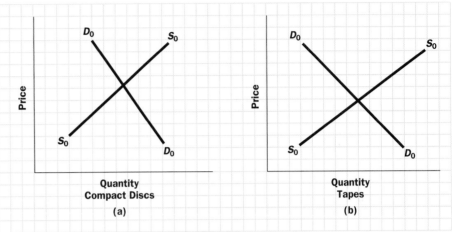

a. On the right-hand diagram, show what happens when rising raw material prices make it costlier to produce tapes.

b. On the left-hand diagram, show what happens to the market for CDs.

14. Consider the market for milk discussed in this chapter (Tables 5–1 through 5–3 and Figures 5–1 and 5–8). Suppose that the government decides to fight kidney stones by levying a tax of 30 cents per quart on sales of milk. Follow these steps to analyze the effects of the tax:

a. Construct the new supply schedule (to replace Table 5–2) that relates quantity supplied to the price that consumers pay.

b. Graph the new supply curve constructed in Review Question 14(a) on the supply-demand diagram depicted in Figure 5–8. What are the new equilibrium price and quantity?

c. Does the tax succeed in its goal of reducing the consumption of milk?

d. How much does the equilibrium price increase? Is the price rise greater than, equal to, or less than the 30-cent tax?

e. Who actually pays the tax, consumers or producers? (This may be a good question to discuss in class.)

15. (More difficult) The demand and supply curves for T-shirts in Touristtown, U.S.A., are given by the following equations:

$$Q = 24,000 - 500P \qquad Q = 6,000 + 1,000P$$

where P is measured in dollars and Q is the number of T-shirts per year.

---

[10] *The New York Times*, December 23, 1981.

a. Find the equilibrium price and quantity algebraically.

b. If tourists decide they do not really like T-shirts that much, which of the following might be the new demand curve?

$$Q = 21,000 - 500P \qquad Q = 27,000 - 500P$$

Find the equilibrium price and quantity after the shift of the demand curve.

c. If, instead, two new stores that sell T-shirts open up in town, which of the following might be the new supply curve?

$$Q = 3,000 + 1,000P \qquad Q = 9,000 + 1,000P$$

Find the equilibrium price and quantity after the shift of the supply curve.

II

THE BUILDING BLOCKS OF DEMAND AND SUPPLY

The next four chapters describe and analyze the basic building blocks with which economists explain how markets work. The two essential elements of any market are its buyers (consumers) and its sellers (producers). As in a piece of machinery, all the parts of a market function together and simultaneously, so there is no logical place to begin the story. Furthermore, the heart of the story is not found in the individual components, but in the way they fit together. The four central micro chapters start off with the separate components, but then assemble them into a working model of how firms determine price and output simultaneously.

Everything is worth what its purchaser will pay for it.

Publilius Syrus (1st century B.C.)

CONSUMER CHOICE: INDIVIDUAL AND MARKET DEMAND

Y ou are about to start a new year in college, and your favorite clothing store is having a sale. So you decide to stock up on jeans. How do you decide how many to buy? How is your decision affected by the price of the jeans and the amount of money you earned in your summer job? How can you get the most for your money? Economic analysis provides some rational ways to make these decisions. Do you think about your decision as an economist would, either consciously or unconsciously? Should you? By the end of the chapter you will be able to consider these questions, and you will have learned a new way to analyze purchase decisions using concepts called "utility" and "marginal analysis."

Chapter 5 introduced you to the idea of supply and demand and how we can use supply and demand curves to analyze how markets determine prices and quantities of products sold. This chapter will enable us to investigate the underpinnings of the demand curve which, as we have already seen, shows us half of the market picture.

Paradox: Should Water Be Worth More Than Diamonds?

When Adam Smith lectured at the University of Glasgow in the 1760s, he introduced the study of demand by posing a puzzle. Common sense, he said, suggests that the price of a commodity must somehow depend on what that good is worth to consumers—on the amount of *utility* that the commodity offers. Yet, Smith pointed out, some cases suggest that a good's utility may have little influence on its price.

Smith cited diamonds and water as examples. He noted that water has enormous value to most consumers; indeed, its availability can be a matter of life and death. Yet water generally is either free or sells at a very low price, whereas diamonds sell for very high prices even though few people would consider them necessities. We will soon be in a position to see how marginal analysis, the powerful method of analysis introduced in this chapter, helps to resolve the paradox.

■ SCARCITY AND DEMAND

When economists use the term "demand," they do not mean mere wishes, needs, requirements, or preferences. Rather, demand refers to actions of consumers who, so to speak, put their money where their mouths are. "Demand" assumes that consumers can pay for the goods in question and that they are also willing to pay out the necessary money. Some of us may, for example, dream of owning a racehorse or a Lear jet, but only a few wealthy individuals can turn such fantasies into effective demands.

Any individual consumer's choices are subject to one overriding constraint that is at least partly beyond that consumer's control: The individual has only a limited income available to spend. This scarcity of income is the obvious reason why less affluent consumers demand fewer computers, trips to foreign countries, and expensive restaurant meals than wealthy consumers do. The scarcity of income affects even the richest of all spenders—the government. The U.S. government spends billions of dollars on the armed services, education, and a variety of other services, but governments rarely if ever have the funds to buy everything they want.

Because income is limited (and thus is a scarce resource), any consumer's purchase decisions for different commodities must be *interdependent*. The number of movies that John can afford to see depends on the amount he spends on new clothing. If Jane's parents have just sunk a lot of money into an expensive addition to their home, they may have to give up a vacation trip. Thus, no one can truly understand the demand curves for movies and clothing, or for homes and vacation trips, without considering demand curves for alternative goods.

The quantity of movies demanded, for example, probably depends not only on ticket prices but also on the prices of clothing. Thus, a big sale on shirts might induce John to splurge on several, leaving him with little or no cash to spend on movies. Therefore, an analysis of consumer demand that focuses on only one commodity at a time leaves out an essential part of the story. Nevertheless, to make the analysis easier to follow, we begin by considering products in isolation. That is, we employ what is called "partial analysis," using a standard simplifying assumption. This assumption requires that all other variables remain unchanged. Later in the chapter and in the appendix, we will tell a fuller story.

■ UTILITY: A TOOL TO ANALYZE PURCHASE DECISIONS

In the American economy, millions of consumers make millions of decisions every day. You decide to buy a movie ticket instead of a paperback novel. Your roommate decides to buy two tubes of toothpaste rather than one tube or three tubes. How do people make these decisions?

Economists have constructed a simple theory of consumer choice based on the hypothesis that each consumer spends her or his income in the way that yields the greatest amount of satisfaction, or *utility*. This seems to be a reasonable starting point, because it says only that people do what they prefer. To make the theory operational, we need a way to measure utility.

A century ago, economists envisioned utility as an indicator of the pleasure a person derives from consuming some set of goods, and they thought that utility could be measured directly in some kind of psychological units (sometimes called *utils*) after somehow reading the consumer's mind. Gradually, they came to realize that this was an unnecessary and, perhaps, impossible task. How many utils did you get from the last movie you saw? You probably cannot answer that question because you have no idea what a util is. Neither does anyone else.

But you may be able to answer a different question like, "How many hamburgers would you give up to get that movie ticket?" If you answer "three," no one can say how many utils you get from seeing a film, but they can say that you get more from the movie than from a single hamburger. When economists approach the issue in this manner, hamburgers, rather than the more vague "utility," becomes the unit of measurement. They can say that the utility of a movie (to you) is three hamburgers.

Early in the 20th century, economists concluded that this indirect way of measuring consumer benefit gave them all they needed to build a theory of consumer choice. One can measure the benefit of a movie ticket by asking how much of some other commodity (like hamburgers) you are willing to give up for it. Any commodity will do for this purpose, but the simplest choice, and the one that we will use in this book, is money.[1]

---

[1] Note to Instructors: You will recognize that, while not using the terms, we are distinguishing here between neoclassical *cardinal utility* and *ordinal utility*. Moreover, throughout the book, *marginal utility in money terms* (or *money marginal utility*) is simply used as a synonym for the *marginal rate of substitution* between money and the commodity.

TOTAL VERSUS MARGINAL UTILITY

The **total utility** of a quantity of a good to a consumer (measured in money terms) is the maximum amount of money that he or she is willing to give in exchange for it.

Thus, we define the **total utility** of some bundle of goods to some consumer as *the largest sum of money that person will voluntarily give up in exchange for those goods.* For example, imagine that you love pizza and are planning to buy four pizzas for a party you are hosting. You are, as usual, a bit low on cash. Taking this into account, you decide that you are willing to buy the four pies if they cost up to $52 in total, but you're not willing to pay more than $52. As economists, we then say that the *total utility* of four pizzas to you is $52, the maximum amount you are willing to spend to have them.

Total utility measures the benefit that you derive from your total purchases of some commodity during some selected period of time. *Total* utility is all that really matters to you. But to understand which decisions most effectively promote total utility, we must consider the related concept of **marginal utility.** This concept does not measure your goal, but rather provides a tool to analyze how much of a commodity that you will buy. It refers to *the addition to total utility that an individual derives by consuming one more unit of any good.* For example, if you consumed two pizzas last month, marginal utility indicates how much additional pleasure you would have received by increasing your consumption to three pizzas instead.

The **marginal utility** of a commodity to a consumer (measured in money terms) is the maximum amount of money that she or he is willing to pay *for one more unit* of that commodity.

Table 6–1 helps to clarify the distinction between marginal and total utility and shows how the two are related. The first two columns show how much *total* utility (measured in money terms) you derive from various quantities of pizza, ranging from zero to eight per month. For example, a single pizza pie is worth (no more than) $15 to you, two are worth $28 in total, and so on. The *marginal* utility is the *difference* between any two successive total utility figures. For example, if you have consumed three pizzas (worth $40.50 to you), an additional pie brings your total utility up to $52. Your marginal utility is thus the difference between the two, or $11.50.

Remember: Whenever we use the terms *total utility* and *marginal utility*, we define them in terms of the consumer's willingness to part with *money* for the commodity, not in some unobservable (and imaginary) psychological units.

THE "LAW" OF DIMINISHING MARGINAL UTILITY

The **"law" of diminishing marginal utility** asserts that additional units of a commodity are worth less and less to a consumer in money terms. As the individual's consumption increases, the marginal utility of each additional unit declines.

With these definitions, we can now propose a simple hypothesis about consumer tastes:

The more of a good a consumer has, the less *marginal* utility an additional unit contributes to overall satisfaction.

TABLE 6–1

Your Total and Marginal Utility for Pizza this Month

(1)	(2)	(3)	(4)
Quantity (Q) Pizzas per month	Total Utility (TU)	Marginal Utility (MU) = (ΔTU/ΔQ)	Point in Figure 6–1
0	$ 0.00		
1	15.00	$15.00	A
2	28.00	13.00	B
3	40.50	12.50	C
4	52.00	11.50	D
5	60.00	8.00	E
6	65.00	5.00	F
7	68.00	3.00	G
8	68.00	0.00	H

NOTE: Each entry in Column (3) is the difference between successive entries in Column (2). This is indicated by zig-zag lines.

Economists use this plausible proposition widely. The idea is based on the assertion that every person has a *hierarchy* of uses for a particular commodity. All of these uses are valuable, but some are more valuable than others. Take pizza, for example. Perhaps you consider your *own* appetite for pizza first—you buy enough pizza to satiate your own personal taste for pizza. But pizza may also provide you with an opportunity to satisfy your social needs. So, instead of eating all the pizza you buy, you decide to have a pizza party. First on your guest list, of course, is your boyfriend or girlfriend. Next priority is your roommate, and, if you feel really flush, you may even invite your economics instructor! Thus, if you buy only one pizza, you eat it yourself. If you buy a second pizza, you share it with your friend. A third is shared with your roommate, and so on.

The point is: Each pizza contributes something to your satisfaction, but each *additional* pizza contributes less (measured in terms of money) than its predecessor because it satisfies a lower-priority use. This, in essence, is the logic behind the **"law" of diminishing marginal utility.**

The third column of Table 6–1 illustrates this concept. The marginal utility (abbreviated MU) of the first pizza is $15; that is, you are willing to pay *up to* $15 for the first pie. The second is worth no more than $13 to you, the third pizza only $12.50, and so on until you are willing to pay only $5 for the sixth (the MU of that pizza is $5).

Figure 6–1, a demand curve, shows a graph of the numbers in the first and third columns of the table. For example, point *D* indicates that the MU of a fourth pizza is $11.50. So, at any higher price, you will not buy a fourth pizza.

Note that the curve for marginal utility is negatively sloped; this again illustrates how marginal utility diminishes as the quantity of the good rises. Like most laws, however, it has exceptions. Some people want even more of some good that is particularly significant to them as they acquire more, as in the case of addiction. Stamp collectors and alcoholics provide good examples. The stamp collector who has a few stamps may consider the acquisition of one more to be mildly amusing. The person who has a large and valuable collection may be prepared to go to the ends of the earth for another stamp. Similarly, an alcoholic who finds

FIGURE 6–1

A Marginal Utility (or Demand) Curve: Your Demand for Pizza This Month

"It's been fun, Dave, but I think we're entering the diminished marginal utility phase of our relationship."

● DO CONSUMERS REALLY BEHAVE "RATIONALLY" AND MAXIMIZE UTILITY?

It may strike you that this chapter's discussion of the consumer's decision process—equating price and marginal utility—does not resemble the thought processes of any consumer you have ever met. Buyers may seem to make decisions much more instinctively and without any calculation of marginal utilities or anything like them. That is true, and yet it need not undermine the pertinence of the discussion.

When you give a command to your computer, you actually activate some electronic switches and start some operations in what is referred to as *binary code.* Most computer users do not know they are doing this and do not care. Yet they are doing it nevertheless, and the analysis of the computation process does not misrepresent the facts by describing this sequence. In the same way, if a shopper divides her purchasing power among various available purchase options in a way that yields the largest possible utility for her money, she *must* be following the rules of marginal analysis, even though she is totally unaware of this choice.

Still, growing experimental evidence points out some persistent deviations between reality and the picture of consumer behavior provided by marginal analysis. Experimental studies by groups of economists and psychologists have turned up many examples of behavior that seem to violate the optimal purchase rule. For example, one such study offered two groups of respondents what were really identical options, presumably yielding similar marginal utilities. Yet, depending on differences in some irrelevant information that was also provided to the respondents, the two groups made very different choices.

One group of subjects received the information in parentheses, and the other received the information in brackets. . . .

[*Problem 1*]. Imagine that you are about to purchase . . . a calculator for ($15)[$125]. The calculator salesman informs you that the calculator you wish to buy is on sale for ($10)[$120] at the other branch of the store, located a 20-minute drive away. Would you make the trip to the other store?

The responses to the two versions of this problem were quite different. When the calculator cost $125 only 29 percent of the subjects said they would make the trip, whereas 68 percent said they would go when the calculator cost only $15.

Thus, in this problem *both* groups were really being told they could save $5 on the price of a product if they took a 20-minute trip to another store. Yet, depending on an irrelevant fact, whether the product was a cheap or an expensive one, the number of persons willing to make the same trip to save the same amount of money was very different. The point is that human purchase decisions are affected by the environment in which the decision is made, and not only by the price and marginal utility of the purchase.

SOURCE: Richard H. Thaler, *Quasi Rational Economics* (New York: Russell Sage Foundation, 1992), pp. 148–150.

---

the first beer quite pleasant may find the fourth or fifth to be absolutely irresistible. Economists generally treat such cases of increasing marginal utility as anomalies. For most goods and most people, marginal utility declines as consumption increases.

Table 6–1 and Figure 6–1 illustrate another noteworthy relationship. Notice that as someone buys more and more units of the commodity, that is, as that person moves further down the table, the total utility numbers get larger and larger, while the marginal utility numbers get smaller and smaller. The reasons should now be fairly clear. The marginal utility numbers keep declining, as the law of diminishing marginal utility tells us. But *total* utility keeps rising so long as marginal utility remains positive. A woman who owns ten cans of tennis balls, other things being equal, is better off (she has higher total utility) than a woman who possesses only nine, as long as the MU of the tenth can is positive. In summary:

As a rule, as a person acquires more of a commodity, total utility increases and marginal utility from that good decreases, all other things being equal. In particular, when a commodity is very scarce, economists expect it to have a high marginal utility, even though it may provide little total utility because people have so little of the item.

USING MARGINAL UTILITY: THE OPTIMAL PURCHASE RULE

Now let us use the concept of marginal utility to analyze consumer choices. As we noted, each consumer has a limited amount of money to spend. Consumers must always choose among the many commodities that compete for their dollars. How can you use the idea of utility to help you understand the purchase choices that best serve your preferences?

You can obviously choose among many different quantities of pizza, any of which will add to your total utility. But which of these quantities will yield the greatest net benefits? If pizza were all that you ever considered buying, in theory the choice would involve a simple calculation. We would need a statistical table that listed all of the alternative numbers of pizzas that you may conceivably buy. The table should indicate the *net* utility that each possible choice yields: that is, the total utility that you would get from that number of pizzas, minus the utility you would lose by having to pay for them. We could then simply read your optimal choice from this imaginary table—the number of pizzas that would give you the highest net utility number.

Even in theory, calculating optimal decisions is, unfortunately, more difficult than that. No real table of net utilities exists; an increase in expenditure on pizzas would mean less money available for clothing or movies, and you must balance the benefits of spending on each of these items against spending on the others. All of this means that we must find a more effective technique to determine optimal pizza purchases (as well as clothing, entertainment, and so on). That technique is *marginal analysis*.

To see how marginal analysis helps consumers determine their optimal purchase decisions, first recall our assumption that you are trying to maximize the total *net* utility you obtain from your pizza purchases. That is, you are trying to select the number of pies that maximizes the total utility the pizzas provide you *minus the total utility you give up with the money you must pay for them.*

We can compare the analysis of the optimal decision process to the process of climbing a hill. First, imagine that you consider the possibility of buying only one pizza. Then suppose you consider buying two pizzas, and so on. If two pizzas give you a higher total net utility than one, you may think of yourself as moving higher up the total net utility hill. Buying more pizzas enables you to ascend that hill higher and higher, until at some quantity you reach the top—*the optimal purchase quantity.* Then, if you buy any more you will have overshot the peak and begun to descend the hill.

Figure 6–2 shows such a hill and describes how your total net utility changes when you change the number of pizzas you buy. It shows the upward-sloping part of the hill, where the number of purchases has not yet brought you to the top. Then it shows the point (*M*) at which you have bought enough pizzas to make your net utility as large as possible (the peak occurs at four pizzas). At any point to the right of *M*, you have overshot the optimal purchase. You are on the downward side of the hill because you have bought more than enough pizzas to best serve your interests; you have bought too many to maximize your net utility.

How does marginal analysis help you to find that optimal purchase quantity, and how does it warn you if you are planning to purchase too little (so that you are still on the ascending portion of the hill) or too much (so that you are descending)? The numerical example in Table 6–1 will help reveal the answers. The marginal utility of, for example, a third pizza is $12.50. This means that the total utility you obtain from three pizzas ($40.50) is exactly $12.50 higher than the total utility you get from two pizzas ($28). Thus, the marginal utility of the third pizza is the amount that this pizza adds to your total utility. As long as marginal utility is a positive number, the more you purchase, the more total utility you will get.

That shows the benefit side of the purchase. But such a transaction also has a debit side—the amount you must pay for the purchase. Suppose that the price is $11 per pizza. Then the net *marginal* utility of the third pizza is marginal utility minus price, $12.50 minus $11, or $1.50. This is the amount that the third pizza adds to your total net utility. (See the third and fourth lines of Table 6–1.) So you really *are* better off with three pizzas than with two.

FIGURE 6-2

Finding Your Optimal Pizza Purchase Quantity: Maximizing Total Net Utility

NOTE: Total Net Utility equals Total Utility minus Total Expenditure (Price × Quantity)

We can generalize the logic of the previous paragraph to show how marginal analysis solves the problem of finding the optimal purchase quantity, given the price of the commodity being purchased.

> **RULE 1:** If marginal net utility is positive, the consumer must be buying too small a quantity to maximize total net utility. Because marginal utility exceeds price, one can increase total net utility by buying one more unit of the product. In other words, a positive marginal net utility means that total net utility is still going uphill. The consumer has not yet bought enough to get to the top of the hill.

> **RULE 2:** No purchase quantity for which marginal net utility is a negative number can ever be optimal. In such a case, a buyer can get a higher total net utility by cutting back the purchase quantity. You would have climbed too far on the net utility hill, passing the topmost point and beginning to descend.

This leaves only one option. The consumer cannot be at the top of the hill if marginal net utility (MU − P) is greater than zero, that is, if MU is greater than P. Similarly, the purchase quantity cannot be optimal if marginal net utility at that quantity (MU − P) is less than zero, that is, if MU is less than P. The purchase quantity can be optimal, giving the consumer the highest possible total net utility, only if:

$$\text{Marginal net utility} = MU - P = 0, \text{ that is, if } MU = P$$

Consequently, the hypothesis that the consumer chooses purchases to make the largest net contribution to total utility leads to the following *optimal purchase rule:*

> It always pays the consumer to buy more of any commodity whose marginal utility (measured in money) exceeds its price, and less of any commodity whose marginal utility is less than its price. When possible, the consumer should buy the quantity of each good at which price (*P*) and marginal utility (*MU*) are exactly equal, that is, at which:

$$MU = P$$

because only these quantities will maximize the *net total utility* that the consumer gains from purchases, given the fact that these decisions must divide available money among all purchases.[2]

Notice that, although the consumer really cares about maximizing total *net* utility (since marginal utility has no intrinsic interest), we have used marginal analysis as a *guide* to the optimum purchase quantity. Marginal analysis serves only as an analytic method—as a means to an end. In Chapter 9, after several other applications of marginal analysis, we will generalize the discussion to show how thinking "at the margin" allows us to make optimal decisions in a wide variety of fields besides consumer purchases.

Let's briefly review graphically how the underlying logic of the marginal way of thinking leads to the optimal purchase rule: MU = P. Refer back to the graph of marginal utilities of pizzas (Figure 6–1). Suppose that Paul's Pizza Parlor currently sells pizzas at a price of $11 (line *PP* in the graph).

At this price, five pizzas (point *E*), for example, is *not* an optimal purchase because the $8 marginal utility of the fifth pizza is less than its $11 price. You would be better off buying only four pizzas since that would save $11 with only a $8 loss in utility—a net gain of $3—from the decision to buy one fewer pizza.

You should note that, in practice, there may not exist a number of pizzas at which MU is *exactly* equal to P. In our example, the fourth pizza is worth $11.50, whereas the fifth pizza is worth $8—neither of them is *exactly* equal to their $11 price. If

---

[2] Economists can equate a dollar price with marginal utility only because they measure marginal utility in money terms (or, as they more commonly state, because they deal with the marginal rate of substitution of money for the commodity). If marginal utility were measured in some psychological units not directly translatable into money terms, a comparison of *P* and *MU* would have no meaning. However, MU could also be measured in terms of any commodity other than money. (Example: How many pizzas are you willing to trade for an additional ticket to a basketball game?)

you could purchase an appropriate (in-between) quantity (say, 4.38 pizzas), then MU would, indeed, exactly equal P. But Paul's Pizza Parlor will not sell you 4.38 pizzas, so you must do the best you can. You buy four pizzas, for which MU comes as close as possible to equality with P.

The rule for optimal purchases states that you should not buy a quantity at which MU is higher than price (points like A, B, and C in Figure 6–1) because a larger purchase would make you better off. Similarly, you should not end up at points E, F, G, and H, at which MU is below price, because you would be better off buying less. Rather, you should buy four pizzas (point D), where P = MU (approximately). Thus, marginal analysis leads naturally to the rule for optimal purchase quantities.

> The decision to purchase a quantity of a good that leaves marginal utility greater than price cannot maximize total net utility, because buying an additional unit would add more to total utility than it would cost. Similarly, it cannot be optimal for the consumer to buy a quantity of a good that leaves marginal utility less than price, because then a reduction in the quantity purchased would save more money than it would sacrifice in utility. Consequently, the consumer can maximize total net utility only if the purchase quantity makes marginal utility as close as possible to equality with price.

Note that price is an objective, observable figure determined by the market, whereas marginal utility is subjective and reflects consumer tastes. Because individual consumers lack the power to influence the price, they must adjust purchase quantities to make the marginal utility of each good equal to the price given by the market.

FROM DIMINISHING MARGINAL UTILITY TO DOWNWARD-SLOPING DEMAND CURVES

We can use the optimal purchase rule to show that the "law" of diminishing marginal utility implies that demand curves typically slope downward to the right, that is, they have negative slopes.[3] To do this, we use the list of marginal utilities in Table 6–1 to determine how many pizzas you would buy at any particular price. For example, we see that at a price of $8, it pays for you to buy five pizzas, because the MU of that fifth pizza ordered is $8. Table 6–2 gives several alternative prices and the optimal purchase quantity corresponding to each price derived in just this way. (To make sure you understand the logic behind the optimal purchase rule, verify that the entries in the right-hand column of Table 6–2 are in fact correct.) This *demand schedule* appears graphically as the *demand curve* shown in Figure 6–1. This demand curve is simply the red marginal utility curve. You can see its negative slope, characteristic of demand curves.

Let's examine the logic underlying the negatively sloped demand curve a bit more carefully. If you are purchasing the optimal number of pizzas, and then the price falls, you will find that your marginal utility for that product is now *above* the newly reduced price. For example, Table 6–1 indicates that at a price of $12.50 per pizza, you would optimally buy three, because the marginal utility (MU) of the fourth pizza is only $11.50. If price falls below $11.50, it then pays to purchase the fourth pizza because its MU exceeds its price. The marginal utility of the next (fifth) pizza is only $8, and so if the price were to remain above $8, it would not pay you to buy that fifth pizza, just as prescribed in the optimal purchase rule.

Note the critical role that the law of diminishing marginal utility plays here. If P falls, a consumer who wishes to maximize total utility must buy more, to the point that MU falls correspondingly. According to the law of diminishing marginal utility, the only way to do this is to increase the quantity purchased.

Although this explanation is a bit abstract, we can easily rephrase it in practical terms. We have noted that individuals put commodities to various uses, each of which has a different priority. For you, buying a pizza for your date has a higher priority than using the pizza to feed your roommate. If the price of pizzas is high, it makes sense for you to buy only enough for the high-priority uses—those that

---

[3] If you need to review the concept of slope, turn back to the Chapter 2 discussion on graphic analysis.

TABLE 6-2

List of Optimal Quantities of Pizza for You to Purchase at Alternative Prices

Price	Quantity of Portions Purchased per Month
$ 3.00	7
5.00	6
8.00	5
11.50	4
12.50	3
13.00	2
15.00	1

NOTE: For simplicity of explanation the prices shown have been chosen to equal the marginal utilities in Table 6–1. In-between prices would make the optimal choices involve fractions of pizzas (say, 2.6 pizzas).

offer high marginal utilities. When price declines, however, it pays to purchase more of the good—enough for some lower-priority uses. The same general assumption about consumer psychology underlies both the law of diminishing marginal utility and the negative slope of the demand curve. They are really two different ways of describing consumers' assumed attitudes.

■ CONSUMER CHOICE AS A TRADE-OFF: OPPORTUNITY COST

We have expressed the optimal purchase rule as a decision about how much of *one* commodity to buy. However, we have already observed that the scarcity of income lurking in the background turns every decision into a trade-off. Given each consumer's limited income, a decision to buy a new car usually means giving up some travel or postponing furniture purchases. The money that the consumer gives up when she makes a purchase—her expenditure on that purchase—is only one measure of the true underlying cost to her.

How Much Does It Really Cost?

The real cost is the *opportunity cost* of the purchase—the commodities that she must give up as a result of the purchase decision. This opportunity cost calculation has already been called for in one of our *Ideas for Beyond the Final Exam*—we must always consider the real cost of our purchase decisions, how much of *other* things they force us to forgo. Any decision to buy implies some such trade-off because scarcity constrains all economic decisions. Though their dilemmas may not inspire much pity, even billionaires face very real trade-offs: Invest $200 million in an office building, or go for the $300 million baseball team?

This last example has one other important implication. The trade-off from a consumer's purchase decision does not always involve giving up another *consumer good*. This is true, for example, of the choice between consumption and saving. Consider a high school student deciding whether to buy a new car or to save the money to pay for college. If he saves the money, it can grow by earning interest, so that the original amount plus interest earned will be available to pay for tuition and board three years later. A decision to cut down on consumption now and put the money into the bank means that the student will be wealthier in the future because of the interest he will earn. This, in turn, will enable the student to afford more of his college expenses at the future date when those expenses arise. So the opportunity cost of a new car today is the forgone opportunity to save funds for the future. We conclude:

From the viewpoint of economic analysis the true cost of any purchase is the opportunity cost of that purchase, rather than the amount of money that is spent on it.

The opportunity cost of a purchase can be either higher or lower than its price. For example, if your computer cost you $1,800, but the purchase required you to take off two hours from your job that pays $20 per hour, the true cost of the computer—that is, the opportunity cost—is the amount of goods you could have bought with $1,840 (the $1,800 price plus the $40 in earnings that the purchase of the computer required you to give up). In this case, the opportunity cost ($,1840, measured in money terms) is higher than the price of the purchase ($1,800). (For an example in which price is higher than opportunity cost, see Review Question 8 at the end of the chapter.)

CONSUMER'S SURPLUS: THE NET GAIN FROM A PURCHASE

The optimal purchase rule, MU (approximately) = *P*, assumes that the consumer always tries to maximize the money value of the total utility from the purchase *minus* the amount spent to make that purchase.[4] Thus, any difference between the price

---

[4] Again, in practice, the consumer can often only approximately equate MU and *P*.

consumers *actually* pay for a commodity and the price they would be *willing* to pay for that item represents a net utility gain in some sense. Economists give the name **consumer's surplus** to that difference, that is, to the net gain in total utility that a purchase brings to a buyer. The consumer is trying to make the purchase decisions that maximize:

Consumer's surplus = Total utility (in money terms) − Total expenditure

Thus, just as economists assume that business firms maximize total profit (equal to total revenue minus total cost), they assume that consumers maximize consumer's surplus, that is, the difference between the total utility of the purchased commodity and the amount that consumers spend on it.

The concept of *consumer's surplus* seems to suggest that the consumer gains some sort of free bonus, or *surplus*, for every purchase. In many cases, this idea seems absurd. How can it be true, particularly for goods whose prices seem to be outrageous?

We hinted at the answer in Chapter 4, where we observed that both parties must gain from a voluntary exchange or else one of them will refuse to participate. The same must be true when a consumer makes a *voluntary* purchase from a supermarket or an appliance store. If the consumer did not expect a net gain from the transaction, he or she would simply not bother to buy. Even if the seller were to "overcharge" by some standard, that would merely reduce the size of the consumer's net gain, not eliminate it entirely. If the seller is so greedy as to charge a price that wipes out the net gain altogether, the punishment will fit the crime: The consumer will refuse to buy, and the greedy seller's would-be gains will never materialize. The basic principle states that every purchase that is not marginal—that is, every purchase except those about which the consumer is indifferent—must yield *some* consumer's surplus.

But how large is that surplus? At least in theory, it can be measured with the aid of a table or graph of marginal utilities (Table 6–1 and Figure 6–1). Suppose that, as in our earlier example, the price of a large pizza is $11 and you purchase four of them. Table 6–3 reproduces the marginal utility numbers from Table 6–1. It shows that the first pizza is worth $15 to you, so at the $11 price, you reap a net gain (surplus) of $15 minus $11, or $4, by buying that pizza. The second pizza also brings you some surplus, but less than the first one does, because the marginal utility diminishes. Specifically, the second pizza provides a surplus of $13 minus $11, or $2. Reasoning in the same way, the third pizza gives you a surplus of $12.50 minus $11, or $1.50. It is only the fourth serving—the last one that you purchase—that offers little or no surplus because, by the optimal purchase rule, the marginal utility of the last unit is approximately equal to its price.

We can now easily determine the total consumer's surplus that you obtain by buying four pizzas. It is simply the sum of the surpluses received from each pizza. Table 6–3 shows that this consumer's total surplus is:

$4 + $2 + $1.50 + $0.50 = $8

This way of looking at the optimal purchase rule shows why a buyer must always gain some consumer's surplus if she buys more than one unit of a good. Note that

Consumer's surplus is the difference between the value to the consumer of the quantity of Commodity *X* purchased and the amount that the market requires the consumer to pay for that quantity of *X*.

Calculating Marginal Net Utility (Consumer's Surplus) from Your Pizza Purchases

TABLE 6-3

Quantity	Marginal Utility	Price	Marginal Net Utility (Surplus)
0	$15.00	$11.00	$4.00
1	13.00	11.00	2.00
2	12.50	11.00	1.50
3	11.50	11.00	0.50
Total			$8.00

the price of each unit remains the same, but the marginal utility diminishes as more units are purchased. The last unit bought yields only a tiny consumer's surplus because MU (approximately) = *P*. But all prior units must have had marginal utilities farther above the MU of the last unit because of diminishing marginal utility.

We can be more precise about the calculation of the consumer's surplus with the help of a graph (Figure 6–3) showing marginal utility as a set of bars. The bars labeled *A*, *B*, *C*, and *D* come from the corresponding points on your marginal utility curve (demand curve) in Figure 6–1. Your consumer's surplus from each pizza equals the marginal utility of that pizza minus the price you pay for it. By representing consumer's surplus graphically, we can determine just how much surplus you obtain from your entire purchase by measuring the area between the marginal utility curve and the horizontal line representing the price of pizzas—in this case, the horizontal line *PP* represents the (fixed) $11 price.

In Figure 6–3, the bar whose upper, right-hand corner is labeled *A* represents the $15 marginal utility you derive from the first pizza; the same interpretation applies to the bars *B*, *C*, and *D*. Clearly, the first serving that you purchase yields a consumer's surplus of $4, indicated by the shaded part of bar *A*. The height of that part of the bar is equal to the $15 marginal utility minus the $11 price. In the same way, the next two shaded areas represent the surpluses offered by the second and third pizzas. The fourth pizza has the smallest shaded area because the height representing marginal utility is (as close as you can get to being) equal to the height representing price. Sum up the shaded areas in the graph to obtain, once again, your total consumer's surplus ($4 + $2 + $1.50 + $0.50 = $8) from your four-serving purchase.

> The consumer's surplus derived from buying a certain number of units of a good is obtained graphically by drawing the person's demand curve as a set of bars whose heights represent the marginal utilities of the corresponding quantities of the good, and then drawing a horizontal line whose height is the price of the good. The sum of the heights of the bars above the horizontal line, that is, the area of the demand (marginal utility) bars above that horizontal line, measures the *total* consumer's surplus that the purchase yields.

FIGURE 6–3

Graphic Calculation of Consumer's Surplus

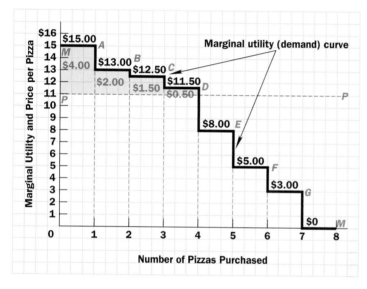

Number of Pizzas Purchased

Resolving the Diamond-Water Paradox

We can now use marginal utility analysis to analyze Adam Smith's paradox (which he was never able to explain) that diamonds are very expensive, whereas water is generally very cheap, even though water seems to offer far more utility. The resolution of the diamond-water paradox is based on the distinction between marginal and total utility.

The *total* utility of water—its role as a necessity of life—is indeed much higher than that of diamonds. But price, as we have seen, is not related directly to *total* utility. Rather, the optimal purchase rule tells us that price tends to equal *marginal* utility. We have every reason to expect the marginal utility of water to be very low, whereas the marginal utility of a diamond is very high.

Given normal conditions, water is comparatively cheap to provide, so its price is generally quite low. Consumers thus use correspondingly large quantities of water. The principle of diminishing marginal utility, therefore, pushes down the marginal utility of water for a typical household to a low level. As the consumer's surplus diagram (Figure 6–3) suggests, this also means that its *total* utility is likely to be high.

On the other hand, high-quality diamonds are scarce (partly because a monopoly keeps them so). As a result, the quantity of diamonds consumed is not large enough to drive down the MU of diamonds very far, so buyers of such luxuries must pay high prices for them. As a commodity becomes more scarce, its *marginal* utility and its market price rise higher, regardless of the size of its *total* utility. Also, as we have seen, because so little of the commodity is consumed, its *total* utility is likely to be comparatively low, despite its large *marginal* utility.

Thus, like many paradoxes, the diamond-water puzzle has a straightforward explanation. In this case, all one has to remember is that:

Scarcity raises price and *marginal* utility, but it generally reduces *total* utility. And although total utility measures the benefits consumers get from their consumption, it is marginal utility that is equal (approximately) to price.

INCOME AND QUANTITY DEMANDED

Our application of marginal analysis has enabled us to examine the relation between the *price* of a commodity and the quantity that will be purchased. Let us next consider briefly how quantity demanded responds to changes in *income*.

As a concrete example, consider what happens to the number of ballpoint pens a consumer will buy when her real income rises. It may seem almost certain that she will buy more such pens than before, but that is not necessarily so. A rise in real income can either increase or decrease the quantity of any particular good purchased.

Why might an increase in income lead a consumer to buy fewer ballpoint pens? People buy some goods and services only because they cannot afford anything better. They may purchase used cars instead of new ones. They may use inexpensive ballpoint pens instead of finely crafted fountain pens or buy clothing secondhand instead of new. If their real income rises, they may then drop out of the used car market and buy brand-new automobiles or buy more fountain pens and fewer ballpoints. Thus, a rise in real income will reduce the quantities of cheap pens and used cars demanded. Economists have given the rather descriptive name **inferior goods** to the class of commodities for which quantity demanded falls when income rises.

> An **inferior good** is a commodity whose quantity demanded falls when the purchaser's real income rises, all other things remaining equal.

The upshot of this discussion is that economists cannot draw definite conclusions about the effects of a rise in consumer incomes on quantity demanded. But for most commodities, if incomes rise and prices do not change, quantity demanded will increase. (Such an item is often called a *normal good*.)

FROM INDIVIDUAL DEMAND CURVES TO MARKET DEMAND CURVES

So far in this chapter we have studied how *individual demand curves* are obtained from the logic of consumer choice. But to understand how the market system works, we must derive the relationship between price and quantity demanded *in the market as a whole*—the **market demand curve**.

> A **market demand curve** shows how the total quantity of some product demanded by *all* consumers in the market during a specified period of time changes as the price of that product changes, holding all other things constant.

MARKET DEMAND AS A HORIZONTAL SUM

If each individual pays no attention to other people's purchase decisions when making his or her own, we can easily derive the market demand curve from consumers' individual demand curves: Simply *add* the negatively sloping individual demand curves *horizontally* as shown in Figure 6–4. The figure gives the individual demand curves *DD* and *ZZ* for two people, Alex and Naomi, and the total (market) demand curve, *MM*. Alex and Naomi are both consumers of the product.

We can derive this market demand curve in the following straightforward way:

Step 1: Pick any relevant price, say, $10.

Step 2: At that price, determine Alex's quantity demanded (9 units) from his demand curve in Panel (a) and Naomi's quantity demanded (6 units) from her demand curve in Panel (b). Note that these quantities are indicated by the line segment labeled *AA* for Alex and that labeled *NN* for Naomi.

FIGURE 6-4

The Relationship between Total Market Demand and the Demand of Individual Consumers within That Market

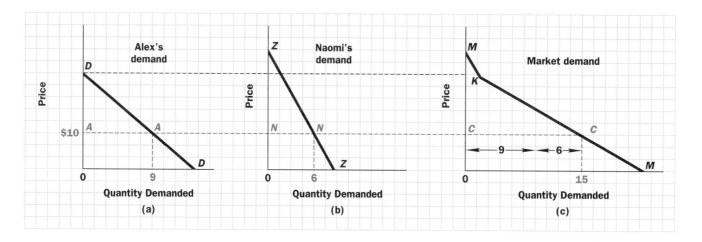

Step 3: Add Naomi's and Alex's quantities demanded at the $10 price (segment *AA* + segment *NN* = 9 + 6 = 15) to yield the total quantity demanded by the market at that price. This gives segment *CC*, with total quantity demanded equal to 15 units, in Panel (c).

Now repeat the process for each alternative price to obtain other points on the market demand curve until the shape of the entire curve *MM* appears. (The sharp angle at point *K* on the market curve occurs because that point corresponds to the price at which Alex, whose demand pattern is different from Naomi's, first enters the market. At any higher price, only Naomi is willing to buy anything.) That is all there is to the adding-up process. (Question: What would happen to the market demand curve if, say, another consumer entered the market?)

THE "LAW" OF DEMAND

The **"law" of demand** states that a lower price generally increases the amount of a commodity that people in a market are willing to buy. Therefore, for most goods, market demand curves have negative slopes.

Just as for the case of an individual's demand curve, we expect the total quantity demanded by the market to move in the opposite direction from price. Economists call this relationship the **"law" of demand.**

Notice that we have put the word *law* in quotation marks. By now you will have observed that economic laws are not always obeyed, and we shall see in a moment that the "law" of demand is not without its exceptions. But first let us see why the "law" usually holds.

Earlier in this chapter, we explained that individual demand curves usually slope downward because of the "law" of diminishing marginal utility. If individual demand curves slope downward, then the preceding discussion of the adding-up process implies that market demand curves must also slope downward. This is just common sense; if every consumer in the market buys fewer pizzas when the price of pizza rises, then the total quantity demanded in the market must surely fall.

But market demand curves may slope downward even when individual demand curves do not, because not all consumers are alike. For example, if a bookstore reduces the price of a popular novel, it may draw many new customers, but few of the customers who already own a copy will buy a second one. Similarly, people differ in their fondness for pizza. True devotees may maintain their pizza purchases even at exorbitant prices, whereas others would not eat pizza even if you gave it to them free of charge. As the price of pizza rises, less enthusiastic pizza eaters drop out of the market entirely, leaving the expensive pie to the more devoted consumers. Thus, the quantity demanded declines as price rises, simply because higher prices induce more people to kick the pizza habit. Indeed, for many commodities, lower prices encourage new customers to come into the *market*, and it is these "fair weather" customers (rather than the negative slope of *individual* demand curves) that account for the law of demand.

This is also illustrated in Figure 6–4, where only Naomi will buy the product at a price higher than *D*. However, at a price below *D*, Alex will also purchase. Hence, below point *K* the market demand curve lies further to the right than it would have if Alex had not entered the market. Put another way, a rise in price from a level below *D* to a level above *D* would cut quantity demanded for two reasons: first, because Naomi's demand curve has a negative slope and, second, because it would drive Alex out of the market.

We conclude, therefore, that the law of demand stands on fairly solid ground. If individual demand curves are downward sloping, then the market demand curve surely will be, too. Further, the market demand curve may slope downward, even when individual demand curves do not.

EXCEPTIONS TO THE LAW OF DEMAND

Nevertheless, exceptions to the law of demand have been noted. One common exception occurs when people judge quality on the basis of price—they perceive a more expensive commodity as offering better quality. For example, many people buy name-brand aspirin, even if right next to it on the drugstore shelf they see an unbranded, generic aspirin with a virtually identical chemical formula, selling at half the price. The consumers who do buy the name-brand aspirin may well use comparative price to judge the relative qualities of different brands. They may prefer Brand *X* to Brand *Y* because *X* is slightly more expensive. If Brand *X* were to reduce its price below that of *Y*, consumers might assume that it was no longer superior and actually reduce their purchases.

Another possible cause of an upward-sloping demand curve is snob appeal. If part of the reason for purchasing a Rolls Royce is to advertise one's wealth, a decrease in the car's price may actually reduce sales, even if the quality of the car remains unchanged. Other types of exceptions have also been noted by economists. But, for most commodities, it seems quite reasonable to assume that demand curves have negative slopes, an assumption that is supported by the data.

This chapter has begun to take us behind the demand curve, to discuss how it is determined by the preferences of the individual consumer. The chapter that follows will explore the demand curve further by examining what determines its shape and the implications of that shape for consumer behavior.

SUMMARY

1. Economists distinguish between total and marginal utility. *Total utility*, or the benefit a consumer derives from a purchase, is measured by the maximum amount of money he or she would give up in order to have the good. Rational consumers seek to maximize (net) total utility, or *consumer's surplus:* the total utility derived from a commodity minus the value of the money spent in buying it.

2. *Marginal utility* is the maximum amount of money that a consumer is willing to pay for an additional unit of a particular commodity. Marginal utility is useful in calculating the set of purchases that maximizes net total utility. This illustrates one of our *Ideas for Beyond the Final Exam.*

3. The *"law" of diminishing marginal utility* is a psychological hypothesis stating that as a consumer acquires more and more of a commodity, the marginal utility of additional units of the commodity decreases.

4. To maximize the total utility obtained by spending money on Commodity *X*, given the fact that other goods can be purchased only with the money that remains after buying

X, the consumer must purchase a quantity of *X* such that the price equals (or approximately equals) the commodity's marginal utility (in monetary terms).

5. If the consumer acts to maximize utility, and if her marginal utility of some good declines when she purchases larger quantities, then her demand curve for the good will have a negative slope. A reduction in price will induce her to purchase more units, leading to a lower marginal utility.

6. Abundant goods tend to have low prices and low marginal utilities regardless of whether their total utilities are high or low. That is why water can have a lower price than diamonds despite its higher total utility.

7. An *inferior good*, such as secondhand clothing, is a commodity that consumers buy less of when they get richer, all other things held equal.

8. Consumers usually earn a surplus when they purchase a commodity voluntarily. This means that the quantity of the good that they buy is worth more to them than the money they give up in exchange. Consumer's surplus is normally positive.

9. As another of our *Ideas for Beyond the Final Exam*, "How Much Does It Really Cost?" tells us, the true economic cost of the purchase of a commodity, *X*, is its opportunity cost, that is, the value of the alternative purchases that the acquisition of *X* requires the consumer to forgo. The money value of the opportunity cost of a unit of good *X* can be higher or lower than the price of *X*.

10. A rise in a consumer's income can push quantity demanded either up or down. For normal goods, the effect of a rise in income raises the quantity demanded; for inferior goods, which are purchased in order to save money, a higher income reduces the quantity demanded.

11. The demand curve for an entire market is obtained by taking a horizontal sum of the demand curves of all of the individuals who buy or consider buying in that market. This sum is obtained by adding up, for each price, the quantity of the commodity in question that every such consumer is willing to purchase at that price.

K E Y   T E R M S

Total utility   96

Marginal utility   96

The "law" of diminishing marginal utility   96

Marginal analysis   99

Optimal purchase rule   100

Consumer's surplus   103

Scarcity and marginal utility   105

Inferior good   105

Market demand curve   105

The "law" of demand   106

Q U E S T I O N S   F O R   R E V I E W

1. Describe some of the different things you do with water. Which would you give up if the price of water were to rise a little? If it were to rise by a fairly large amount? If it were to rise by a very large amount?

2. Which gives you greater *total* utility, 12 gallons of water per day or 20 gallons per day? Why?

3. At which level do you get greater *marginal* utility: 12 gallons per day or 20 gallons per day? Why?

4. Suppose that you wanted to measure the marginal utility of a commodity to a consumer by directly determining the consumer's psychological attitude or strength of feeling for the commodity rather than by seeing how much money the consumer would give up for the commodity. Why would you find it difficult to get such a psychological measurement?

5. Some people who do not understand the optimal purchase rule argue that if a consumer buys so much of a good that its price equals its marginal utility, she could not possibly be behaving optimally. Rather, they say, she would be better off quitting while she was ahead, that is, buying a quantity such that marginal utility is much greater than price. What is wrong with this argument? (*Hint:* What opportunity would the consumer then miss? Is it maximization of marginal or total utility that serves the consumer's interests?)

6. What inferior goods do you purchase? Why do you buy them? Do you think you will continue to buy them when your income is higher?

7. Which of the following items are likely to be normal goods for a typical consumer? Which are likely to be inferior goods?

    a. Expensive perfume

    b. Paper plates

    c. Secondhand clothing

    d. Overseas trips

8. Emily buys an air conditioner that costs her $600. Because the air in her home is cleaner, this saves her $150 in curtain cleaning costs over the lifetime of the air conditioner. In money terms, what is the opportunity cost of the air conditioner?

9. Suppose that strawberries sell for $2 per basket. Jim is considering whether to buy zero, one, two, three, or four baskets. On your own, create a plausible set of total and marginal utility numbers for the different quantities of strawberries (like we did for pizza in Table 6–1) and arrange them in a table. From your table, calculate how many baskets Jim would buy.

10. Draw a graph showing the consumer's surplus Jim would get from his strawberry purchase and check your answer with the help of your marginal utility table.

11. Consider a market with two consumers, Jasmine and Jim. Draw a demand curve for each of the two consumers and use those curves to construct the demand curve for the entire market.

●   **APPENDIX** ▌ **ANALYZING CONSUMER CHOICE GRAPHICALLY: INDIFFERENCE CURVE ANALYSIS**

The consumer demand analysis presented in this chapter, although correct as far as it goes, has one shortcoming: By treating the consumer's decision about the purchase of each commodity as an isolated event, it conceals the fact that consumers must *choose* because of their limited budgets. The foregoing analysis does not explicitly indicate the hard choice behind every purchase decision—the sacrifice of some goods to obtain others.

The idea is included implicitly, of course, because the purchase of any commodity involves a trade-off between that good and money. If you spend more money on rent, you have less to spend on entertainment. If you buy more clothing, you have less money for food. But to represent the consumer's *choice* problem explicitly, economists have invented two geometric devices, the *budget line* and the *indifference curve*, which are described in this appendix.

GEOMETRY OF AVAILABLE CHOICES: THE BUDGET LINE

Suppose, for simplicity, that only two commodities are produced in the world: cheese and rubber bands. The decision problem of any household is then to allocate its income between these two goods. Clearly, the more it spends on one, the less it can have of the other. But just what is the trade-off? A numerical example will answer this question and also introduce the graphical device that economists use to portray the trade-off.

Suppose that cheese costs $2 per pound, boxes of rubber bands sell at $3 each, and a consumer has $12 at his disposal. He obviously has a variety of choices, as displayed in Table 6–4. For example, if he buys no rubber bands, he can go home with six pounds of cheese, and so on. Each of the combinations of cheese and rubber bands that the consumer can afford can be shown in a diagram in which the axes measure the quantities purchased of each commodity. In Figure 6–5, pounds of cheese are measured along the vertical axis, the number of boxes of rubber bands is measured along the horizontal axis, and a labeled point represents each of the combinations enumerated in Table 6–4. This budget line *AE* shows all the different combinations of cheese and rubber bands that the consumer can buy with $12 if cheese costs $2 per pound and a box of rubber bands costs $3. For example, point *A* corresponds to spending everything on cheese; point *E* corresponds to spending everything on rubber bands. At intermediate points on the budget line (such as *C*), the consumer buys some of both goods (at *C*, two boxes of rubber bands and three pounds of cheese), which together use up the $12 available.

FIGURE 6–5

A Budget Line

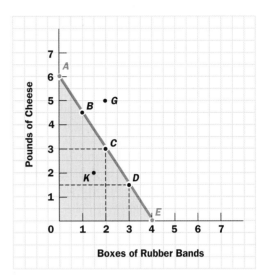

Boxes of Rubber Bands

If a straight line connects points *A* through *E*, the red line in the diagram, it traces all possible ways to divide the $12 between the two goods. For example, at point *D*, if the consumer buys three boxes of rubber bands, he will have only enough money left to purchase $1\frac{1}{2}$ pounds of cheese. This is readily seen to be correct from Table 6–4. Line *AE* is therefore called the *budget line*.

> The *budget line* for a household graphically represents all possible combinations of two commodities that it can purchase, given the prices of the commodities and some fixed amount of money at its disposal.

PROPERTIES OF THE BUDGET LINE

Let us now use *r* to represent the number of boxes of rubber bands purchased by the consumer and *c* to indicate the amount of cheese that he acquires. Thus, at $2 per pound, he spends on cheese a total of $2 times the number of pounds of cheese bought, or $2c. Similarly, he spends $3r on rubber bands, making a total of $2c

Alternative Purchase Combinations for a $12 Budget				TABLE 6–4
Boxes of Rubber Bands (at $3 each)	Expen diture on Rubber Bands	Remaining Funds	Pounds of Cheese (at $2 each)	Label in Figure 6–5
0	$ 0	$12	6	A
1	3	9	4.5	B
2	6	6	3	C
3	9	3	1.5	D
4	12	0	0	E

plus $3r, which must equal $12, if he spends the entire $12 on the two commodities. Thus, $2c + 3r = 12$ is the equation of the budget line. It is also the equation of the straight line drawn in the diagram.[5]

Note also that the budget line represents the *maximum* amounts of the commodities that the consumer can afford. Thus, for any given purchase of rubber bands, it indicates the greatest amount of cheese that his money can buy. If the consumer wants to be thrifty, he can choose to end up at a point *below* the budget line, such as *K*. Clearly, then, the choices he has available include not only those points on the budget line, *AE*, but also any point in the shaded triangle formed by that line and the two axes. By contrast, points above the budget line, such as *G*, are not available to the consumer given his limited budget. A bundle of five pounds of cheese and two boxes of rubber bands would cost $16, which is more than he has to spend.

CHANGES IN THE BUDGET LINE

The position of the budget line is determined by two types of data: the prices of the commodities purchased and the income at the buyer's disposal. We can complete our discussion of the graphics of the budget line by examining briefly how a change in either prices or income affects the location of that line.

Obviously, any increase in the income of the household increases the range of options available to it. Specifically, *increases in income produce parallel shifts in the budget line*, as shown in Figure 6–6. The reason is simple: An increase in available income of, say, 50 percent, if spent entirely on these two goods, would permit the family to purchase exactly 50 percent more of *either* commodity. Point *A* in Figure 6–5 would shift upward by 50 percent of its distance from the origin, whereas point *E* would move to the right by 50 percent.[6] Figure 6–6 shows three such budget lines corresponding to incomes of $9, $12, and $18, respectively.

Finally, we can ask what happens to the budget line when the price of some commodity changes. In Figure 6–7, when the price of the rubber bands *decreases*, the budget line moves outward, but the move is no longer parallel because the point on the cheese axis remains fixed. Once again, the reason is fairly straightforward. A 50 percent reduction in the price of rubber bands (from

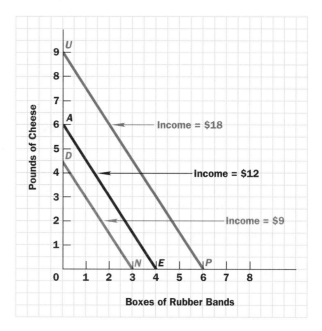

FIGURE 6-6

The Effect of Income Changes on the Budget Line

$3.00 to $1.50) permits the consumer to buy twice as many boxes of rubber bands with his $12 as before: Point *E* moves rightward to point *H*, where the buyer can obtain eight boxes of rubber bands. However, since the price of cheese has not changed from point *A*, the amount of cheese that can be bought for $12 is unaffected. This gives the general result that *a reduction in the price of one of the two commodities swings the budget line*

FIGURE 6-7

The Effect of Price Changes on the Budget Line

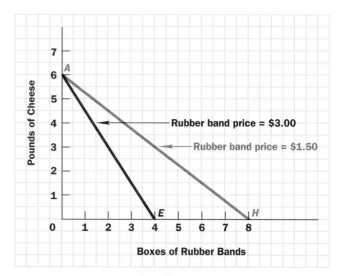

---

[5] You may have noticed one problem that arises in this formulation. If every point on the budget line, *AE*, is a possible way for the consumer to spend his money, he must be able to buy *fractional* boxes of rubber bands. Perhaps the purchase of $1\frac{1}{2}$ boxes can be interpreted to include a down payment of $1.50 on a box of rubber bands to be purchased on the next shopping trip!

[6] An algebraic proof is simple. Let *M* (which is initially $12) be the amount of money available to the household. The equation of the budget line can be solved for *c*, obtaining $c = -(3/2)r + M/2$. This is the equation of a straight line with a slope of $-3/2$ and a vertical intercept of $M/2$. A change in *M*, the quantity of money available, will not change the *slope* of the budget line; it will lead only to parallel shifts in that line.

outward along the axis representing the quantity of that item while leaving the location of the other end of the line unchanged. Thus a fall in the price of rubber bands from $3.00 to $1.50 swings the price line from *AE* to red line *AH*. This happens because at the higher price, $12 buys only four boxes of rubber bands, but at the lower price, it can buy eight boxes.

■ WHAT THE CONSUMER PREFERS: PROPERTIES OF THE INDIFFERENCE CURVE

The budget line indicates what choices are *available* to the consumer, given the size of his income and the commodity prices fixed by the market. Next, we must examine the consumer's *preferences* in order to determine which of these available possibilities he will choose.

After much investigation, economists have determined what they believe to be the minimum amount of information they need about a purchaser in order to analyze his choices. Economists only need know how a consumer *ranks* alternative bundles of available commodities. Suppose, for instance, that the consumer can choose between two bundles of goods, Bundle *W*, which contains three boxes of rubber bands and one pound of cheese, and Bundle *T*, which contains two boxes of rubber bands and three pounds of cheese. The economist wants to know for this purpose only whether the consumer prefers *W* to *T* or *T* to *W*, or whether he is *indifferent* about which one he gets. Note that the analysis requires no information about *degree* of preference—whether the consumer is wildly more enthusiastic about one of the bundles or just prefers it slightly.

Graphically, the preference information is provided by a group of curves called *indifference curves* (Figure 6–8). Any point on the diagram represents a combination of cheese and rubber bands. (For example, point *T* on indifference curve I_b represents two boxes of rubber bands and three pounds of cheese.) Any two points on the same indifference curve (for example, *S* and *W*, on indifference curve I_a) represent two combinations of the goods that the consumer likes equally well. If two points, such as *T* and *W*, lie on different indifference curves, the consumer prefers the one on the higher indifference curve.

An *indifference curve* is a line connecting all combinations of the commodities that are equally desirable to the consumer.

But before we examine these curves, let us see how to interpret such a curve. A single point on an indifference curve says nothing about preferences. For example, point *R* on curve *I* simply represents the bundle of goods composed of four boxes of rubber bands and $\frac{1}{2}$ pound of cheese. It does *not* suggest that the consumer is indifferent between $\frac{1}{2}$ pound of cheese and four boxes of rubber bands. For the curve to indicate anything, one must consider at

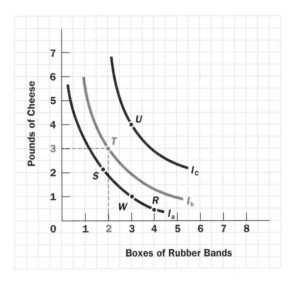

FIGURE 6-8

Three Indifference Curves for Cheese and Rubber Bands

least two of its points, for example, points *S* and *W*. An indifference curve, by definition, represents all such combinations that provide equal utility to the consumer.

We do not know yet which bundle, among all of the bundles he can afford, the consumer prefers; this analysis indicates only that a choice between certain bundles will lead to indifference. Before using indifference curves to analyze the consumer's choice, one must examine a few of its properties. Most important is the fact that:

As long as the consumer desires *more* of each of the goods in question, *every* point on a higher indifference curve (that is, a curve farther from the origin in the graph) will be preferred to *any* point on a lower indifference curve.

In other words, among indifference curves, *higher is better*. The reason is obvious. Given two indifference curves, say, I_b and I_c in Figure 6–8, the higher curve will contain points lying above and to the right of some points on the lower curve. Thus, point *U* on curve I_c lies above and to the right of point *T* on curve I_b. This means that the consumer gets more rubber bands *and* more cheese at *U* than at *T*. Assuming that he desires both commodities, the consumer must prefer *U* to *T*.

Because every point on curve I_c is, by definition, equal in desirability to point *U*, and the same relation holds for point *T* and all other points along curve I_b, the consumer will prefer *every* point on curve I_c to *any* point on curve I_b.

This at once implies a second property of indifference curves: *They never intersect*. This is so because if an indifference curve, say, I_b, is anywhere above another, say, I_a, then I_b must be above I_a everywhere, since every point on I_b is preferred to every point on I_a.

Another property that characterizes the indifference curve is its *negative slope*. Again, this holds only if the consumer wants more of both commodities. Consider two points, such as S and R, on the same indifference curve. If the consumer is indifferent between them, one point cannot represent more of *both* commodities than the other point. Since point S represents more cheese than point R, R must offer more rubber bands than S, or the consumer would not be indifferent about which she gets. This means that any movement toward the one with the larger number of rubber bands implies a decrease in the quantity of cheese. The curve will always slope downhill toward the right, a negative slope.

A final property of indifference curves is the nature of their curvature—the way *they round toward the axes*. They are drawn "bowed in"—they flatten out (their slopes decrease in absolute value) as they extend from left to right. To understand why this is so, we must first examine the economic interpretation of the slope of an indifference curve.

THE SLOPES OF INDIFFERENCE CURVES AND BUDGET LINES

In Figure 6–9, the average slope of the indifference curve between points M and N is represented by RM/RN. RM is the quantity of cheese that the consumer gives up in moving from M to N. Similarly, RN is the

increased number of boxes of rubber bands acquired in this move. Because the consumer is indifferent between bundles M and N, the gain of RN rubber bands must just suffice to compensate him for the loss of RM pounds of cheese. Thus, the ratio RM/RN represents the terms on which the consumer is just willing—*according to his own preference*—to trade one good for the other. If RM/RN equals 2, the consumer is willing to give up (no more than) two pounds of cheese for one additional box of rubber bands.

> The *slope of an indifference curve*, referred to as the *marginal rate of substitution* between the commodities, represents the maximum amount of one commodity that the consumer is willing to give up in exchange for one more unit of another commodity.

The slope of the budget line, BB, in Figure 6–9 is also a rate of exchange between cheese and rubber bands. But it no longer reflects the consumer's subjective willingness to trade. Rather, the slope represents the rate of exchange that *the market* offers to the consumer when he gives up money in exchange for cheese and rubber bands. Recall that the budget line represents all commodity combinations that a consumer can get by spending a fixed amount of money. The budget line is thus a curve of constant expenditure. At current prices, if the consumer reduces his purchase of cheese by amount DE in Figure 6–9, he will save just enough money to buy an additional amount, EF, of rubber bands, since at points D and F he is spending the same total number of dollars.

> The *slope of a budget line* is the amount of one commodity that the market requires an individual to give up in order to obtain one additional unit of another commodity without any change in the amount of money spent.

The slopes of the two types of curves, then, are perfectly analogous in their meaning. The slope of the indifference curve indicates the terms on which the *consumer* is willing to trade one commodity for another, whereas the slope of the budget line reports the *market* terms on which the consumer can trade one good for another.

It is useful to carry our interpretation of the slope of the budget line one step further. Common sense suggests that the market's rate of exchange between cheese and rubber bands should be related to their prices, p_c and p_r, and it is easy to show that this is so. Specifically, the slope of the budget line is equal to the ratio of the prices of the two commodities. The reason is straightforward. If the consumer gives up one box of rubber bands, he has p_r more dollars to spend on cheese. But at a lower price of cheese, this money will enable him to buy a greater quantity of cheese—that is, his cheese purchasing power will be inversely related to its price. Because the price of cheese is p_c per pound, the additional p_r dollars permit him to buy p_r/p_c more pounds of cheese. Thus, the slope of the budget line is p_r/p_c.

FIGURE 6–9

Slopes of a Budget Line and an Indifference Curve

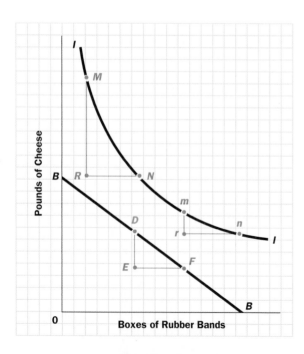

Before returning to our main subject, the study of consumer choice, we pause briefly and use our interpretation of the slope of the indifference curve to discuss the third of the properties of the indifference curve—its characteristic curvature—which we left unexplained earlier. The shape of indifference curves means that the slope decreases with movement from left to right. In Figure 6–9, at point m, toward the right of the diagram, the consumer is willing to give up far less cheese for one more box of rubber bands (quantity rm) than he is willing to trade at point M, toward the left. This is because at M he initially has a large quantity of cheese and few rubber bands, whereas at m his initial stock of cheese is low and he has many rubber bands. In general terms, the curvature premise on which indifference curves are usually drawn asserts that consumers are relatively eager to trade away a commodity of which they have a large amount but are more reluctant to trade goods of which they hold small quantities. This psychological premise underlies the curvature of the indifference curve.

We can now use our indifference curve apparatus to analyze how the consumer chooses among the combinations that he can afford to buy, that is, the combinations of rubber bands and cheese shown by the budget line. Figure 6–10 brings together in the same diagram the budget line from Figure 6–5 and the indifference curves from Figure 6–8.

TANGENCY CONDITIONS

Because, according to the first of the properties of indifference curves, the consumer prefers higher curves to lower ones, he will go to the point on the budget line that lies on the highest indifference curve attainable.

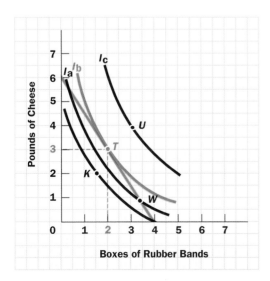

FIGURE 6-10

Optimal Consumer Choice

This will be point T on indifference curve I_b. He can afford no other point that he likes as well. For example, neither point K below the budget line nor point W on the budget line gets him on such a high indifference curve. Further, any point on an indifference curve above I_b, such as point U, is out of the question because it lies beyond his financial means. We end up with a simple rule of consumer choice:

> Consumers will select the most desired combination of goods obtainable for their money. The choice will be that point on the budget line at which the budget line is tangent to an indifference curve.

We can see why only the point of tangency, T (two boxes of rubber bands and three pounds of cheese), will give the consumer the largest utility that his money can buy. Suppose that the consumer were instead to consider buying $3\frac{1}{2}$ boxes of rubber bands and one pound of cheese. This would put him at point W on the budget line and on the indifference curve I_a. But then, by buying fewer rubber bands and more cheese (a move upward and to the left on the budget line), he could get to another indifference curve, I_b, that would be higher and hence more desirable without spending any more money. It clearly does not pay to end up at W. Only the point of tangency, T, leaves no room for improvement.

At a point of tangency, where the consumer's benefits from purchasing cheese and rubber bands are maximized, the slope of the budget line equals the slope of the indifference curve. This is true by the definition of a point of tangency. We have just seen that the slope of the indifference curve is the marginal rate of substitution between cheese and rubber bands, and that the slope of the budget line is the ratio of the prices of rubber bands and cheese. We can therefore restate the requirement for the optimal division of the consumer's money between the two commodities in slightly more technical language:

> Consumers will get the most benefit from their money when they choose combinations of commodities whose marginal rates of substitution equal the ratios of their prices.

It is worth reviewing the logic behind this conclusion. Why is it not advisable for the consumer to stop at a point like W, where the marginal rate of substitution (slope of the indifference curve) is less than the price ratio (slope of the budget line)? Instead, by moving upward and to the left along his budget line, he can take advantage of market opportunities to obtain a commodity bundle that he likes better. This will always be true, for example, if the amount of cheese the consumer is *personally* willing to exchange for a box of rubber bands (the slope of the indifference curve) is greater than the amount of cheese for which the box of rubber bands trades *on the market* (the slope of the budget line).

CONSEQUENCES OF INCOME CHANGES: INFERIOR GOODS

Next, consider what happens to the consumer's purchases after a rise in income. We know that a rise in income produces a parallel outward shift in the budget line, such as the shift from *BB* to *CC* in Figure 6–11. The quantity of rubber bands demanded rises from three to four boxes, and the quantity demanded of cheese also increases. This moves the consumer's equilibrium from tangency point *T* to tangency point *E* on a higher indifference curve.

FIGURE 6-11

Effects of a Rise in Income When Neither Good Is Inferior

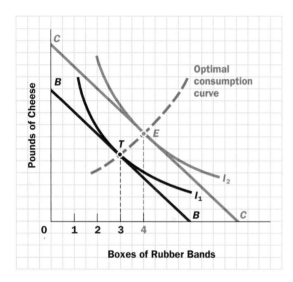

A rise in income may or may not increase the demand for a commodity. In Figure 6–11, the rise in income does lead the consumer to buy more cheese *and* more rubber bands, but indifference curves need not always be positioned in a way that yields this sort of result. In Figure 6–12, as the consumer's budget line rises from *BB* to *CC*, the tangency point moves leftward from *H* to *G*, so that when his income rises he actually buys *fewer* rubber bands. This implies that rubber bands are an *inferior good.*

CONSEQUENCES OF PRICE CHANGES: DERIVING THE DEMAND CURVE

Finally, we come to the main question underlying demand curves: How does a consumer's choice change if the price of one good changes? We explained earlier that a reduction in the price of a box of rubber bands causes the budget line to swing outward along the horizontal axis while leaving its vertical intercept unchanged. In Figure 6–13, we depict the effect of a decline in the price of rubber

FIGURE 6-12

Effects of a Rise In Income When Rubber Bands Are an Inferior Good

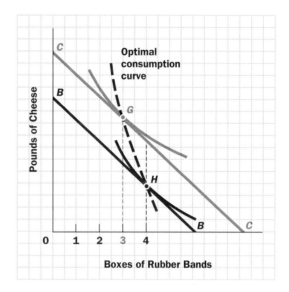

FIGURE 6-13

Consequences of Price Changes

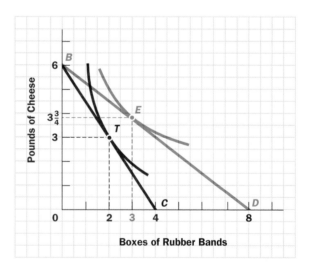

bands on the quantity of rubber bands demanded. As the price of rubber bands falls, the budget line swings from *BC* to *BD*. The tangency points, *T* and *E*, also move in a corresponding direction, causing the quantity demanded to rise from two to three boxes. The price of rubber bands has fallen, and the quantity demanded has risen, so the demand curve for rubber bands is negatively sloped. The desired purchase of rubber bands increases from two to three boxes, and the desired purchase of cheese also increases, from three pounds to $3\frac{3}{4}$ pounds.

The demand curve for rubber bands can be constructed directly from Figure 6–13. Point T shows that the consumer will buy two boxes of rubber bands when the price of a box is $3.00. Point E indicates that when the price falls to $1.50, quantity demanded rises to three boxes of rubber bands.[7] These two pieces of information are shown in Figure 6–14 as points t and e on the demand curve for rubber bands. By examining the effects of other possible prices for rubber bands (other budget lines emanating from point B in Figure 6–13), we can find all the other points on the demand curve in exactly the same way. The demand curve is derived from the indifference-curve diagram by varying the price of the commodity to see the effects of all other possible prices.

The indifference curve diagram also brings out an important point that the demand curve does not show. A change in the *price of rubber bands* also has consequences for the *quantity of cheese demanded* because it affects the amount of money left over for cheese purchases. In the example illustrated in Figure 6–13, the decrease in the price of rubber bands increases the demand for cheese from 3 to $3\frac{3}{4}$ pounds.

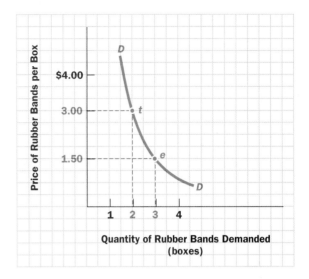

FIGURE 6–14

Deriving the Demand Curve for Rubber Bands

SUMMARY

1. Indifference-curve analysis permits economists to study the interrelationships of the demands for two (or more) commodities.

2. The basic tools of indifference-curve analysis are the consumer's *budget line* and *indifference curves.*

3. A budget line shows all combinations of two commodities that the consumer can afford, given the prices of the commodities and the amount of money the consumer has available to spend.

4. The budget line is a straight line whose slope equals the ratio of the prices of the commodities. A change in price changes the slope of the budget line. A change in the consumer's income causes a parallel shift in the budget line.

5. Two points on an indifference curve represent two combinations of commodities such that the consumer does not prefer one combination over the other.

6. Indifference curves normally have negative slopes and are "bowed in" toward the origin. The *slope of an indifference curve* indicates how much of one commodity the consumer is willing to give up in order to get an additional unit of the other commodity.

7. The consumer will choose the point on her budget line that gets her to the highest attainable indifference curve. Normally this will occur at the point of tangency between the two curves. This point indicates the combination of commodities that gives her the greatest benefits for the amount of money she has available to spend.

8. The consumer's demand curve can be derived from her indifference curve.

KEY TERMS

Budget line   109

Indifference curve   111

Marginal rate of substitution   112

Slope of an indifference curve   112

Slope of a budget line   112

---

[7] How do we know that the price of rubber bands corresponding to the budget line BD is $1.50? Because the $12.00 total budget will purchase at most eight boxes (point D), the price per box must be $12.00/8 = $1.50.

1. John Q. Public spends all of his income on gasoline and hot dogs. Draw his budget line under several conditions:

   a. His income is $80 and one gallon of gasoline and one hot dog each cost $1.60.

   b. His income is $120 and the two prices remain the same.

   c. His income is $80, hot dogs cost $1.60 each, and gasoline costs $1.20 per gallon.

2. Draw some hypothetical indifference curves for John Q. Public on a diagram identical to the one you constructed for the preceding question.

   a. Approximately how much gasoline and how many hot dogs will Mr. Public buy?

   b. How will these choices change if his income increases to $120, as in the previous question? Is either good an inferior good?

   c. How will these choices change if gasoline prices fall to $1.20 per gallon, as in the previous question?

3. Explain the information that the *slope* of an indifference curve conveys about a consumer's preferences. Use this relationship to explain the typical U-shaped curvature of indifference curves.

A high cross elasticity of demand [between two goods indicates that they] compete in the same market. [This can prevent a supplier of one of the products] from possessing monopoly power over price.

U.S. Supreme Court, DuPont cellophane decision, 1956

DEMAND AND ELASTICITY

In this chapter we continue our study of demand and demand curves, which we began in the previous chapter. We focus here on how we can measure the extent to which quantity demanded responds to price changes, and what such responsiveness implies about the revenue that producers will receive if they change prices. In particular, we introduce and explain an important concept called *elasticity* that economists use to examine the relationship between quantity demanded and price.

Issue: Will Taxing Cigarettes Make Teenagers Stop Smoking?

In 1997, President Bill Clinton proposed legislation that would have forced tobacco companies to raise cigarette prices. Although this proposal was eventually rejected by Congress in 1998, public health experts believe that such increases are a major weapon in the effort to cut teenage smoking. Imagine yourself on a panel of consultants helping a congressional committee draft new legislation to deal with this issue. As the youngest member of the group, you are asked your opinion about how effective a big tax increase on cigarettes would be in getting young people to stop smoking. How would you respond? What sorts of statistical data, if any, would you use to help find your answer? And how might you go about analyzing the relevant numbers?

We shed light on such questions in this chapter, where we deal with topics such as the shape of the demand curve and its implications for the effects of a price change on quantity demanded and on the amount of revenue suppliers can earn from consumers. As often happens in economics, we will see that careful investigation brings out some surprises. This is true in the case of taxes to discourage teenage smoking. A tax on cigarettes may actually benefit teenagers'—and other citizens'—health. And it will, of course, benefit government finances by bringing in more tax money. Nothing surprising so far. But the surprise is this: the more

effective the tax turns out to be in curbing teenage smoking, the less beneficial it will be to the government's finances, and vice versa: the more it benefits the government, the less it will contribute to health.

The concept of elasticity of demand will make this and other related matters clearer.

■ ELASTICITY: THE MEASURE OF RESPONSIVENESS

Governments, business firms, supermarkets, consumers, and law courts need a way to measure how responsive demand is to price changes. Economists measure the responsiveness of quantity demanded to price changes via a concept called *elasticity*. Marketers sometimes use estimated elasticities to decide how to price their products, whether to add new product models, and other questions. A relatively flat demand curve like Figure 7–1(b) indicates that consumers respond sharply to a change in price—the quantity they demand falls by 2.5 units (from 4 units to 1.5 units) when price rises $10. They demand or buy much less of the product when price rises even a little bit. Such a "touchy" curve is called *elastic* or *highly elastic*. A relatively steep demand curve like Figure 7–1(a), which indicates that consumers respond hardly at all to a price change, is called *inelastic*. In this graph, a $10 price rise cuts quantity demanded by only one unit.

Two Hypothetical Demand Curves for Film | FIGURE 7–1

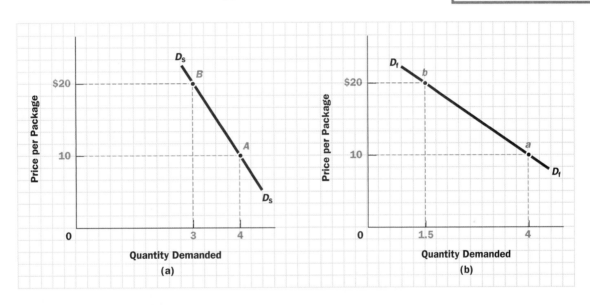

NOTE: Quantities are in millions of packages of film per year.

The precise measure used for this purpose is called the **price elasticity of demand,** or sometimes simply the **elasticity of demand.** We define elasticity of demand as the ratio of the *percentage* change in quantity demanded to the associated *percentage* change in price.

Thus, demand is called *elastic* if, say, a 10 percent rise in price reduces quantity demanded by *more* than 10 percent. Demand is called *inelastic* if such a rise in price reduces quantity demanded by *less* than 10 percent.

Why do we need these definitions to analyze the responsiveness to price shown by a particular demand curve? At first, it may seem that the *slope* of the demand curve conveys the needed information: Curve D_sD_s is much steeper than curve D_fD_f in Figure 7–1, so any given change in price appears to correspond to a much smaller change in quantity demanded in Figure 7–1(a) than in Figure 7–1(b). For this reason, it is tempting to call demand in Panel (b) "more elastic." But slope will not do the job, because the slope of any curve depends on the particular units of measurement (as we showed in Chapter 2), and economists use no standardized units of measurement. Cloth output may be measured in yards or in meters, milk in quarts or liters, and coal in tons or hundred-weights. Figure 7–2(a) brings out the point explicitly. In this graph, we return to the pizza example from Chapter 6, measuring quantity demanded in terms of pizzas and price in dollars per pizza. A fall in price

The **(price) elasticity of demand** is the ratio of the *percentage* change in quantity demanded to the *percentage* change in price that brings about the change in quantity demanded.

from $15 to $11 per large pizza (points *A* and *B*) raises quantity demanded at Paul's Pizza Parlor from 280 pizzas to 360 per week, that is, by 80 pizzas.

| FIGURE 7–2 | **The Sensitivity of Slope to Units of Measurement at Paul's Pizza Parlor** |

Now look at Figure 7–2(b), which provides *exactly* the same information, but measures quantity demanded in *slices* of pizzas rather than whole pizzas (assuming one pizza yields eight slices). Thus, the same price change as before increases quantity demanded, from 8 × 280 = 2,240 slices to 8 × 360 = 2,880 slices—that is, by 640 slices, rather than by 80 pizzas.

Visually, the increase in quantity demanded looks eight times as great in Panel (b) as in Panel (a), but all that has changed is the unit of measurement. The 640-unit increase in Figure 7–2(b) represents the same increase in quantity demanded as the 80-unit increase in Figure 7–2(a). Just as you get different numbers for a given rise in temperature, depending on whether you measure it in Celsius or Fahrenheit, so the slopes of demand curves differ, depending on whether you measure quantity in pizzas or in pizza slices. Clearly, then, slope does not really measure responsiveness of quantity demanded to price, because the measure changes whenever the units of measurement change.

Economists created the elasticity concept precisely in response to this problem. Elasticity measures responsiveness on the basis of *percentage* changes in price and quantity rather than on *absolute* changes. The elasticity formula solves the units problem because percentages are unaffected by units of measurement. If the government defense budget doubles, it goes up by 100 percent, whether measured in millions or billions of dollars. If a person's height doubles between the ages of 2 and 18, it goes up 100 percent, whether measured in inches or centimeters. The elasticity formula given earlier expresses both the change in quantity demanded and the change in price as *percentages*.[1]

---

[1] The remainder of this section involves fairly technical computational issues. On a first reading you may prefer to go directly to the new section that begins at the bottom of the next page.

Further, elasticity calculates the change in quantity demanded *as a percentage of the average of the two quantities*: the quantity demanded *before* the change in price has occurred (Q_0) and the quantity demanded *after* the price change (Q_1). In our example, the number of pizzas sold per week rises by 80, which is 25 percent of the average (320) of 280 (Q_0) and 360 (Q_1), the "before" and "after" sale of pizzas. This is a useful compromise between viewing the change in quantity demanded (80 pizzas) as a percentage of the initial quantity (280) or as a percentage of the final quantity (360).

Similarly, the change in price is expressed as a percentage of the average of the "before" and "after" prices, so that, in effect, it represents elasticity at the price halfway between those two prices. That is, the price falls by \$4 (from \$15 to \$11). Because \$4 is (approximately) 31 percent of the average of \$15 (P_0) and \$11 (P_1) (\$13), we say that in this case a 31 percent fall in price led to a 25 percent rise in quantity of pizza demanded.

To summarize, the elasticity formula has two basic attributes:

■ Each of the changes with which it deals is measured as a *percentage* change.

■ Each of the percentage changes is calculated in terms of the average values of the before and after quantities and prices.

In addition, economists usually adjust the price elasticity of demand formula a third way. Note that when the price *increases*, the quantity demanded usually *declines*. So, when the price change is a positive number, the quantity change will normally be a negative number, and when the price change is a negative number, the quantity change will normally be a positive number. This means that the ratio of the two percentage changes will be a negative number. However, we customarily express elasticity as a positive number. Hence:

■ Each percentage change is taken as an "absolute value," meaning that the calculation drops all minus signs.[2]

We can now state the formula for price elasticity of demand, keeping all three features of the formula in mind:

$$\text{Price elasticity of demand} = \frac{\text{Change in quantity demanded, expressed as a percentage of the average of the before and after quantities}}{\text{Corresponding percentage change in price}}$$

In our example:

$$\text{Elasticity of demand for pizzas} =$$
$$-\frac{(Q_1 - Q_0)/\text{average of } Q_0 \text{ and } Q_1}{(P_1 - P_0)/\text{average of } P_0 \text{ and } P_1} = -\frac{80/320}{-4/13} = \frac{25\%}{31\%} = 0.8 \text{ (approximately)}$$

PRICE ELASTICITY OF DEMAND AND THE SHAPES OF DEMAND CURVES

We noted earlier that looks can be deceiving in some demand curves because their units of measurement are arbitrary. Economists have provided the elasticity formula to overcome that problem. Nonetheless, the shape of a demand curve does convey some information about its elasticity. Let us see what information some demand curve shapes give, with the aid of Figure 7–3.

---

[2] This third attribute of the elasticity formula—the removal of all minus signs—applies only when the formula is used to measure the responsiveness of *quantity demanded* to a change in *price*. Later in the chapter, we will show that similar formulas are used to measure the responsiveness between other pairs of variables. For example, the elasticity of supply uses a similar formula to measure the responsiveness of quantity supplied to price. In such other uses, it is not customary to drop minus signs when calculating elasticity. The reasons will become clearer later in the chapter.

| FIGURE 7-3 | **Demand Curves with Different Elasticities** |

PERFECTLY INELASTIC DEMAND CURVES   Panel (a) depicts a completely vertical demand curve. Such a curve is called *perfectly inelastic* throughout because its elasticity is zero at every point on the curve. Because quantity demanded remains at 90 units no matter what the price, the percentage change in quantity is always zero, and hence in this case the elasticity (which equals percentage change in quantity divided by percentage change in price) is always zero. Thus, in this case, consumer purchases do not respond at all to any change in price.

Vertical demand curves like this occur when a commodity is very inexpensive. For example, you probably will not buy more rubber bands if their prices fall. The demand curve may also be vertical when consumers consider the item in question an absolute necessity. For example, if your roommate's grandfather has a heart attack, the family will buy whatever medicine the doctor prescribes, regardless of the price, and will not purchase any more even if the price falls.

PERFECTLY ELASTIC DEMAND CURVES   Panel (b) of Figure 7–3 shows the opposite extreme: a horizontal demand curve. This curve is said to be *perfectly elastic* (or *infinitely elastic*). At any price above $0.75, quantity demanded will drop to zero; that is, the percentage change in quantity demanded will be infinitely large. Perfect elasticity typically occurs when many producers sell a product and consumers can switch easily from one seller to another if the former raises his price. For example, suppose you and the other students in the economics class are required to buy a newspaper every day to keep up with economic events. If newsdealer X, from whom you have been buying the newspaper, raises the price from 75 cents to 80 cents, while the competitor, Y, across the street keeps the old price, then X may lose all her newspaper customers to Y. This is likely to be true whenever an acceptable rival product is available at the going price (75 cents in the diagram). In cases where no one will pay more than the going price, the seller will lose all of her customers if she raises her price by even a penny.

(SEEMINGLY SIMPLE) STRAIGHT-LINE DEMAND CURVES   Panel (c) of Figure 7–3 depicts a case between these two extremes: a *straight-line* demand curve that runs neither vertically nor horizontally. Though the *slope* of a straight-line demand curve remains constant throughout its length, its *elasticity* does not. For example, the elasticity of demand between points *A* and *B* in Figure 7–3(c) is as follows:

$$\frac{\text{Change in } Q \text{ as a percentage of average } Q}{\text{Change in } P \text{ as a percentage of average } P} = \frac{2/3}{2/5} = \frac{66.67\%}{40\%} = 1.67$$

But the elasticity of demand between points *A'* and *B'* is as follows:

$$\frac{2 \text{ as percentage of } 6}{2 \text{ as a percentage of } 2} = \frac{33.33 \text{ percent}}{100 \text{ percent}} = 0.33$$

The general point is that:

> Along a straight-line demand curve, the price elasticity of demand grows steadily smaller as you move from left to right. That is because the quantity keeps getting larger, so that a given *numerical* change in quantity becomes an ever smaller *percentage* change. But the price keeps going lower, so that a given numerical change in price becomes an ever larger percentage change.

UNIT-ELASTIC DEMAND CURVES If the elasticity of a straight-line demand curve varies from one part of the curve to another, what does a demand curve with the same elasticity throughout its length look like? For reasons explained in the next section, it has the general shape indicated in Figure 7–3(d). That panel shows a curve with elasticity equal to 1 throughout (a *unit-elastic* demand curve). A unit-elastic demand curve bends in the middle toward the origin of the graph—at either end, it moves closer and closer to the axes but never touches or crosses them.

As we have noted, a curve with an elasticity greater than 1 is called an *elastic demand curve* (one for which the percentage change in quantity demanded will be greater than the percentage change in price); a curve whose elasticity is less than 1 is known as an *inelastic* curve. When elasticity is exactly 1, economists say that the curve is *unit-elastic*.

Real-world price elasticities of demand seem to vary considerably from product to product. Moderate luxury goods, such as expensive vacations, are generally more price elastic than goods like milk and shirts, which are considered necessities. Products with close substitutes, like Coke and Pepsi, tend to have relatively high elasticities because if one soft drink gets expensive, consumers will switch to the other. Also, the elasticities of demand for goods that business firms buy, such as raw materials and machinery, tend to be higher on the whole than those for consumers' goods. This is because competition forces firms to buy their supplies wherever they can get them most cheaply. The exception occurs when a firm requires a particular input for which no reasonable substitutes exist or the available substitutes are substantially inferior. Table 7–1 gives actual statistical estimates of elasticities for some industries in the economy.

Estimates of Price Elasticities

TABLE 7-1

Product	Price Elasticity
Industrial chemicals	0.4%
Shoe repairs and cleaning	0.4
Food, tobacco, and beverages	0.5
Newspaper and magazines	0.5
Data processing, precision and optical instruments	0.7
Medical care and hospitalization insurance	0.8
Metal products	1.1
Purchased meals (excluding alcoholic beverages)	1.6
Electricity (household utility)	1.9
Boats, pleasure aircraft	2.4
Public transportation	3.5
China, tableware	8.8

SOURCES: H. S. Houthakker and Lester D. Taylor, *Consumer Demand in the United States*, 2d ed. (Cambridge, Mass.: Harvard University Press, 1970), pp. 153–158; and Joachim Möller, "Income and Price Elasticities in Different Sectors of the Economy—An Analysis of Structural Change for Germany, the U.K., and U.S." (University of Regensburg, December 1998). Thanks to Professor Möller for the early release of his estimates.

■ PRICE ELASTICITY OF DEMAND: ITS EFFECT ON TOTAL REVENUE AND TOTAL EXPENDITURE

Aside from its role as a measure of the responsiveness of demand to a change in price, elasticity serves a second very important purpose. As a real illustration at the end of this chapter will show, a firm often wants to know whether a rise in price will increase or decrease its total revenue—the money it obtains from sales to its customers. The price elasticity of demand provides a simple guide to the answer:

If demand for the seller's product is elastic, a price increase will decrease total revenue. If demand is exactly unit-elastic, a rise in price will leave total revenue unaffected. If demand is inelastic, a rise in price will raise total revenue. The opposite changes will occur when price falls.

A corresponding story must hold true about the expenditures made by the *buyers* of the product. After all, the expenditures of the buyers are exactly the same thing as the revenues of the seller.

These relationships between elasticity and total revenue hold because total revenue (or expenditure) equals price times quantity demanded, $P \times Q$, and a fall in price has two opposing effects on that arithmetic product. It decreases P, and, if the demand curve is negatively sloped, it increases Q. The first effect *decreases* revenues by cutting the amount of money that consumers spend on each unit of the good. But the second effect *increases* revenues by raising the number of units of the good that the firm sells.

The net effect on total revenue (or total expenditure) depends on the elasticity. If price goes down 10 percent and quantity demanded increases 10 percent (a case of *unit elasticity*), the two effects just cancel out: $P \times Q$ remains constant. On the other hand, if price goes down 10 percent and quantity demanded rises 15 percent (a case of *elastic* demand), $P \times Q$ increases. Finally, if a 10 percent price fall leads to only a 5 percent rise in quantity demanded (*inelastic* demand), $P \times Q$ falls.

We can easily see the relationship between elasticity and total revenue in a graph. First, note that:

The total revenue (or expenditure) represented by any point on a demand curve (any price-quantity combination), such as point S in Figure 7–4, equals the area of the rectangle under that point (the area of rectangle ORST in the figure). This is true because the area of a rectangle equals its height times width, OR times RS. That is, clearly, price times quantity, which is exactly total revenue.

FIGURE 7–4

An Elastic Demand Curve

To illustrate the connection between elasticity and consumer expenditure, Figure 7–4 shows an elastic portion of a demand curve, *DD*. In this figure, when price falls, quantity demanded rises by a greater percentage, increasing total expenditure. At a price of $6 per unit, the quantity sold is four units, so total expenditure is $4 \times \$6 = \$24$, represented by the vertical rectangle whose upper right-hand corner is point *S*. When price falls to $5 per unit, 12 units are sold. Consequently, the new expenditure ($\$60 = \$5 \times 12$), measured by the rectangle 0*UVW*, exceeds the old.

In contrast, Figure 7–3(d), the unit-elastic demand curve, shows constant expenditures even though price changes. Total spending is $140 whether the price is $20 and seven units are sold (point *S*), or the price is $10 and 14 units are sold (point *T*).

This discussion also indicates why a unit-elastic demand curve must have the shape depicted in Figure 7–3(d), hugging the axes closer and closer but never touching or crossing them. When demand is unit elastic, total expenditure must be the same at every point on the curve. It must equal $140 at point *S* and point *T* and point *U*. Suppose that at point *U* (or some other point on the curve), the demand curve were to touch the horizontal axis, meaning that the price would equal zero.

Then total expenditure would be zero, not $140. Therefore, if the demand curve remains unit elastic all along its length, it can never cross the horizontal axis (where $P = 0$). By the same reasoning, it cannot cross the vertical axis (where $Q = 0$). Because the slope of the demand curve is negative, the curve simply must get closer and closer to the axes as it moves away from its middle points, as illustrated in Figure 7–3(d).

All this indicates why demand elasticity is so important for business decisions. A firm should not jump to the conclusion that a price increase will automatically add to its profits, for it may find that consumers take their revenge by cutting back on their purchases. For example, when Heinz's Pet Products Co. raised the prices of its 9-Lives cat food a few years ago, its market share plummeted from 23 percent to 15 percent as customers flocked to other brands. In fact, if its demand curve is elastic, a firm that raises price will end up selling so many fewer units that its total revenue will actually fall, even though it makes more money than before on each unit it sells.

Price *cuts* can also be hazardous—if the elasticity of demand is low. For example, among adult smokers cigarettes have an estimated price elasticity of approximately 0.4, meaning that we can expect a 10 percent drop in price to induce only a 4 percent rise in demand. This may explain why, when Philip Morris cut the price of Marlboros by about 18 percent, the company's profits dropped by 25 percent within months. Thus, the strategic value to a business firm of a price rise or a price cut depends very much on the elasticity of demand for its product. But elasticity only tells us how a price change affects a firm's revenues; later, we'll consider the impact of costs on the firm's output decisions.

Issue Revisited: Will a Cigarette Tax Decrease Teenage Smoking Significantly?

We're back to the issue with which we began this chapter: Will a tax on cigarettes, which increases their price, effectively reduce teenage smoking? We can express the answer in terms of the price elasticity of demand for cigarettes by teenagers. If that demand elasticity is high, the tax will be effective, because a small increase in cigarette taxes will lead to a sharp cut in purchases by teenagers. The opposite will clearly be true if this demand elasticity number is small.

Young people *are* more sensitive to price increases than adult smokers. The estimates on teenagers' price elasticity of demand for cigarettes range from about 0.7 all the way up to 1.65.[3] This means that if, for example, a tax on cigarettes raised their price 10 percent, the number of teenage smokers would fall by somewhere between 7 and 16.5 percent. If these elasticity estimates are accurate, we can expect that a significant tax on cigarettes that results in a significant price increase would cause a higher percentage of teenagers than adults to stop smoking.

We said earlier in the chapter that if a cigarette tax program failed to curb teen smoking, it would benefit the government's tax collectors a great deal. On the other hand, if the program successfully curbed teenage smoking, then government finances would benefit only a little. The logic of this should now be clear. If teen cigarette demand were inelastic, the tax program would fail to make a dent in teen smoking. That would mean that many teenagers would continue to

[3] Sources: *Economic Report of the President 1997*, Washington, D.C.: U.S. Government Printing Office, February 1997; David R. Francis, "Demographic Groups Differ in Response to Substance Abuse Policies," *The NBER Digest*, National Bureau of Economic Research, September 1998, www.nber.org, who cites Frank Chaloupka and Rosalie Liccardo Pacula, "An Examination of Gender and Race Differences in Youth Smoking Responsiveness to Price and Tobacco Control Policies," NBER Working Paper No. 6541; Barry Meier, "Proposed Cigarette Deal Doesn't Force Rise in Price," *New York Times*, October 9, 1998, p. A14; Daniel Seligman, "Keeping Up: A Case for the Three-Day Week, How to Really Stop Smoking, the Mob Cuts Prices, and Other Matters," *Fortune*, July 30, 1990, who cites Michael Grossman, City University of New York.

buy cigarettes and government tax revenue would grow as a result of the rise in tax rate. But when elasticity is high, a price rise *decreases* total revenue (in this case, the amount of tax revenues collected) because quantity demanded falls by a greater percentage than the price rises. That is, with an elastic demand, relatively few teen smokers will remain after the tax increase, so there will be few of them to pay the new taxes. The government will "lose out." Of course, in this case the tax seeks to change behavior, so the government would no doubt rejoice at its small revenues!

WHAT DETERMINES DEMAND ELASTICITY?

What kinds of goods have elastic demand curves, meaning that quantity demanded responds strongly to price? What kinds of goods have inelastic demand curves? Several factors influence consumers' sensitivity to price changes.

NATURE OF THE GOOD *Necessities*, such as basic foodstuffs, normally have relatively inelastic demand curves, meaning that the quantities consumers demand of these products respond very little to price changes. For example, people buy roughly the same quantity of potatoes even when the price of potatoes rises. One study estimated that the price elasticity of demand for potatoes is just 0.3, meaning that when their price rises 10 percent, the quantity of potatoes purchased falls only 3 percent. In contrast, many *luxury goods*, such as restaurant meals, have rather elastic demand curves. One estimate found that the price elasticity of demand for restaurant meals is 1.6, so that we can expect a 10 percent price rise to cut purchases by 16 percent.

AVAILABILITY OF CLOSE SUBSTITUTES If consumers can easily obtain a good substitute for a product whose price increases, they will switch readily. Thus, when the market offers close substitutes for a given product, its demand will be more elastic. Substitutability is often a critical determinant of elasticity. The demand for gasoline is inelastic because we cannot easily run a car without it, but the demand for *any particular brand* of gasoline is extremely elastic, because other brands will work just as well. This example suggests a general principle: the demand for narrowly

"Why does it have to be us who prove that price elasticity really works?"

defined commodities (such as romaine lettuce) is more elastic than the demand for more broadly defined commodities (such as vegetables).

FRACTION OF INCOME ABSORBED   The fraction of income absorbed by the purchase of a particular item also affects its elasticity. Very inexpensive items tend to have inelastic demand curves. Who will buy fewer rubberbands if their price rises ten percent? But some families will be forced to postpone buying new cars, or will buy used cars instead, if auto prices go up by ten percent.

PASSAGE OF TIME   The time period is relevant because the demand for many products is more elastic in the long run than in the short run. For example, when the price of home heating oil rose in the 1970s, some homeowners switched from oil heat to gas heat. Very few of them switched immediately, however, because they needed to retrofit their furnaces to accommodate the other fuel. So the short-term demand for oil was quite inelastic. As time passed and more homeowners had the opportunity to purchase and install new furnaces, the demand curve gradually became more elastic.

■ ELASTICITY AS A GENERAL CONCEPT

So far we have looked only at how quantity demanded responds to price changes—that is, the *price* elasticity of demand. But elasticity has a more general use in measuring how any one economic variable responds to changes in another. From our earlier discussion we know that a firm will be keenly interested in the price elasticity of its demand curve, but its interest in demand does not end there. As we have noted, quantity demanded depends on other things besides price. Business firms will be interested in consumer responsiveness to changes in these variables as well.

INCOME ELASTICITY

For example, quantity demanded depends on consumer incomes. A business firm's managers will, therefore, want to know how much a change in consumer income will affect the quantity of its product demanded. Fortunately, an elasticity measure can be helpful here too. An increase in consumer incomes clearly raises the amounts of most goods that consumers will demand. To measure the response, economists use the **income elasticity of demand,** which is the ratio of the percentage change in quantity demanded to the percentage change in income. For example, foreign travel is quite income elastic, with middle and higher income people traveling abroad much more extensively than poor people do. In contrast, blue jeans, worn by rich and poor alike, show little demand increase as income increases.

> **Income elasticity of demand** is the ratio of the percentage change in quantity demanded to the percentage change in income.

PRICE ELASTICITY OF SUPPLY

Economists also use elasticity to measure other responses. For example, to measure the response of quantity *supplied* to a change in price, we use the *price elasticity of supply*—defined as the ratio of the percentage change in quantity supplied to the percentage change in price. The logic and analysis of all such elasticity concepts are, of course, perfectly analogous to those for price elasticity of demand.

CROSS ELASTICITY OF DEMAND

Consumers' demands for many products are substantially affected by the quantities and prices of *other* available products. Some goods make other products more desirable; some products decrease consumer demand for other goods.

Some products just naturally go together. For example, cream and sugar increase the desirability of coffee, and vice versa. The same is true of mustard or ketchup and hamburgers. In some extreme cases, neither product ordinarily has any use without the other—automobiles and tires, shoes and shoelaces, and so on. Such goods, each of which makes the other more valuable, are called **complements.**

> Two goods are called **complements** if an increase in the quantity consumed of one increases the quantity demanded of the other, all other things remaining constant.

The demand curves of complements are interrelated; specifically, a rise in the price of coffee is likely to reduce the quantity of sugar demanded. Why? When coffee prices rise, people drink less coffee and therefore demand less sugar to sweeten it. The opposite will be true of a fall in coffee prices. A similar relationship holds for other complementary goods.

At the other extreme, some goods make one another *less* valuable. These are called **substitutes.** Ownership of a motorcycle, for example, may decrease one's desire for a bicycle. If your pantry is stocked with cans of tuna fish, you are less likely to rush out and buy cans of salmon. As you may expect, demand curves for substitutes are also related, but in the opposite direction. When the price of motorcycles falls, people may demand fewer bicycles, so the quantity demanded falls. When the price of salmon goes up, people may eat more tuna.

Economists use another elasticity measure to determine whether two products are substitutes or complements: their **cross elasticity of demand.** This measure is defined much like the ordinary price elasticity of demand, only instead of measuring the responsiveness of the quantity demanded of, say, coffee, to a change in its own price, cross elasticity of demand measures how quantity demanded of one good (coffee) responds to a change in the price of another, say, sugar. For example, if a 20 percent rise in the price of sugar reduces the quantity of coffee demanded by 5 percent (a change of *minus* 5 percent in quantity demanded), then the cross elasticity of demand will be:

$$\frac{\text{Percentage change in quantity of coffee demanded}}{\text{Percentage change in sugar price}} = \frac{-5\%}{20\%} = -0.25$$

Obviously, cross elasticity is important for business firms, especially where rival firms' prices are concerned. Northwest Airlines, for example, knows all too well that it will lose customers if it does not match price cuts by Continental or United. Coke and Pepsi provide another clear case in which cross elasticity of demand is crucial. But firms other than direct competitors may well take a substantial interest in cross elasticity. For example, the prices of VCRs and video rentals may profoundly affect the quantity of theater tickets that consumers demand.

The cross elasticity of demand measure underlies the following rule about complements and substitutes:

> If two goods are substitutes, a rise in the price of one of them tends to raise the quantity demanded of the other; so their cross elasticities of demand will normally be positive. If two goods are complements, a rise in the price of one of them tends to decrease the quantity demanded of the other item, so their cross elasticities will normally be negative. Notice that, because cross elasticities can be positive or negative, we do *not* customarily drop minus signs as we do in a calculation of the ordinary price elasticity of demand.

This result is really a matter of common sense. If the price of a good rises and buyers can find a substitute, they will tend to switch to the substitute. If the price of Japanese cameras goes up and the price of American cameras does not, at least some people will switch to the American product. Thus, a *rise* in the price of Japanese cameras causes a *rise* in the quantity of American cameras demanded. Both percentage changes are positive numbers and so their ratio, the cross elasticity of demand, is also positive.

On the other hand, if two goods are complements, a rise in the price of one will discourage both its own use and use of the complementary good. Automobiles and car radios are obviously complements. A large increase in automobile prices will depress car sales, and this in turn will reduce sales of car radios. Thus, a positive percentage change in the price of cars leads to a negative percentage change in the quantity of car radios demanded. The ratio of these numbers, the cross elasticity of demand for cars and radios, is therefore negative.

In practice, courts of law often evaluate cross elasticity of demand to measure whether particular firms face strong competition that can prevent them from overcharging consumers—hence, the quote from the U.S. Supreme Court at the

---

Two goods are called **substitutes** if an increase in the quantity consumed of one cuts the quantity demanded of the other, all other things remaining constant.

The **cross elasticity of demand** for Product X to a change in the price of another product, Y, is the ratio of the percentage change in quantity demanded of X to the percentage change in the price of Y that brings about the change in quantity demanded.

opening of this chapter. The quotation is one of the earliest examples of the courts using the concept of cross elasticities. It tells us that if two rival products exhibit a high cross elasticity of demand, for example, between McDonald's and Burger King, then neither firm can raise its price much without losing customers to the other. If this is so, no one can legitimately claim that either firm has a monopoly. If a rise in Firm X's price causes its consumers to switch in droves to a competitor's product, Y, then the cross elasticity of demand for Product Y with respect to the price of X will be high. That, in turn, means that competition is really powerful enough to prevent Firm X from raising its price arbitrarily. This is why cross elasticity is used so often in litigation before courts or government regulatory agencies when the degree of competition is an important issue. The cross elasticity issue keeps coming up whenever firms are accused of acting like monopolists. For example, in 1997 a dispute arose between Litton and Honeywell, the two main manufacturers of the mechanisms that guide the flight of aircraft. In 1998 the issue reappeared in a lawsuit in which Rolite, an ash recycling firm, sued Waste Management, a waste removal company, charging monopolistic behavior by the latter.

■ CHANGES IN DEMAND: MOVEMENTS ALONG THE DEMAND CURVE VERSUS SHIFTS IN THE DEMAND CURVE

Demand is obviously a complex phenomenon. We have studied in detail the dependence of quantity demanded on price, and we have noted that quantity demanded depends also on *other* variables such as consumers' incomes and the prices of complementary and substitute products. Because of changes in these *other* variables (which we formerly held constant while we were studying only the effect of changes in price), demand curves often do not keep the same shape and position as time passes. Instead, they shift about. Chapter 5 showed that shifts in demand curves affect both quantity and price predictably.

Public policy and business discussions often make vague references to "changes in demand." By itself, this expression does not mean anything. Remember from our discussion in Chapter 5 that we must distinguish between a response to a price change— *which shows up as a movement along the demand curve*—and a change in the relationship between price and quantity demanded—*which produces a shift in the demand curve* (in effect, it moves the curve itself).

When price falls, quantity demanded generally rises. This is a movement *along* the demand curve. On the other hand, an effective advertising campaign may result in people buying more goods at *any given price.* This would cause a rightward *shift* of the demand curve. Such a shift can be caused by a change in the value of any of the variables other than price that affect quantity demanded. Although the distinction between a shift in a demand curve and a movement along it may at first seem trivial, the difference is very significant in practice. Let us pause for a moment to consider how changes in some of these other variables shift the demand curve.

DEMAND SHIFTERS

As an example, consider the effect of a change in consumer income on the demand curve for sweaters. In Figure 7–5(a) (next page), the black curve D_0D_0 is the original demand curve for sweaters. Now suppose that parents start sending more money to their needy sons and daughters in college. If the price of sweaters remained the same, those students are likely to use some of their increased income to buy more sweaters. For example, if the price were to remain at $35, quantity demanded might rise from 40,000 sweaters (point R) to 60,000 (point S). Similarly, if price had been $28, and remained at that level, the rise in income might produce a corresponding change from T to U. In other words, we would expect the rise in income to *shift* the entire demand curve to the right from D_0D_0 to D_1D_1. In exactly the same way, a fall in consumer income can be expected to lead to a leftward shift in the demand curve for sweaters, as shown in Figure 7–5(b).

● HOW LARGE IS A FIRM'S MARKET SHARE? CROSS ELASTICITY AS A TEST

A firm's "market share" is often a crucial element in antitrust lawsuits (see Chapter 20) for a simple reason. If the firm supplies no more than, say, 20 percent of the industry's output, courts and regulators presume that the firm is not a monopoly, as its competitors account for most of the industry's sales. On the other hand, if the defendant firm in the lawsuit accounts for 90 percent of the industry's output, courts may have good reason to worry about monopoly power (which we cover in Chapter 12).

Thus court cases often provide lively debates in which the defendant firms try to prove that they have very small market shares, while the plaintiffs seek to establish the opposite. Each side knows how much the defendant firm actually produces and sells, so what do they find to argue about? The dispute is about *the size of the total relevant market,* which clearly affects the magnitude of the firm's market *share.* Ambiguity arises here because different firms do not produce identical products. For instance, are Rice Krispies in the same market as Cheerios? And how about Quaker Oatmeal, which users eat hot? What about frozen waffles? Are all of these products part of the same market? If they are, then the overall market is big, and each seller therefore has a smaller share. But if these products are in different markets, the opposite will be true.

Many observers argue, as the Supreme Court did in the famous DuPont cellophane case (and, more recently, as was argued when Rolite sued Waste Management in 1998), that one of the proper criteria for

determining the borders of the relevant market is *cross elasticity of demand.* If two products have a high and positive cross elasticity, they must be close enough substitutes to compete closely; that is, they must be in the same market. But how large must the cross elasticity be before the court decides that two products are in the same market? Although the law has established no clear elasticity benchmark to determine whether a particular firm is in a relevant market, several courts have determined that a very high cross elasticity number clearly indicates effective competition between them, meaning that the two items must be in the same market.

| FIGURE 7-5 | **Shifts in a Demand Curve** |

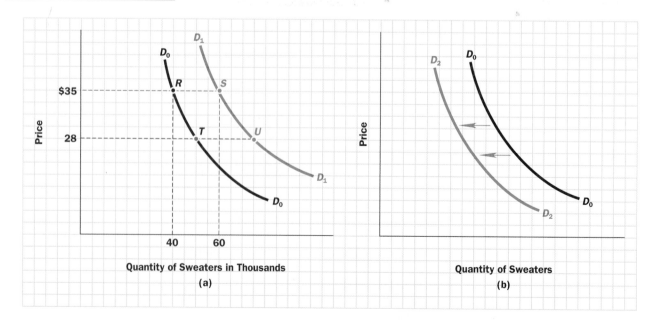

We can analyze other variables that affect quantity demanded in the same way. For example, increased television advertising for sweaters may lead to a rightward (outward) shift in the demand curve for sweaters, as in Figure 7–5(a). The same thing might occur if the price of a substitute product, such as jackets, were to increase, because that would put sweaters at a competitive advantage. If two goods are substitutes, a rise in the price of one of them will tend to shift the demand curve for the other one outward (to the right). Similarly, if a complementary product (perhaps matching pants to go with the sweaters) becomes more expensive, we expect the demand curve for sweaters to shift to the left, as in Figure 7–5(b). In summary:

> We expect a demand curve to shift to the right (outward) if consumer incomes rise, if tastes change in favor of the product, if substitute goods become more expensive, or if complementary goods become cheaper. We expect a demand curve to shift to the left (inward) if any of these factors goes in the opposite direction.

THE TIME PERIOD OF THE DEMAND CURVE AND ECONOMIC DECISION MAKING

One more important feature of a demand curve does not show up on a graph. A demand curve indicates, at each possible price, the quantity of the good that is demanded *during a particular time period*. That is, all of the alternative prices considered in a demand curve must refer to the *same* time period. Economists do not compare a price for a particular item of $10 in January with a price of $8 in September.

This feature imparts a peculiar character to the demand curve and complicates statistical calculations. Actual observed historical data show different prices and quantities only for different dates. Why, then, do economists adopt this apparently peculiar approach? The answer is that the demand curve's time dimension arises inescapably from the logic of decision making.

When a business seeks to price one of its products for, say, the following six months, it must consider the range of alternative prices available for that six-month period and the consequences of each of these possible prices. For example, if management is reasonably certain that the best price for the six-month period lies somewhere between $3.50 and $5.00, it should perhaps consider each of four possibilities, $3.50, $4.00, $4.50, and $5.00, and estimate how much it can expect to sell at each of these potential prices during the six-month period. The result of these estimates may appear in a format similar to that of the following table:

Potential Six-Month Price	Expected Quantity Demanded
$3.50	75,000
4.00	73,000
4.50	70,000
5.00	60,000

This table supplies managers with information that they need to make optimal pricing decisions. It also contains precisely the information an economist uses to draw a demand curve.

> The demand curve describes a set of hypothetical quantity responses to a set of potential prices, but the firm can only actually charge one price. All of the points on the demand curve refer to alternative possibilities for the *same time* period—the period for which the decision is to be made.

Thus, a demand curve of the sort just described is not just an abstract notion that is useful primarily in academic discussions. Rather, it offers precisely the information that businesses need to make rational decisions. However, as already noted, the fact that all points on the demand curve are hypothetical possibilities for the same period of time causes problems for statistical estimation of demand curves. These problems are discussed in the appendix to this chapter.

◼ REAL-WORLD APPLICATION: POLAROID VERSUS KODAK

Let's look at an example from the real world to show how the elasticity concept helps to resolve a concrete problem rather different from those we have been discussing.

In 1989, a lengthy trial resulted in a judgment against the photographic products manufacturing company Eastman-Kodak for patent infringement of technology that rival firm Polaroid had designed. The court then set out to determine the amount of money Kodak owed Polaroid for its patent infringement during the ten-year period (1976 to 1986) when Kodak had sold very similar instant cameras and film. The key issue was how much profit Polaroid had lost as a result of Kodak's entry into the field of instant photography. Both price elasticity of demand and cross elasticity of demand played crucial roles.

The courts needed accurate estimates of the price elasticity of demand to determine whether the explosive growth in instant camera sales from 1976 to 1979 was mainly attributable to the fall in price that resulted from Kodak's competition or was, rather, attributable to Kodak's reputation and its access to additional retail outlets. If the latter were true, then Polaroid might actually have *benefited* from Kodak's entry rather than *losing* profits, because Kodak's presence in the market would have increased the total number of potential customers aware of and eager to try instant cameras.

After 1980, instant camera and film sales began to drop sharply. On this issue, the *cross elasticity of demand* between instant and conventional (35-millimeter) cameras and film was crucial to the explanation. Why? Because the decline in the instant camera market occurred just as the prices of 35-millimeter cameras, film, developing, and printing all began to fall significantly. If the decline in Polaroid's overall sales was attributable to the decreasing cost of 35-millimeter photography, then Kodak's instant photography activity was *not* to blame. Consequently, the amount that Kodak would be required to pay to Polaroid would decrease significantly. On the other hand, if the cross elasticity of demand between conventional photography prices and the demand for instant cameras and film was low, then the cause of the decline in Polaroid's sales might well have been Kodak's patent-infringing activity— *adding* to the damage compensation payments to which Polaroid was entitled.

Yet a third elasticity issue was central to the trial. How much would Polaroid's total revenue have increased as a result of the film-price increase it claimed it *would* have adopted in the absence of illegal competition from Kodak? The crux of the matter was the price elasticity of demand for instant camera film. Polaroid tried to show that this elasticity figure was low, to support its contention that the rise in price would have raised its revenues a great deal—meaning that Kodak had damaged it quite severely. Kodak, on the other hand, offered statistical evidence suggesting that demand for instant film—then a novelty and something of a luxury good—was highly elastic, to support its own claim that a higher price would have brought in little, if any, additional revenue.

On the basis of its relevant elasticity calculations, Polaroid at one point claimed that Kodak was obligated to pay it $9 *billion* or more. Kodak claimed that it owed Polaroid only (!) something in the neighborhood of $450 million. A lot of money was at stake! The judge's verdict came out with a number very close to Kodak's figure.[4]

IN CONCLUSION

In this chapter we have continued our study of the demand side of the market. Rather than focusing on what underlies demand formation, as we did in the chap-

---

[4] William Baumol was a witness in the case, testifying on behalf of Kodak.

ter before this, we sought to apply demand analysis to business decisions. Most notably, we described and analyzed the economist's measure of the responsiveness of consumer demand to changes in price, and we showed how this determines the effect of a firm's price change on the revenues of that enterprise. We illustrated how these concepts throw light not only on business sales and revenues, but also on a number of rather different issues, such as smoking and health, the effectiveness of competition among business firms as studied by law courts, and the determination of penalties for patent infringement. In the next chapter we turn to the supply side of the market and move a step closer to completing the framework we need in order to understand how markets work.

S U M M A R Y

1. To measure the responsiveness of the quantity demanded to price, economists calculate the *elasticity of demand*, which is defined as the percentage change in quantity demanded divided by the percentage change in price.

2. If demand is *elastic* (elasticity is greater than 1), then a rise in price will reduce total expenditures. If demand is *unit elastic* (elasticity is equal to 1), then a rise in price will not change total expenditures. If demand is *inelastic* (elasticity is less than 1), then a rise in price will increase total expenditure.

3. Demand is not a fixed number. Rather, it is a relationship showing how quantity demanded is affected by price and other pertinent influences. If one or more of these other variables change, the demand curve will shift.

4. Goods that make each other more desirable (hot dogs and mustard, wristwatches and watch straps) are called *comple-*

ments. When consumers want less of one good as they get more of another (steaks and hamburgers, Coke and Pepsi), economists call those goods *substitutes*.

5. *Cross elasticity of demand* is defined as the percentage change in the quantity demanded of one good divided by the percentage change in the price of another good. Two substitute products normally have a positive cross elasticity of demand. Two complementary products normally have a negative cross elasticity of demand.

6. A rise in the price of one of two substitute products can be expected to *shift the demand curve* of the other product to the right. A rise in the price of one of two complementary goods is apt to shift the other's demand curve to the left.

7. All points on a demand curve refer to the *same* time period—the time during which the price will be in effect.

K E Y   T E R M S

(Price) elasticity of demand   119

Elastic, inelastic, and unit-elastic demand curves   123

Income elasticity of demand   127

Complements   127

Substitutes   128

Cross elasticity of demand   128

Shift in a demand curve   129

Q U E S T I O N S   F O R   R E V I E W

1. What variables besides price and advertising are likely to affect the quantity demanded of a product?

2. Describe the probable shifts in the demand curves for:

   a. Airplane trips when airlines' on-time performance improves

   b. Automobiles when airplane fares rise

   c. Automobiles when gasoline prices rise

   d. Electricity when the average temperature in the United States falls during a particular year

      (*Note:* The demand curve for electricity in Maine and the demand curve for electricity in Florida should respond in different ways. Why?)

3. Taxes on particular goods discourage their consumption. Economists therefore say that such taxes "distort consumer demands." In terms of the elasticity of demand for the commodities in question, what sort of goods would you choose to tax to achieve the following objectives?

   a. Collect a large amount of tax revenue

   b. Distort demand as little as possible

   c. Discourage consumption of harmful commodities

   d. Discourage production of polluting commodities

4. Explain why elasticity of demand is measured in *percentages*.

5. Explain why the elasticity of demand formula normally eliminates minus signs.

6. Give examples of commodities whose demand you expect to be elastic and some whose demand you expect to be inelastic.

7. Explain why the elasticity of a straight-line demand curve varies from one part of the curve to another.

8. A rise in the price of a certain commodity from $15 to $20 reduces quantity demanded from 20,000 to 5,000 units. Calculate the price elasticity of demand.

9. If the price elasticity of demand for gasoline is 0.3, and the current price is $1.20 a gallon, what rise in the price of gasoline will reduce its consumption by 10 percent?

10. A rise in the price of a product whose demand is elastic will reduce the total revenue of the firm. Explain.

11. Name some events that will cause a demand curve to shift.

12. Which of the following product pairs would you expect to be substitutes, and which would you expect to be complements?

 a. Shoes and sneakers

 b. Gasoline and sport utility vehicles

 c. Bread and butter

 d. Instant camera film and regular camera film

13. For each of the previous product pairs, what would you guess about the products' cross elasticity of demand?

 a. Do you expect it to be positive or negative?

 b. Do you expect it to be a large or small number? Why?

14. Explain why the following statement is true: "A firm with a demand curve that is inelastic at its current output level can always increase its profits by raising its price and selling less." (*Hint:* Refer back to the discussion of elasticity and total expenditure/total revenue on pages 124–125.)

● **APPENDIX** ▌ **STATISTICAL ANALYSIS OF DEMAND RELATIONSHIPS**

The peculiar time dimension of the demand curve, in conjunction with the fact that many variables other than price influence quantity demanded, makes it surprisingly hard to derive a product's demand curve from statistical data. Specialists can and often do derive such estimates, but the task is full of booby traps and usually requires quite advanced statistical methods and interpretation. This appendix seeks to warn you about the booby traps. It implies, for example, that if you become the marketing manager of a business firm after you graduate from college, and you need demand analysis, you will need experts to do the job. The appendix will also show you some mistakes to look for as you interpret the results, if you have reason to doubt the qualifications of the statisticians you hire to calculate or forecast your demand curve.

The most obvious way to go about estimating a demand curve statistically is to collect a set of figures on prices and quantities sold in different periods, like those given in Table 7–2. These points can then be plotted on a diagram with price and quantity on the axes, as shown in Figure 7–6. We can then draw in a line (the dotted line *TT*) that connects these points (labeled Jan., Feb., and so on) reasonably well to represent the prices and quantities sold in the months indicated. This line may appear to approximate the demand curve, but unfortunately, line *TT*, which summarizes the historical data, may bear no relationship to the true demand curve.

You may notice at once that the prices and quantities represented by the historical points in Figure 7–6 refer to different periods of time, and that each point on the graph represents an *actual* (not hypothetical) price and quantity sold at a particular period of time (for example,

January). The distinction is significant. Over the entire period covered by the historical data (January through May), the true demand curve, which is what an economist really wants, may well have shifted because of changes in some of the other variables affecting quantity demanded.

The actual events may appear as shown in Figure 7–7. In January, the demand curve was given by *JJ*, but

---

FIGURE 7-6

Plot of Historical Data on Price and Quantity

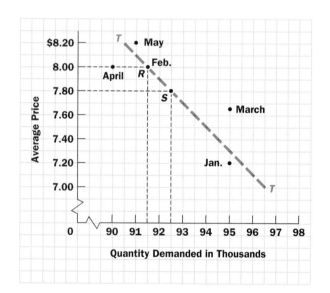

TABLE 7-2 **Historical Data on Price and Quantity**

	January	February	March	April	May
Quantity Sold	95,000	91,500	95,000	90,000	91,000
Price	$7.20	$8.00	$7.70	$8.00	$8.20

FIGURE 7-7

**Plot of Historical Data and
True Demand Curves for
January, February, and March**

by February the curve had shifted to *FF*, by March to *MM*, and so on. This figure shows a separate and distinct demand curve for each of the relevant months, and none of them need have any resemblance to the plot of historical data, *TT*.

In fact, the slope of the historical plot curve, *TT*, can be very different from the slopes of the true underlying demand curves, as is the case in Figure 7–7. This means that the decision maker can be seriously misled if she selects her price on the basis of the historical data. She may, for example, think that demand is quite insensitive to changes in price (as line *TT* seems to indicate), so she may reject the possibility of a price reduction. In fact, the true demand curves show that a price reduction would increase quantity demanded substantially, because they are much more elastic than the shape of the estimated curve in Figure 7–6 would suggest.

For example, if she were to charge a price of $7.80 rather than $8.00 in February, the historical plot would lead her to expect a rise in quantity demanded of only 1,000 units. (Compare point *R*, with sales of 91,500 units, and point *S*, with sales of 92,500 units, in Figure 7–6.) However, the true demand curve for February

(line *FF* in Figure 7–7) indicates an increase in sales of 2,500 units (from point *R*, with sales of 91,500 units, to point *W*, with sales of 94,000 units). A manager who based her decision on the historical plot, rather than on the true demand curve, might be led into serious error. Nevertheless, it is astonishing how often people make this mistake in practice, even when using apparently sophisticated techniques.

AN ILLUSTRATION: DID THE ADVERTISING PROGRAM WORK?

Some years ago one of the nation's largest producers of packaged foods conducted a statistical study to judge the effectiveness of its advertising expenditures, which amounted to nearly $100 million a year. A company statistician collected year-by-year figures on company sales and advertising outlays and discovered, to his delight, that they showed a remarkably close relationship to one another: quantity demanded rose as advertising rose. The trouble was that the relationship seemed just too perfect. In economics, data about demand and any one of the elements that influence it almost never show such a neat pattern. Human tastes and other pertinent influences are just too variable to permit such regularity.

Suspicious company executives asked one of the authors of this book to examine the analysis. A little thought showed that the suspiciously close statistical relationship between sales and advertising expenditures resulted from a disregard for the principles just presented. The investigator had in fact constructed a graph of *historical* data on sales and advertising expenditure, analogous to *TT* in Figures 7–6 and 7–7 and therefore not necessarily similar to the truly relevant relationship.

The stability of the relationship actually arose from the fact that, in the past, the company had based its advertising outlays on its sales, automatically allocating a fixed percentage of its sales revenues to advertising. The *historical* relationship between advertising and demand therefore described only the company's budgeting practices, not the effectiveness of its advertising program. If the firm's management had used this curve in planning future advertising campaigns, it might have made some regrettable decisions. *The moral of the story:* Avoid the use of purely historical curves like *TT* in making economic decisions.

CHAPTER

8

Of course that's only an estimate. The actual cost
will be somewhat more.

Auto mechanic to customer

PRODUCTION, INPUTS, AND COST: BUILDING BLOCKS FOR SUPPLY ANALYSIS

Suppose you take a summer job working on Naomi's

Natural Farm, where, among other things, she raises a

small herd of hogs.[1] When you get there, you find that

Naomi has bought land and built her barns, and pur-

chased two-years' worth of all the ingredients, except corn,

in the organic feed she gives the pigs. She has also pur-

chased all the other farm supplies she needs, so she is

left with only one decision about her farm input purchases:

How much corn should she buy? In this chapter, we

explore this kind of decision and answer the question,

what input choice constitutes the most profitable way for

a business firm to produce its output?

[1] In 1992, women operated 145,000 farms in the United States, and 50,000 of them had sales of $10,000 or more (U.S. Census Bureau, *Statistical Abstract of the United States: 1998*, 118th ed., Washington, D.C., 1998).

When firms make their supply (output) decisions, they weigh the costs of supplying their products against the expected revenue they can earn from selling the products in the marketplace. Thus, they examine the likely demand for the products they create. We have already studied demand in the last two chapters. But to understand the firm's decisions about the supply side of markets, we must also study the firm's production costs. A firm's costs depend on the quantities of labor, raw materials, machinery, and other inputs that it buys, and on the prices it pays for each input. Just how does the firm decide how much of each input to buy? This chapter examines how businesses can select optimal input combinations, that is, the combinations that enable firms to produce whatever output they decide upon at minimum cost as they seek to maximize profitability. We will discuss the firm's decisions about output and price in the next chapter.

To make the analysis of optimal input quantities easier to follow, we approach this task in two stages, based on a very important economic distinction: the short run and the long run. The first part of the chapter deals with a simpler, short-run case in which the firm can vary the quantity of only one input, while all other input quantities are already determined. This assumption vastly simplifies the analysis and enables us to answer three key questions:

- How does the quantity of input affect the quantity of output?
- How can the firm select the optimal quantity of an input?
- How do these input decisions give the firm the cost information it needs?

In the second part of the chapter, we go over the same territory for the case in which the firm can vary the quantities of several inputs at once. Many new insights emerge from this multi-input analysis, but they will be easier to absorb after you have mastered the single-input analysis.[2]

Issue: Are Larger Firms More Efficient?

Modern industrial societies enjoy cost advantages as a result of automation, assembly lines, and sophisticated machinery, all of which often reduce production costs dramatically. But if equipment with such enormous capacity requires a very large investment, small companies will be unable to reap many of these benefits of modern technology. Only large firms will be able to take advantage of the associated cost savings. Where firms can take advantage of such *economies of scale*, as economists call them, production costs per unit will decline as output expands.

But this relationship between large size and low costs does not fit every industry. Sometimes the courts must decide whether a giant firm should be broken up into smaller units. The most celebrated case of this kind involved American Telephone and Telegraph Company, which had a monopoly of the nation's phone service for nearly 50 years. In 1982, AT&T settled a government antitrust suit by agreeing to divest 22 operating units, informally known today as

---

[2] Some instructors may prefer to postpone this part until later in the course.

the "Baby Bells."[3] Government agencies and analysts who urged a breakup of AT&T argued that such a giant firm has great economic power and deprives consumers of the benefits of competition. But those who opposed the breakup, including AT&T itself, pointed out that if AT&T's large size brought significant economies of scale, then smaller firms would be much less efficient producers than the larger one, so that if AT&T were replaced by several smaller companies, costs to consumers would have to be correspondingly higher. Who was right? To settle the issue, the courts needed to know whether significant economies of scale affected AT&T's business before the divestiture.

Sometimes data like those shown in Figure 8–1 are offered to the courts when they consider such cases. These data, provided by AT&T, indicate that as the volume of telephone messages rose after 1942, the capital cost of long-distance communication by telephone dropped enormously and continued to drop consistently for more than 40 years, even as demand for long-distance services increased dramatically. In fact, the dollar cost per circuit mile of long-distance calls had fallen below 8 percent of its 1942 level. Economists maintain that, while this graph may be valid evidence of efficiency and innovation in the telecommunications industry, it does *not* constitute legitimate evidence, one way or another, about the presence of economies of scale. At the end of this chapter, we will study precisely what is wrong with the evidence presented in Figure 8–1 and what sort of evidence really would prove whether a very large firm can indeed produce more efficiently as a result of economies of scale.

| FIGURE 8-1 |

Historical Costs for Long-Distance Telephone Transmissions

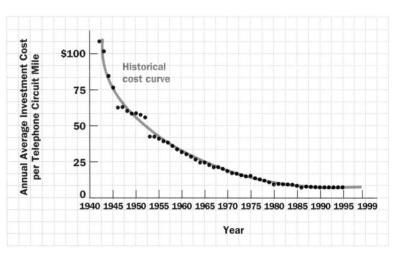

NOTE: Figures are in dollars per year.
SOURCE: AT&T. Recent figures are estimates.

■ SHORT-RUN VERSUS LONG-RUN COSTS: WHAT MAKES AN INPUT VARIABLE?

As firms make input and output decisions, their actions are limited by previous commitments to equipment, plant, and other production matters. At any point in time, many input choices are *precommitted* by past decisions. If, for example, a firm

---

[3] AT&T is a descendant of the original Bell Telephone Company, affectionately known as "Ma Bell." The company relinquished the use of the name Bell when it divested itself of 22 regional companies in 1982. These companies were reorganized into the "Baby Bells"—seven regional phone companies called NYNEX, Bell Atlantic, Ameritech, BellSouth, Southwestern Bell Corporation, USWest, and Pacific Telesis Group. Ironically, in the 1990s several of these "Baby Bells"—for example, Bell Atlantic and NYNEX—merged once again.

purchased machinery a year ago, it has committed itself to that production decision for the remainder of the machine's economic life, unless the company is willing to take the loss involved in replacing that equipment sooner. An economist would say that these temporarily unalterable capital commitments are not variable for the time period in question. Firms that employ unionized labor forces may also incur costs that are temporarily not variable if labor contracts commit the firms to employing a certain number of employees, or to use employees for a required number of weeks per year. Costs are not variable for some period if they are caused by a longer-term financial commitment, such as a contract to buy a raw material, lease a warehouse, or invest in equipment that cannot be resold or transferred without substantial loss of the investment. Even if the firm has not paid for these commitments ahead of time, legally it must still pay for the contracted goods or services.

THE ECONOMIC SHORT RUN VERSUS THE ECONOMIC LONG RUN

A two-year-old machine with a nine-year economic life is an inescapable commitment and therefore represents a cost that is not variable for the next seven years. But that investment is not an unchangeable commitment in plans that extend *beyond* those seven years, because by then it may benefit the firm to replace the machine in any case. Economists summarize this notion by speaking of two different "runs" (or periods of time) for decision making: the **short run** and the **long run.**

The **short run** is a period of time during which some of the firm's cost commitments will *not* have ended.

The **long run** is a period of time long enough for all of the firm's commitments to come to an end.

These terms recur time and again throughout this book. In the short run, firms have relatively little opportunity to change production processes in order to adopt the most efficient way of producing their current outputs, because plant sizes have largely been predetermined by past decisions. Though managers may be able to hire more workers to work overtime and may be able to buy more supplies, they can't easily increase factory size, even if sales turn out to be much greater than expected. Over the long run, however, all such inputs, including plant size, become adjustable.

Consider, as an example, the case of Naomi's Natural Farm and the amount of organic corn that she feeds her hogs. Ultimately—that is, in the long run—Naomi can buy more piglets, feed them different grains, buy more land and buildings, and so on. But suppose for the moment that Naomi's only *current* choice is how much corn to feed the pigs. Once she has constructed the barn in which the animals are sheltered, she has relatively little discretion over its capacity. She can build an addition, but that project may be considerably more expensive than building a bigger barn to begin with. Cutting the size of the barn to save heating bills is even more costly. Over a somewhat longer planning horizon, however, Naomi will need to replace the original building, and she will be free to decide all over again how large a barn to construct.

Much the same is true of big industrial firms. Companies have little control over their plant and equipment capacities in the short run. But with some advance planning, they can acquire different types of machines, redesign factories, and make other choices. For instance, General Motors continued producing the Chevrolet Caprice and other big, rear-wheel drive cars at its plant in Arlington, Texas, for the 1995 and 1996 model years even though the vehicles were not selling well. That was partly because the company knew it would need time to convert the plant to manufacture its popular full-size pickup trucks, which were in short supply. By the 1997 model year, however, GM engineers were able to convert the plant to truck production.

Note that the short run and long run do not refer to the same time periods for all firms; rather, those periods vary in length, depending on the nature of the firm's commitments. If, for example, the firm can change its workforce every week, its machines every two years, and its factory every 20 years, then 20 years will be the long run, and any period less than 20 years will constitute the short run.

FIXED COSTS AND VARIABLE COSTS

This distinction between the short run and the long run also determines which of the firm's costs rise or fall with a change in the amount of output the firm produces. Some costs cannot be varied, *no matter how long the period in question.* These are called

Data of the sort provided in Table 8–1 (see section below) do not represent a farmer's subjective opinion; rather they are objective information that an agricultural scientist can supply from experimental evidence. Now, we don't claim to be experts on hogs, and the data in Table 8–1 (and the following graphs) are not necessarily true-to-life. But we have attempted to approximate the reality of raising hogs on a small organic farm. According to the National Pork Producers Council (www.nppc.org), average hog market weight is 250 pounds, and it takes about $3\frac{1}{2}$ pounds of feed to produce one pound of live hog weight. Thus, a 250-pound porker will have eaten almost 900 pounds of feed. Since hogs are marketed at an age of about five months, this works out to about 180 pounds of feed per month, or an average of 45 pounds of feed per week. The illustrative numbers that we have used in our example of Naomi's Natural Hogs are (we hope) a reasonable approximation of this information.

fixed costs, and they arise when some types of inputs can be bought only in big batches or when inputs have a large productive capacity. For example, there is no such thing as a "mini" automobile assembly line capable of producing two cars a week, and except for extreme luxury models, it is impractical to turn out automobiles without an assembly line. So the fixed cost of automobile manufacturing includes the cost of the smallest (least expensive) assembly line that the firm can acquire. These costs are called *fixed* because the total amount of money spent in buying the assembly line does not vary, whether it is used to produce ten cars a day or 100, so long as the output quantity does not exceed the assembly line's capacity.

In the short run, there are other costs that behave very much as fixed costs do; in other words, they are predetermined by previous decisions and are *temporarily* fixed. But in the longer run, firms can change both their capital and labor commitments. So, in the long run, more costs become **variable.** We will have more to say about fixed and variable costs as we examine other key input and cost relationships.

A **fixed cost** is the cost of an input whose quantity does not rise when output goes up, one that the firm requires to produce any output at all. The total cost of such indivisible inputs does not change when the output changes. Any other cost of the firm's operation is called a **variable cost.**

PRODUCTION, INPUT CHOICE, AND COST WITH ONE VARIABLE INPUT

Although, in reality, all businesses use many different inputs, we will begin our discussion with the short-run case in which there is *only a single input that is variable,* that is, in which the quantities of all other inputs will not be changed. In doing so, we are trying to replicate in our theoretical analysis what physicists or biologists do in the laboratory when they conduct a *controlled* experiment: changing just one variable at a time to enable us to see the influence of one variable in isolation. Thus, we will study the effects of variation in the quantity of one input under the assumption that all other inputs remain unchanged—that is, other things being equal.

TOTAL, AVERAGE, AND MARGINAL PHYSICAL PRODUCTS

We begin the analysis with the first of the firm's three main questions: the relationship between the quantity of inputs utilized and the quantity of production. Naomi has studied how much weight her hogs gain as she uses various amounts of corn. The relevant data are displayed in Table 8–1.

TABLE 8–1

Total Physical Product Schedule for Naomi's Natural Farm

Corn Input (100-lb. bags)	Pork Output (lbs.)
0	0.0
1	14.0
2	36.0
3	66.0
4	100.0
5	130.0
6	156.0
7	175.0
8	184.0
9	185.4
10	180.0
11	165.0
12	144.0

FIGURE 8-2

Total Physical Product with Different Quantities of Corn for Naomi's Natural Farm

The table begins by confirming the commonsense observation that hogs cannot be raised without food. Thus, output is zero when Naomi provides zero corn input (see the first line of the table). After that, the table shows the increase in pork output that additional corn yields. After nine bags of corn per week, more corn actually reduces output.

For instance, with an input of four 100-pound bags of corn per week (for her small hog herd), output is 100 pounds. Eventually, however, Naomi will reach a saturation point beyond which additional corn will not add to the pigs' growth and actually may cause some of them to become ill.

TOTAL PHYSICAL PRODUCT   The data in Table 8–1 appear graphically in Figure 8–2, which is called a **total physical product (TPP)** curve. This curve reports how much pork Naomi can produce with different quantities of corn, holding the quantities of all other inputs constant.

AVERAGE PHYSICAL PRODUCT   To understand more about how the quantity of corn she feeds her hogs contributes to their growth, Naomi can use two other physical product relationships given in Table 8–2. **Average physical product (APP)** measures output per unit of input; it is simply total physical product divided by the quantity of variable input used. On Naomi's farm, it is total pork output in pounds divided by the number of bags of corn. APP is shown in Column (4) of Table 8–2. For example, since four 100-pound bags of corn yield 100 pounds of pork, the APP of four bags of corn is 100/4, or 25 pounds of pork per bag of corn.

MARGINAL PHYSICAL PRODUCT   To decide how much corn to feed her hog herd, Naomi must know how much *additional* pork output to expect from each *additional* bag of corn. This concept is known as **marginal physical product (MPP)**, and she can calculate it from the data on total physical product using the same method we introduced to derive marginal utility from total utility in Chapter 6. For example, the marginal physical product of the fourth bag of corn is the total output of pork when Naomi uses four bags of corn *minus* the total output when she uses three bags (100 − 66 = 34 pounds). We calculate the other MPP entries in the third column of Table 8–2 in exactly the same way. Figure 8–3 displays these numbers in a graph called a *marginal physical product curve*.

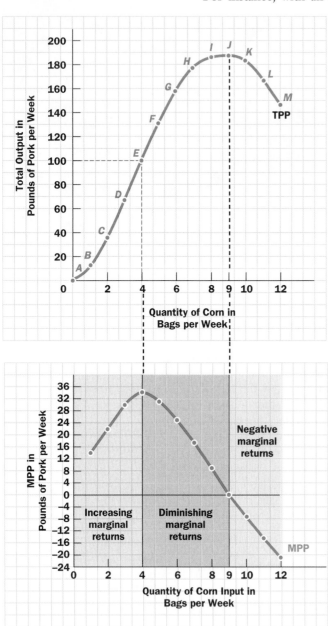

FIGURE 8-3

Naomi's Marginal Physical Product (MPP) Curve

MARGINAL PHYSICAL PRODUCT AND THE "LAW" OF DIMINISHING MARGINAL RETURNS

The shape of the marginal physical product curve in Figure 8–3 has important implications for Naomi's hog raising. Compare the TPP curve in Figure 8–2 with the MPP curve in Figure 8–3. The MPP curve can be described as the curve that reports the *rate* at which the TPP curve is changing—that is, it tells us how much of an increase in pork output results from each additional bag of corn she feeds the hogs. Thus, until input reaches four bags of corn, the marginal physical product of corn *increases* when Naomi feeds more corn. This means that TPP increases at an increasing rate between points *A* and *E* in Figure 8–2. Between four bags and nine bags, the MPP *decreases* but still has *positive* values throughout (that is, it lies above the

Naomi's Schedules for Total Physical Product, Marginal Physical Product, Average Physical Product, and Marginal Revenue Product of Corn

(1)	(2)	(3)	(4)	(5)
Corn Input (bags)	Total Physical Product (pork output in lbs.)	Marginal Physical Product (lbs. of pork per bag)	Average Physical Product (lbs. of pork per bag)	Marginal Revenue Product
0	0.0		—	
		14.0		$ 10.50
1	14.0		14.0	
		22.0		16.50
2	36.0		18.0	
		30.0		22.50
3	66.0		22.0	
		34.0		25.50
4	100.0		25.0	
		30.0		22.50
5	130.0		26.0	
		26.0		19.50
6	156.0		26.0	
		19.0		14.25
7	175.0		25.0	
		9.0		6.75
8	184.0		23.0	
		1.4		1.05
9	185.4		20.6	
		−5.4		−4.05
10	180.0		18.0	
		−15.0		−11.25
11	165.0		15.0	
		−21.0		−15.75
12	144.0		12.0	

TABLE 8-2

horizontal axis). Consequently, in this range, TPP is still increasing (MPP > 0), but at a decreasing rate (MPP is falling). That is, in this region, between points E and J in Figure 8–2, each additional bag of corn adds to pork output, but it adds less than the previous bag added. Beyond nine bags, to the right of point J on Figure 8–2, the MPP of corn actually becomes *negative*: This means that the total physical product curve starts to decrease—additional corn actually makes some of the hogs sick.

Figure 8–3 is divided into three zones to illustrate these three cases. Note that the marginal returns to corn increase at first and then diminish. This is the typical pattern, and parallels what we had to say about the utility of consumption in Chapter 6. Each additional unit adds some productivity, but at a decreasing rate. In the left zone of Figure 8–3 (the region of increasing marginal returns), each additional bag of corn adds more to TPP than the previous bag did.

> The "law" of diminishing marginal returns, which has played a key role in economics for two centuries, states that an increase in the amount of any one input, *holding the amounts of all others constant,* ultimately leads to lower marginal returns to the expanding input.[4]

The so-called *law* rests simply on observed facts; economists did not deduce the theorem analytically. Returns to a single input usually diminish because of the "law" of variable input proportions. When the quantity of one input increases while all others remain constant, the variable input whose quantity increases gradually becomes more and more abundant relative to the others. (For example, the proportion of corn increases and the proportions of other feed, such as soybean meal, decreases.) As Naomi uses more and more corn with fixed quantities of other feed,

The firm's **total physical product (TPP)** is the amount of output it obtains in total from a given quantity of input.

The **average physical product (APP)** is the total physical product (TPP) divided by the quantity of input. Thus, APP = TPP/X where X = the quantity of input.

The **marginal physical product (MPP)** of an input is the increase in total output that results from a one-unit increase in the input, holding the amounts of all other inputs constant.

---

[4] The "law" is generally credited to Anne Robert Jacques Turgot (1727–1781), one of the great comptrollers-general of France before the revolution, whose liberal policies, it is said, represented the old regime's last chance to save itself. With characteristic foresight, the king fired Turgot.

the pigs' diet becomes unbalanced so that adding yet more corn does little good and eventually harms them. At this point, the marginal physical product of corn becomes *negative*.

Many real-world cases seem to display the law of variable input proportions. In China, for instance, farmers have been using increasingly more fertilizer as they try to produce larger grain harvests to feed the country's burgeoning population. Although that country's consumption of fertilizer is four times higher than it was 15 years ago, its grain output has increased by only 50 percent. This certainly suggests that fertilizer use has reached the zone of diminishing returns.

THE OPTIMAL QUANTITY OF AN INPUT AND DIMINISHING RETURNS

We can now address the second question that all firms must ask as they make production decisions: How can the firm select the optimal quantity of an input? For this purpose, look again at the first and third columns of Table 8–2, which show the farm's marginal physical product schedule. We will assume that a 100-pound bag of the special organic corn that the farm uses costs $10, and that Naomi can sell her hogs for 75 cents per pound (she gets top dollar for these pasture-raised, "natural" hogs).[5]

Now suppose that Naomi is considering using just one bag of corn. Is this optimal? That is, does this maximize her profits? The answer is no, because the marginal physical product of a second bag of corn is 22 pounds of pork, the second entry in marginal physical product Column (3) of Table 8–2. At a price of $0.75 per pound, this extra output would add $16.50 to revenue. Since the added revenue exceeds the $10 cost of the second bag of corn, the farm comes out ahead by $16.50 minus $10, or $6.50.

The **marginal revenue product (MRP)** of an input is the additional revenue that the producer earns from the increased sales when it uses an additional unit of the input.

MARGINAL REVENUE PRODUCT AND INPUT PRICES   The additional *money revenue* that a firm receives when it increases the quantity of some input by one unit is called the input's **marginal revenue product.** If Naomi's hogs sell at a fixed price of $0.75 per pound, the marginal revenue product (MRP) of the input equals its marginal physical product (MPP) multiplied by the output price:

$$\text{MRP} = \text{MPP} \times \text{Price of output}$$

For example, we have just shown that the marginal revenue product of the second bag of corn is $16.50, which we obtained by multiplying the MPP of 22 pounds by the price of $0.75 per pound. The other (MRP) entries in Column (5) of Table 8–2 are calculated in the same way. The MRP concept enables us to formulate a simple rule for the optimal use of any input. Specifically:

When the marginal revenue product of an input exceeds its price, it pays the firm to use more of that input. Similarly, when the marginal revenue product of the input is less than its price it pays the firm to use less.

Let's test this rule in the case of Naomi's hogs. We have observed that two bags of corn cannot be enough because the MRP of a second bag ($16.50) exceeds its price ($10). What about a third bag? Table 8–2 shows that the MRP of the third bag ($0.75 × 30 = $22.50) also exceeds its price; thus, stopping at three bags also is not optimal. This remains true through the seventh bag of corn, because its MRP of $14.25 still exceeds its $10 price. The same cannot be said of an eighth

---

[5] More hog facts: In 1997 the average price of hogs was $53 per hundredweight (hundred pounds). But we have assumed here that Naomi, along with many real-world farmers, raises a small herd of premium, organic pigs, so she gets at least $75 per hundredweight (75 cents per pound). In 1997, corn cost $2.42 per bushel (a bushel of corn weighs 56 pounds), or approximately five cents per pound. But Naomi's hogs eat only the best—we assume that the special, hybrid organic corn that she feeds her pampered herd costs 10 cents a pound, or $10 per 100-pound bag.

bag, however. The eighth bag is not a good idea because its MRP, only $6.75, is less than its $10 cost. Thus, the optimal quantity of corn for Naomi to purchase each week is seven bags, yielding a total output of 175 pounds of pork.

Notice the crucial role of diminishing returns in this analysis. When the marginal *physical* product of corn begins to decline, the money value of that product falls, as well; that is, the marginal *revenue* product also declines. The producer always profits by expanding input use until diminishing returns set in and reduce the MRP to the price of the input. So Naomi should stop *increasing* her corn purchases when MRP falls to the price of corn.

A common expression suggests that it does not pay to continue doing something "beyond the point of diminishing returns." As we see from this analysis, quite to the contrary, it normally *does* pay to do so! The firm has employed the proper amount of input only when diminishing returns reduce the marginal revenue product of the input to the level of its price, because then the firm will be wasting no opportunity to *add* to its total profit. Thus, the optimal quantity of an input is that at which MRP equals its price (*P*). In symbols:

$$MRP = P \text{ of input}$$

The logic of this analysis is exactly the same as in our discussion of marginal utility and price in Chapter 6. Naomi is trying to maximize *profits*—the difference between the *total* revenue her corn input yields and the *total* cost of buying that input. To do so, she must increase her corn usage up to the point where its price equals its marginal revenue product, just as an optimizing consumer keeps buying until price equals marginal utility.

INPUT QUANTITIES AND TOTAL, AVERAGE, AND MARGINAL COST CURVES

We turn now to the third of the three main questions that a firm must ask: How do we derive the firm's cost relationships from the input decisions that we have just explained? We will need these cost relationships to analyze the firm's output and pricing decisions in Chapter 9, where we will study the last of the main components of our analysis of the market mechanism: How much of its product or service should the profit-maximizing firm produce?

The most desirable output quantity for the firm clearly depends on the way in which costs change when output varies. Economists typically display and analyze such information in the form of *cost curves*. Indeed, since we will use marginal analysis again in our discussion, we will need three different cost curves: *the total cost curve, the average cost curve, and the marginal cost curve.*

These curves follow directly from the nature of production. The technological production relationships for hog farming—hog physiology and the best animal husbandry practices—dictate the amount of corn that Naomi uses to produce a given quantity of pork. This technological relationship appears in Figure 8–2. From these data on corn usage and the price of corn, Naomi can determine how much it will cost to produce some given amount of pork. Therefore, the relevant cost relationships depend directly on the production relationships we have just discussed. The calculation of the firm's total costs from its physical product schedule assumes that the firm cannot influence the price of corn and, for simplicity, we will continue for now to assume that the quantities of all inputs other than corn are fixed.

The method is simple: For each quantity of output, record from Table 8–1 or Figure 8–2 the amount of corn required to produce it. Then multiply that quantity of corn by its price.

TOTAL COSTS In addition to the cost of corn, Naomi must spend money on other inputs, such as soybean meal, electricity to light the barn, and so on. Furthermore, her costs must include the *opportunity costs* of any inputs that Naomi herself contributes (such as soybeans that she grew herself, which she could have sold to other farmers instead of feeding to her pigs). Because we are simplifying matters by focusing exclusively on corn input for now, however, let us assume for the next several pages that all other inputs are free. Later, we will bring in the costs of the other inputs.

Because corn costs $10 per bag, the data in Table 8–1 lead directly to the total costs shown in Table 8–3. For example, the fourth row of Table 8–1 indicates that Naomi needs three bags of corn to produce 66 pounds of pork. At $10 per bag, this input costs $30, which is the fourth entry in Column (3) of Table 8–3. The other numbers in Table 8–3 are derived similarly. In general:

> The total product curve specifies the input quantities needed to produce any given output. From those input quantities and the prices of the inputs, we can determine the *total cost* (TC) of producing any level of output. Thus, the relationship of total cost to output is determined by the technological production relationships between inputs and outputs and by input prices.

TOTAL, AVERAGE, AND MARGINAL COST CURVES   Two other cost curves—the average cost (AC) and marginal cost (MC) curves—provide information crucial for our analysis. We can calculate these curves directly from the total cost curve, just as Table 8–2 calculated average and marginal physical product from total physical product. For any given output, *average cost* is defined as total cost divided by quantity produced. For example, Table 8–3 shows that the total cost of producing 100 pounds of pork is $40, so that the average cost is $40/100, or $0.40 per pound per week.

Similarly, we define the *marginal cost* as the increase in total cost that arises from the production of an additional pound of pork. For example, the marginal cost of the 100th pound of pork is the difference between the total cost of producing 100 pounds ($40) and the total cost of producing 99 pounds (say, $39.71), although the table doesn't show this number); this difference equals approximately $0.29. Figure 8–4 shows all three curves, the total, average, and marginal cost curves. The TC curve is generally assumed to rise fairly steadily as the firm's output increases. After all, Naomi cannot expect to produce 100 pounds of pork at a lower total cost than she could produce 80 pounds. The AC curve and the MC curve both look roughly like the letter ∪—first going downhill, then gradually turning uphill again. We will explore the reason for and implications of this ∪-shape later in the chapter.

So far, we have ignored the money that Naomi must spend on inputs other than corn. Of course, she cannot obtain these other inputs free, so, because the quantities of these inputs are assumed to be fixed in the short run, their costs should be treated as constants—as positive numbers rather than as zero. In the following discussion, we will treat all of these other costs as fixed.

TOTAL FIXED COST AND AVERAGE FIXED COST CURVES   Although variable costs are only part of total costs (which include fixed and variable costs), variable cost curves have the same general shape as the total cost curve shown in Figure 8–4(a). In contrast, the curves that record *total fixed costs* (TFC) and *average fixed costs* (AFC) have very special shapes, illustrated in Figure 8–5. By definition, TFC remains the same whether the firm produces a little or a lot—so long as it produces anything at all. As a result, any TFC curve is horizontal like the one in Figure 8–5(a). It has the same height at every output.

FIGURE 8-4

Naomi's Total, Average, and Marginal Costs

(a)

(b)

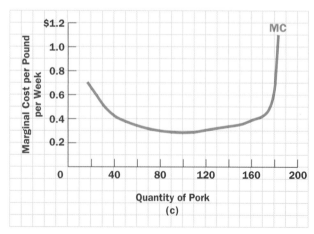

(c)

NOTE: Quantity is in pounds per week.

A Portion of Naomi's Total Cost Schedule

TABLE 8-3

(1)	(2)	(3)
Pork Output (lbs. per week)	Corn Input (bags per week)	Total Cost (cost of corn per week)
0	0	$ 0
14	1	10
36	2	20
66	3	30
100	4	40
130	5	50
156	6	60
175	7	70
184	8	80

NOTE: This schedule is obtained from the production data in Table 8–1, assuming that corn is the only variable input.

Fixed Costs: Total and Average

FIGURE 8-5

Average fixed cost, however, gets smaller and smaller as output increases, because AFC (which equals TFC/Q) falls as output (the denominator) rises for constant TFC. Business people typically put the point another way: Any increase in output spreads the fixed cost (which they often call "overhead") among more units, meaning less of it is carried by any one unit. For example, suppose that Naomi's hog operation incurs a fixed cost of $20 per week. When she produces only 10 pounds of pork, the entire $20 of fixed cost must be borne by that 10 pounds; that is, the average fixed cost is $2 per pound. But if she produces 20 pounds of pork, the average fixed cost falls to $1 for each pound of output (Table 8–4).

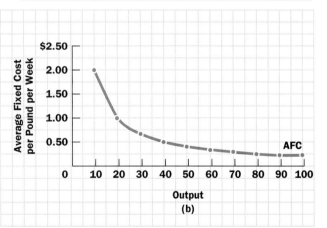

NOTE: Output is in pounds of pork per week.

However, AFC can never reach zero. Even if the farm were to produce a million pounds of pork per week, each unit would have to bear, on the average, one millionth of the TFC—which is still a positive number (though minuscule). It follows that the AFC curve gets lower and lower as output increases, moving closer and closer to the horizontal axis but never crossing it. This pattern appears in Figure 8–5(b).

TABLE 8-4

Naomi's Total and Average Fixed Costs

Output per Period (lbs. per week)	Total Fixed Cost (TFC)	Average Fixed Cost (AFC)
0	$20	$ 0
10	20	2.00
20	20	1.00
30	20	0.67
40	20	0.50
50	20	0.40
60	20	0.33
70	20	0.29
80	20	0.25
90	20	0.22
100	20	0.20

Having divided costs into fixed costs (FC) and variable costs (VC), we can express corresponding rules for total and average costs:[6]

$$TC = TFC + TVC \qquad AC = AFC + AVC$$

THE LAW OF DIMINISHING MARGINAL PRODUCTIVITY AND THE U-SHAPED AVERAGE COST CURVE

The preceding discussion of fixed and variable costs enables us to consider the configuration of the average cost curve and the production implications of its typical ∪-shape. Curve AC in Figure 8–4(b) is roughly ∪-shaped: The left-hand portion of the curve is downward-sloping and the right-hand portion is upward-sloping. AC declines when output increases in the left-hand portion of the curve for two reasons.

The first reason makes intuitive sense and pertains to fixed costs and the fact that they are divided over more units of product as output increases. As Figure 8–5(b) shows, the average *fixed*-cost curve always falls as output increases, and it falls very sharply at the left-hand end of curve AFC. Since AC equals AFC plus average variable costs (AVC), the AC curve for virtually any product contains a fixed-cost portion, AFC, which falls steeply at first when output increases. So, as these fixed costs are spread over more product units as output increases, the AC curve for any product should have a downward-sloping portion such as *CD* in Figure 8–4(b), which is characterized by decreasing average cost.

The second reason why the AC curves have a downward-sloping section relates to changing input proportions. As the firm increases the quantity of one input while holding other inputs constant, the marginal physical product relationship tells us that MPP will first rise; this means that average costs will decrease. If Naomi is using very little corn relative to the amounts of other inputs, a rise in the quantity of corn will, at first, yield increasing additions to output (in the range of increasing marginal physical product of corn illustrated in the left-hand part of Figure 8–3). As the quantity produced increases, the average cost of output falls.

Now look at any point to the right of point E in Figure 8–4(b). Average cost rises as output increases along this section of the curve. Why does the portion of the curve with decreasing AC end? To gain a percentage rise in output, Naomi must use ever more corn relative to output, so the curve begins to turn upward because

---

[6] The reader may wonder if there is such a thing as a marginal fixed cost. The answer is yes, but it doesn't matter because marginal fixed cost must generally equal zero. By definition, an increase in output never adds anything to total fixed cost. For example, for both two and three units of output, TFC must be the same, so that $MFC_3 = TFC_3 - TFC_2 = 0$.

the law of (eventually) diminishing returns holds when any one input quantity increases while other input quantities remain the same. Thus as we expand the use of one input (the quantity of corn) while holding all others constant, average costs fall first, and then eventually rise.

Note that, although it may not seem very important in our simple example, increasing administrative costs are also an important source of increasing average cost in practice. Sheer size makes firms more complicated to run. Large firms tend to be relatively bureaucratic, impersonal, and costly to manage. As a firm becomes very large and loses top management's personal touch, bureaucratic costs ultimately rise disproportionately. This change ultimately drives average cost upward as well.

The output at which average costs stop decreasing and begin to rise varies from industry to industry. Other things being equal, the greater the relative size of fixed costs, the higher will be the output at which the switch-over occurs.[7] For example, it occurs at a much larger volume of output in automobile production than in farming, which is why no farms are as big as even the smallest auto producer. Automobile producers must be larger than farms because the fixed costs of automobile production are far greater than those in farming, so spreading the fixed cost over an increasing number of units of output keeps AC falling far longer in auto production than in farming. Thus, although firms in both industries may have ∪-shaped AC curves, the bottom of the ∪ occurs at a far larger output in auto production than in farming.

> **The AC curve for a typical firm is U-shaped. We can attribute its downward-sloping segment to increasing marginal physical products or to the fact that the firm spreads its fixed costs over larger and larger outputs. Similarly, we can attribute the upward-sloping segment to decreasing marginal physical products from a single variable input, and to the disproportionate rise in administrative cost that occurs as firms grow large.**

THE AVERAGE COST CURVE IN THE SHORT AND LONG RUN

We observed as we started this chapter that some inputs are variable and some are precommitted, depending on the pertinent time horizon. It follows that:

> **The average (and marginal and total) cost curve depends on the firm's planning horizon. The average (and total) cost curve for the long run differs from that for the short run because, in the long run, all input quantities become variable.**

We can, in fact, be much more specific about the relationships between the short-run and long-run average cost (AC) curves. Consider, as an example, the capacity of Naomi's farm. In the short run, after she has built her barn, she can choose, at most, only the number of pigs that she can crowd into its capacity. But, in the long run, she can also choose among barns of different sizes.

If she constructs a smaller barn, her AC curve looks like curve *SL* in Figure 8–6. That means that if she is pleasantly surprised as sales grow to 100 pounds per week, average cost will be $0.40 per pound (point *V*). She may then wish she had built the bigger barn with an AC curve of *BG*, which would have enabled her to cut cost per pound to $0.35 (point *W*). In the short run, though, Naomi can do nothing about this decision; the AC curve remains *SL*. Similarly, had she built the larger barn, the short-run AC curve would be *BG*, and the farm would be committed to this cost curve even if her sales were to decline sharply.

---

[7] Empirical evidence confirms this view, though it suggests that the bottom of the ∪ is often long and flat. That is to say, a considerable range of outputs often fall between the regions of decreasing and increasing average cost. In this intermediate region, the AC curve is approximately horizontal, meaning that, in that range, AC does not change when output increases.

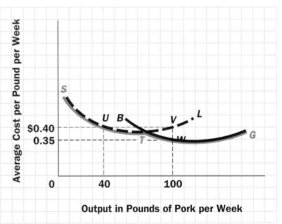

FIGURE 8–6

Short-Run and Long-Run Average Cost Curves

In the long run, however, Naomi must replace the barn, and she is free to decide all over again how big it should be. If Naomi expects sales of 100 pounds per week, she will construct the larger barn and have an average cost of $0.35 per pound of pork (point *W*). Similarly, if she expects sales of only 40 pounds, she will arrange for the smaller building with average costs of $0.40 (point *U*).

In sum, in the long run, a firm will select the plant size (that is, the short-run AC curve) that is most economical for the output level that it expects to produce. The long-run average cost curve then consists of all of the *lower* segments of the short-run AC curves. In Figure 8–6, this composite curve is the red curve, *STG*. The long-run average cost curve shows the lowest possible short-run average cost corresponding to each output level.

MULTIPLE INPUT DECISIONS: THE CHOICE OF OPTIMAL INPUT COMBINATIONS[8]

Up to this point we have simplified our analysis by assuming that the firm can change the quantity of only one of its inputs. We come next to the more realistic, but more complicated, case in which the firm can and does decide on the quantities of several inputs—such as labor, land, and capital—at once. We will once again examine the three basic and closely interrelated issues: production levels, optimal input quantities, and the firm's production costs. But this time, we will allow the firm to select the quantities of *many* inputs. By expanding our analysis in this way, we can study a key issue: how a firm, by its choice of production method (also called its production technology), can make up for decreased availability of one input by using more of another. We will end by returning to the three fundamental cost curves (total cost, average cost, and marginal cost). These cost curves will once again help us to understand the relationship between a firm's pricing and output decisions and its production relationships—that is, the connection between input and output quantities.

SUBSTITUTABILITY: THE CHOICE OF INPUT PROPORTIONS

Just as we found it useful to start the analysis with physical output or product in the one-variable-input case, we will start with physical production in the multiple-variable-input case. Firms can choose among alternative types of technology to produce any given product. Many people mistakenly believe that management really has very little choice when selecting its input proportions. Technological considerations alone, they believe, dictate such choices. For example, a particular type of furniture-cutting machine may require two operators working for an hour on a certain amount of wood to make five desks—no more and no less. But this is an overly narrow view of the matter. Whoever first said that there are many ways to skin a cat saw things more clearly.

The furniture manufacturer can choose among several alternative production processes for making desks. For example, simpler and cheaper machines may be able to change the same pile of wood into five desks using more than two hours of labor. Still more workers can eventually do the job with simple hand tools, using no machinery at all. The firm will seek the method of production that is *least costly*.

In advanced industrial societies, where labor is expensive and machinery is cheap, it may pay to use the most automated process. For example, Caterpillar, an American heavy-vehicle and machinery producer, curbed its high labor costs by investing in computers that enabled it to manufacture twice as many truck engines with the same number of people. But in less developed countries, where machinery is scarce and labor abundant, making things by hand may be the most economical solution. An interesting example can be found in India, where company records are often still handwritten, not computerized, as is widely true in America.

---

[8] Instructors may want to teach this part of the chapter (up to page 155) now, or they may prefer to wait until they come to Chapters 17 and 18 on the determination of wages, interest rates, profit, and rent.

● BLAME THE USUAL SUSPECTS: SUPPLY AND DEMAND

The hog market is cyclical. The National Pork Producers Council explains: "If supplies are low and/or demand is high, prices will be high, and vice versa. When prices are high, more sows are bred and more pigs are produced. When . . . they reach market, supplies increase and prices fall." For instance, hog prices were high in 1997. Farmers responded by raising more hogs in 1998. The result, according to the *New York Times,* was that ". . . a glut in the number of hogs being raised sent hog prices plummeting to Depression-era lows." And many economists argued that the traditional forces of supply and demand largely explained the plunging prices.

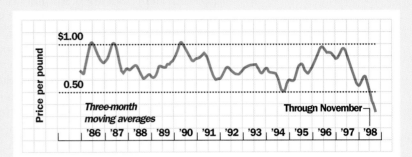

To try to manage the risk inherent in these fluctuating prices, hog producers can buy what amounts to insurance contracts on the Chicago Mercantile Exchange (called Lean Hogs and Pork Bellies contracts) and the Mid-American Exchange (Lean Hogs contracts).

SOURCE: "Pork Facts 1998/1999," National Pork Producers Council (www.nppc.org), and David Barboza, "The Great Pork Gap," *The New York Times,* January 7, 1999, Business Day, pp. 1 and 17.

"ROBERTS, WHAT'S ALL THIS TALK I HEAR ABOUT PORK BELLIES?"

We conclude that firms can generally substitute one input for another. A firm can produce the same number of desks with less labor, *if* it is prepared to sink more money into machinery. But whether it *pays* to make such a substitution depends on the relative costs of labor and machinery. Several general conclusions follow from this discussion.

■ Normally, a firm can choose among different technological options to produce a particular volume of output. Technological considerations rarely fix input proportions immutably.

■ Given a target production level, a firm that cuts down on the use of one input (say, labor) will normally have to increase its use of another input (say, machinery). This is what we mean when we speak of *substituting* one input for another.

■ The combination of inputs that represents the *least costly* way to produce the desired level of output depends on the relative prices of the various inputs.

THE PRODUCTION FUNCTION AND SUBSTITUTABILITY

To help select the combination of inputs to produce the desired output at least cost, economists have invented a concept they call the **production function.** The production function summarizes the technical and engineering information about the relationship between a firm's output and *all* of its inputs. It indicates, for example, just how much pork Naomi's Natural Farm can produce with given amounts of land, labor, corn, and so on. If, as we normally assume, the firm can produce the desired amount of output in many ways, the production function lays out all input combinations that will do the job.

The **production function** indicates the *maximum* amount of product that any particular collection of inputs is capable of producing.

If a firm needs only two inputs (which are enough for our purposes to give you the idea of the basic principles), a production function can be represented graphically (which we do in the appendix to this chapter) or by a simple table. For example, such a table can show various combinations of quantities of two inputs, say soybean meal and corn, with any combination capable of yielding 120 pounds of pork per week. In Table 8–5(b), for example, the production function can indicate that 4.7 bags of corn per week and no soy meal can produce the 120 pounds of pork on Naomi's farm, but that 3.5 bags of corn and half a bag of soy meal will also do the job. Such a table can also tell her that, at the other extreme, she can raise the 120 pounds of pork without any corn by using 3.7 bags of soy meal.

Which will she choose? Naturally, she prefers the cheapest combination. The least-cost option can be found directly with the help of such a table and the relevant input-price information (for example, that corn costs $10 per bag while soy meal is priced at $20). The total cost for each way of producing 120 pounds of pork is calculated, as before, by multiplying the input quantities by the input prices and adding them together. To illustrate, consider the three options just mentioned for the production of 120 pounds of pork:

> **Option A:** 4.7 bags of corn @ $10 per bag = $47
>
> **Option B:** 3.5 bags of corn @ $10 per bag + 0.5 bags of soybean meal @ $20 per bag = $35 + $10 = $45
>
> **Option C:** 3.7 bags of soy meal @ $20 per bag = $74

These calculations tell us that, of the three input combinations capable of producing 120 pounds of pork, the lowest total cost, $45, is obtained by Option B, the use of 3.5 bags of corn and 0.5 bags of soy meal per week. Other possible feed combinations that produce the 120 pounds of pork can, of course, be evaluated in exactly the same way, enabling Naomi to determine the most economical way to produce that output quantity. Similar calculations (Table 8–5a) also enable Naomi to determine the least expensive way to produce 80 pounds of pork. It looks like the cheapest way Naomi can produce 80 pounds of pork is to use 2.3 bags of corn and 0.7 bags of soy meal ($10 × 2.3 + $20 × 0.7 = $37).

Of course, outputs of 80 and 120 pounds per week are not the only production levels that Naomi should consider. She also should consider, for example, the least costly way to produce 60 pounds, 180 pounds, and so on. The total cost of producing *any* given quantity of output equals the sum of the cost-minimizing quantities of each of the inputs, with each input quantity multiplied by the price of that input.

Using the procedures just outlined, Naomi can calculate the minimum cost of producing *any* quantity of output. Let's suppose now that she has done this, completing the information that she needs to plot her *total cost curve*. As before, dividing the total cost for each output by the quantity of output then gives the corresponding *average cost*, that is, the cost per unit of output. Similarly, she can derive the marginal cost curve from the total cost figures, just as we did in an earlier section.

TABLE 8–5	**Alternative Input Combinations for Production of Given Output Quantities**

(a) Ways to Produce 80 Pounds of Pork per Week			(b) Ways to Produce 120 Pounds of Pork per Week		
Corn (bags per week)	Soy Meal (bags per week)	Total Cost* (per week)	Corn (bags per week)	Soy Meal (bags per week)	Total Cost* (per week)
3.8	0	$38	4.7	0	$47
3.0	0.5	40	3.5	0.5	45
2.3	0.7	37	2.8	1.2	52
1.5	2.1	57	2.0	2.8	76
0	3	60	0	3.7	74

*Total cost is calculated from the formula TC = Price of corn × Quantity of corn + Price of soy meal × Quantity of soy meal, with corn priced at $10 per bag and soy meal at $20 per bag.

THE MARGINAL RULE FOR OPTIMAL INPUT PROPORTIONS

Choosing the input proportions that minimize the cost of producing a given output is really a matter of common sense. To understand why, let us turn, once again, to our concrete example. As before, Naomi is considering whether to feed her hogs more corn and less soy meal, or vice versa. The two feeds are substitutes; if the pigs get more soy meal, they need less corn. *But the feeds are not perfect substitutes.* Soy meal provides more protein but fewer carbohydrates than corn, so Naomi gains a considerable benefit by providing the pigs with a balance of the two. If their diet contains too much of one feed and too little of the other, the output of pork will suffer. In other words, it is reasonable to assume *diminishing returns* to excessive substitution of either type of feed for the other.

We continue to assume that corn costs $10 per 100-pound bag, as in our earlier example, although the same size bag of soy meal costs twice as much. Given the $10 and $20 prices for corn and soy, how much of each feed should Naomi use? To answer this question, she must compare the prices of each feed with information on what each of them yields—their marginal physical products. Let's say that the marginal physical product (MPP) of a bag of corn is about 20 pounds of meat, and the marginal physical product of an additional bag of soy meal is about 30 pounds. What should Naomi do? Naomi should cut down on soy meal and increase her use of corn. Why? Because soy meal costs twice as much as corn, but its marginal yield is much less than twice as much meat—only 50 percent more. Obviously, it pays to spend more on the type of feed that yields more pork output per dollar than the other feed does. The corn provides a marginal yield of 20 pounds for $10, or two pounds per dollar. The soy yields 30 pounds of pork for $20, that is, 1.5 pounds per dollar. Clearly her marginal dollar gives her more pork if she invests it in corn than if she uses it to buy soy. So it will pay her to reduce the money she spends on the latter and use that money to buy more of the former.

MARGINAL ANALYSIS What makes this example work out the way it does is that *the ratio of the marginal product of soy meal to the price of soy meal is less than the ratio of the marginal product of corn to the price of corn.* This means, as we have seen, that Naomi gets more for her money—at the margin—by spending on corn rather than on soy meal. This illustrates one of the *Ideas for Beyond the Final Exam* that we see throughout the book: To minimize costs or maximize profits, producers must learn to examine cost relationships at the margin. To generalize, a firm can interpret the ratio:

$$\frac{\text{MPP of any input}}{\text{Price of that input}}$$

as the marginal product obtained by spending an additional $1 on the input. It always pays to reduce spending on Input A if its MPP per dollar is less than the MPP per dollar of Input B. That dollar should be spent on Input B instead. Such a move must *always* reduce the firm's cost of producing some given amount of output. By switching away from the input with the *lower* marginal product per dollar and buying more of the input with the *higher* marginal product per dollar, the firm can reduce the money it spends without reducing its output.

The Importance of Thinking at the Margin

We have thus derived the basic rule for determining the most economical way to produce any given output:

A firm can reduce the cost of producing a given output by using less of some input, A, and making up for it by using more of another input, B, whenever the ratio of the marginal physical product of A to the price of A is less than the ratio of the marginal physical product of B to the price of B, that is, whenever:

$$\frac{\text{MPP}_a}{P_a} < \frac{\text{MPP}_b}{P_b}$$

The opposite will be true if the MPP per dollar spent on A is higher than the MPP per dollar spent on B. Putting these two together, we conclude that input

● BEYOND FARMS AND FIRMS: THE GENERAL RULE FOR OPTIMAL INPUT PROPORTIONS

We have just discussed how a firm can determine the most economical input combination for any given level of output. This analysis does not apply only to business enterprises. Nonprofit organizations like your own college are interested in finding the least costly ways to accomplish a variety of tasks (for example, maintaining the grounds and buildings); government agencies seek to meet their objectives at minimum costs; even in the home, we can find many ways to "skin a cat." Thus, our present analysis of *cost minimization* is widely applicable.

proportions *cannot* be optimal if the ratios of the marginal physical products to the prices for any two inputs differ, that is:

The proportions of any two inputs, A and B, used by the firm can be optimal only if:

$$\frac{MPP_a}{P_a} = \frac{MPP_b}{P_b}$$

This rule, as we have noted, is simply common sense. If a unit of Input A has a marginal product that is, say, three times as big as that of Input B, the firm should be willing to pay exactly three times as much money for an additional unit of A as it pays for a unit of B, no more and no less.

But what if the market happens to set input prices so that this isn't true, meaning that the two fractions are unequal at the current input prices? Suppose that the market price of A happens to be twice as large as that of B, as in our hog-raising example. What can Naomi do about it? In this case, she should buy less of A (soy meal, in our example) and more of B (corn). That will not change the market *prices* of corn and soy meal, but it will change *the marginal physical products* of the two inputs because of the law of diminishing returns. As Naomi buys more corn and less soy meal, the marginal product of corn will fall and the marginal product of soy meal will rise. When Naomi has switched just enough money from soy meal to corn, the ratio of their marginal products will rise from $30 \div 20 = 1.5$ up to, say, $36 \div 18 = 2$. At that point, the ratio of the prices of the two inputs will be equal to the ratio of their marginal products, satisfying the rule for cost minimization.

CHANGES IN INPUT PRICES AND OPTIMAL INPUT PROPORTIONS

The commonsense reasoning behind the rule for optimal input proportions leads to an important conclusion. Let's say that Naomi is producing 120 pounds of output at minimum cost. But suppose that the price of corn rises, while the price of soy meal remains the same. That will cause a violation of the optimal-purchase rule:

$$\frac{MPP_{corn}}{P_{corn}} = \frac{MPP_{soy\ meal}}{P_{soy\ meal}}$$

To restore optimality, the MPP of corn must also rise to match the rise in corn price. But, by the "law" of diminishing returns, the MPP of corn is *higher* only when

---

● INPUT SUBSTITUTION IN THE FOREST

After Congress outlawed logging in much of the Redwood National Forest, Louisiana Pacific Corporation (one of the world's largest lumber producers) lost access to one of its essential inputs: old-growth timber from which the company made building materials. But CEO Harry Merlo was pragmatic about the situation, and turned his attention to trees that were not under the watchful eye of conservationists. One likely candidate, the aspen—a so-called *waste-species*—immediately came to his attention. Aspens grow quickly and they appear plentifully in forests stretching the width of North America. Fortunately, Merlo had kept himself abreast of the latest technology in the building industry.

Canadian lumber mills have long had the capability of trimming small trees into sheets and then gluing and pressing the sheets together. Merlo observed this process, and he conceived some innovative ideas of his own. He correctly figured that alternating the grain of the layered sheets would add to overall strength. The result was waferwood, which turned out to be cheaper and stronger than plywood. It could be used as siding and, when combined with other engineered lumber, used to create I-beams for floor joists and roof rafters.

Thus, when Louisiana Pacific was priced out of the market for its old input (old-growth timber), it substituted a new input, aspen wood, for one that was no longer available.

SOURCE: "Let's Go for Growth," *Fortune*, March 7, 1994, p. 60.

---

the use of corn is lower. Thus, a rise in the price of corn leads the farmer to use *less* corn and, if she still wants to produce 120 pounds of pork, to use *more* soy meal. In general we have the commonsense result that:

> As any one input becomes more costly relative to competing inputs, the firm is likely to substitute one input for another; that is, to use less of the input that has become more expensive and to use more of competing inputs.

This general principle of input substitution applies in industry just as it does on Naomi's farm. For real-world application of the analysis, see the accompanying box, "Input Substitution in the Forest."

■ ECONOMIES OF SCALE

We are now beginning to put together the tools we need to address the question posed at the beginning of this chapter: Does a large firm benefit from substantial **economies of scale** that allow it to operate more efficiently than smaller firms? To answer this question, we need a precise definition of this concept.

An enterprise's scale of operation arises from the quantities of the various inputs that it uses. The production function illustrates what happens when the firm doubles its scale of operations. For example, suppose that the production function for Naomi's Natural Farm indicates that with 1.5 bags of corn and 2.1 bags of soy meal, output is 80 pounds of pork (assuming soy meal and corn are the only two inputs).[9]

Production is said to involve **economies of scale,** also referred to as **increasing returns to scale,** if, when all input quantities are doubled, the quantity of output is *more* than doubled.

---

[9] This assumption is necessary because the table deals with only two inputs and the definition requires that *all* inputs be doubled simultaneously. To be true to the definition, if *labor, corn, land, and machinery* were all used by the farmer, their quantities would all have to double.

● **POLICY DEBATE**   │   **SHOULD WATER BE PROVIDED TO WESTERN FARMERS AT SUBSIDIZED PRICES?**

Farmers in the western United States use a great deal of water. California alone used more than 29 billion gallons of irrigation water per day in 1995 (about 22 percent of total U.S. irrigation water).* Because most of the area's climate is high desert, agriculture there requires artificial irrigation—indeed, water is critical. Yet western farmers and ranchers pay very low prices for the water they use. For example, government controls keep the price of water used for agriculture artificially low, so that California farmers pay only about 1/30th of the price that urban residents pay for water. Even during a recent drought, farmers in that state continued to use vast quantities of water, while residents in the cities were forced to ration.

This situation has given rise to an intense debate between farmers and environmentalists. There is no question that water is scarce in the western states, and there are some predictions of a looming shortage of disastrous proportions. It is also clear that farmers pay a price that is much lower than the true marginal cost of water, particularly because that cost includes a very high *opportunity cost,* that is, the value of the other uses of water that must be forgone as a result of its extensive employment in agriculture.

As analysis from this chapter shows, a low price for an input increases the amount that producers use, and there is little doubt that the low price of water substantially increases its use by western farmers. Environmentalists and economists have joined forces in arguing

that western water users should pay prices that cover its true marginal cost. Indeed, it has been suggested that at such a price any shortage would simply disappear.

The farmers, on the other hand, say that long practice entitles them to continued low water prices and that low prices in the past induced them to invest extensively in their agricultural properties, so that a price increase now would be tantamount to confiscating their investments. Moreover, they argue that a sharp rise in the price of this critical input would destroy a way of life that is valuable for society. The politicians undoubtedly feel caught in the middle, as the debate continues.

*U.S. Geological Survey (http://water.usgs.gov, accessed April 1999).

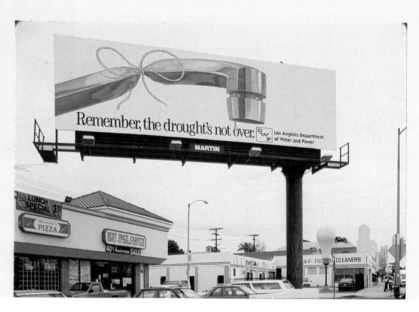

Now suppose that Naomi were to increase both inputs by 33.33 percent—to two bags of corn and 2.8 bags of soy meal. Output would rise by 50 percent (to 120 pounds). Because output goes up by a greater percentage than the increase in each of the inputs, Naomi's production function displays *increasing returns to scale* (also known as economies of scale), at least in this range.

Economies of scale affect operations in many modern industries. Where they exist, they give larger firms cost advantages over smaller ones and thereby foster large firm sizes. Automobile production and telecommunications are two common examples of industries that enjoy significant economies of scale. Predictably, firms in these industries are, indeed, huge.

Technology generally determines whether or not a specific economic activity is characterized by economies of scale. One particularly clear example of a way in which this can happen is provided by warehouse space. Imagine two warehouses, each shaped like perfect cubes with the length, width, and height of Warehouse 2 twice as large as those of Warehouse 1. Now remember your high-school geometry. The surface area of any side of a cube is equal to the square of its length. Therefore, the amount of material needed to build Warehouse 2 will be 2^2, or four times as great as that needed for Warehouse 1. However, because the volume of a cube is equal to the cube of its length, Warehouse 2 will have 2^3, or eight times as much storage space as Warehouse 1. Thus, in a cubic building multiplying the inputs by four leads to eight times the storage space—an example of strongly increasing returns to scale.

This example is, of course, oversimplified. It omits such complications as the need for stronger supports in taller buildings, the increased difficulty of moving goods in and out of higher stories, and the like. Still, the basic idea is correct, and the example shows why, up to a point, the very nature of warehousing creates technological relationships that lead to economies of scale.

Our definition of economies of scale, though based on the production function, relates closely to the shape of the *long-run* average cost curve. Notice that the definition requires that a doubling of *every* input must bring about more than a doubling of output. If all input quantities are doubled, total cost must double. But if output *more* than doubles when input quantities are doubled, then cost per unit (average cost) must decline. In other words:

Production functions with economies of scale lead to long-run average cost curves that decline as output expands.

Figure 8–7(a) depicts a decreasing average cost curve, but this is only one of three possible shapes that the long-run average cost curve can take. Panel (b) shows the curve for *constant* returns to scale. Here, if all input quantities double, both total cost (TC) and the quantity of output (Q) double, so average cost (AC = TC/Q) remains *constant*. Finally, output may increase, but less than double, when all inputs double. This is a case of *decreasing* returns to scale, which leads to a *rising* long-run average cost curve like the one depicted in Panel (c). The figure reveals a close association between the slope of the AC curve and the nature of the firm's returns to scale.

Three Possible Shapes for the Long-Run Average Cost Curve | FIGURE 8-7

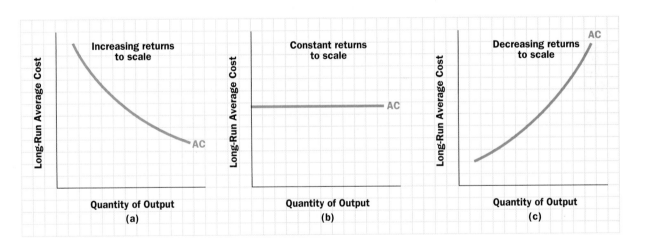

Note that the same production function can display increasing returns to scale in some ranges, constant returns to scale in other ranges, and decreasing returns to scale in yet others. This is true of all the ∪-shaped average cost curves we have shown, for example, Figure 8–4(b).

THE "LAW" OF DIMINISHING RETURNS AND RETURNS TO SCALE

Earlier in this chapter, we discussed the "law" of diminishing marginal returns. Is there any relationship between economies of scale and the phenomenon of diminishing returns? At first, the two ideas may seem contradictory. After all, if a producer gets diminishing returns from his inputs as he uses more of each of them, doesn't it follow that by using more of *every* input, he must encounter decreasing returns to scale? In fact, the two principles do not contradict one another, for they deal with fundamentally different issues.

- *Returns to a single input.* This analysis asks the question, how much does output expand if a firm increases the quantity of just *one* input, *holding all other input quantities unchanged?*

- *Returns to scale.* Here the question is, how much does output expand if *all* inputs are increased *simultaneously* by the same percentage?

The "law" of diminishing returns pertains to the first question, because it examines the effects of increasing only one input at a time. It is plausible that the firm will encounter diminishing returns as this one input becomes relatively abundant. Thus, for example, the addition of too much soy meal relative to a given quantity of corn will contribute too much protein and too few carbohydrates to the pigs, yielding diminishing returns.

Returns to scale pertain to proportionate increases in *all* inputs and therefore answer the second question. If Naomi doubles the quantities of both corn and soy meal, the hogs' diet need not become unbalanced. Thus, the "law" of diminishing returns (to a single input) is compatible with *any* sort of returns to scale. In summary:

Returns to scale and returns to a single input (holding all other inputs constant) refer to two distinct aspects of a firm's technology. A production function that displays diminishing returns to *a single input* may show diminishing, constant, or increasing returns when *all input quantities are increased proportionately.*

HISTORICAL COSTS VERSUS ANALYTICAL COST CURVES

In Chapter 6, we noted that all points on a demand curve pertain to the *same* period of time. Decision makers must use this common time period because the demand curve illustrates alternative choices *for a given period of time.* The same is true of a cost curve. All points on a cost curve pertain to exactly the same time period because the graph examines the cost of each alternative output level that the firm can choose for that period.

It follows that a graph of historical data on prices and quantities at *different points in time* is normally *not* the cost curve that the decision maker needs. This observation will help to resolve the problem posed at the beginning of the chapter about whether declining historical costs were evidence of economies of scale.

All points on any of the cost curves used in economic analysis refer to the same period of time.

One point on an auto manufacturer's cost curve may show, for example, how much it would cost the firm to produce 2.5 million cars during 1999. Another point on the same curve may show what would happen to the firm's costs if, *instead*, it were to produce 3 million cars in 1999. Such a curve is called an *analytical cost curve* or, when there is no possibility of confusion, simply a *cost curve.* This curve must be distinguished from a diagram of *historical costs*, which shows how costs have changed from year to year.

The different points on an analytical cost curve represent *alternative possibilities*, all for the same time period. In 1999, the car manufacturer will produce either 2.5 million or 3 million cars (or some other amount), but certainly not both. Thus, at most, only one point on this cost curve will ever be observed. The company may, indeed, produce 2.5 million in 1999 and 3 million in 2000, but the 2000 data are not relevant to the 1999 cost curve. By the time 2000 comes around, the cost curve may have shifted, so the 1999 cost figure will not apply to the 2000 cost curve either.

A different sort of graph can, of course, indicate year by year how costs and outputs have varied. Such a graph, which gathers together the statistics for a number of different periods, is not, however, a *cost curve* as that term is used by economists. An example of such a diagram of historical costs appeared in Figure 8–1.

Why do economists rarely use historical cost diagrams and instead deal primarily with analytical cost curves, which are more abstract, harder to explain, and more difficult to estimate statistically? The answer is that analysis of real policy

---

● **CLOSER TO HOME: THE DIMINISHING MARGINAL RETURNS TO STUDYING**

The "law" of diminishing marginal returns crops up a lot in ordinary life, not just in the world of business. Consider Jason and his study habits: He has a tendency to procrastinate and then cram for exams the night before he takes them, pulling "all-nighters" regularly. How may an economist speak of his payoff from an additional hour of study in the wee hours of the morning, relative to Colin's (who studies for two hours every night)?

problems—such as the desirability of having a single supplier of telephone services for the entire market—leaves no choice in the matter. Rational decisions require analytical cost curves. Let's see why.

Resolving the Economies of Scale Issue

Recall the problem that we introduced early in the chapter. We examined the AT&T divestiture and concluded that in order to determine whether it made sense to break up such a large company, economists would have to know whether or not the industry provided economies of scale. Among the data offered as evidence was a graph that showed a precipitous drop in the capital cost of long-distance communications as the volume of calls rose after 1942. But we did not answer a more pertinent question: Why didn't such information constitute legitimate evidence about the presence of economies of scale?

As this section shows, to determine whether a single supplier can provide telephone service more cheaply in 1999 than a number of smaller firms can, we must compare the costs of *both large-scale and small-scale production in 1999.* It does no good to compare the cost of a large supplier in 1999 with its own costs as a smaller firm back in 1942, because that cannot possibly supply the needed information. The cost situation in 1942 is irrelevant for today's decision between large and small suppliers because no small firm today would use the obsolete techniques of 1942.

Since the 1940s, great technical progress has taken the telephone industry from ordinary open-wire circuits to microwave systems, telecommunications satellites, coaxial cables of enormous capacity, and now to fiber optics. All of this means that the *entire* analytical cost curve of telecommunications must have shifted downward quite dramatically from year to year. Innovation must have reduced not only the cost of large-scale operations *but also the cost of smaller-scale operations.* Until decision makers compare the costs of large and small suppliers *today,* they cannot make a rational choice between single-firm and multifirm production. It is the analytical cost curve, all of whose points refer to the same period, that, by definition, supplies this information.

FIGURE 8-8

Declining Historical Cost Curve with the Analytical Average Cost Curve also Declining in Each Year

Quantity of Output

FIGURE 8-9

Declining Historical Cost Curve with U-Shaped Analytical Cost Curves in Each Year

Quantity of Output

Figures 8–8 and 8–9 show two extreme hypothetical cases, one that entails true economies of scale and one that does not. Both are based on the same historical cost data (in black) with their very sharply declining costs. (This curve is reproduced from Figure 8–1.) They also show (in red and blue) two possible average cost curves, one for 1942 and one for 2000. In Figure 8–8, the analytical AC curve has shifted downward very sharply from 1942 to 2000, as technological change reduced all costs. Moreover, both of the AC curves slope downward to the right, meaning that, in either year, a larger firm has lower average costs. Thus, the situation shown in Figure 8–8 really does entail scale economies, so that one large firm can serve the market at lower cost than many small ones.

But now look at Figure 8–9, which shows exactly the same historical costs as Figure 8–8. Here, however, both analytical AC curves are U-shaped. In particular, the 2000 AC curve has its minimum point at an output level, *A,* that is less than one-half of the current output, *B,* of the large supplier. Thus, the shape of the analytical cost curves does *not* show economies of scale. This means that, for the situation shown in Figure 8–9, a smaller company can produce more cheaply than a large one. In this case, one cannot justify domination of the market by a single large firm on the grounds that its costs are lower—despite the sharp downward trend of historical costs. In sum, the behavior of historical costs reveals nothing about the cost advantages or disadvantages of a single large firm. More generally:

Because a diagram of historical costs does not compare the costs of large and small firms *at the same point in time,* it cannot be used to determine whether an industry provides economies of large-scale production. Only the analytical cost curve can supply this information.

In the case of telephone service, some estimates indicate that economies of large-scale production do indeed exist. Presumably because of this, almost 20 years after the Bell telephone system breakup, the typical firm providing long-distance telephone service is still very large, with AT&T, MCI, and Sprint in the vanguard. Yet half a dozen or so other smaller firms still compete in this arena. It is perhaps ironic that some of the "Baby Bell" local telephone companies that were broken away from AT&T by the courts in 1982 have recombined, and others are seeking to merge in order to obtain cost and other advantages of larger size.

COST MINIMIZATION IN THEORY AND PRACTICE

Lest you be tempted to run out and open a business, confident that you now understand how to minimize costs, we should point out that business decisions are a good deal more complicated than we have indicated here. Rare is the business executive who knows for sure what his or her production function looks like, or the exact shapes of his or her marginal physical product schedules, or the precise nature of his or her cost curves. No one can provide an instruction book for instant success in business. What we have presented here is, instead, a set of principles that constitutes a guide to the logic of good decision making.

Business management has been described as the art of making critical decisions on the basis of inadequate information, and our complex and ever-changing world often leaves people no alternative but educated guesses. Actual business decisions will at best approximate the cost-minimizing ideal outlined in this chapter. Certainly, practicing managers will make mistakes, but when they do their jobs well and the market system functions smoothly, the approximation may prove amazingly good. Although no system is perfect, inducing firms to produce at the lowest possible cost is undoubtedly one of the jobs the market system does best.

1. A firm's total cost curve shows its lowest possible cost of producing any given quantity of output. This curve is derived from the input combination that the firm uses to produce any given output and the prices of the inputs.

2. The *marginal physical product (MPP)* of an input is the increase in total output resulting from a one-unit increase in that input, holding the quantities of all other inputs constant.

3. The *"law" of diminishing marginal returns* states that if a firm increases the amount of one input (holding all other input quantities constant), the marginal physical product of the expanding input will eventually begin to decline.

4. To maximize profits, a firm must purchase an input up to the point at which diminishing returns reduce the input's *marginal revenue product (MRP)* to equal its price (MRP = MPP × price).

5. The *long run* is a period sufficiently long for the firm's plant to require replacement and for all of its current contractual commitments to expire. The *short run* is any period briefer than that.

6. *Fixed costs* are costs whose total amounts do not vary when output increases. All other costs are called *variable costs*. Some costs are variable in the long run but not in the short run.

7. At all levels of output, the total fixed cost (TFC) curve is horizontal and the average fixed cost (AFC) curve declines toward the horizontal axis but never crosses it.

8. TC = TFC + TVC   AC = AFC + AVC.

9. It is usually possible to produce the same quantity of output in a variety of ways by substituting more of one input for less of another. Firms normally seek the least costly way to produce any given output.

10. A firm that wants to minimize costs will select input quantities at which the ratios of the *marginal physical product* of each input to its price—its MPP per dollar—are equal for all inputs.

11. The *production function* shows the relationship between inputs and output. It indicates the maximum quantity of output obtainable from any given combination of inputs.

12. If a doubling of all the firm's inputs *just* doubles its output, the firm is said to have *constant returns to scale*. If a doubling of all inputs leads to *more than* twice as much output, it has *increasing returns to scale* (or *economies of scale*). If a doubling of inputs produces *less than* a doubling of output, the firm has *decreasing returns to scale*.

13. With increasing returns to scale, the firm's long-run average costs are decreasing; constant returns to scale are associated with constant long-run average costs; decreasing returns to scale are associated with increasing long-run average costs.

14. Economists cannot tell if an industry offers economies of scale (increasing returns to scale) simply by inspecting a diagram of historical cost data. Only the underlying analytical cost curve can supply this information.

Short run   140

Long run   140

Fixed cost   141

Variable cost   141

Total physical product (TPP)   142

Average physical product (APP)   142

Marginal physical product (MPP)   142

Marginal revenue product (MRP)   144

Production function   151

Economies of scale (increasing returns to scale)   155

1. A firm's total fixed cost is $360,000. Construct a table of its total and average fixed costs for output levels varying from zero to 6 units. Draw the corresponding TFC and AFC curves.

2. With the following data, calculate the firm's AVC and MVC and draw the graphs for TVC, AVC, and MVC. Why is MVC the same as MC?

Quantity	Total Variable Costs
1	$ 40,000
2	80,000
3	120,000
4	176,000
5	240,000
6	360,000

3. From the figures in Review Questions 1 and 2, calculate TC and AC for each of the output levels from 1 to 6 units and draw the two graphs.

4. If a firm's commitments in 2001 include machinery that will need replacement in five years, a factory building rented for twelve years, and a three-year union contract specifying how many workers it must employ, when, from its point of view in 2001, does the firm's long run begin?

5. If the marginal revenue product of a gallon of oil used as input by a firm is $1.20 and the price of oil is $1.07 per gallon, what can the firm do to increase its profits?

6. A firm hires two workers and rents 15 acres of land for a season. It produces 150,000 bushels of crop. If it had doubled its land and labor, production would have been 325,000 bushels. Does it have constant, decreasing, or increasing returns to scale?

7. Suppose that wages are $20,000 per season per person and land rent per acre is $3,000. Calculate the average cost of

150,000 bushels and the average cost of 325,000 bushels, using the figures in Review Question 6. (Note that average costs increase when output increases.) What connection do these figures have with the firm's returns to scale?

8. Naomi has stockpiled a great deal of corn. Suppose now that she buys more piglets, but not more corn, and divides the corn she has evenly among the larger number of piglets. What is likely to happen to the marginal physical product of corn? What, therefore, is the role of input proportions in the determination of marginal physical product?

9. Labor costs $10 per hour. Nine workers produce 180 bushels of product per hour, while ten workers produce 196 bushels. Land rents for $1,000 per acre per year. With ten acres worked by nine workers, the marginal physical product of an acre of land is 1,400 bushels per year. Does the farmer minimize costs by hiring nine workers and renting

ten acres of land? If not, which input should he use in larger relative quantity?

10. Suppose that Naomi's total costs increase by $12 per week at every output level. Show in Table 8–2 how this affects her total and average costs.

11. (More difficult) A firm experiences a sudden increase in the demand for its product. In the short run, it must operate longer hours and pay higher overtime wage rates to satisfy this new demand. In the long run, however, the firm can install more machines instead of operating fewer machines for longer hours. Which do you think will be lower, the short-run or the long-run average cost of the increased output? How is your answer affected by the fact that the long-run average cost includes the new machines the firm buys, while the short-run average cost includes no machine purchases?

● **APPENDIX** ▌ **PRODUCTION INDIFFERENCE CURVES**

To describe a production function—that is, the relationship between input combinations and the size of a firm's total output—economists use a graphic device called the *production indifference curve* instead of the sort of numerical information described in Table 8–5 in the chapter.

> A *production indifference curve* (sometimes called an *isoquant*) is a curve in a graph showing quantities of *inputs* on its axes.

Each indifference curve indicates *all* combinations of input quantities just capable of producing a *given* quantity of output; thus, a separate indifference curve corresponds to each possible quantity of output. These production indifference curves are perfectly analogous to the consumer indifference curves discussed in the appendix to Chapter 6.

Figure 8–10 represents different quantities of labor and capital capable of producing given amounts of wheat. The figure shows three indifference curves: one for the production of 220,000 bushels of wheat, one for 240,000 bushels, and one for 260,000 bushels. The indifference curve labeled 220,000 bushels indicates that a farm can generate an output of 220,000 bushels of wheat using *any one* of the combinations of inputs represented by points on that curve. For example, it can employ ten years of labor and 200 acres of land (point *A*) or the labor-capital combination shown by point *B* on the same curve. Because it lies considerably below and to the right of point *B*, point *A* represents a productive process that uses more labor and less land.

Points *A* and *B* can be considered *technologically* indifferent because each represents a bundle of inputs just capable of yielding the same quantity of finished goods. However, the word "indifference" in this sense does not

FIGURE 8–10

A Production Indifference Map

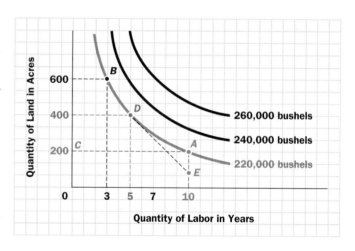

mean that the producer will be unable to decide between input combinations *A* and *B*. Input prices will permit the producer to arrive at a decision.

The production indifference curves in a diagram such as Figure 8–10 constitute a complete description of the production function. For each combination of inputs, they show how much output can be produced. Since production indifference curves are drawn in two dimensions, they represent only two inputs at a time. In more realistic situations, firms are likely to need more than two inputs, so, to study the subject, economists must conduct an algebraic analysis. Still, all the principles we need to analyze such a situation can be derived from the two-variable case.

CHARACTERISTICS OF THE PRODUCTION INDIFFERENCE CURVES, OR ISOQUANTS

Before discussing input pricing and quantity decisions, we first examine what is known about the shapes of production indifference curves.

Characteristic 1: *Higher curves correspond to larger outputs.* Points on a higher indifference curve represent larger quantities of *both* inputs than the corresponding points on a lower curve. Thus, a higher curve represents a larger *output.*

Characteristic 2: *An indifference curve will generally have a negative slope.* It goes downhill as we move toward the right. This means that if a firm reduces the quantity of one input, and it does not want to cut production, it must use more of another input.

Characteristic 3: *An indifference curve is typically assumed to curve inward toward the origin near its middle.* This shape reflects the "law" of diminishing returns to a single input. For example, in Figure 8–10, points *B*, *D*, and *A* represent three different input combinations capable of producing the same quantity of output. At point *B*, the firm uses a large amount of land and relatively little labor, whereas the opposite is true at point *A*. Point *D* is intermediate between the two.

Now consider the choice among these input combinations. When the farmer considers moving from point *B* to point *D*, he gives up 200 acres of land and instead hires two additional years of labor. Similarly, the move from *D* to *A* involves giving up another 200 acres of land. This time, however, hiring an additional two years of labor does not make up for the reduced use of land. Diminishing returns to labor as the farmer hires more and more workers to replace more and more land means that the farm now needs a much larger quantity of additional labor, five person-years rather than two, to make up for the reduction in the use of land. Without such diminishing returns, the indifference curve would have been a straight line, *DE*. The curvature of the indifference curve through points *D* and *A* reflects diminishing returns to substitution of inputs.

THE CHOICE OF INPUT COMBINATIONS

A production indifference curve describes only the input combinations that *can* produce a given output; it indicates the technological possibilities. To decide which of the available options suits its purposes best, a business needs the corresponding cost information: the relative prices of the inputs.

The budget line in Figure 8–11 represents all equally costly input combinations for a firm. For example, if farmhands are paid $9,000 a year and land rents for $1,000 per acre a year, then a farmer who spends $360,000 can hire 40 farmhands but rent no land (point *K*), or he can rent 360 acres but have no money left for farmhands (point *J*). It is undoubtedly more sensible to pick some intermediate point on his budget line at which he divides the $360,000 between the two inputs. The slope of the budget line represents the amount of land the farmer must give up if he wants to hire one more worker without increasing his budget.

FIGURE 8–11

A Budget Line

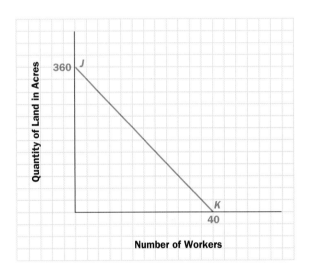

If the prices of the inputs do not change, then the slope of the budget line will not change anywhere in the graph. It will be the same at every point on a given budget line, and it will be the same on the $360,000 budget line as on the $400,000 budget line or on the budget line for any other level of spending. For if the price of hiring a worker is nine times as high as the cost of renting an acre, then the farmer must rent nine fewer acres to hire an additional farmhand without changing the total amount of money he spends on these inputs. Thus, the slope will be acres given up per added farmhand = −9/1 = −9.

So, with input prices given, the slope of any budget line does not change and the slopes of the different budget lines for different amounts of expenditures are all the same. Two results follow: (1) the budget lines are straight lines because their slopes remain the same throughout their length, and (2) because they all have the same slope, the budget lines in the graph will all be parallel, as in Figure 8–12.

FIGURE 8-12

Cost Minimization

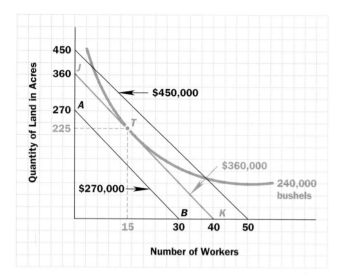

A firm that is seeking to minimize costs does not necessarily have a fixed budget. Instead, it wants to produce a given quantity of output (say, 240,000 bushels) with *the smallest possible budget.*

Figure 8–12 combines the indifference curve for 240,000 bushels from Figure 8–10 with a variety of budget lines similar to *JK* in Figure 8–11. The firm's problem is to find the lowest budget line that will allow it to reach the 240,000-bushel indifference curve. Clearly, an expenditure of $270,000 is too little; no point on the budget line, *AB*, permits production of 240,000 bushels. Similarly, an expenditure of $450,000 is too much, because the firm can produce its target level of output more cheaply. The solution is at point *T* where the farmer uses 15 workers and 225 acres of land to produce the 240,000 bushels of wheat. In general:

> The least costly way to produce any given level of output is indicated by the point of tangency between a budget line and the production indifference curve corresponding to that level of output.

COST MINIMIZATION, EXPANSION PATH, AND COST CURVES

Figure 8–12 shows how to determine the input combination that minimizes the cost of producing 240,000 bushels of output. The farmer can repeat this procedure exactly for any other output quantity, such as 200,000 bushels or 300,000 bushels. In each case, we draw the corresponding production indifference curve and find the lowest budget line that permits the farm to produce that much. For example, in Figure 8–13, budget line *BB* is tangent to the indifference curve for 200,000 units of

output; budget line *JK* is, again, tangent to the indifference curve for 240,000 bushels; and budget line *B'B'* is tangent to the indifference curve for 300,000 units of output. This gives us three tangency points: *S*, which gives the input combination that produces a 200,000-bushel output at lowest cost; *T*, which gives the same information for a 240,000-bushel output; and *S'*, which indicates the cost-minimizing input combination for the production of 300,000 bushels.

FIGURE 8-13

The Firm's Expansion Path

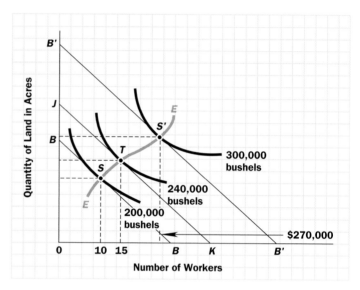

This process can be repeated for as many other levels of output as we like. For each such output we draw the corresponding production indifference curve and find its point of tangency with a budget line. Red curve *EE* in Figure 8–13 connects all these cost-minimizing points; that is, it is the locus of *S*, *T*, *S'*, and all other points of tangency between a production indifference curve and a budget line. Curve *EE* is called the firm's expansion path.

> The *expansion path* is the locus of the firm's cost-minimizing input combinations for all relevant output levels.

Point *T* in Figure 8–12 shows the quantity of output (given by the production indifference curve through that point) and the total cost (shown by the tangent budget line). Similarly, we can determine the output and total cost for every other point on the expansion path, *EE*, in Figure 8–13. For example, at point *S*, output is 200,000 and total cost is $270,000. This is precisely the sort of information we need to find the firm's total cost curve; that is, it is just the sort of information contained in Table 8–3, it is the source of the total cost curve and the average and marginal cost curves in Figure 8–4. Thus:

The points of tangency between a firm's production indifference curves and its budget lines yield its expansion path, which shows the firm's cost-minimizing input combination for each pertinent output level. This information also yields the output and total cost for each point on the expansion path, which is just what we need to draw the firm's cost curves.

EFFECTS OF CHANGES IN INPUT PRICES

Suppose that the cost of renting land increases and the wage rate of labor decreases. This means that the budget lines will differ from those depicted in Figure 8–12. Specifically, with land now more expensive, any given sum of money will rent fewer acres, so the intercept of each budget line on the vertical (land) axis will shift *downward*. Conversely, with labor cheaper, any given sum of money will buy more labor, so the intercept of the budget line on the horizontal (labor) axis will shift to the *right*. Figure 8–14 depicts a series of budget lines corresponding to a $1,500 per acre rental rate for land and a $6,000 annual wage for labor. If input prices change, the combination of inputs that minimizes costs will normally change. In this diagram, the land rent at $1,500 per acre is more than it was in Figure 8–12, whereas labor costs $6,000 per year (less than in Figure 8–12). As a result, these budget lines are less steep than those shown in Figure 8–12, and point *E* now represents the least costly way to produce 240,000 bushels of wheat.

To assist you in seeing how things change, Figure 8–15 combines, in a single graph, budget line *JK* and tangency point *T* from Figure 8–12 with budget line *WV* and tangency point *E* from Figure 8–14. When land becomes more expensive and labor becomes cheaper, the budget lines (such as *JK*) become less steep than they were previously (see *VW*). As a result, the least costly way to produce 240,000 bushels shifts from point *T* to point *E*, at which the firm uses more labor and less land. As common sense suggests, when the price of one input rises in comparison with that of another, it will pay the firm to use less of the more expensive input and more of the other.

FIGURE 8–14

Optimal Input Choice at a Different Set of Input Prices

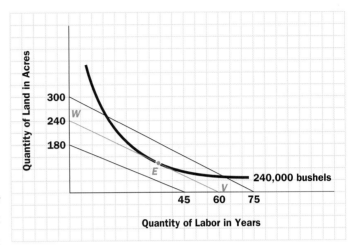

FIGURE 8–15

How Changes in Input Prices Affect Input Proportions

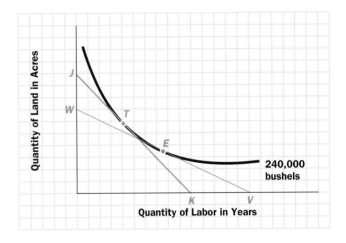

In addition to substituting one input for another, a change in the price of an input may induce the firm to alter its level of output. This is a subject that we will cover in the next chapter.

SUMMARY

1. A production function can be described by a series of *production indifference curves*, each of which shows all the input combinations capable of producing a specified amount of output.

2. As long as each input has a positive marginal physical product, production indifference curves will have negative slopes and the higher curves will represent larger amounts of output than the lower curves. Because of diminishing returns, these curves characteristically bend toward the origin near the middle.

3. The optimal input combination for any given level of output is indicated by the point of tangency between a budget line and the corresponding production indifference curve.

4. The firm's *expansion path* shows, for each of its possible output levels, the combination of input quantities that minimizes the cost of producing that output.

5. Total cost for each output level can be derived from the production indifference curves and the budget lines tangent

to them along the expansion path. These figures can be used to determine the firm's total cost, average cost, and marginal cost curves.

6. When input prices change, firms will normally use more of the input that becomes relatively less expensive and less of the input that becomes relatively more expensive.

Production indifference curve   162

Budget line   163

Expansion path   164

QUESTIONS FOR REVIEW

1. Compound Consolidated Corporation (CCC) produces containers using two inputs: labor and glue. If labor costs $10 per hour and glue costs $5 per gallon, draw CCC's budget line for a total expenditure of $100,000. In this same diagram, sketch a production indifference curve indicating that CCC can produce no more than 1,000 containers with this expenditure.

2. With respect to Review Question 1, suppose that wages rise to $20 per hour and glue prices rise to $6 per gallon. How are CCC's optimal input proportions likely to change? (Use a diagram to explain your answer.)

3. What happens to the expansion path of the firm in Review Question 2?

Business is a good game. . . . You keep score with money.

Nolan Bushnell, founder of Atari
(an early video game maker)

OUTPUT, PRICE, AND PROFIT: THE IMPORTANCE OF MARGINAL ANALYSIS

Suppose you become president of a firm that makes video games. One of your most critical decisions will be how many video games to produce and at what price to offer them for sale. The owners of the company want to make as much profit as possible. This chapter explores how to make logical decisions that help to attain that goal.

With this chapter, we cap off our discussion of the fundamental building blocks of microeconomics. Chapters 6 and 7 dealt with the behavior of consumers, the first of the two main protagonists. Then Chapter 8 introduced the other leading member of the cast: the firm. The firm's two main roles are, first, to produce its product efficiently and, second, to sell it at a profit. The previous chapter described production decisions. Now we turn to the selling decisions.

An **optimal decision** is one which, among all the decisions that are actually possible, is best for the decision maker. For example, if profit is the sole objective of some firm, the price that makes the firm's profit as large as possible is optimal for that company.

Throughout Part II, we have described how firms and consumers can make **optimal decisions,** meaning that their decisions go as far as possible, given the circumstances, to promote the consumer's and producer's goals. In this chapter, we will continue to assume that business firms seek primarily to maximize total profit, just as we assumed that consumers maximize utility.

As in the previous three chapters, marginal analysis helps us to determine what constitutes an optimal decision. Because that method of analysis is so useful, this chapter summarizes and generalizes what we have learned about the methods of marginal analysis, showing also how this analysis applies in many other situations in which optimality is an issue.

Marginal analysis leads to some surprising conclusions that show how misleading unaided "common sense" can sometimes be. Here is an example. Suppose a firm suffers a sharp increase in its rent or some other fixed cost. How should the firm react? Some would argue that the firm should raise product prices to cover the higher rent; others would argue that it should cut its price in order to increase its sales enough to pay the higher rent. We will see in this chapter that both of these answers are incorrect! A profit-maximizing firm faced with a rent increase should neither raise nor lower its price.

Two Puzzles

Price and output decisions can sometimes perplex even the most experienced business people, as the following real-life illustrations show.[1] At the end of the chapter, we will see how marginal analysis helped solve the problems.

Case 1: Making Profits by Selling Below Costs   Ordinary good sense is not necessarily the best guide in business decisions. Our first illustrative case indicates that it is possible for a firm to make a profit by selling at a price that is apparently below its cost!

In a recent legal battle between two manufacturers of pocket calculators, Company B accused Company A of selling 10 million sophisticated calculators at a price of $12, which A allegedly knew was too low to cover costs. B claimed that A was doing this only to drive B out of business. At first, Company A's records, as revealed to the court, appeared to confirm B's accusations. The cost of materials, labor, advertising, and other direct costs of the calculator came to $10.30 per calculator. Company A's accountants also assigned to this product its share of the company's annual expenditure on overhead—such items as general administration, research, and the like—which amounted to $4.25 per calculator.

The $12 price clearly did not cover the $14.55 cost attributed to each calculator. Yet economists representing Company A were able to convince the court that

---

[1] The following cases are disguised to protect the confidentiality of the firms involved.

manufacturing the calculator was a profitable activity for Company A, so there was no basis on which to conclude that its only purpose was to destroy B. At the end of the chapter, we will explain just how this was possible.

Case 2: Pricing a Six-Pack of Soda Managers at one of America's largest soft drink manufacturers became concerned when a rival company introduced a cheaper substitute for one of their leading products. As a result, some of the market leader's managers advocated reducing the price of a six-pack from $1.50 to $1.35. This stimulated a heated debate. Everyone agreed to the price cut if it could be shown to be unlikely to reduce the company's profits. Although some of the managers maintained that the cut made sense because of the additional sales it would stimulate, others held that the price cut would hurt the company by slashing profit per unit of output. The company had reliable information about costs, but didn't know much about the shape of its demand curve. At this point a group of consultants (including one of the authors of this book) was called in to offer suggestions. We will see how economic analysis helped them to solve the problem, even though the vital demand elasticity figures were unavailable.

■ PRICE AND QUANTITY: ONE DECISION, NOT TWO

When your company introduces a new line of video games, the marketing department has to decide what price to charge and the number of games to produce. These crucial decisions strongly influence the firm's labor requirements, consumer response to the product, and, indeed, the company's future success.

When the firm selects a *price* and a *quantity* of output that maximize profits, it seems that it must choose two numbers. In fact, however, the firm can pick only one. Once it has selected the *price*, the *quantity* it can sell is up to consumers. Alternatively, the firm may decide how many units it would like to sell, but then the market will determine the *price* at which this quantity can be sold. Clearly, the firm's dilemma explicitly illustrates the powerful role that consumers play in the market. Management gets two numbers by making only one decision because the firm's demand curve tells it, for any quantity it may decide to market, the highest possible price its product can bring.

To illustrate, we return to Chapter 8's hog-farming example. Naomi's Natural Farm sells organic pork to local restaurants and food markets, and Naomi is trying to figure out how to make more money on her hog operation. Now, whether or not she is aware of it, Naomi faces a demand curve for her hogs, *DD* in Figure 9–1. The curve shows the quantity demanded at each price. For example, the

FIGURE 9–1

Demand Curve for Naomi's Natural Hogs

curve shows that at a price of $222 per hog (point *e*), Naomi's customers will demand five hogs. If Naomi gets greedy and tries to charge the high price of $250 per hog (point *a* on the curve), she can sell only one hog. On the other hand, if she wants to sell eight hogs, she can find the required number of customers only by offering the hogs at the lower price of $201 each (point *h*). In summary:

> **Each point on the demand curve represents a price-quantity pair. The firm can pick any such pair. But it can never pick the price corresponding to one point on the demand curve and the quantity corresponding to another point, because such an output could not be sold at the selected price.**

Throughout this chapter, then, we will not discuss price and output decisions separately, for they are actually two different aspects of the same decision. To analyze this decision, we will make a strong assumption about the behavior of business firms—the assumption that firms strive for the largest possible total profit to the exclusion of any other goal. Although not literally correct, this seems to be a useful simplification of a much more complex reality. As with other chapters, we will present this theoretical and intentionally simplified case first, and then we will let some of those "other things being equal" variables change.

We will therefore assume throughout this chapter (and for most of the book) that the firm has only one objective. It wants to make its total profit as large as possible. Our analytic strategy will seek to determine what output level (or price) achieves this goal. But you should keep in mind that many of our results depend on this simplifying assumption, so the conclusions will not apply to every case. Our decision to base the analysis on the profit-maximizing assumption gives us sharper insights, but we pay with some loss of realism.

■ TOTAL PROFIT: KEEP YOUR EYE ON THE GOAL

The **total profit** of a firm is its net earnings during some period of time. It is equal to the total amount of money the firm gets from sales of its products (the firm's total revenue) minus the total amount that it spends to make and market those products (total cost).

How Much Does It Really Cost?

Economic profit equals net earnings, in the accountants sense, minus the *opportunity* costs of capital and of any other inputs supplied by the firm's owners.

Total profit, then, is the firm's goal. By definition, total profit is the difference between what the company earns in the form of sales revenue and what it pays out in the form of costs:

$$\text{Total profit} = \text{Total revenue} - \text{Total costs}$$

OPPORTUNITY COST   Total profit defined in this way is called **economic profit** to distinguish it from an accountant's definition of profit. The two concepts of profit differ because an economist's total cost counts the *opportunity* cost of any capital, labor, or other inputs supplied by the firm's owner. For example, let's say that Alex, who owns a small business, earns just enough to pay him the money that his labor and capital could have earned if they had been sold to others (say, $60,000 per year). Then, as we saw in Chapter 4, economists say that he is earning zero economic profit. (Alex is just covering all his costs, including his opportunity costs.) In contrast, most accountants would say his profit is $60,000, referring to the difference between his gross receipts and his gross costs.

To see how total profit depends on output, we must study how the two components of total profit, total revenue (TR) and total cost (TC), behave when output changes. It should be obvious that both total revenue and total cost depend on the output-price combination the firm selects; we study these relationships next.

TOTAL, AVERAGE, AND MARGINAL REVENUE

We can calculate total revenue directly from the demand curve because, by definition, it is the product of price times the quantity that consumers will buy at that price:

$$TR = P \times Q$$

Table 9–1 shows how we derive the total revenue schedule from the demand schedule for Naomi's natural hogs. The first two columns simply express Figure

TABLE 9-1

Demand for Naomi's Natural Hogs, Her Total Revenue Schedule, and Her Marginal Revenue Schedule

Number of Hogs per Season	Price = Average Revenue per Hog	Total Revenue per Season	Marginal Revenue per Hog
0	—	$ 0	
			$250
1	$250	250	
			236
2	243	486	
			222
3	236	708	
			208
4	229	916	
			194
5	222	1,110	
			180
6	215	1,290	
			166
7	208	1,456	
			152
8	201	1,608	
			138
9	194	1,746	
			104
10	185	1,850	

Total Revenue Curve for Naomi's Natural Hogs

FIGURE 9-2

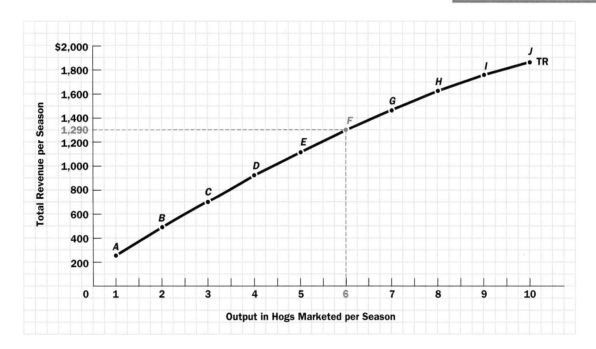

9–1's demand curve in tabular form. The third column gives, for each quantity, the product of price times quantity. For example, if Naomi sells seven hogs at a price of $208 per hog, her seasonal sales revenue will be 7 hogs × $208 per hog = $1,456.

Figure 9–2 displays Naomi's total revenue schedule in graphical form as the black TR curve. This graph shows precisely the same information as the demand curve in Figure 9–1, but in a somewhat different form. For example, point *f* on the demand curve in Figure 9–1, which shows a price-quantity combination of *P* = $215 per hog and *Q* = 6 hogs per season, appears as point *F* in Figure 9–2 as a total revenue of $1,290 per season ($215 per hog times 6 hogs). Similarly, each point on the TR curve in Figure 9–2 corresponds to the similarly labeled point in Figure 9–1.

We can speak of the relationship between the demand curve and the TR curve in a slightly different and more useful way. Because the product price is the revenue

FIGURE 9-3

Cost Curves for Naomi's Natural Hogs

(a) Total Cost

(b) Average Cost

(c) Marginal Cost

NOTE: Output is in hogs per season.

per unit that the firm receives, we can view the demand curve as an **average revenue (AR)** curve. Average revenue and total revenue (TR) are related to one another in a simple way.[2] Specifically:

$$AR = TR/Q = P \times Q/Q = P$$

Therefore, average revenue and price are two names for the same thing. The reason should be clear. If a supermarket sells candy bars at the same price, say, $1, to each and every customer who wants one, then the average revenue that the store derives from the sale of all these candy bars must also be $1.

Finally, the last column of Table 9–1 shows the **marginal revenue (MR)** for each level of output. Marginal revenue provides us with an analytic tool that we will explain presently. This concept (analogous to marginal utility and marginal cost) refers to the addition to total revenue that results from raising output by one unit. Thus, in Table 9–1, we see that when output rises from two to three hogs, total revenue goes up from $486 to $708, so marginal revenue is $708 minus $486, or $222.

TOTAL, AVERAGE, AND MARGINAL COST

The revenue side is, of course, only half of the firm's profit picture. We must turn to the cost side for the other half. As we saw in the previous chapter, average cost (AC) and marginal cost (MC) are obtained directly from total cost (TC) in exactly the same way that average and marginal revenue were calculated from total revenue.

Figure 9–3 plots the numbers in Table 9–2 and thus shows the total, average, and marginal cost curves for the hog operation. As we learned in the previous chapter, the shapes of the curves depicted here are considered typical. The shapes mean that, in any given industry, there is some size of firm that is most efficient in producing the output. Smaller enterprises lose any advantages that derive from a large volume of production, and so their average cost (the cost per unit of output) will be greater than that of a firm operating at the most efficient size of output. Similarly, firms that are too large will suffer from difficulties of supervision and coordination, and perhaps from bureaucratic controls, so that their costs per unit of output will also be higher than those of a firm of the most efficient size.

MAXIMIZATION OF TOTAL PROFIT

We now have all the tools we need to answer our central question: What combination of output and price will yield the largest possible total profit? To study how total profit depends on output, we bring together in Table 9–3 the total revenue and total cost schedules from the two previous tables. The last column in Table 9–3—called, appropriately enough, total profit—is just the difference between total revenue and total cost at each level of output.

---

[2] See the appendix to this chapter for a general discussion of the relationship between totals and averages.

Naomi's Total, Average, and Marginal Costs

TABLE 9-2

Hogs per Season	Total Cost per Season	Marginal Cost per Hog	Average Cost per Hog
0	$ 0		—
		$ 300	
1	300		$300
		159	
2	459		229
		123	
3	582		194
		123	
4	705		176
		141	
5	847		169
		159	
6	1,006		168
		180	
7	1,185		169
		226	
8	1,411		176
		335	
9	1,746		194
		459	
10	2,205		220

NOTE: Numbers in the table are rounded for simplicity, and thus may not add up exactly.

The **average revenue (AR)** is total revenue (TR) divided by quantity.

Marginal revenue, often abbreviated MR, is the addition to total revenue resulting from the addition of one unit to total output. Geometrically, marginal revenue is the slope of the total revenue curve. Its formula is $MR_1 = TR_1 - TR_0$, and so on.

Because we assume that Naomi's objective is to maximize profits, it is simple enough to determine the level of production she will choose. By producing and selling six hogs per season, Naomi's hog operation earns the highest level of profits it is capable of earning—$285 per season. Any higher or lower rate of production would lead to lower profits. For example, profits would drop to $271 if output were increased to seven hogs. If Naomi were to make the mistake of producing 10 hogs per season, she would actually suffer a net loss.

MARGINAL ANALYSIS You will likely have noticed a recurrent theme in this chapter, which is a cornerstone of any economic analysis and thus one of our *Ideas for Beyond the Final Exam.* In any decision about whether to expand an activity, it is always the marginal cost and marginal benefit that are the relevant factors. A calculation based on average figures is likely to lead the decision maker to miss all sorts of opportunities, some of them critical.

More generally, if one wants to make optimal decisions, marginal analysis should be used in the planning calculations. This is true whether the decision applies to a business firm seeking to maximize total profit or minimize the cost of the output it has selected, to a consumer trying to maximize utility, or to a less developed country striving to maximize per-capita output. It applies as much to decisions on input

The Importance of Thinking at the Margin

Total Revenues, Costs, and Profit for Naomi's Natural Hogs

TABLE 9-3

Hogs per Season	Total Revenue (TR)	Total Cost (TC)	Total Profit (TP)
0	$ 0	$ 0	$ 0
1	250	300	−50
2	486	458	28
3	708	582	126
4	916	705	211
5	1,110	846	264
6	1,290	1,005	285
7	1,456	1,185	271
8	1,608	1,410	198
9	1,746	1,746	0
10	1,850	2,204	−354

NOTE: Numbers are rounded for simplicity, and thus may not match some numbers in Table 9–2.

proportions and advertising as to decisions about output levels and prices. Indeed, this is such a general principle of economics that it is one of the *Ideas for Beyond the Final Exam.*

FIGURE 9-4

Profit Maximization: A Graphical Interpretation

PROFIT MAXIMIZATION: A GRAPHICAL INTERPRETATION

We can present the same information on a graph. In Panel (a) of Figure 9–4, we bring together into a single diagram the relevant portion of the total revenue curve from Figure 9–2 and the total cost curve from Figure 9–3. Total profit, which is the difference between total revenue and total cost, appears in the diagram as the vertical distance between the TR and TC curves. For example, when output is four units, total revenue is $916 (point *A*), total cost is $705 (point *B*), and total profit is the distance between points *A* and *B*, or $211.

In this graphical view of the problem, Naomi wants to maximize total profit, which is the vertical distance between the TR and TC curves. Panel (b) of Figure 9–4 shows the curve of total profit—that is, TR minus TC. We see that it reaches its maximum value, about $285, at an output level of six units per week. This is the same conclusion we reached by looking at Table 9–3.

The total profit curve in Figure 9–4(b) is shaped like a hill. Though such a shape is not inevitable, we expect a hill shape to be typical for the following reason: if a firm produces nothing, it certainly earns no profit. At the other extreme, a firm can produce so much output that it swamps the market, forcing price down so low that it loses money. Only at intermediate levels of output—something between zero and the amount that floods the market—will the company earn a positive profit. Conse-

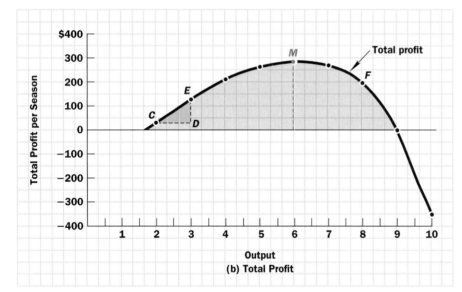

NOTE: Output is in hogs per season.

quently, the total profit curve will rise from zero (or negative) levels at a very small output to positive levels at intermediate outputs; finally, it will fall to negative levels when output gets too large.

■ MARGINAL ANALYSIS AND MAXIMIZATION OF TOTAL PROFIT

We see from Figure 9–4 and Table 9–3 that many levels of output may yield a positive profit, but the firm is not aiming for just any level of profit. It wants the largest possible profit. If management knew the exact shape of its profit hill, that is, if it had Table 9–3, choosing the optimal level of output would be a simple task indeed.

It would only have to locate the point, such as *M* in Figure 9–4(b), that defined the top of its profit hill. However, management rarely if ever has so much information, so a different technique for finding the optimum is required. That technique is marginal analysis—the same set of tools we used to analyze the firm's input purchase decisions in Chapter 8 and the consumer's buying decisions in Chapters 6 and 7.

This time we will use a concept known as **marginal profit** to solve Naomi's problem. Referring back to Table 9–3, we see that an increase in Naomi's output from two to three hogs would raise total profit from $28 to $126; that is, it would generate $98 in additional profit. We call this the marginal profit resulting from the addition of the third unit. Similarly, marginal profit from the seventh unit would be:

Marginal profit is the addition to total profit resulting from one more unit of output.

Total profit from 7 units − Total profit from 6 units = $271 − $285 = −$14.

The marginal rule for finding the optimal level of output is easy to understand:

If the marginal profit from increasing output by one unit is positive, then output should be increased. If the marginal profit from increasing output by one unit is negative, then output should be decreased. Thus, an output level can maximize total profit only if marginal profit is neither positive nor negative, that is, if it equals zero at that output.

On Naomi's Natural Farm, the marginal profit from the third unit of output (a third hog) is $98. This means that going from the second to the third unit adds $98 to profit, so it pays to produce the third unit. But marginal profit from the seventh unit is $271 − $285, or −$14, so the farm should not produce the seventh hog because that would reduce total profit by $14. Only where marginal profit is neither positive nor negative (as is approximately true for the sixth unit of output) can total profit be as big as possible, because neither increasing nor reducing output can add to total profit.

The profit hill in Figure 9–4(b) is a graphical representation of the condition that marginal profit should be as close to zero as possible. Marginal profit is defined as the additional profit that accrues to the firm when output rises by one unit. So when output is increased, say, from two units to three units, the distance *CD* in Figure 9–4(b), total profit rises by $98 (the distance *DE*) and marginal profit is therefore *DE/CD* (see the blue triangle in the graph). This is precisely the definition of the slope of the total profit curve between points *C* and *E*. In general:

Marginal profit is the slope of the total profit curve.

With this geometric interpretation in hand, we can easily understand the logic of the marginal profit rule. At a point such as *C*, where the total profit curve is rising, marginal profit (which equals slope) is positive. Profit cannot be maximal at such a point, because we can increase profits by moving farther to the right. A firm that decided to stick to point *C* would be wasting the opportunity to increase profits by increasing output. Similarly, the firm cannot be maximizing profits at a point like *F*, where the slope of the curve is negative, because there marginal profit (which, again,

"Basic economics—sometimes the parts are worth more than the whole."

equals slope) is negative. If it finds itself at a point like *F,* the firm can raise its profit by decreasing its output.

Only at a point such as *M,* where the total profit curve is neither rising nor falling, can the firm possibly be at the top of the profit hill rather than on one of the sides of the hill. Point *M* is precisely where the slope of the curve—and hence the marginal profit—is zero, or as near as possible to zero. Thus:

An output decision cannot be optimal unless the corresponding marginal profit is zero.

The firm is not interested in marginal profit for its own sake, but rather for what it implies about total profit. Marginal profit is like the needle on the temperature gauge of a car: the needle itself is of no concern to anyone, but failure to watch it can result in serious consequences.

One common misunderstanding of marginal analysis is the idea that it seems foolish to go to a point where marginal profit is zero. "Isn't it better to earn a positive marginal profit?" This notion springs from a confusion between the quantity one is seeking to maximize (total profit) and the gauge that indicates whether such a maximum has in fact been attained (marginal profit). Of course, it is better to have a positive total profit than a zero total profit. In contrast, a zero value on the marginal profit gauge merely indicates that all is well, that total profit is at its maximum.

MARGINAL REVENUE AND MARGINAL COST: GUIDES TO OPTIMIZATION

An alternative version of the marginal analysis of profit maximization can be derived from the cost and revenue components of profit. For this purpose, refer back to Figure 9–4, where we used total revenue (TR) and total cost (TC) curves to construct the profit hill. There is another way of finding the profit-maximizing solution.

We want to maximize the firm's profit, which is measured by the vertical distance between the TR and TC curves. This distance, we see, is not maximal at an output level such as two units, because there the two curves are growing farther apart. If we move farther to the right, the vertical distance between them (which is total profit) will increase. Conversely, we have not maximized the vertical distance between TR and TC at an output level such as eight units, because there the two curves are coming closer together. We can add to profit by moving farther to the left (reducing output). The conclusion from the graph, then, is that total profit—the vertical distance between TR and TC—is maximized only when the two curves are neither growing farther apart nor coming closer together, that is, when their slopes are equal.

Marginal revenue and marginal cost curves, which we learned about earlier in the chapter, will help us understand this concept better. For precisely the same reason that marginal profit is the slope of the total profit curve, marginal revenue is the slope of the total revenue curve, because it represents the increase in total revenue resulting from the sale of one additional unit. Again, for the same reason, marginal cost is equal to the slope of the total cost curve. This interpretation of marginal revenue and marginal cost, respectively, as the slopes of the total revenue and total cost curves permits us to restate the geometric conclusion we have just reached in an economically significant way:

Profit can be maximized only at an output level at which marginal revenue is (approximately) equal to marginal cost. In symbols:

$$MR = MC$$

The logic of the MR = MC rule for profit maximization is straightforward.[3] When MR is not equal to MC, profits cannot possibly be maximized because the

---

[3] You may have surmised by now that just as Total profit = Total revenue − Total cost, it must be true that Marginal profit = Marginal revenue − Marginal cost. This is, in fact, correct. It also shows that when Marginal profit = 0, we must have MR = MC.

firm can increase its profits either by raising its output or by reducing it. For example, if MR = \$236 and MC = \$159, an additional unit of output adds \$236 to revenues but only \$159 to costs. Hence, the firm can increase its net profit by \$77 by producing and selling one more unit. Similarly, if MC exceeds MR, say, MR = \$152 and MC = \$226, then the firm loses \$74 on its marginal unit, so it can add \$74 to its profit by reducing output by one unit. Only when MR = MC (or comes as close as possible to equaling MC), is it impossible for the firm to add to its profit by changing its output level.

Table 9–4 reproduces marginal revenue and marginal cost data for Naomi's Natural Farm from Tables 9–1 and 9–2. The table shows, as must be true, that the MR = MC rule leads us to the same conclusion as Figure 9–4 and Table 9–3. If she wants to maximize her profits, Naomi should produce and sell six hogs per season. The marginal revenue of the sixth hog is \$180 (\$1,290 from the sale of six hogs less \$1,110 from selling five) whereas the marginal cost is only \$159 (\$1,006 − \$847). Therefore, the firm should produce the sixth unit. The seventh hog, however, brings in only \$166 in marginal revenue while its marginal cost is \$180—clearly a losing proposition. Only at six units of output does MR come closest to equaling MC (MR equals MC *exactly* at an output level of about 6.5 hogs, but in the real world Naomi can't produce half a hog!).

Because the graphs of marginal analysis will prove so useful in later chapters, Figure 9–5(a) shows the MR = MC condition for profit maximization graphically. The black curve labeled MR in the figure is the marginal revenue schedule from Table 9–4. The red curve labeled MC is the marginal cost schedule. They intersect at point *E*, which is therefore the point where marginal revenue and marginal cost are equal. The optimal output for Naomi is six units.[4] Figures 9–5(b) and 9–5(c), respectively, are reproductions of the TR and TC curves from the upper panel of Figure 9–4 and the total profit curve from the lower panel of that figure. Note how MC and MR intersect near the same output at which the distance of TR above TC is greatest, which is also the output at which the profit hill reaches its peak.

FINDING THE OPTIMAL PRICE FROM OPTIMAL OUTPUT

At the start of this chapter, we set two goals: to determine the profit-maximizing output and also the profit-maximizing price. So far, we have found the profit-maximizing output, the output level at which MR = (approximately) MC (six hogs per season in our example). That leaves us with the task of determining the profit-maximizing price.

Fortunately, this requires only one more easy step. As we said at the beginning of the chapter, once the firm has selected the output it wants to produce and sell, the demand curve determines the price it must charge to induce consumers to buy that amount of product. Consequently, if we know that the profit-maximizing output is six hogs, the demand curve in Figure 9–1 tells us what price Naomi must charge to sell that profit-maximizing output. To sell an average of six hogs per season, she must price them at \$215 (point *f*). The demand curve tells us that this is the only price at which this quantity will be demanded by customers.

> Once the profit-maximizing output quantity has been determined with the help of the MR = MC rule, it is easy to find the profit-maximizing price with the help of the demand curve. Just use that curve to find out at what price the optimal quantity will be demanded.

---

[4] We must note one important qualification. Sometimes marginal revenue and marginal cost curves do not have the nice shapes depicted in Figure 9–5(a), and they may intersect more than once. In such cases, although it remains true that MR = MC at the output level that maximizes profits, there may be other output levels at which MR is also equal to MC but at which profits are not maximized.

TABLE 9–4

Naomi's Marginal Revenue and Marginal Cost

Hogs per Season	Marginal Revenue	Marginal Cost
0	—	—
1	\$250	\$300
2	236	159
3	222	124
4	208	124
5	194	141
6	180	159
7	166	180
8	152	226
9	138	335
10	104	459

NOTE: Marginal revenue and marginal costs are per hog, per season.

Profit Maximization: Another Graphical Interpretation

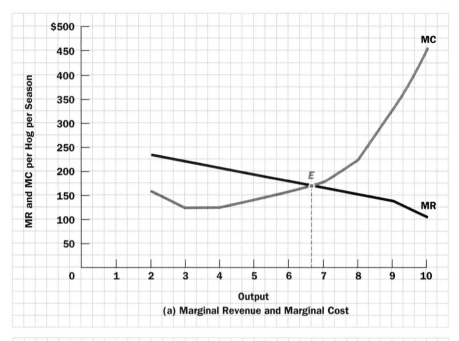

(a) Marginal Revenue and Marginal Cost

(b) Total Revenue, Total Cost

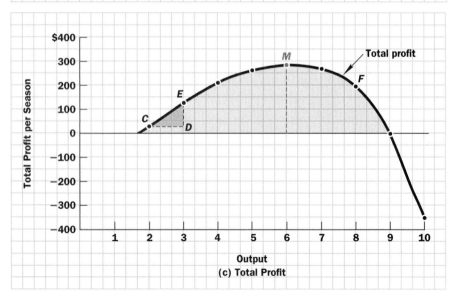

(c) Total Profit

NOTE: Output is in hogs per season.

● **POLICY DEBATE** ▌ **PROFIT AND THE NEW MARKET ECONOMIES**

The collapse of communism after its catastrophic failure to produce economic abundance has led the nations of eastern Europe and elsewhere to turn to the market mechanism. They hope that the market will soon bring them the sort of prosperity achieved by the industrialized countries.

The market, as we know, is driven by the profit motive, and in a free market, profits are not determined by a government agency but by demand and cost conditions, as described by the demand and cost curves. Many citizens of these new market economies are appalled by the sizes of the profits that the free market affords to successful businesspeople, and they are upset by the greed that these entrepreneurs display. There are pressures to put limits on these profits.

The same thing has happened in Great Britain and elsewhere as firms formerly owned by the government have been sold to private individuals and returned to the market. In Britain, a number of the privatized firms were initially monopolies, and the government has chosen to protect consumers by putting ceilings on prices but not on profits in order to provide the firms with appropriate incentives. Yet when some of these firms proved to be quite profitable, the British government agencies reduced the price ceilings

in order to cut those profits, a move that was attacked sharply not only by the firms themselves but also by some British economists. The debate in the United Kingdom and elsewhere amounts to this: Should severe limits be placed on profits as a matter of fairness and to improve the ethical climate of society, or should this be avoided because ceilings on profits undermine the incentives for business success and therefore prevent the market mechanism from delivering the economic abundance of which it is capable?

GENERALIZATION: THE LOGIC OF MARGINAL ANALYSIS AND MAXIMIZATION

The logic of marginal analysis of profit maximization that we have just studied can be generalized, because essentially the same argument was already used in Chapters 6 and 8 and it will recur in a number of the chapters that follow. To avoid having to master the argument each time all over again, it is useful to see how it can be applied in problems other than the determination of the firm's profit-maximizing output.

The general issue is this: Decision makers often are faced with the problem of selecting the magnitude of some variable, such as how much to spend on advertising, or how many bananas to buy, or how many school buildings to construct. Each of these acts brings benefits, so that the larger the number selected by the decision maker, the larger the total benefits that will be derived. But, unfortunately, as larger numbers are selected, the associated costs also grow. The problem is to take the trade-off properly into account and calculate at what point the net gain—the difference between the total benefit and the total cost—will be greatest. Thus, we have the following general principle:

If a decision is to be made about the quantity of some variable, then to maximize:

Net benefit = Total benefit − Total cost

the decision maker must select a value of the variable at which:

Marginal benefit = (approximately) Marginal cost

For example, if a community were to determine that the marginal benefit from building an additional school was greater than the cost of an additional school, it would clearly be better off if it built another school. On the other hand, if it were building so many schools that the marginal benefit was less than the marginal cost, it would be better off with a more limited construction program. Only if the marginal benefit and cost are as close as possible to being equal will the community have the optimal number of schools.

We will apply this same concept in later chapters. Again and again, we analyze a quantitative decision that brings together both benefits and costs and we always conclude that the optimal decision occurs at the point where the marginal benefit equals the marginal cost. The logic is the same whether we are considering the net gains to a firm, to a consumer, or to society as a whole.

APPLICATION: FIXED COST AND THE PROFIT-MAXIMIZING PRICE

We can now use our analytic framework to offer a surprising insight. Suppose there is a rise in the firm's fixed cost; say, that the property taxes on Naomi's Natural Farm double. What will happen to the profit-maximizing price and output? Should she raise her price to cover the increased cost, or should she produce a larger output even if that requires a drop in price? The answer is surprising: Neither!

> When a firm's fixed cost increases, its profit-maximizing price and output remain completely unchanged, so long as it pays the firm to stay in business.

In other words, there is nothing that the firm's management can do to offset the effect of the rise in fixed cost. Management must just put up with it. This is surely a case where common sense is not a reliable guide to the right decision.

Why is this so? Remember that, by definition, a fixed cost does not change when output changes. The increase in Naomi's fixed costs is the same whether business is slow or booming, whether production is two hogs or 200. This is illustrated in Table 9–5, which also reproduces Naomi's total profits from Table 9–3. The third column of the table shows that total fixed cost has risen from zero to $100 per season. As a result, total profit is $100 less than it would have been otherwise—no matter what the firm's output. For example, when output is four units, we see that total profit falls from $211 (second column) to $111 (last column).

Now, because profit is reduced by the same amount at every output level, whatever output was most profitable before the increase in fixed costs must still be

| TABLE 9-5 | **Total Profit before and after a Rise in Fixed Cost** |

Hog Output per Season	Total Profit without Fixed Costs	Total Fixed Costs per Season	Total Profit with Fixed Costs
0	$ 0	$100	$−100
1	−50	100	−150
2	28	100	−72
3	126	100	26
4	211	100	111
5	264	100	164
6	285	100	185
7	271	100	171
8	198	100	98
9	0	100	−100
10	−354	100	−454

most profitable. In Table 9–5, we see that $185 is the largest entry in the last column, which shows profits after the rise in fixed cost. This highest possible profit is attained, as it was before, when output is at six units. In other words, the firm's profit-maximizing price and quantity will remain exactly as they were before.

All of this is shown in Figure 9–6, which displays the firm's total profit hill before and after the rise in fixed cost (reproducing Naomi's initial profit hill from Figure 9–4). We see that the cost increase simply moves the profit hill straight downward by $100, so the highest point on the hill is just lowered from point *M* to point *N*. But the top of the hill is shifted neither toward the left nor toward the right. It remains at the six-hog output level, just as Table 9–5 indicated.

FIGURE 9-6

Fixed Cost Does Not Affect Profit-Maximizing Output

Puzzle Resolved: Marginal Analysis in Real Decision Problems

We can now put the marginal analysis of profit determination to work to unravel the puzzles with which we began this chapter. These are both examples drawn from reality, and reality never works as neatly as a textbook illustration. In particular, neither example involves a mechanical application of the MR = MC rule. However, as these cases show, the underlying reasoning does shed useful light on real problems.

Case 1: The "Unprofitable" Calculator

Our first case study concerned a firm that was apparently losing money on calculator sales because its $12 price was less than the $14.55 average cost that the company's accountants assigned to the product. This $14.55 figure included $10.30 of costs caused directly by manufacture and marketing of the calculators plus a $4.25 per-calculator share of the company's overall general expenses ("overhead"). Accused of deliberately selling below cost in order to drive a competitor out of business, the company turned to marginal analysis to show that this was not true. The calculators were indeed a profitable line of business.

To demonstrate this fact, the company's witness explained that if the sales were really unprofitable, the company would have been able to raise its net earnings by *ceasing* production and sale of the calculators. A moment's consideration shows, however, that the opposite would have happened: profits would have decreased if the company gave up its annual sale of 10 million calculators.

The company's revenues would have been reduced by $12 for each of the 10 million units sold—a (marginal) revenue reduction of $120 million. But how much cost would it have saved? The answer is that the cost outlay actually caused by the production of each calculator was only the $10.30 in direct cost. The company president would not have been fired if the product were discontinued, and general expenditures on new product research probably would even have increased. Thus, none of the company's overhead would have been saved by ending calculator production. Rather, the (marginal) cost saving would have been the direct cost of $10.30 per calculator times the 10 million calculator output—a total cost saving of $103 million.

Thus, elimination of the product would have reduced total profit by $17 million per year—the $103 million cost saving minus the $120 million in revenue forgone. In other words, continued production of the calculators was not causing losses; on the contrary, it was contributing $17 million in profits every year. The court concluded that this reasoning was correct and used this conclusion in its decision.

This case illustrates a point that is encountered frequently. The calculator producer was selling its product at a price that appeared not to cover costs but really did. The same sort of issue frequently faces a firm considering the introduction of a new product or the opening of a new branch office. In many such cases, the new operation may not cover average costs, as measured by standard accounting methods. Yet to follow the apparent implications of those cost figures would amount to throwing away a valuable opportunity to add to the net earnings of the firm (because added [or marginal] revenues exceed added [or marginal] costs) and, perhaps, to contribute to the welfare of the economy. Only marginal analysis can reveal whether the contemplated action is really worthwhile.

Case 2: The Soda-Pricing Problem   Our second problem dealt with a firm's choice between keeping the price of a brand of soda at $1.50 per six-pack or reducing it to $1.35 when a competitor entered the market. The trouble was that to know what to do, the firm needed to know its demand curve (and hence its marginal revenue curve). However, the firm did not have enough data to determine the shape of its demand curve. How, then, could a rational decision be made?

As we indicated, the debate among the firm's managers finally reached agreement on one point: the price should be cut if, as a result, profits were not likely to decline, that is, if marginal profit were not negative. Fortunately, the firm was able to obtain the data needed to determine whether marginal profit was positive. Initial annual sales were 10 million units, and the firm's engineers maintained emphatically that marginal costs were very close to constant at $1.20 per six-pack over the output range in question. Instead of trying to determine the actual increase in sales that would result from the price cut, the team of consultants decided to try to determine the minimum increase in quantity demanded that would be required to avoid a decrease in profits.

It was clear that, if profits were not to decline, the firm needed additional revenue at least as great as the additional cost of supplying the added volume. That is, MR had to exceed MC. The consultants knew that total revenues at the initial price of $1.50 per six-pack were $15 million ($1.50 per unit times 10 million units). Letting Q represent the (unknown) quantity of six-packs that would be sold at the proposed new price of $1.35, the economists compared the added revenue with the added cost of providing the Q new units. Because MC was constant at $1.20 per unit, the added cost amounted to:

$$\text{Added cost} = \$1.20 \times (Q - 10 \text{ million})$$

This was to be compared with the added revenue:

$$\text{Added revenue} = \text{New revenue} - \text{Old revenue} = \$1.35Q - \$15 \text{ million}$$

No loss would result from the price change if the added revenue was greater than or equal to the added cost. The minimum Q necessary to avoid a loss therefore was that at which added revenue equaled added cost, or:

$$1.35Q - 15 \text{ million} = 1.2Q - 12 \text{ million}$$

or:

$$0.15Q = 3 \text{ million}$$

This would be true if, and only if, Q, the quantity sold at the lower price, would be:

$$Q = 20 \text{ million units.}$$

In other words, this calculation showed that the firm could break even from the 15-cent price reduction only if the quantity of its product demanded rose at least 100 percent (from 10 million to 20 million units). Because past experience indicated that such a rise in quantity demanded was hardly possible, the price reduction proposal was quickly abandoned. Thus, the logic of the MR = MC rule, plus a little ingenuity, enabled the consultants to deal with a problem that at first seemed baffling—even though they had no estimate of marginal revenue.

CONCLUSION: THE FUNDAMENTAL ROLE OF MARGINAL ANALYSIS

We saw in Chapter 8 how marginal analysis helps us to understand the firm's input choices. Similarly, in Chapters 6 and 7, it cast indispensable light on the consumer's purchase decisions. In this chapter, it enabled us to analyze output and pricing decisions. The logic of marginal analysis applies not only to economic decisions by consumers and firms but also to those of governments, universities, hospitals, and other organizations. In short, the analysis applies to any individual or group that must make optimal choices about the use of scarce resources. Thus, one of the most important conclusions that can be drawn from this chapter, a conclusion brought out vividly by the two examples we have just discussed, is the importance of thinking "at the margin"—one of our *Ideas for Beyond the Final Exam*.

The Importance of Thinking at the Margin

A real-life example far removed from profit maximization will illustrate how marginal criteria are useful in decision making. For some years before women were admitted to Princeton University (and to several other colleges), administrators cited the cost of the proposed admission of women as a major obstacle. They had decided in advance that any women coming to the university would constitute a net addition to the student body because, for a variety of reasons involving relations with alumni and other groups, it was not feasible to reduce the number of male students. Presumably on the basis of a calculation of average cost, some critics spoke of cost figures as high as $80 million.

To economists it was clear, however, that the relevant figure was the *marginal cost*, the addition to total cost that would result from the admission of the additional students. The women students would, of course, bring to Princeton additional tuition fees (marginal revenues). If these fees were just sufficient to cover the amount that they would add to costs, the admission of the women would leave the university's financial picture unaffected.

A careful calculation showed that the admission of women would add far less to the university's financial problems than the average cost figures indicated. One reason was that women's course preferences then were characteristically different from men's, and hence women frequently selected courses that were undersubscribed in exclusively male institutions. Therefore, the admission of 1,000 women to a formerly all-male institution could be expected to require fewer additional classes than if 1,000 more men had been admitted.[5] More important, it was found that a number of classroom buildings were underutilized. The cost of operating these buildings was nearly fixed—their total utilization cost would be changed only slightly by the influx of women. The marginal cost for classroom space was therefore almost zero and certainly well below the average cost (the cost per student).

For all of these reasons, it turned out that the relevant marginal cost was much smaller than the figures that had been bandied about earlier. Indeed, this cost was something like a third of the earlier estimates. There is little doubt that this careful marginal calculation played a critical role in the admission of women to Princeton and to some other institutions that subsequently made use of the calculations in the Princeton analysis. More recent data, incidentally, confirmed that the marginal calculations were amply justified.

THE THEORY AND REALITY: A WORD OF CAUTION

We have now completed two chapters describing how business managers can make optimal decisions. Can you go to Wall Street or Main Street and find executives calculating marginal cost and marginal revenue to decide how much to produce? Not

---

[5] See Gardner Patterson, "The Education of Women at Princeton," *Princeton Alumni Weekly* 69 (September 24, 1968).

● DO FIRMS REALLY MAXIMIZE PROFITS?

Naturally, many people question whether firms really try to maximize profits to the exclusion of all other goals. Japanese companies, for instance, often promote well-known corporate priorities such as lifetime employment for workers and a preference for doing business with other Japanese companies.

Besides, businesspeople are like other human beings: Their motives are varied and complex. Given the choice, many executives may prefer to control the *largest* firm rather than the most profitable one. Some may be fascinated by technology and therefore may spend so much on R&D that it cuts down on profit. Some may want to conduct business in the most environmentally benign manner. Others may be motivated by a desire to "do good" and therefore may give away some of the stockholders' money to hospitals and colleges. Different managers within the same firm may not always agree with one another on goals, so that it may not even make sense to speak about "the" goal of the firm. Thus, any attempt to summarize the objectives of management in terms of a single number (profit) is bound to be an oversimplification.

In addition, the exacting requirements for maximizing profits are tough to satisfy. In deciding how much to invest, what price to set for a product, or how much to allocate to the advertising budget, the range of available alternatives is enormous. Also, information about each alternative is often expensive and difficult to acquire. As a result, when a firm's management decides on, say, an $18 million construction budget, it rarely compares the consequences of that decision in any detail with the consequences of all the possible alternatives—such as budgets of $17 million or $19 million. But unless all the available possibilities are compared, management cannot be sure that it has chosen the one that brings in the highest possible profit.

Often, management's concern is whether the decision's results are likely to be acceptable—whether its risks will be acceptably low, whether its profits will be acceptably high—so that the company can live satisfactorily with the outcome. Such analysis cannot be expected to bring in the maximum possible profit. The decision may be good, but some unexplored alternative may be even better.

Decision making that seeks only solutions that are acceptable has been called *satisficing,* to contrast it with optimizing (profit maximization). Some analysts, such as Nobel Prize winner Herbert Simon of Carnegie-Mellon University, have concluded that decision making in industry and government is often of the satisficing variety.

But even if this is true, it does not necessarily make profit maximization a bad assumption. Recall our discussion of abstraction and model-building in Chapter 1. A map of Los Angeles that omits hundreds of roads is no doubt "wrong" if interpreted as a literal description of the city. Nonetheless, by capturing the most important elements of reality, it may help us understand the city better than a map that is cluttered with too much detail. Similarly, we can learn much about the behavior of business firms by assuming that they try to maximize profits, even though we know that not all of them act this way all of the time.

"It's true that more is not necessarily better, Edward, but it frequently is."

very often—though in some important applications they do. Nor can you find consumers in stores using marginal analysis to decide what to buy. Like consumers, successful businesspeople often rely heavily on intuition and "hunches" that cannot be described by any set of rules. In fact, in a 1993 survey of CEOs conducted by *Inc.* magazine, nearly 20 percent of the respondents admitted to using guesswork to price their first product or service.

However, we have not sought a literal description of business behavior but rather a model to help us analyze and predict this behavior. The four chapters that we have just completed constitute the core of microeconomics. We will find ourselves returning again and again to the principles learned in these chapters.

SUMMARY

1. A firm can choose the quantity of its product that it wants to sell or the price that it wants to charge. But it cannot choose both because price affects the quantity demanded.

2. In economic theory, we usually assume that firms seek to maximize profits. This should not be taken literally but rather interpreted as a useful simplification of reality.

3. Marginal revenue is the additional revenue earned by increasing sales by one unit. Marginal cost is the additional cost incurred by increasing production by one unit.

4. Maximum profit requires the firm to choose the level of output at which marginal revenue is equal to (or most closely approximates) marginal cost.

5. Geometrically, the profit-maximizing output level occurs at the highest point on the total profit curve. There the slope of the total profit curve is zero (or as close to zero as possible), meaning that marginal profit is zero.

6. A change in fixed cost will not change the profit-maximizing level of output.

7. It may pay a firm to expand its output if it is selling at a price greater than marginal cost, even if that price happens to be below average cost.

8. Optimal decisions must be made on the basis of marginal cost and marginal revenue figures, not average cost and average revenue figures. This is one of the *Ideas for Beyond the Final Exam*.

KEY TERMS

Optimal decision 168	Total revenue (TR) 170	Profit maximization 174
Total profit 170	Average revenue (AR) 172	Marginal analysis 174
Economic profit 170	Marginal revenue (MR) 172	Marginal profit 175

QUESTIONS FOR REVIEW

1. "It may be rational for the management of a firm not to try to maximize profits." Discuss the circumstances under which this statement may be true.

2. Suppose that the firm's demand curve indicates that at a price of $12 per unit, customers will demand two million units of its product. Suppose that management decides to pick both price and output; the firm produces 3 million units of its product and prices them at $20 each. What will happen?

3. Suppose that a firm's management would be pleased to increase its share of the market, but if it expands its production the price of its product will fall. Will its profits necessarily fall? Why or why not?

4. Why does it make sense for a firm to seek to maximize total profit rather than to maximize marginal profit?

5. A firm's marginal revenue is $133 and its marginal cost is $90. What amount of profit does the firm fail to pick up by refusing to increase output by one unit?

6. Calculate average revenue (AR) and average cost (AC) in Table 9–3. How much profit does the firm earn at the output at which AC = AR? Why?

7. A firm's total cost is $800 if it produces one unit, $1,400 if it produces two units, and $1,800 if it produces three units of output. Draw up a table of total, average, and marginal costs for this firm.

8. Draw an average and marginal cost curve for the firm in the preceding question. Describe the relationship between the two curves.

9. A firm has the demand and total cost schedules given in the following table. If it wants to maximize profits, how much output should it produce?

Quantity	Price	Total Cost
1	$6	$ 1.00
2	5	2.50
3	4	6.00
4	3	7.00
5	2	11.00

●   **APPENDIX**   ▮ **THE RELATIONSHIPS AMONG TOTAL, AVERAGE, AND MARGINAL DATA**

You may have surmised that there is a close connection between the average revenue curve and the marginal revenue curve and that there must be a similar relationship between the average cost curve and the marginal cost curve. After all, we derived our average revenue figures from the total revenues and also calculated our marginal revenue figures from the total revenues at the various possible output levels; a similar relationship applied to costs. In fact:

Marginal, average, and total figures are inextricably bound together. From any one of the three, the other two can be calculated. The relationships among total, average, and marginal figures are exactly the same for any variable—such as revenue, cost, or profit—to which the concepts apply.

To illustrate and emphasize the wide applicability of marginal analysis, we switch our example from profits, revenues, and costs to a noneconomic variable. As we are about to see, the same concepts can also be applied to human body weights. We switch to this example because calculation of weights is more familiar to most people than calculation of profits, revenues, or costs, and we can use it to illustrate several fundamental relationships between average and marginal figures.

In Table 9–6, we begin with an empty room. (The total weight of occupants is equal to zero.) A person weighing 100 pounds enters; total, marginal and average weight are all, then, 100 pounds. If the person is followed by a person weighing 140 pounds (marginal weight equals 140 pounds), the total weight increases to 240 pounds, average weight rises to 120 pounds (240/2), and so on.[6]

TABLE 9–6

Weights of Persons in a Room (in pounds)

Number of Persons in a Room	Total Weight	Average Weight	Marginal Weight
0	0	—	
1	100	100	100
2	240	120	140
3	375	125	135
4	500	125	125
5	600	120	100
6	660	110	60

---

[6] Note that in this illustration "persons in room" is analogous to units of output, "total weight" is analogous to total revenue or cost, and "marginal weight" is analogous to marginal revenue or cost in the discussions of marginal analysis in the body of the chapter.

The rule for converting totals to averages, and vice versa, is:

Rule 1a. Average weight equals total weight divided by number of persons.

Rule 1b. Total weight equals average weight times number of persons.

This rule naturally applies equally well to cost, revenue, profit, or any other variable.

We calculate marginal weight from total weight using the same subtraction process already used to calculate marginal cost and marginal revenue. Specifically:

Rule 2a. The marginal weight of, say, the third person equals the total weight of three people minus the total weight of two people.

For example, when the fourth person enters the room, total weight rises from 375 to 500 pounds, and hence the corresponding marginal weight is 500 − 375 = 125 pounds, as is shown in the last column of Table 9–6. We can also do the reverse—calculate total from marginal weight—through an addition process.

Rule 2b. The total weight of, say, three people equals the (marginal) weight of the first person who enters the room plus the (marginal) weight of the second person, plus the (marginal) weight of the third person.

You can verify Rule 2b by referring to Table 9–6 which shows that the total weight of three persons, 375 pounds, is indeed equal to 100 + 140 + 135 pounds, the sum of the preceding marginal weights. A similar relation holds for any other total weight figure in the table, as you should verify.

In addition to these familiar arithmetic relationships, there are two other useful relationships.

Rule 3. With an exception (fixed cost) discussed in the previous chapter, the marginal, average, and total figures for the first person must all be equal.

This rule holds because when there is only one person in the room whose weight is X pounds, the average weight will obviously be X, the total weight must be X, and the marginal weight must also be X (because the total must have risen from zero to X pounds). Put another way, when the marginal person is alone, he or she is obviously also the average person and also represents the totality of all relevant persons.

Our final and very important relationship is:

Rule 4. If marginal weight is lower than average weight, then average weight must fall when the number of persons increases. If marginal weight exceeds average weight, average weight must rise when the number of persons increases. If marginal and average weight are equal, the average weight must remain constant when the number of persons increases.

These three possibilities are all illustrated in Table 9–6. Notice, for example, that when the third person enters the room, the average weight rises from 120 to 125 pounds. That is because this person's (marginal) weight is 135 pounds, which pulls up the average, as Rule 4 requires. Similarly, when the sixth person—who is a 60-pound child—enters the room, the average falls from 120 to 110 pounds because marginal weight, 60 pounds, is below average weight.

It is essential to avoid a common misunderstanding of this rule. It does not state, for example, that if the average figure is rising, the marginal figure must be rising. When the average rises, the marginal figure may rise, fall, or remain unchanged. The arrival of two persons, both well above average, will push the average up in two successive steps even if the second new arrival is lighter than the first. We see such a case in Table 9–6, where average weight rises successively from 100 to 120 to 125, while the marginal weight falls from 140 to 135 to 125.

GRAPHICAL REPRESENTATION OF MARGINAL AND AVERAGE CURVES

We have shown how, from a curve of total profit (or total cost or total anything else), one can determine the corresponding marginal figure. We noted several times in the chapter that the marginal value at any particular point is equal to the slope of the corresponding total curve at that point. But for some purposes, it is convenient to use a graph that records marginal and average values directly rather than deriving them from the curve of totals.

We can obtain such a graph by plotting the data in a table of average and marginal figures, such as Table 9–6. The result looks like the graph shown in Figure 9–7. Here we have indicated the number of persons in the room on the horizontal axis and the corresponding average and marginal figures on the vertical axis. The solid dots represent average weights; the small circles represent marginal weights. Thus, for example, point *A* shows that when two persons are in the room, their average

weight is 120 pounds, as recorded on the third line of Table 9–6. Similarly, point *B* on the graph represents information provided in the next column of the table, that is, that the marginal weight of the third person who enters the room is 135 pounds. We have connected these points into a marginal curve and an average curve, represented, respectively, by the solid and the broken curves in the diagram. This is the representation of marginal and average values economists most frequently use.

Figure 9–7 illustrates two of our rules. Rule 3 says that for the first unit, the marginal and average values will be the same; that is precisely why the two curves start out together at point *C*. The graph also depicts Rule 4 between points *C* and *E*, where the average curve is rising, the marginal curve lies above the average. (Notice, however, that over part of this range, the marginal curve falls even though the average curve is rising; Rule 4 says nothing about the rise or fall of the marginal curve.) We see also that over range *EF*, where the average curve is falling, the marginal curve is below the average curve, again in accord with Rule 4. Finally, at point *E*, where the average curve is neither rising nor falling, the marginal curve meets the average curve: the average and marginal weights are equal at that point.

| FIGURE 9–7 |

The Relationship between Marginal and Average Curves

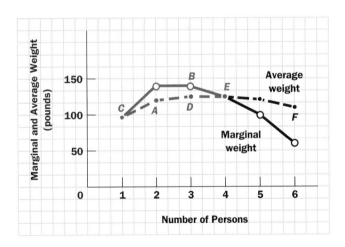

QUESTIONS FOR REVIEW

1. Suppose that the following table is your record of exam grades in your Principles of Economics course:

Exam Date	Grade	Comment
September 30	65	A slow start
October 28	75	A big improvement
November 26	90	Happy Thanksgiving!
December 13	85	Slipped a little
January 24	95	A fast finish!

Use these data to make up a table of total, average, and marginal grades for the five exams.

2. From the data in your table, illustrate each of the rules mentioned in this appendix. Be sure to point out an instance where the marginal grade falls but the average grade rises.

III

MARKETS, FROM COMPETITION TO MONOPOLY: VIRTUES AND VICES

So far, we have talked only about firms in general without worrying about the sorts of markets in which they operate. To understand the different types of competition a firm can face, it is necessary, first, to explain clearly what we mean by the word "market." Economists do not reserve the term only to mean an organized exchange operating in a specific location. In its more general and abstract usage the word *market* refers to a set of sellers and buyers whose activities affect the price at

which a *particular commodity* is sold. For example, two separate sales of General Motors stock in different parts of the country can be considered to take place in the same market, whereas sales of bread in one stall of a market square and sales of carrots in the next stall, may, in our sense, occur in totally different markets.

Economists distinguish among different kinds of markets according to how many firms they include, whether the products of the different firms are identical or somewhat different, and how easy it is for new firms to enter the markets. *Perfect competition* is at one extreme (many small firms selling an identical product, with easy entry), and *pure monopoly* (a single firm) is at the other extreme. In between are hybrid forms—called *monopolistic competition* (many small firms each selling slightly different products) and *oligopoly* (a few large rival firms)—that share some of the characteristics of both perfect competition and monopoly.

Perfect competition is far from the typical market form in the U.S. economy. Indeed, it is quite rare. Pure monopoly—literally *one* firm—is also infrequently encountered. Most of the products you buy are no doubt supplied by oligopolies or monopolistic competitors—terms that we will define precisely in Chapter 13.

Competition . . . brings about the only . . . arrangement of social production which is possible. . . . [Otherwise] what guarantee [do] we have that the necessary quantity and not more of each product will be produced, that we shall not go hungry in regard to corn and meat while we are choked in beet sugar and drowned in potato spirit, that we shall not lack trousers to cover our nakedness while buttons flood us in millions?

Friedrich Engels

THE FIRM AND THE INDUSTRY UNDER PERFECT COMPETITION

Industries differ dramatically in the number and typical sizes of their firms. Some, such as commercial fishing, encompass a great many very small firms. Others, like automobile manufacturing, are composed of a few industrial giants. This chapter deals with a very special type of market structure—called *perfect competition*—in which firms are numerous and small. We begin by comparing alternative market forms and defining perfect competition precisely. But first, once again, we set out our puzzle.

Puzzle: Pollution Reduction Incentives That Actually Increase Pollution

Many economists and other citizens concerned about the environment believe that society can obtain cleaner air and water cheaply and effectively by requiring polluters to pay for the damages they cause. (See Chapter 22 for more details.) Yet people often view pollution charges as just another tax, and that word can spell political poison. Some politicians—reasoning that they can get a donkey to move just as effectively by offering it a carrot as by poking it with a stick—have proposed *paying* firms to cut down polluting emissions.

At least some theoretical and statistical evidence indicates that such a system of bribes (or subsidies) does work, *at least up to a point.* Individual polluting firms will, indeed, respond to government payments for decreased emissions by reducing their pollution. But, over the long haul, it turns out that society will end up with more pollution than before! Subsidy payments to the firms actually exacerbate pollution problems. How is it possible that subsidies induce each firm to pollute less but in the long run lead to a rise in total pollution? The analysis in this chapter will supplement your own common sense sufficiently to supply the answer.

■ PERFECT COMPETITION DEFINED

Perfect competition occurs in an industry when that industry is made up of many small firms producing homogeneous products, when information is perfect, and when there is no impediment to the entry or exit of firms.

You can appreciate just how special perfect competition is by considering this comprehensive definition. A market is said to operate under **perfect competition** when the following four conditions are satisfied:

■ *Numerous small firms and customers.* Competitive markets contain so many buyers and sellers that each one constitutes a negligible portion of the whole: so small, in fact, that each player's decisions have no effect on price. This requirement rules out trade associations or other collusive arrangements in which firms work together to influence price.

■ *Homogeneity of product.* The product offered by any seller is identical to that supplied by any other seller. (For example, No. 1 red winter wheat is a homogeneous product; different brands of toothpaste are not.) Because products are homogeneous, consumers do not care from which firm they buy, so competition is more powerful.

■ *Freedom of entry and exit.* New firms desiring to enter the market face no impediments that previous entrants can avoid. So new firms can easily come in and compete with older firms. Similarly, if production and sale of the good proves unprofitable, no barriers prevent firms from leaving the market.

■ *Perfect information.* Each firm and each customer is well informed about available products and prices. They know whether one supplier is selling at a lower price than another.

These exacting requirements are rarely if ever found in practice. One example that comes close to the perfectly competitive standard is a market for common stocks. On any given day, literally millions of buyers and sellers trade AT&T stock; all of the shares are exactly alike; anyone who wishes to sell his or her AT&T stock can enter the market easily, and most relevant company and industry information is readily available (and virtually free of charge) in the daily newspapers or on the Internet. Many farming and fishing industries also approximate perfect competition. But it is hard to find many other examples. Our interest in the perfectly competitive model surely does not lie in its ability to describe reality.

Why, then, do we spend time studying perfect competition? The answer takes us back to the central theme of this book. Only under perfect competition does the market mechanism perform best. If we want to learn what markets do well, we can put the market's best foot forward by beginning with perfect competition.

As Adam Smith suggested some two centuries ago, perfectly competitive firms use society's scarce resources with maximum efficiency. Also, as Friedrich Engels (Karl Marx's closest friend and coauthor) suggested in the opening quotation of this chapter, only perfect competition can ensure that the economy turns out just those varieties and relative quantities of goods that match consumer preferences. By studying perfect competition, we can learn just what an *ideally functioning* market system can accomplish. This is the topic of this chapter and the next one. Then, in Chapters 12 and 13, we will consider other market forms and see how they deviate from the perfectly competitive ideal. Still later chapters (especially Chapter 14 and the chapters in Parts IV and V) will examine many important tasks that the market does *not* perform at all well, even under perfect competition. These chapters combined should provide a balanced assessment of the virtues and vices of the market mechanism.

■ THE COMPETITIVE FIRM

To discover what happens in a perfectly competitive market, we must deal separately with the behavior of *individual firms* and the behavior of the *industry* that is constituted by those firms. One basic difference between the firm and the industry under competition relates to *pricing*:

> **Under perfect competition, the firm has no choice but to accept the price that has been determined in the market. We say that it is a price taker.**

Under perfect competition, the firm is a **price taker.** It has no choice but to accept the price that has been determined in the market.

The idea that no firm in a perfectly competitive market can exert any control over product price follows from our stringent definition of perfect competition. The presence of a vast number of competitors, each offering identical products, forces each firm to meet but not exceed the price charged by the others. With two important exceptions, the firm under perfect competition behaves exactly as we described and analyzed in Chapters 8 and 9. The two exceptions are the special shape of the competitive firm's demand curve and the freedom of entry and exit, along with their effects on the firm's profits. We will consider each of these special features of perfect competition in turn, beginning with the demand curve.

THE FIRM'S DEMAND CURVE UNDER PERFECT COMPETITION

In Chapter 9, we always assumed that the firm faced a downward-sloping demand curve; if a firm wished to sell more (without increasing its advertising or changing its product specifications), it had to reduce product price. The competitive firm is an exception to this general principle.

> **A perfectly competitive firm faces a *horizontal* demand curve. This means that it can sell as much as it wants at the prevailing market price. It can double or triple its sales without reducing the price of its product.**

How is this possible? The answer is that the competitive firm is so insignificant relative to the market as a whole that it has absolutely no influence over price. The farmer who sells his corn through a commodities exchange in Chicago must accept the current quotation his broker reports to him. Because there are thousands of farmers, the Chicago price per bushel will not budge because Farmer Al decides he doesn't like the price and stores a truckload of corn rather than taking it to the grain elevator.

● THE GARDEN STATE: FARM INCOME IN A COMPETITIVE MARKET

Because farmers are *price takers,* they simply have to live with the price that is determined by the market's supply and demand. Here is an example.

With the month's first drops of rain on Monday, many farmers relaxed a bit about the year's longest and most intense dry spell, and got back to the problem that plagues them rain or shine: earning enough from their crops to stay afloat.

And that boils down to the farmer's golden rule: entwined as they are, prices are still far more variable than weather.

"The quality of the produce does not have anything to do with your income," explained Mark Malench, a 38-year-old farmer who grows lettuce, peppers, eggplant and more than a dozen other crops on his family's 60-acre spread in Vineland [New Jersey]. "It's supply and demand." . . . [And] it was competition, not weather, that almost ruined the blueberry market. . . . "There were just a lot of people out there with berries at the same time," said Dennis G. Doyle, the general manager of the Tru-Blu Cooperative in New Lisbon, where nearly half of New Jersey's 145 blueberry farmers sell. But, he said, that's just part of the high-risk business of farming. "We're near Atlantic City and people ask me if I go much," Mr. Doyle said. "I say no. The risk isn't great enough."

The bottom line for farmers is the price they sell their crops for, which varies not only because of the weather, but also according to competition from other growers.

SOURCE: *The New York Times,* August 16, 1998.

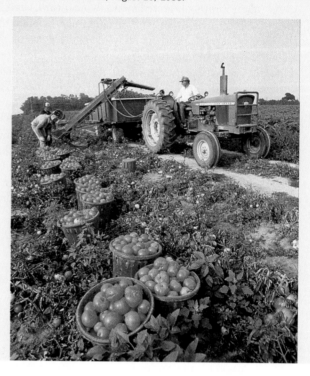

Thus, the demand curve for Farmer Al's corn is as shown in Figure 10–1(a); the price he is paid in Chicago will be $3 per bushel whether he sells one truckload (point *A*) or two (point *B*) or three (point *C*). This is because that $3 price is determined by the intersection of the *industry's* supply and demand curves shown in the right-hand portion of the graph, Panel (b).

Notice that, in the case of perfect competition, the downward-sloping industry demand curve in Figure 10–1(b) leads to the horizontal demand curve for the individual firm in Figure 10–1(a). Also notice that the height of that horizontal firm demand curve will be the height of the intersection point, *E*, of the industry supply and demand curves. And the firm's demand will generally not resemble the demand curve for the industry.

SHORT-RUN EQUILIBRIUM FOR THE PERFECTLY COMPETITIVE FIRM

We already have sufficient background to study the decisions of a firm operating in a perfectly competitive market. Remember from Chapter 9 that profit maximization requires the firm to pick an output level that makes its *marginal cost equal to its marginal*

FIGURE 10–1

Demand Curve for a Firm under Perfect Competition

revenue: MC = MR. The only feature that distinguishes the profit-maximizing equilibrium for the competitive firm from that of any other type of firm is its horizontal demand curve. We know from Chapter 9 that the firm's demand curve is also its average revenue curve because the average revenue a firm gets from selling a commodity is equal to the price of the commodity. Because the demand curve is horizontal, the competitive firm's marginal revenue curve is a horizontal straight line that coincides with its demand curve; hence, MR = Price *(P)*. It is easy to see why this is so.

If the price does not depend on how much the firm sells (which is exactly what a horizontal demand curve means), then each *additional* unit sold brings in an amount of revenue (the *marginal* revenue) exactly equal to the market price. So marginal revenue always equals price under perfect competition because the firm is a price taker. Once we know the shape and position of a firm's marginal revenue curve, we can use this and the marginal cost curve to determine its optimal output and profit, as shown in Figure 10–2. As usual, the profit-maximizing output is that at which MC = MR (point *B*). The demand curve, *D*, is horizontal because the firm's output is too small to affect market price. This particular competitive firm produces 50,000 bushels of corn per year—the output level at which MC and MR both equal the market price, $3. Thus:

> Because it is a price taker, the *equilibrium* of a profit-maximizing firm in a perfectly competitive market must occur at an output level at which marginal cost equals price. This is because a horizontal demand curve makes price and MR equal and, therefore, both must equal marginal cost according to the profit maximizing principle. In symbols:

$$MC = P$$

This idea is illustrated in Table 10–1, which gives the firm's total and marginal revenue, total and marginal cost, and total profit for different output quantities. We see from Column (6) that total profit is maximized at an output of about 50,000 bushels where total profit is $37,500. An increase in output from 40,000 to 50,000 bushels incurs a marginal cost ($26,500) that approximately equals the corresponding marginal revenue ($30,000), confirming that 50,000 bushels is the profit-maximizing output.[1]

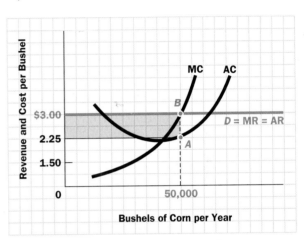

FIGURE 10–2

Short-Run Equilibrium of the Competitive Firm

TABLE 10–1

Revenues, Costs, and Profits of a Competitive Firm

(1) Total Quantity	(2) Total Revenue	(3) Marginal Revenue	(4) Total Cost	(5) Marginal Cost	(6) Total Profit
0	$ 0				
		$30			
10	30		$ 32		$ −2
		30		$ 24	
20	60		56		4
		30		11.5	
30	90		67.5		22.5
		30		18.5	
40	120		86		34
		30		26.5	
50	150		112.5		37.5
		30		56.5	
60	180		169		11
		30		93	
70	210		262		−52

NOTE: Quantity is in thousands of bushels; dollars are in thousands.

---

[1] To calculate marginal costs and marginal revenues accurately, we should increase output one bushel at a time instead of proceeding in leaps of 10,000 bushels. But that would require too much space! In any event, our failure to make a more careful calculation in terms of individual bushels explains why we are unable to find the output at which MR and MC are *exactly* equal.

SHORT-RUN PROFIT: GRAPHIC REPRESENTATION

Our analysis so far tells us how a firm can pick the output that maximizes its profit. But even if it succeeds in doing so, the firm may conceivably find itself in trouble. If the demand for its product is weak or its costs are high, even the firm's most profitable option may lead to a loss. In the short run, the demand curve can either be high or low relative to costs. To determine whether the firm is making a profit or incurring a loss, we must compare *total* revenue (TR = $P \times Q$) with *total* cost (TC = $AC \times Q$). Because Q is common to both of these, this equation tells us that the process is equivalent to comparing P with AC.

We can therefore show the firm's profit in Figure 10–2, which includes the firm's *average cost* (AC) curve. By definition, profit per unit of output is revenue per unit (P) minus cost per unit (AC). We see in Figure 10–2 that average cost at 50,000 bushels per year is only $2.25 per bushel (point *A*), whereas *average revenue* (AR) is $3 per bushel (point *B*). The firm makes a profit of AR − AC = $0.75 per bushel, which appears in the graph as the vertical distance between points *A* and *B*.

Notice that in addition to showing the *profit per unit*, Figure 10–2 can be used to show the firm's *total profit*. Total profit is the profit per unit ($0.75 in this example) times the number of units (50,000 per year). Therefore, total profit is represented by the *area* of the shaded rectangle whose height is the profit per unit ($0.75) and whose width is the number of units (50,000).[2] In this case, profits are $37,500 per year. In general, total profit at any output is the area of the rectangle whose base equals the level of output and whose height equals AR − AC.

> The MC = *P* condition gives us the output that maximizes the perfectly competitive firm's profit. It does not, however, tell us whether the firm is making a profit or incurring a loss. To determine this, we must compare price (average revenue) with average cost.

THE CASE OF SHORT-TERM LOSSES

The market is obviously treating the farmer in Figure 10–2 rather nicely. But what if the corn market were not so generous in its rewards? What if, for example, the market price were only $1.50 per bushel instead of $3? Figure 10–3 shows the equilibrium of the firm under these circumstances. The cost curves are the same in this diagram as they were in Figure 10–2, but the demand curve has shifted down to correspond to the market price of $1.50 per bushel. The firm still maximizes profits by producing the level of output at which marginal cost is equal to price—point *B* in the diagram. But this time "maximizing profits" really means minimizing losses, as shown by the shaded rectangle.

At the optimal level of output (30,000 bushels per year), average cost is $2.25 per bushel (point *A*), which exceeds the $1.50 per bushel price (point *B*). The firm therefore runs a loss of $0.75 per bushel times 30,000 bushels, or $22,500 per year. This loss, which is represented by the area of the gold rectangle in Figure 10–3, is the best the firm can do. If it selected any other output level, its loss would be even greater.

FIGURE 10–3

Short-Run Equilibrium of the Competitive Firm with a Lower Price

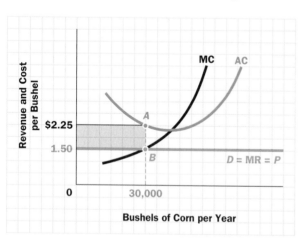

SHUTDOWN AND BREAK-EVEN ANALYSIS

Of course, any firm will accept only a limited amount of loss before it stops production. If losses get too big, the firm can simply go out of business. To understand the logic of the choice between shutting down and remaining in operation, we must return to the distinction between costs that are variable in the short run and those that are not. Remember from Chapter 8 that costs are not variable if the

---

[2] Recall that the formula for the area of a rectangle is area = height × width.

firm cannot escape them in the short run, either because of a contract (say, with the landlord or a union) or because it has already bought the item whose cost is not variable (for example, a machine).

If the firm stops producing, its revenue will fall to zero. Its short-run variable costs will also fall to zero. But its costs that are not variable will remain. If the firm is losing money, sometimes it will be better off continuing to operate until its obligations to pay the nonvariable costs expire; sometimes it will do better by shutting down and producing nothing. Two rules govern the decision:

Rule 1. The firm will make a profit if total revenue (TR) exceeds total cost (TC). In that case, it should not plan to shut down, either in the short run or in the long run.

Rule 2. The firm should continue to operate in the short run if TR exceeds total short-run variable cost (TVC). It should nevertheless plan to close in the long run if TR is less than TC.

The first rule is self-evident. If the firm's revenues cover its total costs, then it does not lose money. The second rule is a bit more subtle. Suppose that TR is less than TC. If our unfortunate firm continues in operation, it will lose the difference between total cost and total revenue, that is:

$$\text{Loss if the firm stays in business} = \text{TC} - \text{TR}.$$

However, if the firm stops producing, both its revenues and short-run variable costs become zero, leaving only the *nonvariable* costs to be paid:

$$\text{Loss if the firm shuts down} = \text{Nonvariable costs} = \text{TC} - \text{TVC}$$

Hence, it is best to keep operating as long as:

$$\text{TC} - \text{TR} < \text{TC} - \text{TVC}$$

or

$$\text{TVC} < \text{TR}$$

That is Rule 2.

We can illustrate Rule 2 by the two cases in Table 10–2. Case A deals with a firm that loses money but is better off staying in business in the short run. If it shuts down, it will lose its entire $60,000 worth of short-run nonvariable cost. But if it continues to operate, total revenue of $100,000 exceeds total variable cost (TVC = $80,000) by $20,000. That means continuing operation contributes $20,000 toward meeting nonvariable costs and reduces losses to $40,000. In Case B, on the other hand, it pays the firm to shut down because continued operation only adds to its losses. If the firm operates, it will lose $90,000 (the last entry in Table 10–2), whereas if it shuts down, it will lose only the $60,000 in nonvariable costs, which it must pay whether it operates or not.

We can also analyze the shutdown decision graphically. In Figure 10–4, the firm will run a loss whether the price is P_1, P_2, or P_3, because none of these prices is

	The Shutdown Decision		TABLE 10-2
	Case A	**Case B**	
Total revenue (TR)	$100	$100	
Total variable cost (TVC)	80	130	
Short-run nonvariable cost	60	60	
Total cost (TC)	140	190	
Loss if firm shuts down (=Short-run nonvariable cost)	60	60	
Loss if firm does not shut down	40	90	

NOTE: Figures are in thousands of dollars.

FIGURE 10–4

Shutdown Analysis

high enough to reach the minimum level of average cost (AC). We can show the *lowest* price that keeps the firm from shutting down by introducing one more short-run cost curve: the average variable cost (AVC) curve. Why is this curve relevant? Because, as we have just seen, it pays the firm to remain in operation if its total revenue (TR) exceeds its total short-run variable cost (TVC). If we divide both TR and TVC by quantity (Q), we get TR/Q = P and TVC/Q = AVC. So, we can state the condition for continued operation equivalently as the requirement that price must exceed AVC. The conclusion is:

The firm will produce nothing unless price lies above the minimum point on the AVC curve.

In Figure 10–4, price P_1 is below the minimum average variable cost. With this price, the firm cannot even cover its variable costs and is better off shutting down (producing zero output). Price P_3 is higher. Although the firm still runs a loss if it sets MC = P at point A (because AC exceeds P_3), it allows the firm to at least cover its short-run variable costs, and so it pays to keep operating in the short run. Price P_2 is the borderline case. If the price is P_2, the firm is indifferent between shutting down and staying in business and producing at a level where MC = P (point B). P_2 is thus the *lowest* price at which the firm will produce anything. As we see from the graph, P_2 corresponds to the minimum point on the AVC curve.

THE COMPETITIVE FIRM'S SHORT-RUN SUPPLY CURVE

Without realizing it, we have now derived the supply curve of the competitive firm in the short run. Why? Recall that a supply curve summarizes in a graph the answers to questions such as, "If the price is so and so, how much output will the firm offer for sale?" We have now discovered two possibilities:

- In the short run, if the price exceeds the minimum AVC, it pays a competitive firm to produce the level of output at which MC equals P. Thus, for any price above point B, we can read the corresponding quantity supplied from the firm's MC curve.

- If the price falls below the minimum AVC, then it pays the firm to produce nothing. Quantity supplied falls to zero, as indicated by vertical line $0P_2$, in Figure 10–4.

Putting these two observations together, we conclude that:

The short-run supply curve of the perfectly competitive firm is that portion of its marginal cost curve that lies above the point where it intersects the average (short-run) variable cost curve, that is, above the minimum level of AVC. If price falls below this level, the firm's quantity supplied drops to zero.

THE COMPETITIVE INDUSTRY

Having completed the analysis of the competitive *firm's* supply decision, we turn our attention next to the competitive *industry*.

THE COMPETITIVE INDUSTRY'S SHORT-RUN SUPPLY CURVE

Again we need to distinguish between the short run and the long run, but the distinction is different here. The short run for the *industry* is defined as a period of time too brief for new firms to enter the industry or for old firms to leave, so the number of firms is fixed. By contrast, the long run for the industry is a period of time long enough for any firm to enter or leave as it desires. In addition, in the long run each firm in the industry can adjust its output to its own long-run costs.[3] We begin our analysis of industry equilibrium in the short run.

With the number of firms fixed, it is a simple matter to derive the supply curve of the competitive industry from those of the individual firms. At any given price, we simply *add up* the quantities supplied by each of the firms to arrive at the industry-wide quantity supplied. For example, if each of 1,000 identical firms in the corn industry supplies 45,000 bushels when the price is $2.25 per bushel, then the quantity supplied by the industry at a $2.25 price will be 45,000 bushels per firm × 1,000 firms = 45 million bushels.

This process of deriving the *market* supply curve from the *individual* supply curves of firms is perfectly analogous to the way we derived the *market* demand curve from the *individual* consumers' demand curves in Chapter 7. Graphically, what we are doing is *summing the individual supply curves horizontally*, as illustrated in Figure 10–5. At a price of $2.25, each of the 1,000 identical firms in the industry supplies 45,000 bushels—point *c* in Panel (a)—so the industry supplies 45 million bushels—point *C* in Panel (b). At a price of $3, each firm supplies 50,000 bushels—point *e* in Panel (a)—and so the industry supplies 50 million bushels—point *E* in Panel (b). We can carry out similar calculations for any other price. By adding up the quantities supplied by each firm at each possible price, we arrive at the industry supply curve *SS* in panel (b).

Derivation of the Industry Supply Curve from the Supply Curves of the Individual Firms

FIGURE 10–5

The supply curve of the competitive industry in the short run is derived by *summing the short-run supply curves of all the firms in the industry horizontally*.

This adding-up process indicates, incidentally, that the supply curve of the industry will shift to the right whenever a new firm enters the industry.

Notice that if the short-run supply curves of individual firms slope upward, then the short-run supply curve of the competitive industry will slope upward as well. We have seen that the firm's supply curve is its marginal cost curve (above the level of minimum average variable cost), so it follows that rising marginal costs lead to an upward-sloping short-run *industry* supply curve.

---

[3] The relationship between short-run and long-run cost curves for the firm was discussed in Chapter 8, pages 149–150.

INDUSTRY EQUILIBRIUM IN THE SHORT RUN

FIGURE 10-6

**Supply-Demand Equilibrium
of a Competitive Industry**

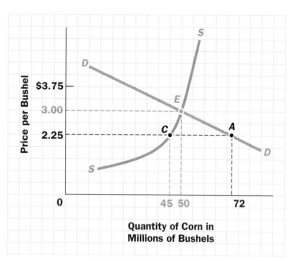

Now that we have derived the industry supply curve, we need only add a market demand curve to determine the price and quantity that will emerge in equilibrium. We do this for our illustrative corn industry in Figure 10–6, where the blue industry supply curve, carried over from Figure 10–5(b), is *SS* and the demand curve is *DD*. The only equilibrium combination of price and quantity is a price of $3 and a quantity of 50 million bushels, at which the supply curve, *SS*, and the demand curve, *DD*, intersect (point *E*). At any lower price, such as $2.25, quantity demanded (72 million bushels, as shown by point *A* on the demand curve) will be higher than the 45-million-bushel quantity supplied (point *C*). Thus, the price will be bid up toward the $3 equilibrium. The opposite will happen at a price such as $3.75, which is above equilibrium.

Note that for the competitive industry, unlike the competitive firm, the demand curve normally slopes downward. Why? Each firm by itself is so small that if it alone were to double its output the effect would hardly be noticeable. But if *every* firm in the industry were to expand its output, that would make a substantial difference. Customers can be induced to buy the additional quantities arriving at the market only if the price of the good falls.

Point *E* is the equilibrium point for the competitive industry, because only at a price of $3 are sellers willing to offer exactly the amount that consumers want to purchase (in this case, 50 million bushels).

Should we expect price actually to reach, or at least to *approximate*, this equilibrium level? The answer is yes. To see why, we must consider what happens when price is not at its equilibrium level. Suppose that the price is lower, say, $2.25. This low price will stimulate customers to buy more; it will also lead firms to produce less than they would at a price of $3. Our diagram confirms that at a price of $2.25, quantity supplied (45 million bushels) is lower than quantity demanded (72 million bushels). Thus, unsatisfied buyers will probably lead sellers to raise their prices, which will force the price *upward* in the direction of its equilibrium value, $3.

Similarly, if we begin with a price higher than the equilibrium price, we may readily verify that quantity supplied will exceed quantity demanded. Under these circumstances, frustrated sellers are likely to reduce their prices, so price will be forced downward. In the circumstances depicted in Figure 10–6, then, in effect, a magnet at the equilibrium price of $3 will pull the actual price in its direction, if for some reason the actual price starts out at some other level.

In practice, in most competitive markets, over a long period of time prices do move toward equilibrium levels. Matters eventually appear to work out as depicted in Figure 10–6. Of course, numerous transitory influences can jolt any real-world market away from its equilibrium point—a workers' strike that cuts production, a sudden change in consumer tastes, and so on.

Yet, as we have just seen, powerful forces push prices back toward equilibrium—toward the level at which the supply and demand curves intersect. These forces are fundamentally important for economic analysis. If no such forces existed, prices in the real world would bear little resemblance to equilibrium prices, and there would be little reason to study supply-demand analysis. Fortunately, the required equilibrating forces do step in as appropriate to bring markets back toward equilibrium.

INDUSTRY AND FIRM EQUILIBRIUM IN THE LONG RUN

The equilibrium of a competitive industry in the long run may differ from the short-run equilibrium that we have just studied for two reasons. First, the number of firms in the industry (1,000 in our example) is not fixed in the long run. Second, as we saw in Chapter 8 (pages 139–141), in the long run firms can vary their plant size and change other commitments that were unchangeable in the short run. Hence, the firm's (and the industry's) long-run cost curves are not the same as the short-run cost curves.

What will lure new firms into the industry or encourage old ones to leave? In a word: *profits*—economic profits that exceed the economy average. Remember that when a firm selects its optimal level of output by setting MC = P, it may wind up with either a profit, as in Figure 10–2, or a loss, as in Figure 10–3. Such profits or losses must be *temporary* for competitive firms, because new firms are free to enter the industry if profits greater than the average are available. For the same reason, old firms will leave if they cannot cover their costs in the long run. Suppose that firms in the industry earn very high profits, in excess of the normal rates of return currently available. Then new companies will find it attractive to enter the business, and expanded production will force the market price to fall from its initial level. Why? Recall that the industry supply curve is the horizontal sum of the supply curves of individual firms. Under perfect competition, new firms can enter the industry *on the same terms as existing firms.* Thus new entrants will have the *same* individual supply curves as old firms. If the market price did not fall, entry of new firms would lead to an increased number of firms, with no change in output *per firm.* Consequently, the total quantity supplied to the market would be higher, and it would exceed quantity demanded—which, of course, would also drive prices down. Thus, the entry of new firms *must* push the price down.

FIGURE 10-7

A Shift in the Industry Supply Curve Caused by the Entry of New Firms

Figure 10–7 shows how the entry process works. In this diagram, the demand curve *DD* and the original (short-run) supply curve S_0S_0 are carried over from Figure 10–6. The entry of new firms seeking high profits *shifts the industry's short-run supply curve outward to the right*, to S_1S_1. The new market equilibrium at point *A* (rather than at point *E*), indicates that price is $2.25 per bushel and that 72 million bushels are produced and consumed. The entry of new firms reduces price and raises total output.

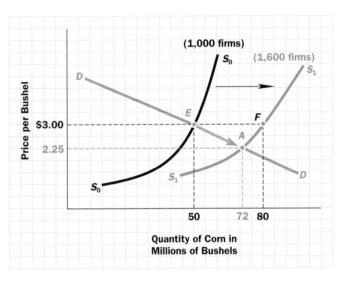

If the price had not fallen, quantity supplied after entry would have been 80 million bushels—point *F*. Why must the price fall in this case? Because the demand curve for the industry slopes downward: consumers will purchase the increased output only at a reduced price.

To see the point at which new entrants stop seeking high profits, we must consider how new firm entry affects existing firms' behavior. At first glance, this notion may seem to contradict the idea of perfect competition; perfectly competitive firms are not supposed to be affected by what competitors do, because no individual firm can influence the industry. Indeed, these corn farmers don't care. But they *do* care very much about the market price of corn and, as we have just seen, the entry of new firms into the corn-farming industry lowers the price of corn.

In Figure 10–8, we juxtapose the diagram of competitive firm equilibrium (Figure 10–2) with the competitive industry equilibrium diagram (Figure 10–7). Before entry, the market price was $3, point *E* in Figure 10–8(b), and each of the 1,000 firms produced 50,000 bushels—the point where marginal cost and price were equal, point *e* in Figure 10–8(a). Each firm faced the horizontal demand curve D_0 in Figure 10–8(a). Firms within the industry enjoyed profits because average costs (AC) at 50,000 bushels per firm were less than price.

Now suppose that 600 new firms are attracted by these high profits and enter the industry. Each faces the cost structure indicated by the AC and MC curves in Figure 10–8(a). As a result of the new entrants' production, the industry supply curve in Figure 10–8(b) shifts to the right, and price falls to $2.25 per bushel. Because the height of the firm's horizontal demand curve is, as we have seen, equal to the industry price, the firm's demand curve must now move down to the red line D_1 *corresponding to the reduced market price.* Firms in the industry react to this demand

| FIGURE 10–8 | **The Competitive Firm and the Competitive Industry** |

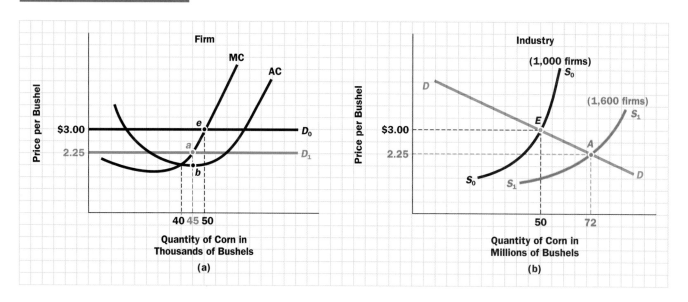

shift and its associated lower price. As we see in Figure 10–8(a), each firm reduces its output to 45,000 bushels (point *a*). But now there are 1,600 firms, so total industry output is 45,000 × 1,600 = 72 million bushels, point *A* in Figure 10–8(b).

At point *a* in Figure 10–8(a), some profits remain available because the $2.25 price exceeds average cost (point *b* is below point *a*). Thus, the entry process is not yet complete. New firms will stop appearing only when all profits have been competed away. The two panels of Figure 10–9 show the competitive firm and the competitive industry in long-run equilibrium. Only when entry shifts the industry supply curve so far to the right—S_2S_2 in Figure 10–9(b)—that each individual firm faces a demand curve that has fallen to the level of minimum average cost—point *m* in Figure 10–9(a)—will all profits be eradicated and entry cease.[4]

| FIGURE 10–9 | **Long-Run Equilibrium of the Competitive Firm and Industry** |

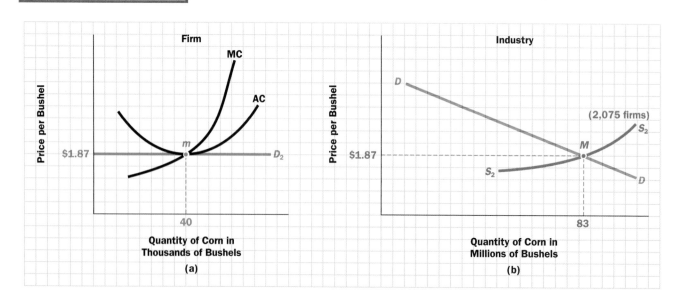

---

[4] If the original short-run equilibrium had involved losses instead of profits, firms would have exited from the industry, shifting the industry supply curve inward, until all losses were eradicated, and we would end up in a position exactly like Figure 10–9. *Exercise:* To test your understanding, draw the version of Figure 10–8 that corresponds to this case.

Notice that at the equilibrium point, *m* in Panel (a), each firm picks its own output level to maximize its profit. This means that for each firm *P* = MC. But free entry also forces AC to equal *P* in the long run—point *M* in Panel (b) of the graph—because if *P* were not equal to AC, firms would either earn profits or suffer losses. That would mean, in turn, that firms would find it profitable to enter or leave the industry, which is not compatible with industry equilibrium. Thus:

> When a perfectly competitive industry is in long-run equilibrium, firms maximize profits so that *P* = MC, and entry forces the price down until it is tangent to the long-run average cost curve (*P* = AC). As a result, in long-run competitive equilibrium it is always true that for each firm:

$$P = MC = AC$$

Thus, even though every firm earns zero profit, profits are at the maximum that is sustainable.[5]

ZERO ECONOMIC PROFIT: THE OPPORTUNITY COST OF CAPITAL

Why would there be any firms in the industry *at all* if in the long run they could make no profits? The answer is that the zero profit concept used in economics does not mean the same thing that it does in ordinary, everyday usage.

We have noted repeatedly that when economists measure average cost, they include the cost of *all* of the firm's inputs, *including the opportunity cost of the capital (the funds) or any other inputs, such as labor, provided by the firm's owners.* Because the firm may not make explicit payments to some of the people who provide it with capital, this element of cost may not be picked up by the firm's accountants. So what economists call zero **economic profit** will correspond to a positive amount of profit as measured by conventional accounting techniques. For example, if investors can earn 15 percent by lending their funds elsewhere, then the firm must earn a 15 percent rate of return to cover its opportunity cost of capital.

> **OPPORTUNITY COST** Because economists consider this 15 percent opportunity cost to be the *cost of the firm's capital*, they include it in the AC curve. If the firm cannot earn at least 15 percent on its capital, funds will not be made available to it, because investors can earn greater returns elsewhere. In order to break even—to earn zero *economic profit*—a firm must earn enough not only to cover the cost of labor, fuel, and raw materials but also the cost of its funds, including the opportunity cost of any funds supplied by the owners of the firm.

Economic profit equals net earnings, in the accountant's sense, minus the opportunity costs of capital and of any other inputs supplied by the firm's owners.

How Much Does It Really Cost?

An example will illustrate how economic profit and accounting profit differ. Suppose that U.S. government bonds pay 8 percent interest, and the owner of a small shop earns 6 percent on her business investment. The shopkeeper might see a 6 percent profit, but an economist would see a 2 percent loss on every dollar she has invested in her business. By keeping her money tied up in her firm, she gives up the chance to buy government bonds and receive an 8 percent return. With this explanation of economic profit, we can understand the logic behind the zero-profit condition for the long-run industry equilibrium.

> Zero profit in the economic sense simply means that firms are earning the normal, economy-wide rate of profit in the accounting sense. This result is guaranteed, in the long run, under perfect competition by freedom of entry and exit.

THE LONG-RUN INDUSTRY SUPPLY CURVE

We have now seen basically what lies behind the supply-demand analysis that we first introduced in Chapter 5. Only one thing remains to be explained. Figures 10–5

---

[5] *Exercise:* Show what happens to the equilibrium of the firm and of the industry in Figure 10–9 if there is a rise in consumer income that leads to an outward shift in the industry demand curve.

through 10–8 depicted short-run industry supply curves and short-run equilibrium. However, because Figure 10–9 describes long-run competitive equilibrium, its industry supply curve must also, of course, pertain to the long run.

How does the long-run industry supply curve relate to the short-run supply curve? The answer is implicit in what we have just discussed. The long-run industry supply curve evolves from the short-run supply curve via two simultaneous processes. First, new firms enter or some existing ones exit, which shifts the short-run industry supply curve toward its long-run position.

Second, and concurrently, as each firm in the industry is freed from its fixed commitments, the cost curves pertinent to its decisions become its long-run cost curves rather than its short-run cost curves. For example, consider a company that was stuck in the short run with a plant designed to serve 20,000 customers, even though it is now fortunate enough to have 25,000 customers. When it is time to replace the old plant, management will want to build a new plant that can serve the larger number of customers more conveniently, efficiently, and cheaply. The reduced cost that results from the larger plant is the pertinent cost to both the firm and the industry in the long run.

Finally, let us note that the long-run supply curve of the competitive industry (S_2S_2 in Figure 10–9) must be identical to the industry's long-run *average* cost curve. This is because in the long run, as we have seen, economic profit must be zero. The price the industry charges cannot exceed the long-run average cost (LRAC) of supplying that quantity because any excess of price over LRAC would constitute a profit opportunity that would attract new firms. Similarly, price cannot be below LRAC because firms would then refuse to supply that output at this price. Therefore, for each possible long-run quantity supplied, the price must equal the industry's long-run average cost. Thus, this long-run industry supply curve is the cost curve relevant for determination of long-run equilibrium price and quantity in a standard supply-demand diagram.

These ideas are illustrated in Figure 10–10, in which the short-run industry supply curve, *SS*, lies above and to the left of the long-run average cost curve, LRAC. Consider any industry output: say, 70 million bushels of corn per year. At that output, the long-run average cost is $1.50 per bushel (point *A*). But if the price charged by farmers were given by the short-run supply curve for that output— that is, $2.62 per bushel (point *B*)—then the firms would earn $1.12 in economic profit on each and every bushel they sold.

Such economic profits would induce other firms to enter the industry, which would force prices downward as the industry supply curve shifted outward. So long as this shift did not take *SS* all the way down to LRAC, some economic profits would remain, and so entry would continue. Thus, *SS* must continue to fall until it reaches the position of the long-run average cost curve. Then and only then will entry cease and long-run equilibrium be attained.

Short-Run Industry Supply and Long-Run Industry Average Cost

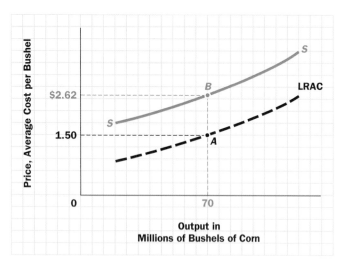

The long-run supply curve of the competitive industry is also the industry's long-run average cost curve. The industry is driven to that supply curve by the entry or exit of firms and by the adjustment of firms already in the industry.

PERFECT COMPETITION AND ECONOMIC EFFICIENCY

Economists have long admired perfect competition as a thing of beauty, like one of King Tutankhamen's funerary masks. (And it's just as rare!) Adam Smith's invisible hand produces results that are considered *efficient* in a variety of senses that we will

POLICY DEBATE

SHOULD GOVERNMENT REGULATORS USE PERFECT COMPETITION AS A GUIDE?

As we have seen here and will discuss further in the next chapter, perfect competition displays the market mechanism at its best. It prevents firms from earning excess profits, it forces firms to produce the output quantity at which AC is as low as possible, and it has other virtues besides.

As we will see in Chapters 12 and 13, markets where monopoly or oligopoly prevail are very different from perfect competition. In monopolistic or oligopolistic markets a few large firms may charge high prices that yield large profits, and they may produce output quantities that do not match consumer preferences. Consequently (see Chapter 20), such industries are often *regulated* by government agencies.

But just what should regulation force monopoly or oligopoly firms to do? Should it force them to behave like perfectly competitive firms? Should it force their prices to equal marginal costs? Should it try to break them up into thousands of tiny enterprises?

No one believes that government regulation should go quite that far. Indeed, there are economists and others who argue that perfect competition is an undesirable and, indeed, impossible goal for such regulated industries. For example, if those industries are characterized by economies of scale, then breaking them into small firms will raise their costs and consumers will have to pay more, not less. Moreover, as we saw in Chapter 8, where there are economies of scale, the average cost curve must go downhill—the larger the firm's output, the lower its average cost. So marginal cost must be below average cost (see the appendix to Chapter 8 for review), and a price equal to marginal cost must also be below average cost. Thus, where there are economies of scale, if the firm is forced to charge a price equal to marginal cost it will be forced to go bankrupt!

Still, many regulators, economists, and others believe that perfect competition is so desirable a state of affairs that regulated firms should be required to come as close to it as possible in their behavior.

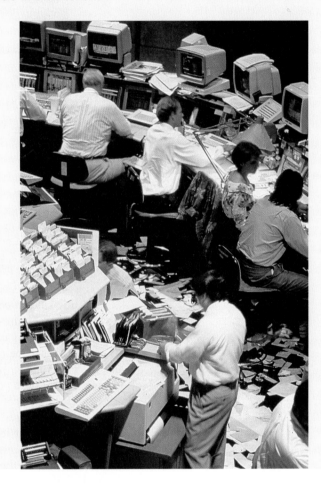

examine carefully in the next chapter. But one aspect of the great efficiency of perfect competition follows immediately from the analysis we have just completed.

We saw earlier that when the firm is in long-run equilibrium, it must have $P = MC = AC$, as indicated by Figure 10–9(a). This implies that the long-run competitive equilibrium of the firm will occur at the lowest point on its long-run AC curve, which is also where that curve is tangent to the firm's horizontal demand curve.

> In long-run competitive equilibrium, every firm produces at the minimum point on its average cost curve. Thus, the outputs of competitive industries are produced at the lowest possible cost to society.

An example will show why it is most efficient if each firm in a competitive industry produces at the point where AC is as small as possible. Suppose the industry is producing 12 million bushels of corn. This amount can be produced by 120 farms each producing 100,000 bushels, or by 100 farms each producing 120,000 bushels, or by 200 farms each producing 60,000 bushels. Of course, the job can also be done instead by other numbers of farms, but for simplicity let us consider only these three possibilities.

TABLE 10-3		**Average Cost for the Firm and Total Cost for the Industry**		
(1)	(2)	(3)	(4)	(5)
Firm's Output	Firm's Average Cost	Number of Firms	Industry Output	Total Industry Cost
60,000	$0.90	200	12,000,000	$10,800,000
100,000	0.70	120	12,000,000	8,400,000
120,000	0.80	100	12,000,000	9,600,000

NOTE: Output is in bushels.

Suppose that the AC figures for the firm are as shown in Table 10–3. Suppose, moreover, that an output of 100,000 bushels corresponds to the lowest point on the AC curve, with an AC of 70 cents per bushel. Which is the cheapest way for the industry to produce its 12-million-bushel output? In other words, what is the cost-minimizing number of firms for the job? Looking at Column (5) of Table 10–3, we see that the industry's total cost of producing the 12-million-bushel output is as low as possible if 120 firms each produce the cost-minimizing output of 100,000 bushels.

Why is this so? The answer is not difficult to see. For any *given* industry output, Q, since Q is constant, *total* industry cost (= AC × Q) will be as small as possible if and only if AC (for *each* firm) is as small as possible, that is, if the number of firms doing the job is such that each is producing the output at which AC is as low as possible.

That this kind of cost efficiency characterizes perfect competition in the long run can be seen in Figures 10–8 and 10–9. Before full long-run equilibrium is reached (Figure 10–8), firms may not be producing in the least costly way. For example, the 50 million bushels being produced by 1,000 firms at points e and E in Figures 10–8(a) and 10–8(b) could be produced more cheaply by more firms, each producing a smaller volume, because the point of minimum average cost lies to the left of point e in Figure 10–8(a). This problem is rectified, however, in the long run by entry of new firms seeking profit. We see in Figure 10–9 that after the entry process is complete, every firm is producing at its most efficient (lowest AC) level—40,000 bushels.

As Adam Smith might have put it, even though each farmer cares only about his or her own profits, the corn-farming industry as a whole is *guided by an invisible hand* to produce the amount of corn that society wants at the lowest possible cost.

Puzzle Resolved: Which Is Better to Cut Pollution— The Carrot or the Stick?

We end by returning to the puzzle with which the chapter began, because we now have all the tools needed to resolve it. Remember that we asked: Should polluters be *taxed* on their emissions, or should they, instead, be offered *subsidies* to cut emissions? A subsidy—that is, a government payment to the firms that comply— would indeed induce firms to cut their emissions. Nevertheless, the paradoxical result is likely to be an *increase* in total pollution. Let us see now why this is so.

In Figure 10–11, we have drawn the industry long-run average cost curve (LRAC), *XX*. We now know that this must also be the industry's long-run supply curve, because if the supply curve lies above (to the left of) LRAC, then economic profits will be earned and entry will drive the supply curve to the right. The opposite would occur if the supply were below and to the right of LRAC.

Now, a tax on business firms clearly raises the long-run average costs of the industry. Suppose that it shifts the LRAC, and thus the long-run supply curve, upward from *XX* to *TT* in the graph. This will move the equilibrium point from *E* to *B* and reduce polluting output from Q_e to Q_b. Similarly, a subsidy reduces average

"So <u>that's</u> where it goes! Well, I'd like to thank you fellows for bringing this to my attention."

cost, and so it shifts the LRAC and the long-run supply curve downward and to the right (from *XX* to *SS*). This moves the equilibrium point from *E* to *A* and raises *polluting output to Q_a.*

Our paradoxical result follows from the presumption that the more output a polluting industry produces, the more pollution it will emit. Under the tax on emissions, equilibrium moves from *E* to *B,* and so the polluting output falls from Q_e to Q_b. Thus, emissions will fall—just as common sense leads us to expect. But, with the subsidy, industry output will *rise* from Q_e to Q_a. Thus, contrary to intuition and despite the fact that each firm emits less, the industry must pollute more!

What explains this strange result? The answer is *entry.* The subsidy will initially bring economic profits to the polluters, and that will attract even more polluters into the industry. In essence, a subsidy encourages more polluters to open up for business. But our graph takes us one step beyond this simple observation. It is true that we end up with more polluting firms, but each will be polluting less than before. Thus, we have one influence leading to more pollution and another influence leading to less pollution. Which of these forces will win out? The graph tells us that if a rise in the polluting good's output always increases pollution, then, in a perfectly competitive industry, subsidies *must* lead to increased pollution on balance.

FIGURE 10-11

Taxes versus Subsidies as Incentives to Cut Pollution

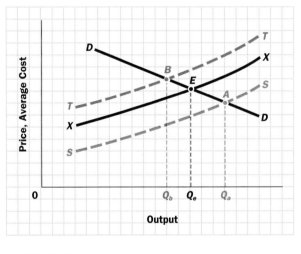

S U M M A R Y

1. *Markets* are classified into several types depending on the number of firms in the industry, the degree of similarity of their products, and the possibility of impediments to entry.

2. The four main market structures discussed by economists are monopoly (single-firm production), oligopoly (production by a few firms), monopolistic competition (production

by many firms with somewhat different products), and *perfect competition* (production by many firms with identical products and free entry and exit).

3. Few, if any, industries satisfy the conditions of perfect competition exactly, although some come close. Perfect competition is studied because it is easy to analyze and because it represents a case in which the market mechanism works well, so that it is useful as a yardstick to measure the performance of other market forms.

4. The demand curve of the perfectly competitive firm is horizontal because its output is so small a share of the industry's production that it cannot affect price. With a horizontal demand curve, price, average revenue, and marginal revenue are all equal.

5. The short-run equilibrium of the perfectly competitive firm is at the level of output that maximizes profits; that is, where MR = MC = price. This equilibrium may involve either a profit or a loss.

6. The short-run supply curve of the perfectly competitive firm is the portion of its marginal cost curve that lies above its average variable cost curve.

7. The industry's short-run supply curve under perfect competition is the horizontal sum of the supply curves of all of its firms.

8. In the long-run equilibrium of the perfectly competitive industry, freedom of entry forces each firm to earn zero *economic profit*, that is, no more than the firm's capital could earn elsewhere (the opportunity cost of the capital).

9. Industry equilibrium under perfect competition is at the point where the industry supply and demand curves intersect.

10. In long-run equilibrium under perfect competition, the firm chooses output such that average cost, marginal cost, and price are all equal. Output is at the point of minimum average cost. The firm's demand curve is tangent to its average cost curve at its minimum point.

11. The competitive industry's long-run supply curve coincides with its long-run average cost curve.

12. Both a tax on the emission of pollutants and a subsidy payment for reductions in those emissions induce firms to cut emissions. However, under perfect competition, a subsidy leads to the entry of more polluting firms and the likelihood of a net increase in emissions by the industry.

KEY TERMS

Market   189

Pure monopoly   190

Monopolistic competition   190

Oligopoly   190

Perfect competition   192

Price taker   193

Horizontal demand curve   193

Short-run equilibrium   194

Variable cost   197

Firm's supply curve   198

Long-run equilibrium   202

Economic profit   203

Opportunity cost   203

Industry supply curve   203

QUESTIONS FOR REVIEW

1. Explain why a perfectly competitive firm does not expand its sales without limit if its horizontal demand curve indicates that it can sell as much as it wants to at the current market price.

2. Explain why a demand curve is also a curve of average revenue. Recalling that when an average revenue curve is neither rising nor falling, marginal revenue must equal average revenue, explain why it is always true that $P = \text{MR} = \text{AR}$ for the perfectly competitive firm.

3. Under what circumstances might you expect the demand curve of the firm to be:

   a. Vertical

   b. Horizontal

   c. Negatively sloping

   d. Positively sloping

4. Explain why $P = \text{MC}$ in the short-run equilibrium of the perfectly competitive firm, whereas in long-run equilibrium $P = \text{MC} = \text{AC}$.

5. Regarding the four attributes of perfect competition—many small firms, freedom of entry, standardized product, and perfect information:

   a. Which is primarily responsible for the fact that the demand curve of a perfectly competitive firm is horizontal?

   b. Which is primarily responsible for the firm's zero economic profits in long-run equilibrium?

6. We indicated in this chapter that the MC curve cuts the AVC (average variable cost) curve at the *minimum* point of the latter. Explain why this must be so. (*Hint:* Because marginal costs are, by definition, entirely composed of variable costs, the MC curve can be considered the curve of *marginal variable costs.* Apply the general relationships between marginals and averages explained in Chapter 9.)

7. Explain why it is not sensible to close a business firm if it earns zero economic profits.

8. If the firm's lowest average cost is $48 and the corresponding average variable cost is $24, what does it pay a perfectly competitive firm to do if:

   a. The market price is $49?

   b. The price is $30?

   c. The price is $8?

9. If the market price in a competitive industry were above its equilibrium level, what would you expect to happen?

10. (More difficult) In this chapter we stated that the firm's MC curve goes through the lowest point of its AC curve and also through the lowest point of its AVC curve. Because the AVC curve lies below the AC curve, how can both of these statements be true? Why are they true? (*Hint:* See Figure 10–4.)

If there existed the universal mind that . . . would register simultaneously all the processes of nature and of society, that could forecast the results of their inter-reactions, such a mind . . . could . . . draw up a faultless and an exhaustive economic plan. . . . In truth, the bureaucracy often conceives that just such a mind is at its disposal; that is why it so easily frees itself from the control of the market.

Leon Trotsky, a leader of the Russian Revolution

THE PRICE SYSTEM AND THE CASE FOR FREE MARKETS

Our study of microeconomics focuses on two crucial questions: What does the market do well, and what does it do poorly? By applying what we learned about demand in Chapters 6 and 7, supply in Chapters 8 and 9, and ideal market functioning in Chapter 10, we can provide a fairly comprehensive answer to the first part of this question. This chapter describes the tasks that the market carries out well—some, indeed, with spectacular effectiveness.

We begin by recalling two important themes from Chapters 4 and 5. First, because all resources are *scarce*, a society must use them efficiently; second, an economy must somehow coordinate the many individual consumers' and producers' actions. Specifically, society must somehow choose:

- How much of each good to produce.
- What input quantities to use in the production process.
- How to distribute the resulting outputs among consumers.

As suggested by the opening quotation (by someone who was certainly in a position to know), these tasks are exceedingly difficult for a centrally planned economy. That overwhelming difficulty surely contributed to the fall of communism in the late 1980s, and the same difficulty shows up in the few remaining centrally planned economies, such as North Korea and Cuba. But for the most part those same tasks appear to be rather simple for a market system. This is why observers with philosophies as diverse as those of Adam Smith and the Russian Revolution's Leon Trotsky have admired the market, and why even those countries that maintain very strong central governments have now moved toward market economies.

Do not misinterpret this chapter as a piece of salesmanship. Here we study the market mechanism at its theoretical very best—when every good is produced under the exacting conditions of perfect competition. Some industries in our economy are reasonable approximations of perfect competition, but many others are as different from this idealized world as the physical world is from a frictionless vacuum tube. Just as the physicist uses the vacuum tube to study the laws of gravity, the economist uses the theoretical concept of a perfectly competitive economy to analyze the virtues of the market. We will spend plenty of time in later chapters studying its vices.

Puzzle: How High Should the Price to Cross the San Francisco–Oakland Bay Bridge Be?

In California, the San Francisco–Oakland Bay Bridge is very heavily traveled. The large volume of toll-paying traffic has probably long since paid for the cost of building this bridge, although that is probably less likely for the nearby San Mateo–Hayward and Dumbarton bridges, which are less crowded. Yet

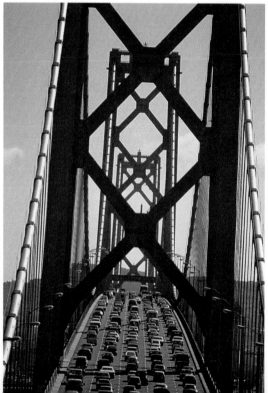

economists argue that the price charged to use the San Francisco–Oakland Bay Bridge should be higher than the prices for the second two. Why may that make sense? Before you have finished reading this chapter, you may even agree with this seemingly unfair proposition.

EFFICIENT RESOURCE ALLOCATION AND PRICING

The fundamental fact of scarcity limits the volume of goods and services that any economic system can produce. In Chapter 4, we illustrated the concept of scarcity with a graphic device called a production possibilities frontier, which we repeat here for convenience as Figure 11–1. The frontier, curve *BC*, depicts all combinations of missiles and milk that a hypothetical society can produce given the limited resources at its disposal. For example, if it decides to produce 300 missiles, it will have enough resources left over to produce no more than 500 billion quarts of milk (point *D*). Of course, it is always possible to produce fewer than 500 billion quarts of milk—at a point, such as *G*, below the production possibilities frontier. But if a society does this, it is wasting some of its potential output; that is, it is not operating efficiently.

In Chapter 4, we defined efficiency rather loosely as the absence of waste. Because this chapter discusses primarily how a competitive market economy allocates resources efficiently, we now need a more precise definition. It is easiest to define an **efficient allocation of resources** by saying what it is not. For example, suppose that we could rearrange our resource allocation so that one group of people would get more of the things it wanted, while no one else would have to give up anything. Then, the failure to change the allocation of resources to take advantage of this opportunity would surely be wasteful—that is, inefficient. When society has taken advantage of every such opportunity for improvement, so that no such possibilities remain for making some people better off without making others worse off, we say that the allocation of resources is efficient.

Because point *G* in Figure 11–1 is below the frontier, there must be points like *E* on the frontier that lie above and to the right of *G*. This means that at *E* we get more of *both* outputs without any increase in input, making it possible to make some people better off without harming anyone. Thus, no point below the frontier can represent an efficient allocation of resources. By contrast, every point on the frontier is efficient because, no matter where on the frontier we start, we cannot get more of one good without giving up some of the other.

This discussion also shows that, normally, many particular allocations of resources will be efficient; in the example, every combination of outputs that is represented by a point on frontier *BC* can be efficient. As a rule, the concept of efficiency cannot tell us which of these efficient allocations is best for society. Yet, as we shall see in this chapter, we can use the concept of efficiency to formulate surprisingly detailed rules to steer us away from situations in which resources would be wasted.

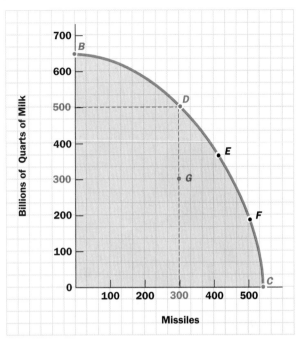

FIGURE 11-1

Production Possibilities Frontier and Efficiency

An **efficient allocation of resources** is one that takes advantage of every opportunity to make some individuals better off in their own estimation while not worsening the lot of anyone else.

PRICING TO PROMOTE EFFICIENCY: AN EXAMPLE

We can use the real example in our opening puzzle about the San Francisco–Oakland Bay Bridge to illustrate the connection between efficiency and the way prices can guide efficient choices. Prices can make all the difference between efficiency and inefficiency. The prices (tolls) that the California Department of Transportation charges drivers to use San Francisco Bay area bridges can make drivers' commutes less time consuming—that is, more efficient. We will see that people nonetheless may well reject the efficient solution.

Figure 11–2 shows a map of the San Francisco Bay area, featuring the five bridges that serve most of the traffic in and around the bay. A traveler going from a location north of Berkeley (point *A*) to Palo Alto (point *B*) can choose among at least three routes:

Route 1: Over the Richmond–San Rafael Bridge, across the Golden Gate Bridge, through San Francisco, and on southward on Highway 101.

Route 2: Across the bay on the San Francisco–Oakland Bay Bridge and on southward on Highway 101 as before.

Route 3: Down the eastern shore of the bay, across the San Mateo–Hayward Bridge or the Dumbarton Bridge, and then on to Palo Alto (shown in red in Figure 11–2).

Let's consider which of these three choices uses society's resources—commuter time, gasoline, and so on—most efficiently. The San Francisco–Oakland Bay Bridge is clearly the most crowded of the five bridges, followed by the Golden Gate Bridge. The first carries 270,000 vehicles per day, and the second 125,000. During rush hours (when more than 20,000 vehicles per hour cross the San Francisco–Oakland

---

FIGURE 11-2

Toll Bridges of the San Francisco Bay Area

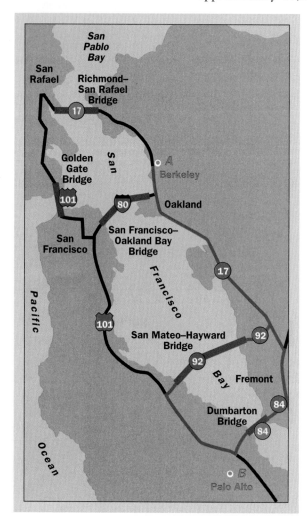

Bay Bridge), delays are frequent and traffic barely crawls across both bridges. In other words, space is scarce, and every car that uses these bridges makes it that much harder for others to get across.

On the other hand, the San Mateo–Hayward and Dumbarton bridges carry approximately 85,000 and 65,000 vehicles per day, respectively. To achieve efficiency, any driver who is indifferent about the two routes should take the one using the least crowded bridges. This would help reduce the amount of travel time wasted by the population as a whole. Specifically, in our illustration, Route 1, using the Golden Gate Bridge, is not a socially desirable way for our driver to get to Palo Alto because it adds too many miles to the trip and because it requires two bridge crossings. Route 2, with its use of the San Francisco–Oakland Bay Bridge, is even worse because of the added delays it causes for everyone else. Route 3, for drivers who are indifferent about these options, is the best choice from the viewpoint of the public interest. This does not mean that it is socially efficient to equalize the traffic among the routes, but it certainly would help travelers get where they are going faster if transportation authorities could induce some drivers to leave the most crowded routes and switch over to some less crowded ones.

Appropriate prices can promote this sort of efficiency in bridge utilization. Specifically, if higher prices (very likely *substantially* higher prices) were charged for drivers to cross the most crowded bridges (on which space is a scarce resource), balanced by lower prices on the uncrowded bridges, then more drivers could be induced to use the uncrowded bridges. This is just the same reasoning that leads economists to advocate low prices for abundant minerals and high prices for scarce ones.

CAN PRICE INCREASES EVER SERVE THE PUBLIC INTEREST?

This discussion raises a point that people untrained in economics always find extremely difficult to accept: Low prices may not always serve the public interest! The reason is pretty clear. If a price, such as the price of crossing a crowded bridge or the price of gasoline, is set "too low," then consumers will receive the "wrong" market signals. Low prices will encourage them to crowd the bridge even more or to consume more oil, thereby squandering society's precious resources.

A striking historical illustration brings out this point. In 1834, a professor of economics at the University of Dublin named Mountifort Longfield lectured about the price system. He offered the following example:

> Suppose the crop of potatoes in Ireland was to fall short in some year one-sixth of the usual consumption. If [there were no] increase of price, the whole . . . supply of the year would be exhausted in ten months, and for the remaining two months a scene of misery and famine beyond description would ensue. . . . But when prices [increase] the sufferers [often believe] that it is not caused by scarcity. . . . They suppose that there are provisions enough, but that the distress is caused by the insatiable rapacity of the possessors . . . [and] they have generally succeeded in obtaining laws against [the price increases] . . . which alone can prevent the provisions from being entirely consumed long before a new supply can be obtained. [1]

You may be intrigued to know that this talk was given some 10 years before the great potato famine, which caused unspeakable misery and death by starvation and

---

[1] Mountifort Longfield, *Lectures on Political Economy Delivered in Trinity and Michaelmas Terms* (Dublin: W. Curry, Jr., and Company, 1834), pp. 53–56.

brought many people from Ireland to the United States. The story of the actual potato famine in Ireland is much more complex than Longfield's discussion indicates. Still, the implications of his lecture about the way the price system works are entirely valid.

We can perhaps rephrase Longfield's reasoning more usefully. If the crop fails, potatoes become scarcer. If society is to use its scarce resources efficiently, stretching out the potato supply to last until the next crop arrives, it must cut back on the consumption of potatoes during earlier months—which is just what rising prices will do automatically if free-market mechanisms are allowed to work. However, if the price is held artificially low, consumers will use society's resources inefficiently. In this case, the inefficiency shows up in the form of famine and suffering when people deplete this year's crop months before the next one is harvested.

It is not easy to accept the notion that higher prices can serve the public interest better than lower ones. Politicians who voice this view are in the position of the proverbial parent who, before spanking a child, announces, "This is going to hurt me much more than it hurts you!" Because advocacy of higher prices courts political disaster, the political system often rejects the market solution when resources suddenly become more scarce.

The way that airport officials price landing privileges at crowded airports offers a good example. Airports become particularly congested at "peak hours," just before 9 A.M. and just after 5 P.M. This is when passengers most often suffer long delays. But many airports continue to charge bargain landing fees throughout the day, even at those crowded hours. That makes it attractive for small corporate jets or other planes carrying only a few passengers to arrive and take off at those hours, worsening the delays. Higher fees for peak-hour landings can discourage such overuse, but they are politically unpopular, and many airports are run by local governments. So we continue to experience late arrivals as a normal feature of air travel.

THE MARKET STRIKES BACK As we saw in our *ideas,* keeping prices low when a rise is appropriate can have serious consequences indeed. We have seen that it can worsen the effects of shortages of food and other vital goods. We know that inappropriately low prices caused nationwide chaos in gasoline distribution after the sudden drop in Iranian oil exports in 1979. In times of war, constraints on prices have even contributed to the surrender of cities under military siege, deterring those who would otherwise have risked smuggling food supplies through enemy lines. Low prices have also discouraged housing construction in cities where rent controls made building a losing proposition. Of course, in some cases it is appropriate to resist price increases—when unrestrained monopoly would otherwise succeed in gouging the public, when taxes are imposed on products capriciously and inappropriately, and when rising prices fall so heavily on poor people that rationing becomes the more acceptable option. But before tampering with the market mechanism we must carefully evaluate the potentially serious and even tragic consequences that artificial restrictions on prices can produce.

Attempts to Repeal the Laws of Supply and Demand: The Market Strikes Back

■ SCARCITY AND THE NEED TO COORDINATE ECONOMIC DECISIONS

Efficiency becomes a particularly critical issue when we concern ourselves with the workings of the economy as a whole, rather than narrower topics such as choosing among bridge routes or deciding on the output of a single firm. We can think of an economy as a complex machine with literally millions of component parts. If this machine is to function efficiently, we must find some way to make the parts work in harmony.

A consumer in Peoria, Illinois, may decide to purchase two dozen eggs, and on the same day thousands of shoppers throughout the country make similar decisions. None of these purchasers knows or cares about the decisions of the others. Yet scarcity requires that these demands must somehow be coordinated with the production process so that the total quantity of eggs demanded does not exceed the total quantity supplied. Consumers, supermarkets, wholesalers, shippers, and

---

● AFTER "SHOCK THERAPY," THE POLISH ECONOMY IS THRIVING

Ten years ago, communism collapsed all over eastern Europe and the former Soviet Union, ending economic central planning and heralding the emergence of a free market in these countries. Nowhere were these changes as dramatic as in Poland, where reforms constituted no less than economic "shock therapy."

Poland's transformation into a market economy, though far from complete, has been nearly as radical as the first postcommunist government hoped. Poland began the decade saddled with a legendarily incompetent, old-fashioned, and badly managed economy, which in its depths managed to run out of things like matches and salt, its paltry living standards bequeathed by a centrally controlled economy. It reached out to the West for help in creating monetary, budget, trade, and legal regimes. It now ranks among Europe's fastest-growing economies, with an annual GDP growth rate of more than 5 percent. Economic liberalization has freed thousands of entrepreneurs to sell, within loose limits, anything they want at whatever price they can get. Today, more than 65 percent of GDP comes from the private sector (up from just 16 percent in 1989), and more than half of Polish workers are employed in private enterprise.

The new, free-market mechanisms are clearly visible on Warsaw streets. Once-empty shelves are now overflowing with goods. Stores sell the latest fashions from Levi Strauss and Benetton. Glitzy billboards symbolize the battle over the consumer's pocketbook.

Despite all the good news, Poland still has much work to do. Many of its publicly owned industries are still backward, business and personal life remains hampered by bureaucratic red tape, and agriculture is 50 years behind the rest of Europe, with 27 percent of Polish workers engaged in farming.

SOURCES: "Survey of Business in Eastern Europe," *The Economist,* November 22, 1997; "Russia Is Not Poland, and That's Too Bad," Week in Review, *New York Times,* August 30, 1998, p. 5; and "Poland and the European Union," *The Economist,* February 28, 1998.

---

chicken farmers must somehow arrive at mutually consistent decisions; otherwise the economic process will deteriorate into chaos, as will millions of other such decisions. A machine cannot run with a few missing parts.

In a planned or centrally directed economy, we can easily imagine how such coordination takes place—though implementation is far more difficult than conception. Central planners set production targets for firms and sometimes tell firms how to meet these targets. In extreme cases, consumers may even be told, rather than asked, what they want to consume.

In contrast, a market system uses *prices* to coordinate economic activity. High prices discourage consumption of the most scarce resources, whereas low prices encourage consumption of comparatively abundant resources. In this way, Adam Smith's invisible hand uses prices to organize the economy's production.

The invisible hand has an astonishing capacity to handle enormously complex coordination problems—even those that remain beyond computer capabilities. Like any mechanism, this one has its imperfections, some of them rather serious. But we should not lose sight of the tremendously demanding task that the market constantly does accomplish—unnoticed, undirected, and in some respects, amazingly well. Let's look at just how the market goes about coordinating economic activity.

THREE COORDINATION TASKS IN THE ECONOMY

We noted in Chapter 4 that any economic system, whether planned or unplanned, must find answers to three basic questions of resource allocation:

- *Output selection.* How much of each commodity should be produced?
- *Production planning.* What quantities of each of the available inputs should be used to produce each good?
- *Distribution.* How should the resulting products be divided among consumers?

These coordination tasks may at first appear to be tailor-made for a regime of government planning like the one that the former Soviet Union used to employ. Yet most economists (even, nowadays, those in the formerly centrally planned economies) believe that it is in exactly these tasks that central direction performs most poorly and, paradoxically, the undisciplined free market performs best.

To understand how the unguided market manages the miracle of creating order out of what might otherwise be chaos, let's look at how each of these questions is answered by a system of free and unfettered markets—the method of economic organization that 18th-century French economists named **laissez faire.** Under laissez faire, the government acts to prevent crime, enforce contracts, and build roads and other types of public works; but it does not set prices and interferes as little as possible with the operation of free markets. How does such an unmanaged economy solve the three coordination problems?

Laissez faire refers to the practice of minimal government interference with the workings of the market system. The term means that people should be left alone in carrying out their economic affairs.

OUTPUT SELECTION   A free-market system decides what should be produced via what we have called the "law" of supply and demand. Where there is a shortage (that is, where quantity demanded exceeds quantity supplied), the market mechanism pushes the price upward, thereby encouraging more production and less consumption of the commodity that is in short supply. Where a surplus arises (that is, where quantity supplied exceeds quantity demanded), the same mechanism works in reverse: the price falls, discouraging production and stimulating consumption.

As an example, suppose that millions of people wake up one morning with a particular craving for omelets. As a result, for the moment, the quantity of eggs demanded exceeds the quantity supplied. But, within a few days, the market mechanism swings into action to meet this sudden change in demand. The price of eggs rises, which stimulates egg production. At first, farmers will simply bring more eggs to market by taking them out of storage. Over a somewhat longer time period, chickens that otherwise would have been sold for meat are kept in the chicken coops laying eggs. Finally, if the high price of eggs persists, farmers begin to increase their flocks, build more cages, and so on. Thus, a shift in consumer demand leads to a shift in society's resources; more eggs are wanted, and so the market mechanism sees to it that more of society's resources are devoted to egg production and marketing.

Similar reactions follow if a technological breakthrough reduces the input quantities needed to produce some item. Electronic calculators are a marvelous example. Just 25 years ago, calculators were so expensive that they could be found only in business firms and scientific laboratories. Then advances in science and engineering reduced their cost dramatically, and the market went to work. With costs sharply reduced, prices fell and the quantity demanded skyrocketed. Electronics firms flocked into the industry to meet this demand, which is to say that more of society's resources were devoted to producing the calculators that were suddenly in such great demand. These examples lead us to conclude that:

Under laissez faire, the allocation of society's resources among different products depends on consumer preferences (demands) and the production costs of the goods demanded. Prices (and the resulting profitability of the different products) vary so as to bring the quantity of each commodity produced into line with the quantity demanded.

Notice that no bureaucrat or central planner arranges resource allocation. Instead, an unseen force guides allocation—the lure of profits, which is the invisible hand that guides chicken farmers to increase their flocks when eggs are in greater demand and guides electronics firms to build new factories when the cost of electronic products falls.

PRODUCTION PLANNING   Once the market has decided on output composition, the next coordination task is to determine just how those goods are going to be produced. The production-planning problem includes, among other things, the division

CORPORATE LEADERS GATHER IN A FIELD OUTSIDE DARIEN, CONNECTICUT, WHERE ONE OF THEM CLAIMS TO HAVE SEEN THE INVISIBLE HAND OF THE MARKETPLACE.

of society's scarce inputs among enterprises. Which farm or factory will get how much of which materials? Of the labor force? Of the produced inputs such as plant and machinery? Such decisions can be crucial. If a factory runs short of an essential input, the entire production process may grind to a halt.

As a matter of fact, no economic system can select inputs and outputs separately. The input distribution between the production of cars and the manufacture of washing machines determines the quantities of cars and washing machines that society can obtain. However, it is simpler to think of input and output decisions as if they occur one at a time.

Once again, under laissez faire it is the price system that apportions fuels and other inputs among different industries in accord with those industries' requirements. The firm that needs a piece of equipment most urgently will be the last to drop out of the market for that product when prices rise. If millers demand more wheat than is currently available, the price will rise and bring quantity demanded back into line with quantity supplied, always giving priority to those users who are willing to pay the most for grain. Thus:

> In a free market, inputs are assigned to the firms that can make the most productive (most profitable) use of them. Firms that cannot make a sufficiently productive use of some input will be priced out of the market for that item.

This task, which sounds so simple, is actually almost unimaginably complex. It is so complex that it has helped to bring down many centrally planned systems. We will return to it shortly, as an illustration of how difficult it is to replace the market by a central planning bureau. But first let us consider the third of our three coordination problems.

DISTRIBUTION OF PRODUCTS AMONG CONSUMERS The third task of any economy is to decide which consumer gets each of the goods that has been produced. The objective is to distribute the available supplies to match differing consumer preferences as well as possible. Coffee lovers must not be flooded with tea while tea drinkers are showered with coffee.

The price mechanism solves this problem by assigning the highest prices to the goods in greatest demand and then letting individual consumers pursue their own self-interests. Consider our example of rising egg prices. As the price of eggs rises, those whose craving for omelets is not terribly strong will begin to buy fewer eggs. In effect, the price acts as a rationing device that apportions the available eggs among consumers who are willing to pay the most for them.

Thus, the price mechanism has an important advantage over other rationing devices: it can respond to individual consumer preferences. If a centrally planned economy rations eggs by distributing the same amount to everyone (say, two eggs per week to each person), then everyone ends up with two eggs whether he likes eggs or detests them. The price system, on the other hand, permits each consumer to set her own priorities. Thus:

THE TRADE-OFF The price system carries out the distribution process by rationing goods on the basis of preferences and relative incomes. Notice the last three words of the previous sentence. The price system *does* favor the rich, and this is a problem that market economies must confront.

However, we may still want to think twice before declaring ourselves opposed to the price system. If equality is our goal, might not a more reasonable solution be to use the tax system to equalize incomes and then let the market mechanism distribute goods in accord with preferences? We take this idea up in Chapter 21, where we discuss tax policy.

The Trade-off between Efficiency and Equality

We have just seen, in broad outline, how a laissez-faire economy addresses the three basic issues of resource allocation: what to produce, how to produce it, and how to distribute the resulting products. Because it performs these tasks quietly, without central direction, and with no apparent concern for the public interest, many radical critics have predicted that such an unplanned system must degenerate into chaos. Yet unplanned, free-market economies are far from chaotic. Quite ironically, it is the centrally planned economies that have often ended up in economic disarray while the invisible hand seems to go on about its business seamlessly. Perhaps the best way to appreciate the free market's accomplishments is to consider how a centrally planned system must cope with the coordination problems we have just outlined. Let us examine just one of them: production planning.

INPUT-OUTPUT ANALYSIS: THE NEAR IMPOSSIBILITY OF PERFECT CENTRAL PLANNING

Of the three coordination tasks of any economy, the assignment of input to specific industries and firms has claimed the most attention of central planners. Why? Because the production processes of the various industries are interdependent. Industry X cannot operate without Industry Y's output, but Industry Y, in turn, needs Industry X's product. The whole economy can grind to a halt if planners do not solve the production-planning problem satisfactorily. In recent years, failure to adapt to this kind of interdependence has had graphic consequences in North Korea, one of the last remaining centrally planned economies. Breakdowns of key economic activities such as the electric supply grid, transportation systems, and other basic industries have each exacerbated the others' failures and created a terrible cycle of economic disaster, contributing to severe famine.

A simple example will further illustrate the point. Unless economic planners allocate enough gasoline to the trucking industry, products will not get to market. And unless they allocate enough trucks to haul gasoline to gas stations, consumers will not be able to get around. Thus, trucking activity depends on gasoline production but gasoline production also depends on trucking activity. We seem to be caught in a circle. Planners must decide both truck and gasoline outputs together, not separately.

Because the output required from any one industry depends on the output from every other industry, planners can be sure that the production of the various outputs is sufficient to meet both consumer and industrial demands only by taking explicit account of the interdependencies among industries. If they change the output target for one industry, they must also adjust every other industry's output target.

For example, if planners decide to provide consumers with more electricity, then more steel must be produced in order to build more electric generators. But an increase in steel output requires more coal to be mined. More mining, in turn, means

● INPUT-OUTPUT EQUATIONS: AN EXAMPLE

Imagine an economy with only three outputs: electricity, steel, and coal, and let E, S, and C represent the dollar values of their respective outputs. Suppose that to produce every dollar's worth of steel, $0.20 worth of electricity is used, so that the total electricity demand of steel manufacturers is $0.2S$. Similarly, assume that coal manufacturers use $0.30 of electricity in producing $1 worth of coal, or a total of $0.3C$ units of electricity. Because E dollars of electricity are produced in total, the amount left over for consumers, after subtraction of industrial demands for fuel, will be E (available electricity) minus $0.2S$ (used in steel production) minus $0.3C$ (used in coal production). Suppose further that the central planners have decided to supply $15 million worth of electricity to consumers. We end up with the electricity output equation:

$$E - 0.2S - 0.3C = 15$$

The planner will also need such an equation for each of the two other industries, specifying for each of them the net amount intended to be left for consumers after the industrial uses of the product. The full set of equations will then be similar to the following:

$$E - 0.2S - 0.3C = 15$$
$$S - 0.1E - 0.06C = 7$$
$$C - 0.15E - 0.4S = 10$$

These are typical equations in an input-output analysis. In practice, however, such an analysis has dozens and sometimes hundreds of equations with similar numbers of unknowns. This, then, is the logic of input-output analysis.

Input-output analysis is a mathematical procedure that takes account of the interdependence among the economy's industries and determines the amount of output each industry must provide as inputs to the other industries in the economy.

that still more electricity is needed to light the mines, to run the elevators, perhaps to operate some of the trains that carry the coal, and so on and on. Any single change in production sets off a chain of adjustments throughout the economy that require still further adjustments.

To decide how much of each output an economy must produce, the planner must use statistics to form a set of equations, one equation for each product, and then solve those equations simultaneously. The simultaneous solution process prevents the circularity of the analysis—electricity output depends on steel production, but steel output depends on electricity production—from becoming a vicious circle. The technique used to solve these complicated equations—**input-output analysis**—was invented by the late economist Wassily Leontief, who won the 1973 Nobel Prize for his work.

The equations of input-output analysis illustrated in the accompanying box, "Input-Output Equations: An Example," take explicit account of the interdependence among industries by describing precisely how each industry's target output depends on every other industry's target. Only by solving these equations simultaneously for the required outputs of electricity, steel, coal, and so on can planners ensure a consistent solution that produces the required amounts of each product—including the amount of each product needed to produce every other product.

The example of input-output analysis that appears in the box is not provided so that you can learn how to apply the technique yourself. Its real purpose is to help you imagine how very complicated the problems facing a central planner can become. Their task, although analogous to the one in the box, is enormously more complex. In any real economy, the number of commodities is far greater than the three outputs in the example. In the United States, some large manufacturing companies deal in hundreds of thousands of items, and the armed forces keep several million different items in inventory.

In this cartoon from a Soviet humor magazine, one construction worker comments to another, "A slight mistake in the plans, perhaps." It is interesting that there were many cartoons making fun of the inefficiencies of the Soviet economy in the humor magazines of the USSR before the collapse of communism.

Planners must thus ultimately make calculations for each single item. It is not enough to plan the right number of bolts in total; they must make sure that the required number of each size is produced. (Try putting 5 million large bolts into 5 million small nuts!) To be sure that their plans will really work, they need a separate equation for every size of bolt and one for every size and type of nut. But then, to replicate the analysis described in the box, they would have to solve several million equations simultaneously! This task would strain even the most powerful computer's capability, if it could do the job at all.

Worse still is the data problem. Each of our three equations requires three pieces of statistical information, making 3 × 3, or 9 numbers in total. The equation for electricity must indicate how much electricity is needed in steel production, how much in coal production, and how much is demanded by consumers, all on the basis of statistical information that is itself subject to error. Therefore, in a five-industry analysis, 5 × 5, or 25 pieces of data are needed; a 100-industry analysis requires 100^2, or 10,000 numbers, and a million-item input-output study might need one trillion pieces of information. Solving data-gathering problems is, therefore, no easy task, to put it mildly. Still other complications arise, but we have seen enough to conclude that:

A full, rigorous central-planning solution to the production problem is a tremendous task, requiring an overwhelming quantity of information and some incredibly difficult calculations. Yet this very complex job is carried out automatically and unobtrusively by the price mechanism in a free-market economy.

WHICH BUYERS AND WHICH SELLERS GET PRIORITY?

Because the supplies of all commodities are limited, some potential customers of a product will end up with none of it. And because demand is not infinite, some potential suppliers of a commodity will find no market available for them. So, which consumers get the scarce commodity, and which firms get to supply the goods? Again, the price mechanism comes to the rescue.

Other things being equal, the price mechanism ensures that those consumers who want a scarce commodity most will receive it, and that those sellers who can supply it most efficiently will get to supply the commodity.

To illustrate, let's look at Figure 11–3, an ordinary supply-demand graph. For simplicity, suppose we are dealing here with a commodity such as a best-selling novel. We assume also that no one buys more than one copy of the book. The

FIGURE 11–3

Supply-Demand Graph Showing that Price Excludes only Buyers and Sellers Who Care the Least

Quantity

demand curve, *DD*, represents the preferences of 6,000 potential customers with widely differing preferences. The first 1,000 of them are willing to pay as much as $70 for the book, as shown by point *A* on the demand curve (though they would, of course, prefer to pay less). Point *B* shows a second group of 1,000 buyers who will purchase the book at a price of $60, but refuse to spend $70 on it (because they care less about the book than the point *A* consumers). Similarly, point *C* represents the demand of a third group of consumers, to whom the book is even less important, so that they are willing to spend only $50 for a copy. And points *E*, *F*, and *G* represent sets of consumers with successively lower desires for the book, until at point *G*, consumers are only willing to pay $20 for the book.

With *SS* the supply curve, the equilibrium point is *E*, where *SS* and *DD* intersect. Under perfect competition, the market price of the book will be $40. Buyers at point *A*, to whom the book is worth $70, will be delighted to buy it for only $40. Similarly, buyers at points *B*, *C*, and *E* will also buy the book. But the consumers at points *F* and *G*, to whom the book is worth less than $40, will not buy the book. We can see in this example that the book will go to the consumers who value it most (in terms of money), and only those who value it least will be deprived of it.

The price mechanism always ranks potential consumers of a good in the order of the intensity of their preference for the good, as indicated by the amount they are willing to spend for it.

The price system's priority to those consumers who assign most importance to a good goes one step further. Suppose that supply increases, with the supply curve shifting to the right, from *SS* to *S'S'* in the figure. Which consumers will get the increased quantity supplied? Answer: Of those consumers in the group of people who were previously denied the commodity, those who want it most intensely will acquire the product. In the graph, the shift in supply moves the equilibrium point from *E* to *F*, so point *F* consumers will now be included in the group of buyers of the book (along with point *A*, *B*, *C*, and *E* consumers), but the point *G* consumers still do not purchase the book. The book is worth more to point *F* consumers ($30) than it is to point *G* consumers, who value it only at $20.

The price system seems to set the right priorities in deciding which prospective consumers of some specific good do receive some of it, and which do not. Only one major imperfection arises in this argument, to which we will return in a moment.

First, however, let's look at Figure 11–3 again, this time from the supplying firm's point of view. Assume that *SS* is the long-run industry supply curve. Point *g* on this curve represents the amount that the industry will supply if the price is $20—that is, it is the amount that will be supplied by firms whose average cost is no higher than $20, so that the price will cover their cost. Similarly, point *f* represents the output of all firms whose average cost is no higher than $30, so that the group of suppliers now includes some firms that are less efficient (they have higher average cost) than those at point *g*. And at point *e* some of the suppliers will have average costs of $40, but none of suppliers will have an average cost higher than that. Using the same reasoning, as we move further along *SS* to points *c*, *b*, and *a*, increasingly inefficient firms will be included among the suppliers.

Now, we examine the supply-demand equilibrium point *e*, at which price is $40. Which suppliers will be able to market their products at this point? Answer: Those at points *g*, *f*, and *e*, but not firms at points *c*, *b*, and *a*, because no firm in the last three groups can cover its costs at the equilibrium price. Once again, the price mechanism does its job. It ranks firms in order of their efficiency, as measured by long-run average costs, and brings business to the more efficient firms, leaving out the least efficient potential suppliers.

All this illustrates yet another of the many desirable features of the price mechanism. But there is one fly in the ointment—at least on the demand side of the story. We saw that consumers in group G were likely to be denied the scarce commodity we are discussing, because they wanted it less than the other consumers. Group G consumers were willing to spend only $20 for the book, whereas the others were willing to spend more for it. But what if some consumers in group G want the book very badly, but are also very poor? This is an important question—one we will encounter again and again. The price mechanism is like a democracy, but one in which the rule is not "one person, one vote," but rather, "one dollar, one vote." In other words, under the price mechanism rich consumers' preferences get much more attention than poor consumers' desires do.

HOW PERFECT COMPETITION ACHIEVES EFFICIENCY

We have indicated how the market mechanism solves the three basic coordination problems of any economy—what to produce, how to produce it, and how to distribute the goods to consumers. Also, we have suggested that these same tasks pose almost insurmountable difficulties for central planners. One critical question remains. Is the allocation of resources that the market mechanism selects *efficient*, according to the precise definition of efficiency presented at the start of this chapter?

EXAMPLE: EFFICIENT RESOURCE ALLOCATION IN OUTPUT SELECTION

The answer, under perfect competition's idealized circumstances, is yes. Because a detailed proof of this assertion for all three coordination tasks is long and time-consuming, we will present the proof only for the first of the three tasks—*output selection*. We will show that, at least in theory, perfect competition does guarantee efficiency in determining the relative quantities of the different commodities that the economy produces.

The proof comes in two steps. First, we derive a criterion for efficient output selection, that is, a test that tells us whether or not production is being carried out efficiently. Second, we show that the prices that emerge from the market mechanism under perfect competition automatically pass this test.

STEP 1: RULE FOR EFFICIENT OUTPUT SELECTION   We begin by stating the rule for efficient output selection:

MARGINAL ANALYSIS Efficiency in the choice of output quantities requires that, for each of the economy's outputs, the marginal cost (MC) of the last unit produced be equal to the marginal utility (MU) of the last unit consumed.[2] In symbols:

$$MC = MU$$

This rule is yet another example of the basic principle of marginal analysis that we learned in Chapter 9.

The efficient decision about output quantities is the one that maximizes the total benefit (total utility) to society, minus the cost to society of producing the output quantities that are chosen. In other words, the goal is to maximize the surplus that society gains—total utility minus total cost. But, as we saw in Chapter 9, to maximize the difference between total utility and total cost, we must find the outputs

The Importance of Thinking at the Margin

---

[2] Recall from Chapter 6 that we measure marginal utility in money terms, that is, the amount of money that a consumer is willing to give up for an additional unit of the commodity. Economists usually call this the marginal rate of substitution between the commodity and money.

that equalize the corresponding marginal figures—marginal utility and marginal cost—to one another, as the preceding efficiency rule tells us.

An example will help us to see explicitly why resource allocation must satisfy this rule to be deemed efficient. Suppose that the marginal utility of an additional pound of beef to consumers is $8, but its marginal cost is only $5. Then the value of the resources that would have to be used up to produce one more pound of beef (its MC) would be $3 less than the money value that consumers would willingly pay for that additional pound (its MU). By expanding the output of beef by one pound, society could get more (in MU) out of the economic production process than it was putting in (MC). We know that the output at which MU exceeds MC cannot be optimal, because society would be better off with an increase in that output level. The opposite is true if the MC of beef exceeds the MU of beef.

We have therefore shown that, if any product's MU is not equal to MC—whether MU exceeds MC or MC exceeds MU—the economy must be wasting an opportunity to achieve a net improvement in consumers' welfare. This is exactly what we mean by saying society is using resources inefficiently. Just as was true at point G in Figure 11–1, if MC does not equal MU for any commodity, it is possible to rearrange production to make some people better off while harming no one else. It follows, then, that efficient output choice occurs only when MC equals MU for every good.[3]

STEP 2: THE PRICE SYSTEM'S CRITICAL ROLE   Next, we must show that under perfect competition, the price system automatically leads buyers and sellers to behave in a way that equalizes MU and MC.

To see this, recall from the previous chapter that under perfect competition it is most profitable for each beef-producing firm to produce the quantity at which the marginal cost equals the price *(P)* of beef:

$$MC = P$$

This must be so because, if the marginal cost of beef were less than the price, the farmer could add to profits by increasing the size of the herd (or the amount of grain fed to the animals). The reverse would be true if the marginal cost of beef were greater than its price. Thus, under perfect competition, the lure of profits leads each producer of beef (and of every other product) to supply the quantity that makes $MC = P.$

We also learned, in Chapter 6, that each consumer will purchase the quantity of beef at which the marginal utility of beef in money terms equals the price of beef:

$$MU = P$$

If consumers did not do this, either an increase or a decrease in their beef purchases would leave them better off.

Putting these last two equations together, we see that the invisible hand enforces the following string of equalities:

$$MC = P = MU$$

But if the MC of beef and the MU of beef both equal the same price, $P,$ then they must equal each other. That is, it must be true that the quantity of beef produced and consumed in a perfectly competitive market satisfies the equation:

$$MC = MU$$

This is precisely our rule for efficient output selection. Because the same must be true of every other product supplied by a competitive industry:

Under perfect competition, producers and consumers will make uncoordinated decisions that we can expect automatically (and amazingly) to produce exactly the

---

[3] *Warning:* As shown in Chapter 14, markets sometimes perform imperfectly because the decision maker faces a different marginal cost from the marginal cost to society. This occurs when the individual who creates the cost can make someone else bear the burden. Example: Firm X's production causes pollution emissions that increase nearby households' laundry bills. In such a case, Firm X will ignore the cost and produce inefficiently large outputs and emissions. We study such problems, called externalities, in Chapters 14 and 22.

quantity of each good that satisfies the MC = MU rule for efficiency. That is, under the idealized conditions of perfect competition, the market mechanism, without any government intervention and without anyone else directing it or planning for it, is capable of allocating society's scarce resources efficiently.

THE INVISIBLE HAND AT WORK

This is truly a remarkable result. How can the price mechanism automatically satisfy all of the exacting requirements for efficiency (that marginal utility equals marginal cost for each and every commodity)—requirements that no central planner can hope to handle because of the masses of statistics and the enormous calculations they entail? This seems analogous to a magician suddenly pulling a rabbit out of a hat!

But, as always, rabbits come out of hats only if they were hidden there in the first place. What really is the mechanism by which our act of magic works? The secret is that the price system lets consumers and producers pursue their own best interests—something they are probably very good at doing. Prices are the dollar costs of commodities to consumers, so in pursuing their own best interests, consumers will buy the commodities that give them the most satisfaction per dollar. But the price the consumer pays is also equal to MC.

Because MC measures the resource cost (in every firm) of producing one more unit of the good, this means that consumers will buy the commodities that give them the most satisfaction for the resources used up in producing them. In other words, the market mechanism leads consumers to squeeze the greatest possible benefit out of the social resources used up in making the goods and services they buy. So, if resources are priced appropriately (P = MC), when consumers make the best use of their money they must also be making the best use of society's resources. That is the way the market mechanism ensures economic efficiency.

> When all prices are set equal to marginal costs, the price system gives correct cost signals to consumers. It has set prices at levels that induce consumers to use society's resources with the same care they devote to watching their own money, because the money cost of a good to the consumer has been set equal to the opportunity cost of the good to society. A perfectly analogous explanation applies to the decisions of producers.

This is the magic of the invisible hand. Unlike central planners, consumers need not know how difficult it is to manufacture a certain product or how scarce the inputs required by the production process are. Everything consumers need to know to make their decisions is embodied in the market price, which, under perfect competition, accurately reflects marginal costs. Similarly, producers do not need to know anything about the psychology and tastes of their individual customers—price movements tell them all they need to know when consumer preferences change.

OTHER ROLES OF PRICES: INCOME DISTRIBUTION AND FAIRNESS

So far we have stressed the role of prices that economists emphasize most: Prices guide resource allocation. But prices also command the spotlight in another role: Prices influence the distribution of income between buyers and sellers. For example, high rents often make tenants poorer and landlords richer.

This rather obvious role of prices draws the most attention from the public, politicians, and regulators, and we should not lose sight of it.[4] Markets serve only those demands that are backed up by consumers' desire and *ability to pay*. The market system may do well in serving poor families, because it gives them more food and clothing than a less efficient economy would provide. But the market system offers far more to wealthy families. Many people think that such an arrangement represents a great injustice, however efficient it may be.

---

[4] Income distribution is the subject of Part IV.

⬤ **POLICY DEBATE** ▌ **USER CHARGES FOR PUBLIC FACILITIES**

At a time when budget cutting is the way to popularity for a politician, the notion of charging users for the services that government once gave away free is under debate. Economists have often advocated such charges for the use of roads, bridges, museums, educational facilities, and the like. Of course, it's true that if the services are provided "free," the public has to pay for them anyhow, though more indirectly through taxes. But if people are asked to pay directly for such services, it can make a big difference.

For example, let's say a road is financed out of general taxes. In this circumstance, it does not matter how many times Sabrina, the owner of an independent trucking firm, uses the road. She pays the same amount whether she uses it twice a year or every day. But if Sabrina has to pay a toll every time she uses the road, she will have a strong incentive to avoid unnecessary use. That is why advocates of pricing to promote economic efficiency propose more substantial *user charges,* not only for roads and bridges but also for admission to national parks, for the use of publicly owned grazing lands, and for the use of the television and radio spectrum by broadcasters.

Opponents of user charges contend that these fees are unfair to poor people. Besides, it is argued, the use of public facilities like libraries, museums, and schools should be encouraged rather than impeded by user charges. For instance, in New York there is no charge to cross the three deteriorating bridges that connect Brooklyn and Queens with Manhattan. But each time user charges are proposed, they are met with the cry, "Should I have to pay an admission fee into my own city?!"

Often, people oppose economists' recommendations for improving the economy's efficiency on the grounds that these proposals are *unfair.* For example, economists frequently advocate higher prices for transportation facilities at the times of day when the facilities are most crowded. Economists propose a pricing arrangement called "peak, off-peak pricing" under which prices for public transportation are higher during rush hours than during other hours.

The rationale for this proposal should be clear from our discussion of efficiency. A seat on a train is a much scarcer resource during rush hours than it is during other times of the day when the trains run fairly empty. Thus, according to the principles of efficiency outlined in this chapter, seats should be more expensive during rush hours to discourage those consumers with no set schedule from riding the trains during peak periods. The same notion applies to other services. Charges for long-distance telephone calls made at night are sometimes lower than those in the daytime. And in some places, electricity is cheaper at night, when demand does not strain the supplier's generating capacity.

Yet the proposal that transportation authorities should charge higher fares for public transportation during peak hours—say, from 8:00 A.M. to 9:30 A.M. and from 4:30 P.M. to 6:00 P.M.—often runs into stiff opposition. Opponents say that most of the burden of such higher fares will fall on lower-income working people who have no choice about the timing of their trips. For example, a survey in Great Britain of economists and members of Parliament found that, while high peak-period fares were favored by 88 percent of the economists, only 35 percent of the Conservative Party members of Parliament and just 19 percent of the Labour Party members of Parliament approved of this arrangement (see Table 11–1). We may surmise that these members of the British Parliament reflected the views of the public more accurately than did the economists. In this case, people simply found the efficient solution unfair, and so they refused to adopt it.

YET ANOTHER FREE-MARKET ACHIEVEMENT: GROWTH VERSUS EFFICIENCY

This chapter has followed the economist's standard approach in evaluating the market mechanism. Economists usually stress efficiency in resource allocation and the role of the market in ensuring such efficiency-the division of resources among alternative uses in a way that misses no opportunity to increase consumer net benefits.

● PEAK/OFF-PEAK PRICES WORK ON THE ISLAND OF SINGAPORE

With incomes per head of $23,000, a population of 3 million, and an area of just 650 square kilometers, Singapore is a very rich, very small country. People want to cruise around in style. Their 370,000 cars (plus 310,000 buses, lorries, vans, and motorbikes) translate into 220 vehicles per road-kilometer, one of the highest densities in the world. If nothing were done, the result would be endless traffic jams.

For the past 20 years, to enter the central restricted zone, covering about seven square kilometers, drivers have had to display a license [which costs] . . . $2 in the morning peak hour, falling to $1.30 at off-peak times. In 1989 authorities extended the peak surcharge to the evening rush hour as well. That reduced evening traffic sharply (see chart) and raised average speeds inside the restricted zone

by 20 percent. Some drivers have switched to off-peak travel and now take buses or trains; through-traffic has declined.

SOURCE: "Singapore's Plan," *The Economist*, December 6, 1997, p. 22.

Prices work
Singapore's cars and taxis travelling through the restricted zone in peak periods, '000

SOURCE: John Polak, Piotr Olszewski, and Yiik-diew Wong.

However, other admirers of the market do not place their main emphasis on the free market's efficiency accomplishments. A very diverse group, including business-people, politicians, economic historians, leaders in formerly communist economies such as Mikhail Gorbachev, and even Marxists, admire the market primarily for a very different reason—the extraordinary growth in output which market economies have achieved and the historically unprecedented abundance that has resulted.

Historians have estimated that before the arrival of the capitalistic market mechanism, output per person grew with glacial slowness. But today, an average American can afford almost *ten* times the quantity of goods and services that an individual's income bought 100 years ago. Undoubtedly, the failure to achieve substantial growth and prosperity (and not just inefficiencies in allocating goods) helped to bring about the fall of communism in eastern Europe. Even Karl Marx stressed this role of the market mechanism and waxed lyrical in his description of its accomplishments. Chapter 15 will return to this subject, indicating what a free market economy can accomplish in terms of economic growth.

Replies to a Questionnaire | TABLE 11–1

Question: In order to make the most efficient use of a city's resources, how should subway and bus fares vary during the day?	Economists	Conservative Party Members of Parliament	Labor Party Members of Parliament
a. They should be relatively low during rush hour to transport as many people as possible at lower costs.	1%	0%	40%
b. They should be the same at all times to avoid making travelers alter their schedules because of price differences.	4	60	39
c. They should be relatively high during rush hour to minimize the amount of equipment needed to transport the daily travelers.	88	35	19
d. Impossible to answer on the data and alternatives given.	7	5	2

SOURCES: Adapted from Samuel Brittan, *Is There an Economic Consensus?* (London: Curtis Brown, Ltd., 1973), p. 93. Copyright Samuel Brittan, 1973. Reproduced by permission of Curtis Brown Ltd.

● EARTHQUAKE, BRIDGE CONGESTION, AND ROUTE SUBSTITUTION

Bridge congestion and route substitution took on graphic proportions after the partial collapse of the San Francisco-Oakland Bay Bridge during the Loma Prieta earthquake that shook the San Francisco area on October 17, 1989. According to one newspaper report:

> The bridge closure forced commuters . . . [who] used it to cross the bay some other way. While many people stayed home the week after the disaster, they now appear to be rejoining the ranks of the daily rush. . . . The result has been major delays on alternative routes, such as the Golden Gate, San Mateo and San Rafael-Richmond bridges.

Just a little over four years later, the North-ridge earthquake in Los Angeles decimated that city's massive freeway system, with the worst damage to bridges on the nation's most heavily traveled road, the Santa Monica Freeway. Many of the more than 300,000 commuters who travel that highway daily switched over to the

city's rail system, where average ridership shot up from 8,000 commuters per day to peaks of 30,000 per day.

SOURCES: *The Boston Globe,* October 31, 1989, p. 15; "New Technology Cuts Time for Bridge Repair," *American City and County,* December 1994, p. 42; "Working Together to Unclog Road," *Public Relations Journal,* May 1994.

San Francisco Bridge Pricing Revisited

Our earlier example of the San Francisco Bay area bridges also raises fairness issues. Recall that we concluded from our analysis that efficient bridge use requires higher tolls on the more crowded bridges. Because this principle seems so clear and rational, it may be interesting to see what the actual bridge tolls were in 1998. Travel on the Golden Gate Bridge required a $3 toll for a round trip, and the San Francisco-Oakland Bay, Dumbarton, Richmond-San Rafael, and San Mateo-Hayward bridges all carried a uniform $2 toll even though, as we saw earlier, average daily traffic on these bridges varies widely, with the San Francisco-Oakland Bay Bridge by far the most crowded.[5]

From an efficiency point of view, the pattern of tolls on the four publicly owned bridges seems quite irrational. The least crowded bridges were assigned the same tolls as the most crowded bridge! The explanation lies in some widely held notions of fairness.

Many people feel that it is fair for those who travel on a particular bridge to pay for its costs. In this view, it would be unjust for those who use the crowded San Francisco-Oakland Bay Bridge to pay more, in order to subsidize the least-crowded Dumbarton Bridge. Naturally, a heavily traveled bridge recoups its building, maintenance, and operating costs more quickly. On the other hand, it is felt that the relatively few users of a less crowded bridge should make a fair contribution toward its costs.

---

[5] Toll schedule and traffic volumes for the San Francisco Bay area bridges from California Department of Transportation, www.dot.ca.gov., October 1998. We should note that CalTrans has encouraged additional efficiency by instituting faster carpool lanes for buses and cars with three or more passengers; such vehicles cross the four publicly owned bridges free of charge between 5 and 10 A.M. and between 3 and 6 P.M.

An economically irrational pattern of tolls does nothing to ease congestion on overcrowded bridges, and thereby contributes to inefficiency. But one cannot legitimately conclude that advocates of such prices are "stupid." Whether this pattern of tolls is or is not desirable must be decided, ultimately, on the basis of the public's sense of what constitutes fairness and justice in pricing. It also depends on the amount that people are willing to pay in terms of delays, inconvenience, and other inefficiencies in order to avoid apparent injustices.

Economics alone cannot decide the appropriate trade-off between fairness and efficiency. It cannot even pretend to judge which pricing arrangements are fair and which are unfair. But it can and should indicate whether a particular pricing decision, proposed because it is considered fair, will impose heavy inefficiency costs on the community. Economic analysis also can and should indicate how to appraise these costs, so that the issues can be evaluated on a rational, factual basis.

■ TOWARD ASSESSMENT OF THE PRICE MECHANISM

We do not mean to imply in our discussion of the case for free markets that the free-enterprise system is an ideal of perfection, without flaw or room for improvement. In fact, it has a number of serious shortcomings that we will explore in subsequent chapters. But recognition of these imperfections should not conceal the price mechanism's enormous accomplishments.

We have shown that, given the proper circumstances, prices are capable of meeting the most exacting requirements of allocative efficiency: requirements that go well beyond any central planning bureau's capacities. Even centrally planned economies use the price mechanism to carry out considerable portions of the task of allocation, most notably in the distribution of consumer goods. No one has invented an instrument for directing the economy that can replace the price mechanism, which no one ever designed or planned for, but which simply grew by itself, a child of the processes of history.

SUMMARY

1. Economists consider an allocation of resources inefficient if it wastes opportunities to change the use of the economy's resources in any way that makes at least some consumers better off without harming anyone. Resource allocation is called efficient if there are no such wasted opportunities.

2. Under perfect competition, the free-market mechanism adjusts prices so that the resulting resource allocation is efficient. It induces firms to buy and use inputs in ways that yield the most valuable outputs per unit of input. It distributes products among consumers in ways that match individual preferences. Finally, it produces commodities whose value to consumers exceeds the cost of producing them and assigns the task of production to the potential suppliers who can produce most efficiently.

3. Resource allocation involves three basic coordination tasks:

   a. How much of each good to produce.

   b. What quantities of available inputs to use in producing the different goods.

   c. How to distribute the goods among different consumers.

4. Efficient decisions about what goods to produce require that the marginal cost (MC) of producing each good be equated to its marginal utility (MU) to consumers. If the MC of any good differs from its MU, then society can improve resource allocation by changing the amount produced.

5. Because the market system induces firms to set MC equal to price, and it induces consumers to set MU equal to price, it automatically guarantees satisfaction of the condition that MC should equal MU.

6. Improvements in efficiency occasionally require some prices to increase in order to stimulate supply or to prevent waste in consumption. This is why price increases can sometimes be beneficial to consumers.

7. In addition to resource allocation, prices also influence income distribution between buyers and sellers.

8. The price mechanism can be criticized on the grounds that it is unfair because it accords wealthy consumers preferential treatment.

Efficient allocation of resources   211

Coordination tasks: 214

   Selecting output   215

   Planning production   215

   Distribution of goods   215

Laissez faire   215

Input-output analysis   218

P = MU requirement of consumer equilibrium   222

MC = P requirement of perfect competition   222

MC = MU efficiency requirement   222

Q U E S T I O N S   F O R   R E V I E W

1. What possible social advantages of price increases accrue in each of the following two cases?

  a. Charging higher prices for electrical power on very hot days when many people use air conditioners.

  b. Raising water prices in drought-stricken areas.

2. Discuss the fairness of the two preceding proposals.

3. Using the concepts of marginal cost (MC) and marginal utility (MU), discuss the nature of the inefficiency in each of the following cases:

  a. An arrangement that offers relatively little coffee and much tea to people who prefer coffee and does the reverse for tea lovers.

  b. An arrangement in which skilled mechanics are assigned to ditch digging and unskilled laborers to repairing cars.

  c. An arrangement that produces a large quantity of trucks and few cars, assuming that both cost about the same amount to produce and to run, but that most people in the community prefer cars to trucks.

4. In reality, which of the following circumstances might give rise to each of the preceding problem situations?

  a. Regulation of output quantities by a government.

  b. Rationing of commodities.

  c. Assignment of soldiers to different jobs in an army.

5. We have said that the economy's three coordination tasks are output selection, production planning, and product distribution. Which of these is done badly in the case described in Review Questions 3a, 3b, and 3c?

6. In a free market, how will the price mechanism deal with each of the inefficiencies described in Review Question 3?

7. Suppose that a given set of resources can be used to make either handbags or wallets, and the MC of a handbag is $19 while the MC of a wallet is $10. If the MU of a wallet is $10 and the MU of a handbag is $30, what can be done to improve resource allocation? What can you say about the gain to consumers?

8. In the early months after the end of communism in eastern Europe, there seems to have been an almost superstitious belief that the free market could solve all problems. What sorts of problems do you think the leaders and the citizens of those countries had in mind? Which of those problems is there good reason to believe the market mechanism actually can deal with effectively? What disappointments and sources of disillusionment should have been expected? Which disappointments have resulted?

The price of monopoly is upon every occasion the highest which can be got.

Adam Smith[1]

MONOPOLY

In Chapters 10 and 11, we described an idealized market system in which all industries are perfectly competitive, and we extolled the beauty of that system. In this chapter, we turn to one of the blemishes—the possibility that some industries may be monopolized—and to the consequences of such a flaw in the market system.

We will indeed find that monopolized markets do not match the ideal performance of perfectly competitive markets. Under monopoly, the market mechanism no longer allocates society's resources efficiently. This suggests that government actions to constrain monopoly may sometimes be able to improve the workings of the market—a possibility that we will study in detail in Chapter 20.

But first, as usual, we start with a real-life puzzle.

---

[1] But Adam Smith's statement is incorrect! See Review Question 7 at the end of the chapter.

Puzzle: Competition in Local Telephone Service Markets?

We are all keenly aware of the strong competition in the market for long-distance telephone service. How can we miss it? Representatives of the firms offering this service—some with familiar names like MCI and Sprint, and some newer and smaller firms with less familiar names—interrupt countless dinners with their telephone sales pitches. But, though vigorous competition has occurred in the market for long-distance phone service since the late 1970s, most areas of the United States still treat *local* telephone service markets as regulated monopolies. People in northern Colorado, however, see a new and innovative trend in telecommunications: competitive local phone markets. The residents in this region can now choose between US West, the established provider, and a new firm, McleodUSA.

The markets for local phone service in northern Colorado and a few other areas around the nation currently contain competing firms, and this phenomenon is on the rise. Soon all consumers may be able to choose from two or more providers of local phone service. This competition potentially promises lower rates, better service, and a wider range of options for phone service. Why is competition possibly arising now in this market? What has allowed this industry, which until recently had been considered by some as a classic example of "natural monopoly," suddenly to offer the beginnings of competition? In this chapter you will learn about the causes and consequences of monopoly and, in the process, learn the answers to these questions.

■ *MONOPOLY* DEFINED

A **pure monopoly** is an industry in which there is only one supplier of a product for which there are no close substitutes and in which it is very hard or impossible for another firm to coexist.

Requirements to meet the definition of **pure monopoly** are quite stringent. First, only one firm may exist in the industry—the monopolist must be "the only game in town." Second, no close substitutes for the monopolist's product may exist. Thus, even a city's sole provider of natural gas is not considered a pure monopoly, because other firms offer close substitutes like heating oil and electricity. Third, there must be some reason why entry and survival of potential competitors is extremely unlikely. Otherwise monopolistic behavior and its excessive economic profits could not persist.

These rigid requirements make pure monopoly a rarity in the real world. The local telephone company and the post office in some small towns may be examples of one-firm industries that face little or no effective competition. But most firms face at least a degree of competition from substitute products. If only one railroad serves a particular town, it still must compete with bus lines, trucking companies, and airlines. Similarly, the producer of a particular brand of beer may be the only supplier of that specific product, but the firm is not a monopolist by our definition. Because many other beers are close substitutes for its product, the firm will lose much of its business if it tries to raise its price far above the prices of other brands. Even the local phone company and the post office face competition in more populous areas.

There is another reason why the unrestrained pure monopoly of economic theory is rarely found in practice. We will learn in this chapter that pure monopoly can have a number of undesirable features. So in markets where pure monopoly might otherwise prevail, the government has intervened to prevent monopolization or to limit the discretion of the monopolist to set its price.

If we do not study pure monopoly for its descriptive realism, why do we study it? Because, like perfect competition, pure monopoly is a market form that is easier to analyze than the more common market structures that we will consider in the next chapter. Thus, pure monopoly is a stepping stone toward more realistic models. Also, we will understand the possible evils of monopoly most clearly if we examine monopoly in its purest form.

SOURCES OF MONOPOLY: BARRIERS TO ENTRY AND COST ADVANTAGES

The key requirement for preservation of a monopoly is exclusion of potential rivals from the market. One way to achieve this is by means of some specific impediment that prevents the establishment of a new firm in the industry. Economists call such impediments *barriers to entry*. Some examples follow.

LEGAL RESTRICTIONS The U.S. Postal Service has a monopoly position because Congress has given it one. Private companies that may want to compete with the postal service directly are prohibited from doing so by law. Local monopolies of various kinds are sometimes established either because government grants some special privilege to a single firm (for example, the right to operate a food concession in a municipal stadium) or prevents other firms from entering the industry (for instance, by licensing only a single cable television supplier).

PATENTS Some firms benefit from a special, but important, class of legal impediments to entry called patents. To encourage inventiveness, the government gives exclusive production rights for a period of time to the inventors of certain products. As long as a patent is in effect, the firm has a protected position and holds a monopoly. For example, Xerox for many years had (but no longer has) a monopoly in plain-paper copying. Most pharmaceutical companies also get monopolies on the drugs they develop. The drug maker Eli Lilly, for instance, has a patent on Prozac, the world's best-selling antidepressant. However, the patent expires in 2003, opening the door to competition from generic drug makers.

CONTROL OF A SCARCE RESOURCE OR INPUT If a certain commodity can be produced only by using a rare input, a company that gains control of the source of that input can establish a monopoly position for itself. Real examples are not easy to find, but the South African diamond syndicate is one.

DELIBERATELY ERECTED ENTRY BARRIERS A firm may deliberately attempt to make entry difficult for others. One way is to start costly lawsuits against new rivals, sometimes on trumped-up charges. Another is to spend exorbitant amounts on advertising, thus forcing any potential entrant to match that expenditure.

LARGE SUNK COSTS Entry into an industry will, obviously, be very risky if it requires a large investment, especially if that investment is sunk—meaning that it cannot be recouped for a considerable period of time. Thus, the need for a large sunk investment discourages entry into an industry. Many analysts therefore consider sunk costs to be the most important type of "naturally imposed" barrier to entry. For example, the high sunk costs involved in jet airplane building helped Boeing enjoy a monopoly in the top end of the long-range, wide-body jet airliner market for many years after the launch of the 747 jumbo jet. But Airbus, which, with European governments' sponsorship has been able to afford the high investments, has encroached on Boeing's territory.

Such barriers can keep rivals out and ensure that an industry is monopolized. But monopoly can also occur in the absence of barriers to entry if a single firm has substantial cost advantages over potential rivals. Two examples of this are technical superiority and economies of scale.

TECHNICAL SUPERIORITY A firm whose technological expertise vastly exceeds that of any potential competitor can, for a period of time, maintain a monopoly position. For example, IBM for many years had little competition in the computer business mainly because of its technological virtuosity. Eventually, however, competitors caught up. More recently, Microsoft has established a commanding position in the software business, especially for operating systems, through a combination of inventiveness and marketing wizardry.

ECONOMIES OF SCALE If mere size gives a large firm a cost advantage over a smaller rival, it is likely to be impossible for anyone to compete with the largest firm in the industry.

NATURAL MONOPOLY

This last type of cost advantage is important enough to merit special attention. In some industries, economies of large-scale production or economies of scope (from simultaneous production of a large number of related items, for example, car motors and bodies, truck parts, and so on) are so extreme that the industry's output can be produced at far lower cost by a single firm than by a number of smaller firms. In such cases, we say there is a **natural monopoly**. Once a firm gets large enough relative to the size of the market for its product, its natural cost advantage may well drive the competition out of business whether or not anyone in the relatively large firm has evil intentions.

A monopoly need not be a large firm if the market is small enough. *What matters is the size of a single firm relative to the total market demand for the product.* Thus, a small bank in a rural town or a gasoline station at a lightly traveled intersection may both be monopolies, even though they are very small firms.

Figure 12–1 shows the sort of average cost (AC) curve that leads to natural monopoly. It has a negative slope throughout, meaning that the more a firm in this industry produces, the lower its average cost will be. Suppose that any firm producing video games has this AC curve and that, initially, there are two firms in the industry. Suppose also that the larger firm is producing 2 million games at an average cost of $2.50 (red point *A*), and the smaller firm is producing 1 million games at an average cost of $3.00 (blue point *B*). Clearly, the larger firm can drive the smaller firm out of business if it offers its output for sale at a price below $3.00 (so the smaller firm can match the price only by running a loss) but above $2.50 (so it can still make a profit). Hence, a monopoly may arise "naturally," even in the absence of barriers to entry.

Once the monopoly is established (producing, say, 2.5 million video games—point *C*) the economies of scale act as a very effective deterrent to entry because no new entrant can hope to match the low average cost ($2.00) of the existing monopoly firm. Of course, the public interest may be well served if the natural monopolist uses its low cost to keep its prices low. The danger, however, is that the firm may raise its price once rivals have left the industry.

Many public utilities operate as *regulated* monopoly suppliers for exactly this reason. It is believed that the technology of producing or distributing their output enables them to achieve substantial cost reductions by producing large quantities. It is therefore often considered preferable to permit these firms to achieve lower costs by having the entire market to themselves, and then to subject them and their prices to regulatory supervision, rather than to break them up into a number of competing firms. We will examine the issue of regulating natural monopolies in detail in Chapter 20. To summarize this discussion:

A **natural monopoly** is an industry in which advantages of large-scale production make it possible for a single firm to produce the entire output of the market at lower average cost than a number of firms each producing a smaller quantity.

FIGURE 12–1

Natural Monopoly

NOTE: Average cost is in dollars per unit; quantity is in millions.

There are two basic reasons why a monopoly may exist: barriers to entry, such as legal restrictions and patents, and cost advantages of superior technology or large-scale operation that lead to natural monopoly. It is generally considered undesirable to break up a large firm whose costs are low because of scale economies. But barriers to entry are usually considered to be against the public interest except where they are believed to offer offsetting advantages, as in the case of patents.

The rest of this chapter analyzes how a monopoly can be expected to behave if its freedom of action is not limited by the government.

■ THE MONOPOLIST'S SUPPLY DECISION

A monopoly firm does not have a "supply curve," as we usually define the term. Unlike a perfect competitor, a monopoly is not at the mercy of the market; the firm does not have to accept the market's price as beyond its control and adjust to it. Instead, it has the power to set the price, or rather to select the price-quantity combination on the demand curve that suits its interests best.

Put differently, a monopolist is not a *price taker* that must simply adapt to whatever price the forces of supply and demand decree. Rather, a monopolist is a *price maker* that can, if so inclined, raise the product price. For any price that the monopolist chooses, the demand curve for the product indicates how much consumers will buy. Thus, the standard supply-demand analysis described in Chapter 5 does not apply to the determination of price or output in a monopolized industry.

The demand curve of a monopoly, unlike that of a perfect competitor, is normally downward sloping, not horizontal. This means that a price rise will not cause the monopoly to lose *all* of its customers. But any increase will cost it *some* business. The higher the price, the less the monopolist can expect to sell.

The market cannot impose a price on a monopolist as it imposes a price on the price-taking competitive firm. But the monopolist cannot select both price and the quantity it sells. In accord with the demand curve, the higher the price it sets, the less it can sell.

In deciding what price best serves the firm's interests, the monopolist must consider whether profits can be increased by raising or lowering the product's price. Because of the downward-sloping demand curve, the sky is not the limit in pricing by a monopolist. Some price increases are not profitable.

In our analysis, we shall assume that the monopolist wants to maximize profits. That does not mean that a monopoly is guaranteed a positive profit. If the demand for its product is low, or if the firm is inefficient, even a monopoly may lose money and eventually be forced out of business. However, if a monopoly firm does earn a positive profit, it may be able to keep on doing so in the long run because there will be no entry that competes the profits away.

We can use the methods of Chapter 9 to determine which price the profit-maximizing monopolist will prefer. To maximize profits, the monopolist must compare marginal revenue (the addition to total revenue resulting from a 1-unit rise in output) with marginal cost (the addition to total cost resulting from that additional unit). Figure 12–2 shows a marginal cost (MC) curve and a marginal revenue (MR) curve for a typical monopolist. Recall that the firm's demand curve (DD) is also its average revenue (AR) curve. That is because if a firm sells Q units of output, selling every unit of output at the price P, then the average revenue brought in by a unit of output must be the price, P, because the average of a bunch of equal numbers must be that same number. Because the demand curve gives the price at which any particular quantity can be sold, it also automatically indicates the AR (= price) yielded by that quantity.

FIGURE 12-2

Profit-Maximizing Equilibrium for a Monopolist

NOTE: Price is in dollars per unit.

■ IS THE SOFTWARE INDUSTRY A NATURAL MONOPOLY?

Some leading economists believe the software industry is prone to monopoly. Three influences may incline the industry in this direction, as an article in *InfoWorld* describes:

"One factor is diminishing costs: while the first copy of a software program costs millions to produce, the cost to produce subsequent copies is negligible. The second factor is the network effect in which the value of software increases by the number of people using it and developers creating applications for it. The third factor is the lock-in effect, in which the cost of switching to another system (installation, training, application compatibility) persuades users to stick with current systems. . . . These forces create natural barriers to entry for newcomers, and Microsoft's operating-system dominance is a prime example."

SOURCE: Lynda Radosevich, "Top of the News: How the Software Industry Creates Monopolies," *InfoWorld* 20 (May 25, 1998).

Notice that the marginal revenue curve is always below the demand curve, meaning that MR is always less than price (*P*). This important fact is easy to explain. The monopoly firm charges the same price to all of its customers. If the firm wants to increase sales by 1 unit, it must decrease the price somewhat to all of its customers. When it cuts the price to attract new sales, all previous customers also benefit. Thus, the additional revenue that the monopolist takes in when sales increase by 1 unit (*marginal revenue*) is the price the firm collects from the new customer *minus the revenue it loses by cutting the price paid by all of its old customers.* This means that MR is necessarily less than price; graphically, it implies that the MR curve is below the demand curve, as in Figure 12–2.

DETERMINING THE PROFIT-MAXIMIZING OUTPUT

Like any other firm, the monopoly maximizes its profits by setting marginal revenue (MR) equal to marginal cost (MC). It selects point *M* in Figure 12–2, where output is 150 units. But point *M* does not tell us the monopoly price because, as we have just seen, price exceeds MR for a monopolist. To learn what price the monopolist charges, we must use the demand curve to find the price at which consumers are willing to purchase the profit-maximizing output of 150 units. The answer, we see, is given by point *P* directly above *M*. The monopoly price is $10 per unit. Not surprisingly, it exceeds both MR and MC (which are equal at $8).

The monopolist depicted in Figure 12–2 is earning a tidy profit. This profit is shown in the graph by the shaded rectangle whose height is the difference between price (point *P*) and average cost (point *C*) and whose width is the quantity produced (150 units). In the example, profits are $6 per unit, or $900.

To study the decisions of a profit-maximizing monopolist:

1. Find the output at which MR = MC to select the profit-maximizing output level.

2. Find the height of the demand curve at that level of output to determine the corresponding price.

3. Compare the height of the demand curve with the height of the AC curve at that output to see whether the net result is an economic profit or a loss.

We can also show a monopolist's profit-maximization calculation numerically. In Table 12–1, the first two columns show the quantity and price figures that constitute the monopolist's demand curve. Column (3) shows total revenue (TR) for each output, which is the product of price times quantity. Thus, for 3 units of output, we have TR = $92 × 3 = $276. Column (4) shows marginal revenue (MR). For example, when output rises from 3 to 4 units, TR increases from $276 to $320, so MR is $320 − $276 = $44. Column (5) gives the monopolist's total cost for each level of output. Column (6) derives marginal cost (MC) from total cost (TC) in the usual way. Finally, by subtracting TC from TR for each level of output, we obtain total profit in Column (7).

The table brings out a number of important points. We note first in Columns (2) and (3) that a cut in price may increase or decrease total revenue. When output rises from 1 to 2 units, P falls from $140 to $107 and TR rises from $140 to $214. But when (between 5 and 6 units of output) P falls from $66 to $50, TR falls from $330 to $300. Next we observe, by comparing Columns (2) and (4), that after the first unit, price always exceeds marginal revenue. Finally, from Columns (4) and (6) we see that MC = MR = $44 when Q is between 3 and 4 units, indicating that this is the level of output that maximizes the monopolist's total profit. That is confirmed in Column (7) of the table, which shows that at those outputs profit reaches its highest level, $110, for any of the output quantities considered in the table.

COMPARING MONOPOLY AND PERFECT COMPETITION

This completes our analysis of the monopolist's price-output decision. At this point it is natural to wonder whether there is anything distinctive about the monopoly equilibrium. But to find out, we need a standard of comparison. Perfect competition provides this standard because, as we learned in Chapters 10 and 11, it is a theoretical benchmark of ideal performance against which other market structures can be judged. By comparing the results of monopoly with those of perfect competition, we will see why economists since Adam Smith have condemned monopoly as inefficient.

A MONOPOLIST'S PROFIT PERSISTS The first difference between competition and monopoly is a direct consequence of barriers to entry in monopoly. Profits such as those shown in Figure 12–2 would be competed away by free entry in a perfectly

A Profit-Maximizing Monopolist's Price-Output Decision

TABLE 12-1

(1) Q	(2) P	Revenue		Cost		Total Profit
		(3) TR = P × Q	(4) MR	(5) TC	(6) MC	(7) TR − TC
0	—	$ 0		$ 10		$−10
			$140		$60	
1	$140	140		70		70
			74		50	
2	107	214		120		94
			62		46	
3	92	276		166		110
			44		44	
4	80	320		210		110
			10		43	
5	66	330		253		77
			−30		45	
6	50	300		298		2

competitive market, because a positive profit would attract new competitors into the business. A competitive firm must earn *zero economic profit* in the long run; that is, it can earn only enough to cover its costs, including the opportunity cost of the owner's capital and labor. But higher profit *can* persist under monopoly—if the monopoly is protected from the arrival of new competitors by barriers to entry. Fate can allow monopolists to grow wealthy at the expense of their consumers. But because people find such accumulations of wealth objectionable, monopoly is widely condemned. As a result, monopolies are regulated by government, which often limits the profits they can earn.

MONOPOLY RESTRICTS OUTPUT TO RAISE SHORT-RUN PRICE   Excess monopoly profit can be a problem. But economists believe that the second difference between competition and monopoly is even more worrisome:

> Compared with the perfectly competitive ideal, the monopolist restricts output and charges a higher price.

To see that this is so, let us conduct the following thought experiment. Imagine that a court order breaks up the monopoly firm depicted in Figure 12–2 (and reproduced as Figure 12–3) into a large number of perfectly competitive firms. Suppose further that the industry demand curve is unchanged by this event and that the MC curve in Figure 12–3 is also the (horizontal) sum of the MC curves of all the newly created competitive firms. These may be unrealistic assumptions, as we will soon explain. However, they make it easy to compare the output-price combinations that would emerge in the short run under monopoly and perfect competition.

Before making our comparison, we must note that under monopoly, the firm and the industry are exactly the same entity. But under perfect competition, any one firm is just a small portion of the industry. So when we measure the performance of monopoly against that of perfect competition, we should compare the monopoly with the entire competitive industry, not with an individual competitive firm. In Figure 12–3, the monopolist's output is point *M* at which MC = MR. The long-run competitive output (point *B*) is greater than the monopoly's because it must be sufficiently large to yield zero economic profit (*P* = AR = AC).

FIGURE 12-3

Comparison of a Monopoly and a Competitive Industry

It is self-evident and not very interesting to observe that the output of the monopolist is virtually certain to be larger than that of a tiny competitive *firm*. The interesting issue is how much product gets into the hands of consumers under the two market forms, that is, how much output is produced by a monopoly as against the quantity provided by a comparable competitive *industry*.

MONOPOLY RESTRICTS OUTPUT TO RAISE LONG-RUN PRICE   As we have seen, monopoly output is determined by the profit-maximization requirement that MC = MR (point *M*). But as we learned in Chapter 10, long-run competitive equilibrium occurs at point *B* in Figure 12–3, where price and average cost are equal and economic profit is zero.

By comparing point *B* with the monopolist's equilibrium (point *M*), we see that the monopolist produces fewer units of output than would a competitive industry with the same demand and cost conditions. Because the demand curve slopes downward, producing less output means charging a higher price. The monopolist's price, indicated by point *P* on the demand curve and directly above *M*, exceeds the price that would result from perfect competition at point *B*. This is the essence of the truth behind the popular view that unregulated monopolists "gouge the public."

We should note that matters will always turn out that way if the average cost curve has a positive slope between the monopoly output level and the competitive output level. That is because we know, in this case, that the MC curve must lie above the AC curve (to review why, see pages 172–180 of Chapter 9). We have also just seen that the MR curve must lie below the demand (AR) curve. It is clear, then, that the point where the MR curve meets the MC curve (the monopoly output) must always lie to the left of the output at which AC and AR meet (the competitive industry output). Consequently, monopoly output will always be the smaller of the two when the curves of the competitive and monopoly industries are identical. With monopoly output lower, its price will always be higher.

MONOPOLY LEADS TO INEFFICIENT RESOURCE ALLOCATION We conclude, then, that a monopoly will charge a higher price and produce a smaller output than will a competitive industry with the same demand and cost conditions. Why do economists find this situation so objectionable? Because, as we learned in Chapter 11, a competitive industry devotes "just the right amount" of society's scarce resources to the production of its particular commodity. Therefore, if a monopolist produces less than a competitive industry, it must be producing too little.

Remember from Chapter 11 that efficiency in resource allocation requires that the marginal utility (MU) of each commodity be equal to its marginal cost. Also, perfect competition guarantees that:

$$MU = P \text{ and } MC = P, \text{ so } MU = MC$$

Under monopoly, consumers continue to maximize their own welfare by setting MU equal to P. But the monopoly producer sets MC equal to MR. Because MR is *below* the market price, P, we conclude that in a monopolized industry:

$$MU = P \text{ and } MC = MR < P \text{ so that } MC < MU$$

Because MU exceeds MC, too small a share of society's resources is being used to produce the monopolized commodity. Consumers would have a net benefit of $MU - MC > 0$ if output were increased above the monopoly level by one unit. Adam Smith's invisible hand is sending out the wrong signals. Consumers are willing to pay an amount for an additional unit of the good (its MU) that exceeds what it costs to produce that unit (its MC). But the monopoly refuses to increase production, because if it raises output by one unit, the revenue it will collect (MR) will be less than the price the consumer will pay for the additional unit (P). The monopolist does not increase production, and resources are allocated inefficiently. To summarize this discussion of the consequences of monopoly:

> Because it is protected from entry, a monopoly firm may earn profits in excess of the opportunity cost of capital. At the same time, monopoly breeds inefficiency in resource allocation by producing too little output and charging too high a price. For these reasons, some of the virtues of laissez-faire evaporate if an industry becomes monopolized.

MONOPOLY IS LIKELY TO SHIFT DEMAND

For one thing, we have assumed that the market demand curve is the same whether the industry is competitive or monopolized. But is this usually so? The demand curve will be the same if the monopoly firm does nothing to expand its market, but that is hardly plausible.

Under perfect competition, purchasers consider the products of all suppliers in an industry to be identical, and so no single supplier has any reason to advertise. But if a monopoly takes over from a perfectly competitive industry, it may very well pay to advertise. If management believes that the touch of the advertising agency can make consumers rush to the market to purchase the product whose virtues have been extolled on television, then the firm will allocate a substantial sum of money to accomplish this feat. Take Kodak, for example. It enjoyed a near monopoly on U.S. film sales from the turn of the century until the 1980s, but that did not stop the company from spending a good deal on advertising. This type of expenditure should shift the demand curve outward. The monopoly's demand curve and that of the competitive industry will then no longer be the same.

The higher demand curve for the monopoly's product may induce it to expand production and therefore reduce the difference between the competitive and the monopolistic output levels indicated in Figure 12–3. But it may also make it possible for the monopoly to charge even higher prices, so the increased output may not constitute a net gain for consumers.

MONOPOLY IS LIKELY TO SHIFT COST CURVES

The advent of a monopoly may also shift the average and marginal cost curves. One reason for higher costs is the advertising we have just been discussing. Another reason is the sheer size of the monopolist's organization, which may lead to bureaucratic inefficiencies, coordination problems, and the like.

On the other hand, a monopolist may be able to eliminate certain types of duplication that are unavoidable for a number of small, independent firms: One purchasing agent may do the input-buying job where many buyers were needed before; a few large machines may replace many small items of equipment in the hands of the competitive firms. In addition, the large scale of the monopoly firm's input purchases may permit it to take advantage of quantity discounts not available to small competitive firms.

If the consolidation achieved by a monopoly does shift down the marginal cost curve, monopoly output will tend to move up closer to the competitive level. The monopoly price will then tend to move down closer to the competitive price.

CAN ANYTHING GOOD BE SAID ABOUT MONOPOLY?

The preceding comparison of monopoly and perfect competition is very artificial. It assumes that all other things will remain the same, even though that is unlikely to happen in reality.

MONOPOLY MAY AID INNOVATION

Some economists have argued that it is misleading to compare the cost curves of a monopoly and a competitive industry *at a single point in time*. Because it is protected from rivals and therefore sure to capture the benefits from any cost-saving methods and new products it can invent, a monopoly has particularly strong motivation to invest in research, these economists argue. If this research bears fruit, the monopolist's costs will be lower than those of a competitive industry in the long run, even if they are higher in the short run. Monopoly, according to this view, may be the handmaiden of innovation. Although the argument is an old one, it remains controversial. The statistical evidence is decidedly mixed.

NATURAL MONOPOLY: WHERE SINGLE-FIRM PRODUCTION IS CHEAPEST

Finally, we must remember that the monopoly depicted in Figure 12–2 is not a natural monopoly, because its average costs increase rather than decrease when its output expands. But some of the monopolies you find in the real world are natural ones. Where a monopoly is natural, costs of production would, by definition, be higher—possibly much higher—if the single large firm were broken up into many smaller firms. (Refer back to Figure 12–1.) In such cases, it may serve society's interests to allow the monopoly to continue because consumers benefit from the economies of large-scale production. But then it may be appropriate to regulate the monopoly by placing legal limitations on its ability to set its prices.

PRICE DISCRIMINATION UNDER MONOPOLY

So far we have assumed that a monopoly charges the same price to all of its customers, but that is not always true. In reality, monopoly firms can sell the same product to different customers at different prices, even if that price difference is unrelated to any special costs that affect some customers but not others. Such a practice is called **price discrimination**. Pricing is also said to be discriminatory if it costs more to supply a good to Customer A than to Customer B, but A and B are nonetheless charged the same price.

We are all familiar with cases of price discrimination. For example, suppose that Matt and Emily both mail letters from Philadelphia, but his goes to New York while hers goes to Seattle. Both pay the same 33-cent postage even though Seattle is much farther than New York from Philadelphia. Bargain airline fares are another example. Passenger C may find herself seated next to Passenger D, who has paid 25 percent more for the same flight.

The airline example shows that price discrimination occurs in industries that are not monopolies. Still, it is far easier for a monopolist to charge discriminatory prices than it is for a firm that is affected by competition, because price discrimination means that sales to some customers are more profitable than sales to others. Such discrepancies in profitability tempt rivals, including new entrants into the industry, to charge the more profitable consumers somewhat lower prices in order to lure them away from the firm that is "overcharging" them. Price discriminators sneeringly call this type of targeted entry *cream skimming*, meaning that entrants go after the best paying customers, leaving the low payers (the "skimmed milk") to the discriminator. But, whether desirable or not, such entry certainly makes it harder to charge higher prices to the more profitable customers.

Price discrimination is the sale of a given product at different prices to different customers of the firm, when there is no difference in the cost of supplying different customers. Prices are also discriminatory if it costs more to supply one customer than another, but they are charged the same price.

Why do firms sometimes engage in price discrimination? You may already suspect the answer: to increase their profits. To see why, let us consider a simple example. Imagine a town with 100 rich families and 1,000 poor ones. The poor families are each willing to buy one video game but cannot afford to pay more than $25. The rich, however, are prepared to buy one per family as long as the price is no higher than $75.

If it cannot price-discriminate, the best the firm can do is to set the price at $25 for everyone, yielding a total revenue of $25 × 1,100 = $27,500. If it charged more, say, $75, it would sell only to the rich and earn just $7,500. If the added cost of producing the 1,000 games for the poorer families is less than the $27,500 − $7,500 = $20,000 in added revenues from the sales to the poor, then the $25 price must be more profitable than the $75 price.

But what if the game maker can charge different prices to the rich and to the poor—and can prevent the poor from reselling their low-priced merchandise to the rich at a markup? Then the revenue obtainable by the firm from the same 1,100 video game output becomes $25 × 1,000 = $25,000 from selling to the poor plus $75 × 100 = $7,500 from selling to the rich, for a total of $32,500. This is clearly a better deal for the firm than the $27,500 revenue obtainable without price discrimination. Profits are $5,000 higher. In general:

> **When a firm charges discriminatory prices, profits are normally higher than when the firm charges nondiscriminatory (uniform) prices.**

We have constructed our simple example to make the two profit-maximizing prices obvious. In practice, that is not so; the monopolist knows that if it sets a price too high, quantity demanded and hence profits will be too low. The discriminating monopolist's problem is determining the profit-maximizing prices to charge to different customer groups. The answer is given by another rule of marginal analysis. For simplicity, suppose that the seller proposes charging two different prices to two customer groups, A and B. Profit maximization requires that the price to Group A and the price to Group B are such that they yield the same *marginal* revenue, that is:

> **The marginal revenue from a sale to a Group A customer must be the same as that from a sale to a Group B customer:**

$$MR_a = MR_b$$

The reasoning is straightforward. Suppose that the sale of an additional video game to a Group A customer brings in MR_a = $18 in revenue although the corresponding sale to a Group B customer adds only MR_b = $15. Such an arrangement cannot possibly be a profit-maximizing solution. By switching 1 unit of sales from B customers to A customers the firm gives up $15 in revenue to gain $18—a net gain of $3 from the same total sales. Because a similar argument holds for any other pair of marginal revenues that are unequal, profit maximizing clearly requires that the marginal revenue from each group of customers be equal.

The equal-marginal-revenue rule enables us to determine the profit-maximizing prices and sales volumes for the two groups of customers diagrammatically. The two panels of Figure 12–4 show the demand curves and corresponding marginal revenue curves for customer groups A and B. Suppose that the firm is selling the quantity Q_a to Group A customers. How much must the firm then sell to Group B customers in order to maximize profits? Our rule gives the answer. The marginal revenue from selling to Group A is equal to M—point V directly above Q_a on the MR curve in Panel (a). The rule tells us that the firm must charge a price to Group B customers that induces them to buy the quantity that yields the same marginal revenue, M. We find this quantity by drawing a horizontal line MM from Panel (a) to Panel (b). The marginal revenues of the two customer groups will clearly be equal where MM cuts the Group B marginal revenue curve—at point W. The profit-maximizing sales volume to Group B will be Q_b, directly below point W.

Unfortunately, that is not quite the end of the story because we have not yet said anything about costs, and we know that profit maximization must take account of costs as well as revenues. But we can deal with the cost issue quite easily, at least if

Prices and Quantities under Price Discrimination | FIGURE 12-4

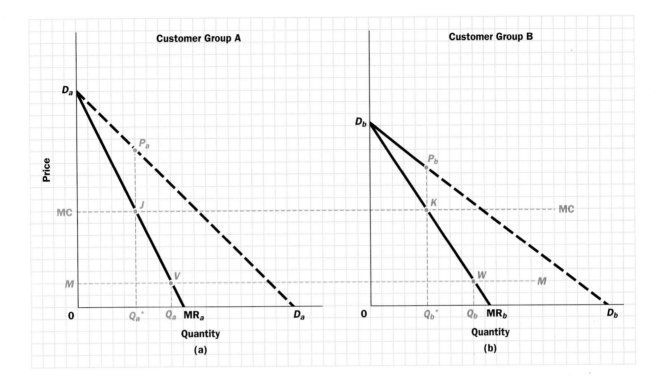

the marginal cost of a video game is the same whether supplied to an A customer or a B customer. Even under price discrimination, we still have the fundamental MR = MC rule for profit maximization in each market segment (see page 179 of Chapter 9). The extended profit-maximization rule under price discrimination must be:

$$MR_a = MR_b = MC$$

Going back to our graph, assume for simplicity that the firm's marginal cost is a fixed number—indicated by the height of the red horizontal marginal cost curve MCMC. Then $MR_a = MR_b = MC$ when the firm sells the quantity Q_a^* to A customers (point J) and the quantity Q_b^* to B customers (point K). Moreover, the demand curve for A customers tells us that selling quantity Q_a^* to this group requires a price of P_a—the red point on demand curve D_aD_a directly above Q_a^*. Similarly, the profit-maximizing price to B customers is P_b on the B demand curve in Figure 12–4(b).

> To determine the profit-maximizing outputs and prices under price discrimination, do the following:
>
> 1. Draw the demand and marginal revenue curves for the different customer groups side by side.
>
> 2. Draw in the pertinent marginal cost as a horizontal line if MC is constant.
>
> 3. Find the profit-maximizing sales quantity for each customer group where the horizontal MC line cuts the MR curve for that group, so that MC = MR for each group.
>
> 4. Determine each customer group's profit-maximizing price by locating the point on the demand curve corresponding to the profit-maximizing quantity.

IS PRICE DISCRIMINATION ALWAYS UNDESIRABLE?

The word *discrimination* is generally used to refer to an undesirable practice. However, *price* discrimination may not always be bad. Most people feel strongly that it is appropriate for the post office to charge the same price for all first-class letters going between two points in the United States, regardless of the differences in delivery costs. Similarly, most people approve of discounts on theater tickets sold to students or to senior citizens, even though those prices are obviously discriminatory. The same is widely agreed about lower doctor's fees for needy patients.

Other reasons, in addition to some standard of fairness or justice, may provide a defense for price discrimination in certain cases. One such case arises when it is impossible without price discrimination for a private firm to supply a product that customers want. For an illustration, go back to our first numerical example of price discrimination. Suppose that the total cost of producing 100 video games is $8,000, and the total cost of producing 1,100 video games is $30,000. Then our firm cannot cover its costs with a uniform, nondiscriminatory price. If it charged $75 to the 100 rich customers willing to pay that much, its $7,500 total revenue would fall short of its $8,000 total cost. Similarly, charging the uniform price of $25 to all 1,100 customers would yield total revenue of only $27,500, which is less than the $30,000 total cost. Thus, *any* uniform price would drive the firm out of business, depriving customers of the consumers' surplus from purchasing the product. But with discriminatory prices, we saw that the firm would earn, $32,500, enabling the firm to cover the $30,000 cost of supplying the requirements of both sets of customers.

It is even possible that price discrimination can make a product cheaper than it would otherwise be for all customers—even those who pay the higher prices. As you may imagine, this can be true only if there are significant economies of scale in the production of the commodity. Thus, suppose that price discrimination permits the firm to offer lower prices to certain customers, thereby attracting some business that it would not otherwise have. The firm's output will therefore increase. But scale economies will then reduce the firm's marginal costs. If marginal cost falls enough, even the "high-priced" customer group may end up paying less than it would in the absence of price discrimination.

The conclusion from this discussion is not that price discrimination is always a good thing. However, it does follow that it is sometimes desirable. In particular, we must recognize that a firm may be unable to cover its costs without price discrimination—a situation that some observers consider to be relatively common.

The Puzzle Resolved: Competitive Local Telephone Service

We conclude our discussion of monopoly by returning to the puzzle that began this chapter: Why are local phone services around the country threatened by competition in an industry that was once considered the very definition of a natural monopoly? The answer is that there has been a change in the way that the federal government proposes to treat this industry.

Until recently, the market for local telephone service was considered a natural monopoly. Local and state governments disallowed competition in these markets because they believed that it would lead to wasteful duplication of large fixed costs and hence to higher prices. Instead, local utility commissions regulated these monopolies to ensure adequate service and reasonable prices. Recent changes in communications technology, however, combined with legislative action, have ripened this market for competition. Computers and satellite technology have reduced the investment costs of providing phone service, and the federal government has improved the prospects for competition with the enactment of the Telecommunications Act of 1996.

The Act overturns state restrictions on competition in local and long-distance telephone service and removes barriers to entry that once kept new firms from entering these markets. Specifically, the act requires existing phone companies to allow new competitors access to their phone lines that connect customers, essentially turning these lines into a *shared* network available to all firms offering phone service. The new competitors must pay an access fee to route their customers' calls over the existing lines, but if the price is not too high, the access will permit competition without requiring new firms to reproduce already existing plants and equipment.

The federal government has taken a legislative approach, turning an industry with huge start-up costs and economies of scale into one that firms may enter with much smaller investments. Thus, these new firms may be able to offer better service at lower rates. For now the issue is in the courts, with the established local monopolies battling prospective entrants over the price to be charged to entrants for access to local facilities.

Your own community may still have a monopoly providing local phone service, but, wherever you live, competition may be on the way. Soon, in addition to those annoying phone calls from long-distance providers, you may also be getting calls from local phone companies attempting to lure you onto their client lists.

S U M M A R Y

1. A *pure monopoly* is a one-firm industry producing a product for which there are no close substitutes.

2. Monopoly can persist only if there are important cost advantages to single-firm operation or barriers to free entry. These barriers may be legal impediments (patents, licensing), the special risks faced by a potential entrant resulting from the need to incur large sunk investments, or the result of "dirty tricks" designed to make things tough for an entrant.

3. One important case of cost advantages is *natural monopoly:* instances where only one firm can survive because of important economies of large-scale production.

4. A monopoly has no supply curve. It maximizes its profit by producing an output at which its marginal revenue equals its marginal cost. Its price is given by the point on its demand curve corresponding to that output.

5. In a monopolistic industry, if demand and cost curves are the same as those of a competitive industry, and if the demand curve has a negative slope and the supply curve a positive slope, then monopoly output will be lower and price will be higher than those of the competitive industry.

6. Economists consider the fact that monopoly output tends to be below the competitive level to constitute an (undesirable) inefficiency.

7. Advertising may enable a monopoly to shift its demand curve above that of a comparable competitive industry's. Through economies such as large-scale input purchases, a monopoly may be able to shift its cost curves below those of a competitive industry.

8. A monopoly may be able to increase its profits by engaging in *price discrimination*—charging higher prices for the same goods to those of its customers who are less resistant to price increases, or failing to charge higher prices to customers whom it costs more to serve.

9. The profit-maximizing discriminatory prices, and corresponding sales volumes, for a firm with several different customer groups can be determined with the help of an extended rule for profit maximization: that the marginal revenue from sales to each customer group must equal the firm's marginal cost.

10. Price discrimination can sometimes be damaging to the public interest, but at other times it can be beneficial. Some firms cannot survive without it, and price discrimination may reduce prices to all customers if there are substantial economies of scale.

11. Any rise in costs generally hurts a monopolist. Because of the negatively sloping demand curve, a monopolist cannot simply pass on cost increases entirely to consumers.

KEY TERMS

Pure monopoly   230

Barriers to entry   231

Patents   231

Natural monopoly   232

Monopoly profits   235

Inefficiency of monopoly   237

Price discrimination   239

QUESTIONS FOR REVIEW

1. Which of the following industries are pure monopolies?

   a. The only supplier of heating fuel in an isolated town

   b. The only supplier of IBM notebook computers in town

   c. The only supplier of instant cameras

   Explain your answers.

2. Suppose that a monopoly industry produces less output than a similar competitive industry. Discuss why this may be considered socially undesirable.

3. If competitive firms earn zero economic profits, explain why anyone would invest money in them. (*Hint:* What is the role of the opportunity cost of capital in economic profit?)

4. The following are the demand and total cost schedules for Company Town Water, a local monopoly:

Output in Gallons	Price per Gallon	Total Cost
50,000	$0.28	$ 6,000
100,000	0.26	15,000
150,000	0.22	22,000
200,000	0.20	32,000
250,000	0.16	46,000
300,000	0.12	64,000

   How much output will Company Town Water produce, and what price will it charge? Will it earn a profit? How much? (*Hint:* You will first have to compute its MR and MC schedules.)

5. Show from the preceding table that for the water company, marginal revenue (per 50,000-gallon unit) is always less than price.

6. Suppose that a tax of $24 is levied on each item sold by a monopolist, and as a result, she decides to raise her price by exactly $24. Why may this decision be against her own best interests?

7. Use Figure 12–2 to show that Adam Smith was wrong when he claimed that a monopoly would always charge "the highest price which can be got."

8. MCI and Sprint have invested vast amounts of money in their fiber-optic networks, which are costly to construct but relatively cheap to operate. If both of them were to go bankrupt, why might this *not* result in a decrease in the competition facing AT&T? (*Hint:* At what price would the assets of the bankrupt companies be offered for sale?)

9. What does your answer to the preceding question tell you about ease or difficulty of entry into telecommunications?

10. A monopoly sells Frisbees to two customer groups. Group A has a downward-sloping straight-line demand curve, whereas the curve for Group B is infinitely elastic. Draw the graph determining the profit-maximizing discriminatory prices and sales to the two groups. What will be the price of Frisbees to Group B? Why? How is the price to Group A determined?

11. A firm cannot break even by charging uniform (nondiscriminatory) prices, but with price discrimination it can earn a small profit. Explain why in this case consumers *must* be better off if the firm is permitted to charge discriminatory prices.

12. It can be proved that, other things being equal, under price discrimination the price charged to some customer group will be higher the less elastic the demand curve of that group is. Why is that result plausible?

. . . neither fish nor fowl.

John Heywood (circa 1565)

BETWEEN COMPETITION AND MONOPOLY

Most productive activity in the United States, as in any advanced industrial society, falls somewhere between the two extreme market forms we have considered so far. So, if we want to understand the workings of the market mechanism in a real, modern economy, we must look somewhere between perfect competition and pure monopoly, at the hybrid market structures: *monopolistic competition* and *oligopoly*. Monopolistic competition is a market structure characterized by many small firms selling somewhat different products. Here each firm's output is so small relative to the total output of closely related and, hence, rival products that the firm does not expect its competitors to respond to or even to *notice* any changes in its own behavior.

Monopolistic competition or something close to it is widespread in retailing: shoe stores, restaurants, and gasoline stations are good examples. Most firms in our economy can be classified as monopolistic competitors, because even though they are small, such enterprises are abundant. We begin the chapter by using the theory of the firm described in Chapter 9 to analyze a monopolistically competitive firm's price-output decisions, then we consider the role of entry and exit, as we did in Chapter 10.

Finally we turn to oligopoly, a market structure in which a few large firms dominate the market. The steel, automobile, and airplane manufacturing industries are good examples of oligopolies, despite the increasing number of strong foreign competitors. Probably the largest share of U.S. economic output comes from oligopolists. Although they are fewer in number than monopolistic competitors, many oligopoly firms are extremely large, with annual sales exceeding the total outputs of most countries in the world and even of some of the smaller industrial European countries (see the accompanying box, "A Global Colossus That Is Richer Than Most Nations").

One critical feature distinguishing an oligopolist from either a monopolist or a perfect competitor is that oligopolists care very much about what other firms in the industry do. The resulting *interdependence* of decisions, we will see, makes oligopoly very hard to analyze, and results in a wide range of behavior patterns. Consequently, economic theory uses not just one but many models of oligopoly (some of which we will review in this chapter), and it is often hard to know which model to apply in any particular situation.

We will also see that the case for free markets is weakened where monopolistic competition or oligopoly occur.

Some Puzzling Observations

We need to study the hybrid market structures considered in this chapter because we cannot explain many economic phenomena via theories of perfect competition or pure monopoly. Here are three examples:

Case 1: Why Are There So Many Retailers? You have seen road intersections with gasoline stations on each corner. Often, two or three of them have no customers at the pumps. There seem to be more gas stations than the number of cars warrant, with a corresponding waste of labor, time, equipment, and other resources. Why—and how—do they all stay in business?

Case 2: Why Do Oligopolists Advertise More Than "More Competitive" Firms? Although some advertising is primarily designed to inform (for example, help-wanted ads), much of the advertising on television, in magazines, and elsewhere is part of a competitive struggle for our business. Many big companies use advertising as a principal weapon as they battle for customers, and advertising budgets can constitute very large shares of their expenditures. Such firms spend literally hundreds of millions of dollars per year on advertising, seeking to leap ahead of rivals. Indeed, in 1997 Procter & Gamble, Philip Morris, and Chrysler each spent more than a billion dollars on ads, and General Motors spent more than two billion. Yet critics often accuse oligopolistic industries containing only a few giant firms of being "uncompetitive." Farming, on the other

● A GLOBAL COLOSSUS THAT IS RICHER THAN MOST NATIONS

General Motors (GM) is the world's largest company in sales and share of global economic output. When strikes shut down its North American operations, as happened in the summer of 1998, the entire American economy feels the blow.

SOURCE: "Keith Bradsher, "Forget Microsoft. G.M. Is Still the Biggest Kid on the Block," *The New York Times*, July 26, 1998, section 4, p. 4.

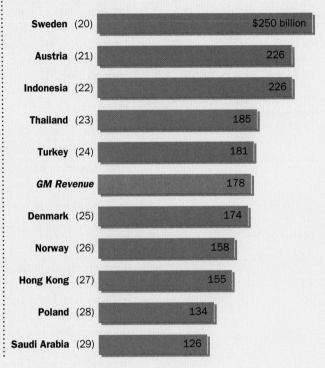

The World's Biggest Company ...

The revenues of the world's biggest corporations and six other selected companies, with their global rank and number of employees, in 1997.

Company	(rank)	Revenue	Employees
GM	(1)	$178 billion	698,000
Ford	(2)	154	364,000
Mitsui	(3)	143	40,000
Mitsubishi	(4)	129	36,000
Shell	(5)	128	105,000
Wal-Mart	(8)	119	825,000
GE	(12)	91	276,000
AT&T	(32)	53	128,000
Boeing	(39)	46	239,000
Intel	(125)	25	64,000
Microsoft	(400)	11	22,000

... Produces More Than Many Nations

GM's revenue and the gross domestic product of 10 nations, ranked globally in 1997.

Nation	(rank)	GDP
Sweden	(20)	$250 billion
Austria	(21)	226
Indonesia	(22)	226
Thailand	(23)	185
Turkey	(24)	181
GM Revenue		178
Denmark	(25)	174
Norway	(26)	158
Hong Kong	(27)	155
Poland	(28)	134
Saudi Arabia	(29)	126

hand, is considered as close to perfect competition as any industry in our economy, but few, if any, individual farmers spend anything at all on advertising.[1] Why do these allegedly "uncompetitive" oligopolists make such heavy use of combative advertising whereas very competitive farmers do not?

Case 3: Why Do Oligopolists Seem to Change Their Prices So Infrequently?   Many prices in the economy change from minute to minute. Every day, newspapers and other media publish the latest prices of commodities such as soybeans, pork bellies, and copper. If you want to buy one of these commodities at 11:45 A.M. today, you cannot use yesterday's price—or even the price from 11:44 A.M. today—because it has probably changed already. Yet prices of products

---

[1] But farmers associations, such as Sunkist and various dairy groups, do spend money on advertising.

such as cars and refrigerators generally change only a few times a year at most, even during fairly rapid inflation. Firms that sell cars and refrigerators know that product and input market conditions change all the time. Why don't they adjust their prices more often? This chapter will offer answers to each of these questions.

■ MONOPOLISTIC COMPETITION

Monopolistic competition refers to a market in which products are heterogeneous but which is otherwise the same as a market that is perfectly competitive.

For years, economic theory told us little about market forms in between the two extreme cases of pure monopoly and perfect competition. Then, during the 1930s, Edward Chamberlin of Harvard University and Joan Robinson of Cambridge University (working separately) partially filled this gap and helped to make economic theory more realistic. The market structure they analyzed is called **monopolistic competition.**

CHARACTERISTICS OF MONOPOLISTIC COMPETITION

A market is said to operate under conditions of monopolistic competition if it satisfies four requirements, three of which are the same as those for perfect competition:

- *Numerous participants*—that is, many buyers and sellers, all of whom are small
- *Freedom of exit and entry*
- *Perfect information*
- *Heterogeneous products*—as far as the buyer is concerned, each seller's product differs at least somewhat from every other's

Notice that monopolistic competition differs from perfect competition in only the last respect. Perfect competition assumes that the products of different firms in an industry are identical, but under monopolistic competition products differ from seller to seller—in quality, packaging, supplementary services offered (such as windshield washing at a gas station), or merely in terms of consumers' perceptions. The attributes that differentiate products need not be "real" in any objective or directly measurable sense. For example, differences in packaging or in associated services can and do distinguish otherwise identical products. On the other hand, two products may perform quite differently in quality tests, but if consumers know nothing about this difference, it is irrelevant.

In contrast to a perfect competitor, a monopolistic competitor's demand curve is negatively sloped. Because each seller's product is different, each caters to a set of customers who vary in their loyalty to the particular product. If the firm raises its price somewhat, it will drive *some* of its customers to competitors' offerings, but customers who strongly favor the firm's product will not switch. If one monopolistic competitor lowers its price, it may expect to attract some trade from rivals. But, because different products are imperfect substitutes, it will not attract away *all* of the rivals' business.

Thus, if Harriet's Hot Dog House reduces its price slightly, it will attract those customers of Sam's Sausage Shop who were nearly indifferent between the two. If Harriet were to cut her prices further, she would gain some customers who have a slightly greater preference for Sam's product. But even a big cut in Harriet's price will not bring her the hard-core sausage lovers who hate hot dogs. Therefore, monopolistic competitors face a negatively sloped demand curve, like that of a monopolist, rather than horizontal, like that of a perfect competitor who will lose all his business if he insists on a higher price than a rival's.

Because consumers see each product as distinct from all others, a monopolistically competitive firm appears to have something akin to a small monopoly. Can we therefore expect it to earn more than zero economic profit? As with a perfect competitor, perhaps monopolistic competitors will obtain economic profits in the short run. But in the long run, high economic profits will attract new entrants into a monopolistically competitive market—not with products *identical* to an existing firm's, but with products sufficiently similar to absorb the excess economic profits.

If McDonald's is thriving at a particular location, it can confidently expect Burger King or some other fast-food outlet to open a franchise nearby shortly. When one seller adopts a new, attractive package, rivals will soon follow suit with slightly different designs and colors of their own. For example, when Coke brought back its curved glass bottle in 1994, Pepsi countered with a new cube-shaped package that fits easily into the refrigerator. In this way, freedom of entry ensures that the monopolistically competitive firm earns no higher return on its capital in the long run than that capital could earn elsewhere: in other words, the firm earns no excess economic profits. Just as under perfect competition, competition will drive price down to equal average cost, including the opportunity cost of capital. In this sense, though its product differs somewhat from everyone else's offering, the firm under monopolistic competition has no more monopoly *power* than one operating under perfect competition.

Let us now examine the process that ensures that competition will drive economic profits down to zero in the long run, even under monopolistic competition, and see what prices and outputs that process fosters.

PRICE AND OUTPUT DETERMINATION UNDER MONOPOLISTIC COMPETITION

The *short-run* equilibrium of the firm under monopolistic competition differs little from equilibrium under monopoly. Because the firm faces a downward-sloping demand curve (labeled *D* in Figure 13–1), its marginal revenue (MR) curve will lie below its demand curve. Like any firm, a monopolistic competitor maximizes profits by producing the output at which marginal revenue equals marginal cost (MC). In Figure 13–1, the profit-maximizing output for a hypothetical gas station is 12,000 gallons per week, and it sells this output at a price of $1 per gallon (point *P* on the demand curve). The firm makes 10 cents per gallon in profits, as depicted by the vertical distance from *C* to *P*.

This analysis, you will note, looks much like Figure 12–2 for a monopoly. The main difference is that monopolistic competitors are likely to face a much flatter demand curve than pure monopolists do, because many products serve as close substitutes for the monopolistic competitor's product. If our gas station raises its price to $1.30 per gallon, most of its customers will go across the street. If it lowers its price to 70 cents, it will have long lines at its pumps.

The gas station depicted in Figure 13–1 is enjoying economic profits. Because average cost at 12,000 gallons per week is only 90 cents per gallon (point *C*), the station makes a profit of 10 cents per gallon on gasoline sales, or $1,200 per week in total, shown by the shaded rectangle. Under monopoly, such profits can persist. But under monopolistic competition they cannot, because economic profits will entice new firms to enter the market. Although the new gas stations will not offer the identical product, they will offer products that are close enough to take away some business from our firm. (For example, they may sell Conoco or Shell gasoline instead of Exxon.)

When more firms enter the market, each firm's demand curve will shift downward (to the left). But how far will it shift? The answer is basically the same as it was under perfect competition. Market entry will cease only when the most that the firm can earn is zero economic profit—exactly the same return the firm can earn elsewhere.

Short-Run Equilibrium of the Firm under Monopolistic Competition

Gallons of Gasoline per Week

FIGURE 13-2

Long-Run Equilibrium of the Firm under Monopolistic Competition

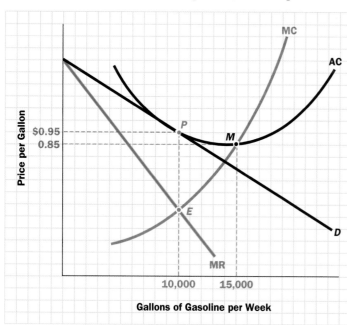

Figure 13–2 depicts the same monopolistically competitive firm as in Figure 13–1 *after* the adjustment to the long-run equilibrium is complete. The demand curve—and hence also the MR curve—has been pushed down so far by the entry of new rivals that when the firm equates MC and MR in order to maximize profits (point *E*), it simultaneously equates price *(P)* and average cost (AC) so that profits are zero (point *P*). As compared to the short-run equilibrium depicted in Figure 13–1, price in long-run equilibrium is *lower* (95 cents per gallon versus $1), *more firms* participate in the industry, and each firm is producing a *smaller* output (10,000 gallons versus 12,000) at a *higher* average cost per gallon (95 cents versus 90 cents).[2] In general:

Long-run equilibrium under monopolistic competition requires that the firm's demand curve be tangent to its average cost curve.

Why? Because if the two curves intersected, firms could produce output quantities at which price would exceed average cost, which means that participants would be earning economic profits that would draw an influx of new close-substitute products. Similarly, if the average cost curve failed to touch the demand curve altogether, the firm would incur an economic loss—it would be unable to obtain returns equal to those that its capital can get elsewhere, and firms would leave the industry.

This analysis of entry is quite similar to the perfectly competitive case. Moreover, the notion that firms under monopolistic competition earn exactly zero economic profits seems to correspond fairly well to what we see in the real world. Gas station operators, whose markets fit the characteristics of monopolistic competition, do not earn notably higher profits than do small farmers, who operate under conditions closer to perfect competition.

THE EXCESS CAPACITY THEOREM AND RESOURCE ALLOCATION

One economically significant difference arises between perfect and monopolistic competition. Look at Figure 13–2 again. The tangency point between the average cost and demand curves, point *P*, occurs along the *negatively sloping portion* of the average cost curve, because *P* is the only point where the AC curve has the same (negative) slope as the demand curve. If the AC curve is ∪-shaped, the tangency point must therefore lie above and to the left of the *minimum point* on the average cost curve, point *M*. In other words, under monopolistic competition, the demand curve hits the average cost curve in a region where average costs are still declining. Average costs have yet to reach their lowest point. By contrast, the perfectly competitive firm's demand curve is horizontal, so tangency must take place at the minimum point on the average cost curve You can easily confirm this by referring back to Figure 10–9(a). This difference leads to the following important conclusion:

Under monopolistic competition in the long run, the firm will tend to produce an output lower than that which minimizes its unit costs, and hence unit costs of the monopolistic competitor will be higher than necessary. Because the level of output that corresponds to minimum average cost is naturally considered to be the firm's optimal capacity, this result has been called the *excess capacity theorem of monopolistic competition*. Thus, monopolistic competition tends to lead firms to have unused or wasted capacity.

---

[2] *Exercise:* Show that if the demand curve fell still further, the firm would incur a loss. What would then happen in the long run?

It follows that if every firm under monopolistic competition were to expand its output, cost per unit of output would be reduced. But we must be careful about jumping to policy conclusions from that observation. It does *not* follow that *every* monopolistically competitive firm *should* produce more. After all, such an overall increase in industry output means that a smaller portion of the economy's resources will be available for other uses; from the information at hand, we have no way of knowing whether that leaves us better or worse off in terms of social benefits.

Yet the situation depicted in Figure 13–2 probably still represents a substantial *inefficiency*. Although it is not clear that society would gain if *every* firm were to achieve lower costs by expanding its production, society *can* save resources if firms combine into a smaller number of larger companies that produce the same total output. For example, suppose that in the situation shown in Figure 13–2, 15 monopolistically competitive firms each sell 10,000 gallons of gasoline per week. The total cost of this output, according to the figures given in the diagram, would be:

Number of firms × Output per firm × Cost per unit = 15 × 10,000 × $.95 = $142,500

If, instead, the number of stations were cut to 10 and each sold 15,000 gallons, total production would be unchanged. But total costs would fall to 10 × 15,000 × $.85 = $127,500, a net saving of $15,000 *without any cut in total output*.

This result does not depend on the particular numbers that we used in our illustration. It follows directly from the observation that lowering the cost per unit must always reduce the total cost of producing *any* given industry output. Society must gain in the sense of getting the same total output as before but at a lower cost. After all, which do you prefer—a dozen cans of soda for 60 cents each or a dozen cans of soda for 35 cents each?

Puzzle Resolved: Explaining the Abundance of Retailers

The excess capacity theorem explains one of the puzzles mentioned at the start of this chapter. The highway intersection with four gas stations, where two could serve the available customers with little increase in customer delays and at lower costs, is a real-world example of excess capacity.

The excess capacity theorem seems to imply that too many sellers participate in monopolistically competitive markets and that society would benefit from a reduction in their numbers. However, such a conclusion may be a bit hasty. Even if a smaller number of larger firms can reduce costs, society may not benefit from the change because it will leave consumers a smaller range of choice. Because all products differ at least slightly under monopolistic competition, a reduction in the number of *firms* means that the number of different *products* falls, as well. We achieve greater efficiency at the cost of greater standardization.

"Why have we come? Because only Earth offers the rock-bottom prices and wide selection of men's, women's, and children's clothing in the styles and sizes we're looking for."

In some cases, consumers may agree that this trade-off represents a net gain, particularly if the variety of products available was initially so great that it only served to confuse them. But for some products, most consumers would probably agree that the diversity of choice is worth the extra cost involved. After all, we would probably save money on clothing if every student were required to wear a uniform. But because the uniform is likely to be too hot for some students, too cool for other students, and aesthetically displeasing to almost everyone else, would the cost saving really be a net benefit?

■ OLIGOPOLY

An **oligopoly** is a market dominated by a few sellers, at least several of which are large enough relative to the total market to be able to influence the market price.

An **oligopoly** is a market dominated by a few sellers, at least several of which are large enough relative to the total market that they may well be able to influence the market price.

In highly developed economies, it is not monopoly, but *oligopoly*, that is virtually synonymous with "big business." Any oligopolistic industry includes a group of giant firms, each of which keeps a watchful eye on the actions of the others. Under oligopoly, rivalry among firms takes its most direct and active form. Here one encounters such actions and reactions as frequent new product introductions, free samples, and aggressive—if not downright nasty—advertising campaigns. A firm's price decision may elicit cries of pain from its rivals, and firms are often engaged in a continuing battle in which they plan strategies day by day and each major decision induces direct responses by rival firms.

Notice that the definition of oligopoly does not mention the degree of product differentiation. Some oligopolies sell products that are essentially identical (such as steel plate from different steel manufacturers), whereas others sell products that are quite different in consumers' eyes (for example, Chevrolets, Fords and Hondas). Some oligopolistic industries also contain a considerable number of smaller firms (example: soft drink manufacturers), but they are nevertheless considered oligopolies because a few large firms carry out the bulk of the industry's business, and smaller participants must follow their larger rivals' lead to survive at the margins of the industry. As shown in the accompanying box, "The Mad Scramble to Differentiate the Product," oligopolistic firms often seek to create unique products—unique, at least, in consumers' perceptions. To the extent that an oligopolistic firm can create a unique product in terms of features, location, or appeal, it protects itself from the pressures of competition that will force down its prices and eat into its sales.

Managers of large, oligopolistic firms who have occasion to study economics are somewhat taken aback by the notion of perfect competition, because it is devoid of all harsh competitive activity as they know it. Remember that under perfect competition, firm managers make no price decisions—they simply accept the prices dictated by market forces and adjust their output accordingly. As we observed at the beginning of the chapter, a perfectly competitive firm does not advertise; it adopts no sales gimmicks; it does not even know who most of its competitors are. But because oligopolists have some degree of influence on market forces, they do not enjoy such luxurious anonymity. They worry about prices, spend fortunes on advertising, and try to understand or even predict their rivals' behavior patterns.

Puzzle Resolved: Why Oligopolists Advertise but Perfectly Competitive Firms Generally Do Not
The two reasons for such divergent behavior should be clear, and they explain the puzzling fact that oligopolists advertise far more than the supposedly far more competitive firms in perfectly competitive markets. First, a perfectly competitive firm can sell all it wants at the current market price, so why should it waste money on advertising? By contrast, General Motors (GM) and Toyota cannot sell all the cars

---

● THE MAD SCRAMBLE TO DIFFERENTIATE THE PRODUCT

Competition is fierce in the world of business, and it's not easy to lure customers away from your rivals. McDonald's hit upon a good thing:

Liberal, Kan.—One recent evening after 9 P.M., Jody Hibbert stopped by the only McDonald's in this west Kansas town for the fourth time that day. She wasn't there for the food.

Like a multitude of Americans, Mrs. Hibbert is hooked on Teenie Beanie Babies. She didn't want to miss getting all 12 of the critters starring in a promotion that is shaping up as one of the most successful marketing campaigns ever. . . . McDonald's Corp. is striking gold by simply repeating a Teenie Beanie Babies promotion that was a hit last spring. This year's babyfest began just two weeks ago and was supposed to last a month. But many metropolitan-area McDonald's were cleaned out of the toys days ago, and even rural pockets like Liberal expect to sell their last ones this weekend. . . .

All this is putting happy faces on McDonald's executives and the company's 2,772 franchisees. "Our cash flow has just been super," says Mark Benzinger, owner of the burger chain's outlet in Liberal. He credits the toys with pushing his sales up more than 30% from a year ago. Other franchisees report similar results.

Last year, the initial Teenie Beanie giveaway overwhelmed McDonald's and its famed marketing department. . . . It didn't anticipate the scramble miniatures would cause. At some restaurants police had to control crowds. Almost overnight about 80 million toys were gobbled up.

SOURCE: The *Wall Street Journal*, June 5, 1998, pp. B1 and B8.

they want at the current price. Because they face negatively sloped (and thus less than perfectly elastic) demand curves, if they want to sell more, they must either reduce prices (to move along the demand curve toward greater quantities) or advertise more (to shift their demand curves outward).

Second, because the public believes that the products supplied by firms in a perfectly competitive industry are identical, if Firm A advertises its product, the advertisement is just as likely to bring customers to Firm B. Under oligopoly, however, consumer products are often *not* identical. Ford advertises to convince consumers that its automobiles are better than Chrysler's or Subaru's. If the advertising campaign succeeds, Chrysler and Subaru will be hurt and probably will respond with more advertising of their own. Thus, the firms in an oligopoly with differentiated products must compete via advertising, whereas perfectly competitive firms gain little or nothing by doing so.

WHY OLIGOPOLISTIC BEHAVIOR IS SO HARD TO ANALYZE

Firms in an oligopolistic industry, in particular the largest of those firms, thus have some latitude in choosing product prices and outputs. Further, to survive and thrive in an oligopolistic environment, firms must take direct account of rivals' responses. Both of these features complicate the analysis of the oligopolistic firm's behavior and prevent unambiguous conclusions about resource allocation under oligopoly. Oligopoly is much more difficult to analyze than other forms of economic organization, because oligopolistic decisions are, by their very nature, *interdependent*. Oligopolists *recognize* that the outcomes of their decisions depend on rivals' responses. For example, Ford managers know that their actions will probably lead to reactions by General Motors, which in turn may require a readjustment in Ford's plans, thereby modifying GM's response, and so on. Where such a sequence of moves and countermoves may lead is difficult enough to ascertain. But the fact that Ford executives know all this in advance, and may try to second-guess or predict GM's reactions as they initially decide on a marketing tactic, makes even that first step difficult, if not impossible, to analyze and predict.

Truly, almost anything can and sometimes does happen under oligopoly. The early railroad kings went so far as to employ gangs of hoodlums who fought pitched battles to prevent rival lines' operations. At the other extreme, oligopolistic firms have employed overt or covert forms of collusion to avoid rivalry altogether—to transform an oligopolistic industry, at least temporarily, into a monopolistic one. In other instances, oligopolistic firms seem to have arranged to live and let live, via price leadership (discussed later) or geographic allocations, dividing up customers by agreement among the firms.

Because of this rich variety of behavior patterns, it should not be surprising that economists use a number of oligopoly models. Because oligopolies in the real world are so diverse, oligopoly models in the theoretical world should also come in various shapes and sizes. Oligopoly theory contains some really remarkable pieces of economic analysis, a few of which we will review in the following sections.

A SHOPPING LIST

An introductory course cannot hope to explain all of the different oligopoly models. This section offers a quick general review of some oligopolistic behavior models. In the remainder of the chapter, we turn our attention to a particularly interesting set of models that use methods such as game theory to predict firm behavior under oligopoly.

IGNORING INTERDEPENDENCE One simple approach to the problem of oligopolistic interdependence is to assume that the oligopolists themselves ignore it—that they behave as if their actions will not elicit reactions from their rivals. Perhaps an oligopolist, finding the "if they think that we think that they think" chain of reasoning too complex, will decide to ignore rivals' behavior. The firm may then just seek to maximize profits, assuming that its decisions will not affect its rivals' strategies. In this case, economists can analyze oligopoly in the same way they look at monopoly, which we described in Chapter 12. Probably no oligopolist totally ignores all of its major rivals' decisions. But many of them seem to do so as they make their more routine decisions, which are nevertheless often quite important.

STRATEGIC INTERACTION Although *some* oligopolists may ignore interdependence *some* of the time, models based on such behavior probably do not offer a general explanation for *most* oligopoly behavior *most* of the time. The reason is simple. Because they operate in the same market, the price and output decisions of soap suds makers Brand X and Brand Y *really are* interdependent.

Suppose, for example, that Brand X, Inc., managers decide to cut its price to $1.05, on the assumption that Brand Y, Inc., will continue to charge $1.12 per box. X decides to manufacture 5 million boxes per year and to spend $1 million per year on advertising. It may find itself surprised when Brand Y, Inc., cuts its price to $1 per box, raises production to 8 million boxes per year, and sponsors the Super Bowl! If so, Brand X's profits will suffer, and the company will wish it had not cut its price in the first place. Most important for our purposes, Brand X managers will learn not to ignore interdependence in the future.

For many oligopolies, then, competition may resemble military operations involving tactics, strategies, moves, and countermoves. Thus, we must consider models that deal explicitly with oligopolistic interdependence.

A **cartel** is a group of sellers of a product who have joined together to control its production, sale, and price in the hope of obtaining the advantages of monopoly.

CARTELS The opposite of ignoring interdependence occurs when all firms in an oligopoly try to do something about their interdependence and agree to set price and output, acting as a monopolist would. In a **cartel**, firms collude directly to coordinate their actions to transform the industry into a giant monopoly.

● VENEZUELAN ACCUSATION AGAINST IRAN HITS OIL PRICES

World oil prices slipped yesterday after Venezuela accused Iran of breaking the Riyadh pact on production.

Luis Giusti, president of Petroleos de Venezuela, said Iran was producing 250,000 barrels a day above the level agreed at the emergency meeting of Saudi Arabia, Mexico and Venezuela in March.

The cuts—ratified by the Organization of Petroleum Exporting Countries but also involving producers from outside the organization—were an attempt to support the oil price. However, the markets have appeared skeptical that the production limits will have a real impact on long-term oil supplies. . . . At the close of trading on London's International Petroleum Exchange, the benchmark August contract for Brent crude was $12.95 a barrel, compared with Friday's close of $13.55.

SOURCE: *Financial Times,* "Commodities and Agriculture," July 7, 1998, p. 34.

A notable cartel is the Organization of Petroleum Exporting Countries (OPEC), which first began making joint decisions in the 1970s. For a while, OPEC was one of the most spectacularly successful cartels in history. By restricting output, the member nations managed to quadruple the price of oil between 1973 and 1974. Then, unlike most cartels, which come apart in internal bickering or for other reasons, OPEC held together through two worldwide recessions and a variety of unsettling political events. It struck again with huge price increases between 1979 and 1980. In the mid-1980s its members began to act in ways that did not promote the interest of the entire industry and oil prices tumbled, but OPEC still dominates the world oil market. (See the accompanying box, "Venezuelan Accusations against Iran Hit Oil Prices," for more recent news of OPEC and oil prices.)

OPEC's early success is hardly the norm. Cartels are difficult to organize and are even more difficult to enforce. Firms find it hard to agree on such things as the amount by which each will reduce its output in order to help push up the price. For a cartel to survive, each member must agree to produce no more output than that assigned to it by the group. Yet once the cartel drives up the price and increases profitability, each member faces the temptation to offer secret discounts that lure some of the very profitable business away from other members. When this happens, or even when members begin to suspect one another of doing so, collusive agreement often begins to come apart. Each member begins suspecting the others and is tempted to cut price first, before the others beat it to the punch.

Cartels, therefore, usually adopt elaborate policing arrangements. In effect, they spy on each member firm to make sure it does not sell more than it is supposed to or shave the price below that chosen by the cartel. This means that cartels are unlikely to succeed or to last very long if the firms sell many, varied products whose prices are difficult to compare and whose outputs are difficult to monitor. In addition, if firms frequently negotiate prices on a customer-by-customer basis and often offer special discounts, a cartel may be almost impossible to arrange.

Many economists consider cartels to be the worst form of market organization, in terms of efficiency and consumer welfare. A successful cartel may end up charging the monopoly price and obtaining monopoly profits. But because the firms do not actually combine operations, cartels offer the public no offsetting benefits in the form of economies of large-scale production. For these and other reasons, open collusion among firms is illegal in the United States, as we will see in Chapter 20, and outright cartel arrangements rarely occur within the United States, though cartels

---

| ● **POLICY DEBATE** | **ACTING ON RECOGNIZED INTERDEPENDENCE VERSUS "TACIT COLLUSION"** |

Antitrust laws unequivocally prohibit price fixing—collusion among competitors in which they agree on their pricing policies (see Chapter 20). But suppose that the firms in an industry, recognizing their interdependence, simply decide to "go along with" each other's decisions? Is this collusion by long distance? Should it be declared illegal? Should the government require such a firm to "make believe" that it does not know how competitors will respond to its price moves? Must firms act as if they were not interdependent? If such requirements make no sense, what should the government require of oligopolistic firms?

The airline industry constantly illustrates this issue and its complexities. In 1992, American Airlines decided that the vast number of different airline fares and discounts hurt all airlines and that the industry needed a simplified fare structure. American offered a new, simplified pricing plan called "value pricing," in the hope that other airlines would copy that structure widely. But a few weeks later, Northwest Airlines introduced a special vacation travel deal that undercut American's pricing. This led to a price war, and American had to withdraw its plan, losing considerable money in the process. In this case, American's rivals did not go along with a price leader's decision.

In a more recent set of events, matters worked out differently. The airlines, which have lost money for years, have been seeking ways to cut costs by reducing wages, firing employees, and so on. As part of these cost-cutting efforts, Delta Airlines announced in early 1995 that it was capping

payments to travel agents for each ticket sold. As it moved first to make the first such cut in 10 years, Delta feared (as we know from its internal memoranda) that if the other airlines did not do the same, travel agents would stop booking passengers on Delta. Everything depended on whether other airlines would support Delta's new policy. They did. Within a week of Delta's announcement, the seven largest airlines each announced (apparently without consulting one another) that they would adopt Delta's ceiling on payments to travel agents. The travel agents sued, charging tacit collusion. The case was settled out of court with a compromise.

are common in some other countries. Only one major exception occurs in the United States: Government regulations have sometimes forced industries such as railroads and gas pipeline transportation to behave as cartels. Regulations prohibit these firms from undercutting the prices set by the regulatory agencies—an exception that we will discuss in Chapter 20.

PRICE LEADERSHIP AND TACIT COLLUSION Overt collusion—in which firms meet to decide on prices and outputs—is quite rare. But some observers think that *tacit collusion*—where firms, without meeting together, do unto their competitors as they hope their competitors will do unto them—occurs quite commonly among oligopolists in our economy. Oligopolists who do not want to rock a very profitable boat may seek to find some indirect way of communicating with one another, signaling their intentions and managing the market accordingly. Each tacitly colluding firm hopes that if it does not make things too difficult for its competitors, its rivals will return the favor. For example, the three main makers of infant formula—Abbott Laboratories, Bristol-Myers Squibb Co., and American Home—were accused of conspiring against competitors by keeping their wholesale prices only a few cents apart. The formula makers denied any wrongdoing. (See the accompanying Policy Debate box, "Acting on Recognized Interdependence versus 'Tacit Collusion'," for another example.)

Under **price leadership,** one firm sets the price for the industry and the others follow.

One common form of tacit collusion is **price leadership,** an arrangement in which one firm in the industry, in effect, makes pricing decisions for the entire group. Other firms are expected to adopt the prices set by the price leader, even though no explicit agreement exists, only tacit consent. Often, the price leader will be the largest firm in the industry. But in some price-leadership arrangements, the leadership role may rotate from one firm to another. For example, analysts suggested that for many years the steel industry conformed to the price-leadership model, with U.S. Steel and Bethlehem Steel assuming the leadership role at different times.

Price leadership *does* overcome some problems that result from oligopolistic interdependence, although it does not provide the only possible way of doing so. If Brand X, Inc., acts as price leader for the soap suds industry, it can predict how Brand Y, Inc., will react to any price increases it announces: Brand Y will match the increases. Similarly, Brand Z executives will be able to predict Brand Y's behavior as long as the price-leadership arrangement holds up.

One problem besetting price leadership is that, although the oligopolists as an industry may benefit by avoiding a damaging **price war,** the *firms* may not benefit equally. The price leading firm may be able to enhance its own profits more easily than any of the other firms in the group can. But if the price leader does not consider its rivals' welfare as it makes price decisions, it may find itself dethroned! Like cartels, such arrangements can easily break down.

In a **price war,** each competing firm is determined to sell at a price that is lower than the prices of its rivals, usually regardless of whether that price covers the pertinent cost. Typically, in such a price war, Firm A cuts its price below Firm B's; then B retaliates by undercutting A, and so on and so on until one or more of the firms surrender and let themselves be undersold.

SALES MAXIMIZATION: AN OLIGOPOLY MODEL WITH INTERDEPENDENCE IGNORED

Early in our analysis of the firm we discussed the profit maximization hypothesis, and we noted that firms have other possible objectives. Among these alternative goals, one has attracted much attention: *sales maximization.*

Modern industrial firms are managed by people who are not the owners of the companies. Paid executives manage the firms, working for the company on a full-time basis. These managers may begin to believe that whatever is good for them as individuals must be good for the company. The owners may be a large and diffuse group of stockholders, most of whom own only a tiny fraction of the outstanding stock. They may take little interest in the company's day-to-day operations and may feel no real sense of ownership. In such a situation, managers' goals may influence company decisions more heavily than the owners' goal of profit maximization.

Some statistical evidence, for example, suggests that management's compensation often relates more directly to company *size,* as measured by sales volume, than to *profit.* The president of a large firm generally fetches a much higher salary—and bigger incentive rewards—than the president of a tiny company. Therefore, firm managers may select price-output combinations that maximize *sales* rather than profits. But does sales maximization lead to different outcomes than profit maximization? We shall see shortly that the answer is yes.

The diagram in Figure 13–3 should be familiar by now. It shows the marginal cost (MC) and average cost (AC) curves for a soap suds firm—in this case Brand X, Inc.—along with its demand and marginal revenue (MR) curves. We have used such diagrams before and thus know that if the company wants to maximize profits, it will select point *A,* where MC = MR. Brand X will produce 2.5 million boxes of soap suds

FIGURE 13-3

Sales-Maximization Equilibrium

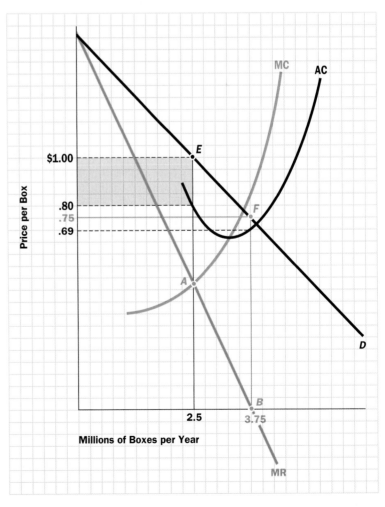

per year and sell them at $1 each (point *E* on the demand curve above *A*). Because average cost at this level of output is only 80 cents per box, X earns 20 cents profit per unit. Total profits are therefore $.20 × 2,500,000 = $500,000 per year. This is the highest attainable profit level for Brand X, Inc.

Now what if Brand X wants to maximize sales revenue instead? In this case, it will want to keep producing until MR falls to *zero*; that is, it will select point *B*. Why? By definition, MR is the *additional* revenue obtained by raising output by 1 unit. If the firm wishes to maximize revenue, then whenever MR is positive, it will want to increase output further, and any time that MR becomes negative, X management will want to decrease output. Only when MR = 0 can management possibly have maximized sales revenue.[3]

Thus, if Brand X, Inc., is a sales maximizer, it will produce 3.75 million boxes of soap suds per year (point *B*), and charge 75 cents per box (point *F*). Because average costs at this level of production are only 69 cents per box, profit per unit is 6 cents and, with 3.75 million units sold, total profit is $225,000. Naturally, this profit is substantially less than what the firm can achieve if it reduces output to the profit-maximizing level. But this is not the goal of X's management. Its sales revenue at point *B* is 75 cents per unit times 3.75 million units, or $2,812,500, whereas at point *A* it was only $2,500,000 (2.5 million units at $1.00 each). We conclude that:

> **If a firm is maximizing sales revenue, it will produce more output and charge a lower price than it would if it were maximizing profits.**

Figure 13–3 clearly shows that this result holds for Brand X, Inc. But does it always hold? The answer is yes. Look again at Figure 13–3, but ignore the numbers on the axes. At point *A*, where MR = MC, marginal revenue must be positive because it equals marginal cost (which, we may assume, is *always* positive—output can never be increased at zero additional cost). At point *B*, MR is equal to zero. Because the marginal revenue curve slopes negatively, the point where it reaches zero (point *B*) must necessarily correspond to a higher output level than does the point where it cuts the marginal cost curve (point *A*). Thus, sales-maximizing firms always produce more than profit-maximizing firms and, to sell this greater volume of output, they must charge lower prices. *Exercise:* In the graph how much below maximum profit is total profit under sales maximization?

Puzzle Resolved: The Kinked Demand Curve Model[4]

Another oligopoly analysis model accounts for the alleged "stickiness" in oligopolistic pricing, meaning that prices in oligopolistic markets change far less frequently than do competitive market prices—one of the puzzling phenomena with which we began this chapter. The prices of corn, soybeans, pork bellies, and silver, all commodities that trade in markets with large numbers of buyers and sellers, change second by second. But products supplied by oligopolists such as cars, televisions, and refrigerators usually change prices only every few months or even more rarely. These products seem to resist frequent price changes, even in inflationary periods.

One reason for such "sticky" prices may be that when an oligopolist cuts its product's price, it can never predict how its rivals will react. One extreme possibility is that Firm Y will ignore Firm X's price cut; that is, Y's price will not change. Alternatively, Y may reduce its price, precisely matching that of Firm X. Accordingly, the model of oligopolistic behavior we discuss next uses two different

---

[3] The logic here is exactly the same as the logic that led to the conclusion that a firm maximized profits by setting *marginal profit* equal to zero. If you need to review, consult Chapter 9, especially pages 175–176.

[4] Variants of this model were constructed by Hall and Hitch in England and by Sweezy in the United States. See R. L. Hall and C. J. Hitch, "Price Theory and Business Behavior," *Oxford Economic Papers* 2 (May 1939): pp. 12–45; and P. M. Sweezy, "Demand under Conditions of Oligopoly," *Journal of Political Economy* 47 (August 1939): pp. 568–573.

demand curves. One curve represents the quantities a given oligopolistic firm can sell at different prices *if competitors match its price moves,* and the other demand curve represents what will happen if competitors stubbornly *stick to their initial price levels.*

Point *A* in Figure 13–4 represents our firm's initial price and output: 1,000 units at $10 each. Two demand curves, *DD* and *dd,* pass through point *A. DD* represents our company's demand if competitors keep their prices fixed, and *dd* indicates what happens when competitors match our firm's price changes.

FIGURE 13-4

The Kinked Demand Curve

The *DD* curve is the more elastic (flatter and more responsive) of the two, and a moment's thought indicates why this should be so. If our firm cuts its price from its initial level of $10 to, say, $8, and if competitors do not match this cut, we would expect our firm to get a large number of new customers—perhaps its quantity demanded will jump to 1,400. However, if its competitors respond by also reducing their prices, its quantity demanded will rise by less—perhaps only to 1,100 (more inelastic demand curve *dd*). Similarly, when it raises its price, our firm may expect a larger sales flight if its rivals fail to match its increase, as indicated by the relative flatness (elasticity) of the curve *DD* in Figure 13–4, as compared to *dd,* the firm's demand curve when rivals do match our firm's price changes.

How does this relate to sticky oligopolistic prices? The economists who designed this model hypothesized that a typical oligopolistic firm has good reason to fear the worst. If it lowers its prices and its rivals do not, its sales will seriously cut into its competitors' volume, and so the rivals will *have* to match the price cut in order to protect themselves. The inelastic demand curve, *dd,* will therefore apply if our firm decides on a price reduction (points below and to the right of point *A*).

On the other hand, if our company chooses to *increase* its price, management will fear that its rivals will continue to sit at their old price levels, calmly collecting customers as they flee from X's higher prices. Thus, the relevant demand curve for price increases (above *A*) will be *DD.*

In sum, our firm will figure that it will face a segment of the elastic demand curve *DD* if it raises its price and a segment of the inelastic demand curve *dd* if it decreases its price. Its true demand curve will then be given by the heavy red line, *DAd.* For obvious reasons, this is called a *kinked demand curve.*

The kinked demand curve represents a "heads you lose, tails you lose" proposition in terms of any potential price changes. If a firm raises its price, it will lose many customers (because in that case its demand is elastic); if it lowers its price, the sales increase will be comparatively small (because then its demand is inelastic). In these circumstances, management will vary its price only under extreme provocation, that is, only if its costs change enormously.

Figure 13–5 illustrates this conclusion graphically. The two demand curves, *dd* and *DD,* are carried over precisely from Figure 13–4. The dashed line labeled MR is the marginal revenue curve associated with *DD,* while the solid line labeled mr is the marginal revenue curve associated with *dd.* The marginal revenue curve relevant to the firm's decision making is MR for any output level below 1,000 units, but mr for any output level above 1,000 units. Therefore, the composite marginal revenue curve facing the firm is shown by the yellow-highlighted line DBCmr with two angles.

FIGURE 13-5

The Kinked Demand Curve and Sticky Prices

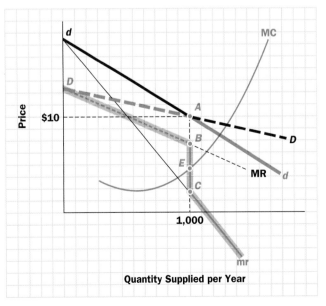

The marginal cost curve drawn in the diagram cuts this composite marginal revenue curve at point *E,* which indicates the profit-maximizing combination of output and price for this oligopolist. Specifically, the quantity supplied at point *E* is 1,000 units, and the price is $10, which we read from demand curve *DAd.*

The unique aspect of this diagram is that the kinked demand curve leads to a marginal revenue curve that takes a sharp plunge between points *B* and *C.* Consequently, even if the MC curve shifts moderately upward or downward, it will still intersect the marginal revenue curve somewhere between *B* and *C* and thus will *not* lead the firm to change its output decision. Therefore, *the firm's price will remain unchanged.* (Try this for yourself in Figure 13–5.) Oligopoly prices are "sticky," then, in the sense that they do not respond to minor cost changes. Only cost changes large enough to push the MC curve out of the *BC* range will lead to price changes.

If this is, in fact, the way oligopolists view their competitors' behavior, we can easily see why they may be reluctant to make frequent price changes. We can also understand why price leadership may arise. The price leader firm can raise prices at will, confident that the firm will not be left out on a limb (a kink?) by other firms' unwillingness to follow. (See the accompanying box, "Will the Internet End 'Sticky Prices'?" for more on price flexibility.)

THE GAME-THEORY APPROACH

In 1944, mathematician John von Neumann (1903–1957) and economist Oskar Morgenstern (1902–1977) contributed a new approach to oligopoly analysis called *game theory.* Game theory is now economists' most widely used approach to analyze oligopoly behavior. The theory approaches the issue of interdependence directly by assuming, for the most part, that each firm's managers proceed on the assumption *that their rivals are extremely ingenious strategic decision makers.* In this model, each oligopolist acts as a competing player in a strategic game.

Game theory uses two fundamental concepts: *strategy* and the *payoff matrix.* A strategy represents a participant's operational plan. In its simplest form, it may refer to just one possible decision, such as "I will add a new car to my product line that features a TV set for the passengers," or "I will cut the price of my car to $19,500." For simplicity's sake, game-theory analysis often focuses on an oligopoly of two firms—a *duopoly.* We illustrate the payoff matrix for a two-person game in Table 13–1.

This matrix reports the profits that each of two rival firms, Firm A and Firm B, can expect to earn—depending on the pricing strategy that each adopts (not knowing the price that the other will offer to customers). The choice open to each firm is either to charge a "high price" or a "low price." The payoff matrix reports the profits that each

---

TABLE 13-1

A Payoff Matrix

		Firm B's Strategy			
		High Price		**Low Price**	
Firm A's Strategy	**High Price**	A gets $10	B gets $10	A gets $−2	B gets $12
	Low Price	A gets $12	B gets $−2	A gets $3	B gets $3

NOTE: Figures are in millions of dollars.

● WILL THE INTERNET END "STICKY PRICES"?

People all over the world have access to the Internet, and companies large and small maintain Internet Web sites. The following excerpt from the British magazine *The Economist* discusses the prospect of more flexible prices that the Internet may offer.

> As shares are bought and sold, the prices on trading screens flicker red and black. Most other prices are far less jumpy. Petrol-pump prices don't change every time the oil price moves, holiday prices and standard hotel rates are fixed for months, and doctors seldom alter their fees. Some claim the Internet could change all that. Prices could flick at the click of a computer mouse. And, they argue, the economy would run more efficiently as a result.
>
> Will the Internet really make prices more flexible? The answer depends on why prices fail to fluctuate with every shift in supply and demand now. Simply put, prices change only when the cost of leaving them unchanged becomes bigger than the expense of adjusting them. In financial markets, prices move all the time because the cost of quoting the "wrong" price can be huge. If market makers failed to raise prices when they were too low, for instance, they would make hefty losses because they would be obliged to sell unlimited amounts of securities on the cheap. And on a market stall, a fruit trader who didn't lower prices when they were too high would have to throw away unsold produce at the end of the day.

> The Internet is unlikely to increase the cost of leaving prices unchanged. . . . But it *will* make it cheaper to change *some* prices. Electronic price-tags can be altered almost costlessly. Digital holiday brochures do not need reprinting. And the Internet makes finding out and comparing prices much easier. Rates for hotel rooms in Honolulu can now be checked from a laptop in London. That, some argue, will make booking a room more like buying shares, where investors plump for the broker quoting the best price, which changes all the time.

SOURCE: *The Economist,* May 16, 1998, p. 86.

---

firm can expect to earn, given its own pricing choice and that of its rival. We read Table 13–1 much like a mileage chart. For example, the upper, left-hand cell indicates that if both firms decide to charge high prices, both A and B will earn $10 million.

We also see that if either firm succeeds in charging a low price when the other does not, the price cutter will actually raise its profit to $12 million (presumably by capturing more sales) and drive its rival to a $2 million loss. However, if *both* firms offer low prices, each will be left with a modest $3 million profit.

How does game theory analyze optimal strategic choice? We may envision the management of Firm A reasoning as follows: "If I choose a high-price strategy, the worst that can happen to me is that my competitor will select the low-price counterstrategy, which will cut my return to −$2 million (the blue number in the first row of the payoff matrix). Similarly, if I select a low-price strategy, the worst possible outcome for me is a $3 million profit (the blue minimum payoff in the second row of the matrix)."

THE MAXIMIN STRATEGY AND THE PRISONERS' DILEMMA How can the managers of Firm A best protect their company from trouble in these circumstances? Game theory suggests that it may be rational to select a strategy based on its *minimum* payoff, just as described earlier. They should pick the strategy that will guarantee them the *highest* minimum payoff (in other words, the best of the bad outcomes). This is called the **maximin criterion,** in which one seeks the *max*imum of the *min*imum payoffs to the various available strategies. In this case, the maximin strategy for each firm is to offer a low price and earn a profit of $3 million (the red-shaded boxes in Table 13–1).

The **maximin criterion** requires you to select the strategy that yields the maximum payoff on the assumption that your opponent does as much damage to you as he or she can.

Notice that each firm's fear of what its rival will do virtually forces it to offer a low price and to forgo the high ($10 million) profit that each could earn if it could trust the other to stick to a high price. This example illustrates why many observers conclude that, particularly where the number of firms is small, firms should not be permitted to confer or exchange information on prices, because consumers would pay for the additional profits provided by successful collusion. The same sort of analysis also helps to explain how competition limits profits and benefits consumers, and why price cartel arrangements are fragile.

A payoff matrix with a pattern like that in Table 13–1 has many other interesting applications. It can show how people can get trapped into making each other (and themselves) worse off. For example, it applies to people driving polluting cars in the absence of laws requiring emission controls. Each does so because she does not trust other drivers to install emission controls voluntarily. (*Exercise:* Make up a payoff matrix that tells this story.)

Still another interpretation applies, one which gave this matrix the name by which it is known to game theorists: "the prisoners' dilemma." Here, instead of a two-firm industry, the underlying scenario is that of two burglary suspects who are captured by the police and interrogated in separate rooms. Each suspect has two strategy options: to deny the charge or to confess. If both deny it, both go free, for the police have no other evidence. But if one confesses and the other does not, the silent prisoner can expect the key to his cell to be thrown away. The *maximin* solution, then, is for both to confess and receive the moderate sentence that this elicits.

OTHER STRATEGIES: THE NASH EQUILIBRIUM We can interpret the maximin strategy as a pessimist's way to deal with uncertainty. A player who adopts this strategy assumes that the worst will always happen: no matter what move he makes, his opponent will adopt the countermove that does him the most damage. The maximin strategy neglects the possibility that opponents will not have enough information to find out the most damaging countermove. It also ignores the possibility of finding common ground, as when two competitors collude to extract monopoly profit from consumers.

A **Nash equilibrium** results when each player adopts the strategy that gives her the highest possible payoff if her rival sticks to the strategy he has chosen.

Other strategies are less pessimistic, yet still rational. One of the most analytically useful strategies leads to what is called a **Nash equilibrium.** Mathematician John Nash devised this strategy, for which he won the Nobel Prize in economics in 1994. The basic idea is simple. In a two-player game, suppose that each firm is trying to decide whether to adopt a red or a blue package for its product. Assume that each firm earns a higher profit if it selects a package color that differs from the other's. Then, if Firm X happens to select a blue package, it will obviously be most profitable for Y to select a red package. Moreover, it will pay each firm to stick with that choice, because red is Y's most profitable response to X's choice of blue, and vice versa.

In general, a Nash equilibrium describes a situation in which both players adopt moves such that each player's move is its most profitable response to the other's move. Often, no such mutually accommodating solution is possible. But where it is possible, if both players realize this and act accordingly, they may both be able to benefit. Thus, note how much worse off both firms would be in the preceding example if Firm Y were determined to damage X, whatever the cost to itself, and adopted a blue package, just like X's.

A **repeated game** is one that is played over again a number of times.

REPEATED GAMES The scenarios described so far involve one-time transactions, as when a tourist passes through a city and makes a purchase at a store that she will never visit again. Most business transactions are different. A firm usually sells its products day after day, often to repeat buyers. It must continuously review its pricing decisions, knowing that its rivals are likely to respond to any change.

Repeated games give players the opportunity to learn something about each other's behavior patterns and, perhaps, to arrive at mutually beneficial arrangements. By adopting some fairly clear pricing behavior pattern, each firm can attain a reputation that elicits desired responses from competitors.

We return to the example of the price war between Firm A and Firm B to show how this works. When we studied the payoff matrix for that game, we saw that in a single play in which neither player knew anything about the other's behavior pattern, each player was likely to feel forced to adopt the maximin strategy. In other words, each firm set a low price for fear that if it adopted the potentially more profitable high price, its rival would adopt a low price and take customers away. In that way, both firms would end up with low prices and low profits.

But when games are repeated, the players may be able to escape such a trap. For example, Firm A can cultivate a reputation for playing a strategy called "*tit for tat.*" Each time Firm B charges a high price, Firm A responds by charging a high price next time. Firm A follows a similar strategy if B's price is low. After a few repetitions, B will learn that A always matches its decisions. B will then see that it is better off sticking to a high price. Firm A, too, benefits from its tit-for-tat approach, which will also lead it, eventually, to set permanently high prices.

THREATS AND CREDIBILITY   A player can also use *threats* to induce rivals to change their behavior. The trouble is that, if carried out, the threat may well damage both parties. For example, a retailer can threaten to double its output and drive prices down near zero if a rival imitates its product. However, the rival is unlikely to believe the threat, because such a low price harms the threatener as much as the threatened. Such a threat is simply not *credible*, with one exception.

The possibility can become a **credible threat** if the threatener takes steps that commit it to carry out the action. For example, if Firm A signed an irrevocable contract committing it to double its output if Firm B copied A's product, then the threat would become credible, and B would be forced to believe it. But A can make other commitments that make its threat credible. For example, it can build a large plant with plenty of excess capacity. The factory may be very expensive to build, but once built, that cost is irrevocable. If the additional cost of turning out the product, once the plant has been built, is very low, then it will pay A to expand its output of the product even at a very low price (if that price exceeds the marginal cost of the item).

A **credible threat** is a threat that does not harm the threatener if it is carried out.

This last possibility leads directly to an important application of game theory: how firms inside an industry ("old firms") can decide strategically how to prevent *new* firms from entering into the industry. To create a credible threat to potential entrants, the old firm may well consider building a bigger factory than it would otherwise want.

Some hypothetical numbers and a typical game theory graph will make the story clear. The old firm faces two options: to build a small factory or a big one. Potential new firms also face two options: open for business (that is, enter the industry) or do not enter. Figure 13–6 shows the four resulting possible decision combinations and the corresponding profits or losses that the two firms may expect in each case.

FIGURE 13–6

Entry and Entry-Blocking Strategy

The graph shows that the best outcome for the old firm is if it builds a small factory and the new firm decides not to enter. In that case, the old firm will earn $6 million, whereas the new firm will earn nothing, because it never starts up.

However, if the old firm *does* decide to build a small factory, it can be pretty sure that the new firm most likely *will* open up for business, because the new firm can then earn $2 million (rather than zero), as shown by the dashed lines. In the process, the old firm's profit will be reduced to $2 million.

On the other hand, if the old firm builds a big factory, its increased output will depress prices and profits. The old firm will now earn

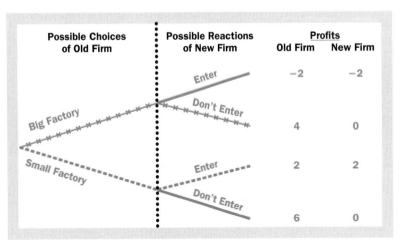

only $4 million if the new firm stays out, as shown by the asterisk line, whereas *each* firm will *lose* $2 million if the new firm enters. Obviously, if the old firm builds a big factory, the new firm will be better off staying out of the business rather than subjecting itself to a $2 million loss.

What size factory, then, should the old firm build? When we consider the firms' interactions, the old firm should clearly build the large factory with its excess capacity—because this decision will keep the new firm out of the industry, leaving the old firm a $4 million profit. The moral of the story: "Wasting" money on excess capacity may not be wasteful to the oligopolist firm if it protects the firm's long-term interest.

Of course, game theory is a much richer topic than we have explained here. For example, game theory also provides tools for economists and business managers to analyze coalitions. It indicates, for cases involving more than two firms, which firms would do well to align themselves together against which others. People other than economists have also used game theory to analyze a variety of complicated problems outside the realm of oligopoly theory. Management training programs employ its principles, as do a number of government agencies (see the accompanying box, "Billion-Dollar Application: Game Theory and FCC Auctions"). Political scientists and military strategists use game theory to formulate and analyze strategy.

MONOPOLISTIC COMPETITION, OLIGOPOLY, AND PUBLIC WELFARE

How well or poorly do monopolistically competitive or oligopolistic firms perform, from the viewpoint of the general welfare?

We have seen that their performance *can* leave much to be desired. For example, the excess capacity theorem showed us that monopolistic competition can lead to inefficiently high production costs. Similarly, because market forces may not sufficiently restrain their behavior, oligopolists' prices and outputs may differ substantially from socially optimal levels. In particular, when oligopolists organize themselves into a successful cartel, prices will be higher and outputs lower than their perfectly competitive counterparts. Moreover, some people believe that misleading advertising by corporate giants often distorts consumer judgments, leading them to buy things they do not need and would otherwise not want. Many social critics feel that such corporate giants wield political power, economic power, and power over the minds of consumers—power that undermines the benefits of Adam Smith's invisible hand.

Because oligopoly behavior varies so widely, the social welfare implications differ from case to case. But some recent economic analysis provides one theoretical case in which oligopolistic behavior and performance quality can be predicted and judged unambiguously.[5] The analysis can also serve as a model for government agencies that are charged with the task of preventing harmful anticompetitive behavior by oligopolistic firms. In this theoretical case, called a **perfectly contestable market,** entry into or exit from the market is costless and unimpeded. Here, the constant threat of the possible entry by new firms forces even the largest existing firm to behave well—to produce efficiently and never to overcharge. Otherwise, the firm will be threatened with replacement by an entrant who offers to serve customers more cheaply and efficiently.

A market is **perfectly contestable** if entry and exit are costless and unimpeded.

We define a market as perfectly contestable if firms can enter it and, if they choose, exit it without losing the money they invested. The crucial issue here is not the amount of capital required to enter the industry, but whether or not an entrant can withdraw the investment if it wishes. For example, if market entry requires investing in highly *mobile* capital (like airplanes, trucks, or river barges—which can be moved around easily), the entrant may be able to exit quickly and cheaply.[6] For

---

[5] See William J. Baumol, John C. Panzar, and Robert D. Willig, *Contestable Markets and the Theory of Industry Structure*, rev. ed. (San Diego: Harcourt Brace Jovanovich, 1988).

[6] Earlier it was thought that air transportation could be classed as a highly contestable industry, but recent evidence suggests that although this judgment is not entirely incorrect, it requires considerable reservations.

● BILLION-DOLLAR APPLICATION: GAME THEORY AND FCC AUCTIONS

When the Federal Communications Commission announced plans to auction off radio spectrum wavelengths for such "personal communications services" as cell phones and pagers, many large companies scrambled to hire game theorists to advise them about strategy in this extremely high-stakes undertaking. The FCC used game theory to design the on-line auction of these so-called *rights to the airways,* and the bidding companies themselves had to figure out how much to pay for the right to service a particular region.

By any measure, the game theorists had their work cut out for them. Each bidder sent its information through its computer, so the FCC had a difficult task in checking out the number and size distribution of the competition. Also, because the commodity being purchased was the latest generation of wireless technology, it was nearly impossible to understand the buying decision completely. Knowing competitors' cost and revenue structures was another hard one, as was gauging future demand for the service. This enormous uncertainty made nimble strategies all important.

The FCC might simply have priced the licenses for the various available regions itself. But by conducting an auction, it placed the decision-making onus on the bidding companies and their hired game theorists. Each bidder had to decide what sectors it could serve most efficiently, and each had to

anticipate competitiors' most likely moves and countermoves. As it turned out, the FCC auctioned off more than 1,000 PCS licenses in nearly 500 cities or regions between August 1996 and January 1997, raising more than $20 billion.

SOURCE: "FCC Plans Spectrum Auction Conference," June 16, 1998, and "Consent in Bid-Rigging Case," November 10, 1998, CNN Financial Network, June 16, 1998 *http://cnnfn.com.*

instance, if a barge operation decides to serve the lower Mississippi River but finds business disappointing, it can easily transfer its boats to, say, the Ohio River.

A profitable market that is also contestable therefore attracts *potential* entrants. Because no barriers to entry or exit exist, firms undertake little risk by going into such a market. If their entry turns out to have been a mistake, they can move to another market without loss.

Because perfect competition requires a large number of firms, all of them small relative to the size of the industry, no industry with economies of large-scale production can be perfectly competitive. However, markets that contain a few relatively large firms may be highly contestable, though they are certainly not perfectly competitive. But no real-world industry is in fact *perfectly* contestable, just as no industry is perfectly competitive.

The constant threat of entry forces oligopolists to perform well. Even monopolists must perform well if they do business in a highly contestable market. In particular, perfectly contestable markets have at least two socially desirable characteristics.

First, freedom of entry eliminates any excess economic profits so that in this respect contestable markets resemble perfectly competitive markets. For example, if the current opportunity cost of capital is 12 percent while the firms in a contestable market are earning a return of 18 percent, then new firms will enter the market, expand the industry's outputs, and drive down the prices of its products to the point at which no firm earns any excess profit. To avoid this outcome, established firms must expand output to a level that precludes excess profit.

Second, inefficient enterprises cannot survive in a perfectly contestable industry because cost inefficiencies invite replacement of the existing firms by entrants who can provide the same outputs at lower cost and lower prices. Only firms operating at the lowest possible cost can survive. In sum, firms in a perfectly contestable market will be forced to operate as efficiently as possible and to charge prices as low as long-run financial survival permits.

The theory of contestable markets has been widely used by courts and government agencies concerned with the performance of business firms (for a recent example, see Chapter 20) and provides workable guidelines for improved or acceptable behavior in industries in which economies of scale mean that only a small number of firms can or should operate.

A GLANCE BACKWARD: COMPARING THE FOUR MARKET FORMS

We have now completed the set of chapters that has taken us through the four main market forms: perfect competition, monopoly, monopolistic competition, and oligopoly. You have probably absorbed a lot of information about the workings of these market forms as you read through Chapters 10 through 13, but you may be confused by the details. Table 13–2 presents an overview of the main attributes of each of the market forms for comparison. It shows that:

- Perfect competition and pure monopoly are concepts useful primarily for *analytical* purposes—we find neither very often in reality. There are very many monopolistically competitive firms, and oligopoly firms account for the largest share of the economy's output.

- Profits are zero in long-run equilibrium under perfect competition and monopolistic competition because entry is so easy that high profits attract new rivals into the market.

- Consequently, AC = AR in long-run equilibrium under these two market forms. In equilibrium, MC = MR for the profit-maximizing firm under any market form. However, under oligopoly, firms may adopt the strategies described by game theory or they may pursue goals other than profits; for example, they may be sales maximizers. Therefore, in the equilibrium of the oligopoly firm, MC may be unequal to MR.

- The behavior of the perfectly competitive firm and industry theoretically leads to an efficient allocation of resources that maximizes the benefits to consumers, given the resources available to consumers. Monopoly, however, can misallocate resources by restricting output in order to raise prices and profits. Under monopolistic competition, excess capacity and inefficiency are apt to result. And under oligopoly, almost anything can happen, so it is impossible to generalize about its vices or virtues.

Attributes of the Four Market Forms

TABLE 13-2

Market Form	Number of Firms in the Market	Frequency in Reality	Entry Barriers	Public Interest Results	Long-Run Profit	Equilibrium Conditions
Perfect competition	Very many	Rare (if any)	None	Good	Zero	MC = MR = AC = AR = P
Pure monopoly	One	Rare	Likely to be high	Misallocates resources	May be High	MR = MC
Monopolistic competition	Many	Widespread	Minor	Inefficient	Zero	MR = MC AR = AC
Oligopoly	Few	Produces large share of GDP	Varies	Varies	Varies	Vary

S U M M A R Y

1. Under *monopolistic competition*, there are numerous small buyers and sellers; each firm's product is at least somewhat different from every other firm's product—that is, each firm has a partial "monopoly" of some product characteristics, and thus a downward-sloping demand curve; there is freedom of entry and exit; and there is perfect information.

2. In long-run equilibrium under monopolistic competition, free entry eliminates economic profits by forcing the firm's demand curve into a position of tangency with its average cost curve. Therefore, output will be below the point at which average cost is lowest. This is why monopolistic competitors are said to have "excess capacity."

3. An oligopolistic industry is composed of a few large firms selling similar products in the same market.

4. Under *oligopoly*, each firm carefully watches the major decisions of its rivals and often plans counterstrategies. As a result, rivalry is often vigorous and direct, and the outcome is difficult to predict.

5. One model of oligopoly behavior assumes that the oligopolists ignore interdependence and simply maximize profits or sales. Another assumes that they join together to form a *cartel* and thus act like a monopoly. A third possibility is *price leadership*, where one firm sets prices and the others follow suit.

6. A firm that maximizes sales will continue producing up to the point where marginal revenue is driven down to zero. Consequently, a sales maximizer will produce more than a profit maximizer and will charge a lower price.

7. If a firm thinks that its rivals will match any price cut but fail to match any price increase, its demand curve becomes "kinked" and its price will be sticky—in other words, it will be adjusted less frequently than would be true under either perfect competition or pure monopoly.

8. *Game theory* provides new tools for the analysis of business strategies under conditions of oligopoly.

9. In a *maximin strategy*, the player takes the strongest possible precautions against the worst possible outcome of any move it selects.

10. A *Nash equilibrium* is one in which each player adopts the move that yields the highest possible payoff to itself, given the move selected by the other player.

11. In *repeated games*, a firm can seek to acquire a reputation that induces the other player to make decisions that do not damage its interests. It may also promote its goals by means of *credible threats*.

12. Monopolistic competition and oligopoly can be harmful to the general welfare. But because behavior varies widely, the implications for social welfare also vary from case to case.

K E Y   T E R M S

Monopolistic competition   248

Excess capacity theorem   250

Oligopoly   252

Oligopolistic interdependence   253

Cartel   254

Price leadership   256

Price war   257

Sales maximization   257

Kinked demand curve   258

Sticky price   259

Game theory   260

Maximin criterion   261

Prisoners' dilemma   262

Nash equilibrium   262

Repeated game   262

Credible threat   263

Perfectly contestable market   264

Q U E S T I O N S   F O R   R E V I E W

1. How many real industries can you name that are oligopolies? How many that operate under monopolistic competition? Perfect competition? Which of these is hardest to find in reality? Why do you think this is so?

2. Consider some of the products that are widely advertised on television. By what kind of firm is each produced—a perfectly competitive firm, an oligopolistic firm, or what? How many major products can you think of that are *not* advertised on TV?

3. In what ways may the small retail sellers of the following products differentiate their goods from those of their rivals to make themselves monopolistic competitors: hamburgers, radios, cosmetics?

4. Pricing of securities on the stock market is said to be carried out under conditions in many respects similar to perfect competition. The auto industry is an oligopoly. How often do you think the price of a share of Ford Motor Company's common stock changes? How about the price of a Ford Taurus? How would you explain the difference?

5. Suppose that Chrysler hires a popular singer to advertise its compact automobiles. The campaign is very successful, and the company increases its share of the compact-car market substantially. What is Ford likely to do?

6. Using game theory, set up a payoff matrix similar to one Chrysler's management might employ in analyzing the problem presented in Review Question 5.

7. Review Question 4 at the end of Chapter 12 presented cost and demand data for a monopolist and asked you to find the profit-maximizing solution. Use these same data to find the sales-maximizing solution. Are the answers different? Explain.

8. A new entrant, Bargain Airways, cuts air fares between Eastwich and Westwich by 20 percent. Biggie Airlines,

which has been operating on this route, responds by cutting fares by 35 percent. What does Biggie hope to achieve?

9. If air transportation were perfectly contestable, why would Biggie Airlines fail to achieve the ultimate goal of its price cut?

10. Which of the following industries are most likely to be contestable?

a. Aluminum production

b. Barge transportation

c. Automobile manufacturing

Explain your answers.

11. Since the deregulation of air transportation, a community served by a single airline is no longer protected by a regulatory agency from monopoly pricing. What market forces, if any, restrict the ability of the airline from raising prices as a pure monopolist would? How effective do you think those market forces are in keeping air fares down?

12. Explain, for a repeated game:

a. Why it may be advantageous to have the reputation of a tough guy who always takes revenge against anyone who harms your interests.

b. Why it may be advantageous to have a reputation of irrationality.

CHAPTER

14

When she was good

She was very, very good,

But when she was bad

She was horrid.

Henry Wadsworth Longfellow

THE MARKET MECHANISM: SHORTCOMINGS AND REMEDIES

What does the market do well, and what does it do poorly? This is the focus of our microeconomic analysis, and we are well on our way toward answers. In Chapters 10 and 11 we explained the workings of Adam Smith's invisible hand, the instrument by which a perfectly competitive economy allocates resources efficiently without any guidance from government. Of course, that perfectly competitive model is just a theoretical ideal, but our observations of the real world confirm the extraordinary accomplishments of the market mechanism. Free-market economies have achieved levels of output, productive efficiency, variety in available consumer goods, and general prosperity that are unprecedented in history—and are now the envy of the formerly planned economies. We will discuss that phenomenal record of production and growth in detail in Chapter 15.

Yet the market mechanism has its weaknesses. In Chapters 12 and 13, we examined one of these defects—the free market's vulnerability to exploitation by large and powerful business firms, which can lead to both an inappropriate concentration of wealth and resource misallocation. Now we take a more comprehensive view of market failures and of some of the things that can be done to remedy them. Clearly, the market does not do everything we want it to do. Amid the vast outpouring of products, we also find appalling poverty, cities choked by traffic and pollution, and hospitals, educational institutions, and artistic organizations in serious financial trouble. Though our economy produces an overwhelming abundance of material wealth, it seems far less capable of reducing social ills and environmental damage. We will examine the reasons for these failings and indicate why the price system *by itself* may not be able to deal with them.

However, recognition of the market's limitations does not imply that the public interest calls for its abandonment. As we will see, many of the imperfections of this economic system are treatable within the market environment, sometimes even making use of the market mechanism to cure its own deficiencies.

Puzzle: Why Are Health-Care Costs in Canada Rising?

Long before the U.S. government made a serious attempt to grapple with the costs of health care, Canada adopted a universal health-care program intended to solve the same problem in that country. For this purpose, the Canadian government imposed strong controls over prices and fees. Each province has one insurance plan that reimburses doctors according to a uniform fee schedule; hospitals are put on predetermined overall budgets; and patients pay very low direct, out-of-pocket costs.

Many observers believe that Canada has created an efficient, user-friendly system, though some critics disagree. But Canadians clearly have not succeeded in containing costs. Despite price controls, Canadian health-care costs have been rising persistently faster than the general inflation rate, just as they have in the United States, where there are no such national rules to rein in rising health-care prices. Does this mean that Canadian health services are especially inefficient or corrupt? There is no evidence for such suspicions. Then why have the Canadians been unable to brake their health care costs? The materials in this chapter will help you to understand the answer, with its important implications for U.S. policy.

■ WHAT DOES THE MARKET DO POORLY?

Although we cannot list all of the market's imperfections, we can list some major areas in which it has been accused of failing:

- Market economies suffer from severe business fluctuations.
- The market distributes income unequally.
- Where markets are monopolized, they allocate resources inefficiently.

- The market deals poorly with the side effects of many economic activities.

- The market cannot readily provide public goods, such as national defense.

- The market may do a poor job of allocating resources between the present and the future.

- The market mechanism makes public and personal services increasingly expensive and this often induces socially damaging countermeasures by government.

We discuss the first three items in the list elsewhere in this book. This chapter deals with the remaining four. To help us analyze these cases, we will first briefly review the concept of efficient resource allocation, discussed in detail in Chapter 11.

■ EFFICIENT RESOURCE ALLOCATION: A REVIEW

The basic problem of resource allocation is deciding how much of each commodity the economy should produce. At first glance, the solution may seem simple: the more, the better! But this is not necessarily so, as one of our *ideas* indicates.

TRUE COST Outputs are not created out of thin air. We produce them from scarce supplies of fuel, raw materials, machinery, and labor. If we use these resources to produce, say, more jeans, then we must take resources away from some other products, such as backpacks. To decide whether increasing the production of jeans is a good idea, we must compare the utility of that increase with the loss of utility in producing fewer backpacks. This, as you recall, means we must consider the opportunity cost of increased output. It is *efficient* to increase the output of jeans only if society considers the additional jeans more valuable than the forgone backpacks.

How Much Does It Really Cost?

To illustrate this idea, we repeat a graph you have seen several times in earlier chapters—a *production possibilities frontier*—but we put it to a somewhat different use. Curve *ABC* in Figure 14–1 is a production possibilities frontier showing the alternative combinations of jeans and backpacks that the economy can produce by reallocating its resources between production of the two goods. Suppose that point *B*, representing the production of 8 million backpacks and 60 million pairs of jeans, constitutes the *optimal* resource allocation. We assume this is the only combination of outputs that best satisfies society's wants among all the possibilities that are *attainable* (given the technology and resources as represented by the production frontier). Two questions are pertinent to our discussion of the price system:

- What prices will get the economy to select point *B*; that is, what prices will yield an *efficient* allocation of resources?

- How can the wrong set of prices lead to a misallocation of resources?

We discussed the first question in detail in Chapter 11, where we saw that:

An efficient allocation of resources requires that each product's price be equal to its marginal cost; that is:

$$P = MC$$

The reasoning, in brief, goes like this: In a free market, the price of any good reflects the money value to consumers of an additional unit, that is, its *marginal utility* (MU). Similarly, if the market mechanism is working well, the *marginal cost* (MC) measures the value (the opportunity cost) of the resources needed to produce an additional unit of the good. That is, MC is the resources cost *caused* by producing another unit of the commodity. Hence, if prices are set equal to marginal costs, then consumers, by using *their own money* in the most effective way to maximize *their own* satisfaction, will automatically be using *society's resources* in the most effective way. In other words, as long

FIGURE 14-1

The Economy's Production Possibilities Frontier for the Production of Two Goods

NOTE: Numbers are in millions per year.

as it sets prices equal to marginal costs, the market mechanism automatically satisfies the MC = MU rule for efficient resource allocation that we studied in Chapter 11.[1] In terms of Figure 14–1, this means that if P = MC for both goods, the economy will automatically gravitate to point B, which we assumed to be the optimal point.

This chapter is devoted mainly to the second question: How can the "wrong" prices cause a *mis*allocation of resources? The answer to this question is not too difficult, and we can use the case of monopoly as an illustration.

The "law" of demand tells us that a rise in a commodity's price normally will reduce the quantity demanded. Suppose, now, that the backpack industry is a monopoly, so the price of backpacks exceeds their marginal cost.[2] This will decrease the quantity of backpacks demanded below the 8 million that we have assumed to be socially optimal (point B in Figure 14–1). The economy will move from point B to a point such as K, where too few backpacks and too many pairs of jeans are being produced for maximal consumer satisfaction. By setting the "wrong" prices, then, the market prevents the most efficient use of the economy's resources.

> If a commodity's price is above its marginal cost, the economy will tend to produce less of that item than would maximize consumer benefits. The opposite will occur if an item's price is below its marginal cost.

In the rest of this chapter, we will encounter several other instances in which the market mechanism may set the "wrong" prices.

■ EXTERNALITIES: GETTING THE PRICES WRONG

We start with the fourth item on our list of market failures (since we have studied the first three in previous chapters): The market deals poorly with the *incidental* side effects of economic activities. This flaw is one of the least obvious yet most consequential of the price system's imperfections.

Many economic activities provide incidental *benefits* to others for whom they are not specifically intended. For example, homeowners who plant beautiful gardens in front of their homes incidentally and unintentionally provide pleasure to neighbors and passers-by, though they receive no payment in return. Economists say that their activity generates a **beneficial externality.** Similarly, some activities incidentally and unintentionally impose *costs* on others. For example, the owners of a motorcycle repair shop create a lot of noise for which they pay no compensation to their neighbors. Economists say these owners produce a **detrimental externality.** Pollution is the classic illustration of a detrimental externality.

To see why externalities cause the price system to misallocate resources, you need only recall that the price system achieves efficiency by rewarding producers who serve consumers well—that is, at the lowest possible cost. This argument breaks down, however, as soon as some of the costs and benefits of economic activities are left out of the profit calculation.

When a firm pollutes a river, it uses up some of society's resources just as surely as when the firm burns coal. However, if the firm pays for coal but not for the use of clean water, we can expect the firm's management to be economical in its use of coal and wasteful in its use of water. By the same token, a firm that provides unpaid benefits to others is unlikely to be generous in allocating resources to the activity, no matter how socially desirable it may be.

In an important sense, the source of the market mechanism's difficulty here lies in society's rules about property rights. Coal mines are *private property;* their owners will not let anyone take coal without paying for it. Thus, coal is costly and

An activity is said to generate a **beneficial** or **detrimental externality** if that activity causes incidental benefits or damages to others not directly involved in the activity and no corresponding compensation is provided to or paid by those who generate the externality.

---

[1] If you need review, consult pages 221–223.

[2] To review why price under monopoly may be expected to exceed marginal cost, you may want to reread pages 236–238.

so is not used wastefully. But waterways are not private property. Because they belong to everyone in general, they belong to no one in particular. Therefore, anyone can use waterways as free dumping grounds for wastes. Because no one pays for the use of the socially valuable dissolved oxygen in a public waterway, people will use that oxygen wastefully. The fact that waterways are exempted from the market's normal control procedures is therefore the source of a detrimental externality.

EXTERNALITIES AND INEFFICIENCY

Using these concepts, we can see precisely why an externality has undesirable effects on the allocation of resources. In discussing externalities, it is crucial to distinguish between *social* and *private* marginal cost. We define **marginal social cost (MSC)** as the sum of two components: (1) **marginal private cost (MPC),** which is the share of an activity's marginal cost that is paid for by the persons who carry out the activity, and (2) *incidental cost*, which is the share paid by others.

> The **marginal social cost (MSC)** of an activity is the sum of its **marginal private cost (MPC)** plus the incidental cost (positive or negative) that is borne by others.

If an increase in a firm's output also increases the smoke its factory spews into the air, then, in addition to direct private costs (as recorded in the company accounts), the expansion of production imposes incidental costs on others. These costs take the form of increased laundry bills, medical expenditures, outlays for air conditioning and electricity, as well as the unpleasantness of living in a cloud of noxious fumes. These are all part of the activity's marginal *social* cost.

Where the firm's activities generate detrimental externalities, its marginal social cost will be greater than its marginal private cost. In symbols, MSC > MPC. Therefore, the firm's output must be too big because, in equilibrium, the market will yield an output at which consumers' marginal utility (MU) is equal to the firm's marginal private cost (MU = MPC). So where there are detrimental externalities, the marginal utility is *smaller* than marginal *social* cost. Society would then necessarily benefit if output of that product were *reduced*. It would lose the marginal utility but save the greater marginal social cost. We conclude that:

> Where a firm's activity causes detrimental externalities, marginal benefits will be less than marginal social costs in a free market. Smaller outputs than those that maximize profits will be socially desirable.

This is because private enterprise has no motivation to take into account any costs to others for which it does not have to pay. In fact, competition *forces* firms to produce at as low a cost as possible, because if they don't, rivals will be able to take their customers away. Thus, competition *compels* firms to make extensive use of resources for which they are not required to pay. This means that goods that cause externalities will be produced in undesirably large amounts, because they have social costs that are not paid by the supplier firms.

These principles can be illustrated with the aid of Figure 14–2. This diagram repeats the two basic curves needed for analysis of the firm's equilibrium: a marginal revenue curve and a marginal cost curve (see Chapter 9). These curves represent the *private* costs and revenues of a particular firm (in this case, a paper mill). The mill maximizes profits by providing 100,000 tons of output, corresponding to the intersection between the marginal private cost and marginal revenue curves (point *A*).

Now suppose that the factory's wastes pollute a nearby waterway, so that its production creates a detrimental externality for which the owners do not pay. Then marginal social cost must be higher than marginal private cost, as shown in the diagram. The output of paper, which is governed by private costs, will be 100,000 tons (point *A*)—an excessive amount from the viewpoint of the public interest, given its environmental consequences.

FIGURE 14-2

Equilibrium of a Firm whose Output Produces a Detrimental Externality (Pollution)

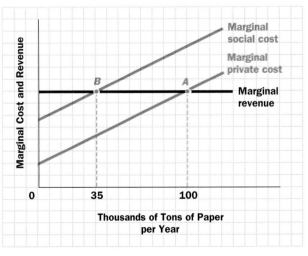

If, instead of being able to impose the external costs on others, the paper mill's owners were forced to pay them, then their private marginal cost curve would correspond to the higher of the two cost curves. Paper output would then fall to 35,000 tons, corresponding to point *B*, the intersection between the marginal revenue curve and the marginal *social* cost curve.

The same sort of diagram shows that the opposite relationship will hold when the firm's activity produces beneficial externalities. The firm will produce less of its beneficial output than it would if it were rewarded fully for its activities' benefits. Beneficial externalities arise when the activities of Firm A create incidental benefits for Firm B or Individual C (and perhaps for many others as well), or when A's activities *reduce* the costs of others' activities. For example, Firm A's research laboratories, while making its own products better, may also incidentally discover new research techniques that reduce other firms' research costs. Thus:

> Where the firm's activity generates beneficial externalities, free markets will produce too little output. Society would be better off with larger output levels.

We can also see these results with the help of a production possibilities frontier diagram similar to that in Figure 14–1. In Figure 14–3, we see the frontier for two industries: electricity generation, which causes air pollution (a detrimental externality), and tulip growing, which makes an area more attractive (a beneficial externality). We have just seen that detrimental externalities make marginal social cost greater than marginal private cost. Hence, if the electric company charges a price equal to its own marginal (private) cost, that price will be less than the true marginal social cost. Similarly, in tulip growing, a price equal to marginal private cost will be above the true marginal cost to society.

We saw earlier in the chapter that an industry that charges a price above marginal social cost will reduce quantity demanded through this high price, and so it will produce an output too small for an efficient allocation of resources. The opposite will be true for an industry whose price is below marginal social cost. In terms of Figure 14–3, suppose that point *B* again represents the efficient allocation of resources, involving the production of *E* kilowatt hours of electricity and *T* dozen tulips.

Because the polluting electricity-generation company charges a price below marginal social cost, it will sell more than *E* kilowatt hours of electricity. Similarly, because tulip growers generate external benefits, and so charge a price above marginal social cost, they will produce less than *T* dozen tulips. The economy will end up with the resource allocation represented by point *K* rather than that at point *B*. There will be too much smoky electricity production and too little attractive tulip growing. More generally:

> An industry that generates detrimental externalities will have a marginal social cost higher than its marginal private cost. If the price is equal to a firm's own marginal private cost, it will therefore be below the true marginal cost to society. The market mechanism thereby tends to encourage inefficiently large outputs of products that cause detrimental externalities. The opposite is true of products that cause beneficial externalities—private industry will provide inefficiently small quantities of these products.

EXTERNALITIES ARE EVERYWHERE

Externalities occur throughout the economy. Many are beneficial. A factory that hires unskilled or semiskilled laborers gives them on-the-job training and provides the external benefit of better workers to future employers. Benefits to others are also generated when firms invent useful but unpatentable products, or even patentable products that can be imitated by others to some degree. We will discuss the externalities of innovation further in the next chapter.

FIGURE 14-3

Externalities, Market Equilibrium, and Efficient Resource Allocation

Tulip Output in Dozens

Electricity Output in Kilowatt Hours

Detrimental externalities are also widespread. Pollution by factories, cars, and trucks cause some of our most pressing environmental problems. The abandonment of buildings causes the quality of neighborhoods to deteriorate and is the source of serious externalities for cities.

Although the market mechanism, acting on its own, does nothing to cure externality problems, there's more to the story. Market economies often have dirty air and rivers and suffer from the effects of improperly disposed toxic wastes, but that does not mean that *non*market economies do any better. The communist countries of eastern Europe and the Soviet Union long were known to have a dismal environmental record. But when communism fell apart in those countries, the horrors of environmental degradation that were revealed were difficult to believe. It became abundantly clear that central planning is not a guaranteed cure for environmental difficulties.

Moreover, the market mechanism does offer us one effective way of dealing with such difficulties. Although markets hardly can be claimed to protect the environment automatically, they do offer us a powerful tool for doing so.

GOVERNMENT POLICY AND EXTERNALITIES

Because of the market's inability to cope with externalities, governments support activities that are believed to generate external benefits. Governments subsidize education, not only because they know it helps promote equal opportunity for all citizens, but also because they believe it generates beneficial externalities. For example, educated people normally commit fewer crimes than uneducated people, so the more we educate people, presumably, the less we will need to spend on crime prevention. Also, academic research that is a by-product of the educational system has often benefited the entire population and has, indeed, been a major contributor to the nation's economic growth. Biotechnology and advanced computing are just two major scientific breakthroughs that have stemmed from university research. We consequently believe that, if education were offered only by profit-making institutions, the outputs of these beneficial services would be provided at less than optimal levels.

Similarly, governments have recently begun to increase fines on companies that contribute heavily to air and water pollution. In recent years, the U.S. Environmental Protection Agency has levied more criminal fines and civil penalties against violators than ever before.

EXTERNALITIES Our *ideas* suggest that standard economic analysis shows the effects of externalities on resource allocation. Externalities are really just failures to price resources such that markets can allocate them efficiently. One effective way to deal with externalities may be to use taxes and subsidies, making polluters pay for the costs they impose on society and paying the generators of beneficial externalities for the incidental benefits of their activities (which can be considered as an offset or deduction from the social cost of the activity).

Externalities: A Shortcoming of the Market Cured by Market Methods

For example, firms that generate beneficial externalities should be given *subsidies* per unit of their output equal to the difference between their marginal social costs and their marginal private costs. Similarly, detrimental externalities should be *taxed* so that the firm will have to pay the entire marginal social cost. In terms of Figure 14–2, after paying the tax, the firm's marginal private cost curve will shift up until it coincides with its marginal social cost curve, so the market price will be set in a manner consistent with efficient resource allocation.

Although this approach works well in principle, it is often difficult to carry out. Social costs are rarely easy to estimate, partly because they are so widely diffused throughout the community (everyone is affected by pollution) and partly because it is difficult to assess many of the costs and benefits (effects on health, unpleasantness of living in smog) in monetary terms. In Chapter 22 on environmental problems, we will continue our discussion of the pros and cons of the economist's approach to externalities and will outline alternative policies for their control.

■ PROVISION OF PUBLIC GOODS

A **public good** is a commodity or service whose benefits are *not depleted* by an additional user and from which it is generally difficult or *impossible to exclude* people, even if the people are unwilling to pay for the benefits.

A **private good** is a commodity characterized by both excludability and depletability.

A commodity is **depletable** if it is used up when someone consumes it.

A commodity is **excludable** if someone who does not pay for it can be kept from enjoying it.

A second area in which market failure occurs is the provision of what economists call **public goods.** These are socially valuable commodities whose provision, for reasons we will explain, cannot be financed by private enterprise, or at least not at socially desirable prices. Thus, government must pay for public goods if they are to be provided at all. Standard examples of public goods range from national defense to coastal lighthouses.

It is easiest to explain the nature of public goods by contrasting them with **private goods,** which are at the opposite end of the spectrum. *Private goods are characterized by two important attributes.* One can be called **depletability.** If you eat an apple or use a gallon of gasoline, there is that much less fruit or fuel in the world available for others to use. Your consumption depletes the supply available for other people, either temporarily or permanently.

But a pure public good is like the legendary widow's jar of oil, which always remained full no matter how many people used it. For example, once snow has been removed from a street, improved driving conditions are available to every driver who uses that street, whether ten or 1,000 cars pass that way. One passing car does not make the road less snow-free for the next driver. The same is true of spraying swamps near a town to kill disease-carrying mosquitoes. The cost of spraying is the same whether the town contains 10,000 or 20,000 persons. A resident of the town who benefits from this service does not deplete its advantages to others.

The other property that characterizes private goods but not public goods is **excludability,** meaning that anyone who does not pay for the good can be excluded from enjoying its benefits. If you do not buy a ticket, you are excluded from the basketball game. If you do not pay for an electric guitar, the storekeeper will not give it to you.

But some goods or services, once provided to anyone, automatically become available to many others whom it is difficult, if not impossible, to exclude from the benefits. When the street is cleared of snow, everyone who uses the street benefits, regardless of who paid for the snowplow. If a country provides a strong military, every citizen receives its protection, even persons who do not want it.

A public good is defined as a good that lacks depletability. Very often, it also lacks excludability. Notice two important implications.

First, because nonpaying users usually cannot be excluded from enjoying a public good, suppliers of such goods will find it *difficult or impossible to collect fees* for the benefits they provide. This is the so-called free-rider problem. How many people, for example, will *voluntarily* cough up $4,400 a year to support our national defense establishment? Yet this is roughly what it costs per American family. Services such as national defense and public health, which are not depletable and where excludability is simply impossible, *cannot* be provided by private enterprise because people will not pay for what they can get free. Because private firms are not in the business of giving services away, the supply of public goods must be left to government authorities and nonprofit institutions.

The second implication we notice is that, because the supply of a public good is not depleted by an additional user, *the marginal (opportunity) cost of serving an additional user is zero.* With marginal cost equal to zero, the basic principle of optimal resource allocation (price equal to marginal cost) calls for provision of public goods and services to anyone who wants them *at no charge.* In other words, not only is it often *impossible* to charge a market price for a public good, it is often *undesirable* as well. Any nonzero price would discourage some users from enjoying the public good; but this would be inefficient, because one more person's enjoyment of the good costs society nothing. To summarize:

It is usually *not possible* to charge a price for a pure public good because people cannot be excluded from enjoying its benefits. It may also be *undesirable* to charge a price for it because that would discourage some people from benefiting, even though using a public good does not deplete its supply. For both of these reasons, government supplies many public goods. Without government intervention, public goods simply would not be provided.

Referring back to our example in Figure 14–1, if backpacks were a public good and their production were left to private enterprise, the economy would end up at point *A*, with zero production of backpacks and a far greater output of jeans than is called for by efficient allocation (point *B*). Usually, communities have not let that happen; today they devote a substantial proportion of government expenditure, indeed the bulk of municipal budgets, to financing of public goods or services believed to generate substantial external benefits. National defense, public health, police and fire protection, and research are among the services governments provide because they offer beneficial externalities or are public goods.

ALLOCATION OF RESOURCES BETWEEN PRESENT AND FUTURE

A third area in which market failure occurs is the division of benefits between today and tomorrow. When a society invests, more resources are devoted to expanding its capacity to produce consumer goods in the future. But if we devote inputs to building new plants and equipment that will add to production tomorrow, those resources then become unavailable for consumption now. Fuel used to make steel for a factory cannot be used to heat homes or drive cars. Thus, the allocation of inputs between current consumption and investment—their allocation between present and future—determines how fast the economy grows.

In principle, the market mechanism should be as efficient in allocating resources between present and future uses as it is in allocating resources among different outputs at any one time. If future demands for a particular commodity, say, personal computers, are expected to be higher than they are today, it pays manufacturers to plan now to build the necessary plant and equipment so they will be ready to turn out the computers when the market expands. More resources are thereby allocated to future consumption.

We can analyze the allocation of resources between present and future with the aid of a production possibilities frontier diagram, such as the one in Figure 14–1. The question now is how much labor and capital to devote to producing consumer goods and how much to devote to construction of factories to produce output in the future. Then, instead of jeans and backpacks, the graph will show consumer goods and number of factories on its axes, but otherwise it will be exactly the same as Figure 14–1.

The profit motive directs the flow of resources between one time period and another, just as it handles resource allocation among different industries in a given period. The lure of profits directs resources to those products *and those time periods* in which high prices promise to make output most profitable. But at least one feature of the process of resource allocation among different time periods distinguishes it from the process of allocation among industries. This is the special role that the *interest rate* plays in allocation among time periods.

THE ROLE OF THE INTEREST RATE

If receipt of a given amount of money is delayed until some future time, the recipient incurs an *opportunity cost*—the interest that the money could have earned if it had been received earlier and invested. For example, if the prevailing interest rate is 9 percent and you can persuade someone who owes you $100 to make that payment one year earlier than originally planned, you come out $9 ahead (because you can take the $100 and invest it at 9 percent). Put another way, if the interest rate is 9 percent and the payment of $100 is postponed for one year, you lose the opportunity to earn $9. Thus, the interest rate determines the opportunity cost to a recipient who gets money at some future date instead of now—the lower the interest rate, the lower the opportunity cost. For this reason, as we will see in greater detail in Chapter 16:

> **Low interest rates will persuade people to invest more now in factories and equipment, because these investments yield a large portion of their benefits in the future. Thus, more resources will be devoted to the future if interest rates are low. Similarly, high interest rates make durable investment, with future benefits, less attractive. Therefore, high interest rates tend to increase the use of resources for current output at the expense of reduced future outputs.**

On the surface, it seems that the price system can allocate resources among different time periods in the way consumers prefer, because the supply of and demand for loans (see Chapter 16), which determine the interest rate, reflect the public's preferences between present and future. Suppose, for example, that the public suddenly became more interested in future consumption (say, people wanted to save more for their retirement years). People would save more money, the supply of funds available for borrowing would increase, and interest rates would tend to fall. This would stimulate investment and add to the future output of goods at the expense of current consumption.

But economists have raised several questions about how effectively the market mechanism allocates resources among different time periods in practice.

HOW DOES IT WORK IN PRACTICE?

One thing that makes economists uneasy is that the interest rate (which is the price that controls resource allocation over time) is also used for a variety of *other* purposes. For instance, sometimes the interest rate is used to deal with business fluctuations. It plays an analogous role in international monetary relations. As a result, governments frequently manipulate interest rates. In doing so, policymakers seem to give little thought to the effects on resource allocation between present and future, so we may well worry whether the resulting interest rates are the most appropriate.

Second, some economists have suggested that, even when the government doesn't manipulate the interest rate, the market may devote too large a proportion of the economy's resources to immediate consumption. One British economist, A. C. Pigou, argued that people suffer from "a defective telescopic faculty"—that they are too shortsighted to give adequate weight to the future. A "bird in the hand" point of view leads people to spend too much on today's consumption and commit too little to tomorrow's investments.

A third reason why the free market may not invest enough for the future is that investment projects, like the construction of a new factory, are much greater risks to the individual investor than to the community as a whole. Even if the original investor goes bankrupt and the factory falls into someone else's hands, it can still go on turning out goods. But the profits will not go to the original investor or his or her heirs. Therefore, the loss to the individual investor will be far greater than the loss to society. For this reason, individual investment for the future may fall short of the socially optimal amounts. Investments too risky to be worthwhile to any group of private individuals may nevertheless be advantageous to society as a whole.

Fourth, our economy shortchanges the future when it despoils irreplaceable natural resources, exterminates whole species of plants and animals, floods canyons, "develops" attractive areas into acres of potential slums, and so on. Worst of all, industry, the military, and individuals bequeath a ticking time bomb to the future when they leave behind lethal and slow-acting toxic residues. For example, nuclear wastes may remain dangerous for hundreds or even thousands of years, but their disposal containers are likely to fall apart long before their contents lose their lethal qualities. Such actions are essentially *irreversible*. If a factory is not built this year, the deficiency in facilities provided for the future can be remedied by building it next year. But a natural canyon, once destroyed, can never be replaced. For this reason:

> **Many economists believe that *irreversible decisions* have a special significance and must *not* be left entirely to the decisions of private firms and individuals, that is, to the market.**

However, some writers have questioned the general conclusion that the free market will not invest enough for the future. They have pointed out that our economy's prosperity has increased fairly steadily from one decade to the next, and that there is reason to expect future generations to have far greater real average incomes and an abundance of consumer goods. Pressures to increase future investment then may be like taking from the poor to give to the rich—a sort of backward Robin Hood redistribution of income.

■ MARKET FAILURE AND GOVERNMENT FAILURE

We have pointed out some of the invisible hand's most noteworthy failures. We seem forced to the conclusion that a market economy, if left entirely to itself, is likely to produce results that are, at least in some respects, far from ideal. We have noted in our discussion, either directly or by implication, some of the things that government can do to correct these deficiencies. But the fact that government often *can* intervene in the economy's operation in a constructive way does not always mean that it actually *will* succeed in doing so. Governments cannot be relied on to behave ideally, any more than business firms can be expected to do so.

It is difficult to make this point in a suitably balanced way. Commentators too often stake out one extreme position or the other. Some people think the market mechanism is inherently unfair and biased by the greed of those who run its enterprises and look to the government to cure all economic ills. Others deplore government intervention and consider the public sector to be the home of every sort of inefficiency, graft, and bureaucratic stultification. The truth, as usual, lies somewhere in between.

Governments, like humans, are inherently imperfect. The political process leads to compromises that sometimes bear little resemblance to rational decisions. For example, legislators' versions of the policies suggested by economic analysis are sometimes mere caricatures of the economists' ideas. (For a satirical editorial illustrating this point, see the accompanying box, "The Politics of Economic Policy.")

Yet often the problems engendered by an unfettered economy are too serious to be left to the free market. The problems of inflation, environmental decay, and the provision of public goods are cases in point. In such instances, government intervention is likely to yield substantial benefits to the general public. However, even when *some* government action is clearly warranted, it may be difficult or impossible to calculate the *optimal* degree of governmental intervention. There is, then, the danger of intervention so excessive that the society might have been better off without it.

But in other areas the market mechanism is likely to work reasonably well, and small imperfections do not constitute adequate justification for government intervention. In any event, *even where government action is appropriate, we must consider marketlike instruments to correct market mechanism deficiencies.* The tax incentives described earlier in our discussion of externalities are an outstanding example of what we have in mind.

■ THE COST DISEASE OF THE SERVICE SECTOR

Next, we consider a problem that is not strictly a *failure* of the market mechanism. But it *is* a case where the market's behavior creates that illusion and often leads to ill-advised *government* action that threatens the general welfare.

DETERIORATING PERSONAL SERVICES

Over the years, general standards of living have increased and our material possessions have multiplied. But at the same time, our communities have experienced a decline in the quality of a variety of public and private services. Not just in the United

● THE POLITICS OF ECONOMIC POLICY

In 1978, Alfred Kahn, a noted economist who served in the administration of President Jimmy Carter, advocated reducing pollution by raising the tax on leaded gasoline and lowering the tax on unleaded gasoline. *The Washington Post,* in an editorial excerpted below, agreed that Kahn's idea was a sound one but worried about what might emerge from Congress:

> If the administration adopts the Kahn plan, recent history offers a pretty clear view of the rest of the story. Mr. Kahn will draft a one-page bill to raise the tax on the one kind of gas and lower it on the other. But the White House political staff will immediately point out that his draft fails to address profound questions of social equity. What about the poor, who buy leaded gas because it's cheaper? What about young people driving old cars? What about the inhabitants of lower Louisiana, who need their outboard motors to get around the swamps and bayous? There will have to be a rebate formula. It will take into account each family's income, the number and ages of its various automobiles and the distance from its front doorstep to the bus stop. The legislative draftsmen at the Energy Department have had a lot of experience with that kind of formula and eventually the 53-page bill will be sent to Congress. . . .
>
> The real fun will start when it arrives at the Senate Finance Committee. First the committee will add tuition tax credits for families with children in private schools. Then, warming to its work, it will vote import quotas on straw hats from Hong Kong, beef from Argentina and automobiles from Japan. . . . [I]t will then add several obscure but pregnant provisions that seem to refer to the tax treatment of certain oil wells in the Gulf states. When the 268-page bill comes to the Senate floor, the administration will narrowly manage to defeat an amendment to improve business confidence by repealing the capital-gains tax and returning to the gold standard.
>
> When the bill gets back to the House, liberal Democrats will denounce it as an outrage and declare all-out war. They will succeed in getting all references to gasoline taxes and the environment stricken—but not, unfortunately, the import quotas or the obscure tax changes for the oil wells. By the time the staff of the Joint Committee on Taxation has straightened out a few technical difficulties, the bill will run to 417 pages and Ralph Nader will be calling on President Carter to veto it. But the feeling at the White House will be that Congress has worked so long and hard on the bill that he has no choice but to sign it. By the time the bill is finally enacted, Mr. Kahn might well wish he had chosen some other instrument of policy.

SOURCE: *The Washington Post,* December 26, 1978. © *The Washington Post.*

SOURCE: William Gropper, *The Senate* (1935). Collection, The Museum of Modern Art, New York. Gift of A. Conger Goodyear.

States, but throughout the world, streets and subways have grown increasingly dirty. Bus, train, and postal services have all been reduced. Amazingly enough, in the 1800s in suburban London, there were twelve mail deliveries per day on weekdays and one on Sundays! We all know what has happened to postal services since then.

Parallel cutbacks have occurred in the quality of private services. Doctors almost never visit patients at home anymore. In many areas a house call, which only 50 years ago was a commonplace event, now almost never occurs. Another example, though undoubtedly a matter for less general concern, is the quality of food served in restaurants. Even some of the most elegant and expensive restaurants serve frozen and reheated meals—charging high prices for what amounts to little more than TV dinners.

PERSONAL SERVICES ARE GETTING MORE EXPENSIVE

Perhaps most distressing of all, and closely connected with the problems just described, is the persistent and dramatic rise in the *cost* of personal services such as education and health care. You are painfully aware of the speed at which college tuitions have been increasing. The cost of a hospital stay has been going up even more rapidly. Worse still, the cost of health care has denied adequate health services to a substantial portion of our population—the poor and even some members of the middle class. These cost increases have made health care a prime subject of debate in political contests, not only in the United States but in virtually every other industrialized country.

Consider these facts: between 1948 and 1999, the Consumer Price Index (an official measure of *overall* price rises in the economy) increased at an average rate of about 3.8 percent per year, whereas the price of physicians' services rose 5.4 percent per year. This difference seems tiny, but compounded over those 51 years it had the effect of increasing the price of a doctor visit 125 percent, measured in dollars of constant purchasing power. During this same period, the price of hospital care skyrocketed: The average price of a hospital room increased at an annual rate of 8.2 percent compounded. This amounts to an almost 900 percent increase since 1948, measured in constant dollars.[3]

Virtually every major industrial nation has tried to prevent health-care costs from rising faster than its economy's rate of inflation, but none has succeeded, as Panel (a) of Figure 14–4 shows. In this graph the bar for each country shows its average yearly rate of increase in real (inflation-adjusted) health-care costs per person between 1960 and 1996. In some countries, real health-care cost has grown even faster than in the United States.

The cost of education has a similar record—costs per pupil in the United States have increased an average of 7.5 percent per year in the past 50 years. And during the approximately 30-year period 1965–1994, U.S. increases in education costs have been *lower* than education cost increases for four of the six top industrial countries, as shown in Panel (b) of Figure 14–4.

These are remarkable statistics, particularly because doctors' earnings barely kept up with the economy's overall inflation rate during this period, and teachers' salaries actually fell behind. Persistent cost increases have also plagued other services such as postal delivery, libraries, and theater tickets. The soaring costs of education, health care, and police and fire protection place a terrible financial burden on municipal budgets.

WHY ARE PERSONAL SERVICES GETTING WORSE BUT COSTING MORE?

What accounts for the ever-increasing costs? Are they attributable to inefficiencies in government management or to political corruption? Perhaps in part to both. But another reason exists—one that cannot be avoided by any municipal administration no matter how pure and efficient—and one that affects the private service industry just as severely as it does the public sector. The common influence underlying all

FIGURE 14-4

International Comparison: Growth Rates of Real per-Capita Health-Care Costs and Real per-Pupil Education Costs

(a) Real per-Capita Health-Care Costs, 1960–1996:

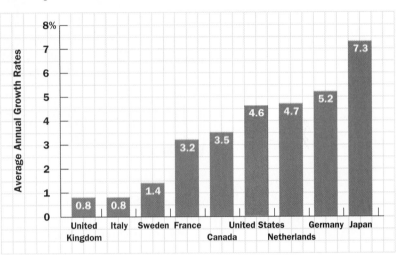

(b) Real per-Pupil Education Costs, 1965–1994:

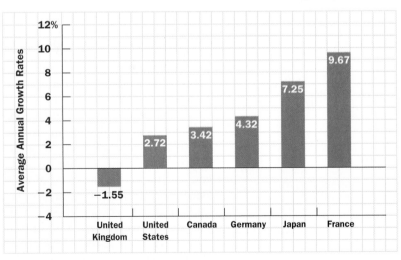

SOURCE: Organization for Economic Cooperation and Development, *OECD Health Data 1997*, CD-ROM (Paris: OECD, 1998); United Nations Educational, Scientific, and Cultural Organization, *Statistical Yearbook* (Paris: UNESCO, various years); and U.S. Department of Education, *Digest of Education Statistics*, http://nces.ed.gov, accessed March 1999.

---

[3] These figures were derived from data provided by the U.S. Department of Labor, Bureau of Labor Statistics, *CPI Detailed Report*, Washington, D.C., http://stats.bls.gov, accessed March 1999; and U.S. Department of Education, *Digest of Education Statistics*, http://nces.ed.gov, accessed March 1999.

BY ROSE FOR BYRD NEWSPAPERS, FREDERICKSBURG, VA.

of these problems of rising cost and deterioration in service quality, which is *economic* in character and expected to grow even more serious with time, has been called the *cost disease of the personal services.*

This "cost disease" stems from the basic nature of personal services. Most such services are *handicrafts*—they require direct contact between those who provide the service and those who consume it. Doctors, teachers, and librarians all engage in activities that require direct, person-to-person contact. Moreover, the quality of the service deteriorates if less time is provided by doctors, teachers, and librarians to each user of their services.

UNEVEN LABOR PRODUCTIVITY GROWTH IN THE ECONOMY

But in other parts of the economy, like manufacturing, no direct personal contact between the consumer and the producer is required. For instance, the buyer of an automobile usually has no idea who worked on it and could not care less how much labor time went into its production. A labor-saving innovation in auto production need not imply a reduction in product quality. As a result, over the years it has proved far easier for technological change to save labor in manufacturing than to save labor in providing services. Labor productivity (output per worker) in U.S. manufacturing and agriculture has increased at an average rate of something like 2 percent a year since World War II, but the productivity of college teaching (crudely measured by number of students taught per teacher) has increased at a rate of only 1 percent per year during that period. And, in elementary and secondary education labor productivity has actually *declined*—the average number of pupils per teacher has fallen from about 27 pupils per teacher in 1955 to 17 pupils per teacher in 1994, partly because classes have become smaller.[4]

These disparate productivity performances have grave consequences for prices. When manufacturing wages rise 2 percent, the cost of manufactured products need not rise because increased output per worker can make up for the rise in wages. But the nature of many services makes it very difficult to introduce labor-saving devices

---

[4] U.S. Department of Education, ibid.

in those parts of the service sector. A 2 percent wage increase for teachers or police officers is not offset by higher productivity and must lead to an equivalent rise in municipal budgets. Similarly, a 2 percent wage increase for hairdressers must lead beauty salons to raise their prices.

In the long run, wages for all workers throughout the economy tend to go up and down together, for otherwise the activity whose wage rate falls seriously behind will tend to lose its labor force. So autoworkers and police officers will see their wages rise at roughly the same rate in the long run. But if productivity on the assembly line advances, even though productivity in the patrol car does not, then police protection must grow ever more expensive, relative to manufacturing, as time goes on. Because productivity improvements are very difficult for most personal services, their costs can be expected to rise faster, year in and year out, than the cost of manufactured products. Over a period of several decades, this difference in the growth rate of costs of the two sectors adds up, making services enormously more expensive compared with manufactured goods. In this way, personal services have grown steadily more expensive compared to goods, and they are likely to continue to do so.

A FUTURE OF MORE GOODS BUT FEWER SERVICES: IS IT INEVITABLE?

If some services continue to get ever more expensive in comparison to goods, the implications for life in the future are profound indeed. The cost disease analysis portends a world in which the typical home contains an abundance of goods—luxuries and furnishings that we can hardly imagine. But it is a home surrounded by garbage and perhaps by violence. The cost disease analysis portends a future in which the services of doctors, teachers, and police officers are increasingly mass produced and impersonal, and in which arts and crafts are increasingly supplied only by amateurs because the cost of professional work in these fields is too high.

If this is the shape of the economy a hundred years from now, it will differ significantly from our own, and some persons will undoubtedly question whether the quality of life has increased in step with greater material prosperity. Some may even ask whether it has increased at all.

Is there anything that can be done to escape this future? The answer is that it is by no means inevitable. To see why, we must first recognize that the problem's source, paradoxically, is the growth in our economy's productivity—or rather, the *unevenness* of that growth. Trash removal costs go up, *not* because garbage collectors become less efficient but because labor in automobile manufacturing becomes *more* efficient, thus enhancing the sanitation worker's potential value on the automotive assembly line. The sanitation worker's wages must go up to keep him at his garbage removal job.

But increasing productivity in goods manufacturing does *not* make a nation poorer. It does *not* make us unable to afford things that we could afford in the past. Indeed, increasing productivity (i.e., more output from each work-hour) means that we can afford more of *all* things—televisions, electric toothbrushes, cell phones, *and* medical care, education, and other services.

> The role of services in our future depends on how we order our priorities. If we value services sufficiently, we can have more and better services—at some sacrifice in the growth rate of manufactured goods. Whether that is a good choice for society is not for economists to say. But society *does* have a choice, and if we fail to exercise it, matters may proceed relentlessly toward a world in which material goods are abundant and many things that most people now consider primary requisites for a high quality of life are scarce.

GOVERNMENT MAY MAKE THE PROBLEM WORSE

How does the cost disease relate to the central topic of this chapter—the market's performance and its implications for the government's economic role? Here the problem is that the market *does* give the appropriate price signals, but government is likely to misunderstand these signals and to make decisions that do not promote the public interest most effectively.

Health care is a good example. The cost disease itself is capable of causing health-care costs (say, per hospital room) to rise faster than the economy's inflation rate because medical care cannot be standardized enough to share the productivity gains offered by automation and assembly lines. As a result, if we want to maintain standards of care in public hospitals, it is not enough to keep health-care budgets growing at the economy's prevailing inflation rate. Those budgets must actually grow *faster* to prevent a decline in quality. For example, when the inflation rate is 4 percent per year, hospitals' budgets may need to increase by 6 percent annually.

In these circumstances, something may seem amiss to a state legislature that increases its hospitals' budgets by only 5 percent per year. Responsible legislators will doubtless be disturbed by the fact that the budget is growing steadily, outpacing the inflation rate, and yet standards of quality at public hospitals are constantly slipping. If the legislators do not realize that the cost disease is causing the problem, they will look for villains—greedy doctors or corrupt or inefficient hospital administrators and so on. The net result, all too often, is a set of wasteful rules that hamper the freedom of action of hospitals and doctors inappropriately or that tighten hospital budgets below the levels that demands and costs would require if they were determined by the market mechanism rather than by government.

In many cases, *price controls* are proposed for sectors of the economy affected by the cost disease—for medical services, insurance services, and the like. But as we know, price controls can, at best, only eliminate the symptoms of the disease, and they often create problems that are sometimes more serious than the disease itself.[5]

Puzzle Resolved: Explaining the Rising Costs of Canadian Health Care

The medical care system in Canada, as in every other industrial country, struggles with the effects of the cost disease. As we have just seen, legislative fiat cannot abolish the productivity-growth patterns that force health-care costs to rise persistently and universally faster than the overall inflation rate. The government-imposed price controls on doctors' fees and hospital budgets have, in fact, led to long waiting lists for Canadians who need high-tech medical procedures and have reduced patients' access to high-priced specialists. The Canadian government has been forced to ease up somewhat on price controls, allowing health-care prices to adapt more closely to costs in order to prevent more serious erosion of medical-care services. The overall quality of service apparently remains high, but the costs have risen persistently faster than the overall inflation rate, just as in the United States.

Panel (a) of Figure 14–4 shows that the U.S. record of health-care costs is not out of line with other industrialized countries. After correcting for differences in the overall inflation rates in the various countries (the U.S. record looks even better if this correction is omitted), we see that our performance is somewhere in the middle—by no means the best, but far from the worst in this sample of nine countries for the 36-year period from 1960 to 1996. (In Panel [b], we see that the same is true of education cost increases—the U.S. growth rate over the 29-year period, 1965 to 1994, falls in the middle of this group of six countries.) The conclusion is that, although a modification in our health-care system may or may not be desirable for other reasons, it is hardly a promising cure for the cost disease. Congress can declare both heart disease and the cost disease of the services to be illegal, but that will do little to cure either disease, and such a law may well impede more effective approaches to the problem.

In sum, the cost disease is not a case where the market performs badly. But it is a case in which the market *appears* to misbehave by singling out certain sectors for particularly large cost increases. Because the market *seems* to be working badly here, government reactions that can be highly damaging to the public interest are likely. That is, "government failure" may occur.

---

[5] See Chapter 5, pages 69–70 and 84–87.

"What really makes this heaven is our great healthcare plan."

■ SOME OTHER SOURCES OF MARKET FAILURE

We have now surveyed the most important imperfections of the market mechanism. But our list is not complete, and it can never be. In this imperfect world, nothing ever works out ideally, and by examining anything with a sufficiently powerful microscope, one can always detect more blemishes. However, some important items were omitted from our list. We will conclude with a brief description of three of them.

IMPERFECT INFORMATION

In our analysis of the virtues of the market mechanism in Chapter 11, we assumed that consumers and producers have all the information they need to make their decisions. But in reality, this is not always the case. When buying a house or second-hand car or selecting a doctor, consumers are vividly reminded of how little they know about what they are purchasing. The old motto "Let the buyer beware" applies. Obviously, if participants in the market are ill-informed, they will not always make the optimal decisions described in our theoretical models. (For more on this issue, see the accompanying box, "Asymmetric Information, Lemons, and Agents.")

Yet not all economists agree that imperfect information is really a failure of the market mechanism. They point out that information, too, is a commodity that costs money to produce. Neither firms nor consumers have complete information because it would be irrational for them to spend the enormous amounts needed to get it. As always, the optimum is a compromise. One should, ideally, stop buying information at the point where the marginal utility of further information is no greater than its marginal cost. With this amount of information, the business executive or the consumer is able to make what we call "optimally imperfect" decisions.

RENT SEEKING

An army of lawyers, expert witnesses, and business executives crowd our courtrooms and pile up enormous costs. Business firms seem to sue each other at the slightest provocation, wasting vast resources and delaying business decisions. Why? Because it is possible to make money by such seemingly unproductive activities—through legal battles over profit-making opportunities.

For example, suppose that a municipality awards a contract to produce electricity to Firm A, offering $20 million in profit. It may be worthwhile for Firm B to spend $5 million in a lawsuit against the municipality and Firm A, hoping that the courts will award it the contract (and thus the $20 million profit) instead.

In general, any source of unusual profit, such as a monopoly, is a temptation for firms to waste economic resources in an effort to obtain control of that source of profit. This process, called **rent seeking** (meaning that the firms hope to obtain earnings without contributing to production), is judged by some observers to be a

Rent seeking refers to unproductive activity in the pursuit of economic profit—in other words, profit in excess of competitive earnings.

● ASYMMETRIC INFORMATION, LEMONS, AND AGENTS

Have you ever wondered why a six-month-old car sells for so much less than a brand-new one? Economists offer one explanation, having to do with *imperfect information*. The problem is that some small percentage of new automobiles are "lemons" that are plagued by mechanical troubles. The new-car dealer probably knows no more than the buyer whether a particular car is a lemon. The information known to the two parties, therefore, is said to be *symmetric*, and there is a low probability that a car purchased from a new-car dealer will turn out to be a lemon.

In the used-car market, however, information is *asymmetric*. The person selling the used car knows very well whether the car is a lemon, but the buyer does not. Moreover, a seller who wants to get rid of a relatively new car is likely to be doing so only because it *is* a lemon. Potential buyers realize that. Hence, if a person is forced to sell a good new car because of an unexpected need for cash, he too will be stuck with a low price because he cannot *prove* that his car really works well. The moral is that asymmetric information also tends to harm the honest seller.

In addition, asymmetric information leads to what are called *principal-agent problems*, whose analysis is a major concern of recent economic research. The issue arises because many critical tasks must be delegated to others. For instance, people who own stock in a corporation delegate the running of the firm to its management team.* U.S. citizens delegate lawmaking to Congress. Union members delegate many decisions to the union leadership. In such cases, the persons who give away part of their decision-making powers are called the *principals,* and those who exercise those powers are called the *agents,* who are, in effect, hired by the principals to perform the jobs in question.

Asymmetric information is crucial here. The principals know only *imperfectly* whether their agents are serving their interests faithfully and efficiently or are instead neglecting or even acting against the principals' interests to pursue selfish interests of their own. Misuse of the principals' property, embezzlement, and political corruption are extreme examples of such dereliction of duty by agents and, unfortunately, they seem to occur often. Among other things, economic analysis studies ways of curing or at least alleviating such problems by arranging for the kind of compensation for agents that bring the agents' interests more closely into line with those of the principals. For example, if the salaries of corporate management are linked to company profits or based on the

market value of company shares, then by promoting the welfare of stockholders, managers will make themselves better off. Shareholders, even though they know only imperfectly what management is doing, can have a fair degree of confidence that management will try to serve their interests well.

*This is an important issue in *takeover battles,* where some outside group tries to gain control of a corporation by buying up a large share of its stock. Because the new owners will be likely to fire the firm's current management, this latter group may fight hard to prevent the takeover even if it is in the interest of the company's stockholders. For more discussion of takeovers, see Chapter 16, page 320.

major source of inefficiency in our economy. (For more on rent seeking, see pages 342–343 of Chapter 17.)

MORAL HAZARD

Another widely discussed problem for the market mechanism is associated with insurance. Economists view insurance—which is the provision of protection against risk—

as a useful commodity, like shoes or information. But insurance also encourages the very risks against which it provides protection. For example, if an individual has a valuable stamp collection that is fully insured against theft, she has little motivation to protect it against burglars. She may, for example, fail to lock it up in a safe-deposit box. This problem—the tendency of insurance to encourage the source of risk—is called **moral hazard,** and it makes a free market in insurance hard to operate.

Moral hazard refers to the tendency of insurance to discourage policyholders from protecting themselves from risk.

THE MARKET SYSTEM ON BALANCE

This chapter, like Chapter 11, has deliberately offered a rather unbalanced assessment of the market mechanism. We spent Chapter 11 extolling the market's virtues and spent this chapter cataloguing its vices. We come out, as in the nursery rhyme, concluding that the market is either very, very good or it is horrid.

There seems to be nothing *moderate* about the quality of performance of a market system. As a means of achieving efficiency in the production of ordinary consumer goods and responding to changes in consumer preferences, it is unparalleled. It is, in fact, difficult to overstate the accomplishments of the price system in these areas. On the other hand, the market has proven itself unable to cope with business fluctuations, income inequality, or the consequences of monopoly. It has proved to be a very poor allocator of resources among outputs that generate external costs and external benefits, and it has shown itself to be completely incapable of arranging for the provision of public goods. Some of the most urgent problems that plague our society—the deterioration of services in the cities, the despoliation of our atmosphere, the social unrest attributable to poverty—can be ascribed in part to one or another of these market system shortcomings.

Most economists conclude from these observations that although the market mechanism is virtually irreplaceable, the public interest nevertheless requires considerable modifications in the way it works. Proposals designed to deal directly with the problems of poverty, monopoly, and resource allocation over time abound in economic literature. All of them call for the government to intervene in the economy, either by supplying directly those goods and services that, it is believed, private enterprise does not supply in adequate amounts, or by seeking to influence the workings of the economy more indirectly through regulation. We discussed many of these programs in earlier chapters; we will explain others in future chapters.

EPILOGUE: THE UNFORGIVING MARKET, ITS GIFT OF ABUNDANCE, AND ITS DANGEROUS FRIENDS

As we said at the end of Chapter 11, economists' analysis of the free market's accomplishments, although valid enough, may fail to emphasize its central contribution. The same can be said of their analysis of the market's shortcomings.

The market's major contribution to the general welfare may well be its stimulation of *productivity*, which has yielded an abundance of consumer goods, contributed to increases in human longevity, created new products, expanded education, and raised standards of living to levels undreamed of in earlier societies. The main shortcoming of the market, in the view of many observers, lies in the arena of justice and injustice, a subject that economists are no more competent to address than anyone else. The perception that markets are cruel and unjust springs from the very heart of the mechanism. The market mechanism has sometimes been described appropriately as the profit system, because it works by richly rewarding those who succeed in introducing attractive new products or in increasing efficiency sufficiently to permit sharp price reductions of other items. At the same time, it is unforgiving to those who fail, subjecting them to bankruptcy and perhaps to poverty.

Both the wealth awarded to those who succeed and the drastic treatment accorded those who fail are main sources of the markets' productive power. But they also generate disenchantment and opposition. This has been true in the newly "marketized" countries of eastern Europe. Predictably, as enterprise in these countries was freed from government control, a number of wildly successful entrepreneurs have earned high incomes, leading to widespread resentment among the populace and calls for restrictions on entrepreneurial earnings. But critics do not seem to realize that a market without substantial rewards to successful entrepreneurs is a market whose engine has been weakened, if not altogether removed.

Indeed, efficient and effectively competitive markets often elicit support from groups who, at the same time, do their best to undermine that competition. For example, regulators who seek to prevent "excessive competition," and politicians in other countries who arrange for the sale of government enterprises to private owners only to constrain decision making by the new owners at every turn, are, in fact, doing their best to keep markets from working. When the general public demands price controls on interest rates, rents, and health-care services, it is expressing its unwillingness to accept the free market's decisions. Businesspeople who are tireless in proclaiming their support for the market system, but who seek to acquire the monopoly power that can distort its activities, are doing the same thing. In short, the market has many professed supporters who genuinely believe in its virtues, but whose behavior poses a constant threat to its effectiveness.

We cannot take for granted the success of the newly introduced market mechanism in eastern Europe. As this book is being written the Russian economy is in turmoil, as are other economies in eastern Europe and several countries in the Far East. Even in the older free-enterprise economies, we cannot just assume that the market will survive unscathed from the dangerous embrace of its most vocal supporters.

SUMMARY

1. There are at least seven major imperfections associated with the market mechanism:

   a. Inequality of income distribution

   b. Fluctuations in economic activity (inflation and unemployment)

   c. Monopolistic output restrictions

   d. *Beneficial* and *detrimental externalities*

   e. Inadequate provision of public goods

   f. Misallocation of resources between present and future

   g. Deteriorating quality and rising costs of personal services

2. Efficient resource allocation is basically a matter of balancing the benefits of producing more of one good against the benefits of devoting the required inputs to some other good's production.

3. A detrimental externality occurs when an economic activity incidentally does harm to others who are not directly involved in the activity; a beneficial externality occurs when an economic activity incidentally creates benefits for others.

4. When an activity causes a detrimental externality, the activity's *marginal social cost* (including the harm it does to others) must be greater than the *marginal private cost* to those who carry on the activity. The opposite will be true when a beneficial externality occurs.

5. If a product's manufacture causes detrimental externalities, its price will generally not include all of the marginal social cost it causes, because part of the cost will be borne by others. The opposite is true for beneficial externalities.

6. The market will therefore tend to overallocate resources to the production of goods that cause detrimental externalities and underallocate resources to the production of goods that create beneficial externalities. This is one of the *Ideas for Beyond the Final Exam*.

7. A *public good* is defined by economists as a commodity (like the guiding beam of a coastal lighthouse) that is not depleted by additional users. In addition, it is often difficult to exclude anyone from the benefits of a public good, even those who refuse to pay for it. A *private good*, in contrast, is characterized by both *excludability* and *depletability*.

8. Free-enterprise firms generally will not produce a public good, even if it is extremely useful to the community, because they cannot charge money for the use of the good.

9. Many observers believe that the market often shortchanges the future, particularly when it makes *irreversible decisions* that destroy natural resources.

10. Because personal services—such as education, medical care, and police protection—are handicraft activities that are therefore not amenable to labor-saving innovations, they suffer from a *cost disease*. That is, their costs tend to rise persistently and considerably faster than costs in the economy as a whole, where more rapid productivity increases offset rising input costs. The result can be a distortion in the supply of services by government or the imposition of unwise price controls because the rising cost is misattributed to greed and mismanagement. This *cost disease of the service sector* is another of our *Ideas for Beyond the Final Exam*.

KEY TERMS

Resource misallocation 270

Production possibilities   271

Externalities (detrimental and beneficial)   272

Marginal social cost (MSC)   273

Marginal private cost (MPC)   273

Public good   276

Private good   276

Depletability   276

Excludability   276

Opportunity cost   277

Irreversible decision   278

Cost disease of the personal services   279

Rent seeking   285

Asymmetric information   286

Principals   286

Agents   286

Moral hazard   286

QUESTIONS FOR REVIEW

1. Specifically, what is the opportunity cost to society of a 100-mile trip of a truck? Why may the price of the gasoline used by the truck not adequately represent that opportunity cost?

2. Suppose that, because of a new disease that attacks coffee plants, far more labor and other inputs are required to harvest a pound of coffee than before. How might that affect the efficient allocation of resources between tea and coffee? Why? How would the prices of coffee and tea react in a free market?

3. Give some examples of goods whose production causes detrimental externalities and some examples of goods that create beneficial externalities.

4. Compare cleaning a dormitory room with cleaning the atmosphere of a city. Which is a public good and which is a private good? Why?

5. Give some other examples of public goods. Discuss in each case why additional users do not deplete them and why it is difficult to exclude people from using them.

6. Think about the goods and services that your local government provides. Which of these are "public goods" as economists use the term?

7. Explain why the services of a lighthouse are sometimes given as an example of a public good.

8. Explain why education is not a very satisfactory example of a public good.

9. In recent decades, college tuition costs have risen faster than the general price level even though the wages of college professors have failed to keep pace with the price level. Can you explain why?

10. A firm holds a patent that is estimated to be worth $20 million. The patent is repeatedly challenged in the courts by a large number of (rent-seeking) firms, each hoping to grab away the patent. In what sense may the rent seekers be "competing perfectly" for the patent? If so, how much will end up being spent in the legal battles? (*Hint:* Under perfect competition, should firms expect to earn any economic profit?)

The Bourgeoisie [i.e., capitalism] cannot exist without constantly revolutionizing the instruments of production. . . . The bourgeoisie, during its rule of scarce one hundred years has created more massive and more colossal productive forces than have all preceding generations together.

Karl Marx and Friedrich Engels
The Communist Manifesto, 1847

MICROECONOMICS OF INNOVATION: PRIME ENGINE OF GROWTH

Human history in the last two centuries has been unlike anything ever experienced before. In the world's industrial countries, the quantity and quality of food, clothing, and comforts have reached levels that were never before dreamed possible. The change has been so revolutionary that it is difficult to grasp. What accounts for this transformation? The answer is growth in *labor productivity*—the fact that the hourly production of a person in the United States today is perhaps 20 times as high as it was in 1800. Just two figures will suggest the magnitude of the achievement. In 1800 about 90 percent of America's labor force had to work on farms, but

Labor productivity refers to the amount of output a worker turns out in an hour (or a week or a year) of labor. It can be measured as gross domestic product (GDP) in a given year divided by the total number of paid work hours during that year. That is, labor productivity is defined as GDP per hour of labor.

all that farm labor barely managed to produce enough food to feed the country adequately. Today less than 3 percent of U.S. workers earn their livings on farms. Yet those relatively few farm workers provide an outpouring of surpluses, which the U.S. government constantly struggles to contain.

Figure 15–1 shows, for five industrialized countries, the impressive growth of **labor productivity** over the past century. It is this spectacular growth in productivity that has transformed living standards. Productivity growth is what has made all the difference and, over the long haul, is what counts most in raising living standards.

FIGURE 15–1

The Growth of Labor Productivity, 1870 to 1996

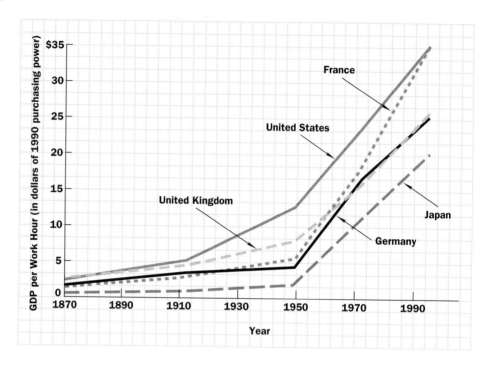

SOURCE: Angus Maddison, "The Nature and Functioning of European Capitalism: A Historical and Comparative Perspective," University of Groningen, Belgium, Oct. 1, 1997, mimeo.

Productivity Growth Is (Almost) Everything in the Long Run

PRODUCTIVITY GROWTH   As we pointed out in our *ideas* in Chapter 1, only rising productivity can raise standards of living in the long run. Over long periods of time, small differences in rates of productivity growth compound like interest in a bank account and can make an enormous difference to a society's prosperity. Nothing contributes more to reduction of poverty, to increases in leisure, and to the country's ability to finance education, public health, environmental improvement, and the arts. By the same token, a slowdown in productivity growth that persists for a substantial number of years can have a devastating effect on living standards.

Innovation is the process by which new products or new methods of production are introduced, including all the steps from the inventor's idea to bringing the new item to market.

Many factors contribute to productivity growth. Most often cited are (1) the education and experience of the labor force that enable the worker to produce more and better goods in a given amount of time; (2) investment in plant and equipment that gives the worker more and better tools with which to do the job; and, above all, **innovation,** the discovery and introduction of new production methods and new products that offer workers productive powers never before imagined. This chapter discusses the economic influences that affect the flow of new products and new technology. In particular, we will investigate what underlies the explosion of the technical change that occurred in the past few centuries in the industrialized countries of the world.

Although we have devoted a lot of attention to the virtues and vices of the market system in earlier chapters, we have barely mentioned what may be its greatest strength. It is the one at which Marx and Engels marveled: Free-market capitalism has proven to be the most powerful engine of economic growth and innovation ever known.

Although the process of *innovation* has yet to be analyzed completely by economists, we can understand some of its crucial features using concepts you have learned in previous chapters—such as marginal cost (Chapter 8), marginal revenue (Chapter 9), and externalities (Chapter 14). Thus, though this chapter deals with a new and critically vital subject, it does not require any new analytic concepts or methods. Indeed, the chapter will help you to review those tools and their uses.

The *Big* Puzzle: Why Do All Rival Economic Systems Trail So Far behind Free Market Growth Rates?

Undoubtedly, the spectacular and unmatched growth rates of the industrialized free-market economies (also called **capitalist** economies) distinguishes them most from *all* other economic systems. In no other system, current or past, has the general public's average income risen anywhere nearly as much or as quickly as it has in North America, western Europe, and Japan. Though the Soviet Union planned its economy and forced its population to invest heavily in factories and hydroelectric dams, its failure to raise the people's standard of living to the level enjoyed by members of the free-market economies undoubtedly played a major role in the USSR's downfall. Great civilizations have amassed extraordinary records of invention and engineering—medieval China and ancient Rome are clear examples. But none has approached the growth record of modern free-market economies. What is the secret of their extraordinary success? Resolution of this economic puzzle is undoubtedly critical to the future prosperity of our planet. The truth is that this puzzle has not yet been solved. But this chapter will offer some clues.

Capitalism is an economic system in which most of the production process is controlled by private firms operating in markets with minimal government control. The investors in these firms (called "capitalists") own the firms.

■ THE FREE MARKET'S GROWTH RECORD

Growth in per-capita income and productivity in free-market economies has been so enormous that we can hardly comprehend its magnitude. In contrast, average growth rates of per-capita incomes probably approximated *zero* for about 1,500 years before the **Industrial Revolution** (around the time of George Washington). In 1776, even the wealthiest consumers in England, then the world's richest country, could purchase only a half-dozen consumers' goods that were not also available in ancient Rome. These new products included (highly inaccurate) hunting guns, (highly inaccurate) watches, paper, window glass, and very little else. And Roman citizens enjoyed a number of amenities, such as hot baths and paved roads, that had practically disappeared long before the American Revolution. In contrast, in the past two centuries, per-capita incomes in the typical capitalist economy have risen by amounts ranging from several hundred to several thousand percent. Recent decades have yielded an unmatched outpouring of new products and services: color television, the computer, jet aircraft, the VCR, the microwave, the hand-held calculator, the cellular telephone, and so on and so on. And the flood of new products continues. Surely part of the reason for the collapse of most of the world's communist regimes was their citizens' desire to participate in the growth miracle of the capitalist economies, the very miracle that Marx and Engels—those high priests of anti-capitalist movements—were among the first economists to discern.

The **Industrial Revolution** is the stream of new technology and the resulting growth of output that began in England toward the end of the 18th century.

We must seek an explanation for this miracle in the activities of industries and the business firms of which they are constituted, for firms produce the increasing flow of goods and services that constitute the capitalist economies' amazing growth. Yet standard microeconomic theory of firms and industries that we discussed in earlier chapters provides no suggestion as to the forces underlying the business decisions that foster such explosive growth. Indeed, as we will see, standard microeconomic theory offers several reasons to expect much less than optimal growth performance in a capitalist economy.

In contrast, this chapter describes some features of competitive markets that literally force businesses to do all they can to contribute to growth.

INNOVATION AND THE GROWTH PROCESS

A primary source of the growth miracle of the past two centuries, undoubtedly, was "the wave of new gadgets,"[1] the surge of innovation that first reached a substantial pace in Britain between 1800 and 1830. Improved education and infrastructure (the combination of facilities, factories, roads and other influences that enable firms to do business more easily) surely made substantial contributions. But innovation clearly was crucial for the explosive growth from 1800 to the present. The Industrial Revolution's inventions helped to end the incredible poverty of earlier centuries that previously prevented societies from spending much on education or on building of infrastructure, plant, and machinery.

We cannot easily grasp the magnitude of that poverty. The following passage from a noted historian suggests how serious the problem was as recently as the 1600s:

> The poor in the towns and countryside lived in a state of almost complete deprivation. Their furniture consisted of next to nothing. . . . Inventories made after death . . . testify almost invariably to the general destitution . . . a few old clothes, a stool, a table, a bench, the planks of a bed, sacks filled with straw. Official reports for Burgundy [in France] between the sixteenth and the eighteenth centuries are full of references to people [sleeping] on straw . . . with no bed or furniture, who were only separated from the pigs by a screen. . . . Paradoxically the countryside sometimes experienced far greater suffering [from famines than the townspeople]. The peasants . . . had scarcely any reserves of their own. They had no solution in case of famine except to turn to the town where they crowded together, begging in the streets and often dying in public squares.[2]

Innovation permitted growing outputs, first in agriculture and mining and then in manufacturing and transportation, that enabled society to invest increasingly in productive plant and equipment and in education. These investments themselves contributed greatly to economic growth. Thus, innovation allowed us to embark on a growth process that itself contributed to further growth.

Two of today's leading analysts of economic growth conclude:

> As yet, no empirical study proves that technology has been the engine of modern-day growth. Still, we ask the reader to ponder the following: What would the century's growth performance have been like without the invention and refinement of methods for generating electricity and using radio waves to transmit sound, without Bessemer's discovery of a new technique for refining iron, and without the design and development of products like the automobile, the airplane, the transistor, the integrated circuit, and the computer?[3]

WHAT IS DIFFERENT ABOUT FREE-MARKET ECONOMIES?

Yet invention alone does not completely answer the great puzzle—why free-market growth has never been rivaled. Some earlier societies had spectacular invention

---

[1] According to the late British economist, T. S. Ashton, "the wave of new gadgets" is how one schoolboy (quite appropriately) described the Industrial Revolution.

[2] Fernand Braudel, *The Structures of Everyday Life: Civilization and Capitalism, 15th–18th Century, Vol. 1* (New York: Harper & Row, 1979), pp. 73–75 and 284–286.

[3] Gene M. Grossman and Elhanan Helpman, "Endogenous Innovation in the Theory of Growth," *Journal of Economic Perspectives* 8 (Winter 1994): p. 32.

records. The Chinese are the outstanding example. Centuries before Columbus came to the New World, the Chinese had invented printing, the compass, complex clockworks, gunpowder, spinning machinery, cotton gins, porcelain, matches, toothbrushes, playing cards, and much more. Other countries in history also achieved a considerable record of new products and new technology. Moreover, Chinese culture and others placed a high value on education, though much of the population was uneducated. Yet, economically, these inventions and this education never produced economic growth anything like that in modern market economies.

We know that substantial markets exist, and have existed, in virtually every economy in the world throughout recorded history. How, then, do modern markets differ, so that they exhibit the capacity to produce growth miracles in a seemingly unending stream? There is no simple answer. Indeed, any proposed answer may well leave out key influences, including political changes, religious beliefs, even historical accidents. However, two features of our economy seem to have played especially crucial roles. The first is free competition—that is, competition not handicapped by tight government regulations or tightly enforced customary rules (like the rules governing the medieval guilds, which prevented gloves-off combat among rival firms). Second, in today's economy, many rival firms use *innovation* as their main weapon with which to battle actual and potential competitors. As in an arms race between two countries, each firm fears that the other will introduce new successful products and therefore it must match the other firm's research and development expenditures. Each feels that at least matching its rival's efforts and spending on innovation is a matter of economic life or death. In such an economy, we can expect a constant stream of innovations, because firms do not dare relax their innovation activities.

INNOVATION VERSUS PRICE AS THE PRIME WEAPON OF COMPETITORS

It is quite clear that innovation is the weapon of choice for competitive battles in substantial sectors of the economy. Price does, of course, matter. But process and product improvements really capture the attention of management. Product lines as diverse as computers and computer software, automobiles, cameras, and machinery all feature constant improvements, which are instantly and widely advertised. Any firm that can come up with a better model than its rivals have will gain an advantage that its competitors cannot match as quickly and easily as a price cut. Dramatic new products also provide substantially greater market advantages than slightly lower prices. Many high-tech industries gain market advantages in exactly this way: computers, medical equipment, aeronautics, automobiles, and so forth.

Of course, not all industries compete via innovation. In fact, most innovations derive from a very few industries in a very few countries. About 80 percent of industrial outlays on new product **research and development**—the means by which firms create new products and prepare them for market, also known as **R&D**—comes from the chemical or machinery and equipment industries. Yet, even in industries where product and process development do not act as the leading instruments of competition, management cannot afford to neglect research and development activities. For if one firm fails to adopt the latest technology—even technology created by others—then rivals can easily take the lead and make disastrous inroads into slower firms' sales.

Thus, especially in high-tech sectors, firms dare not leave innovation to chance. Rather, competitive markets force firms to systematize the innovation process and (in the immortal words of W. C. Fields) "to remove all elements of chance" from the undertaking.[4] Many business firms today routinely budget for R&D, systematically decide how to promote and price their innovations, and even systematically determine what kinds of products the company's laboratories should invent. (See the

Research and development (R&D) is the activity of firms, universities, and government agencies that seeks to invent new products and processes and to improve those inventions so that they are ready for the market or other uses.

---

[4] This phrase is uttered when Fields seeks to lure a novice into a card game, whereupon his intended victim questions the morality of "games of chance." Fields hastens to reassure him: "Young man, when you play with me, all elements of chance have been removed!"

● INNOVATIONS IN BIG FIRMS

Thousands of police can attest to the value of Stephanie Kwolek's breakthrough research in para-aramid fibers. The fruits of her inventiveness can be found in mooring ropes, fiber-optic cables, aircraft parts, canoes, and—most important—in lightweight bullet-resistant vests. Born in New Kensington, Pennsylvania, Kwolek received her B.S. in chemistry from the Carnegie Institute of Technology in 1946. That same year she went to work as a chemist at the Buffalo, New York, operations of E. I. Du Pont de Nemours & Company. "I really wanted to study medicine," Kwolek recalled, "but I didn't have enough money to enter medical school. I joined Du Pont as a temporary measure, but the work turned out to be so interesting that I stayed on."

Kwolek's earliest work, together with that of colleagues, pioneered low-temperature processes for the preparation of condensation polymers. These processes made possible the preparation of hundreds of new polymers and found applications in the future preparation of Lycra® spandex fiber and Nomex® and Kevlar® aramid fibers.

Later, as she searched for a fiber to reinforce radial tires, she unexpectedly discovered a new class of polymers—the liquid crystalline polyamides. This technology, which involved the formation and spinning of liquid crystalline solutions of extended-chain aromatic polyamides into fibers with very high strength and very high stiffness, became the foundation of the Kevlar® fiber. The latter fiber, which is five times stronger than steel on an equal weight basis, is the fiber of choice for bullet-resistant vests. The many unique applications of Kevlar® generate hundreds of millions of dollars in sales worldwide each year.

Kwolek moved to the Pioneering Research Laboratory at Du Pont's Experimental Station in Wilmington, Delaware, in 1950. She retired in 1986 as a research associate but continues to consult for Du Pont and has served on the committees of the National Research Council of the National Academy of Sciences. Her name appears on 17 patents issued between 1961 and 1986.

SOURCE: "Inventure Place," National Inventors Hall of Fame, www.invent.org, accessed on November 10, 1998.

accompanying box, "Innovations in Big Firms" for an example of the fruits of such routinized R&D efforts in big firms.)

Of course, we can analyze this kind of orderly business-firm innovation activity using the standard tools of the theory of the firm much more easily than we can the "Eureka! I have found it!" process, in which the classic lone inventor working in a basement or garage happens to come up with a brilliant invention. Business-firm innovation is easier to analyze because R&D budgets and decisions look a lot like other business decisions, such as how much to produce or how much to spend on advertising. We can study all of these standard business decisions using the same tools of marginal analysis.

HOW MUCH WILL THE PROFIT-MAXIMIZING FIRM SPEND ON INNOVATION?

So, competition forces many firms in the economy to keep up their R&D expenditures. Some of the money spent on R&D will lead to spectacular successes. Other such spending will yield only modest advances, and some R&D outlays will fail outright. Taken as a whole, we can expect that the more money firms spend on R&D, the more innovation will take place and the faster the economy will grow. The key questions are, how much can we expect firms to spend on R&D, and how will competition affect that amount?

We have encountered the general answer to these questions over and over again when we studied how basic marginal analysis addresses business decisions in Chapters 8, 9, and 10.

If the firm seeks to maximize its profits, it will expand its spending on R&D up to the point at which its anticipated marginal cost of R&D equals its anticipated marginal revenue from R&D.

A level of R&D spending (call it X dollars) at which marginal revenue is, for example, *greater* than marginal cost cannot possibly represent the profit-maximizing amount for the company to spend on R&D. If MR exceeds MC, the company can increase profits by spending more than X dollars on R&D. The opposite will be true if MR < MC. Then the firm can increase its profit by decreasing R&D spending. So X dollars cannot be the optimal level of spending if either MR > MC or MR < MC. It follows that the profit-maximizing level of spending on R&D can only be an amount, say Y dollars, at which MR = MC. You will recognize this argument, for we have repeated it many times when we discussed other business decisions, such as those on price and quantity of output, in earlier chapters.

This analysis tells us everything, and nothing, about the R&D decision. It tells us everything, because its conclusion is correct. If the firm is a profit maximizer, and if we know its MR and its MC curves for R&D investment, then the MR = MC rule does, in theory, tell us exactly how much the firm must invest in R&D to attain its objective. But the discussion so far tells us nothing about the shape of "typical" marginal revenue and marginal cost curves for R&D. Nor does it tell us how competitive pressures affect these curves—the competition that plays such an important role in R&D decisions. Nor have we discussed how business behavior contributes to economic growth. Before dealing with these crucial matters, however, let us first apply the standard theory of the firm and the industry to see what such tools tell us about innovation.

THE PROFITS OF INNOVATION

Many discussions of innovation start off with the assumption that innovators expect to earn very high profits. And huge rewards do accrue to those who introduce unusually successful innovations. We have all heard of innovators like Thomas Edison, Alexander Graham Bell, and, more recently, Bill Gates, Steven Jobs, and others in the computer industry, who have acquired great riches from their ability to invent, or bring innovations to market and sell their products. But for every successful innovator, many others have plowed their family savings into new gadgets and lost all they have spent. Quite possibly, inventors on average earn zero economic profits, or even lose money.

This possibility appears even more clearly when we consider business investment in R&D, which is the focus of this chapter. We have just seen that profit-maximizing firms earn zero *marginal* profit (where, by definition, marginal profit = MR − MC), because the firm will invest to the point at which MR = MC. But we can take the analysis further if new firms can enter freely into invention activity, as must be true if the industry is perfectly competitive.

As we saw in Chapter 10, an industry under perfect competition entry will occur until economic profits are zero in equilibrium. Said another way, perfectly competitive industries permit firms to earn just what they need to pay investors for the funds they provide. This must be so because if a typical firm in one industry earns more than firms in other industries, investors will put more money into the more profitable industry. Any excess (economic) profit will expand industry output, thereby driving prices down and eliminating economic profits.

Because there are some barriers to entry into innovation, we cannot be certain that economic profits to invention will tend *exactly* toward zero. But we can still expect them to be very low on average. In other words, although inventive activity sometimes pays off enormously well, large R&D investments also can fail spectacularly, so that the average comes out close to zero. In particular, a large firm with a big R&D division may work simultaneously on many possible innovations. The "law of averages" suggests that some of these efforts will fail and some will succeed. So we can expect zero economic profit even in industries with a great deal of innovative activity.

Does this conclusion fit the facts? Although we have no systematic study of all inventive activities, high-tech industries provide a useful illustration—especially the computer industry, where many founders have made fortunes and received much publicity. According to one recent assessment, however:

> "The computer industry hasn't made a dime. . . . Intel and Microsoft make money, but look at all the people who were losing money all the world over. It is doubtful the industry has yet broken even," said Peter Drucker in a recent interview . . . but is it true? Paul Gompers

"You will never catch up with the new technology."

of the Harvard Business School and Alon Brav of the University of Chicago . . . looked at companies that went public from 1975 to 1992, most of which were high-tech firms, and found their rate of return to be about average [i.e., zero economic profit], once they adjusted for risk and company size.[5]

REDUCING RISK BY SHARING TECHNOLOGY

Low average profits from innovation arise largely from the inherent riskiness of the activity—the high likelihood that investments in apparently promising innovations will go down the drain. Recent marketing literature suggests that only about 6 to 7 percent of new products ever make it all the way to the marketing stage. We would expect firms to try to minimize their risks, and they do. For example, management may not fund research in their laboratories on inventions that they judge to be impractical. However, managers have also proven amazingly shortsighted in some cases, as when the Western Union Telegraph Company turned down the newly invented telephone.

Firms also try to protect themselves by joining together to share risks. After all, each partner in a five-firm partnership has to supply only one-fifth of the funds needed to bring an innovation to completion. Such partnerships are called "research joint ventures," and there are many of them (see the accompanying box, "Collaboration, Rather Than Competition, in Innovation," for an example).

A lesser-known phenomenon occurs when many firms try to reduce their risks by **trading technology.** It may seem to you that when a business firm succeeds in producing a promising new invention, it will do all it can to bar its competitors' access to the new technology in order to retain its competitive advantage over rivals. But this is often not true. Fearing that their own laboratories may conceivably fail in all R&D undertakings in a particular period, while competitors may possibly have better luck, firms often enter into agreements with their competitors to *share* all successful future innovations for a specified time period—say, the next five years. Such agreements reduce risk for *both* technology-sharing firms.

In photography, for example, one camera manufacturer may introduce an improved automatic focus device, another an automatic light adjustment, and a third may invent a way to make the camera more compact. Each of these three firms can keep its invention to itself. But if two of them get together and agree to produce cameras combining both their new features, then they will be able to market a product clearly superior to what either could have produced alone. They will also be in a far better position to meet competition from the third camera manufacturer.

Many firms and industries engage in this practice of **cross licensing.** For example, the Perkin-Elmer Corporation manufactures and sells scientific instruments (notably those using precision optics such as microscopes) throughout the world. Since World War II, Perkin-Elmer has entered into technology-transfer agreements with domestic and foreign firms. In 1960, for example, Perkin-Elmer agreed to share technology with the Hitachi Corporation, and a modified version of that agreement continued for decades. The contract required the two firms to supply *a full menu* of their technical developments periodically. Either firm was authorized to produce any product designed in this way, with full technical assistance from the other. Each firm agreed to pay a royalty rate of 6 to 7.5 percent for items invented by the other firm. The agreement required reciprocal technical training as well, although the company requesting such training paid its own employees' travel and living expenses.

In another example, IBM cross-licenses patents with *each* of its major competitors. Such a contract usually covers some well-defined field, such as semiconductors or input-output devices. In the negotiation of such a contract the firms compare what prospective technological changes each has to offer and agree to make up any difference in patent value via a monetary "balance payment," bargaining over the amount. Contracts normally run over several years and entitle

Technology trading is an arrangement in which a firm voluntarily makes its privately owned technology available to other firms either in exchange for access to the technology of the second company or for an agreed-upon fee.

Cross licensing of patents occurs when each of two firms agrees to let the other use some specified set of its patents, either at a price specified in their agreement or in return for access to the other firm's patents.

---

[5] "The Rewards of Investing in High Tech," *Federal Reserve Bank of Boston Regional Review* 6 (Fall 1996): p. 14.

● COLLABORATION, RATHER THAN COMPETITION, IN INNOVATION

Even some of the largest companies in the world find that collaboration, rather than competition, can sometimes give them an advantage in the global economy. Cargill and Monsanto, two firms that are active in the global market for agricultural products, recently announced a joint venture that will produce and market better animal feeds around the world.

Cargill is a producer and marketer of agricultural products, pharmaceuticals, and food ingredients with 79,000 employees in 72 countries. Monsanto is a global marketer of agricultural, food, and industrial products with 21,000 employees around the world. Even though both of these companies are large by any measure, they decided to pool their strengths: Monsanto has relatively greater expertise in genomics and biotechnology, and Cargill has a comprehensive distribution and marketing network. Together they plan to use the latest in biotechnology research to create and market better animal feeds around the world.

The Monsanto-Cargill joint venture will allow the two firms to develop new products and introduce them more rapidly to the market, perhaps reducing hunger around the world—and earning greater profits, too.

SOURCE: "Cargill and Monsanto Announce Global Feed and Processing Biotechnology Joint Venture," www.asgrow.com/corporate/cargill.html, accessed January 11, 1999.

each firm to use the other firm's current patents in a particular field, as well as any other patents obtained during the life of the contract.

One technology-exchange study looked at a sample of 11 American steel minimills of the 40 U.S. firms that are now world leaders in steel productivity. It found that *all but one* of the sample firms regularly and routinely exchanged information with the others: "sometimes, workers of competing firms were trained (at no charge), firm personnel were sent to competing facilities to help set up unfamiliar equipment, and so on."[6] The trade in know-how often included exchanges between direct rivals and, though engineers and technicians normally carried out the exchanges, upper management knew about and approved the technology transfers.[7]

Indeed, business firms provide their technology to others for a profit so commonly that MIT runs an annual seminar that teaches firms how they can earn more from their technology-rental business.

A KINKED REVENUE CURVE MODEL OF SPENDING ON INNOVATION

Our discussion thus far leaves one basic question unanswered. If innovation takes so much effort and money, if it is so risky, and if the economic profits expected from innovation approach zero, why do firms do it? Why doesn't every firm refuse to participate in this unattractive game? The answer, at least in part, is that competitive markets leave them no choice. If firms do not keep up with competitors in terms of product attractiveness and improved process efficiency that lowers costs, they will

---

[6] Eric Von Hippel, *The Sources of Innovation* (New York: Oxford University Press, 1988), p. 79.

[7] In fields such as aircraft and semiconductor production, the U.S. Department of Defense has reportedly played an important role in encouraging automatic cross licensing. See Robert Merges and R. R. Nelson, "On Limiting or Encouraging Rivalry in Technical Progress: The Effect of 'Patent-Scope Decisions,'" in R. R. Nelson, *The Sources of Economic Growth* (Cambridge, Mass.: Harvard University Press, 1996), pp. 134–137.

● **BETTING ON INNOVATION**

In the world of business, the word "innovation" usually refers to a product that contains *new* capabilities and features. Apple Computer has turned this conventional wisdom on its head with the new iMac.

The iMac computer has received much attention for its appearance. With its smoothly rounded corners, translucent shell, and lollipop colors, the iMac appeals to anyone who is tired of the boxy beige machines that sit on everyone's desk. Certainly, the iMac's low price is important to most computer buyers. Beyond the price and outward appearances, though, one of the most significant differences between the iMac and virtually every other computer on the market is in the floppy disk drive: the iMac doesn't have one! Apple had good reasons for leaving out a floppy drive, but some industry analysts thought the company was taking a big risk.

The gamble seems to have paid off. Almost as soon as it hit the market, to almost universal praise, the iMac has sold like hotcakes.

SOURCES: Henry Bortman, "Does the Floppy Have a Future?" *Macworld Online*, September 1998, http://macworld.zdnet.com; Adam Engst, "With the iMac, Apple Shows It's Thinking Different," *MacWEEK*, June 1, 1998, http://www.zdnet.com; and Andrew Gore, "iMac: Groundbreaking Consumer Offering Lives Up to Its Hype," *Macworld Online*, November 1998, http://macworld.zdnet.com.

lose out to their rivals and end up losing money. Clearly, firms prefer zero economic profits—profits that yield normal competitive returns to investors—to negative profits and investor flight.

We can make the technological scenario more explicit with the help of a microeconomic model very similar to one we encountered in Chapter 13—the kinked demand curve model that we used to explain why prices tend to "stick" in oligopoly markets. We saw the underlying mechanism: an asymmetry in the firm's expectations about its competitors. The firm hesitates to lower its price for fear that its rivals will match the price cut, so that the firm will end up with a few new customers, but dramatically reduced revenues. On the other hand, it fears that if it increases its price, the others will *not* follow suit, so that it will be left all by itself with an overpriced product. Thus, such a firm normally will set its price at the industry level, no more and no less, and leave it there unless the competitive situation changes drastically.

The innovation story is similar. Think about an industry with, say, five firms of roughly equal size. Company X sees that each of the other firms spends about $20 million a year on R&D. Company X will not dare to spend much less than $20 million on its own R&D because if it does so its next product model may lack new features as attractive as those of rival products. On the other hand, Company X sees little point in raising the ante to, say, $30 million because it knows the others will simply follow suit.

The story is described graphically in Figure 15–2, which shows an MC curve and two MR curves. For simplicity, we have drawn the MC curve as a straight line. The MR curves, however, reflect two possible competitor responses. If each time Company X expands its spending, *its rivals do the same*, then any improvements in X's product is likely to face comparable competitive products. Thus, the MR resulting from X's enhanced R&D will be quite low (curve *mAr*), because Company X will fail to pull ahead of its rivals. On the other hand, if competitors let X increase its R&D spending *without increasing their own*, then X can expect its increased product quality to put it well ahead of the others, and so its MR from R&D spending will be relatively high (curve *MCR*).

A **ratchet** is an arrangement that permits some economic variable, such as investment or advertising, to increase, but prevents that variable from subsequently decreasing.

In Figure 15–2, Company X expects mixed reactions from its competitors. They will follow its lead in *increasing* R&D but will not follow any decreases. The result will be the Z-shaped red curve, *MCAr*, with a vertical break between points *A* and *C* at the current level of R&D investment ($20 million in the example). The explanation is simple. If each firm in the industry spends $20 million a year, and Company X were suddenly to decrease R&D spending—say, to $7 million per year—it has good reason to fear that competitors would *not* match that cut. With its product quality declining (because it is spending so much less on R&D) and no competitor's product doing so (because competitors are still spending $20 million), Company X can expect to lose a good deal of revenue. It will find itself moving backward along the "not matched" MR curve *MCR*, to point *S*. However, if Company X decides to increase its R&D spending above $20 million, it will not gain much revenue (it will move along the low "matched" MR curve *mAr*), because its rivals will feel threatened and will match the increase.

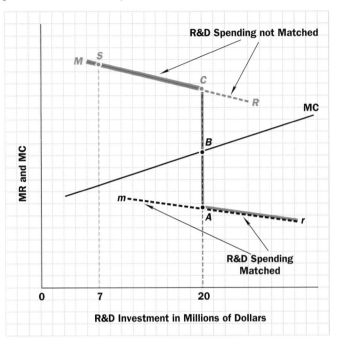

FIGURE 15-2

Competition and R&D Investment

But that's not the end of the story. All five firms in the industry will continue to invest the same amount until one of them enjoys a research breakthrough leading to a wonderful new product (as happens from time to time, particularly in high-tech industries). That fortunate firm will then expand its investment in the breakthrough product, because doing so will pay off even if the other firms in the industry match the increase. The MR curve for the breakthrough firm will rise, and its MC = MR point will move to the right, to an amount larger than $20 million. Now Company X's Z-shaped marginal revenue curve will have shifted to the right, from its original position, $M_1B_1R_1$, to $M_2B_2R_2$ in Figure 15–3. Other companies in the industry will follow to some degree. So now the industry norm will no longer be a $20 million investment per year but may instead be something like $25 million per firm. No firm will dare to drop back to the old level, fearing that no other company will follow such a retrenchment move. Again, the common story of armaments races among countries parallels the story of innovation battles among firms. The MR = MC equilibrium point will now be B_2, at $25 million of R&D spending.

FIGURE 15-3

Competition and R&D Investment after a Research Breakthrough by One Firm

The process we have just described assumes that competition forces firms in the industry to keep up with one another in their R&D investment. But once they have caught up, the investment level remains fairly level until one firm breaks ranks and increases its spending, and all other firms follow behind. Such an arrangement is described as a **ratchet,** in analogy to the mechanical device that prevents a wound-up spring from suddenly unwinding. This arrangement holds technological spending steady, permits it under certain circumstances to move forward, but generally does not allow it to retreat. Thus, we can expect R&D spending to expand from time to time, but once the new level is reached, the ratchet—enforced by the competitive market—prevents firms from retreating to the previous lower level.

Such ratcheting acts as a critical part of the mechanism that produces the extraordinary growth records of free enterprise economies and differentiates them from all other known economic systems. Competitive pressures force firms to run as fast as they can in the innovation race just to keep up with the others.

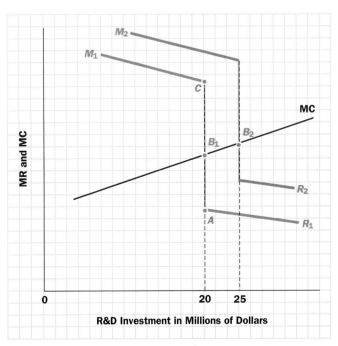

■ THREE GROWTH-CREATING PROPERTIES OF INNOVATION

Thus, we expect the market mechanism to force firms to devote at least a steady stream of resources to innovative activities. With luck, such level R&D efforts will yield a fairly constant flow of innovations within industries. But a steady flow of innovation does not mean that GDP remains constant. Rather, *an unchanging rate of innovation* can be expected to result in *steady growth of the economy's output*. Here we must take note of three critical features of innovation that can, so to speak, magnify the contribution that technical change makes to an economy's GDP:

- *Many innovations create cumulative changes.* Rather than merely replacing older technology, many innovations *add* to what was previously available. Thus, they increase an economy's store of technical knowledge, as when computers improve the precision of chemical processes, the new invention supplementing the old.

- *Innovation offers a public good.* An innovation, once created, usually does not contribute only to the output of the firm that discovered the breakthrough. At little or no additional cost, the new technology can also add to the outputs produced by other enterprises, often in other industries. This public-good property of technical knowledge enables those who adopt the innovation (with or without the inventor's permission) to adopt it more cheaply.

- *Innovations enjoy an accelerator feature.* A level stream of innovation usually means that output will not stay level but will grow. Like stepping on the accelerator of a car, a steady unchanging pressure makes an automobile move forward more rapidly.

Let's look at each of these growth-creating properties in turn.

CUMULATIVE INNOVATION

Some innovation merely replaces older technology, as the automobile replaced the horse and buggy. But probably more often innovation creates new features or applications for the previous technology. Computers' new features, which constantly appear on the market, do not merely replace previous technology; those features make computers faster, more reliable, and more versatile. CD-ROM drives supplement floppy disk drives and hard drives but do not make them obsolete. Automatic focus devices became part of an older camera design rather than replacing the entire device.

The economy's stock of technical knowledge keeps expanding as new information is added to old. A steady stream of innovations accumulates and builds the volume of technical knowledge, as society discovers new applications for the new developments. Both coal and technical knowledge contribute to output. But when a ton of coal is used to create a product, it cannot be used over again. A second ton of coal must be mined and used up to make more of the product. But once technical knowledge is created, it can be used over and over again without ever being depleted.

THE PUBLIC GOOD PROPERTY OF INNOVATION

In Chapter 14, we used the term "public good" to describe any good—that is, any input or output—that is not depleted when used once, but rather can be used over and over with little or no additional cost.[8] Such goods are available to the entire public, not just to a single individual. For instance, Thomas Edison and his colleagues worked for many months and used up much material before they finally found a way to create a viable light bulb. They did not have to repeat that outlay to produce a second light bulb. If Edison licensed the technology to another firm, that firm would not need to repeat the expensive research that yielded the first light bulb. R&D expenses need not be repeated when the firms use knowledge repeatedly to produce output. Innovation is like the oil lamp in the ancient Hanukkah

[8] For review of the concept of public goods, see Chapter 14, pages 274–275.

legend: a lamp that miraculously replenished its fuel and could provide light day after day without any additional oil.

THE ACCELERATOR PROPERTY OF INNOVATION

Each successful innovation adds to the nation's GDP, either by permitting firms to create more products with a given quantity of resources (a **process innovation**) or by making new and more valuable products available (a **product innovation**). Thus, an economy in which R&D produces a steady output of one innovation per month will obtain a GDP that is higher each month than it was in the previous month. The economy's ability to produce output will *grow constantly*, even though the innovation flow that fuels output growth remains *steady* at one invention per month.[9] This acceleration relationship applies to innovation generally, so that if the competitive market mechanism described in the previous figures leads firms to devote a constant *level* of resources to R&D, we would expect continued *growth* of GDP to result.

Of course, as noted, the ratchet principle encourages firms to *increase* expenditures on innovation, not just to leave them level. The acceleration principle tells us about the effects of this too. It says that if the level of R&D spending were to increase just once, for example, and then stay at that new higher level forever, the *growth rate* of GDP would also move upward. GDP would then grow at a faster rate forever. This process is illustrated in Figure 15–4, where we imagine that in the 21st century the level of R&D spending had been expected to be constant at the moderate level indicated by horizontal line, R_1. With this amount of R&D, GDP growth appears as the upward slope of the GDP line, Y_1. But if it turns out that R&D spending is at the higher level rate R_2 instead, then GDP will follow the path Y_2. The upward slope of Y_2 is greater than that of Y_1, meaning that with a higher *level* of expenditure on R&D we will get faster *growth* of GDP.

All of this reinforces the role of the competitive market mechanism and its stimulation of innovation as a contributor to the extraordinary growth that characterizes the world's free-enterprise economies.

A **process innovation** is an innovation that changes the way in which a commodity is produced.

A **product innovation** is the introduction of a good or service that is entirely new or involves major modifications of earlier products.

FIGURE 15–4

Higher R&D Spending Accelerates GDP Growth

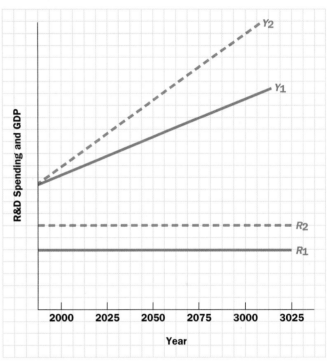

■ DO FREE MARKETS SPEND ENOUGH ON R&D ACTIVITIES?

Business firms, the U.S. government, universities, and others spend a good deal on research and innovation. In 1997 more than $200 billion (about 2.5 percent of total GDP) was spent on these activities, with business firms spending three-quarters of that amount (about $151 billion, or 2.2 percent of total business GDP). Is this too small or too large a share of GDP? That is, would the general public benefit or lose if more resources were devoted to innovation?

As usual, a trade-off arises. If we devote more resources to innovation this year, smaller amounts will be left over to produce cars, build dormitories, or expand movie theaters. With smaller supplies of these items, their prices will rise and they will cost us more. On the other hand, if we devote more resources to innovation, we will probably get better and cheaper products in the future. So, as with any investment,

---

[9] Note, however, that in the nearly 40-year period, 1950–1987, while the number of scientists and engineers engaged in R&D increased fivefold (from less than 200,000 to nearly 1 million), real GDP per capita only doubled. (See Charles Jones, "R&D-based models of Economic Growth," *Journal of Political Economy*, Vol. 103, No. 4, August 1995, pages 759–784.)

R&D investment entails a trade-off between the present and the future. More R&D spending means that consumers get less to consume this year, but they will get more and better products in the future. The question is, how much is enough?

It surely would be irrational to spend no resources on innovation. It would be even more irrational to devote all of GDP to this activity because that would leave nothing for consumption and everyone would starve. But these are silly extremes. What intermediate figure is best for the nation, and does the free market automatically approximate this level of expenditure?

INNOVATION AS A BENEFICIAL EXTERNALITY

Many economists believe private enterprise does *not* devote enough resources to innovation, because the acquisition of new technical knowledge generates large *externalities*. Recall that an externality is an effect of a business transaction that benefits or hurts persons other than those who directly take part in the transaction.[10] For example, if some manufacturer decides to buy a lot more electric power from the local public service utility, you may have to breathe dirtier air and spend more money on laundry. Here, the electric utility company and its customer firm are the participants in the transaction, and you are among the people who suffer from the damaging externality. A detrimental externality is part of the true social cost of producing a commodity—the electricity in this example. This means that the utility will not pay all the costs its electricity generation causes because, inadvertently or deliberately, it can shift part of the cost over to you—which you pay in the form of higher doctor or laundry bills. Because lower costs lead firms to produce higher outputs, the ability to escape part of the cost of its operation will lead the utility to overproduce electricity. The result is excessive electricity production and too much pollution in the air.

But sometimes externalities *benefit* innocent third parties, so that those who carry out the transaction do not reap all the benefits. For example, suppose your roommate, an advanced engineering student, comes up with a more efficient battery that turns out to benefit laptop computer manufacturers, the makers of electric cars, and many others. Your roommate may get a prize for her work, or may even receive a royalty payment from the companies that license her innovation. But she will not get all of the benefits. This is true of most innovations: They benefit the innovator to some degree, but large parts of the benefits also go to others. Such beneficial externalities mean that a firm that invests in R&D can expect less of the profits than it would if it could keep all of the benefits of the innovation.

Consequently, many economists believe that the free market does not induce private firms to invest the socially optimal amount in innovation. They believe that many innovations whose benefits would exceed their costs are never carried out because any firm that spent the money to produce the innovation would get only part of the benefit, and that part would be insufficient to cover its costs. Thus, governments finance a good deal of innovation and research activity, carried out by research institutions such as universities.

Basic research refers to research that seeks to provide scientific knowledge and general principles rather than coming up with any specific marketable inventions.

Applied research is research whose goal is to invent or improve particular products or processes, often for profit, though the military and health industries provide examples of not-for-profit applied research.

The externality problem is probably most severe for what is called **basic research**, that is, research that deals with science and general principles rather than with improvement of a specific product. (Research of the latter sort, which is directly related to commercial or other uses, is called **applied research**.) For example, research on the nature of electricity and magnetism may yield enormous economic benefits in the near or distant future, but for the moment it only satisfies physicists' curiosity. Few business firms will finance such research. But the economy would be much less productive in the long run if no one conducted such research. That is why the governments of the United States and a number of other industrial countries provide money to finance such basic research, and why economists generally favor such funding.

So what is the bottom line? Do externalities make spending on R&D in market economies lower than it should be to promote the public interest best? Economists are still debating this issue and no settled answer has appeared.

---

[10] For review, see Chapter 14, pages 271–273.

EFFECTS OF PROCESS RESEARCH ON AMOUNTS OF GOODS PRODUCED AND ON THEIR PRICES

As a last example of how microeconomic analysis can deal with innovation, let's consider the effects of innovation on outputs and prices. We will consider a single monopoly firm that makes decisions independently of other enterprises' activities and decisions.

Innovation, as we saw, is often divided into two types: product innovations, which consist of the introduction of a new item such as a photocopying machine or a video camera, and process innovations, which entail an improvement in the way in which commodities are produced, making them cheaper to buy. Here we will discuss only process innovations because, it turns out, they are easier to analyze.

A successful *process* innovation can be expected to expand the output of the product that uses the process, and to reduce the price of that product, for a very simple reason: A process innovation can be expected to lead to a downward shift in the firm's marginal and average cost curves. But because it involves no change in the product, it will not cause any change in the demand curve.

A standard graph familiar from earlier chapters can demonstrate these results. Figure 15–5 shows MR and DD (demand), the firm's marginal revenue and demand (average revenue) curves for the production of widgets. The graph also shows MC_1, the marginal cost curve of widgets *before* the process innovation, and MC_2, the new marginal cost curve *after* the innovation is adopted. MC_2 is naturally lower than MC_1 because the innovation has reduced the cost of making widgets. We see that before the innovation the quantity produced by our profit-maximizing firm is Q_1, the quantity at which MR = MC_1 (at point E_1). Price at this output is P_1, the point on the DD curve (the demand curve) above quantity Q_1. After the process innovation, the marginal cost curve shifts downward to MC_2. That new marginal cost curve meets the downward-sloping MR curve at point E_2, which lies to the right of E_1. This means that the profit-maximizing output quantity must increase from Q_1 to Q_2, and therefore, because of the downward slope of the demand curve, price must fall from P_1 to P_2. Thus, we have shown, as suggested earlier, that:

FIGURE 15-5

Effect of Process Innovations on Prices and Outputs

> A cost-cutting process innovation increases the output and decreases the price of the product a profit-making firm supplies with the help of the innovation.

The Puzzle Revisited: Extraordinary Growth in Free-Market Economies

In this chapter we have seen that innovation is a large part of the reason for the extraordinary productivity and growth of free-market economies. We have traced the economy's stream of innovation to the tough competition among business firms, in which those firms use new products and new processes as their most powerful weapons in their battle to win customers. Certainly, this stream of innovations sheds light on what is probably the most spectacular feature of free-enterprise economies—their unparalleled growth and the unprecedented standards of living they provide. And, as one of our *Ideas for Beyond the Final Exam* notes, that explosive growth of productivity is (almost) all that counts in the long run.

SUMMARY

1. The growth records and per-capita incomes achieved by market economies far exceed those attained by any other form of economic organization. Innovation is one of the main sources of that economic growth.

2. *Innovation* in free-market economies is stimulated by competition among business firms, which try to outdo one another in the attractiveness of their new and improved products and in the efficiency of their productive processes. Firms pursue these goals through investment in *research and development (R&D)*.

3. As in any other decision, a profit-maximizing firm will invest in R&D up to the point at which the expected MR equals the MC of that expenditure.

4. Competition can force firms to set their R&D spending at levels corresponding to those of their rivals.

5. The typical level of R&D spending in an industry will sometimes increase, but it will rarely decline because no firm dares to be the firm to cut back on such spending.

6. Firms often seek to reduce the risks of their R&D activities by making agreements with other firms to share one another's technology. They also often sell their technology to others.

7. If new inventions appear at a constant, steady rate we can expect steady growth of the economy's productive capacity.

8. Many economists believe that private investment in innovation will be below the socially optimal level, because the externalities from innovation mean inventors do not obtain all the benefits of their innovations. However, some economists believe that these externalities, which are largely made up of improvements in the living standards of society's noninventors, are a good thing. This may mean that private investment in innovation is, in fact, not far from the socially optimal level.

9. Process innovations can be shown by MR = MC analysis to increase outputs and decrease prices, even in monopoly firms.

KEY TERMS

Labor productivity   292

Innovation   292

Capitalism   293

Industrial Revolution   293

Research and development (R&D)   295

Technology trading   298

Cross licensing   298

Ratchet   301

Process innovation   303

Product innovation   303

Basic research   304

Applied research   304

QUESTIONS FOR REVIEW

1. To understand how much the free-enterprise economy has increased living standards, try to envision the daily life style of a middle-class family in a major American city just after the Civil War, when the average purchasing power is estimated to have been less than one-ninth of today's. What do you think they ate? How much clothing did they own? What were their living quarters like? What share of their budgets was available for vacations and entertainment?

2. Name five common products introduced since you were born.

3. Name some companies that advertise that their products are "new" or "improved."

4. Explain why firms in an industry that spends a large amount of money on advertising may feel locked into their current advertising budgets, with no one firm daring to cut its expenditure. Describe the analogy with competition in innovation.

5. Alexander Graham Bell beat Elisha Grey to the patent office by several hours, so that Bell obtained the patent on the telephone. Imagine how much that patent turned out to be worth. How much do you think Grey got for his effort and expenditure on development of the invention? How does that help explain the possibility that *average* economic profits from innovation are close to zero?

6. If average economic profits from investment in innovation are close to zero, why would many people be anxious to invest in innovation?

7. Explain how firms that share their technology with competitors benefit by improving their ability to compete against new entrants.

8. What are the possible advantages to the general welfare when firms make their technology automatically available to others (while, of course, charging a price for use of the technology)?

9. Why may it be unprofitable for a firm to spend much more on R&D than its competitors do?

10. Define the following terms:

    a. externality

    b. public good

    c. ratchet

    Explain the applicability of these concepts to innovation.

11. From the point of view of the general welfare, do you think spending on R&D in the United States is too low? Too high? Just about right? Why?

The action of the stock market must necessarily be puzzling at times since otherwise everyone who studies it only a little bit would be able to make money in it.

B. Graham, D. L. Dodd, and S. Cottle, authors of the classic textbook on securities analysis

REAL FIRMS AND THEIR FINANCING: STOCKS AND BONDS

A firm does more than select inputs, outputs, and prices, the topics of previous chapters. In this chapter we discuss how real firms finance their activities—notably with stocks and bonds—from the viewpoint of both firms and investors. The latter may be of special interest to you, because a very large proportion of the nation's college graduates invest money in the stock and bond markets, and you may well do so too.

But before describing these markets, we will offer our usual opening puzzle and a broad picture of the different types of firms that make up U.S. business, focusing on individually owned enterprises, partnerships, and corporations.

Puzzle: The Stock Market's Unpredictability

The stock market is something of an enigma. No other economic activity is reported in such detail in so many newspapers and followed with such concern by so many people. Yet few activities have so successfully eluded prediction of their future. There is no shortage of well-paid "experts" prepared to forecast the future of the market or a particular stock. But there are real questions about what these experts deliver.

For example, a famous study of leading analysts' predictions of company earnings (on which they based their stock-price forecasts) reports:

> [W]e wrote to 19 major Wall Street firms . . . among the most respected names in the investment business.
>
> We requested—and received—past earnings predictions on how these firms felt earnings for specific companies would behave over both a one-year and a five-year period. These estimates . . . were . . . compared with actual results to see how well the analysts forecast short-run and long-run earnings changes. . . .
>
> Bluntly stated, the careful estimates of security analysts (based on industry studies, plant visits, etc.) do very little better than those that would be obtained by simple extrapolation of past trends. . . .
>
> For example . . . the analysts' estimates were compared [with] the assumption that every company in the economy would enjoy a growth in earnings approximating the long-run rate of growth of the national income. It often turned out that . . . this naïve forecasting model . . . would make smaller errors in forecasting long-run earnings growth than . . . [did] the professional forecasts of the analysts. . . .
>
> When confronted with the poor record of their five-year growth estimates, the security analysts honestly, if sheepishly, admitted that five years ahead is really too far in advance to make reliable projections. They protested that, although long-term projections are admittedly important, they really ought to be judged on their ability to project earnings changes one year ahead.
>
> Believe it or not, it turned out that their one-year forecasts were even worse than their five-year projections.[1]

It has been said that an investor may as well pick stocks by throwing darts at the stock market page—it is far cheaper to buy a set of darts than to obtain the apparently useless advice of a professional analyst. Indeed, there have been at least two experiments, one by a U.S. senator and one by *Forbes* magazine, in which stocks picked by dart-throwing actually outperformed the mutual funds, the stocks of which are selected by experts.

Later in this chapter we will suggest an explanation for this poor performance.

■ FIRMS IN THE UNITED STATES

Firms are typically divided into three groups: *individual proprietorships* (businesses with one owner), *partnerships*, and *corporations*. Corporations play a crucial role in the U.S. economy. Revenues of the top 500 corporations totaled more than $6 trillion in 1999, two-thirds of the country's gross domestic product (GDP). Almost all large American firms are corporations. General Motors alone raised $189 billion in revenues in 1999, and Wal-Mart and Exxon Mobil took in $167 billion and $164 billion, respectively. The combined revenues of just these three firms amount to considerably more than the GDPs of Australia, Austria, Belgium, the Netherlands,

---

[1] Burton G. Malkiel, *A Random Walk Down Wall Street* (New York: W. W. Norton, 1990), pp. 140–141.

Sweden, Switzerland, and many, many other countries. With some exceptions, these giant firms are primarily found in industries that are *oligopolies*, a market form we analyzed in Chapter 13.

But although a huge chunk of America's output comes from corporations, only 20 percent of American firms are incorporated, because most firms are small. Even corporations are often quite small—almost 40 percent have business receipts of less than $100,000. But by far the greatest number of firms (counting all firms large and small, and including the corner grocery store and shoe repair shop) are individual or family proprietorships. Of the 23 million business firms in the United States, about 17 million are proprietorships, 4.6 million are corporations, and 1.6 million are partnerships.[2]

The nation's small business firms have a disproportionately small share of U.S. GDP. The earnings of these small firms are also very risky. The average new firm is reported to last less than seven years. When making economic decisions, the buyer is not the only one who must beware!

Let's take a closer look at the three forms of business organization and what leads those who organize a firm to choose one form rather than another.

PROPRIETORSHIPS

Most small retail firms, farms, and many small factories are **proprietorships.** A proprietorship involves fewer legal complications than any other form of business organization. To start a proprietorship, an individual simply decides to go into business and opens a new firm or takes over an existing one. This is a major advantage of the proprietorship form of organization.

But the main attraction of the proprietorship is probably the owner's ability to be his or her own boss and the firm's sole decision maker. The owner does not have to consult any partners or stockholders when he or she wants to expand or change the company's product line or modify its advertising policy. A proprietorship also has tax advantages, particularly compared with a corporation. A proprietor's income is taxed only once. If the same firm were to incorporate, its income would be taxed twice—once as the firm's income (the corporate income tax) and again as the owner's income. (We'll discuss corporate taxation in detail later in this chapter).

On the other hand, a major disadvantage makes it almost impossible to organize large-scale enterprises as proprietorships: The owner of a proprietorship has **unlimited liability** for the debts of the firm. If the company goes out of business, leaving unpaid bills, the former owner can be forced to pay them out of personal savings. The owner may have to sell the family home, private collections of stamps or paintings, or any other personal assets (even those unrelated to the business) so that the proceeds can be used to pay off the company's debts.

SUMMARY   There are three main advantages of the individual proprietorship:

- Full control remains in the hands of the owner.
- The proprietorship is subject to few legal complications.
- Owners generally pay fewer taxes.

Its two main disadvantages are that:

- The owner has unlimited liability for the debts of the company.
- Raising substantial funds for the firm can be difficult.

PARTNERSHIPS

In terms of amount of capital, **partnerships** tend to be larger than proprietorships but smaller than corporations. However, the largest partnerships greatly exceed the smallest corporations in financing and influence. For example, some of the most prestigious law firms and investment banks are partnerships.

> A **proprietorship** is a business firm owned by a single person.

> **Unlimited liability** is a legal obligation of a firm's owner(s) to pay back company debts with whatever resources he or she owns.

> A **partnership** is a firm whose ownership is shared by a fixed number of proprietors.

---

[2] U.S. Bureau of the Census, *Statistical Abstract of the United States: 1999*, 119th ed. (Washington, D.C.: U.S. Government Printing Office, 1999).

The partnership's advantage over a proprietorship is that it combines a number of people's funds and expertise to form a company larger than any single owner could have financed or managed alone. A partnership may also bring together a variety of specialists, as often happens in a medical practice. In addition, partnership, like proprietorship, offers freedom from double taxation.

But the partnership has disadvantages, too—some of them substantial. Decision making in a partnership may be harder than in any other type of firm. The sole proprietor need consult no one before acting; the corporation appoints officers who are authorized to make decisions for the company. But in a partnership, it may be necessary for *every* partner to agree before any steps are taken, and that is the primary difficulty of this form of enterprise. A partnership has been compared to two people in a horse costume, each supplying two of the legs, each prepared to go in a different direction, and each unable to move without the other.

Furthermore, partners, like sole proprietors, have unlimited liability. They can lose personal possessions to pay off company debts. Finally, the partnership suffers from unique legal complications. A partnership agreement is like a marriage contract entered into exclusively for the financial advantage of the participants, so considerable haggling about the terms can take place. Also, under the law, if a partner dies or decides to leave the firm, the partnership may have to be dissolved and haggling about the contract may begin anew.

SUMMARY   The benefits of the partnership to the owners of the firm are that:

- They gain access to larger quantities of capital.
- They enjoy protection from double taxation.

Its disadvantages are that:

- Many if not all partners must agree to major decisions.
- Partners share unlimited liability for the company's obligations.
- Legal complications, including automatic dissolution of the partnership, arise when *any* change in ownership occurs.

CORPORATIONS

A **corporation** is a firm that has the legal status of a fictional individual. This fictional individual is owned by a number of persons, called its *stockholders,* and is run by a set of elected officers and a board of directors, whose chairman is often also in a powerful position.

Limited liability is a legal obligation of a firm's owners to pay back company debts only with the money they have already invested in the firm.

Most big firms are **corporations,** a form of business organization whose legal status differs significantly from that of a proprietorship or a partnership. Though it seems strange, a corporation is an *individual* in the eyes of the law. Therefore, its earnings, like those of other individuals, are taxed. This leads to double taxation of the stockholders. That is, corporate earnings are taxed twice, once when they are earned by the company and a second time when they go to investors in the form of dividends (and are subject to personal income tax).

But this disadvantage is counterbalanced by an important advantage: any corporate debt is regarded as that fictitious individual's obligation, not any one stockholder's liability. So stockholders benefit from the protection of **limited liability**—they can lose no more money than they have invested in the firm.

Limited liability is the main secret of the success of the corporate organizational form. Thanks to that provision, individuals throughout the world are willing to invest money in firms whose operations they do not understand and whose management personnel they do not know. Each shareholder receives in return a claim on the firm's profits, and, at least in principle, a portion of the company's ownership.

Corporations are directed by hired managers: a chairman of the board of directors, a president, various vice presidents, and so on. These executives are, legally, employees of the firm's owners—the people who, as we will see, hold stock in the corporation. This arrangement has a great advantage: It prevents the quarrels and indecision that are often problems for partnerships. On the other hand, because the managers are hired personnel, they cannot always be trusted to do what is best for the owners. Managers are often accused of looking after their own interests even if that means sacrificing those of the stockholders (the owners). This problem has recently received much attention in discussions of *takeovers*—that is, purchase of control of a corporation by outsiders—a subject we will examine later in this chapter.

Corporations escape one other problem that troubles partnerships. As we saw, if one partner wants to leave a firm, the remaining owners may have to reorganize the entire enterprise. But in a corporation, any owner who wants to quit just sells her stock, and the corporation goes on exactly as before. In this way, at least in theory, a corporation can continue forever.

SUMMARY   Benefits of the corporate form to the owners are that:

- They benefit from limited liability.

- They gain access to large quantities of capital.

- They enjoy ease of operation with the help of hired management.

- Permanence: The firm is not dissolved or reorganized each time an owner leaves.

Its disadvantages are that:

- Double taxation: The owners' income is taxed twice.

- Hired managers may act in their own interests rather than the owners'.

THE EFFECT OF DOUBLE TAXATION ON CORPORATE EARNINGS

Does a person end up earning less by investing in a corporation than in a company that is equally risky but not subject to double taxation? Paradoxically, the answer is that investors, on average, will *not* lose anything by choosing the corporation. The tax will not and cannot put one type of investment at a disadvantage in comparison with any other.

How is this possible? How does the effect of the additional tax on a corporate stock disappear before it reaches the stockholder? Two processes achieve this act of magic.

First, corporations must avoid some investment opportunities that partnerships and proprietorships can afford to take on. For example, suppose that the market rate of interest to firms is 9 percent, and a new product is expected to bring a 12 percent return to a manufacturer. An individual proprietor can afford to produce the new item—borrowing the necessary funds at 9 percent and keeping the 3 percent additional return on the new item for himself. But a large corporation *cannot* afford to produce the new item. To compete for funds with the proprietorship, it must also pay investors 9 percent, which means that it will have to choose investments that promise to earn at least 14 percent—because about 35 percent of the 14 percent return will be siphoned off in corporate taxes.

Thus, double taxation keeps corporate business out of economic activities that offer real, but limited, earnings. This may cause economic inefficiency, because many firms will avoid activities that can benefit society. For instance, corporations may find it too costly to open retail outlets in slum areas or to run trains to isolated rural areas—activities that may be profitable in the absence of the tax.

A second fail-safe mechanism protects investors in corporate stocks from earning lower returns than they would on other equally risky *securities*.[3] Suppose that two otherwise identical securities, A and B, each offer a return of $60 per year, but A is subject to a 50 percent tax whereas B is not. *Question:* If the market price of Security B is $1,000, what will the market price of A be? *Answer:* The price of A will be only $500, exactly half the price of Security B. Why? Because it brings in only $30 per year after taxes, exactly half of what Security B returns, investors will pay only half as much for A as they will for the untaxed security. But at $500 and $1,000 respectively, investors in either security will earn the same rate of return after taxes. That is, $30 is 6 percent of $500 and $60 is 6 percent of $1,000 so either firm provides the same 6 percent return on investment.

---

[3] Stocks and bonds are also called securities.

Double taxation of corporate earnings tends to restrict corporations' activities, keeping them out of relatively low-profit operations. However, double taxation does not mean that the individual investor earns less by putting money into a corporation than by putting it into other businesses.

■ FINANCING CORPORATE ACTIVITY

When a corporation needs money to add to its plant or equipment, or to finance other types of real investment, it may reinvest its own earnings (rather than paying them out as dividends to stockholders), print and sell new stock certificates or new bonds, or take out a loan. We will consider each of these three options in detail (in reverse order of their actual use by corporations).

LOANS

A company can obtain money by borrowing it from banks, insurance companies, or other private firms. It may also sometimes obtain assistance from a U.S. government agency, which will either lend funds directly to the corporation or serve as guarantor, promising to make sure a loan is repaid. For example, loans may be arranged with the help of the national defense agencies if they want a private firm to undertake the design and production of an expensive new weapons system. Small business firms, too, are eligible for various forms of assistance in borrowing.

STOCKS AND BONDS

Stocks and bonds are a subject of interest to millions of Americans. How can a firm obtain money in exchange for such printed paper? Doesn't the process seem a bit like counterfeiting? If done improperly, there are grounds for the suspicion. But, carried out appropriately, it is a perfectly reasonable economic process. First, let's define our terms.

A **common stock** of a corporation is a piece of paper that gives the holder of the stock a share of the ownership of the company.

Common stock represents partial ownership of a corporation. For example, if a company issues 100,000 shares, then a person who owns 1,000 shares owns 1 percent of the company and is entitled to 1 percent of the company's *dividends*, the corporation's annual payments to stockholders. This shareholder's vote counts for 1 percent of the total votes in an election of corporate officers or in a referendum on corporate policy.

A **bond** is simply an IOU by a corporation that promises to pay the holder of the bond a fixed sum of money at the specified *maturity* date and some other fixed amount of money (the *coupon* or the *interest payment*) every year up to the date of maturity.

Bonds differ from stocks in several ways. First, the purchaser of a corporation's stock *buys* a share of its ownership and some control over its affairs, whereas a bond purchaser simply *lends* money to the firm and obtains no part of its ownership. Second, whereas stockholders have no idea how much they will receive when they sell their stocks, or how much they will receive in dividends each year, bondholders know with a high degree of certainty how much money they will be paid if they hold their bonds to maturity (the date the firm has promised to repay the loan). For instance, a bond with a face value of $1,000 and an $80 *coupon* (the firm's annual interest payment to the bondholder) that matures in 2007 will provide $80 per year every year until 2007, and the firm will repay the bondholder's $1,000 in 2007. Unless the company goes bankrupt, this repayment schedule is guaranteed. Third, bondholders legally have a *prior claim* on company earnings, which means the stockholders receive no money until the firm has paid its bondholders. For all these reasons, bonds are considered less risky investments than stocks.

An important exception are so-called junk bonds—very risky bonds that became popular in the 1980s. They were used heavily by people trying to purchase enough of a corporation's stock to acquire control of that firm. We will say more later about such "takeover" activities and the use of junk bonds to finance them.

To return to our question at the beginning of this section, a new issue of stocks and bonds is generally not like counterfeiting. As long as the funds obtained from the sale of the new securities are used effectively to increase a firm's profit-earning capacity, these funds will automatically yield any required repayment and appropriate interest and dividends to purchasers. But occasionally this does not happen. One of the favorite practices of the more notorious 19th-century market manipulators was "watering" company stocks—issuing stocks with little or nothing to back them up. The term is originally derived from the practice of some cattle dealers who would force their animals to drink large quantities of water just before bringing them to be weighed for sale.

SIMILARITIES BETWEEN STOCKS AND BONDS   In reality, the differences between stocks and bonds are not as clear-cut as just described. Two relevant misconceptions are worth noting. First, the ownership represented by a few shares of a company's stock may be more symbolic than real. A person who holds 0.002 percent of AT&T stock—which, by the way, is a *very large* investment—exercises no real control over AT&T's operations.

In fact, many economists believe that the ownership of large corporations is so diffuse that stockholders or stockholder groups rarely have *any* effective control over management. In this view, a corporation's management is a largely independent decision-making body; as long as it keeps enough cash flowing to stockholders to prevent discontent and *organized* rebellion, management can do anything it wants within the law. Looked at in this way, stockholders, like bondholders, merely provide loans to the company. The only real difference between the two groups, according to this interpretation, is that stockholders' loans are riskier and therefore entitled to higher payments.

Second, contrary to appearance, bonds actually *can* be a very risky investment. Persons who try to sell their bonds before maturity may find that the market price happens to be low; so if they need to raise cash in a hurry, they may incur substantial losses. Also, bondholders may be exposed to losses from inflation. Whether the $1,000 promised to the bondholder at the 2007 maturity date represents substantial (or very little) purchasing power depends on what happens to the general price level in the meantime (i.e., how much price inflation occurs). No one can predict the price level this far in advance with any accuracy. Finally, a firm can issue bonds with little backing; that is, the firm may own little valuable property that it can use as a guarantee of repayment to the lender—the bondholder. This was often true of the junk bonds of the 1980s, and it helps to explain their high risk.

BOND PRICES AND INTEREST RATES   What makes bond prices go up and down? A straightforward relationship exists between bond prices and *interest rates:* whenever one goes up, the other *must* go down.

For example, suppose that Sears Roebuck issued some 15-year bonds when interest rates were comparatively low, so the company had to pay only 6 percent to sell the bonds. People who invested $1,000 in those Sears bonds received a contract that promised them $60 per year for 15 years plus the return of their $1,000 at the end of that period. Suppose, however, that interest rates *rise*, so new 15-year bonds of similar companies now pay 12 percent. An investor with $1,000 can now buy a bond that offers $120 per year. Obviously, no one will now pay $1,000 for a bond that promises only $60 per year. Consequently, the market price of the old Sears bonds must fall.

This example is not entirely hypothetical. Until a few years ago, bonds issued much earlier—at interest rates of 6 percent or lower—were still in circulation. In the 1980s' markets, when interest rates were well *above* 6 percent, such bonds sold for prices far below their original values.

> When interest rates *rise,* the prices of previously issued bonds with lower interest earnings must fall. For the same reason, when interest rates *fall,* the prices of previously issued bonds must rise.

It follows that as interest rates change because of changes in monetary policy or other reasons, bond prices fluctuate. That is one reason why bonds can be a risky investment.

CORPORATE CHOICE BETWEEN STOCKS AND BONDS   If a corporation chooses to finance the construction of new factories and equipment through the issue of new stocks or bonds, how does it determine whether bonds or stocks suit its purposes?

Two considerations are of prime importance. Although issuing bonds generally exposes a firm to more risk than issuing stocks, the corporation usually expects to pay more money to stockholders over the long run. In other words, to the firm that issues them, bonds are cheaper but riskier. The decision about which is better for the firm therefore involves a trade-off between the two considerations of expense and risk.

Why are bonds risky to a corporation? When it issues $20 million in new bonds at 10 percent, a company commits itself to pay out $2 million every year of the bond's life, whether business is booming or the firm is losing money. If the firm is unable to meet its obligation to bondholders in some year, bankruptcy may result.

Stocks do not burden the company with any such risk, because the firm does not promise to pay stockholders *any* fixed amount. Stockholders simply receive whatever is left of the company's net earnings after payments to bondholders. If nothing is left to pay the new stockholders in some years, legally speaking, that is just their bad luck. The higher risk faced by stockholders is the reason they normally obtain higher average payments than bondholders.

> To the firm that issues them, bonds are riskier than stocks because they commit the firm to make a fixed annual payment, even in years when it is losing money. For the same reason, stocks are riskier than bonds to the buyers of securities. Therefore, stockholders expect to be paid more money than bondholders.

PLOWBACK, OR RETAINED EARNINGS

Plowback (or **retained earnings**) is the portion of a corporation's profits that management decides to keep and invest back into the firm's operations rather than paying dividends to stockholders. Corporations may also buy back shares from stockholders.

The final major source of funds for corporations, in addition to loans and the issue of stocks and bonds, is **plowback** or **retained earnings.** For example, if a company earns $30 million after taxes and decides to pay only $10 million in dividends and reinvest the remaining $20 million in the firm, that $20 million is called "plowback."

When business is profitable, corporate managers will often prefer plowback to other sources of funding. For one thing, plowback usually involves lower risk. Also, plowback, unlike other sources of funding, does not come under the scrutiny of the Securities and Exchange Commission (SEC), the government agency that regulates stocks.[4] And, of course, plowback does not depend on the availability of eager customers for new company stocks and bonds. An issue of new securities can be a disappointment if there is little public demand when they are offered. But plowback runs no such risk.

Above all, a plowback decision generally does not call attention to the degree of success of management's operations, as a new stock issue does. When stock is issued, the SEC, potential buyers, and their professional advisers may all scrutinize the company carefully. No management has a perfect record, and the process may reveal things management would prefer to be overlooked.

Another reason for plowback's attractiveness is that issuing new stocks and bonds is usually an expensive and lengthy process. The SEC requires companies to gather masses of data in a *prospectus*—a document that describes a company's financial condition—before any new issue is approved.

Figure 16–1 shows the relative importance of each of the different funding sources to U.S. corporations. It indicates that plowback is by far the most important source of corporate financing, constituting about 64 percent of total corporate financing in 1999. New bond issues and other forms of borrowing supplied about 31 percent of the total, and stock sales actually contributed a *negative* amount of funding (−24.7 percent), because corporations reduced the number of their stocks in the public's hands by buying some back.

FIGURE 16-1

Sources of New Funds, U.S. Corporations, 1999

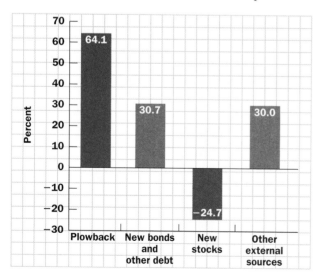

SOURCE: U.S. Bureau of the Census, *Statistical Abstract of the United States 1999*, 119th ed. (Washington, D.C.: U.S. Government Printing Office, October 1999).

[4] The Securities and Exchange Commission, established in 1934, protects the interests of people who buy securities. It requires firms that issue stock and other securities to provide information about their financial condition, and it regulates the issue and trading of securities.

FROM THE INVESTOR'S VIEWPOINT: BUYING STOCKS AND BONDS

Although investors can purchase stocks and bonds through any brokerage firm, not all brokers charge the same fees. Bargain brokerage houses advertise in the newspapers' financial pages, offering investors very little service—no advice, no research, no other frills—other than merely buying or selling what the customer wants them to, at lower fees than those charged by higher-service brokerage firms.

Many investors are not aware of the various ways in which they can purchase (or sell) stocks. Two noteworthy arrangements are (a) a *market order* purchase, which simply tells the broker to buy a specified quantity of stock at the best price the market currently offers, and (b) a *limit order*, which is an agreement to buy a given amount of stock when its price falls to a specified level. If the investor offers to buy at $18, then the broker will purchase shares if and when the market price falls to $18 per share or less.

The most recent shareowners survey by the *New York Stock Exchange* (NYSE) estimated that in 1995 there were 69.3 million individual stockholders in the United States (about one out of every four Americans). Of these 69.3 million, just under 40 percent (27.4 million) held stock directly. The rest had a more indirect stake in the market, with their money invested through various *institutional investors*, such as mutual funds, pension plans, and employer-based savings accounts.[5]

SELECTING A PORTFOLIO: DIVERSIFICATION

A person or organization's holdings of securities from several different corporations is called a *portfolio* of investments. A portfolio tends to be far less risky than any of the individual securities it contains. The secret is **portfolio diversification:** not putting all of your eggs in one basket.

If, for example, Alex divides his holdings among Companies A, B, and C, then his portfolio may perform satisfactorily even if Company A goes broke. Moreover, suppose that Company A specializes in producing luxury items, which do well in prosperous periods but very badly during recessions, whereas Company B sells cheap clothing, whose cyclical demand pattern differs greatly from that of Company A. If Alex holds stock in both companies, his overall risk is less than if he owned stock in only one. All other things being equal, a portfolio containing many different types of securities tends to be less risky than a portfolio with fewer types of securities.

Increasingly, institutional investors, such as **mutual funds,** have adopted portfolios composed of broad ranges of stocks typifying those offered by the entire stock

Portfolio diversification means including a number and variety of stocks, bonds, and other such items in an individual's portfolio. If the individual owns airline stocks, for example, diversification requires the purchase of a stock or bond in a very different industry, such as a breakfast cereal producer.

A **mutual fund,** in which individual investors can buy shares, is a private investment firm that holds a portfolio of securities. Investors can choose among a large variety of different mutual funds, such as stock funds, bond funds, and so forth.

"To hell with a balanced portfolio. I want to sell my Fenwick Chemical and sell it _now._"

---

[5] New York Stock Exchange, *Shareownership 1998*, www.nyse.com, accessed March 1999.

An **index fund** is a mutual fund that chooses a particular stock price index and then buys the stocks (or most of the stocks) that are included in the index. The value of an investment in an index fund depends on what happens to the prices of all the stocks in that index.

A **stock price index,** such as the S&P 500, is an average of the prices of a large set of stocks. These stocks are selected to represent the price movements of the entire stock market, or some specified segment of the market, and the chosen set is rarely changed.

market. Mutual funds now are among the largest U.S. investors of securities. They offer portfolios of various groups of domestic stocks, foreign stocks, and bonds. Small investors can easily put their money into these funds, thereby reducing the risks of owning individual stocks and ensuring that the overall market does not significantly outperform their portfolios. Mutual fund transactions can be carried out by telephone or over the Internet, and investors can also easily check on the past performance of the different funds and obtain other pertinent information.

One kind of mutual fund, called an **index fund,** buys the securities used in one of the standard **stock price indexes** (such as Standard & Poor's 500 or the broader Wilshire 5000 Index). A stock price index is an average of the prices of a group of stocks—weighted by the size of each company—that are believed to be representative of the overall stock market. When you invest in an index fund, the return on your money will therefore reflect the performance of the whole market, rather than any one or a few securities that you or your broker might have selected instead.

Institutional money managers increasingly use computers to decide on their portfolios and to buy or sell huge portfolios of stocks simultaneously and rapidly. Since 1982, some traders have also allowed their computers to decide when to jump in and make massive sales or purchases. This is called *program trading.* In 1998 program trading accounted for about 16 percent of total NYSE volume and a considerable amount elsewhere. Program trading is controversial, and some observers have argued that it has aggravated price fluctuations, especially during the stock market crash of October 1987.

FIGURE 16-2

Excerpt from a Stock-Price Table

52 Weeks Hi	52 Weeks Lo	Stock	Sym	Div	Yld %	PE	Vol 100s	Hi	Lo	Close	Net Chg

-G-G-G-

40⅞	28⅜	GATX	GMT	1.20	3.4	12	1100	36⅛	35⅛	35⅝	− ³⁄₁₆
12⅜	7⅞	G&L Rlty				dd	7	7⅞	7⅞	7⅞	...
19¹¹⁄₁₆	14⅞	G&L Rlty pfA		2.56	16.5	...	3	15½	15½	15½	...
19¼	14	G&L Rlty pfB		2.45	16.6	...	2	14¾	14¾	14¾	...
37	23	GC Cos	GCX		...	dd	65	27⅛	26½	26¾	− ½
12½	3⅞	GP Strategs	GPX		...	341	5⅛	5⅜	5⅜	5⅞	+ ¹⁄₁₆
44⅞	23⁷⁄₁₆	GPU Inc	GPU	2.18f	7.6	9	2330	29⅜	28⅛	28⁹⁄₁₆	− ¾
78½	55¹³⁄₁₆	GTE	GTE	1.88	2.7	17	17270	69⅜	67¹⁄₁₆	68¾	+ 2
25⅜	14¾	Gabelli A	GBL		...	186	25¼	24¹¹⁄₁₆	25¼	+ ⅛
11⅞	8¹⁵⁄₁₆	GabelliConv	GCV	.80a	8.3	...	10	9¹⅛	9⅜	9¹¹⁄₁₆	− ¹⁄₁₆
26	23¾	GabelliConv pf		2.00	8.4	...	6	23⅞	23⅞	23⅞	...
12⅜	10³⁄₁₆	GabelliTr	GAB	1.08	9.1	...	854	11¹⁵⁄₁₆	11¾	11⅞	+ ⅛
25⁹⁄₁₆	20½	GabelliTr pf		1.81	8.2	...	38	22	21¾	22	+ ⅛
19¾	13¼	GabelliMlti	GGT	e	...	390	15½	15⅜	15¼	...
25⅜	22	GabelliMlti pf		1.98	8.5	...	5	23½	23¼	23¼	− ¼
⅞	⁹⁄₁₆	GabelliMlti rt wi			...	20	⅝	⅝	⅝	+ ¹⁄₁₆
10⅜	7¾	GabelliUt	GUT	.60	7.4	...	118	8⅛	7¹⁵⁄₁₆	8¹⁄₁₆	+ ¹⁄₁₆
25¾	20¼	GblsRsdntl	GBP	2.12	8.3	15	2863	25⅞	25¼	25½	− ⅝
24½	16¾	GblsRsdntl pfA		2.08	10.9	...	34	19¼	19%	19%	...
6¹⅛	4	▲ Gainsco	GNA	.07	1.4	...	201	4¹⁵⁄₁₆	4¹³⁄₁₆	4⅞	+ ¹⁄₁₆
5½	1¼	▲ GaleyLord	GNL		...	dd	218	2⅜	2¼	2⅜	+ ⅛
58¹¹⁄₁₆	16½	▲ GalileoInt	GLC	.36	1.4	13	5858	26⁹⁄₁₆	25½	26¹⁄₁₆	− ⅛
39¾	23¾	Gallagr	AJG	.92	2.4	22	959	39¹³⁄₁₆	38¼	38¾	+ ¾
29¼	16⅜	GallaherGp	GLH	1.57e	7.6	...	404	21	20⅝	20⅝	...
83⅝	58⁹⁄₁₆	▲ Gannett	GCI	.84	1.3	10	6477	63¹⁵⁄₁₆	61¹¹⁄₁₆	62¹¹⁄₁₆	+ ¼
53¾	30¹³⁄₁₆	Gap Inc	GPS	.09	.3	25	52503	32¹³⁄₁₆	31¹⁄₁₆	32⅜	+ 1

SOURCE: *Wall Street Journal,* June 15, 2000, p. C5.

FOLLOWING A PORTFOLIO'S PERFORMANCE

Newspapers carry daily information on stock and bond prices. Figure 16–2 is an excerpt from the stock market page of the *Wall Street Journal.* We have highlighted the stock listing for the clothing retailer, Gap Inc. In the first two columns, before the company name, the report gives the stock's highest and lowest price in the last year. Gap Inc. stock is reported to have ranged between $30\frac{13}{16}$ and $53\frac{3}{4}$. After the stock's name and symbol (GPS), the annual dividend per share ($.09) appears. Following that is the yield, or the dividend as a percentage of the closing price (.3 percent).

The next column reports the *price earnings* (P/E) ratio (25 for Gap Inc.). This figure is the price per share divided by the company's net earnings per share in the previous year, and it is often taken as a basic measure indicating whether the stock's current price overvalues or undervalues the company. However, no simple rule enables us to interpret the P/E figures—for example, a very risky firm or a slowly growing firm with a low P/E may be considered overvalued, although a safe, rapidly growing firm with a high P/E may still be a bargain.

The next column indicates the number of shares traded on the previous day (5,250,300), an indication of whether that stock is actively traded. Finally, the last four figures indicate yesterday's highest price ($32\frac{13}{16}$), lowest price ($31\frac{1}{16}$), the price of the last transaction of the day ($32\frac{3}{8}$), and the change in that price from the previous day (+1).

Figure 16–3, this time from the *New York Times,* gives similar information about bonds. Notice that a given company may have several different bonds differing in maturity date and coupon (annual interest payment). For example, AT&T offers five different bonds. The highlighted one is labeled ATT $7\frac{1}{2}$ 06, meaning that these bonds pay an annual interest rate of 7.5 percent (the coupon) on their face value and that their maturity (redemption) date is 2006. Next, the current yield is reported as 7.4 percent. This is simply the coupon divided by the price. Because that yield, 7.4 percent, is slightly lower than the coupon, 7.5 percent, the bond must be selling at a price a little above its face value, so the return per dollar is correspondingly lower. The remaining information in the table, as in the previous figure, tells us the trading volume for the bond, the previous day's closing price, and the change in price from the day before.

STOCK EXCHANGES AND THEIR FUNCTIONS

The New York Stock Exchange—"The Big Board"—is perhaps the world's most prestigious stock market. Located on Wall Street in New York City, it is "*the* establishment" of the securities industry. The NYSE deals with only the best-known and most heavily traded securities—more than 3,000 companies in all. Approximately 1,300 of the leading brokerage firms hold "seats" on the stock exchange, which enable them to trade directly on the exchange floor. (In the NYSE's early years, members sat in assigned seats during roll call; the term lost its literal meaning with the advent of continuous trading in 1871.) Seats are traded on the open market; in February of 1999, for example, a seat on the exchange went for $2 million.

Someone who wants to buy a stock on the New York Stock Exchange must use a broker, who will in turn deal with a firm that has a seat on the exchange. Suppose that you live in Florida and want to buy 200 shares of General Motors stock. The broker you approach may be employed by a firm that holds a seat on the exchange, or he may work through another firm that holds one. The exchange broker who is to fill your order then contacts a third person called a *specialist*, who also works on the exchange floor and handles GM stock.

The specialist usually owns some GM stock of her own which she will offer to sell if no other sellers are available at the moment. In addition, the specialist usually receives a number of *limit orders* from investors offering to sell specified quantities of GM stock at specified prices. There may, for example, be one offer to sell 5,000 shares at any price above $75 and another offer to sell 1,200 shares at any price above $90. Similarly, the specialist is likely to have several limit orders to buy at various specified prices.

The floor broker brings your order to the specialist, who determines a price that she believes more or less balances supply and demand as indicated by her recent sales and purchases and her limit orders. At this price, the specialist will fill your order from one of the limit orders to sell (she must do so whenever possible) or from her personal inventory of General Motors stock. The price determination process we have just described is sometimes called the *auction market* process. The New York Stock Exchange expedites this "auction" by using an elaborate electronic system to link member firms directly to the appropriate specialists or floor brokers.

The New York Stock Exchange handles a little over half of all stock market transactions in the United States (measured in *dollar* volume). A number of *regional* exchanges—such as the Chicago, Pacific, Philadelphia, Boston, and Cincinnati Stock Exchanges—deal in many of the stocks handled on the NYSE but mainly serve large institutional customers such as banks, insurance companies, and mutual funds. These regional exchanges together handle about 9 percent of the total stock traded. The *American Stock Exchange*, another traditional stock market exchange located a few blocks away from the NYSE, carries out about 1 percent of total stock market transactions.

The remainder (about 42 percent) of all stock transactions are carried out "over the counter" via the institution called *NASDAQ* (the automated quotation system of the National Association of Securities Dealers). NASDAQ, which has become a major force in the industry since its inception in 1971, deals with stocks that are not listed on the traditional exchanges; it has no physical trading floor and all transactions are carried out on a computer network. NASDAQ handles the stocks of nearly 5,400 companies, including such giants as Intel and Microsoft.[6]

NASDAQ is a "dealer market" in which a number of securities dealers compete with one another in stock sales and purchases. More than 500 such dealer firms are active "market makers" on NASDAQ, buying and selling for their own accounts. The dealers charge no commissions and post (electronically) the prices at which they are willing to buy and sell a given stock. The market makers earn the excess of the

---

FIGURE 16-3

Excerpt from a Bond-Price Table

Company	Cur. Yld	Vol	Price	Chg
AES Cp 8s8	8.8	15	905/8	− 3/8
ATT 51/s01	5.2	10	981/4	+ 15/32
ATT 71/s02	7.1	35	100	+ 1/8
ATT 61/202	6.6	10	981/4	− 5/8
ATT 63/404	6.9	4	981/8	+ 1
ATT 55/s04	6.0	163	941/2	− 1/2
ATT 71/206	7.4	49	101	+ 5/8
ATT 81/s22	8.1	228	100	+ 1/2
ATT 81/s24	8.2	108	993/8	+ 1
ATT 8.35s25	8.3	5	1011/8	− 11/2
ATT 61/229	7.6	45	851/2	+ 3/8
ATT 85/s31	8.6	251	1001/8	− 1/8
ARetire 53/402	cv	10	66	...
Amresco 10s03	18.9	30	53	+ 1/4
ARch 91/s11	8.4	1	1083/8	− 3/4

SOURCE: *The New York Times*, June 20, 2000, p. C21.

---

[6] *Wall Street Journal Almanac 1999* (New York: Ballantine Books, 1998), p. 288; and NASDAQ, www.nasdaq.com, accessed March 1999.

● **YOU ARE THERE** | **AN EVENT ON THE TRADING FLOOR OF THE NEW YORK STOCK EXCHANGE**

You are standing on the trading floor of the New York Stock Exchange, a crowded and noisy set of rooms cluttered with people, hundreds of computer monitors, and other paraphernalia. It is a high-tech space in a 93-year-old architectural relic of bygone days. Around the floor are 17 stations, or "trading posts," presided over by *specialists*, each assigned responsibility for trading a particular set of stocks.

Suddenly the floor's frenetic activity focuses on one specialist's post. News has just come in that one of the companies whose stock she handles has earned more in the previous quarter than was expected. Brokers crowd around her, calling out orders to buy and sell the company's stock, as its price rises rapidly in the wake of the good news. Deals are completed verbally, as clerks record the trades and enter them into the computerized tape, making the information instantly available all over the globe.

SOURCE: Murray Teitelbaum, Communications Division, New York Stock Exchange.

selling price over the buying price, called *the spread*. They also may profit from changes in the prices of the securities they hold.

In the last few years, the established stock markets have faced competition from another source. With the rapid growth of the Internet, people are beginning to buy and sell stocks directly through their home computers. Some observers predict that such trading, though currently very limited in volume, will grow by leaps and bounds.

REGULATION OF THE STOCK MARKET

Both the government and the industry itself regulate the U.S. securities markets. At the base of the regulatory pyramid, stock brokerage firms maintain compliance departments to oversee their own operations. At the next level, the New York Stock Exchange, the American Stock Exchange, NASDAQ, and the regional exchanges are responsible for monitoring their member firms' business practices, funding adequacy, compliance, and integrity. They also use sophisticated computer surveillance systems to scrutinize trading activity. The *Securities and Exchange Commission* (SEC) is the federal government agency that oversees the market's self-regulation.

One example of these self-imposed rules is the steps markets adopted after the October 1987 stock market crash to cushion future price falls. In 1988 the NYSE and other stock markets adopted a series of rules called *circuit breakers*, which halted all equities trading for one hour if the Dow Jones Industrial Average fell 250 points from the previous day's level and an additional two hours if the Dow Jones fell another 150 points on the same day. These levels were later increased and the duration of the trading halts shortened to half an hour for a 350-point drop and one hour for a 550-point drop on the same day. Circuit breakers were designed to head off a panic among market participants and forestall a crash like the one in 1987, but when they were finally tested during the October 1997 stock market plunge, they were criticized as out of date and more disruptive than helpful. A new series of circuit breakers, inaugurated in April 1998, are based on *percentage* drops in the Dow Jones, rather than point drops. Under the new rules, much steeper drops are required to activate the circuit breakers.

STOCK EXCHANGES AND CORPORATE CAPITAL NEEDS

Although corporations often raise needed funds by selling stock, they do not normally do so through the stock exchanges. New stock issues usually are handled by a special type of bank called an *investment bank*. In contrast, the stock markets trade almost exclusively in "secondhand securities"—stocks in the hands of individuals and others who bought them earlier and now wish to sell them.

Thus, the stock market does not provide funds to corporations needing financing to expand their productive activities. The markets provide money only to persons who already hold previously issued stocks.

Yet stock exchanges have two critically important functions for corporate financing. First, by providing a secondhand market for stocks, they make individual investment in a company much less risky. Investors know that if they need the money, they can always sell their stocks to other investors or to the specialist at the current market price. This reduction in risk makes it far easier for corporations to issue new stocks.

Second, the stock market determines the current price of the company's stocks. That, in turn, determines whether it will be hard or easy for a corporation to raise money by selling new stocks.

Some people believe that a company's stock price is closely tied to its operational efficiency, its effectiveness in meeting consumer demands, and its diligence in going after profitable innovation. In this view, firms that use funds effectively will usually have comparatively high stock prices. In this way the stock market tends to channel the economy's funds to the firms that can make best use of the money. In sum:

If a firm has a promising future, its stock will tend to command a high price on the stock exchanges. Its high stock price will increase the firm's ability to raise capital by permitting it to amass a large amount of money through the sale of a comparatively small number of new stock shares. Thus, *the stock market helps to allocate the economy's resources to firms that can best use those resources.*

However, other people are skeptical about the claim that the price of a company's stock is closely tied to efficiency. These observers believe that the demand for stock is disproportionately influenced by short-term developments in a company's profitability and that the market pays little attention to management decisions affecting the company's long-term earnings growth. These critics sometimes suggest that the stock market is similar to a gambling casino in which hunch, rumor, and superstition have a critical influence on prices. (We will see more about this later in the chapter.)

Whether or not stock prices are an accurate measure of a company's efficiency, if a company's stock price is very low in comparison with the value of its plant, equipment, and other assets, or when a company's earnings seem low compared to their potential level, that company becomes a tempting target for a **takeover** attempt. This may be because the firm's current management is believed not to be very competent or perhaps because the demand for a company's stocks is inordinately influenced by short-term developments, such as temporarily low profits.

A *takeover* occurs when a group of outside financiers buys a sufficient amount of company stock to gain control of the firm. Often, the new controlling group will simply fire the current management and substitute a new chairman, president, and other top officers (see the accompanying box, "The Surge in Takeovers").

A **takeover** is the acquisition by an outside group (the raiders) of a controlling proportion of a company's stock. When the old management opposes the takeover attempt, it is called a *hostile takeover attempt.*

■ SPECULATION

Securities dealings are sometimes viewed with suspicion because they are thought to be an instrument of **speculation.** When something goes wrong in the stock market—when, say, prices suddenly fall—observers often blame speculators. Editorial writers, for example, often use the word *speculators* as a term of strong disapproval, implying that those who engage in the activity are parasites who produce no benefits for society and often cause considerable harm. (See the accompanying box, "How

Individuals who engage in **speculation** deliberately invest in risky assets, hoping to obtain profits from future changes in the prices of these assets.

● THE SURGE IN TAKEOVERS

Small groups of individuals or enterprises sometimes buy enough stock to gain control or take over a company. When the purchaser is another firm, this process is called a "merger" or "acquisition." Periodically, bursts of takeover activity have resulted in a very large rise in the number of mergers and acquisitions (there have been five such merger "waves" in the 20th century). For example, corporate "raiders" shook up the stock market and the managements of a number of corporations in the 1980s by trying to take over firms. This boom in takeovers slackened during the recession of the early 1990s, but has since surged again. In 1998 a record $1.6 trillion in mergers took place, with such headline-making deals as the $73.7 billion takeover of Mobil Oil by Exxon, a deal that created one of the largest corporations in the world (and put back together two of the biggest pieces from the 1911 breakup of John D. Rockefeller's Standard Oil). As this book was being written, takeover activity was still on a hot streak.*

An attempt to acquire a company by a group of "raiders" that is unfriendly to current management is called a *hostile takeover*. Naturally, the officers of that corporation will try to fight the takeover, because they do not want to lose their high-paying jobs. They can fight back in many ways, for example, by trying to arrange for a "friendly takeover" by a group of investors they like better. They may also deliberately sabotage the company—often by selling some of its most valuable parts in order to make what is left of the firm less attractive to the takeover group. Management may seek to bribe the takeover group to go away by offering a very high price for the already-acquired stock. Indeed, groups often attempt takeovers in the hope that management will be forced to offer them such a bribe (called *greenmail*).

In the 1980s, when a large number of takeover battles broke out, the issue received a good deal of publicity and set off a heated debate over the pros and cons of legal restrictions on such activity. People who argue against strong legal restrictions point out that takeover is the most effective means to rid companies of incompetent managements, thus keeping the economy at peak efficiency. They also argue that this activity helps "create stockholder value," or drive the price of an undervalued company's stock up to its true economic value.

But advocates of stricter regulations or restrictions upon takeovers argue that the process can hurt bystander stockholders, as when management pays a large bribe to the takeover group or sells off a valuable part of the company. Moreover, those seeking to buy a large percentage of the company's shares will try to do so as secretly as possible, hoping to obtain the stock cheaply. Critics claim that in the process, the raiders, in effect, cheat those who sell them stock.

Opponents of takeovers also point out that the time bright, talented people take in planning and carrying out the strategies and counterstrategies uses up a valuable resource that could be better used elsewhere. In this view, takeover activity absorbs some of the nation's most capable individuals in financial manipulation rather than productive and innovative activity. These critics are wrong, however, when they argue that the billions of dollars changing hands in a takeover battle tie up the nation's capital wastefully or "use up" the economy's credit supply. A takeover process in fact ties up little or no capital (machinery, factories, and the like). The money and credit used are simply transferred from one group of persons to another.

Sometimes, takeovers are financed by "junk bonds," that is, the raiders issue bonds to raise the money they need to acquire control of the target corporation. These bonds are frequently backed only by the profits that the raiders *expect* to grow out of their acquisition. Such profits may arise from more efficient management. The new owners may also sell off valuable portions of the corporation's activities (one of its successful products, for example) which they purchased cheaply because the corporation's stock price was low before the takeover.

Junk bonds backed only by such earnings prospects after the takeover are risky because those promised profits may never materialize. A takeover financed in this way is called a "leveraged buyout" because the raider risks little of his or her own money in the process. Instead, the raider's limited resources are levered upward with other people's money, supplied by junk bond purchasers. Critics of leveraged buyouts note that they may leave firms saddled with burdensome financial obligations to these junk bond purchasers.

Most of the very recent mergers have not been hostile contests that resulted in heavy debt. Corporate mergers in the mid to late 1990s seem more often to have had the goal of creating bigger companies that were believed to be better able to face increasing global competition. Recent deals have been financed to a greater extent with corporate stock of the acquiring company, rather than borrowed money.

Economic Report of the President, 1999 (Washington, D.C.: U.S. Government Printing Office, February 1999).

to Lose Billions: Betting on Derivatives" for a description of a particularly risky speculative instrument, the *derivative*.)

Economists disagree vehemently with this judgment. They argue that speculators perform two vital economic functions:

■ Speculators sell *protection from risk* to other people, much as a fire insurance policy offers protection from risk to a homeowner.

■ Speculators help to smooth out price fluctuations by purchasing items when they are abundant (and cheap) and holding them and reselling them when they are scarce (and expensive). In that way, speculators play a vital economic role in helping to alleviate and even prevent shortages.

Some examples from outside the securities markets will help clarify the role of speculators. Say a Broadway ticket broker attends a preview of a new musical comedy and suspects it will be a hit. He decides to speculate by buying a large block of tickets for future performances. In that way, he takes over part of the producer's risk, while the comedy's producer reduces her inventory of risky tickets and receives some hard cash. If the show opens and is a flop, the broker will be stuck with the tickets. If the show is a hit, he can sell them at a premium, if the law allows (and be denounced as a speculator or a "scalper").

Similarly, speculators enable farmers (or producers of metals and other commodities whose future price is uncertain) to decrease their risk. Let's say Jasmine and Jim have planted a large crop of wheat but fear its price may fall before harvest time. They can protect themselves by signing a contract with a speculator for future delivery of the crop at an agreed-upon price. If the price then happens to fall, the speculator, not Jasmine and Jim, will suffer the loss. Of course, if the price rises, the speculator will reap the gain—but that is the nature of risk bearing. The speculator who has agreed to buy the crop at a preset price, regardless of market conditions at the time of the sale, has, in effect, sold an insurance policy to Jasmine and Jim. Surely this is a useful function.

THE WALL STREET JOURNAL

"Don't laugh—she's called the last five Dow Jones turnarounds right on the nose."

● HOW TO LOSE BILLIONS: BETTING ON DERIVATIVES

erivatives, one of the fastest growing areas of finance, are complex financial instruments so named because they "derive" their value from the price movements of an underlying investment, such as a group of stocks, bonds, or commodities. Businesses buy these very risky contracts in an effort to hedge or ensure against sudden changes in interest rates or currency values. They also can be used to speculate in the markets.

A number of recent spectacular financial failures have been closely tied to the use of derivatives. First was the nearly $2 billion loss and resulting bankruptcy of Orange County, California. Then came the collapse of a 233-year-old British investment bank, Barings PLC, after one of its employees (a 28-year-old "rogue" futures trader named Nicholas Leeson) "bet the ranch" on the movement of the Japanese stock market (and lost $1.46 billion). The latest astounding near-meltdown involved a private investment fund called Long-Term Capital Management, the management of which

happens to include two Nobel Prize–winning economists. The firm is a so-called hedge fund that uses derivatives to place (or hedge) million- and billion-dollar bets on movements in such financial instruments as Russian treasury bonds and Danish mortgages. In the fall of 1998 the firm was reported to have lost upwards of $4 billion (and had to be bailed out by its bankers) when its statistical models failed to predict the movement of global markets.

SOURCE: "Wall Street Struggles to Save Big Fund," *Washington Post*, September 24, 1998.

The speculators' second role is perhaps even more important. In effect, they accumulate and store goods in periods of abundance and make goods available in periods of scarcity. Suppose that a speculator has reason to suspect that next year's crop of a storable commodity will not be nearly as abundant as this year's. She will buy some now, when it is cheap, for resale when it becomes scarce and expensive. In the process, she will smooth out the swing in prices by adding her purchases to the total market demand in the low-price period (which tends to bring the price up), and bringing in her supplies during the high-price period (which tends to push the price down).[7]

Thus, the successful speculator will help to relieve matters during periods of extreme shortage. Speculators have sometimes even helped to relieve famine by releasing supplies they had deliberately hoarded for such an occasion. Of course, speculators are cursed for their high prices on such occasions. But those who curse them do not understand that prices would have been even higher if the speculators' foresight and avid pursuit of profit had not provided for the emergency. On the securities market, famine and severe shortages are not an issue, but the fact remains that successful speculators tend to reduce price fluctuations by increasing demand for stocks when prices are low and contributing to supply when prices are high.

Far from aggravating instability and fluctuations, to earn a profit speculators *iron out* fluctuations by buying when prices are low and selling when prices are high.

Puzzle Resolved: Unpredictable Stock Prices as "Random Walks"

The beginning of this chapter cited evidence that the best professional securities analysts have a forecasting record so miserable that investors may do as well predicting earnings by hunch, superstition, or any purely random process as they would by following professional advice. (See the accompanying box, "Football and Financial Forecasting" to learn about one crazy way of predicting the stock market's performance: the outcome of the Super Bowl.)

---

[7] For a diagrammatic analysis of this role of speculation, see Review Question 7 at the end of the chapter.

● FOOTBALL AND FINANCIAL FORECASTING

The following excerpt from Floyd Norris' column in the business section of *The New York Times* suggests some of the gimmicks that stock market analysts turn to in a desperate effort to predict stock prices.

In years gone by, when people thought that stocks went both up and down and that market timing was therefore important, market seers searched for indicators that would point the way to determining whether a certain time was a good one to be in the market.

There were indicators based on dividends and on profits, on Federal Reserve actions and on bond yields. Even skirt lengths were tried. (In very speculative markets, hem lines rise along with share prices.) But the indicator that seemed to work the best was one that was so clearly irrelevant that no one could take it seriously: the Super Bowl indicator.

Now, investors are far less interested in market timing than they were 20 years ago—a time when stock prices were below where they had been more than a decade earlier and when few thought that stocks were sure to rise over long periods of time. Now, after the best 20 years in stock market history, the general belief is that one need not pay attention to much of anything regarding value. If you buy and hold for a long period, you will do well. As a result, indicators receive far less attention.

But the Super Bowl indicator has continued to perform, albeit with less publicity. It holds—in its current version, for like many indicators it has been tweaked along the way—that if a team from the old National Football League wins the Super Bowl, stocks will rise over the next year. But if a team from the old American Football League prevails, the stock market is in trouble.

In 1998, the Super Bowl indicator got it wrong: The Denver Broncos (from the old AFL) beat the Green Bay Packers (an original NFL team), but the stock market went ahead and had a fantastic year anyway. The following year, the Broncos did it again—beating the Atlanta Falcons, 34–19, but Wall Street had another spectacular year. Is the Super Bowl indicator dead?

SOURCE: Floyd Norris, "Market Place," *The New York Times,* January 22, 1998.

Does this mean that analysts are incompetent people who do not know what they are doing? Not at all. Rather, there is fairly strong evidence that they have undertaken a task that is basically impossible.

How can this be so? The answer is that to make a good forecast of *any* variable—be it GDP, population, fuel usage, or stock market prices—there must be something in the past whose behavior is closely related to the future behavior of the variable whose path we wish to predict. If a 10 percent rise in this year's consumption always produces a 5 percent rise in next year's GDP, this fact can help us predict future GDP on the basis of current observations. But if we want to forecast the future of a variable whose behavior is completely unrelated to the behavior of *any* current or past variable, there is no objective evidence that can help us make that forecast. Throwing darts or gazing into a crystal ball are no less effective than analysts' calculations.

There is a mass of statistical evidence that the behavior of stock prices is largely unpredictable. In other words, the behavior of stock prices is essentially *random;* the paths they follow are what statisticians call **random walks.** A random walk is like the path followed by a sleepwalker. All we know about his position after his next step is that it will be given by his current position plus whatever random direction his next haphazard step will carry him. The relevant feature of randomness, for our purposes, is that it is by nature *unpredictable,* which is just what the word *random* means.

The time path of a variable such as the price of a stock is said to constitute a **random walk** if its magnitude in one period (say, May 2, 2000) is equal to its value in the preceding period (May 1, 2000) plus a completely random number. That is: Price on May 2, 2000 = Price on May 1, 2000 + Random number, where the random number (positive or negative) can be obtained by a roll of dice or some such procedure.

If the evidence that stock prices approximate a random walk stands up to research in the future as it has so far, it is easy enough to understand why stock market predictions are as poor as they are. Analysts are trying to forecast behavior that is basically random; in effect, they are trying to predict the unpredictable.

Two questions remain. First, does the evidence that stock prices follow a random walk mean that investment in stocks is a pure gamble and never worthwhile? Second, how does one explain the random behavior of stock prices?

To answer the first question, it is false to conclude that investment in stocks is generally not worthwhile. The statistical evidence is that, over the long run, stock prices *as a whole* have had a fairly marked upward trend, perhaps reflecting the long-term growth of the economy. Thus, the random walk does not proceed in just any direction—rather, it represents a set of erratic movements *around a basic upward trend in stock prices.*

Moreover, it is not in the *overall* level of stock prices that the most pertinent random walk occurs, but in the performance of one company's stock compared with another's. For this reason, professional advice may be able to predict that investment in the stock market is likely to be a good thing over the long haul. But, if the random walk evidence is valid, there is no way professionals can tell us *which* of the available stocks is most likely to go up—that is, which combination of stocks is best for the investor to buy.

The only appropriate answer to the second question is that no one is sure of the explanation. There are two widely offered hypotheses—each virtually the opposite of the other. The first asserts that stock prices are random because clever professional speculators are able to foresee almost perfectly every influence that is *not* random. For example, suppose that a change occurs that makes the probable earnings of some company higher than had previously been expected. Then, according to this view, the professionals will instantly become aware of this change and immediately buy enough to raise the price of the stock accordingly. Then the only thing for that stock price to do between this year and next is wander randomly, because the professionals cannot predict random movements, and hence they cannot force current stock prices to anticipate them. The other explanation of random behavior of stock prices is at the opposite pole from the view that all nonrandom movements are wiped out by supersmart professionals. This view is that people who buy and sell stocks have learned that they cannot predict future stock prices. As a result, they react to *any* signal, however irrational and irrelevant it appears. If the president catches cold, stock prices fall. If an astronaut's venture is successful, prices go up. According to this view, investors are, in the last analysis, trying to predict not the prospects of the economy or of the company whose shares they buy, but the supply and demand behavior of other investors, which will ultimately determine the course of stock prices. Because all investors are equally in the dark, their groping can only result in the randomness that we observe.

Just a normal day at the nation's most important financial institution...

The classic statement of this view of stock market behavior was provided in 1936 by English economist John Maynard Keynes, a successful professional speculator himself:

> Professional investment may be likened to those newspaper competitions in which the competitors have to pick out the six prettiest faces from a hundred photographs, the prize being awarded to the competitor whose choice most nearly corresponds to the average preferences of the competitors as a whole; so that each competitor has to pick not those faces which he himself finds prettiest, but those which he thinks likeliest to catch the fancy of the other competitors, all of whom are looking at the problem from the same point of view. It is not a case of choosing those which, to the best of one's judgment, are really the prettiest, nor even those which average opinion genuinely thinks the prettiest. We have reached the third degree where we devote our intelligences to anticipating what average opinion expects the average opinion to be. And there are some, I believe, who practice the fourth, fifth and higher degrees.[8]

This may help to explain the impressive rise of the stock market from a Dow Jones index of 800 in 1982 to 2,700 in 1987, a 700-point fall in two consecutive trading days in October 1987, then several sharp fluctuations followed by a remarkably sustained upward trend since then.

SUMMARY

1. The three basic types of firms are *corporations, partnerships,* and individual *proprietorships.* Most U.S. firms are individual proprietorships, but most U.S. manufactured goods are produced by corporations.

2. Individual proprietorships and partnerships have tax advantages over corporations. But corporate investors have greater risk protection because they have *limited liability—* they cannot be asked to pay more of the company's debts than they have invested in the firm.

3. Higher taxation of corporate earnings tends to limit the things in which corporations can invest and may lead to inefficiency in resource allocation.

4. A *common stock* is a share in a company's ownership. A *bond* is an IOU for money lent to a company by the bondholder. Many observers argue that a stock purchase also really amounts to a loan to the company—a loan that is riskier than a bond purchase.

5. If interest rates rise, bond prices will fall. In other words, if some bond amounts to a contract to pay 8 percent and the market interest rate goes up to 10 percent, people will no longer be willing to pay the old price for that bond.

6. Corporations finance their activities mostly by *plowback* (that is, by retaining part of their earnings and putting it back into the company). They also obtain funds by sales of stocks and bonds and through more traditional loans.

7. If stock prices correctly reflect the future prospects of different companies, it is easier for promising firms to raise money because they are able to sell each stock they issue at favorable prices.

8. Bonds are relatively risky for the firms that issue them, but they are fairly safe for their buyers, because they are a commitment by those firms to pay fixed annual amounts to the bondholders whether or not the companies make money that year. But stocks, which do not promise any fixed payment, are relatively safe for the companies and risky for their owners.

9. A portfolio is a collection of stocks, bonds, and other assets of a single owner. The greater the number and variety of securities and other assets a portfolio contains, the less risky it is.

10. A corporation is said to be taken over when an outside group buys enough stock to get control of the firm's decisions. *Takeovers* are a useful way to get rid of incompetent management or to force management to be efficient. However, the process is costly and leads to wasteful defensive and offensive activities.

11. *Speculation* affects stock market prices, but (contrary to widespread belief) speculation actually tends to *reduce* the frequency and size of price fluctuations. Speculators are also useful to the economy because they undertake risks that others wish to avoid, thereby, in effect, providing others with insurance against risk.

12. Statistical evidence indicates that individual stock prices behave randomly (in other words, unpredictably).

---

[8] John Maynard Keynes, *The General Theory of Employment, Interest, and Money* (New York: Harcourt Brace, 1936), p. 156.

```
           Q U E S T I O N S   F O R   R E V I E W
```

1. Why would it be difficult to run General Motors as a partnership or an individual proprietorship?

2. Do you think it is fair to tax a corporation more than a partnership doing the same amount of business? Why or why not?

3. If you hold shares in a corporation and management decides to plow back the company's earnings some year instead of paying dividends, what are the advantages and disadvantages to you?

4. Suppose that interest rates are 6 percent in the economy and a safe bond promises to pay $3 a year in interest forever. What do you think the price of the bond will be? Why?

5. Suppose in the economy in the previous example, interest rates suddenly fall to 3 percent. What will happen to the price of the bond that pays $3 per year?

6. If you want to buy a stock, when might it pay you to use a market order? When will it pay to use a limit order?

7. Show in diagrams that if a speculator were to buy when price is high and sell when price is low, he would increase price fluctuations. Why would it be in his best interest *not* to do so? (*Hint:* Draw two supply-demand diagrams, one for the high-price period and one for the low-price period. How would the speculator's activities affect these diagrams?)

8. If stock prices really are a random walk, can you nevertheless think of good reasons for getting professional advice before investing?

9. Hostile takeovers often end up in court when managements attempt to block them and raiders accuse the managements of selfishly sacrificing the stockholders' interests. The courts often look askance at "coercive" offers by raiders—an offer to buy, say, 20 percent of the company's stock by a certain date from the first stockholders who offer to sell. By contrast, they take a more favorable attitude toward "noncoercive" offers to buy any and all stock supplied at announced prices. Do you think the courts are right to reject "coercive offers" but prevent management from blocking "noncoercive" offers? Why?

10. In "program trading," computers decide when to buy or sell stocks on behalf of large, institutional investors. The computers then carry out those transactions with electronic speed. Critics claim that this is a major reason why stock prices rose and fell sharply in the 1980s. Is this plausible? Why or why not?

IV

THE DISTRIBUTION OF INCOME

In Part IV we examine how a market economy distributes its income. As we will see, the market works through the price mechanism, with the prices of the inputs of the production process—the land, the labor, the capital—determined by supply and demand. We will see that the market also assigns a central role to marginal productivity.

In Chapter 17, we will study the payments made for the use of capital (interest), land (rent), and the reward to entrepreneurs (profits). Because most people earn their incomes primarily from wages and salaries, and because these payments constitute nearly three-quarters of U.S. national income, our analysis of the payments

327

to labor (wages) merits a separate chapter (Chapter 18). In Chapter 19 we turn to some important problems in the distribution of income—poverty, inequality, and discrimination. We save the discussion of the pricing of exhaustible natural resources, as part of the income of land, for Chapter 22 in Part V.

Rent is that portion of the produce of the earth which
is paid to the landlord for use of the original
and indestructible powers of the soil.

David Ricardo (1772–1823)

PRICING THE FACTORS OF PRODUCTION

In Chapter 14 we saw that the market mechanism cannot be counted on to distribute income in accord with ethical notions of "fairness," and we listed this as one of the
market's shortcomings. There is much more to say about
how income is distributed in a market economy, and we
turn to that subject in this chapter.

The market mechanism distributes income through
its payments to the factors of production. Everyone owns
some *factors of production*—which are simply the inputs
used in the production process. Many of us have only our
own labor; but some of us also have funds that we can
lend, land that we can rent, or natural resources that we
can sell. We sell these factors on markets at prices determined by supply and demand. So the distribution of

Factors of production are the broad categories, land, labor, capital, exhaustible natural resources, and entrepreneurship, into which we divide the economy's different productive inputs.

Entrepreneurship is the act of starting new firms, introducing new products and technological innovations, and, in general, taking the risks that are necessary in seeking out business opportunities.

income in a market economy is determined by the prices of the **factors of production** and by the amounts that are employed. For example, if wages are low and unequal and unemployment is high, then many people will be poor.

It is useful to group the factors of production into five broad categories: land, labor, capital, exhaustible natural resources, and a rather mysterious input called **entrepreneurship.** In this chapter, we will look at three of them—the interest paid to capital, the rent of land, and the profits earned by entrepreneurs—saving labor for Chapter 18 and natural resources for Chapter 22.

But first, because there is a great deal of misperception about the distribution of income among workers, capitalists, and landlords, let's see how much these three groups actually earn. In 1998, interest payments in the United States accounted for about 6.5 percent of national income; land rents were minuscule, making up only 2 percent; corporate profits accounted for about 12 percent; and income of other business proprietors made up about 8 percent.[1] In total, the returns to all the factors of production that we deal with in this chapter amounted to about one-quarter of national income. Where did the rest of it go? The answer is that close to three-quarters of national income was composed of employee compensation—wages and salaries. The huge share of labor in national income is one of the reasons why the next chapter is devoted entirely to this subject.

There are many other serious misunderstandings about the nature of income distribution and about what government can do to influence it, and discussions of the subject are often emotional. That's because the distribution of income is the one area in economics in which any one individual's interests almost inevitably conflict with those of someone else. By definition, if I get a larger slice of the total income pie, then you end up with a smaller slice.

■ THE PRINCIPLE OF MARGINAL PRODUCTIVITY

The **marginal physical product (MPP)** of an input is the increase in output that results from a one-unit increase in the use of the input, holding the amounts of all other inputs constant.

The **marginal revenue product (MRP)** of an input is the money value of the additional sales that a firm obtains by selling the marginal physical product of that input.

By now it will not surprise you to learn that economists analyze factor prices in terms of supply and demand. The supply sides of the markets for the various factors differ enormously, so we must discuss each factor market separately. But we can use one basic principle, the *principle of marginal productivity*, to explain how much of any input a profit-maximizing firm will *demand*, given the price of that input. To review the principle, we must first recall two concepts from Chapter 8: **marginal physical product (MPP)** and **marginal revenue product (MRP).**[2]

Table 17–1 helps us review these two concepts by recalling Naomi's Natural Farm, which has to decide how much corn to feed the hogs. The *marginal physical product* (MPP) column tells us how many additional pounds of pork each additional bag of corn will yield. For example, according to the table, the fourth bag increases output by 34 pounds. The *marginal revenue product* (MRP) column tells us how many dollars this marginal physical product is worth. In Table 17–1, we assume Naomi's prized, natural hogs sell at 75 cents a pound, so the marginal revenue product of the fourth bag of corn is $0.75 per pound times 34 pounds, or $25.50 (last column of the table).

> The **marginal productivity principle** states that in competitive factor markets, the profit-maximizing firm will hire or buy the quantity of any input at which the marginal revenue product equals the price of the input.

The basic logic behind this principle is both simple and powerful. We know that the firm's profit from acquiring an additional unit of an input is the input's marginal revenue product minus its marginal cost (the price of the additional unit of

---

[1] National income and product tables, U.S. Department of Commerce, Bureau of Economic Analysis, www.bea.doc.gov., accessed May 1999.

[2] Instructors may prefer to postpone the multi-input analysis until later in the course.

Naomi's Natural Farm Schedules for TPP, MPP, APP, and MRP of Corn

TABLE 17-1

(1) Input of Corn in 100-Pound Bags	(2) TPP: Total Physical Product Hog Output	(3) MPP: Marginal Physical Product per Bag	(4) APP: Average Physical Product per Bag	(5) MRP: Marginal Revenue Product per Bag
0	0.0 lbs.			
		14.0 lbs.		$10.50
1	14.0		14.0 lbs.	
		22.0		16.50
2	36.0		18.0	
		30.0		22.50
3	66.0		22.0	
		34.0		25.50
4	100.0		25.0	
		30.0		22.50
5	130.0		26.0	
		26.0		19.50
6	156.0		26.0	
		19.0		14.25
7	175.0		25.0	
		9.0		6.75
8	184.0		23.0	
		1.4		1.05
9	185.4		20.6	
		−5.4		−4.05
10	180.0		18.0	
		−15.0		−11.25
11	165.0		15.0	
		−21.0		−15.75
12	144.0		12.0	

input). If the input's marginal revenue product is greater than its price, it will pay the profit-seeking firm to hire more of that input because an additional unit of input brings the firm revenue over and above its cost. The firm should purchase that input up to the amount at which diminishing returns reduce the MRP to the level of the input's price. By similar reasoning, if MRP is less than price, then the firm is using too much of the input. We see in Table 17–1 that about seven bags is the optimal amount of corn for Naomi to use each week, because an eighth bag brings in a marginal revenue product of only $6.75, which is less than the $10 cost of buying the bag.

One corollary of the principle of marginal productivity is obvious: the quantity of any input demanded depends on its price. The lower the price of corn, the more it pays the farm to buy. In our example, it pays Naomi to use between seven and eight bags when the price per bag is $10. But if corn were more expensive, say, $20 per bag, that high price would exceed the value of the marginal product of either the sixth or seventh bag. It would, therefore, pay the firm to stop at five bags of corn. Thus, *marginal productivity analysis shows that the quantity demanded of an input normally declines as the input price rises.* The "law" of demand applies to inputs just as it applies to consumer goods.

■ INPUTS AND THEIR DERIVED DEMAND CURVES

We can, in fact, be much more specific about how much of each input a profit-maximizing firm will demand, for the marginal productivity principle tells us precisely how to derive the demand curve for any input from its marginal revenue product (MRP) curve.

Figure 17–1 graphs the MRP schedule from Table 17–1, showing the marginal revenue product for corn (MRP_c) rising and then declining as Naomi feeds more and more corn to her hogs. In the figure, we focus on three possible prices for a bag of corn: $20, $15, and $10. The optimal purchase rule requires Naomi to keep increasing the use of corn until its MRP is reduced to the price of corn. At a price of $20 per bag, we see that the quantity demanded is about 5.6 bags of corn per

FIGURE 17–1

Marginal Revenue Product Schedule for Naomi's Natural Farm

Bags of Corn per Week

FIGURE 17–2

A Shift in the Demand Curve for Corn

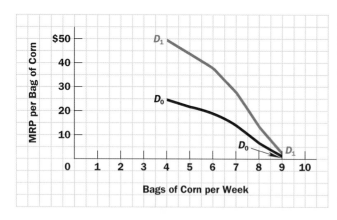

Bags of Corn per Week

week (point *A*) because at that point, MRP equals price. Similarly, if the price of corn is $15 per bag, quantity demanded is about 6.8 bags per week (point *B*). Finally, at a price of $10 per bag, the quantity demanded would be about 7.7 bags per week (point *C*). Points *A*, *B*, and *C* are therefore three points on the demand curve for corn. By repeating this exercise for any other price, we learn that:

The demand curve for any input is the downward-sloping portion of its marginal revenue product curve.[3]

The demand for corn or labor (or for any other input) is called a **derived demand** because it is derived from the underlying demand for the final product (hogs in this case). For example, suppose that a surge in demand drives organic hog prices to $1.50 per pound. Then, at each level of corn usage, the marginal revenue product will be twice as large as when hogs brought 75 cents a pound. This effect appears in Figure 17–2 as an upward shift of the (derived) demand curve for corn, from $D_0 D_0$ to $D_1 D_1$, even though the marginal physical product curves have not changed. Thus, an outward shift in demand for pork leads to an outward shift in the demand for corn.[4] We conclude that, in general:

An outward shift in the demand curve for any commodity causes an outward shift of the derived demand curve for all factors utilized in the production of that commodity.

Similarly, an inward shift in the demand curve for a commodity leads to inward shifts in the demand curves for factors used in producing that commodity.

This completes our discussion of the *demand* side of the analysis of input pricing. The most noteworthy feature of the discussion is the fact that the same marginal productivity principle serves as the foundation for the demand schedule for each and every type of input. In particular, as we will see in the next chapter, the marginal productivity principle serves as the basis for the determination of the demand for *labor*—that crucial input whose financial reward plays so important a role in an economy's standard of living. On the demand side, one analysis fits all.

The supply side for each input, however, entails a very different story. Here we must deal with each of the main production factors individually. We must do this in order to see how each input's earnings depend on the interaction of demand *and* supply. We begin with *interest payments*, which is what we call the return on capital. First, we must define a few key terms.

The **derived demand** for an input is the demand for the input by producers as determined by the demand for the final product that the input is used to produce.

---

[3] Why is the demand curve restricted to only the *downward-sloping portion* of the MRP curve? The logic of the marginal productivity principle dictates this. For example, if the price of corn were $15.00 per bag, Figure 17–1 shows that there are two input quantities for which MRP = *P*: (approximately) 1.5 bags (point *D*) and 6.8 bags (point *B*). But point *D* cannot be the optimal stopping point because the MRP of a second bag ($16.50) is greater than the cost of the third bag ($15.00), so that the firm makes more money by expanding its input use beyond 1.5 bags per week. A similar profitable opportunity for expansion occurs any time the MRP curve slopes upward at the current price, because that means that an increase in the quantity of input used by the firm will raise MRP above the input's price. It follows that a profit-maximizing firm will always demand an input quantity that is in the range where MRP is diminishing.

[4] To make the diagram easier to read, the (irrelevant) upward-sloping portion and the negative portion of each curve have been omitted.

■ INVESTMENT, CAPITAL, AND INTEREST

Though people sometimes use the words *investment* and *capital* as if they were interchangeable, the distinction between them is important. Economists define **capital** as the inventory (or stock) of plant, equipment, and other productive resources held by a business firm, an individual, or some other organization. **Investment** is the amount by which capital *grows*. So, when economists use the word investment, they do not mean just the transfer of money. The higher the level of investment, the *faster* the amount of capital that the investor possesses grows. We can describe the relation between investment and capital by the analogy of filling a bathtub: The accumulated water in the tub is analogous to the *stock* of capital, whereas the flow of water from the faucet (which adds to the tub's water) is like the *flow* of investment. Just as the faucet must be turned on for more water to accumulate, the capital stock increases only when investment continues. If investment ceases, the capital stock stops growing (but does not disappear). In other words, if investment is zero, the capital stock does not fall to zero but remains constant (just as when you turn off the faucet the tub doesn't suddenly empty, but rather the level of the water stays the same).

The process of building up capital by investing and then using this capital in production can be divided into five steps. They are listed below and are summarized in Figure 17–3.

> **Capital** refers to an inventory (*a stock*) of plant, equipment, and other (generally durable) productive resources held by a business firm, an individual, or some other organization.
>
> **Investment** is the *flow* of resources into the production of new capital. It is the labor, steel, and other inputs devoted to the *construction* of factories, warehouses, railroads, and other pieces of capital during some period of time.

The Investment Production Process

FIGURE 17–3

Step 1. The firm decides to enlarge its stock of capital.

Step 2. It raises the funds to finance its expansion, either from outside sources such as banks or by holding onto some of its own earnings rather than paying them out to company owners.

Step 3. The firm uses these funds to hire the inputs to build factories, warehouses, and the like. This step is the act of *investment.*

Step 4. After the investment is completed, the firm ends up with a larger stock of capital.

Step 5. The firm uses the capital (along with other inputs) either to expand production or to reduce costs. At this point, the firm starts earning *returns* on its investment.

Notice that investors put *money* into the investment process, either their own or funds they borrow from others. Then, through a series of steps, firms transform the funds into physical inputs suitable for production use. If investors borrow the funds, they must someday return those amounts to the lender with some payment for their use. This payment is called **interest,** and it is calculated as an annual percentage of the amount borrowed. For example, if an investor borrows $1,000 at an interest rate of 12 percent per year, the annual interest payment is $120.

> **Interest** is the payment for the use of funds employed in the production of capital; it is measured as a percentage per year of the value of the funds tied up in the capital.

"I can't sleep. I just got this incredible craving for capital."

THE DEMAND FOR FUNDS

The rate of interest is the *price* at which funds can be rented (borrowed). Just like other factor prices, interest rates are determined by supply and demand.

On the demand side of the market for loans are borrowers—people or institutions that, for one reason or another, wish to spend more than they currently have. Individuals or families borrow to buy homes or automobiles or other expensive products. Sometimes, as we know, they borrow because they want to consume more than they can afford, which can get them into financial trouble. But often, borrowing makes good sense as a way to manage their finances when they experience a temporary drop in income. It also makes sense to borrow money to buy an item like a home that will be used for many years; this long product life makes it appropriate for people to pay for the item as it is used, rather than all at once when it is purchased.

Businesses use loans primarily to finance investment. To the business executive who borrows funds to finance an investment and pays interest in return, the funds really represent an intermediate step toward the acquisition of the machines, buildings, inventories, and other forms of physical capital that the firm will purchase.

The marginal productivity principle governs the quantity of funds demanded, just as it governs the quantity of corn demanded for hog feed. Specifically:

> **Firms will demand the quantity of borrowed funds that makes the marginal revenue product of the investment financed by the funds just equal to the interest payment charged for borrowing.**

One noteworthy feature of capital distinguishes it from other inputs, like corn, for example. When Naomi feeds corn to her hogs, it is used once and then it is gone. But a blast furnace, which is part of a steel company's capital, normally lasts many years. The furnace is a *durable* good; and because it is durable, it contributes not only to today's production but also to future production. This fact makes calculating the marginal revenue product more complex for a capital good than for other inputs.

To determine whether the MRP of a capital good is greater than the cost of financing it (that is, to decide whether an investment is profitable), we need a way to compare money values received at different times. To make such comparisons, economists and business people use a calculation procedure called *discounting*. We will explain discounting in detail in the appendix to this chapter, but you need not master this technique in an introductory course. There are really only two important attributes of discounting to learn here:

- **A sum of money received at a future date is worth less than the same sum of money received today.**

- **This difference in values between money today and money in the future is greater when the rate of interest is higher.**

We can easily understand why this is so. To illustrate our first point, consider what you could do with a dollar that you received today rather than a year from today. If the annual rate of interest were 10 percent, you could lend it out (for example, by putting it in a savings account) and receive $1.10 in a year's time—your original $1.00 plus 10 cents interest. For this reason, money received today is worth more than the same number of dollars received later.

Now for our second point. Suppose the annual rate of interest was 15 percent instead. In this case, $1.00 invested today would grow to $1.15 (rather than $1.10) in a year's time, which means that $1.15 received a year from today would be equivalent to $1.00 received today, and so $1.10 a year in the future must now be worth less than $1.00 today. But when the interest rate is 10 percent per year, $1.10 to be received a year from today is equivalent to $1 of today's money. This illustrates the second of our two points.

The rate of interest is a crucial determinant of the economy's level of investment. That is, it strongly influences the amount of current consumption that consumers will choose to forgo in order to use the resources to build machines and factories that can increase the output of consumers' goods in the future. The interest rate is crucial in determining the allocation of society's resources between present and future—an issue that we discussed in Chapter 14 (pages 277–279). Let us see, then, how the market sets interest rates.

THE DOWNWARD-SLOPING DEMAND CURVE FOR FUNDS

The two attributes of discounting discussed above are all we need to explain why the quantity of funds demanded declines as interest rates rise, that is, why the demand curve for funds has a negative slope.

Remember that the demand for borrowed funds, like the demand for all inputs, is a *derived demand*, derived from the desire to invest in capital goods. But firms will receive part—perhaps all—of a machine or factory's marginal revenue product in the future. Hence, the value of the MRP *in terms of today's money* shrinks as the interest rate rises. Why? Because future returns to investment in a machine or factory must be *discounted* more when the rate of interest rises, as our illustration of the second point about discounting showed. The consequence of this shrinkage is that a machine that appears to be a good investment when the interest rate is 10 percent may look like a terrible investment if interest rates rise to 15 percent. That is, the higher the interest rate, the fewer machines a firm will demand, because investing in the machines would use up money that could earn more interest in a savings account. Thus, the demand curve for machines and other forms of capital will have a negative slope—the higher the interest rate, the smaller the quantity that firms will demand.

> As the interest rate on borrowing rises, more and more investments that previously looked profitable start to look unprofitable. The demand for borrowing for investment purposes, therefore, is lower at higher rates of interest.

Note that, although this analysis clearly applies to a firm's purchase of capital goods such as plant and equipment, it may also apply to the company's land and labor purchases. Firms often finance both of these expenditures via borrowed funds, and these inputs' marginal revenue products may accrue only months or even years after the inputs have been bought and put to work. (For example, it may take quite some time before newly acquired agricultural land will yield a marketable crop.) Thus, just as in the case of capital investments, a rise in the interest rate will reduce the quantity demanded of investment goods like land and labor, just as it cuts the derived demand for investment in plant and equipment.

FIGURE 17-4

The Derived Demand Curve for Loans

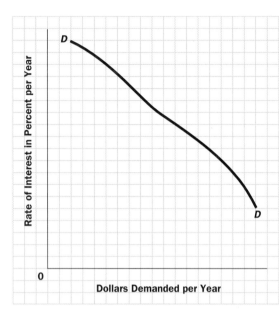

Figure 17–4 depicts a derived demand schedule for loans, with the interest rate on the vertical axis as the loan's cost to a borrower. Its negative slope illustrates the conclusion we have just stated:

The higher the interest rate, the less people and firms will want to borrow to finance their investments.

THE SUPPLY OF FUNDS

Somewhat different relationships arise on the supply side of the market for funds—where the suppliers or *lenders* are consumers, banks, and other business firms. Funds lent out are usually returned to the owner (with interest) only over a period of time. Loans will look better to lenders when they bear higher interest rates, so the supply schedule for loans rather naturally may be expected to slope upward—at higher rates of interest, lenders supply more funds. Such a supply schedule appears as the curve *SS* in Figure 17–5, where we also reproduce the demand curve, *DD*, from Figure 17–4. Here, the free-market interest rate is 12 percent.

However, not all supply curves for funds slope uphill to the right like curve *SS*. Suppose, for example, that Mario is saving to buy a $10,000 boat in three years, and that if he lends money out at interest in the interim, he must save $3,000 a year to reach his goal. If interest rates were higher, he could get away with saving less than $3,000 each year and still reach his $10,000 goal. (The higher interest payments would, of course, contribute the difference.) So his saving (and lending) may decline as a result of the rise in interest rate. This argument only applies fully to savers, like Mario, with a fixed accumulation goal. But similar considerations affect the calculations of other savers.

Generally, we expect the quantity of loans supplied to rise at least somewhat when the interest reward rises, so the supply curve will have a positive slope, like *SS* in Figure 17–5. However, for reasons similar to those indicated in Mario's example,

FIGURE 17-5

Equilibrium in the Market for Loans

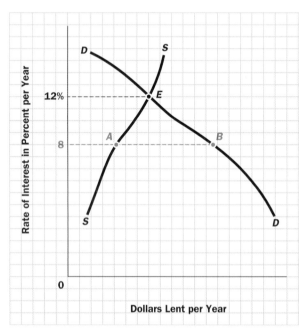

the increase in the economy's saving that results from a rise in the interest rate is usually quite small. That is why we have drawn the supply curve so steep. The rise in the amount supplied by some lenders is partially offset by a decline in the amounts lent by savers with fixed goals (like Mario, who is putting money away to buy a boat, or Kathryn, who is saving for a mountain bike).

Having examined the relevant demand and supply curves, we are now in a position to discuss the determination of the equilibrium rate of interest. This is summed up in Figure 17–5, in which the equilibrium is, as always, at point *E*, where quantity supplied equals quantity demanded. We conclude, again, that the equilibrium interest rate on loans is 12 percent in the example in the graph.

THE ISSUE OF USURY LAWS: ARE INTEREST RATES TOO HIGH?

People have often been dissatisfied with the market mechanism's determination of interest rates. Fears that interest rates, if left unregulated, would climb to exorbitant levels have made usury laws (which place upper limits on money-lending rates) quite popular in many times and places. Attempts to control interest payments date back to biblical days, and in the Middle Ages the influence of the church even led to total prohibition of interest payments in much of Europe. In the United States, the patchwork of state usury laws was mostly dismantled during the 1980s when the banking industry was deregulated.

Unscrupulous lenders often manage to evade usury laws by charging interest rates even higher than the free-market equilibrium rate. But even when usury laws are effective, they interfere with the operation of supply and demand and, as we will demonstrate, they often harm economic efficiency.

Look at Figure 17–5 again, but this time assume it depicts the supply of bank loans to consumers. Consider what happens if a usury law prohibits interest rates higher than 8 percent per year on consumer loans. At 8 percent, the quantity supplied (point *A* in Figure 17–5) falls short of the quantity demanded (point *B*). This means that many applicants for consumer loans are being turned down even though banks consider them to be creditworthy.

Who gains and who loses from this usury law? The gainers are the lucky consumers who get loans at 8 percent even though they would have been willing to pay 12 percent. The losers come on both the supply side and the demand side: the consumers who would have been willing and able to get credit at 12 percent but who are turned down at 8 percent, and the banks that could have made profitable loans at rates of up to 12 percent if there were no interest-rate ceiling.

This analysis explains why usury laws can be politically popular. Few people sympathize with bank stockholders; and the consumers who get loans at lower rates are, naturally, pleased with the result of usury laws. Other consumers, who would like to borrow at 8 percent but cannot because quantity supplied is less than quantity demanded, are likely to blame the bank for refusing to lend, rather than blaming the government for outlawing mutually beneficial transactions.

Yet concern over high interest rates can be rational. It may, for example, be appropriate to combat homelessness by making financing of housing cheaper for poor people. But it may be much more rational for the government to subsidize the interest on housing for the poor rather than declaring high interest rates illegal, in effect pretending that those costs can simply be legislated away, as a usury ceiling tries to do.[5]

THE DETERMINATION OF RENT

The second main factor of production is land. Rent, the payment for the use of land, is another price which, when left to the market, often seems to settle at politically unpopular levels. Rent controls are a popular solution. We discussed the effects of rent controls in Chapter 5 (pages 83–85), and we will say a bit more about them later in this chapter. But our main focus here is the determination of rents by free markets.

The market for land is characterized by a special feature on the supply side. Land is a factor of production whose quantity supplied is (roughly) unchanging: the same quantity is available at every possible price. Indeed, classical economists used this notion as the working definition of land. And the definition seems to fit, at least approximately. Although people may clear land, drain swamps, fertilize it, build on it, or convert it from one use (a farm) to another (a housing development), human effort cannot change the total land supply, or at least not very much.

What does this fact tell us about how the market determines land rents? Figure 17–6 helps to provide an answer. The vertical supply curve *SS* means that no matter what the level of rents, there are only 1,000 acres of land in a small hamlet called Littleville. The demand curve *DD* slopes downward and is a typical marginal revenue product curve, predicated on the notion that the use of land, like everything else, is subject to diminishing returns. The free-market price is determined, as usual, by the intersection of the supply and demand curves at point *E*. In this example,

---

[5] The law also sometimes concerns itself with discrimination in lending against women or members of ethnic minority groups. Strong evidence suggests sex and race discrimination in lending. For example, married women have been denied loans without the explicit permission of their husbands, even where the women had substantial independent incomes.

FIGURE 17-6

Determination of Land Rent in Littleville

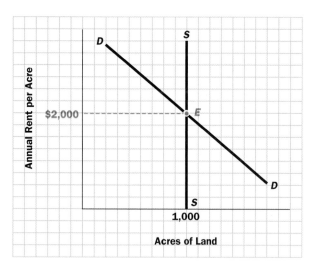

each acre of land in Littleville rents for $2,000 per year. The interesting feature of this diagram is that, because quantity supplied is rigidly fixed at 1,000 acres whatever the price:

The market level of rent is entirely determined by the market's demand side.

If, for example, a major university relocates to Littleville, attracting more people who want to live there, the DD curve will shift outward, as depicted in Figure 17–7. Equilibrium in the market will shift from point E to point A. The same 1,000 acres of land will be available, but now each acre will command a rent of $2,500 per acre. The landlords will collect more rent, though society gets no more of the input—land—from the landlords in return for its additional payment.

The same process also works in reverse, however. If the university shuts its doors and the demand for land declines as a result, the landlords will suffer even though they did not contribute to the decline in the demand for land. (To see this, simply reverse the logic of Figure 17–7. The demand curve begins at D_1D_1 and shifts to D_0D_0.)

This discussion shows the special feature of rent that leads economists to distinguish it from payments to other factors of production. An **economic rent** is an "extra" payment for a factor of production (such as land) that does not change the amount of the factor that is supplied. Society is not compensated for a rise in its rent payments by any increase in the quantity of land it obtains. Economic rent is thus that portion of the factor payment that exceeds the minimum payment necessary to induce any of that factor to be supplied.

As late as the end of the 19th century, the idea of economic rent exerted a powerful influence far beyond technical economic writings. An American journalist, Henry George, was nearly elected mayor of New York in 1886, running on the platform that all government should be financed by a "single tax" levied on landlords who, he said, are the only ones who earn incomes without contributing to the productive process. George said that landlords reap the fruits of economic growth without contributing to economic progress. He based his logic on the notion that landowners do not increase the supply of their factor of production—the quantity of land—when rents increase.

FIGURE 17-7

A Shift in Demand with a Vertical Supply Curve

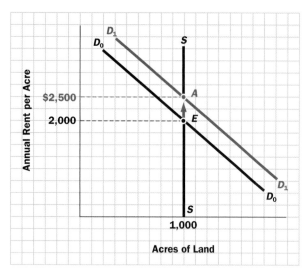

LAND RENTS: COMPLICATED VERSION

If all plots of land were identical, our previous discussion would be virtually all there is to the theory of land rent. But plots of land *do* differ—in geographical location, topography, nearness to marketplaces, soil quality, and so on. The classical economists took this into account in their analysis of rent determination—a remarkable 19th-century piece of economic logic still considered valid today.

The basic notion is that capital invested on any piece of land must yield the same return as capital invested on any other piece that is actually in use. Why? If it were not so, capitalists would bid against one another for the more profitable pieces of land. This would go on until the rents they would have to pay for these parcels were driven up to a point that eliminated their advantages over other parcels.

Suppose that a farmer produces a crop on one piece of land for $160,000 per year in labor, fertilizer, fuel, and other nonland costs, while a neighbor who is no more efficient produces the same for $120,000 on a second piece of land. The rent on the second parcel must be *exactly* $40,000 per year higher than the rent on the first, because otherwise production on one plot would be cheaper than on the other. If, for example, the rent difference were only $30,000 per year, it would be $10,000

Economic rent is the portion of the earnings of a factor of production that exceeds the minimum amount necessary to induce any of that factor to be supplied.

cheaper to produce on the second plot of land. No one would want to rent the first plot and every grower would instead bid for the second plot. Rent on the first plot would be forced down by lack of customers, and rent on the second would be driven up by eager bidders. These pressures would come to an end only when the rent difference reached $40,000, so that both plots became equally profitable.

At any given time, some low-quality pieces of land are so inferior that it does not pay to use them at all—remote deserts are a prime example. Any land that is exactly on the borderline between being used and not being used is called **marginal land.** By this definition, marginal land earns no rent because if its owner charged any for it, no one would willingly pay to use it.

We now combine these two observations—that the difference between the costs of producing on any two pieces of land must equal the difference between their rents and that zero rent is charged on marginal land—to conclude that:

> **Rent on any piece of land will equal the difference between the cost of producing the output on that land and the cost of producing it on marginal land.**

That is, competition for the superior plots of land will permit landlords to charge prices that capture the full advantages of their superior parcels.

This analysis helps us to understand more completely the effects of an outward shift in the demand curve for land. Suppose population growth raises demand for land. Naturally, rents will rise. But we can be more specific than this. In response to an outward shift in the demand curve, two things will happen:

- *It will now pay to employ some land whose use was formerly unprofitable.* The land that was previously on the zero-rent margin will no longer be on the borderline, and some land that is so poor that it was formerly not even worth considering will now just reach the borderline of profitability. The settling of the American West illustrates this process strikingly. Land that once could not be given away is now quite valuable.

- *People will begin to exploit already-used land more intensively.* Farmers will use more labor and fertilizer to squeeze larger amounts of crops out of their acreage, as has happened in recent decades. Urban real estate that previously held two-story buildings will now be used for high-rise buildings.

These two events will increase rents predictably. Because the land that is considered marginal *after* the change must be inferior to the land that was marginal previously, rents must rise by the difference in yields between the old and new marginal lands. Table 17–2 illustrates this point. We deal with three pieces of land: A, a very productive piece; B, a piece that was initially considered only marginal; and C, a piece that is inferior to B but nevertheless becomes marginal when the demand curve for land shifts upward and to the right.

Marginal land is land that is just on the borderline of being used, i.e., any land the use of which would be unprofitable if the farmer had to pay even a penny of rent.

| | | Nonrent Costs and Rent on Three Pieces of Land | | **TABLE 17-2** |

Type of Land	Nonland Cost of Producing a Given Crop	Total Rent	
		Before	After
a. A tract that was better than marginal before and after	$120,000	$80,000	$ 92,000
b. A tract that was marginal before but is attractive now	200,000	0	12,000
c. A tract that was previously not worth using but is now marginal	212,000	0	0

The crop costs $80,000 more when produced on B than on A, and $12,000 more when produced on C than on B. Suppose, initially, that demand for the crop is so low that Farmer Jones does not plant crops in C. Farmer Jones is on the fence about whether to plant crops in field B. Because field B is marginal, it is just on the margin between being used and left idle—it will command no rent. We know that the rent on A will be equal to the $80,000 cost advantage of A over B. Now suppose demand for the crop increases enough so that plot C is now marginal land. Then field B commands a rent of $12,000, the cost advantage of B over C. Plot A's rent now must rise from $80,000 to $92,000, the size of its cost advantage over C, the newly marginal land.

In addition to the quality differences among pieces of land, a second influence pushes land rents up: increased intensity of use of land that is already under cultivation. As farmers apply more fertilizer and labor to their land, the marginal productivity of land increases, just as factory workers become more productive when more is invested in their equipment. Once again, the landowner can capture this productivity increase in the form of higher rents. (If you do not understand why, refer back to Figure 17–7 and remember that the demand curves are marginal revenue product curves—that is, they indicate the amount that capitalists are willing to pay landlords to use their land.) Thus, we can summarize the theory of rent as follows:

> As the use of land increases, landlords receive higher payments from two sources:
>
> ■ Increased demand leads the community to employ land previously not good enough to use; the advantage of previously used land over the new marginal land increases, and rents go up correspondingly.
>
> ■ Land is used more intensively; the marginal revenue product of land rises, thus increasing the ability of the producer who uses the land to pay rent.

GENERALIZATION: ECONOMIC RENT SEEKING

Economists refer to the payments to land as "rents," but land is not the only scarce input with a fixed supply, at least in the short run. Toward the beginning of this century some economists realized that the economic analysis of rent can be applied to inputs *other* than land. As we will see, this extension yielded some noteworthy insights.

The concept of rent can be used to analyze such common phenomena as lobbying in the U.S. Congress by industrial groups, lawsuits between rival firms, and battles over exclusive licenses (as for a television station). Such interfirm battles can waste very valuable economic resources—for example, the time that executives, bureaucrats, judges, lawyers, and economists spend preparing and trying cases. Because this valuable time could have been used in production, such activities entail large *opportunity costs*. Rent analysis offers insights into the reasons for these battles and provides a way to assess what *quantity* of resources people waste as they seek economic rents for scarce resources.

How is economic rent—which is a payment to a factor of production above and beyond the amount necessary to get the factor to make its contribution to production—relevant in such cases? Gordon Tullock, an economist also trained in legal matters, coined the phrase "rent seeking" to describe the search and battle for opportunities to charge or collect those payments above and beyond the amount necessary to create the source of the income.

An obvious source of such rents is a monopoly license. For example, a license to operate the only television station in town will yield enormous advertising profits, far above the amount needed for the station to operate. No wonder rent seekers swoop down when such licenses become available. Similarly, the powerful lobby for U.S. sweetener producers, including corn and beet growers as well as cane sugar farmers, pressures Congress to impede cane sugar imports, because free importation would cut prices (and rents) substantially.

How much of society's resources will be wasted in such a process? Rent seeking theory can give us some idea. Consider a race for a monopoly cable TV license

● LAND PRICES AROUND THE WORLD

Supply and demand do not equalize prices when the commodity, such as land, cannot be transferred from one geographic market to another. For instance, in the late 1980s, when property values in Japan hit their peak, the average price of residential land in Tokyo was $3,000 per square meter (about 11 square feet), compared to $110 in Toronto and $70 in Washington, D.C. The world's highest rents on commercial property can be found in Hong Kong, where a square meter of office space will cost you over $1,200, compared to $800 in New York, $400 in Stockholm, and $300 in Istanbul.

SOURCE: Steven K. Mayo, "Land Prices, Land Markets, and the Broader Economy," *Land Lines,* March 1998, Lincoln Institute of Land Policy, www.lincolninst.edu; and *The Economist,* September 12, 1998, p. 116.

which, once awarded, will keep competing stations from operating. But nothing prevents *anyone from entering the race* to grab the license. Anyone can hire the lobbyists and lawyers or offer the bribes needed in the battle. Thus, although the cable business itself may not be competitive, the process of fighting for the license is competitive.

Of course, we know from the analysis of long-run equilibrium under perfect competition (Chapter 10, pages 200–203) that in such markets, economic profits approximate zero—in other words, revenues just cover costs. So, if owners expect a cable license to yield, say, $900 million over its life in rent, rent seekers (i.e., companies competing to gain the license in the first place) are likely to waste something near that amount as they fight for the license.

Why? Suppose ten bidders each have an equal chance at winning the license. To each bidder, that chance should be worth about $90 million—one chance in ten of getting $900 million. If the average bidder spends, say, only $70 million on the battle, each will still value the battle for the license at $90 million minus $70 million. This will tempt an 11th bidder to enter and raise the ante to, say, $80 million in lobbying fees, hoping to grab the rent. This process stops only when all of the excess rent available has been wasted on the rent-seeking process.

We can use the concept of economic rent, then, to divide the payment for any input into two parts. The first part is simply the minimum payment needed to acquire the input: for example—the cost of producing a ball bearing or the compensation people require in exchange for the unpleasantness, hard work, and loss of leisure involved in performing labor. The owner needs at least this first part of the factor payment to supply any amount of the input willingly. If workers do not receive at least this first part, they will not supply any of their labor.

The second part of the payment is a *bonus* that does not go to every input, but only to inputs of particularly high quality. Payments to workers with exceptional natural skills are a good example. These bonuses are like the extra payment for a better piece of land and so are called *economic rents.* Indeed, like the rent of land, an increase in the amount of economic rent paid to an input may not increase the *quantity* of that input supplied. This second part of the payment—the economic rent—is pure gravy. The skillful worker is happy to have it as an extra. But it is not a deciding consideration in the choice of whether or not to work.

Shaquille O'Neal

AN APPLICATION OF RENT THEORY: SHAQUILLE O'NEAL'S SALARY

A basketball player like Shaquille O'Neal (star center for the champion Los Angeles Lakers) would seem to have little in common with a plot of farmland. Yet to an economist, the same analysis—the theory of economic rent—explains how the market arrives at the amounts paid to each of these "factors of production." To understand why, we first note that there is only one Shaquille O'Neal. That is, he is a scarce input whose supply is fixed just like the supply of land. Because he is in fixed supply, the price of his services is determined in a way similar to that of land rents.

A moment's thought shows how the general notion of economic rent applies both to land and to O'Neal. The total quantity of land available for use is the same whether rent is high, low, or zero; only limited payments to landlords are necessary to induce them to supply land to the market. So, by definition, a considerable proportion of the payments to landholders for their land is economic rent—payments above and beyond those necessary for landlords to provide land to the economy. O'Neal is (almost) similar to land in this respect. His athletic talents are somewhat unique and cannot be reproduced. What determines the payment to such a factor? Because the quantity supplied of such a unique, nonreproducible factor is absolutely fixed, and therefore unresponsive to price, the analysis of rent that we summarized in Figure 17–6 applies: *The position of the demand curve alone determines the price.*

Figure 17–8 portrays a hypothetical "Shaquille O'Neal market." The (mostly) vertical supply curve *TUR* represents the fact that no matter what wage he is paid, there is only one Shaquille O'Neal. Demand curve *DD* is a marginal productivity curve of sorts, but not quite the kind we encountered earlier in the chapter. Because the question, "What would be the value of a second unit of Shaquille

O'Neal?" is nonsensical, we construct the demand curve by considering only the *portion* of his time demanded at various wage levels. The curve indicates that at an annual salary of $50 million no employer can afford even a little bit of Shaq. At a lower salary of, say, $35 million per year, however, two-thirds of his time will be demanded. At $30 million per year, O'Neal's full time is demanded; and at lower wage rates, like $25 million, the demand for his time exceeds the amount of it that is for sale.

Equilibrium is at point *E* in the diagram, where the supply of and demand for his time are equal. His annual salary here is $30 million. Now we can ask: How much of that salary is economic rent? According to the economic definition of rent, the answer is: only part of it. Because the supply schedule is only partly vertical, part of O'Neal's financial reward is necessary to get him to supply his services, as is undoubtedly true in reality. Thus, it is not true that every penny he earns is rent.

This is why we said that top athletes such as O'Neal are *almost* good examples of pure rent. For, in fact, if his salary were low enough, O'Neal might well prefer to live off his savings rather than work. Suppose, for example, that $250,000 per year is the lowest salary at which Shaq would offer even one minute of his services, and that his labor supply then increases with his wage up to an annual salary of $1,500,000, at which point he is willing to work full time. Then, although his equilibrium salary will still be $30 million per year, not all of it will be rent, because some of it (at least $250,000) is required to get him to supply any services at all.

The portion of O'Neal's compensation that is not pure rent corresponds to the upward-sloping portion, *TU*, of his labor-supply curve. Thus, only part of the supply curve, *TUR* in Figure 17–8, is vertical—that portion above the $1,500,000 salary that will lead him to supply all his available time. And his equilibrium compensation level, *E*, will consist partly of rent (portion *UE*) and partly of a payment, *SU*, that is not rent.

This same analysis applies to any factor of production whose supply curve is not horizontal, as in Figure 17–9, in which we see that at any price above $5, suppliers are willing to provide some units of the input, that is, at any price above point *S*, quantity supplied is greater than zero. Yet the supply-demand equilibrium point yields a price of $7—well above the minimum price at which some input supply would be forthcoming. The difference must constitute a rent to the input suppliers, who get paid more than the minimum amount required to induce them to supply it.

Almost all employees earn some rent. What sorts of factors earn no rent? Only those factors that can be reproduced by a number of producers at constant cost earn no rents. For instance, no ball bearing supplier will ever receive any rent on a ball bearing, at least in the long run, because any desired number of them can be produced at (roughly) constant costs—say, one cent each. If one supplier tried to charge a price above one cent, another manufacturer would undercut the first supplier and take its customers away. Hence, the competitive price includes no rent.

RENT CONTROLS: THE MISPLACED ANALOGY

Why is the analysis of economic rent important? Because only economic rent can be taxed away without reducing the quantity of the input supplied. And here common English gets in the way of sound reasoning. Many people feel that the *rent* they pay to their landlord is economic rent. After all, their apartments will still be there if they pay $1,500 per month, or $500, or $100. This view, although true in the short run, is quite myopic.

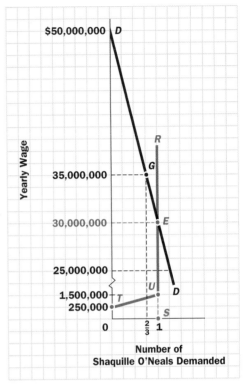

FIGURE 17–8

Hypothetical Market for Shaquille O'Neal's Labor

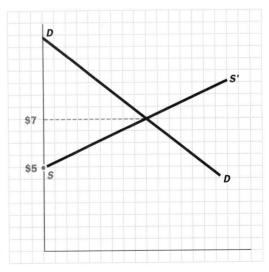

FIGURE 17–9

Rent When the Supply Curve Is Not Vertical

Like the ball-bearing producer, the owner of a building cannot expect to earn *economic rent* because too many other potential owners whose costs of construction are roughly the same as her own will also offer apartments. If the market price temporarily included some economic rent—that is, if price exceeded production costs plus the opportunity cost of the required capital—other builders would start new construction that would drive the price down. Thus, far from being in perfectly *inelastic* (vertical) supply, like raw land, buildings come rather close to being in perfectly *elastic* (horizontal) supply, like ball bearings. As we have learned from the theory of rent, this means that builders and owners of buildings cannot collect economic rent in the long run.

Because apartment owners collect very little economic rent, payments by tenants in a free market must be just enough to keep those apartments on the market. (This is the definition of zero economic rent.) If rent controls push these prices down, the apartments will start disappearing from the market.[6] Among other unfortunate results, we can therefore expect rent controls to contribute to homelessness—though it is, of course, not the only influence behind this distressing phenomenon.

PAYMENTS TO ENTREPRENEURSHIP: ARE PROFITS TOO HIGH OR TOO LOW?

We turn next to business profits, the discussion of which often seems to elicit more passion than logic. With the exception of some economists, almost no one thinks that profit rates are at about the right level. Critics point accusingly at some giant corporations' billion-dollar profits and argue that they are unconscionably high. They call for much stiffer profits taxes. On the other hand, the Chambers of Commerce, National Association of Manufacturers, and other business groups complain that regulations and "ruinous" competition keep profits too low, and they constantly petition Congress for tax relief.

The public has many misconceptions about the nature of the U.S. economy, but probably none is further from reality than popular perceptions of what American corporations earn in profits. Try the following experiment. Ask five of your friends who have never had an economics course what fraction of the nation's income they imagine is pure profit to companies. Although the correct answer varies from year to year, business profits in 1998 made up about 10 percent of gross domestic product (GDP) (before taxes).[7] A comparable percentage of the prices you pay represents before-tax profit. Most people think this figure is much, much higher—as we saw in the box in Chapter 3 on page 42.

As you have no doubt noticed by now, economists are reluctant to brand factor prices as "too low" or "too high" in some moral or ethical sense. Rather, they are likely to ask first: What is the market equilibrium price? Then they will ask whether there are any good reasons to interfere with the market solution. This analysis, however, is not so easily applied to the case of *profits*, because it is hard to use supply and demand analysis when you do not know what factor of production earns profit.

In both a bookkeeping and an economic sense, *profits are the residual.* They are what remains from the selling price after all other factors have been paid.

But what production factor earns this reward? What factor's marginal productivity constitutes the profit rate?

---

[6] None of this is meant to imply that temporary rent controls in certain locations cannot have desirable effects in the short run. In the short run, the supply of apartments and houses really is fixed, and large shifts in demand can hand windfall gains to landlords—gains that are true economic rents. Controls that eliminate such windfalls should not cause serious problems. But knowing when the "short run" fades into the "long run" can be tricky. "Temporary" rent control laws have a way of becoming rather permanent.

[7] *Economic Report of the President 1999* (Washington, D.C.: U.S. Government Printing Office, February 1999).

● **A FISTFUL OF DOLLARS: ENTREPRENEURSHIP IN POLAND**

It would be rare in Western Europe, but in the continent's post-communist half it is commonplace; entrepreneurs start off with a fistful of dollars and become multi-millionaires a few years later. . . .

Take Univex, a Polish firm established in 1990 to import consumer electronics. It had practically no starting capital, but managed to persuade its customers to pay in advance. Univex now employs 500 people, including a bunch of managers "head-hunted" from western multinationals, and has annual sales of probably more than $50 million. . . . Its line of business has been transformed, too. The founders, two Polish engineers, have developed a range of ingenious products, sold widely in the West, including a tiny digital voice recorder that transfers its contents to a computer, allowing voicemail to be sent easily over the Internet. The company's shambolic-looking assembly line is reminiscent of an East Asian sweat shop, but its "brain room," where the product developers work, feels like Silicon Valley. This combination of low labor costs and technical ingenuity is the secret of Univex's success.

Start-ups are the engine of Poland's post-communist boom. . . . [By one calculation] private firms have trebled their share in industrial output since the transition began, from 16 percent of gross sales at the end of 1989 to 45 percent in 1995—an annual growth rate of more than a fifth.

SOURCE: "Survey of Business in Eastern Europe, *The Economist,* November 22, 1997, p. 10.

WHAT ACCOUNTS FOR PROFITS?

Economic profit, as we learned in Chapter 10, is the amount a firm earns *over and above the payments for all inputs,* including the interest payments for the capital it uses and the opportunity cost of any capital provided by the owners of the firm. The payment that firm owners receive to compensate them for the opportunity cost of their capital (that in common parlance is considered profit) is closely related to interest rates. In an imaginary (and dull) world in which everything was certain and unchanging, capitalists who invested money in firms would simply earn the market rate of interest on their funds. Profits beyond this level would be competed away. Payment for capital below this level could not persist, because capitalists would withdraw their funds from firms and deposit them in banks. Capitalists in such a world would be mere moneylenders.

But the real world is not at all like this. Some capitalists are much more than moneylenders, and the amounts they earn often exceed going interest rates by a huge margin (see the accompanying box, "A Fistful of Dollars: Entrepreneurship in Poland"). These active capitalists who seek out or even create earnings opportunities are called *entrepreneurs.* We can credit such creative individuals for the constant change that characterizes business firms and for preventing operations of the firm from stagnating. Because entrepreneurs constantly seek to do something new, it is difficult to provide a general description of their activities. However, we can list three primary ways in which entrepreneurs can and do drive profits above "normal" interest rate levels.

MONOPOLY POWER   If entrepreneurs can establish monopolies with some or all of their products, even for a short while, they can use that monopoly power to earn monopoly profits. We analyzed the nature of these monopoly earnings in Chapter 12.

RISK BEARING   Entrepreneurs often engage in financially risky activities. For example, when a firm prospects for oil, it must drill exploratory wells hoping to find petroleum at the bottom. But many such exploratory wells only end up as dry holes, and the costs then bring no return. Of course, lucky investors do find oil and are rewarded handsomely—more than the competitive return on the firm's capital. The extra income thus pays the firm for bearing risk.

A few lucky individuals make out well in this process, but many suffer heavy losses. How well can we expect risk takers to do, on the average? If, on the average, one exploratory drilling out of ten pays off, do we expect its return to be exactly 10 times as high as the interest rate, so that the *average* firm will earn exactly the normal rate of interest? The answer is that the payoff will be *more* than 10 times the interest rate

Economic profit is the total revenue of a firm minus all of its costs including the interest payments and opportunity costs of the capital it obtains from its investors.

if investors dislike gambling, that is, if they prefer to avoid risk. Why? Because investors who are risk averse will not be willing to put their money into a business that faces such odds—10 to 1—unless the market provides compensation for the financial peril.

In reality, however, nothing guarantees that things always work out this way. Some people love to gamble and tend to be overly optimistic. They may plunge into projects to a degree unjustified by the odds. Average payoffs to such gamblers in risky undertakings may end up below the interest rate. The successful investor will still make a good profit, just like the lucky winner in Las Vegas. But the average participant will have to pay for the privilege of bearing risk.

RETURNS TO INNOVATION   The third major source of profits is perhaps the most important of all for social welfare. The first entrepreneur able to innovate and market a desirable new product or employ a new cost-saving machine will garner a higher profit than what an uninnovative (but otherwise similar) business manager would earn. Innovation differs from invention, because whereas **invention** generates new ideas, **innovation** takes the next step by putting the new idea into practical use. Businesspeople are rarely inventors, but they are often innovators.

When an entrepreneur innovates, even if her new product or new process is not protected by patents, she will be one step ahead of her competitors. She will be able to capture much of the market, either by offering customers a better product or by supplying the product more cheaply. In either case, she will temporarily find herself with some monopoly power as her competitors weaken, and she will receive monopoly profit for her initiative.

However, this monopoly profit, the reward for innovation, will only be temporary. As soon as the idea's success becomes evident to the world, other firms will find ways of imitating it. Even if they cannot turn out precisely the same product or the same process, they must find close substitutes in order to survive. In this way, new ideas spread through the economy, and in the process the innovator's special profits come to an end. The innovator can only resume earning special profits by finding still another promising idea.

> The market system forces entrepreneurs to keep searching for new ideas, to keep instituting innovations, and to keep imitating new ideas even if they did not originate those innovations or ideas. This process lies at the heart of the growth of the capitalist system. It is one of the secrets of its extraordinary dynamism.

We explored these issues of innovation and growth performance in free markets more fully in Chapter 15.

TAXING PROFITS

Thus, we can consider profits in excess of market interest rates as the return on entrepreneurial talent. But this is not really very helpful, because no one can say exactly what entrepreneurial talent is. Certainly we cannot measure it; nor can we teach it in a college course, though business schools may try. We do not know whether the observed profit rate provides more than the minimum reward necessary to attract entrepreneurial talent into the market. This relationship between observed profit rates and minimum necessary rewards is crucial when we start to consider the policy ramifications of taxes on profits—a contentious issue, indeed.

Consider a profits tax on oil companies. If oil companies earn profits well above the minimum required to attract entrepreneurial talent, those profits contain a large element of economic rent. In that case, we could tax away these excess profits (rents) without fear of reducing oil production. On the other hand, if oil company profits do not include economic rents, then a windfall profits tax can seriously curtail oil exploration and, hence, production.

This example illustrates the general problem of deciding how heavily governments should tax profits. Critics of big business who call for high, if not confiscatory, profits taxes seem to believe that profits are mostly economic rent. But if they are wrong—if, in fact, most of the observed profits are necessary to attract people into entrepreneurial roles—then a high profits tax can be dangerous. Such a tax

Invention is the act of generating an idea for a new product or a new method for making an old product.

Innovation, the next step, is the act of putting the new idea into practical use.

would threaten the very lifeblood of the capitalist system. Business lobbying groups claim, predictably enough, that current tax policy creates precisely this threat. Unfortunately, neither group has offered much evidence for its conclusion.

■ CRITICISMS OF MARGINAL PRODUCTIVITY THEORY

The theory of factor pricing described in this chapter once again uses supply-demand analysis. Factor pricing theory also relies heavily on the principle of marginal productivity to derive the shape and position of the demand curve for various inputs. Indeed, some economists often refer to the analysis (rather misleadingly) as *the marginal productivity theory of distribution*, when it is, at best, only a theory of the demand side of the pertinent market.

Over the years, factor pricing analysis has been subject to attack on many grounds. One frequent accusation, which is largely (but not entirely) groundless, is the assertion that marginal productivity theory merely attempts to justify the income distribution that the capitalist system yields—in other words, that it is a piece of pro-capitalist propaganda. According to this argument, when marginal productivity theory claims that each factor is paid exactly its marginal revenue product, this is only a sneaky way of saying that each factor is paid exactly what it deserves. These critics claim that the theory legitimizes the gross inequities of the system—the poverty of many and the great wealth of the few.

The argument is straightforward but wrong. Payments are made not to factors of production, but rather to the people who happen to own them. If an acre of land earns $2,000 because that is its marginal revenue product, this does not mean, nor is it meant to imply, that the landlord *deserves* any particular payment, because he may even have acquired the land by fraud.

Second, an input's marginal revenue product (MRP) does not depend only on "how hard it works" but also on how much of it happens to be employed—because, according to the "law" of diminishing returns, the more that is employed, the lower its MRP. Thus, a factor's MRP is not and cannot legitimately be interpreted as a measure of the intensity of its "productive effort." In any event, what an input deserves, in some moral sense, may depend on more than what it does in the factory. For example, workers who are sick or have many children may be considered more deserving, even if they are no more productive.

On these and other grounds, no economist today claims that marginal productivity analysis shows that distribution under capitalism is either just or unjust. It is simply wrong to claim that marginal productivity theory is pro-capitalist propaganda. The marginal productivity principle is just as relevant to organizing production in a socialist society as it is in a capitalist one.

Other critics have attacked marginal productivity theory for using rather complicated reasoning to tell us very little about the really urgent problems of income distribution. In this view, it is all very well to say that everything depends on supply and demand and to express this in terms of many complicated equations (many of which appear in more advanced books and articles). But these equations do not tell us what to do about such serious distribution problems as malnutrition among the indigenous populations in Latin America or poverty among minority groups in the United States.

Though it does exaggerate somewhat, there is some truth to this criticism. We have seen in this chapter that the theory does provide some insights on real policy matters, though not as many as we would like. Later in the book we will see that economists do have useful things to say about the problems of poverty and underdevelopment. But very little of what we can say about these issues arises out of marginal productivity analysis.

Perhaps, in the end, what should be said for marginal productivity theory is this: As the best model we have at the moment, marginal productivity theory offers us *some* valuable insights into the way the economy works, and until we find a more powerful model, we are better off using the tools that we do have.

SUMMARY

1. A profit-maximizing firm purchases the quantity of any input at which the price of the input equals its *marginal revenue product (MRP)*. Consequently, the firm's demand curve for an input is the downward-sloping portion of that input's MRP curve.

2. Investment in a firm is the amount that is added to the firm's capital, which is its plant, equipment, inventory, and other productive inputs that tie up the company's money.

3. Interest rates are determined by the supply of and demand for funds. The demand for funds is a derived demand, because these funds are used to finance business *investment.* Thus, the demand for funds depends on the marginal productivity of *capital.*

4. A dollar obtainable sooner is worth more than a dollar obtainable later because of the *interest* that can be earned on that dollar in the interim.

5. Increased demand for a good that needs land to produce it will drive up the prices of land either because inferior land will be brought into use or because land will be used more intensively.

6. Rent controls do not significantly affect the supply of land, but they do tend to reduce the supply of buildings.

7. *Economic rent* is any payment to the supplier of a factor of production that is greater than the minimum amount needed to induce any of the factor to be supplied.

8. Factors of production that are unique in quality and difficult or impossible to reproduce will tend to be paid relatively high economic rents because of their scarcity.

9. Factors of production that are easy to produce at a constant cost and that are provided by many suppliers will earn little or no economic rent.

10. Economic profits over and above the cost of capital are earned (a) by exercise of monopoly power, (b) as payments for bearing risk, and (c) as the earnings of successful *innovation.*

11. The desirability of increased taxation of profits depends on its effects on the supply of entrepreneurial talent. If most profits are economic rents, then higher profits taxes will have few detrimental effects. But if most profits are necessary to attract *entrepreneurs* into the market, then higher profits taxes can weaken the capitalist system.

KEY TERMS

Factors of production   330

Entrepreneurship   330

Marginal productivity principle   330

Marginal physical product (MPP)   330

Marginal revenue product (MRP)   330

Derived demand   332

Capital   333

Investment   333

Interest   333

Discounting   334

Usury law   336

Economic rent   338

Marginal land   339

Profit   344

Entrepreneurs   345

Economic profit   345

Risk bearing   345

Invention versus innovation   346

QUESTIONS FOR REVIEW

1. A profit-maximizing firm expands its purchase of any input up to the point where diminishing returns have reduced the marginal revenue product so that it equals the input price. Why does it not pay the firm to "quit while it is ahead," buying so small a quantity of the input that the input's MRP remains greater than its price?

2. Which of the following inputs do you think include relatively large economic rents in their earnings?

   a. Nuts and bolts

   b. Petroleum

   c. A champion racehorse

   Use supply-demand analysis to explain your answer.

3. Three machines are employed in an isolated area. They each produce 2,000 units of output per month, the first requiring $20,000 in raw materials, the second $25,000, and the third $28,000. What would you expect to be the monthly charge for the first and second machines if the services of the third machine can be hired at a price of $9,000 a month? What parts of the charges for the first two machines are economic rent?

4. Economists conclude that a tax on the revenues of firms will be shifted in part to consumers of the products of those firms in the form of higher product prices. However, they believe that a tax on the rent of land usually cannot be shifted and must be paid entirely by the landlord. What explains the difference?

5. Many economists argue that a tax on apartment buildings is likely to reduce the supply of apartments, but that a tax on all land, including the land on which apartment buildings stand, will not reduce the supply of apartments. Can you explain the difference? How is this answer related to the answer to Review Question 4?

6. Distinguish between investment and capital.

7. If you have a contract under which you will be paid $10,000 two years from now, why do you become richer if the rate of interest falls?

8. What is the difference between interest and profit? Who earns interest, in return for what contribution to production? Who earns economic profit, in return for what contribution to production?

9. Do you know any entrepreneurs? How do they earn a living? How do they differ from managers?

10. Explain the difference between an invention and an innovation. Give an example of each.

11. "Marginal productivity does not determine how much a worker will earn—it determines only how many workers will be hired at a given wage. Therefore, marginal productivity analysis is a theory of demand for labor, not a theory of distribution." What, then, do you think determines wages? Does marginal productivity affect their level? If so, how?

12. (More difficult) American savings rates are among the lowest of any industrial country. This has caused concern about our ability to finance new plants and equipment for U.S. industry. Some politicians and others have advocated lower taxes on saving as a remedy. Do you expect such a program to be very effective? Why?

13. If rent constitutes only 2 percent of the incomes of Americans, why may the concept nevertheless be significant?

14. Litigation in which one company sues another often involves costs for lawyers and other court costs literally amounting to hundreds of millions of dollars per case. What does rent have to do with the matter?

●	**APPENDIX**	▌	**DISCOUNTING AND PRESENT VALUE**

Frequently, in business and economic problems, it is necessary to compare sums of money received (or paid) at different dates. Consider, for example, the purchase of a machine that costs $11,000 and will yield a marginal revenue product of $14,520 two years from today. If the machine can be financed by a two-year loan bearing 10 percent interest, it will cost the firm $1,100 in interest at the end of each year, plus $11,000 in principal repayment at the end of the second year. (See the table that follows.) Is the machine a good investment?

COSTS AND BENEFITS OF INVESTING IN A MACHINE

	End of Year 1	End of Year 2
Benefits		
Marginal revenue product of the machine	$ 0	$14,520
Costs		
Interest	1,100	1,100
Repayment of principal on loan	0	11,000
Total Cost	1,100	12,100

The total costs of owning the machine over the two-year period ($1,100 + $12,100 = $13,200) are less than the total benefits ($14,520). But this is clearly an invalid comparison, because the $14,520 in future benefits are not worth $14,520 in terms of today's money. Adding up dollars received (or paid) at different dates is a bit like adding apples and oranges. The process that has been invented for making the magnitudes of payments at different dates comparable to one another is called *discounting*, or *computing the present value* of a future sum of money.

To illustrate the concept of present value, let us ask how much $1 received a year from today is worth *in terms of today's money*. If the rate of interest is 10 percent, the answer is about 91 cents. Why? Because if we invest 91 cents today at 10 percent interest, it will grow to 91 cents plus 9.1 cents in interest = 100.1 cents in a year. That is, at the end of a year a payment of $100 will leave the recipient about as well off as he would have been if he had instead received $91 now. Similar considerations apply to any rate of interest. In general:

If the rate of interest is i, the present value of $1 to be received in a year is:

$$\frac{\$1.00}{(1 + i)}$$

This is so, because in a year

$$\frac{\$1.00}{(1 + i)}$$

will grow to

$$\frac{\$1.00}{1 + i} \times (1 + i) = \$1$$

What about money to be received two years from today? Using the same reasoning, and supposing the interest rate is 10 percent so that $1 + i = 1.1$, $1.00 invested today will grow to $1.00 times $(1.1) = \$1.10$ after one year and will grow to $1.00 times (1.1) times $(1.1) = \$1.00$ times $(1.1)^2 = \$1.21$ after two years. Consequently, the present value of $1.00 to be received two years from today is:

$$\frac{\$1.00}{(1 + i)^2} = \frac{\$1.00}{1.21} = 82.64 \text{ cents}$$

A similar analysis applies to money received three years from today, four years from today, and so on.

The general formula for the present value of $1.00 to be received N years from today when the rate of interest is i is:

$$\frac{\$1.00}{(1 + i)^N}$$

The present value formula is based on the two variables that determine the present value of any future flow of money: the rate of interest (i) and how long you have to wait before you get it (N).

Let us now apply this analysis to our example. The present value of the $14,520 revenue is easy to calculate because it all comes two years from today. Since the rate of interest is assumed to be 10 percent $(i = 0.1)$ we have:

$$\text{Present value of revenues} = \frac{\$14,520}{(1.1)^2}$$
$$= \frac{\$14,520}{1.21}$$
$$= \$12,000$$

The present value of the costs is a bit trickier in this example because costs occur at two different dates.

The present value of the first interest payment is:

$$\frac{\$1,100}{(1 + i)} = \frac{\$1,100}{1.1} = \$1,000$$

And the present value of the final payment of interest plus principal is:

$$\frac{\$12,100}{(1 + i)^2} = \frac{\$12,100}{(1.1)^2} = \frac{\$12,000}{1.21} = \$10,000$$

Now that we have expressed each sum in terms of its present value, it is permissible to add them up. So the present value of all costs is:

$$\text{Present value of costs} = \$1,000 + \$10,000$$
$$= \$11,000$$

Comparing this figure to the $12,000 present value of the revenues clearly shows that the machine really is a good investment. We can use the same calculation procedure for all investment decisions.

SUMMARY

1. To determine whether a loss or a gain will result from a decision whose costs and returns will come at several different periods of time, we must discount all the figures represented by these gains and losses to obtain their present value.

2. For this, we use the present value formula for X dollars receivable N years from now:

$$\text{Present value} = \frac{X}{(1 + i)^N}$$

3. We then combine the present values of all the returns and all the costs. If the sum of the present values of the returns is greater than the sum of the present values of the costs, then the decision to invest will promise a net gain.

KEY TERMS

Discounting   349
Present value   349

QUESTIONS FOR REVIEW

1. Compute the present value of $1,000 to be received in three years if the rate of interest is 11 percent.

2. A government bond pays $100 in interest each year for three years and also returns the principal of $1,000 in the third year. How much is it worth in terms of today's money if the rate of interest is 8 percent? If the rate of interest is 12 percent?

Octavius (a wealthy young Englishman):
"I believe most intensely in the dignity of labor."
The chauffeur: "That's because you never done any."
George Bernard Shaw, *Man and Superman*, Act II

LABOR: THE HUMAN INPUT

Labor costs account, by far, for the largest share of gross domestic product (GDP). As noted in the previous chapter, the earnings of labor amount to almost three-quarters of national income. Wages also represent the primary source of personal income to the vast majority of Americans. For more than a century, wages were the centerpiece of the American dream. In almost every decade, the purchasing power of a typical worker's earnings grew substantially, and the U.S. working class evolved into a comfortable middle class—the envy of the world and an irresistible lure for millions of immigrants. Then, something changed fundamentally in ways economists do not yet fully understand.

Figure 18–1 shows that average real wages (adjusted for inflation) stopped their upward march around

"But if I haven't given you a raise in five years, Pottsburg, why should you think I'd give you one now?"

FIGURE 18–1

Index of Long-Run Trends in Real (Inflation-Adjusted) Wages, Real Compensation (Wages Plus Benefits), and Hours Worked per Week, 1909–1999

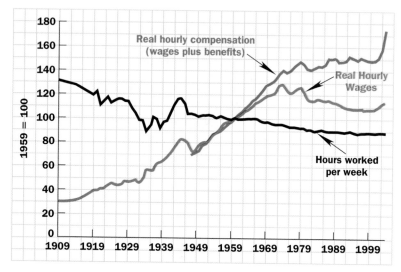

SOURCES: Constructed by the authors from data in U.S. Census Bureau, *Historical Statistics of the United States, Colonial Times to 1970* (Washington, D.C.: U.S. Government Printing Office, 1975); and *Economic Report of the President* (Washington, D.C.: U.S. Government Printing Office, various years).

1973 and, by some (disputed) calculations, even declined. In contrast, *total compensation* did not fall, as shown by the blue line in the graph, which represents wages *plus fringe benefits*—including such things as health insurance, retirement payments, and education subsidies that employers provide to their employees). But compensation *growth* did slow markedly.[1] The graph also shows that average hours worked per week have declined by about 30 percent during this century, even when wages and compensation were increasing. (The big drop in hours worked during the 1930s was a consequence of the Great Depression, and the sharp rise in hours worked during the 1940s was caused by World War II.)

Slowing wage growth has been accompanied by an expanding *income gap* between the rich and the poor. Today, high-income families in the United States earn almost twenty times as much as low-income families—and the disparity is rising. Figure 18–2 shows how dramatically the disparity has grown. Back in 1967, the richest one-fifth of American households accounted for nearly 44 percent of all household income generated in the United States, while the poorest one-fifth accounted for only 4 percent. By 1998, the income share of the lowest fifth of households had actually slipped a little to about 3.6 percent, while the richest fifth's income share had risen to nearly 50 percent.[2]

In Germany, by contrast, the ratio between low-wage and high-wage families is only 2.5. As one economist recently said of the United States, "We are the most unequal industrialized country in terms of income and wealth, and we're growing

---

[1] The sharp increases in compensation over the years reflect, at least in part, the rising cost of services such as health care, rather than an increase in the quantity and quality of benefits provided to workers. We explored the reasons for the rising costs of services in Chapter 14, and they form the basis of one our central *Ideas for Beyond the Final Exam* (why the costs of education and health care keep growing).

[2] U.S. Census Bureau, www.census.gov, accessed on June 8, 2000.

unequal faster than the other industrialized countries."[3] With nearly one-fifth of its children living below the poverty line, the United States is second only to Mexico in child poverty rates among the industrialized countries of the world.[4]

Along with this, the prospective gap between your incomes as future college graduates and those of your contemporaries who have not attended college has widened sharply. For instance, in 1970 male college graduates earned about 45 percent more than their high school-educated counterparts, and female college grads earned about 80 percent more than their high school-educated counterparts. By 1998, college educated men and women were taking in twice as much as men and women with only high-school educations.[5] This "college premium" will likely give you a huge financial advantage in terms of your family life, leisure activities, health benefits, retirement conditions, in short, virtually every aspect of your existence.

These developments also have profound and distressing implications for the future of our society as a whole. We are not sure what is behind these trends, nor do we quite know what can be done about them. But we will discuss some of the possible causes later in the chapter.

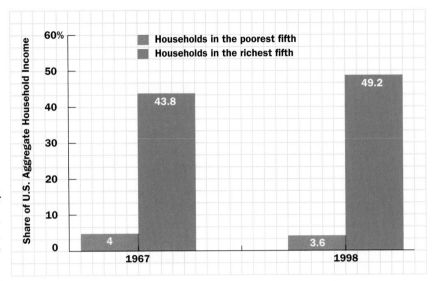

FIGURE 18-2

Income Inequality in America: Not Getting Any Better

SOURCE: U.S. Census Bureau, www.census.gov, accessed June 2000.

Issue: Do Cheap Foreign Labor and Technological Progress Contribute to Lagging Wages?

Throughout the history of the successful free-enterprise economies, workers have usually identified two economic enemies: first, the competition of underpaid foreign laborers and their underpriced exported products, and second, labor-saving technological progress that eliminates jobs. Either or both of these may be able to hold down wages in the United States and other industrial economies, and many economists believe that the peril is real (though they argue about which one is the greater danger). Many workers worry about the future of their jobs and incomes, especially in light of trade legislation that seems to export jobs to other countries. But as obvious as these explanations of lagging wages may seem, as

[3] "Studies Show Major Economic Division," Reuters, April 17, 1995 (from *The New York Times*). For more information on this issue, see Edward N. Wolff, *Top Heavy: A Study of Increasing Inequality of Wealth in America* (New York: Twentieth Century Fund, 1995).

[4] Federal Interagency Forum on Child and Family Statistics, *America's Children: Key National Indicators of Well-Being, 2000,* July 2000, www.childstats.gov; and Dale Russakoff, "Report Paints Brighter Picture of Childrens' Lives," *Washington Post,* July 14, 2000, p. A01.

[5] U.S. Census Bureau, *Median Earnings of Full-Time, Year-Round Workers by Selected Characteristics: 1998,* www.census.gov.

is often true in economics, things are less straightforward when we dig beneath the surface.

The second side of the issue is the role of technical progress and labor-saving innovation, which has played a key part in U.S. economic history. After all, saying that productivity has risen spectacularly is just another way of saying that fewer workers are needed to produce a given amount of output. Is this a major threat to jobs in the United States? These two issues—foreign competition and technological progress— are among the most crucial that face economic analysis and policy, and although economists continue to gather valuable evidence on these questions, we are still a long way from being able to claim that we know the answers. This chapter, however, will report some of the things we do know, or think we know, about the subject.

WAGE DETERMINATION IN COMPETITIVE LABOR MARKETS

To begin to understand labor issues, we must first investigate how wages are determined in a free-market economy. In a completely free labor market, wages (the price of labor) would be determined by supply and demand, just like any other price. On the demand side, we would find that the demand curve for labor is derived like the demand curve for any other input—by labor's marginal revenue product, in the manner described in the previous chapter for the economy's other inputs. But the labor market has a number of distinctive features on the supply side.

The labor market is also generally far from perfectly competitive. Nonetheless, we start our investigation by describing the theory of competitive labor markets in which the buyers are large numbers of tiny firms and the sellers are individual workers who act independently of one another. In this model, both buyers and sellers are too small to have any choice but to accept the wage rate determined by the impersonal forces of supply and demand.

THE DEMAND FOR LABOR AND THE DETERMINATION OF WAGES

> **MRP_L, the marginal revenue product of labor,** is the increase in the employer's total revenue that results when he hires an additional unit of labor.

Much of what we can say about the demand for labor was already said about the demand for inputs in general in earlier chapters. Workers are hired (primarily) by profit-maximizing firms, which hire an input quantity at which the input's price (the market wage) equals its marginal revenue product (MRP). In this chapter, we will use the symbol MRP_L as an abbreviation of the **marginal revenue product of labor.** Recall that the marginal revenue product is the addition to the firm's revenue that it obtains by hiring one additional unit of input—in this case, one additional worker. So, MRP_L is equal to the additional amount that worker produces (the worker's marginal physical product) multiplied by the price of that product. In other words, to determine how much additional money that worker brings in, we multiply the amount she produces by the price of the commodity she produces.[6]

If the MRP_L is above the price of labor (the wage), by the usual reasoning of marginal analysis, the firm can increase its profit by hiring at least one more worker either to produce more output or to substitute for some other input. The reverse is true when the MRP_L is less than its wage. Thus, the derived demand and, consequently,

---

[6] To review, see Chapter 8, pages 144–145.

the demand curve for labor are determined by labor's marginal revenue product. Such a demand curve is shown as blue curve *DD* in Figure 18–3. The figure also includes a red supply curve, labeled *SS*. In a competitive labor market, equilibrium will be established at the wage that equates the quantity supplied with the quantity demanded. In this figure, equilibrium occurs at point *E*, where demand curve *DD* crosses supply curve *SS*. The equilibrium wage is $300 per week and equilibrium employment is 500,000 workers.

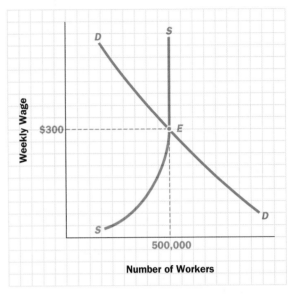

FIGURE 18–3

Equilibrium in a Competitive Labor Market

If nothing interferes with the free labor market operation (such as minimum wages or unions—which we will consider later), equilibrium will be at point *E*, where the supply and demand curves intersect. In this example, because 500,000 workers will be employed at a wage of $300 per week, the total income of the workers will be $300 × 0.5 million = $150 million.

INFLUENCES ON MRP$_L$: SHIFTS IN THE DEMAND FOR LABOR

The conclusion that the demand curve for labor is one and the same as labor's MRP curve is only the beginning of the story. The next question is: What influences affect MRP$_L$? The answers cast light on a number of important developments in the labor market.

Some obvious factors can change labor's MRP. For example, increased education can improve the ability of the labor force to follow complex instructions and to master difficult technology, thus raising a worker's MRP. Economists use the term **investment in human capital** to refer to spending on increased education and on other means to increase the knowledge and skills of the labor force. Such spending is analogous to investment in the firm's plant and equipment because both of them are outlays today that lead to more production.

Investment in human capital is any expenditure on an individual that increases that person's future earning power or productivity.

Workers can also improve their skills through experience, called *on-the-job training*, and in a variety of other ways that add to the information they possess and increase their mental and physical dexterity.

Because the demand for labor is a *derived demand*, anything that improves the market for the goods and services that labor produces can shift the labor demand curve upward. In particular, in a period of economic prosperity consumers will have more to spend; their demand for products will shift upward and this in turn will raise the price of the worker's product, thereby shifting the MRP curve upward. The result will be a rise in the demand for labor. That, of course, is why unemployment is always low when the economy is undergoing a period of prosperity.

TECHNICAL CHANGE, PRODUCTIVITY GROWTH, AND THE DEMAND FOR LABOR

Another critical influence upon the MRP$_L$ is the quality and quantity of the *other* inputs used in the workers' productive activity. Especially important is the technology of the workers' equipment. Innovation that improves machinery, power sources, and other productive instruments adds to the amount that can be produced by a given amount of labor. Thus, technical change that increases labor productivity plays a crucial role in determining the level of wages and the level of employment.

Technical change that increases the worker's productivity has two effects that work in opposite directions. First, increased productivity clearly implies an increase in the worker's marginal physical product—the quantity of widgets that an additional worker can produce will rise. On the other hand, because of the resulting reduction in labor cost and the increased output of widgets, we can expect that when productivity rises, widget prices will fall. Now recall that:

Marginal revenue product of labor in widget production = price of widgets multiplied by the worker's marginal widget output, that is:

$$MRP = P(\text{of widgets}) \times MPP.$$

Because a rise in productivity raises MPP but reduces P we cannot be sure of the net effect on MRP, that is, the net effect on the demand curve for labor.

However, experience shows us how a rise in productivity will affect both wages and the demand for labor. In the very short run, a rise in labor productivity (that is, of labor-saving technology) often causes a downward shift in the demand for labor, which holds down wages. If firms can meet the current demand for their products with 10 percent fewer workers than they needed last year, they will be tempted to "downsize," which is a polite way of saying that they will fire some workers. This does not always happen, but it does sometimes occur, so workers' widespread fear of labor-saving technology is, to some degree, justified.

Productivity Growth Is (Almost) Everything in the Long Run

PRODUCTIVITY GROWTH   However, in the long run, rising productivity has always improved the standard of living for both workers and the owners of other factors of production. As we indicated in one of our *Ideas for Beyond the Final Exam,* in the long run nothing contributes more to the economic well-being of the nation than rising productivity. Today workers enjoy far longer lives, better health, more education, and more luxury goods than they did a century ago or in any previous period in history. The fact that an hour of labor today can produce a large multiple of what our ancestors could create in an hour increases everyone's average income, including the workers who constitute so large a part of it. In the short run, labor-saving technological change sometimes cuts employment and holds down wages. But, historically, in the long run it has not reduced employment. It has raised workers' incomes and increased real wages spectacularly since the Industrial Revolution.

THE SERVICE ECONOMY AND THE DEMAND FOR LABOR

Although productivity growth has not led to any long-term upward trend in unemployment, it *has* cut jobs drastically in some parts of the economy, sending the labor force to other economic sectors for employment. Agriculture is the prime example. At the time of the American Revolution, probably more than 90 percent of the U.S. labor force had agricultural jobs and eked out what today would be considered a meager standard of living. In Europe only a century earlier, farm productivity was so low that famines and starvation were frequent occurrences. Yet today, with less than 3 percent of the nation's labor working on farms, the United States produces such a surplus of products that it sometimes seems unmanageable. It is this dramatic increase in farm productivity that has forced farm employment to drop from about 90 percent to less than 3 percent of the labor force. At first, farm workers shifted to manufacturing, as growing U.S. incomes led to a sharp rise in demand for industrial products. Then productivity in manufacturing took off, and workers again had to go elsewhere for their jobs.

Now, in its turn, increased productivity in manufacturing has moved workers into the service sector of the economy. Indeed, it has transformed the United States into a "service economy," meaning that nearly three-quarters of the labor force is employed in services such as telecommunications, software design, health care, teaching, and restaurant services.

Some observers have argued that this has happened to the United States because other countries are stealing away our manufacturing business base. But the facts show that this is simply untrue. As Figure 18–4 reports, the service sector has become dominant in *all* the major industrial economies. No industrial economy has been able to avoid this development by stealing manufacturing markets away from the others. More relevant to our concerns here is another worry: that the workers driven from manufacturing into the service sector of the economy have predominantly become low-paid dishwashers and hamburger flippers That is true in some cases, but the majority of new service jobs created in the past half-century are in the information sector of the economy, which includes computation, research, and teaching, among other jobs, requiring education and specialized skills. Many economists attribute the rising relative compensation of college-educated workers to such developments.

The Growing Share of Service Sector Jobs in Nine Countries, 1967–1997   FIGURE 18-4

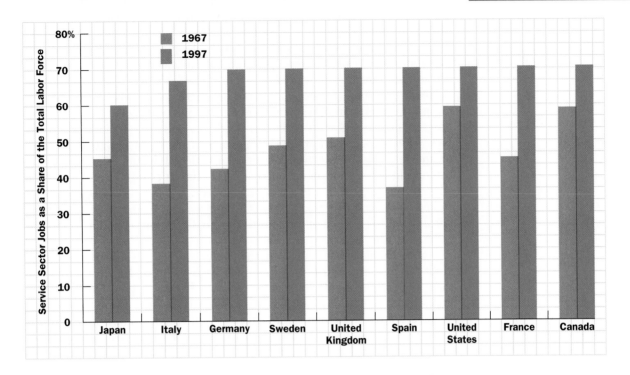

SOURCES: Organization for Economic Cooperation and Development, *OECD in Figures, 1999*, www.oecd.org, accessed June 8, 2000.

■ THE SUPPLY OF LABOR

Having discussed the demand for labor, we turn next to its supply. Several significant labor supply trends have characterized recent decades in the United States. First, there has been a continuation of the expansion of the total labor force that has been going on throughout the country's history. Much of this is ascribable to sheer growth of the nation's population through birth and immigration. With more people living in the country the number of job seekers and jobholders has grown—from about 60 million jobholders right after the Second World War to more than 134 million today. Second, the proportion of the population with jobs has also grown (from about 58 percent after World War II to 67 percent today). This is referred to as a rise in *labor force participation*. Third, new groups of workers have entered the labor force. This is particularly true of women, who today hold proportionately more jobs (46 percent of the workforce) than they did in earlier decades (except during wartime). Finally, in addition to the trends in sheer numbers of workers, the labor supply picture has been affected by a protracted and substantial relative decline in union membership. That is, there has been a significant fall in the share of American workers who belong to unions, the organizations whose stated purpose is to protect their interests. Because unions seek to bargain for all the workers in a firm or industry, thus eliminating competition among workers over jobs and wages, we will consider them later in the chapter, after we have finished our discussion of wage determination in labor markets that are fully competitive. First, we consider some other supply-side influences.

RISING LABOR-FORCE PARTICIPATION

One significant development in the supply of labor in the industrial countries is the increase in the number of family members who hold jobs. For instance, in 1997, 66 percent of American married-couple families had *two* wage earners, compared with only 40 percent in 1970.[7] It used to be that the "head of the household" (usually the husband) was ordinarily the only breadwinner. Today, married women also hold jobs. This phenomenon is in part attributable to lagging wages, so that both heads of the family are forced to seek gainful employment if the household's economic aspirations are to be realized. Rapidly rising medical costs and costs of education add to these financial pressures.

But participation in the labor force has increased for other reasons: the moves toward the liberation of women from their traditional role in the family, along with progress in the education of minorities that has increased their job opportunities. Not so long ago, an African American executive in a major business firm was unheard of, and an employed wife was considered disgraceful because it implied that her husband could not support her properly. Today this has changed drastically, though discrimination is by no means a thing of the past. In many firms top jobs, beyond the "token black" and the "token woman," have gone to members of these groups. It is not unusual for women and minorities to hold positions superior to those of many employees who are white and male.

These changes have affected the labor market in several ways that, some observers have suggested, may have held back wages, at least for a time. First, the sheer increase in supply of workers tends to depress wages. This is, of course, an implication of standard supply-demand analysis. Just draw the usual supply-demand graph for a labor market and you will readily confirm that when the supply curve of labor shifts to the right, the price of labor (that is, the wage) can be expected to fall. Second, it has been argued that a combination of discrimination and the initial lack of experience of these new entrants into the labor market (which temporarily reduced their MRP_L) had a similar effect. Discrimination against women or black or Hispanic workers in the labor market means that in order to get jobs workers from these groups must offer special incentives to prospective employers. This can force them to accept wages lower than those paid to white male employees with comparable ability for the performance of similar tasks. Lack of experience can have a similar effect, but for a reason that is less objectionable. If workers acquire skill through experience on the job (on-the-job

THE ECONOMY IS CREATING TENS OF THOUSANDS OF NEW JOBS

THAT'S THE GOOD NEWS

SO WHAT'S THE BAD NEWS?

TO SUPPORT A FAMILY YOU'LL NEED THREE

---

[7] U.S. Census Bureau, *Current Population Survey*, www.census.gov, accessed February 1999.

training) then, on the average, inexperienced workers can be expected to have lower productivity than more experienced workers. Because their MRP_L is comparatively low, the demand curve for the inexperienced will also be low, and lower wages will tend to follow.

AN IMPORTANT LABOR SUPPLY PUZZLE

For most commodities, increases in their prices leads to an increase in the quantities supplied, and price declines reduce amounts supplied: that is, supply curves slope upward. But the striking historical trends in labor supply tell a very different story. Supply has tended to fall when wages rose and to rise when wages fell. Throughout the first three-quarters of this century, real wages rose, as Figure 18–1 clearly showed. Yet labor asked for and received *reductions* in the length of the workday and workweek. At the beginning of the century, the standard workweek was 50 to 60 hours (with virtually no vacations). Since then, labor hours have generally declined to an average workweek of about 35 hours.

But in the two most recent decades, as real wages have fallen, the number of family members who leave the home each day to earn wages has increased. And, in the last few years there has been a rise in overtime work, that is, workers laboring more than the standard number of hours in their firms. Thus, reduced real wages appear to have induced people to increase the quantity of labor they supply.

Where has the commonsense view of this matter gone wrong? Why, as hourly wages rose for 75 years, did workers not sell more of the hours they had available instead of pressing for a shorter and shorter workweek? And why, in recent years, have they sold more of their labor time as real wage rates stopped rising?

To answer these questions it is helpful to follow the economic analysis of labor supply and make use of a simple observation: Given the fixed amount of time in a week, a person's decision to *supply labor* to firms is simultaneously a decision to *demand leisure* time for himself. Assuming that, after deducting the necessary time for eating and sleeping, a worker has 90 usable hours in a week, then a decision to spend 40 of those hours working is simultaneously a decision to demand 50 of them for other purposes.

The supply curve of labor, like that of any other input or commodity, tells us how the quantity supplied is affected by the market price of the item in question. Here we are investigating how the quantity of labor supplied is affected by its price, that is, by the level of wages. The interpretation of the supply of labor as the opposite of the worker's demand for leisure offers us a very substantial insight into the relation between wage and labor supply. Economists say that a rise in wages has two effects on the worker's demand for leisure: the substitution effect and the income effect. We will see that they tell us a good deal about the labor market.

SUBSTITUTION EFFECT The substitution effect of a rise in the price of any good is the resulting switch of customers to a substitute product whose price has not risen. A rise in the price of fish, for example, can lead consumers to buy more meat. The same is true of wages and the demand for leisure. When the wage rate rises, leisure becomes more expensive relative to other commodities that consumers can buy. For instance, if you decide not to work overtime this weekend, the price you pay for that increase in leisure (the opportunity cost) is the wage you have to give up as a result of the decision. So a rise in wages makes leisure more expensive. This leads us to expect that a wage increase will induce workers to buy *less* leisure time (and *more* of other things). Thus:

The substitution effect of higher wages leads most workers to want to work more.

INCOME EFFECT A rise in the price of any good, other things equal, clearly increases the real incomes of sellers of the good and reduces the real incomes of buyers of the good. That change in income affects the amount of the good (as well as the amounts of other items) that the individual demands. This *indirect* effect of a price change on demand is called the income effect of the price change and it is especially important in the case of wages. Higher wages make consumers richer. We expect this increased wealth to raise the demand for most goods, *including leisure*. So:

> **The income effect of higher wages leads most workers to want to work less (i.e., demand more leisure), whereas the income effect of lower wages make them want to work more.**

Putting these two effects together, we conclude that some workers may react to an increase in their wage rate by working more, whereas others may react by working less. Still others will have little or no discretion over their work hours. In terms of the market as a whole, therefore, higher wages can lead to either a larger or a smaller quantity of labor supplied.

Statistical studies of this issue in the United States have arrived at the following conclusions:

- The response of labor supply to wage changes is not very strong for most workers.

- For low-wage workers, the substitution effect seems clearly dominant, so they work more when wages rise.

- For high-wage workers, the income effect just about offsets the substitution effect, so they do not work more when wages rise.

FIGURE 18–5

A Typical Labor Supply Schedule

Figure 18–5 depicts these approximate "facts." It shows labor supply rising (slightly) as wages rise up to point *A*, *as substitution effects outweigh income effects*. Thereafter, labor supply is roughly constant as wages rise and income effects become just as important as substitution effects up to point *B*. At still higher wages, above point *B*, income effects may overwhelm substitution effects, so that rising wages can even cut the quantity of labor supplied.

Thus, it is even possible that when wages are raised high enough, further wage increases will lead workers to purchase more leisure and therefore to work less (see the accompanying box, "Is Time More Precious Than Money?"). The supply curve of labor is then said to be *backward-bending*, as illustrated by the broken portion of the curve above point *B*.

Does this theory of labor supply apply to college students? A study of the hours worked by students at Princeton University found that it does.[8] Estimated substitution effects of higher wages on the labor supply of Princeton University students were positive and income effects were negative, just as the theory predicts. Apparently, substitution effects outweighed income effects by a slim margin, so that higher wages attracted a somewhat greater supply of labor. Specifically, a 10 percent rise in wages increased the hours of work of the Princeton student body by about 3 percent.

THE LABOR SUPPLY PUZZLE RESOLVED

We can now answer our earlier question: Why is it that, historically, rising wages have reduced labor supply and falling wages have increased it? We know that any wage increase sets in motion *both* a substitution effect *and* an income effect. If only the substitution effect operated, then rising wages would indeed cause people to work longer hours because the high price of leisure makes leisure less attractive. But this reasoning leaves out the income effect.

Rising wages enable the worker to provide for the family with fewer hours of work. So the worker can afford to purchase more leisure without a cut in living standards.

---

[8] Mary P. Hurley, "An Investigation of Employment among Princeton Undergraduates during the Academic Year," senior thesis submitted to the Department of Economics, May 1975.

● THE INCOME EFFECT: IS TIME MORE PRECIOUS THAN MONEY?

Plagued by stress, a growing number of people say they think time is becoming more precious than money and they're trying to slow down. . . . Five years before the end of what has been called the American Century, Americans say they have become worn down. But the exhaustion represents a paradox. They are extraordinarily stressed out even though they make more money, have more leisure time, spend more on recreation and enjoy more time-saving and efficient technology than adults did a generation or two ago. The reasons underlying this paradox are varied. Many Americans, especially married women, are working longer at their jobs now than they were then—although they have cut back on the amount of work they do around their homes. The anxieties wrought by the increasingly competitive global economy also have put many on edge, not to mention the fact that work-related intrusions via fax, E-mail or cellular phones can take place anywhere, from a kitchen to the family minivan.

In addition, . . . there's the thesis of economist Steffan Linder, whose book called *The Harried Leisure Class* argued that affluence itself engendered "an increasing scarcity of time." His argument: Productivity increases the "value" of time spent at work, and folks who want to maximize their worth then feel they should work more.

Now, though, a growing number of citizens have begun to unplug their lives from a system they feel leaves them little or no time to recharge. They have begun to retreat . . . into their private corners and demand at least some quiet time. In a comprehensive new quality-of-life poll conducted by U.S.

News and the advertising agency Bozell Worldwide Inc., half of all Americans say they have taken steps in the past five years that could simplify their lives—steps as dramatic as moving to communities with a less hectic way of life, cutting back their hours at work, lowering their commitments or expectations and declining promotions.

SOURCE: Excerpted from John Marks, "Time Out: Plagued by Stress, a Growing Number of People Say They Think Time Is Becoming More Precious Than Money and They're Trying to Slow Down," *U.S. News and World Report*, December 11, 1995, pp. 84–96.

Thus, the income effect of increasing wages induces workers to work fewer hours. Similarly, falling wages reduce the worker's income. To preserve the family's living standard, the worker must seek additional hours of work; and the worker's spouse may have to leave their children in day care and take a job.

Thus, it is the strong income effect of rising wages that may account for the fact that labor supply has responded in the "wrong" direction, with workers working ever-shorter hours as real wages rose and longer hours as wages fell.

■ WHY DO WAGES DIFFER?

Earlier in the chapter, we saw how wages are determined in a free-market economy: In a competitive labor market the equilibrium wage occurs where quantity supplied equals quantity demanded (refer back to Figure 18–3). In reality, of course, no single wage level applies to all workers. Some workers are paid very well, whereas others are forced to accept meager earnings. We all know that certain groups in our society (the young, the disadvantaged, the uneducated) earn relatively low wages and that some of our most severe social ills (poverty, crime, drug addiction) are related to this fact. But why are some wages so low while others are so high? The explanation is important, because it can help us determine what to do to help poorly paid workers increase their earnings and move up toward the income levels of the more fortunate suppliers of labor. Because the issue is so significant, we will discuss it in some detail.

In the most general terms, the explanation of wage differences is the fact that there is not one labor market but many—each with its own supply and demand curves and its own equilibrium wage. Supply-demand analysis implies that wages are relatively high in markets where demand is high relative to supply, as in Figure 18–6(a). This can happen if qualified workers are scarce or if the demand for a product is great (because labor demand is a derived demand). On the other hand, wages are comparatively low in markets where labor supply is high relative to demand, as in Figure 18–6(b). This can also be true if product demand is weak or if workers are not very productive. This is hardly startling news and doesn't tell us what we need to know about wage differentials. To make the analysis useful, we must breathe some life into the supply and demand curves.

| FIGURE 18-6 | **Wage Differentials** |

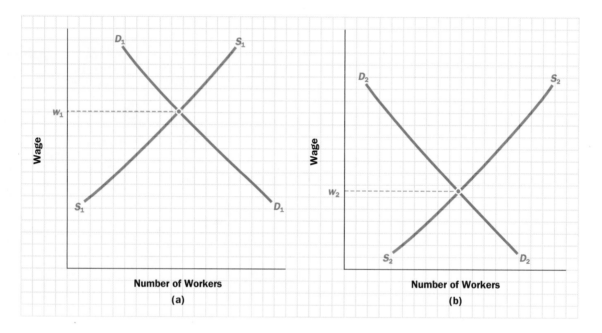

LABOR DEMAND IN GENERAL

We start with demand. Why is the demand for labor greater in some markets than in others? Because the marginal revenue product of workers depends on their *marginal physical product* (MPP), variables that influence MPP_L will influence wages. Each worker's marginal physical product depends, of course, on his or her own *abilities* and *degree of effort* on the job. But, as we have seen, the influence of these characteristics is supplemented by the *other factors of production* that workers use to produce output. Workers in American industry are more productive than workers in many other countries at least partly because they have generous supplies of machinery, natural resources, and technical know-how with which to work. As a consequence, they earn high wages. In other words, the marginal product of labor is raised by an abundance of efficient machinery and other inputs that increase the worker's effectiveness.

The marginal product of some workers can also be increased relative to that of others by superior education, training, and experience. We will go into greater detail later about the role of education in wage determination.

LABOR SUPPLY IN GENERAL

Turning next to differences in the supply of labor to different areas, industries, or occupations, it is clear that *the size of the available working population* relative to the magnitude of industrial activity in a given area is of major importance. This helps explain why wages rose so high in sparsely populated Alaska when the Alaskan oil pipeline created many new jobs, and why wages have been and remain so low in Appalachia, where industry is dormant.

Second, the *nonmonetary* attractiveness of any job will also clearly influence the supply of workers to it. (The monetary attractiveness is the wage itself, which governs movements *along* the supply curve.) Jobs that people find pleasant and satisfying—such as teaching in suburban schools—will attract a large supply of labor and will consequently pay a relatively low wage. In contrast, a premium will have to be paid to attract workers to jobs that are onerous, disagreeable, or dangerous—such as washing the windows of skyscrapers.

Finally, the amount of ability and training needed to enter a particular job or profession is relevant to its supply of labor. Brain surgeons and professional ice skaters earn generous incomes because there are few people as highly skilled as they, and because it is time-consuming and expensive to acquire these skills even for those who have the ability.

ABILITY AND EARNINGS: THE RENT COMPONENT OF WAGES

In considering the effects of ability on earnings, it is useful to distinguish between skills that can be duplicated easily and skills that cannot. If Jill Jones has an ability that Sandra Smith cannot acquire, even if she undergoes extensive training, then the wages that Jones earns will contain an element of *economic rent*. We saw this to be true in the case of basketball star Shaquille O'Neal's earnings in Chapter 17.[9]

Indeed, the salaries of professional athletes provide particularly clear examples of how economic rents can lead to huge wage differentials. Virtually anyone with moderate athletic ability can be taught to jump and shoot a basketball. But in most cases, no amount of training will teach the player to play basketball like Shaq. His high salary is a reward for his unique ability.

But many of the abilities that the market rewards generously—such as those of doctors and lawyers—clearly can be duplicated. Here the theory of rent does not apply, and we need a different explanation of the high wages that these skilled professionals earn. Once again, however, part of our analysis from Chapter 17 finds an immediate application because the acquisition of skills, through formal education and other forms of training, has much in common with business investment decisions. Why? Because the decision to gain more education in the hope of increasing future earnings involves a sacrifice of *current* income for the sake of *future* gain—precisely the hallmark of an investment decision.

INVESTMENT IN HUMAN CAPITAL

The idea that education is an investment is likely to be familiar even to students who have never thought explicitly about it. You made a conscious decision to go to college rather than to enter the labor market, and you are probably acutely aware that this decision is now costing you money—lots of money. Your tuition payments may be only a minor part of the total cost of going to college. Think of a high school friend who chose not to go to college and is now working. The salary that he or she is earning could, perhaps, have been yours. You are deliberately giving up this possible income in order to acquire more education.

In this sense, your education is an *investment* in yourself—a *human investment*. Like a firm that devotes some of its money to building a plant that will yield profits at some future date, you are investing in your own future, hoping that your college education will help you earn more than your high school-educated friend or enable you to find a more pleasant or prestigious job when you graduate. Economists call activities such as going to college investments in human capital because such activities give the human being many of the attributes of a capital investment.

Doctors and lawyers earn such high salaries partly because of their many years of training. That is, part of their wages can be construed as a *return on their (educational)*

---

[9] See the previous chapter, pages 342–343.

investments, rather than as economic rent. Unlike the case of Shaquille O'Neal, any number of people conceivably *could* become surgeons if they found the job sufficiently attractive to endure the long years of training that are required. Few, however, are willing to make such large investments of their own time, money, and energy. Consequently, the few who do become surgeons earn very generous incomes.

Economists have devoted quite a bit of attention to the acquisition of skills through human investment. An entire branch of economic theory—called *human capital theory*—analyzes an individual's decisions about education and training in exactly the same way as we analyzed a firm's decision to buy a machine or build a factory in the previous chapter. Though educational decisions can be influenced by love of learning, desire for prestige, and a variety of other factors, human capital theorists find it useful to analyze a schooling decision as if it were made purely as a business plan. The optimal length of education, from this point of view, is to stay in school until the marginal revenue (in the form of increased future income) of an additional year of schooling is exactly equal to the marginal cost.

One implication of human capital theory is that college graduates should earn substantially more than high school graduates to compensate them for their extra investments in schooling. Do they? Will your college investment pay off? Many generations of college students have supposed that it would, and recent data strongly confirm they were right. Indeed, as we noted earlier, the gap between the wages of workers with a college degree and those with a high school education has been widening. College graduates now earn twice as much as their high-school-educated peers.

> **The large income differentials earned by college graduates provide an excellent "return" on the tuition payments and sacrificed earnings that they "invested" while in school.**

Human capital theory emphasizes that jobs that require more education *must* pay higher wages if they are to attract enough workers, because people insist on a financial return on their human investments. But the theory does not address the other side of the question: What is it about more-educated people that makes firms willing to pay them higher wages? Put differently, the theory explains why the supply of educated people is limited, but does not explain why the *demand* is substantial even at high wages.

Most human capital theorists complete their analyses by assuming that students in high schools and colleges acquire particular skills that are productive in the marketplace, thereby raising the marginal revenue products of those workers. In this view, educational institutions are factories that take less productive workers as their raw materials, apply doses of training, and create more productive workers as outputs. This view of what happens in schools makes educators happy and accords well with common sense. However, a number of social scientists doubt that this is quite how schooling raises earning power.

EDUCATION AND EARNINGS: DISSENTING VIEWS

Just why do jobs with stiffer educational requirements typically pay higher wages? The commonsense view that educating people makes them more productive is not universally accepted.

EDUCATION AS A SORTING MECHANISM One alternative view denies that the educational process teaches students anything directly relevant to their subsequent performance on jobs. In this view, people differ in ability when they enter the school system and differ in more or less the same way when they leave. What the educational system does, according to this theory, is to *sort* individuals by ability. Skills like intelligence and self-discipline that lead to success in schools, it is argued, are closely related to the skills that lead to success in jobs. As a result, the abler individuals stay in school longer and perform better. Prospective employers know this, and consequently seek to hire those whom the school system has suggested will be the most productive workers.

THE DUAL LABOR MARKET THEORY   Another view of the linkages among education, ability, and earnings is part of a much broader theory of how the labor market operates—the theory of *dual labor markets*. Proponents of this theory suggest that there are two very different types of labor markets with relatively little mobility between them.

The "primary labor market" is where most of the economy's "good jobs" are—jobs like business management, computer programming, and skilled crafts that are interesting and offer considerable possibilities for career advancement. The educational system helps decide which individuals get assigned to the primary labor market and, for those who make it, greater educational achievement does indeed offer financial rewards.

The privileged workers who wind up in the primary labor market are offered opportunities for additional training on the job; they augment their skills by experience and by learning from their fellow workers; and they progress in successive steps to more responsible, better-paying positions. Where jobs in the primary labor market are concerned, dual labor market theorists believe that education really is productive. But they also think that admission to the primary labor market depends in part on social position, and that firms probably care more about steady work habits and punctuality than about reading, writing, and arithmetic.

Everything is quite different in the "secondary labor market"—where we find all the "bad jobs." Jobs like cleaning and fast-food services, which are often the only ones inner-city residents can find, offer low pay, few fringe benefits, and virtually no training to improve the workers' skills. They are dead-end jobs with little or no hope for promotion or advancement. As a result, lateness, absenteeism, and pilferage are expected as a matter of course, so that workers in the secondary labor market tend to develop the bad work habits that confirm the prejudices of those who assigned them to inferior jobs in the first place.

In the secondary labor market, increased education leads neither to higher wages nor to increased protection from unemployment—benefits generally offered elsewhere in the labor market. For this reason, workers in the secondary market have little incentive to invest in education.

In sum, we have a well-established fact—that people with more education generally earn higher wages—but little agreement on what accounts for this fact. Probably, there is some truth to all of the proposed explanations.

THE EFFECTS OF MINIMUM WAGE LEGISLATION

As we have observed, the "labor market" is really composed of many submarkets for labor of different types, each with its own supply and demand curves. One particular labor market always seems to have higher unemployment than the labor force as a whole: the job market for teenagers.

Figure 18–7 shows that teenage unemployment rates have consistently been much higher than the overall unemployment rate, and black teenagers have fared worse than white teenagers. For the most part, however, the three unemployment rates have moved up and down together, as this chart shows. It indicates that whenever the unemployment rate for all workers goes up or down, the teenage (defined here as a person aged 16 to 19 years) unemployment rate almost always moves in the same direction, but more dramatically.

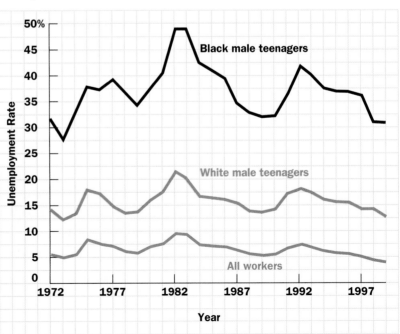

FIGURE 18-7

The Teenage Unemployment Problem

SOURCE: *Economic Report of the President* (Washington, D.C.: U.S. Government Printing Office, various years).

Thus, when things are generally bad, things are much, much worse for teenage workers, and especially for black teenage workers. Despite social and legislative pressures against race discrimination, efforts to improve the quality of education available to children in the inner cities, and many related programs, there has been no relative improvement in black teenage unemployment in recent years.

One reason is that teenagers generally have not completed their educations and have little job experience, hence their marginal revenue products tend to be relatively low. Until recently, many economists argued that this fact, together with minimum wage laws that prevent teenagers from accepting wages commensurate with their low marginal revenue products, is the main cause of high teenage unemployment. The reasoning is that legally imposed high wages make it too expensive to hire teenagers. Recent studies of the data suggest, however, that a rise in minimum wage produces little, if any, cut in demand for teen labor.

We should also note that inflation has eaten into the real value of the minimum wage over the years. Figure 18–8 shows clearly that after 48 years of sporadic increases in the nominal minimum wage rate, the real (inflation-adjusted) rate has remained virtually unchanged.

FIGURE 18-8

The Minimum Wage, 1950–1999

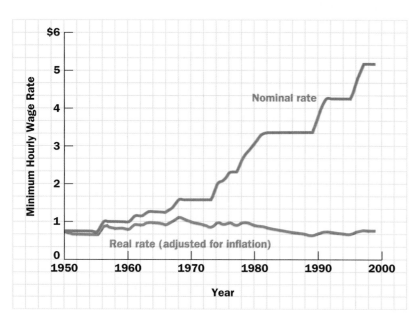

NOTE: Nominal rates deflated by CPI (1950 = 100).

SOURCE: U.S. Bureau of the Census, *Statistical Abstract of the United States,* (Washington, D.C.: U.S. Government Printing Office, various years), and U.S. Bureau of Labor Statistics, http://stats.bls.gov/, accessed June 2000.

"As far as I'm concerned, they can do what they want with the minimum wage, just as long as they keep their hands off the maximum wage."

■ UNIONS AND COLLECTIVE BARGAINING

Our analysis of competitive labor markets has so far not dealt with one rather distinctive feature of the markets for labor: The supply of labor is not at all competitive in many labor markets; instead it is controlled by a labor monopoly, a **labor union.**

Although they are significant, unions in the United States are not nearly as important as is popularly supposed. For example, most people who are unfamiliar with the data are astonished to learn that about 14 percent of American workers belong to unions. This percentage is much lower than it was in the heyday of unionism in the mid-1950s, when about a quarter of all workers were union members. Figure 18–9 shows that in 1930, unions had enrolled just under 7 percent of the U.S. labor force, and by 1933 this figure had slipped to barely above 5 percent. Unionization took off with President Franklin D. Roosevelt's New Deal, reaching almost 16 percent of the labor force by 1939. It then drifted irregularly upward to a peak of about 25 to 26 percent of all workers in the mid-1950s, from which it has since fallen more or less steadily back to just under 14 percent in 1998. Since the 1950s, the unionization rate has fallen with few interruptions.

Why has the extent of unionization in the United States been declining? One reason is the shift of the U.S. labor force (like that of every other industrial country) into service industries and out of manufacturing, where unions traditionally had their base. In addition, deregulation forced airlines, trucking companies, and firms in other industries to compete more intensely, and it may thus have influenced the firms to hire less expensive nonunion labor.

In addition, American workers' preferences seem to have shifted away from unions. The increasing share of women in the labor force may have contributed to this trend, because women have traditionally been less prone than men to join unions.

Finally, American unions have been under increasing pressure in the 1990s owing to stronger competition both at home and from abroad. In response, firm after firm has closed plants and eliminated jobs. The downsizing trend has made it even more difficult for unions to win concessions that improve the economic positions of their members. That, in turn, has reduced the attractiveness of union membership.

Unionization is much less prevalent in the United States than it is in most other industrialized countries. For example, 33 percent of German workers and 90 percent of Swedish workers belong to unions.[10] The differences are quite striking and doubtless have something to do with our tradition of "rugged individualism."

The main sector of the U.S. economy in which the unions are still fairly healthy is government employment. City, state, and federal employees join unions in relatively large numbers (about 37 percent of public-sector workers are union members). Perhaps this higher union participation arises because the job opportunities for public-sector employees are controlled by political forces, and politicians find it far harder to resist the unions than private firms do.[11] However, here too, the

A **labor union** is an organization made up of a group of workers (usually with the same specialization, such as plumbing or costume design, or in the same industry). The unions represent the workers in negotiations with employers over issues such as wages, vacations, and sick leave.

FIGURE 18–9

Unionization in the United States, 1930–1999

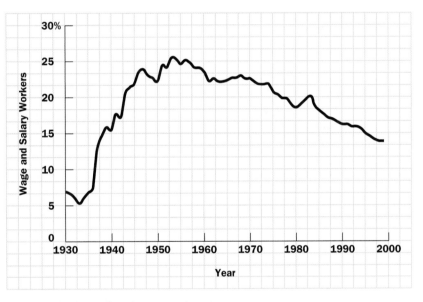

SOURCES: U.S. Department of Labor, Bureau of Labor Statistics, *Employment and Earnings* (Washington, D.C.: U.S. Government Printing Office, January issues, various years); and http://stats.bls.gov, accessed June 2000.

---

[10] Unpublished data provided by William McMichael, Division of Foreign Labor Statistics, U.S. Department of Labor, February 1998.

[11] U.S. Census Bureau, *Statistical Abstract of the United States: 1998*, 118th ed. (Washington, D.C.: U.S. Government Printing Office, 1998).

● **THE WAY IT WAS**

The calamitous Triangle Shirtwaist Factory fire of 1911, in which 146 women and girls lost their lives, was a landmark in American labor history. It galvanized public opinion behind the movement to improve conditions, hours, and wages in the sweatshops. Pauline Newman went to work in the factory, located on what is now New York University's campus, at the age of eight. Many of her friends lost their lives in the fire. She went on to become an organizer and executive of the newly formed International Ladies Garment Workers' Union. In her words:

> We started work at seven-thirty in the morning, and during the busy season we worked until nine in the evening. They didn't pay you any overtime and they didn't give you anything for supper money. . . .
>
> The employers didn't recognize anyone working for them as a human being. You were not allowed to sing. . . . We weren't allowed to talk to each other. . . . If you went to the toilet and you were there longer than the floor lady thought you should be, you would be laid off for half a day and sent home. And, of course, that meant no pay. You were not allowed to have your lunch on the fire escape in the summertime. The door was locked to keep us in. That's why so many people were trapped when the fire broke out. . . .
>
> You were expected to work every day if they needed you and the pay was the same whether you worked extra or not.
>
> Conditions were dreadful in those days. We didn't have anything. . . . There was no welfare, no pension, no unemployment insurance. There was nothing. . . . There was so much feeling against unions then. The judges, when one of our girls came before him, said to her: "You're not striking against your employer, you know, young lady. You're striking against God," and sentenced her to two weeks.
>
> I wasn't at the Triangle Shirtwaist Factory when the fire broke out, but a lot of my friends were. . . . The thing that bothered me was the employers got a lawyer. How anyone could have *defended* them! Because I'm quite sure that the fire was planned for insurance purposes. And no one is going to convince me otherwise. And when they testified that the door to the fire escape was open, it was a lie! It was never open. Locked all the time. One hundred and forty-six people sacrificed, and the judge fined Blank and Harris seventy-five dollars!

The Triangle Factory, now part of New York University

THE PROBLEM PERSISTS

The following excerpt from *Time* magazine shows that unsafe working conditions continue to produce tragedies, even in this day and age:

---

unions are under siege as more and more government services are contracted out to private businesses. For example, the state of New Jersey used the threat of turning highway toll collection over to private enterprise as an effective bargaining chip in 1995 negotiations with the toll-collectors' union.

THE DEVELOPMENT OF UNIONISM IN AMERICA

Serious unionism in the United States is not much more than a century old. The current union structure began to take shape in 1881 with the founding of the American Federation of Labor (AFL) by Samuel Gompers. Working conditions then were incredibly bad by today's standards, and unscrupulous practices by many employers fostered the growth of unions (see the accompanying box, "The Way It Was").

Gompers strongly believed that unions should be nonpolitical organizations seeking more pay, better working conditions, longer vacations, and so on. He also believed that unions should be organized along craft lines—carpenters in one union, plumbers in another—rather than trying to include all types of workers within a given industry. The AFL grew steadily from about 1900 until the 1920s, went into decline during the Roaring Twenties, but then grew rapidly thanks to the favorable legislation of the Roosevelt administration in the 1930s. The National

Nobody who worked at the Imperial Food Products plant in Hamlet, North Carolina, had much love for the place. The job—cooking, weighing and packing fried chicken parts for fast-food restaurants—was hot, greasy and poorly paid. The conveyor belts moved briskly, and the rest breaks were so strictly timed that going to the bathroom at the wrong moment could lead to dismissal. But in the sleepy town of 6,200 there was not much else in the way of work. So most of the plant's 200 employees, predominantly black and female, were thankful just to have the minimum-wage job. Until last week, that is.

The morning shift had just started when an overhead hydraulic line ruptured, spilling its volatile fluid onto the floor. Gas burners under the frying vats ignited the vapors and turned the 30,000-sq.-ft. plant into an inferno of flame and thick, yellow smoke. Panicked employees rushed for emergency exits only to find several of them locked. "I thought I was gone, until a man broke the lock off," says Letha Terry, one of the survivors. Twenty-five of Terry's fellow employees were not so lucky. Their bodies were found clustered around the blocked doorways or trapped in the freezer.

The disaster brought to light the mostly invisible body count of the American workplace. By some estimates, more than 10,000 workers die each year from on-the-job injuries—about 30 every day. Perhaps 70,000 more are permanently disabled. The fire also exposed the weaknesses of measures for ensuring job safety. The 11-year-old Imperial Food Products plant had never been inspected. Like a lot of American workplaces, it fell through the gaping cracks of a system in which there are too few inspectors, penalties are mostly trifling and the procedures for reporting dangerous conditions can leave workers to choose between risking their jobs and risking their lives.

SOURCE: Excerpted from Joan Morrison and Charlotte Fox Zabusky, *American Mosaic: The Immigrant Experience in the Words of Those Who Lived It* (New York: E. P. Dutton, 1980), reprinted by permission of the publisher, E. P. Dutton, Inc.; and Richard Lacayo, "Death on the Shop Floor: A Murderous Fire in a North Carolina Poultry Plant Underscores the Dangers of America's Workplaces," *Time,* September 16, 1991, p. 28.

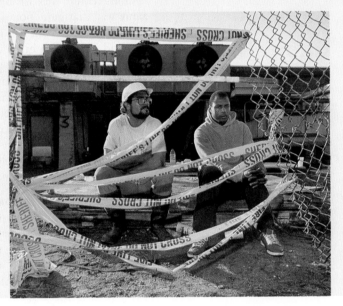

Labor Relations Act (Wagner Act) in 1935 guaranteed workers the right to form unions and to choose unions to represent them in collective bargaining. It also set up the National Labor Relations Board (NLRB) to protect labor from "unfair labor practices" by employers. Today the NLRB oversees elections in firms to determine which union will represent the workers. It can also force employers to take back workers who it considers to have been fired unjustly.

The favorable public attitude toward unions soured somewhat after World War II, perhaps because of the rash of strikes that took place in 1946. One result of these strikes was the Taft-Hartley Act of 1947, which specified and outlawed certain "unfair labor practices" by unions and which sought to shift some of labor's power back to management. Specifically, the act severely limited **closed shops** that hire only union members; permitted state governments to ban the **union shop,** an arrangement that *requires* employees to join the union; and provided for court injunctions to delay strikes that threaten the national interest for an 80-day "cooling-off" period.

Today, the character of American unionism is still somewhat unsettled. Unions are struggling very hard to make inroads into labor markets that by tradition have not been unionized—such as the agricultural and white-collar office markets. They have achieved notable successes in organizing teachers, government employees, and many other types of white-collar workers. Between 1983 and 1997, the number of

A **closed shop** is an arrangement that permits only union members to be hired.

A **union shop** is an arrangement under which nonunion workers may be hired, but then must join the union within a specified period of time.

managerial and professional workers belonging to unions increased from 20 million to 32 million.[12]

U.S. labor unions are very different from those in Europe and Japan. For one thing, U.S. unions are strongly committed to capitalism and have rarely espoused socialism—unlike their western European counterparts. American unions also often see themselves as adversaries of management, unlike Japanese unions. This country's century-long tradition of hostile labor-management relations has impeded current attempts to emulate the Japanese model of labor-management cooperation. However, several U.S. plants that are owned and run by Japanese companies reportedly have achieved an unprecedented degree of trust and support between the labor force and management. There are other cases though in which such firms have had extremely poor labor relations. In general, U.S. labor still seems to feel that American employers are all too likely to adopt unfair practices unless they are restrained by powerful unions.

UNIONS AS LABOR MONOPOLIES

Unions require that we alter our economic analysis of the labor market in much the same way that monopolies required us to alter our analysis of the goods market (see Chapter 12). Remember that a monopoly seller of goods selects the point on its demand curve that maximizes its profits. Much the same idea applies to a union, which is, after all, a monopoly seller of labor. It too faces a demand curve—derived this time from the marginal revenue product schedules of firms—and can choose the point on that curve that suits it best.

The problem for the economist trying to analyze union behavior—and perhaps also for the union leader trying to select a course of action—is how to decide which point on the demand curve is "best." There is no obvious single goal analogous to profit maximization that clearly delineates what a union should do. Instead there are a number of *alternative* goals that sound plausible.

ALTERNATIVE UNION GOALS   The union leadership may, for example, decide that the size of the union is pretty well fixed and try to force employers to pay the highest wage they will pay without firing any of the union members. But this is a high-risk strategy for a union. Firms forced to pay such high wages will be at a competitive disadvantage compared with firms that have nonunion labor, and they may even be forced to shut down. Alternatively, union leaders may assign priority to increasing the size of their union. They may even try to make employment as large as possible by accepting a wage just above the competitive level. One way, but certainly not the only way, to strike a balance between the conflicting goals of maximizing wages and maximizing employment is to maximize the product of the two—which is the total earnings of all workers taken together.

The basic conclusion of these alternative possible goals for unions is this: Even if unions, as monopoly sellers of labor, have the power to push wages above the competitive level, they can normally only achieve such wage increases by reducing the number of jobs, because the demand curve for labor is downward sloping. Just as monopolists must limit their outputs to push up their prices, so unions must restrict employment to push up wages.

In some exceptional cases, however, a union may be able to achieve wage gains without sacrificing employment. To do this, the union must be able to exercise effective control over the demand curve for labor. Figure 18–10 illustrates such a possibility. Union actions push the demand curve outward from D_0D_0 to D_1D_1, simultaneously raising both wages and employment. Typically, this is difficult to do. One way to do it is by *featherbedding*—forcing

---

FIGURE 18–10

Union Control over the Demand Curve

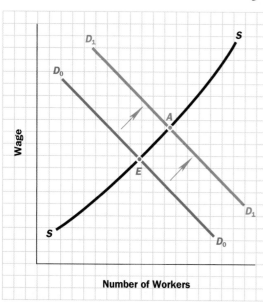

Wage

Number of Workers

---

[12] U.S. Census Bureau, *Statistical Abstract of the United States*, various years (Washington, D.C.: U.S. Government Printing Office).

management to employ more workers than it really needs.[13] Quite the opposite technique is to institute a campaign to raise worker productivity, which some unions seem to have been able to do. Alternatively, the union can try to raise the demand for the company's product either by flexing its political muscle (for example, by obtaining legislation to reduce foreign competition) or by appealing to the public to buy union products.

HAVE UNIONS REALLY RAISED WAGES? To what extent do union members actually earn higher wages than nonmembers? The consensus would probably surprise most people. Economists estimate that most union members' wages are about 15 percent above those of nonmembers who are otherwise identical (in skills, geographical locations, and so on). Though certainly not negligible, we can hardly consider this a huge differential. Narrowing the gap even further is the fact that nonunion workers do not have to pay the dues that are required of union members.

This 15 percent differential does not mean, however, that unions have raised wages no more than 15 percent. Some observers believe that union activity has also raised wages of nonunion workers by forcing nonunion employers to compete harder for their workers. If so, the differential between union and nonunion workers will be less than the amount by which unions raised wages overall.

MONOPSONY AND BILATERAL MONOPOLY

Our analysis thus far oversimplifies matters in several important respects. For one thing, it envisions a market situation in which one powerful union is dealing with many powerless employers: We have assumed that the labor market is monopolized on the selling side but competitive on the buying side. Some industries more or less fit this model. The giant Teamsters' union negotiates with a trucking industry consisting of thousands of firms, most of them quite small and powerless. Similarly, most of the unions within the construction industry are much larger than the firms with which they bargain.

But many cases simply do not fit the model. The huge auto manufacturing corporations do not stand idly by while the United Automobile Workers (UAW) picks its favorite point on the demand curve for auto workers. Nor does the steelworkers' union sit across the bargaining table from representatives of a perfectly competitive industry. In these and other industries, although the union certainly has a good deal of monopoly power over labor supply, the firms also have some **monopsony** power over labor demand. This means that the firms may deliberately reduce the quantity of labor they demand as a way to force down the equilibrium level of wages. We can calculate the profit-maximizing restriction in the quantity of labor the same way we determined a monopolist's profit-maximizing restriction of output in Chapter 12.

Analysts find it difficult to predict the wage and employment decisions that will emerge when both the buying and selling side of a market are monopolized—a situation called **bilateral monopoly**. The difficulties here are similar to those we encountered in considering the behavior of oligopolistic industries in Chapter 13. Just as one oligopolist is acutely aware that rivals are likely to react to anything the oligopolistic employer does, a union dealing with a monopsony employer knows that any move it makes will elicit a countermove by the firm, and this knowledge makes the first decision that much more complicated. In practice, the outcome of bilateral monopoly depends partly on economic logic, partly on the relative power of the union and man-

A **monopsony** is a market situation in which there is only one buyer.

A **bilateral monopoly** is a market situation in which there is both a monopoly on the selling side and a monopsony on the buying side.

---

[13] The best-known example of featherbedding involved the railroad unions, which for years forced management to keep "firemen" in the cabs of diesel engines, in which there were no burning fires. Similarly, the musicians' union in New York City forces Broadway producers who use certain theaters to employ a minimum number of musicians—whether or not they actually play music. Of course, it is not only unionized labor that has tried to create an artificial demand for its services. Lawyers, doctors, and business firms, among others, have sought ways to induce consumers to buy more of their products and services. *Exercise:* Can you think of ways in which they have done this?

agement, partly on the skill and preparation of the negotiators, and partly on luck. (For an example of the bargaining process that can occur in a bilateral monopoly in the real world, see the accompanying box, "Bargaining in a Bilateral Monopoly: Millionaires versus Billionaires.")

Still, we can be a bit more concrete about the outcome of the wage determination process under bilateral monopoly. A monopsonist employer unrestrained by a union will use its market power to force wages down below the competitive level, just as a monopoly seller uses its market power to force prices higher. It accomplishes this by reducing its demand for labor below what would otherwise be the profit-maximizing amount, thereby cutting both wages and the number of workers employed.

However, a union may be in a position to prevent this from happening. It can deliberately set a floor on wages, pledging its members not to work at all at any wage level below this floor. So, a union may force the monopsony employer to pay higher wages and, simultaneously, to hire more workers than the employer otherwise would.

Even though we can hardly find examples of industries that are pure monopsonists in their dealings with labor, these conclusions do bear some importance in reality. The fact is that large, oligopolistic firms do often engage in one-on-one wage bargaining with the unions of their employees, and there is reason to believe that the resulting bargaining process closely resembles the workings of the bilateral monopoly model that we just described.

COLLECTIVE BARGAINING AND STRIKES

The process by which unions and management settle on the terms of a labor contract is called *collective bargaining*. Unfortunately, nothing as straightforward as a supply-demand diagram can tell us what wage level will emerge from a collective bargaining session.

Furthermore, actual collective bargaining sessions range over many more issues than wages. For example, fringe benefits such as pensions, health and life insurance, overtime pay, seniority privileges, and work conditions are often crucial issues. Many labor contracts specify in great detail the rights of labor and management to set work conditions—and also provide elaborate procedures for resolving grievances and disputes. This list could go on and on. The final contract that emerges from collective bargaining may well run to many pages of fine print.

With the issues so varied and complex, and with the stakes so high, it is no wonder that both labor and management employ skilled professionals who specialize in preparing for and carrying out these negotiations. The bargaining in these sessions is often heated, with outcomes riding as much on personalities and the skills of the negotiators as on cool-headed logic and economic facts. Negotiations may last well into the night, with each side making threats and seeming to try to wear out the other side. Unions, for their part, generally threaten strikes or work slowdowns. Firms counter that they would rather face a strike than give in, or they may even threaten to close the plant without a strike. (This is called a *lockout*.)

MEDIATION AND ARBITRATION   When the public interest is seriously affected, or when the union and firm reach an impasse, government agencies may well send in a *mediator*, whose job is to try to speed up the negotiation process. As an impartial observer, the mediator sits down with both sides separately to discuss their problems and then tries to persuade each to make concessions. At some stage, when an agreement looks possible, she or he may call them back together for another bargaining session in the mediator's presence. Mediators, however, have no power to force a settlement. Their success hinges on their ability to smooth ruffled feathers and to find common ground.

Sometimes in cases in which unions and firms simply cannot agree but neither wants a strike, differences are finally settled by *arbitration*—the appointment of an impartial individual empowered to settle the issues that negotiation could not resolve. This happens often, for example, in wage negotiations in professional sports

● BARGAINING IN A BILATERAL MONOPOLY: MILLIONAIRES VERSUS BILLIONAIRES

The 1998–1999 labor dispute between the National Basketball Association and the National Basketball Players Association lasted 191 days before the two sides reached a settlement—and it seems that the owners, not the players, won the match in "sudden death overtime."

The relationship between professional basketball players and the owners' association is classic example of *bilateral monopoly*—a market with a monopoly on the selling side and a monopsony on the buying side. The players' union controls the sale of professional basketball talent, and the owners have a virtual monopsony on the purchase of that talent.* A labor dispute in a bilateral monopoly market is often won by the side with the craftiest negotiator and the greatest ability to wait for the right deal. In the case of pro basketball, the owners seem to have held those advantages. With only hours to go before the entire season was to be canceled, NBA commissioner David Stern and Billy Hunter, the executive director of the player's union, reached an agreement that allowed them to salvage an abbreviated season. While Stern claimed that he had given too many concessions to the players, *Sports Illustrated* believes that Stern was the shrewdest negotiator. The agreement makes the NBA the only professional sports league with a maximum salary: under the new agreement, the maximum salary in the first year of a new contract will be $14 million, and only players with ten seasons of experience will be eligible. For the average NBA player, who earns much less than superstars like Shaquille O'Neal or Scottie Pippen, the agreement spells out a pay scale based on seniority, preventing 22-year-old newcomers from negotiating eight-figure salaries. The team owners won other victories, such as the ability to retain their draft choices for longer periods before those players became eligible for free agency and a reduction in total league revenues paid to players.

Although the players' union won a few concessions, such as an increase in the minimum salary that is paid to league benchwarmers, the team owners seem to have gotten a better bargain. It is not surprising that the players were more eager to settle the dispute, because they collectively sacrificed a half billion in salary during the strike, while the team owners saved the same amount by not paying their players. The owners were further emboldened by their television contracts, which guaranteed that they were paid, even while the season was on hold.

*But not a pure monopsony, because American basketball players can join teams in other countries.

SOURCE: Steve Springer, "Season's Greetings: How Much They're Losing; Owners Get TV Money, But Might Not Keep It," *Los Angeles Times*, December 18, 1998; Phil Taylor and Jackie MacMullan, "Pro Basketball: To The Victor Belong the Spoils," *Sports Illustrated*, January 18, 1999; and United Press International, "Report: NBA Labor Impasse Resolved," January 6, 1999.

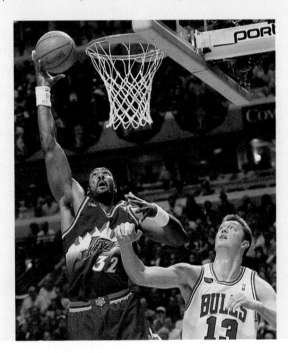

or for municipal jobs such as police and firefighters. For instance, a federal arbitrator was called in to resolve the labor dispute between American Airlines and its flight attendants' union. In fact, in some vital sectors in which a strike is too injurious to the public interest, the labor contract or the law may stipulate that there must be *compulsory arbitration* if the two parties cannot agree. However, both labor and management are normally reluctant to accept this procedure.

STRIKES   Most collective bargaining situations do not lead to strikes. But the right to strike, and to take a strike, remain fundamentally important tools in the bargaining process. Imagine, for example, a firm bargaining with a union that was prohibited from striking. The union's bargaining position would probably be quite weak. On the other hand, a firm that always capitulated rather than suffer a strike would be virtually at the mercy of the union. So strikes—or, more precisely, the possibility of strikes—serve an important economic purpose.

Fortunately, however, the incidence of strikes is not nearly so common as many

FIGURE 18-11

Work-Time Lost in the United States because of Strikes, 1948–1999

SOURCE: U.S. Department of Labor, Bureau of Labor Statistics, *Monthly Labor Review,* various issues, and http://stats.bls.gov.

people believe. Figure 18–11 reports the percentage of work time lost as a result of strikes in the United States from 1948 to 1998. This fraction varies greatly from year to year, but is never very large. The worst year for strikes was 1946, and it is probably no coincidence that the Taft-Hartley law was enacted the following year. The fraction of total work time lost has been under one-tenth of 1 percent since 1970 and has now dwindled to insignificance at about *one-hundredth of 1 percent.* Despite the headline-grabbing nature of major national strikes, the total amount of work time lost to strikes is truly trivial—far less, for example, than the time lost to coffee breaks! Compared with other nations, the United States suffers more from strikes than, say, Japan, but it has many fewer strikes than such countries as Italy and Canada (see Figure 18–12).

FIGURE 18-12

The Incidence of Strikes in Eight Industrial Countries, 1991–1995

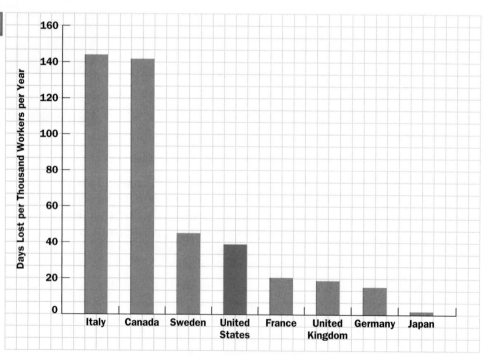

NOTE: Five-year averages (1991–1995), except for Italy (1991–1994) and the United Kingdom (1992–1995).

SOURCE: International Labour Office, *1996 Yearbook of Labour Statistics,* Geneva: 1996.

Issue Revisited: Foreign Competition, Technology, and American Jobs: Are Union Fears Justified?

Unions have actively taken up the issues we discussed at the beginning of this chapter. Early in the 1990s trade agreements worldwide seemed to threaten U.S. workers' jobs—union jobs in particular. But historical evidence raises questions about these union fears.

First, we must recognize that although one effect of cheap foreign products may be to hold down American dollar wages, these inexpensive products also help to raise *real* wages. Lower product prices also mean that U.S. wages command more goods per dollar. If cars, televisions, and foods become cheaper because of imports, a given wage can buy larger quantities of these items. Besides, in comparison with most other industrial economies, the U.S. imports a relatively small proportion of its GDP, yet wages in those other countries have risen faster than those in the United States for many decades. Indeed, historically, real wages in the United States grew most rapidly when wages in the countries from which the United States received many of its imports were much further behind U.S. wages than they are now. In other words, when foreign labor was really cheap, U.S. wages were growing most rapidly.

The second part of the story, related to technological progress, also raises questions. Labor-saving innovation has played a leading role in the economic history of the United States. In the course of the past century, the productivity of the U.S. labor force has grown more than 12-fold. This means that 11 out of 12 U.S. workers could have been fired without any loss in production. Yet unemployment in the United States has shown no rising trend over this period. As we write this book, the U.S. unemployment rate is the lowest it has been in 30 years. Evidently, technological progress, which has stimulated the demand for products, has not cut the demand for the workers who turn out those products. That is because, by making goods and services cheaper and better, technical progress has always stimulated the demand for the improved commodities. But increased demand for goods and services translates into a demand for labor. Thus, in terms of demand for labor, there are two sides to technical progress. And in the long run, throughout our history, its effects have generally included rising real wages, but no trend toward increased unemployment.

SUMMARY

1. In a free market, the wage rate and the level of employment are determined by the interaction of supply and demand. Workers in great demand or short supply command high wages. Conversely, low wages go to workers who are in abundant supply or to workers who have skills that are not in great demand.

2. The demand curve for labor, like the demand curve for any factor of production, is derived from the marginal revenue product curve. It slopes downward because of the "law" of diminishing marginal returns.

3. The demand curve for labor can be shifted upward by an increase in education or on-the-job training that raise the workers' marginal physical products or by a rise in demand for those products that raises their price and therefore also increases labor's MRP.

4. Labor-saving innovations may either raise or lower worker's wages and available jobs in the short run. But because they are tantamount to increased productivity, in the long run they generally raise the incomes of workers along with those of other members of the community.

5. The supply of labor is determined by free choices made by individuals. The supply curve can be shifted so that more labor is supplied at any given wage level if there are devel-

opments such as increased labor force participation, as when women find it more desirable to hold jobs.

6. Because of conflicting *income and substitution effects*, the quantity of labor supplied may rise or fall as a result of an increase in wages. Historical data show that hours of work per week have fallen as wages have risen, suggesting that income effects may be dominant in the long run.

7. Some valuable skills are virtually impossible to duplicate. People who possess such skills will earn *economic rents* as part of their wages.

8. But most skills can be acquired by means of *investment in human capital*, such as education.

9. *Human capital theory* assumes that people make educational decisions in much the same way as businesses make investment decisions, and it tacitly assumes that people learn things in school that increase their productivity in jobs.

10. Other theories of the effects of education on earnings deny that schooling actually raises productivity. For example, one view is that the educational system primarily sorts people according to their abilities.

11. According to the theory of *dual labor markets*, there are two distinct types of labor markets, with very little mobility

between them. The primary labor market contains the "good" jobs where wages are high, prospects for advancement are good, and higher education pays off. The secondary labor market contains the "bad" jobs with low wages, little opportunity for promotion, and little return to education.

12. Less than 14 percent of all American workers belong to *unions*, which we can think of as monopoly sellers of labor. Compared with many other industrialized countries, unions in the United States are younger, less widespread, and less political.

13. For the most part, unions probably force wages to be higher and employment to be lower than they would be in a competitive labor market.

14. *Collective bargaining* agreements between labor and management are complex documents covering much more than employment and wage rates.

15. Strikes play an important role in collective bargaining as a way of dividing the fruits of economic activity between big business and big labor. Fortunately, strikes are not nearly so common as is often supposed.

16. For about two decades Americans have experienced three noteworthy trends: (a) a decline in union membership of more than 30 percent, (b) a steady fall in real wages partly offset by rising fringe benefits, and (c) a rise in the income gap between well-paid and poorly paid workers.

KEY TERMS

Marginal revenue product of labor (MRP$_L$) 354

Investment in human capital 355

Income and substitution effects 359

Backward-bending supply curve 360

Economic rent 363

Human capital theory 364

Dual labor markets 365

Minimum wage law 366

Labor union 367

Taft-Hartley Act (1947) 369

Closed shop 369

Union shop 369

Monopsony 371

Bilateral monopoly 371

Collective bargaining 372

Mediation 372

Arbitration 372

QUESTIONS FOR REVIEW

1. Colleges are known to pay rather low wages for student labor. Can this be explained by the operation of supply and demand in the local labor markets? Is the concept of monopsony of any use? How might things differ if students formed a union?

2. College professors are highly skilled (or at least highly educated!) laborers. Yet their wages are not very high. Is this a refutation of the marginal productivity theory?

3. The following table shows the number of pizzas that can be produced by a large pizza parlor employing various numbers of pizza chefs.

Number of Chefs	Number of Pizzas per Day
1	40
2	64
3	82
4	92
5	100
6	92

a. Find the marginal physical product schedule of chefs.

b. Assuming a price of $9 per pizza, find the marginal revenue product schedule.

c. If chefs are paid $100 per day, how many chefs will this pizza parlor employ? How would your answer change if chefs' wages rose to $125 per day?

d. Suppose the price of pizza rises from $9 to $12. Show

what happens to the derived demand curve for chefs.

4. Discuss the concept of the financial rate of return to a college education. If this return is less than the return on a bank account, does that mean you should quit college? Why might you wish to stay in school anyway? Are there circumstances under which it might be rational not to go to college, even when the financial returns to college are very high?

5. It seems to be a well-established fact that workers with more years of education typically receive higher wages. What are some possible reasons for this?

6. Approximately what fraction of the American labor force belongs to unions? (Try asking this question of a person who has never studied economics.) Why do you think this fraction is so low?

7. What are some reasonable goals for a union? Use the tools of supply and demand to explain how a union might pursue its goals, whatever they are. Consider a union that has been in the news recently. What was it trying to accomplish?

8. "Strikes are simply intolerable and should be outlawed." Comment on this statement.

9. In which of the following industries is wage determination most plausibly explained by the model of perfect competition? The model of pure monopoly? The model of bilateral monopoly?

a. Odd-job repairs in private homes

b. Manufacture of low-priced clothing for children

c. Steel manufacturing.

10. In a bitter strike battle between Eastern Airlines and several of its unions, it was clear from the beginning that the airline was in serious financial trouble. The airline was, indeed, eventually forced to close down at the cost of many jobs.

Discuss what might nevertheless have led the unions to hold out so tenaciously.

11. Can you think of some types of workers whose marginal products probably were raised by computerization? Are there any whose marginal products were probably reduced? Can you characterize the difference between the two types of jobs in general terms?

12. European labor unions have traditionally had a strong socialistic orientation. How would you guess this is likely to be affected by the movement of countries in eastern Europe toward market economies?

13. What, if anything, do you think is the effect of long-term unemployment on crime rates? What about short-term unemployment?

14. Since about 1980, GDP per capita (that is, the average real income per person) in the United States has risen fairly substantially. Yet real wages have failed to rise. What do you think may explain this?

CHAPTER

19

The white man knows how to make everything,
but he does not know how to distribute it.

Sitting Bull

POVERTY, INEQUALITY, AND DISCRIMINATION

The last two chapters analyzed how factor prices— wages, rents, and interest rates—are determined in a market economy. One reason for concern with this issue is that these payments determine the *incomes* of the people who own the factors, and income is a primary determinant of well-being. The study of factor pricing is, therefore, an indirect way to learn about how the market *distributes income* among individuals.

In this chapter, we turn to the problem of income distribution more directly. Specifically, we seek answers to the following questions: How unequal are incomes in the United States, and why? How can society decide rationally on how much equality it wants? And, once this decision is made, what policies are available to pursue this goal?

Issue: Ending Welfare As We Know It

For decades, America's main programs for the poor were widely decried as "the welfare mess," a vague term indicating that the programs were too bureaucratic, too expensive, and too ineffective. Some critics went so far as to claim that welfare hurts the very people it was designed to help by, for example, encouraging out-of-wedlock births and fostering a culture of dependence on the state. When candidate Bill Clinton campaigned on a promise to "end welfare as we know it" in 1992, many Americans shared his dissatisfaction with the system.

About four years later, Clinton's campaign pledge turned into reality when Congress passed and the president signed into law a complete overhaul of the federal welfare system. This so-called welfare reform abolished Aid to Families with Dependent Children (AFDC), which had been the main program providing cash grants to poor families since the 1930s. Its replacement, called Temporary Assistance to Needy Families (TANF), limits a family's eligibility for welfare checks to two years at a time and five years over a lifetime. Before recipients reach these time limits, they are supposed to have found jobs. The former federal guarantee of a minimum income is, therefore, now a thing of the past. The new law also gives states much greater freedom to design their own welfare systems as they see fit, thereby greatly reducing federal influence over welfare.

The new welfare law is highly controversial. Critics argue that it will throw many needy families to the wolves when their benefits run out. Supporters argue that it will give them "a hand up, instead of a handout"—and will save the taxpayers money to boot.

Are the criticisms of the new welfare law justified? Or would criticism be more aptly directed at the old system? As we shall see in this chapter, the debate over welfare reform is a classic example of the trade-off between equality and efficiency that we introduced in Chapter 1. Some liberals argue that society should adopt extremely generous programs to reduce discrimination, increase income equality, or eradicate poverty regardless of the potential side effects these policies might have. Some conservatives, on the other hand, seem so obsessed with these undesirable side effects, whether real or imagined, that they ignore the benefits of redistribution or of antidiscrimination programs.

Economists prefer to avoid absolutes and to think in terms of trade-offs: To reap gains on one front, society often must make sacrifices on another. A policy is not necessarily ill conceived simply because it has an undesirable effect on income

The Trade-off between Efficiency and Equality

inequality, *if* it makes a sufficiently important contribution to efficiency. But policies

with very bad distributive consequences may deserve to be rejected, even if they

would raise the nation's total output.

Admitting that there is a trade-off between equality and efficiency, that welfare

spending may alleviate poverty but reduce economic efficiency, may not be the best

way to win votes. But it does face the facts. And in that way, it helps us make the

inherently political decisions about what should be done. If we are to understand

these complex issues, a good place to start is, as always, with the facts.

■ THE FACTS: POVERTY

In 1962, social critic Michael Harrington published a little book called *The Other America*, which had a profound effect on American society. Harrington's "other Americans" were the poor who lived in the land of plenty. Ill-clothed in the richest country on earth, inadequately nourished in a nation where obesity was a problem, infirm in a country with some of the world's highest health standards, these people lived an almost unknown existence in their dilapidated hovels, according to Harrington. To make matters worse, this deprivation often condemned the children of the "other Americans" to repeat the lives of their parents. There was, Harrington argued, a "cycle of poverty" that could be broken only by government action.

The work of Harrington and others touched the hearts of many Americans who, it seemed, really had no idea of the abominable living conditions of some others in the country. Within a few years, the growing outrage over the plight of the poor had crystallized into a "War on Poverty," which President Lyndon Johnson declared in 1964.

COUNTING THE POOR: THE POVERTY LINE

The **poverty line** is an amount of income below which a family is considered "poor."

As part of this program, the government adopted an official definition of poverty: The poor were those families with incomes below $3,000 in 1964. This dividing line between the poor and nonpoor was called the **poverty line,** and a goal was established: to get all Americans above the poverty line by the nation's bicentennial in 1976. (The goal was not met.) The poverty line was subsequently modified to account for differences in family size and other considerations, and it is now also adjusted each year to reflect changes in the cost of living. In 1998, the poverty line for a family of four was $16,600, and 12.7 percent of all Americans remained in poverty by official definitions.

Who are the poor? Relative to their proportions in the overall population, they are more likely to be black than white and female than male. They are less educated and in poorer health than the population as a whole. About 40 percent of the poor are children.

America made substantial progress toward eliminating poverty in the decade from 1963 to 1973; the percentage of people living below the poverty line dropped from 20 percent to 11 percent (see the red line in Figure 19–1). But thereafter, slower economic growth and cutbacks in social welfare programs reversed the trend. By 1983, the poverty rate was back to what it had been in the 1960s. Since then, the poverty rate has increased and decreased with no clear trend, but it is still well above its 1970s low.

The rise in poverty since the 1970s worries many people, especially because poverty nowadays seems often to be associated with homelessness, illegitimacy, drug

| FIGURE 19–1 | **Progress in the War on Poverty** |

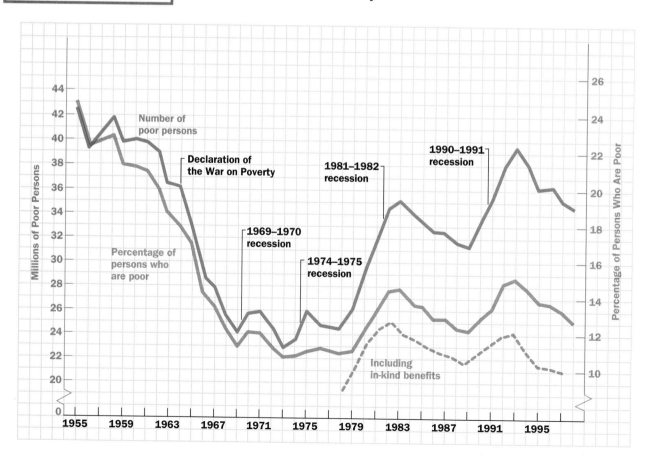

SOURCE: For 1959–1997, U.S. Bureau of the Census. For 1955–1958, estimates kindly provided by Gordon M. Fisher.

● THE POOREST PLACE IN AMERICA

The town has no public parks or swimming pools, no movie theaters, no shopping malls, not even a McDonald's or a Wal-Mart. In fact, business in Lake Providence, Louisiana, is so bad that even the pawnshop has shut down. "The only recreation we have," says a resident, "is poor people's fun: drinking, drugs, fighting, and sex." Restless teenagers mill around narrow streets lined with burned-out houses and dilapidated trailer parks. . . . If there is a poorer place in America, the Census Bureau cannot find it. . . .

The 1990 census found that the median annual household income in Block Numbering Area 9903, which covers the southern two-thirds of Lake Providence and three-quarters of its population, was only $6,536—less than half the official poverty level of $14,764 for a family of four and the lowest in the United States. Two years later, a Children's Defense Fund study found that in East Carroll Parish, where Lake Providence is located, 70.1 percent of children younger than 18, or 2,409, were living in poverty, the highest rate in the nation—and this amid staggeringly high rates of infant mortality, teenage pregnancy, and drug use.

Meanwhile, jobs are scarce, low paying, and seasonal. For most of the year, hundreds of families subsist on welfare: A single mother with one child gets $123 a month. . . . For many the only available work is backbreaking minimum-wage jobs in the nearby cotton fields. . . .

Inevitably, almost everyone who can escape from Lake Providence does so. "I'd rather shoot myself than stay here. It would be a wasted life," says Karva Henderson, who graduated from Lake Providence's High School in June. She plans to go to college and wants never to return.

SOURCE: Jack E. White, "The Poorest Place in America," *Time*, August 15, 1994, pp. 35–36.

dependency, and ill health—all symptoms of a growing underclass whose lives are no better, and are in many respects worse, than the people Harrington wrote about in 1962.

However, some critics argue that the official data badly overstate the number of poor persons. Some even go so far as to claim that poverty would be considered a thing of the past if the official definition (based on cash income) were amended to include the many goods that the poor receive in kind: public education, public housing, health care, food, and the like.

These criticisms prompted the Census Bureau to develop several experimental measures of poverty that include the value of goods given in kind. If these new measures are accepted as valid, fewer people are classified as poor, but the basic patterns of recent years are the same: Poverty has gone up and down since the late 1970s with no clear trend. (See the broken red line in Figure 19–1.)

ABSOLUTE VERSUS RELATIVE POVERTY

This debate raises a fundamental question: How do we define "the poor"? Continuing economic growth will eventually pull almost everyone above any arbitrarily established poverty line. Does this event mark the end of poverty? Some would say yes. But others would insist that the biblical injunction is right: "The poor ye have always with you" (Deuteronomy 15:11).

We can define poverty two ways. The more optimistic definition uses an *absolute concept of poverty*: If you fall short of a certain minimum standard of living, you are poor; once you pass this standard, you are no longer poor. The second definition relies on a *relative concept of poverty*: The poor are those who fall too far behind the average income.

Each definition has its pros and cons. The basic problem with the absolute poverty concept is that it is arbitrary. Who sets the line? Most of the people of Bangladesh would be delighted to live a bit below the U.S. poverty line and would consider themselves quite prosperous. Similarly, the standard of living that we now call "poor" would probably not have been considered so in America in 1900, and certainly not in Europe during the Middle Ages. Different times and different places apparently call for different poverty lines.

Because the concept of poverty seems to be culturally, not physiologically, determined, it must be a relative concept. For example, the European Union places the poverty line at one-half the national average income. Under this definition, the poverty line automatically rises as a nation grows richer.

Once we move from an absolute to a relative concept of poverty, any sharp distinction between the poor and the nonpoor starts to evaporate. Instead, we begin to think of a parade of people from the poorest soul to the richest billionaire. The "poverty problem" then becomes an issue of disparities in income that are "too large." At least in part, the poor are so poor because the rich are so rich. If we follow this line of thought far enough, we are led away from the narrow problem of *poverty* toward the broader problem of *income inequality*.

THE FACTS: INEQUALITY

Nothing in the market mechanism guarantees equality of incomes. On the contrary, the market system tends to breed inequality, because the basic source of its great efficiency is its system of rewards and penalties. The market is generous to those who succeed in operating efficient enterprises that respond to consumer demands; it ruthlessly penalizes those who are unable or unwilling to satisfy consumer demands efficiently.

Its financial punishment of those who try and fail can be particularly severe. At times the market even brings down the great and powerful. Robert Morris, once perhaps the wealthiest resident of the American colonies, ended up in a debtors prison. In more recent decades, the financial travails of the Hunt brothers of Texas and Donald Trump of New York, once among America's richest people, have been highly publicized.

Most people have a pretty good idea that the gulf between the rich and the poor is wide. But few have any concept of where they stand in the income distribution. For example, during the 1995 congressional debate over cutting taxes for "the middle class," one member of Congress with an annual income in excess of $150,000 declared himself a member of the "middle class," if not indeed of the "lower-middle class"!

Table 19–1 offers some statistics on the 1998 income distribution in the United States. But before looking at them, try the following experiment. First, write down what you think your family's before-tax income was in 1998. (If you do not know, take a guess.) Next, try to guess what percentage of American families had incomes *lower* than this. Finally, if we divide America into three broad income classes—rich, middle class, and poor—to which group do you think your family belongs?

Now that you have written down answers to these three questions, look at the income distribution data for 1998 in Table 19–1. If you are like most college students, these figures may surprise you. First, if we adopt the tentative definition that the lowest 20 percent are the "poor," the highest 20 percent are the "rich," and the middle 60 percent are the "middle class," many fewer of you belong to the celebrated "middle class" than thought they did. In fact, the cut-off point that defined membership in the "rich" class in 1998 was only about $86,000 before taxes, an income level exceeded by the parents of many college students. (Your parents may be shocked to learn that they are rich!)

Next, use Table 19–1 to estimate the fraction of U.S. families that have incomes lower than your family's. (The caption has instructions to help you do this.) Most students who come from households of moderate prosperity feel instinctively that they stand somewhere near the middle of the income distribution; so they estimate about half, or perhaps a little more. In fact, the median income among American families in 1998 was only about $46,750.

Distribution of Family Income in the United States in 1998

TABLE 19-1

Income Range	All Families in This Range	Families in This and Lower Ranges
Less than $5,000	2.7%	2.7%
$5,000 to $9,999	3.8	6.5
$10,000 to $14,999	5.3	11.8
$15,000 to $24,999	12.3	24.1
$25,000 to $34,999	12.7	36.8
$35,000 to $49,999	16.8	53.6
$50,000 to $74,999	21.6	75.2
$75,000 to $99,999	11.7	86.9
$100,000 or more	13.1	100.0

NOTE: If your family's income falls close to one of the end points of the ranges indicated here, you can approximate the fraction of families with income *lower* than yours by just looking at the last column. If your family's income falls within one of the ranges, you can interpolate the answer. Example: Your family's income was $60,000. This is 40 percent of the way from $50,000 to $75,000, so your family was richer than roughly 0.40 × 21.6 percent = 8.6 percent of the families in this class. Adding this to the percentage of families in lower classes (53.6 percent in this case) gives the answer—about 62.2 percent of all families earned less than yours.

SOURCE: U.S Bureau of the Census.

This exercise has perhaps brought us down to earth. America is not nearly as rich as Madison Avenue would like us to believe. Let us now look past the average level of income and see how the pie is divided. Table 19–2 shows the shares of income accruing to each fifth of the population in 1998, and several earlier years. In a perfectly equal society, all the numbers in this table would be "20 percent," because each fifth of the population would receive one-fifth of the income. In fact, as the table shows, this is far from true. In 1998, for example, the poorest fifth of all households had under 4 percent (3.6%) of the total income, whereas the richest fifth had 49.2 percent, almost 14 times as much.

DEPICTING INCOME DISTRIBUTIONS: THE LORENZ CURVE

Statisticians and economists use a convenient tool to portray data graphically like those in Table 19–2. The device, called a *Lorenz curve*, appears in Figure 19–2. To construct a Lorenz curve, we first draw a square whose vertical and horizontal dimensions both represent 100 percent. Then we record the percentage of households (or persons) on the horizontal axis and the percentage of income that

Income Shares in Selected Years

TABLE 19-2

Income Group	1998	1990	1980	1970
Lowest fifth	3.6	3.9	4.3	4.1
Second fifth	9.0	9.6	10.3	10.8
Middle fifth	15.0	15.9	16.9	17.4
Fourth fifth	23.2	24.0	24.9	24.5
Highest fifth	49.2	46.6	43.7	43.3

SOURCE: U.S Bureau of the Census.

FIGURE 19-2

A Lorenz Curve for the United States

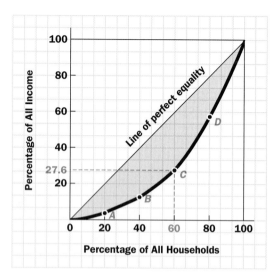

these households (or persons) receive on the vertical axis, using all the data that we have. For example, point *C* in Figure 19–2 depicts the fact (known from Table 19–2) that in 1998, the bottom 60 percent (the three lowest fifths) of American families received 27.6 percent of the total income. Similarly, points *A*, *B*, and *D* represent the other information contained in Table 19–2. We can list four important properties of a Lorenz curve:

- It begins at the origin because zero families naturally have zero income.

- It always ends at the upper-right corner of the square because 100 percent of the nation's families must receive all of the nation's income.

- If income were distributed equally, the Lorenz curve would be a straight line connecting these two points (the thin, solid line in Figure 19–2). This is because, with everybody equal, the bottom 20 percent of the families would receive 20 percent of the income, the bottom 40 percent would receive 40 percent, and so on.

- In a real economy, with significant income differences, the Lorenz curve will "sag" downward from this line of perfect equality. It is easy to see why this is so. If there is any inequality at all, the poorest 20 percent of families must get less than 20 percent of the income. This corresponds to a point below the equality line, such as point *A*. Similarly, the bottom 40 percent of families must receive less than 40 percent of the income (point *B*), and so on.

By itself, the Lorenz curve tells us little. To interpret it, we must know what it looked like in earlier years or what it looks like in other countries. The historical data in Table 19–2 on the previous page show that:

The distribution of income in the United States has grown substantially more unequal since about 1980.

"The poor are getting poorer, but with the rich getting richer it all averages out in the long run."

Specifically, the share of the poorest fifth is now the lowest, and the share of the richest fifth is now about the highest since the government began collecting data in 1947. America is not a very class-conscious society, and for years only specialists paid much attention to data like those in Table 19–2. But income inequality has recently become a big social issue, as more and more American families sense that they are losing ground to the people at the top. There is particular, and well-justified, concern that the real earnings of wage earners below the middle have fallen dramatically in the past two decades.

Comparing the United States with other countries is much harder because no two nations use precisely the same definition of income distribution. The Luxembourg Income Study is the leading international effort to produce comparable data for many countries. In its latest comparison of the income distributions of 19 (mostly European) countries, Finland and Austria had the most equal income distributions, with Sweden, Norway, and Belgium close behind. The United States stood out as having the most inequality. Thus, it appears that:

The United States has rather more income inequality than most other industrialized countries.

■ SOME REASONS FOR UNEQUAL INCOMES

Let us now formulate a list of the *causes* of income inequality. Here are some that come to mind.

DIFFERENCES IN ABILITY   Everyone knows that people have different capabilities. Some can run faster, ski better, calculate figures more quickly, type more accurately, and so on. Hence, it should not be surprising that some people are more adept at earning income. Precisely what sort of ability is relevant to earning income is a matter of intense debate among economists, sociologists, and psychologists. The talents that make for success in school seem to have some effect, but hardly an overwhelming one. The same is true of innate intelligence—"IQ" (see the accompanying box, "How Important Is the Bell Curve?"). It is clear that some types of inventiveness are richly rewarded by the market, as is that elusive characteristic called "entrepreneurial ability." Also, it is obvious that poor health often impairs earning ability.

DIFFERENCES IN INTENSITY OF WORK   Some people work longer hours than others, or labor more intensely when they are on the job, leading to income differences that are largely voluntary.

RISK TAKING   Most people who acquire large sums of money do so by taking risks—by investing their money in the stock market, in a small start-up company, or in some other uncertain venture. Those who gamble and succeed become wealthy. Those who try and fail go broke. Most others prefer not to take such chances and end up somewhere in between. This is another way in which income differences arise voluntarily.

COMPENSATING WAGE DIFFERENTIALS   Some jobs are more arduous than others, or more dangerous, or more unpleasant for other reasons. To induce people to take these jobs, some sort of financial incentive normally must be offered. For example, factory workers who work the night shift normally receive higher wages than those who work during the day.

SCHOOLING AND OTHER TYPES OF TRAINING   Chapter 18 analyzed schooling and other types of training as "investments in human capital." The term refers to the idea that workers can sacrifice *current* income in order to improve their skills so that their *future* incomes will be higher. When this is done, income differentials naturally rise. Although it is generally agreed that differences in schooling are an important cause of income differentials, this particular cause has both voluntary and involuntary aspects. Young men or women who *choose* not to go to college have made

---

● **HOW IMPORTANT IS THE BELL CURVE?**

In 1994, social critic Charles Murray and the late Richard Herrnstein, a psychologist, created a furor with a book claiming that genetically inherited intelligence is an overwhelmingly important determinant of economic success. The book's title, *The Bell Curve,* was a reference to the shape of the distribution of observed test scores on conventional IQ tests (see chart), which show most people clustered near the middle of the distribution, with small minorities on either end.

Critics of government antipoverty programs were quickly attracted to the book's central message: that the poor are poor in large measure because they are not very smart. Among the most stunning claims made by Herrnstein and Murray was that much of the observed economic gap between blacks and whites could be attributed to the fact that blacks' IQs were, on average, lower than those of whites.

Although *The Bell Curve* received a blitz of media attention, social scientists generally ignored it or gave the analysis low marks. No one seriously doubts that intelligence contributes to economic success, nor that genetics has some bearing on intelligence. But the scientific evidence on the strength of each link is in great dispute. Many experts on IQ,

for example, argue that environmental factors may be more important than genetics in determining intelligence and that "true" intelligence may differ from measured IQ. Furthermore, few if any economists believe that cognitive ability is the main ingredient in economic success.

The bottom line, according to most scholars, is that the black-white IQ gap does not go very far in explaining racial income inequalities. Nor can we be certain that much of the measured IQ gap is biologically, rather than culturally, determined.

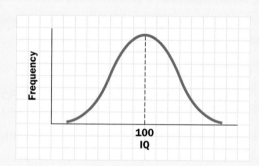

voluntary decisions that affect their incomes. But many never get the choice: Their parents simply cannot afford to send them. For them, the resulting income differential is not voluntary.

WORK EXPERIENCE It is well-known to most people and well-documented by scholarly research that more experienced workers earn higher wages.

INHERITED WEALTH Not all income is derived from work. Some is the return on invested wealth, and part of this wealth is inherited. Although this cause of inequality applies to few people, many of America's super-rich got that way through inheritance. And financial wealth is not the only type of capital that can be inherited; so can human capital. In part this happens naturally through genetics: High-ability parents tend to have high-ability children, although the link is an imperfect one. But it also happens partly for economic reasons: Well-to-do parents send their children to the best schools, thereby transforming their own *financial* wealth into *human* wealth for their children. This type of inheritance may be much more important than the financial type.

LUCK No observer of our society can fail to notice the role that chance plays. Some of the rich and some of the poor got there largely by good or bad fortune. A farmer digs for water, but strikes oil instead. A construction worker is unemployed for a whole year because of a recession that he had no part in creating. Two skilled programmers work hard, but only one develops the "killer app" that makes him rich. The list could go on and on. Many large income differentials arise purely by chance.

■ THE FACTS: DISCRIMINATION

Some of the factors we have just listed lead to income differentials that are widely accepted as "just." For example, most people believe it is fair for people who work harder to receive higher incomes. Other factors on our list ignite heated debates. For example, some people view income differentials that arise purely by chance as perfectly acceptable. Others find these same differentials intolerable. However, almost no one is willing to condone income inequalities that arise from discrimination.

The facts about discrimination are not easy to come by. **Economic discrimination** occurs when equivalent factors of production receive different payments for equal contributions to output. But this definition is hard to apply in practice because we cannot always tell when two factors of production are "equivalent."

Economic discrimination occurs when equivalent factors of production receive different payments for equal contributions to output.

Few people would call it "discrimination" if a woman with only a high school diploma receives a lower salary than a man with a college degree. Even if a man and a woman have the same education, the man may have 10 more years of work experience than the woman. If they receive different wages for this reason, is that discriminatory?

In principle, we should compare men and women whose *productivities* are equal. If women receive lower wages than men who do the same work, we would then attribute the difference to discrimination. But discrimination normally takes much more subtle forms than paying unequal wages for equal work. For instance, employers can simply relegate women to inferior jobs, thus justifying lower salaries.

One clearly *incorrect* way to measure discrimination is to compare the different groups' typical incomes. Table 19–3 displays such data for white men, white women, black men, and black women in 1998. Virtually everyone agrees that the amount of discrimination is less than these differentials suggest, but far greater than zero. Precisely how much is a topic of continuing economic research. Several studies suggest that about half of the observed wage differential between black and white men, and at least half of the differential between white women and white men, arises from discrimination in the labor market (though more might be due to discrimination in education, and so on). Other studies have reached somewhat different conclusions. Although no one denies the existence of discrimination, its quantitative importance is a matter of ongoing controversy and research.

■ THE ECONOMIC THEORY OF DISCRIMINATION[1]

Let us see what economic theory tells us about discrimination. In particular, consider the following two questions:

1. Must *prejudice*, which we define as arising when one group dislikes associating with another group, lead to *discrimination* (unequal pay for equal work)?

2. Do "natural" economic forces tend either to erode or to exacerbate discrimination over time?

Median Incomes in 1998

TABLE 19-3

Population Group	Median Income	Percentage of White Male Income
White males	$27,646	100
Black males	19,321	70
White females	14,617	53
Black females	13,137	48

NOTE: For persons 15 years old and older.
SOURCE: U.S. Bureau of the Census.

---
[1] This section may be omitted in shorter courses.

As we shall see now, the analysis we have provided in previous chapters sheds light on both these issues.

DISCRIMINATION BY EMPLOYERS

Most attention seems to focus on discrimination by employers, so let us start there. What happens if, for example, some firms refuse to hire blacks? Figure 19–3 will help us find the answer. Panel (a) pertains to firms that discriminate; panel (b) pertains to firms that do not. There are supply and demand curves for labor in each market, based on the analysis of Chapter 18. We suppose the two demand curves to be identical.

| FIGURE 19-3 | **Wage Discrimination** |

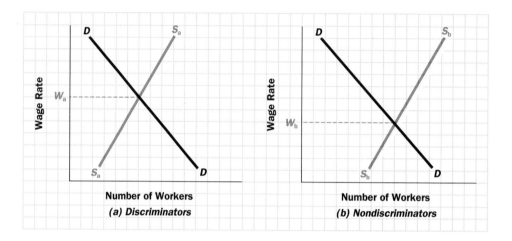

(a) Discriminators

(b) Nondiscriminators

However, the supply curve in market (b) must be farther to the right than the supply curve in market (a) because both whites *and* blacks can work in market (b), whereas only whites can work in market (a). The result is that wages will be lower in market (b) than in market (a). Because all the blacks are forced into market (b), we conclude that employers discriminate against them.

But now consider the situation from the *employers'* point of view. Firms in market (a) of Figure 19–3 pay more for labor (W_a is greater than W_b), so they pay for the privilege of discriminating. The nondiscriminatory firms in market (b) have a cost advantage. As we learned in earlier chapters, in the face of effective competition, these nondiscriminatory firms will tend to capture more and more customers. The discriminators will gradually be driven out of business. If, on the other hand, many of the firms in market (a) have protected monopolies, they will be able to remain in business. But they will pay for the privilege of discriminating by earning lower monopoly profits than they otherwise could (because they pay higher wages than they need to).

DISCRIMINATION BY FELLOW WORKERS

Thus, competitive forces tend to reduce discrimination over time *if* employers are the source of discrimination. Such optimistic conclusions do not follow, however, if workers, rather than employers, are prejudiced. Consider what happens, for example, if men object to having women as their supervisors. If male workers do not give their full cooperation, female supervisors will be less effective than male supervisors and hence will earn lower wages. Here prejudice does lead to discrimination. Furthermore, in this case, firms that put women into supervisory positions will be at a competitive disadvantage relative to firms that do not. So market forces will not erode discrimination.

● ARE WOMEN BETTER WORKERS?

Economist Audrey Freedman argues that female employees can be a better bargain than male employees, even though only women request pregnancy leaves and it is mainly women who miss workdays for child-care reasons.

It is undeniable . . . that women, not men, take pregnancy leaves. It is also undeniable that women are the primary nurturers in a family. They are the most likely to be responsible for the care and support of children, as well as their elderly parents. If we stop there . . . women in business are more costly than men.

But the built-in bias of that analysis is the failure to account for far more costly drains on corporate productivity from behavior that is more characteristic of men than of women.

For example, men are more likely to be heavy users of alcohol. This gender-related habit causes businesses to suffer excessive medical costs, serious performance losses, and productivity drains. Yet, the male-dominated corporate hierarchy most often chooses to ignore these "good old boy" habits.

Drug abuse among the fast-movers of Wall Street seems to be understood as a normal response to the pressures of taking risks with other people's money. The consequences in loss of judgment are tolerated. They are not calculated as a male-related cost of business.

Apart from performance problems at high levels, alcohol and drug abuse cause costly accidents. We never think of them, however, as risks primarily associated with male employees. In addition, in our culture, lawlessness and violence are found far more often among men than women. The statistics on criminals and prison population are obvious, yet we seem to be unable to recognize these as primarily male behaviors.

A top executive of a major airline once commented to me that his company's greatest problem is machismo in the cockpit—pilots and copilots fighting over the controls. There is an obvious solution: Hire pilots from that half of the population that is less susceptible to the attacks of rage that afflict macho males.

SOURCE: Audrey Freedman, "Those Costly 'Good Old Boys,'" *The New York Times,* July 12, 1989, p. A23. Copyright, 1989 by the New York Times Company. Reprinted by permission.

STATISTICAL DISCRIMINATION

A final type of discrimination, called **statistical discrimination,** may be the most stubborn of all and can exist even when there is no prejudice. Here is an important example. It is, of course, a biological fact that only women can give birth. It is also a fact that most working women who have babies leave their jobs for a while to care for their newborns. Employers know this. What they cannot know, however, is *which* women of child-bearing age will leave the labor force for this reason.

Statistical discrimination is said to occur when the productivity of a particular worker is estimated to be low just because that worker belongs to a particular group (such as women).

Suppose three candidates apply for a job that requires a long-term commitment. Susan plans to quit after a few years to raise a family. Jane does not plan to have any children. Jack is a man. If he knew all the facts, the employer might not want Susan, but would be equally happy with Jane or Jack. But the employer cannot differentiate between Susan and Jane. He therefore presumes that either one, being a young woman, is more likely than Jack to quit to raise a family. So he hires Jack, even though Jane is just as good a prospect. Jane is discriminated against.

Lest it be thought that this example actually justifies discrimination against women on economic grounds, it should be noted that most women return to work within six months after childbirth. Furthermore, women typically have less absenteeism and job turnover for nonpregnancy health reasons than men do. The accompanying box, "Are Women Better Workers?" (on page 391) argues that employers often fail to take these other sex-related differences into account and thus mistakenly favor men.

THE ROLES OF THE MARKET AND THE GOVERNMENT

In terms of the two questions with which we began this section, we conclude that different types of *discrimination* lead to different answers. Prejudice will often, but not always, lead to economic discrimination, and discrimination may occur even in the absence of prejudice. Finally, the forces of competition tend to erode some, but not all, of the inequities caused by discrimination.

However, the victims of discrimination are not the only losers. Society also loses whenever discriminatory practices impair economic efficiency. Hence, most observers believe that we should not rely on market forces *alone* to combat discrimination. The government has a clear role to play.

■ THE OPTIMAL AMOUNT OF INEQUALITY

FIGURE 19-4

The Optimal Distribution of Income

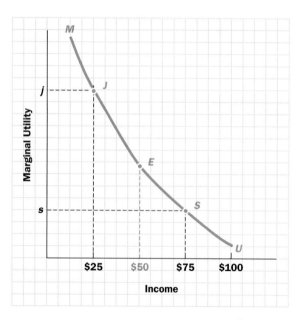

We have seen that substantial income inequality exists in America, and we have noted some reasons for it. Let us now ask a question that is loaded with value judgments, but to which economic analysis can contribute nonetheless: *How much inequality is the ideal amount?* We shall not, of course, be able to answer this question definitively. Rather, our objective is to see the type of analysis that is relevant. We begin in a simple setting in which we can easily obtain the answer. Then we shall see how the real world differs from this simple model.

Consider a society in which two people, Smith and Jones, are to divide $100 between them. The objective is to maximize *total utility*. Suppose Smith and Jones are alike in their ability to enjoy money; technically, we say that their *marginal utility* schedules are identical.[2] This identical marginal utility schedule is depicted in Figure 19–4. We will now prove the following result: *The optimal distribution of income is to give $50 to Smith and $50 to Jones*, which is represented by point E in Figure 19–4.

We prove it by showing that, if the income distribution is unequal, we can improve things by moving closer to equality. So suppose that Smith has $75 (point *S* in the figure) and Jones has $25 (point *J*). Then we can see that Smith's *marginal utility* (which is *s*) is *less* than Jones's (which is *j*). This is a simple consequence of the law of diminishing marginal utility: Because Smith has more money, his marginal utility of money is lower.

---

[2] If you need to refresh your memory about marginal utility, see Chapter 6, especially pages 96–98.

"There is a perfect example of what is wrong with this country today."

"There is a perfect example of what is wrong with this country today."

If we take $1 away from Smith, he *loses* the low marginal utility, *s*, that a dollar gives him. When we transfer that dollar to Jones, he *gains* the high marginal utility, *j*, that a dollar gives him. On balance, society's total utility rises by $j - s$ because Jones's gain exceeds Smith's loss. Therefore, a distribution with Smith getting only $74 is better than one in which he gets $75. Because the same argument shows that a $73/$27 distribution is better than $74/$26, and so on, we have proven our result: a $50/$50 distribution—point *E*—is best.

Now in this example there is nothing special about the fact that we assumed only two people or that exactly $100 was available. Any number of people and dollars would do as well. What really *is* crucial is our assumption that the same amount of money would be available no matter how we chose to distribute it. Thus, we have proved the following general result:

> To maximize total utility, the best way to distribute any *fixed* amount of money among people with identical marginal utility schedules is to divide it equally.

■ THE TRADE-OFF BETWEEN EQUALITY AND EFFICIENCY

As soon as we seek to apply this analysis to the real world, two major difficulties arise. First, people have different marginal utility schedules. Thus, *some* inequality can probably be justified. The second problem is much more formidable.

> The total amount of income in society is *not* independent of how we try to distribute it.

To see why, consider an extreme example. Ask yourself what would happen if we tried to achieve perfect equality by putting a 100 percent income tax on all income and then dividing the tax receipts equally among the population. No one would have any incentive to work, to invest, to take risks, or to do anything else to earn money, because the rewards for all such activities would disappear. The nation's total production would fall drastically. Although the example is extreme, the principle is universal; indeed, it is the basic idea behind supply-side economics.

THE TRADE-OFF Policies that redistribute income reduce the rewards of high-income earners while raising the rewards of low-income earners. Hence, they reduce the incentive to earn high income. This gives rise to a trade-off that is one of the most fundamental in all of economics, and one of our *Ideas for Beyond the Final Exam*.

When we take measures to increase the amount of economic equality, we normally reduce economic efficiency—that is, we reduce society's total output. In trying to divide the pie more equally, we may inadvertently reduce its size.

The Trade-off between Equality and Efficiency

Because of this trade-off, equal incomes are not optimal in practice. On the contrary:

The optimal income distribution will always involve *some* inequality.

But this stark fact does not mean that attempts to reduce inequality are misguided. We should learn two things from this analysis:

1. **There are better and worse ways to promote equality. In pursuing further income equality (or fighting poverty), we should seek policies that do the least possible harm to incentives.**

2. **Equality is bought at a price. Thus, like any commodity, we must rationally decide how much to "purchase." We will probably want to spend some of our potential income on equality, but certainly not all of it.**

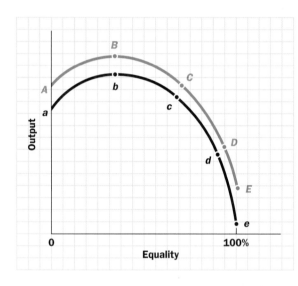

FIGURE 19–5

The Trade-off between Equality and Efficiency

Figure 19–5 illustrates both of these lessons. The curve *abcde* represents possible combinations of total output and income equality that are obtainable under the present system of taxes and transfers. If, for example, point *c* is the current position of the economy, raising taxes on the rich to finance more transfers to the poor, which is one of the things President Clinton did in 1993, might move us downward to the right toward point *d*. Equality then increases, but the nation's output falls as the rich react to higher marginal tax rates by producing less. Similarly, reducing the tax rate on capital gains, as the Republican Congress did in 1997, might move us upward to the left toward point *b*. Notice that, to the left of point *b*, output falls as inequality rises. Here there is no trade-off, perhaps because very poorly paid workers are less productive due to inadequate investment in human capital, poor nutrition, or just a general sense of disaffection.

The curve *ABCDE* represents possible combinations of output and equality under some new, more efficient redistributive policy. It is more efficient in the sense that for any desired level of equality, we can get more output with the policy represented by *ABCDE* than with the policy represented by *abcde*. The movements from points *C* and *c* toward points *D* and *d* represent two alternative policies for equalizing income distribution. The policy that leads to *D* is better because it is more efficient.

The first lesson is obvious: We should stick to the higher of the two curves. If we find ourselves at any point on curve *abcde*, we can always improve things by moving up to the corresponding point on curve *ABCDE*, that is, by changing policies. By picking the most efficient redistributive policy, we can have more equality *and* more output. In the rest of this chapter, we discuss alternative policies and try to indicate which ones damage incentives least.

The second lesson is that neither point *B* nor point *E* would normally be society's optimal choice. At point *B*, we are seeking the highest possible output with utter disregard for whatever inequality might accompany it. At point *E*, we are forcing complete equality, even if work incentives vanish and a minuscule total output is the result.

It is astonishing how much confusion is caused by a failure to understand these two lessons. Proponents of greater equality often feel obliged to deny that the programs they advocate will hurt incentives at all. Sometimes these vehement denials are so patently unrealistic that they undermine the very case the egalitarians are trying to make. Conservatives who oppose such policies also undercut the strength of their case by making outlandish claims about the efficiency losses from redistribution.

Neither side, it seems, is willing to acknowledge the fundamental trade-off between equality and efficiency depicted in Figure 19–5. As a result, the debate generates more heat than light. Because these debates will likely continue for the rest of your lives, we hope that some understanding of this trade-off stays with you well *Beyond the Final Exam.*

But merely understanding the trade-off will not tell you what to do. Look at Figure 19–5. We know that the optimal amount of equality lies between points *B* and *E*, but we do not know what it actually is. Is it more like point *D*, with greater equality and less output than we now have? Or is it more like a movement back toward point *B*? Everyone will have a different answer to this question, because it is basically one of value judgments. Just how much is more equality worth to you?

Arthur Okun, onetime chairman of the Council of Economic Advisers, put the issue graphically. Imagine that money is liquid, and that you have a bucket to use to transport money from the rich to the poor. But the bucket leaks. (These are the efficiency losses from redistribution.) As you move the money, some gets lost. Will you use the bucket if only 1 cent is lost for each $1 you move? Probably everyone would say yes. But what if each $1 taken from the rich results in only 10 cents for the poor? Only the most extreme egalitarians will still say yes. Now try the hard questions. What if 20 to 40 cents is lost for each $1 that you move? If you can answer questions like these, you can decide how far down the hill from point *B* you think society should travel, for you will have expressed your value judgments in quantitative terms.

■ POLICIES TO COMBAT POVERTY

Let us take it for granted that the nation has a commitment to reduce poverty. What policies can promote this goal? Which of these does the least harm to incentives, and hence is most efficient?

EDUCATION AS A WAY OUT

Education is often advertised as one of the principal ways to escape from poverty. No doubt many people have used this route successfully, and still do.[3]

However, delivering quality education to poor children is no simple matter. Many of them, especially in the inner cities, are ill-equipped to learn and attend schools that are ill-equipped to teach. Despite some gratifying progress in recent years, dropout rates remain dismayingly high. An astonishing number of youths leave the public school system without even acquiring basic literacy. All of these problems are familiar; none is easy to solve.

In truth, our educational system must serve many goals, and the alleviation of poverty is not the major one. If it were, we would almost certainly spend more money on preschool and inner-city kids and less on college education than we do today. Furthermore, education is not a particularly effective way to lift *adults* out of poverty. Its effects are delayed for a generation or more.

THE WELFARE DEBATE

By contrast, a variety of programs collectively known as "welfare" are specifically designed to alleviate poverty, meant to help adults as well as children, and intended to have quick effects. As mentioned at the start of this chapter, the best known and most heavily criticized of these programs used to be *Aid to Families with Dependent Children*. AFDC provided direct cash grants to families that had children but no breadwinner, generally because the father was absent or unknown and the mother could not or did not work.

AFDC was attacked as a classic example of an inefficient redistributive program. Why? One major reason was that it provided no incentive for these mothers to earn income. Once monthly earnings passed a few hundred dollars, welfare payments

---

[3] The role of education as a determinant of income was considered at length in the previous chapter.

were reduced by $1 for each $1 that the family earned as wages. Thus, if a member of the family got a job, the family was subjected to a 100 percent marginal tax rate! Little wonder, then, that many welfare recipients did not look very hard for work.

TEMPORARY ASSISTANCE TO NEEDY FAMILIES (TANF)   The 1996 welfare reform tackled the work-incentive problem by using a stick rather than a carrot. Instead of reducing the marginal tax rate on earnings, the new system—*Temporary Assistance to Needy Families, or TANF*—compels welfare recipients to work by cutting off their benefits after two years. Effective marginal tax rates under TANF vary tremendously both by income level and by state, because the 50 states have a great deal of flexibility in designing their own programs.

It is far too early to tell how successful this new approach will be. Early results have been favorable, but the years since welfare reform have seen a booming economy with plentiful jobs. Critics worry about how well the TANF program will work when jobs are less easy to find.

FOOD STAMPS   Another welfare program that burgeoned in the 1970s and was cut back several times in the 1980s and 1990s is *food stamps*, under which poor families can buy stamps which they can exchange for food. The dollar amount of the stamps they receive, and how much they pay for them, depends on the family's income. The poorer the family, the less it must pay for the stamps. The program made headlines in 1993 when newspapers reported that a stunning 10 percent of all Americans were receiving food stamps. That percentage has fallen in the economic boom since the early 1990s, but the program was nonetheless cut back in 1996 to save money.

TRANSFERS IN KIND   In addition to TANF and food stamps, the government provides many poor people with a number of important goods and services, either at no charge or at prices that are well below market levels. Medical care under the Medicaid program and subsidized public housing are two notable examples.[4] These programs significantly enhance the living standards of the poor. However, most of them offer benefits that decline as family income rises. Taken as a whole, all the antipoverty programs put some poor families in a position where they are taxed extremely heavily if their earnings rise. When this occurs, the incentive not to work becomes quite powerful.

WELFARE REFORM AND THE TRADE-OFF

The debate over welfare reform is a good illustration of the two questions that are central to the trade-off between equality and efficiency

First come value judgments: How much equality should society buy? Congressional backers of the 1996 welfare reform argued that the government was spending too much money to reduce inequality, and so America should move from a point like *c* to a point like *b* in Figure 19–5. Opponents of welfare cutbacks argued that we were spending too little and allowing excessive amounts of inequality to persist.

The second question pertains more to means than to ends. Critics of the old welfare system argued that it was a terribly inefficient way to redistribute income, for reasons like those we have just discussed. It was more like *abcde* in Figure 19–5 than *ABCDE*. They believe that the new TANF system will do a better job. Time will tell.

THE NEGATIVE INCOME TAX

How can we do the job better? Can we design a simple structure that gets income into the hands of the poor without destroying their incentives to work? The solution suggested most frequently by economists is called the *negative income tax (NIT)*.

Table 19–4 illustrates how an NIT works. A particular NIT plan is defined by picking two numbers: a minimum income level below which no family is allowed to

---

[4] The *Medicaid* programs pay for the health care of low-income people; *Medicare* is available to all seniors, regardless of income.

fall (the "guarantee") and a rate at which benefits are "taxed away" as income rises. The table considers a plan with a $6,000 guaranteed income and a 50 percent tax rate. Thus, a family with no earnings (top row) would receive a $6,000 payment (a "negative tax") from the government. A family earning $2,000 (second row) would have the basic benefit reduced by 50 percent of its earnings. Thus, because half its earnings is $1,000, it would receive $5,000 from the government plus the $2,000 earned income for a total income of $7,000.

Notice in Table 19–4 that, with a 50 percent tax rate, the increase in total income as earnings rise is always *half* of the increase in earnings. Thus, families always have some incentive to work. Notice also that there is a level of income at which benefits cease—$12,000 in this example. This "break-even" level is not a third number that policymakers can select freely. Rather, it is dictated by the choices of the guarantee and the tax rate. In our example, $6,000 is the maximum possible benefit, and benefits are reduced by 50 cents for each $1 of earnings. Hence, benefits will be reduced to zero when 50 percent of earnings is equal to $6,000—which occurs when earnings are $12,000. The general relation is:

$$\text{Guarantee} = \text{Tax rate} \times \text{Break-even level}$$

The fact that the break-even level is completely determined by the guarantee and the tax rate creates a vexing problem. To make a real dent in the poverty problem, the guarantee must be placed fairly close to the poverty line. But then any moderate tax rate will push the break-even level way above the poverty line. This means that families who are not considered "poor" (though they are certainly not rich) will also receive benefits. For example, a low tax rate of $33\frac{1}{3}$ percent means that some benefits are paid to families whose income is as high as three times the guarantee level.

The solution seems obvious: raise the tax rate to bring the guarantee and the break-even level closer together. But then the incentive to work shrinks, and with it the principal rationale for the NIT in the first place. So the NIT is no panacea. Difficult choices must still be made.

THE NEGATIVE INCOME TAX AND WORK INCENTIVES The NIT should increase work incentives for welfare recipients. However, we have just seen that a number of families who are now too well off to collect welfare inevitably would become eligible for NIT payments. For these people, the NIT imposes work disincentives by subjecting them to the relatively high NIT tax rate. Government-sponsored experiments in the 1960s found that recipients of NIT benefits did in fact work less than nonrecipients, but only slightly.

Largely because of its superior work incentives, economists believe that an NIT is a more efficient way to redistribute income than the existing welfare system. In terms of Figure 19–5, the NIT is curve *ABCDE*, whereas the present system is curve *abcde*. If this view is correct, then replacing the current welfare system with an NIT would lead to both more equality *and* more efficiency. But this does not mean that equalization would become cost free. The curve *ABCDE* still slopes downward: By increasing equality, we still diminish the nation's output.

THE NEGATIVE INCOME TAX AND REALITY The NIT is often mistakenly viewed as an "academic" idea that does not exist in practice. But, in fact, America has two important programs that strongly resemble an NIT. One is the Food Stamp program. Food stamp benefits decline as earnings rise, and food stamps are used like cash in many poor neighborhoods. Hence food stamp benefits look very much like the NIT plan illustrated in Table 19–4.

The second program is an important feature of the income tax code called the Earned Income Tax Credit (EITC). It works as follows. As earnings rise from zero to some upper limit ($9,500 in 1999 for a worker with two children), the federal government supplements the earnings of the working poor by giving them what amounts to a grant that is proportional to their earnings. But once earnings pass a second threshold, the government starts taking this grant back, just as an NIT would. The EITC was made substantially more generous in 1993, and it is now America's biggest income-support program.

TABLE 19–4

Illustration of a Negative Income Tax Plan

Earnings	Benefits Paid	Total Income
$ 0	$6,000	$ 6,000
2,000	5,000	7,000
4,000	4,000	8,000
6,000	3,000	9,000
8,000	2,000	10,000
10,000	1,000	11,000
12,000	0	12,000

■ OTHER POLICIES TO COMBAT INEQUALITY

If we take the broader view that society's objective is not just to eliminate poverty but to reduce income disparities, then the fact that many nonpoor families would receive benefits under an NIT is perhaps not a serious drawback. After all, unless the plan is outlandishly generous, these families' incomes will still fall well below the average. Still, the NIT is largely thought of as an antipoverty program, not as a tool for general income equalization.

THE PERSONAL INCOME TAX

By contrast, the federal personal income tax is thought to promote equality. Indeed, it is probably given far more credit for this than it actually deserves. Because the income tax is *progressive*, it takes a larger share of income from the rich than from the poor. Thus, incomes *after* tax are distributed more equally than incomes *before* tax.[5] This point is illustrated by the two Lorenz curves in Figure 19–6, which show a slight equalization due to the progressive income tax. These curves, however, are not drawn accurately to scale. If they were, they would lie almost on top of each other because research shows that the degree of equalization attributable to the tax is rather modest.

DEATH DUTIES AND OTHER TAXES

Taxes on inheritances and estates levied by both states and federal government also equalize incomes. In this case they seem clearly aimed at limiting the incomes of the rich, or at least at limiting their ability to transfer this largesse from one generation to the next. But the amount of money involved is too small to make much difference to the overall income distribution. Total receipts from estate and gift taxes by all levels of government provide under 1 percent of total tax revenues.

Nonetheless, the federal estate tax became a hot political issue in 2000. The Republican Congress sought to repeal it, and presidential candidate George W. Bush made phasing out the estate tax part of his tax-cut proposal.

Most experts agree that the many other taxes in the U.S. system—including sales taxes, payroll taxes, and property taxes—are decidedly regressive as a group. On balance, the evidence seems to suggest that:

The U.S. tax system as a whole is only slightly progressive.

FIGURE 19–6

The Effect of Progressive Income Taxation on the Lorenz Curve

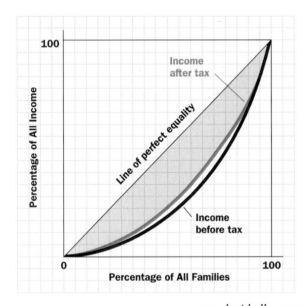

■ POLICIES TO COMBAT DISCRIMINATION

The policies we have just considered are all based on taxes and transfer payments—on moving dollars from one set of hands to another. A quite different approach has been used to fight discrimination: governments have made it *illegal* to discriminate.

Perhaps the major milestone in the war against discrimination was the *Civil Rights Act of 1964*, which outlawed many forms of discrimination and established the *Equal Employment Opportunity Commission (EEOC)*. When you read in a want ad that the company is "an equal opportunity employer," the firm is proclaiming its compliance with this and related legislation.

Originally, policymakers thought that they could attack the problem by outlawing discrimination in rates of pay and in hiring standards, and by devoting resources to enforcing these provisions. Although progress in reducing discrimination by race and sex undoubtedly was made between 1964 and the early 1970s, many people felt the pace was too slow. One reason was that discrimination in the labor market

---

[5] For definitions of progressive, proportional, and regressive taxes, see Chapter 21, page 435.

● POLICY DEBATE   SHOULD AFFIRMATIVE ACTION BE ABOLISHED?

Affirmative action has always been controversial. But it became a particularly hot political issue in the mid 1990s, as conservative politicians reacted to what they perceived to be one of the chief grievances of the "angry white male."

A number of critics believe that affirmative action has outlived its usefulness. It is time, they say, to rely on "race blind" standards that judge each person on his or her individual merits. Any other system of selection is unfair, they insist, especially when affirmative action programs devolve into rigid quotas by race or sex—as they frequently do.

Although no federal laws were changed, an important 1995 Supreme Court ruling in *Adarand v. Pena* set new and tougher standards for federal affirmative action programs. This ruling prompted President Clinton to order a comprehensive review of federal programs that favored minorities in such matters as hiring and awarding contracts. Although a few programs were cut back or eliminated, the review generally concluded that the United States was still so far from being a "color blind" society that affirmative action was still

needed, and the president continued to defend affirmative action against Republican efforts to eliminate it.

Some state governments, however, went much farther than the federal government. California and Texas, for example, abolished several affirmative action programs at their state universities. (In California, this action followed a contentious statewide referendum on the matter.) When they did, minority enrollments plummeted so dramatically that a few opponents of affirmative action had well-publicized second thoughts.

The issue remains open. Few people actually like affirmative action—it offends many peoples' sense of fairness. But a majority of Americans continue to believe it is necessary to redress a centuries-long imbalance.

proved to be more subtle than was first thought. Officials rarely could find proof that unequal pay was being given for equal work, because determining when work was "equal" turned out to be a formidable task.

So a new approach was added to the antidiscrimination arsenal. Firms and other organizations with suspiciously small representations of minorities or women in their workforces were required not just to end discriminatory practices but also to demonstrate that they were taking **affirmative action** to remedy this imbalance. That is, they had to *prove* that they were making efforts to locate members of minority groups and females and then to hire them if they proved to be qualified.

This approach to fighting discrimination was controversial from the start, and remains so to this day. Critics claim that affirmative action really means quotas and compulsory hiring of unqualified workers simply because they are black or female. If this is so, it exacts a toll on economic efficiency. Proponents counter

Affirmative action refers to active efforts to locate and hire members of underrepresented groups.

that without affirmative action, discriminatory employers would simply claim they were unable to find qualified minority or female employees.

The difficulty revolves around the impossibility of deciding who is "qualified" and who is not based on *purely objective criteria.* What one person sees it as government coercion to hire an unqualified applicant to fill a quota, another sees as a discriminatory employer being forced to mend his or her ways. Nothing in this book, or anywhere else, will teach you which view is correct in any particular instance.

The controversy over affirmative action is another excellent example of the trade-off between equality and efficiency. Putting more women and members of minority groups into high-paying jobs would certainly make the income distribution more equal. Supporters of affirmative action seek this result. But if affirmative action disrupts industry and requires firms to replace "qualified" white males with other, "less qualified" workers, the nation's productivity will suffer. Opponents of affirmative action are disturbed by these potential efficiency losses. How far should these programs be pushed? A good question, but one without a good answer.

■ A LOOK BACK

We have now completed three chapters on the distribution of income. So this may be an opportune moment to pause and see how this analysis relates to our central theme: *What does the market do well, and what does it do poorly?*

We have learned that a market economy relies on the marginal productivity principle to assign an income to each individual. In so doing, the market attaches high prices to scarce factors and low prices to abundant ones, and therefore guides firms to use society's resources *efficiently.* This is one of the market's great strengths.

However, by attaching high prices to some factors and low prices to others, the market mechanism often creates a distribution of income that is quite unequal. Some people wind up fabulously rich, whereas others wind up miserably poor. For this reason, the market has been widely criticized for centuries for doing a rather poor job of distributing income in accord with commonly held notions of *fairness* and *equity.*

On balance, most observers feel that the criticism is justified: The market mechanism is extraordinarily good at promoting efficiency but not very good at promoting equality. As we said at the outset, the market has both virtues and vices.

SUMMARY

1. President Lyndon Johnson declared the War on Poverty in 1964, and within a decade the fraction of families below the official *poverty line* had dropped substantially. However, the poverty rate is higher today that it was in the early 1970s.

2. In the United States today, the richest 20 percent of households receive about 49 percent of the income, while the poorest 20 percent of households receive under 4 percent. These numbers reflect a considerable increase in inequality since about 1980. The U.S. income distribution also appears to be more unequal than those of most other industrial nations.

3. Individual incomes differ for many reasons. Differences in native ability, in the desire to work hard and to take risks, in schooling and experience, and in inherited wealth all account for income disparities. Discrimination also plays a role. All of these factors, however, explain only part of the inequality that we observe. A portion of the rest is due simply to good or bad luck, and the balance is unexplained.

4. Prejudice against a minority group may lead to discrimination in rates of pay, or to segregation in the workplace, or to both. However, discrimination may also arise even when there is no prejudice (this is called *statistical discrimination*).

5. There is *a trade-off between the goals of reducing inequality and enhancing economic efficiency:* Policies that help on the equality front normally harm efficiency, and vice versa.

6. Because of this trade-off, there is an *optimal degree of inequality* for any society. Society finds this optimum in the same way that a consumer decides how much to buy of different commodities: the trade-off tells us how costly it is to "purchase" more equality, and preferences then determine how much should be "bought." However, because people have different value judgments about the importance of equality, they disagree over the ideal amount of equality.

7. Whatever goal for equality is selected, society can gain by using more efficient redistributive policies because such

policies let us buy any given amount of equality at a lower price in terms of lost output. Economists claim, for example, that a *negative income tax* is preferable to our current welfare system on these grounds.

8. But the negative income tax is no panacea. Its primary virtue lies in the way it preserves incentives to work. But if this is done by keeping the tax rate low, then either the minimum guaranteed level of income will have to be low or many non-poor families will become eligible to receive benefits.

9. The goal of income equality is also pursued through the tax system, especially through the progressive federal income tax and death duties. But other taxes are typically regressive, so the tax system as a whole is only slightly progressive.

10. *Economic discrimination* has been attacked by making it illegal, not through the tax and transfer system. But simply declaring discrimination to be illegal is much easier than actually ending discrimination. The trade-off between equality and efficiency applies once again: Strict enforcement of *affirmative action* will certainly reduce discrimination and increase income equality, but it may do so at a cost in terms of economic efficiency.

KEY TERMS

Poverty line   382

Absolute and relative concepts of poverty   383

Lorenz curve   385

Economic discrimination   389

Statistical discrimination   391

Optimal amount of inequality   392

Trade-off between equality and efficiency   393

Temporary Assistance to Needy Families (TANF)   396

Food stamps   396

Negative income tax (NIT)   396

Earned income tax credit (EITC)   397

Civil Rights Act of 1964   398

Equal Employment Opportunity Commission (EEOC)   398

Affirmative action   399

QUESTIONS FOR REVIEW

1. Discuss the "leaky bucket" analogy (page 395) with your classmates. What maximum amount of income would you personally allow to leak from the bucket in transferring money from the rich to the poor? Explain why people differ in their answers to this question.

2. Continuing the leaky bucket example, explain why economists believe that replacing the present welfare system with a negative income tax would help reduce the leak.

3. Suppose you were to design a negative income tax system for the United States. Pick a guaranteed income level and a tax rate that seem reasonable to you. What break-even level of income is implied by these choices? Construct a version of Table 19–4 for the plan you have just devised.

4. Following is a complete list of the distribution of income in Disneyland. From these data, construct a Lorenz curve for Disneyland.

Donald Duck	$ 100,000
Mickey Mouse	172,000
Minnie Mouse	68,000
Pluto	44,000
Ticket taker	16,000

How different is this from the Lorenz curve for the United States (Figure 19–2)?

5. Take a piece of graph paper and construct Lorenz curves for the United States for 1997 and 1980. (The data are in Table 19–2.) What do you learn from comparing these two curves?

6. Suppose the War on Poverty were starting anew and you were part of a presidential commission assigned the task of defining the poor. Would you choose an absolute or a relative concept of poverty? Why? What would be your specific definition of poverty?

7. Discuss the concept of the "optimal amount of inequality." What are some of the practical problems in determining how much inequality really is optimal?

8. A number of conservative politicians and economists advocate replacing the progressive income tax with a "flat tax" that would apply the same, low tax rate to all income above a certain exempt amount. One argument against making this change is that the distribution of income has grown much more unequal since the 1970s. Does the evidence support that view? Is it a decisive argument against a flat tax? How is the trade-off between equality and efficiency involved here?

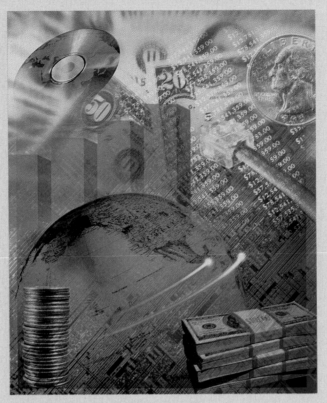

V

THE GOVERNMENT AND THE ECONOMY

e come now to the ways in which governments seek to manage market processes. As we saw in Chapter 11, we have good reason to believe that the market mechanism generally promotes the public interest and does so very effectively. But Chapters 12 and 14 pointed out that the invisible hand does not always work perfectly. Some market failures may justify some governmental attempts to correct market operations. In Part V, we describe some kinds of governmental intervention and the logic that underlies them. You should keep in mind that governments can also make mistakes—we can find examples

403

of governmental failure as well as market failures. When this happens, the government's cure for a market imperfection can sometimes prove worse than the disease. In other cases, however, there is reason to believe that government intervention does promote society's interests.

Three imperfections of the market mechanism drive the governmental actions described in this part. The first type of market failure results when some firm possesses market power that allows it to obtain monopoly profits (as we described in Chapter 12), generally by restricting output and charging higher prices than those firms would earn in otherwise similar competitive markets. If the government doesn't intervene, these firms can use their monopoly power to distort prices and outputs in ways that undermine economic efficiency and harm consumers. Externalities arise as a second major source of market imperfection—the benefits that firms generate for which they are not compensated, or the damage they do for which they do not have to pay. Environmental degradation—as when a firm faces no penalty even if it pours pollutants into the water we drink or fouls the air we breathe—is one clear consequence of such externalities. The third major reason for government intervention is the income inequality and widespread poverty that can occur in a free-market economy.

In Part V, we discuss what governments *can* do, and what, in fact, they *do* about these market weaknesses. We will even discuss a set of problems for which the economists' solution is to *extend* the market's role rather than constrain it—in other words, to allow the market to cure itself.

CHAPTER

20

. . . the one law you can't repeal is supply and demand.

William Safire
The New York Times, July 13, 1998

LIMITING MARKET POWER: REGULATION AND ANTITRUST

To protect the interests of the public when industries are, or threaten to become, monopolistic or oligopolistic, government in the United States uses two basic tools. *Antitrust policy* seeks to prevent acquisition of *monopoly power* and to ban certain monopolistic practices. All business firms are subject to the antitrust laws. In addition, some industries are also *regulated* by rules that constrain firms' pricing and other decisions. Generally, only firms suspected of having the power to act like monopolists are regulated.

THE PUBLIC INTEREST ISSUE: MONOPOLY POWER VERSUS MERE SIZE

Economies of scale are savings that are obtained through increases in quantities produced. Scale economies occur when an X percent increase in input use raises output by *more than* X percent, so that the more the firm produces, the lower its per-unit costs become.

Monopoly power (or market power) is the ability of a business firm to raise the prices of its products above competitive levels and to keep those prices high for a substantial amount of time.

We learned in Chapters 12 and 13 that when an industry is a monopoly or an oligopoly, the result may not be as desirable in terms of the public interest as it would be if the industry were perfectly competitive. Yet for many industries anything like perfect competition is an impossible goal. This is true, notably, when the industry's technology provides **economies of scale,** meaning, you will remember, that the more of its product that a firm supplies the lower the cost of supplying a unit of that product will be. Scale economies therefore mean that in competition between a large firm and a small one, the big one can usually win. As a result, industries with scale economies usually end up having a small number of firms, each of which has a large share of the industry's sales. In other words, such an industry is usually fated to be a monopoly or an oligopoly.

But what is so bad about that? The answer is that sometimes it is not bad at all, but in other cases the public interest will be threatened because some or all of the firms in the industry will possess **monopoly power.** Monopoly power (or market power) is usually defined as the ability of a firm to raise and keep the prices of its products substantially above the levels at which those products would be priced in competitive markets. That is, if a firm has monopoly power it can charge high prices and get away with it—the market will not punish it for doing so. In a competitive industry, in contrast, the market will punish a high-price firm by the loss of its customers to rivals with lower prices. Thus, monopoly power is undesirable for several reasons, some of them obvious:

■ *High prices reduce the wealth of consumers.* The use of monopoly power is obviously undesirable to consumers because no one likes to pay high prices for purchased commodities. Such high prices may make the firm with monopoly power rich and make the consumers of its products poor. Such effects on the distribution of wealth are generally considered undesirable.

■ *High prices lead to resource misallocation.* Economists give greater emphasis to a second undesirable effect of prices that exceed the competitive level. As we saw in Chapter 14, such prices tend to reduce the quantities of the products that consumers demand. This means that smaller quantities of labor, raw materials, and other inputs will be devoted to production of these high-priced products relative to the quantities that would *best* serve consumer interests. More of those inputs will therefore be transferred to the products of competitive industries. The result will be *underproduction* of the products priced at monopoly levels and *overproduction* of the products of competitive industries. So, as a result of the exercise of monopoly power, the economy does not produce the mix of outputs that best serves the public interest.

■ *Monopoly power creates an obstacle to efficiency and innovation.* In addition, a firm with monopoly power is a firm that does not face much effective competition. It does not have as much reason to fear loss of business to others. Where this is so, there is little incentive for management to make the effort to produce efficiently with a minimum of waste or to undertake the expenses and risks of innovation. The result is that products may have poorer quality than they would if the company possessed no monopoly power, and there will be waste in the production process.

Efficiency problems inherent in monopoly power are among the main reasons for governmental intervention controlling business firms' behavior and other attributes. The critical problem is control of monopoly power and prevention of acts by firms that are designed either to give them (or enhance) monopoly power, or to curb the use of that power to exploit the public.

There is a widespread misconception that all big firms have monopoly power, so that the primary purpose of antitrust or regulatory activity should be to break up as many large firms and to constrain the pricing of all large firms that cannot be broken into smaller ones. But this is an invalid conclusion. It is true that firms that have a very small share of their industry's sales cannot wield market power. For reasons studied in Chapter 11, such small firms are price takers, not price makers. They must simply accept the price determined by supply and demand in a competitive market, or the prices determined by larger firms in their industry if those large firms do have market power. But though firms with small market shares never have market power, the converse is untrue. Large firms do not always have market power.

This may be true for many reasons. In an oligopoly with fierce rivalry, each firm may be prevented by the actions of its competitors from raising price above competitive levels. For example, Coca-Cola and Pepsi each have a very large share of the soft drink market. But it is well known that there is no love between the two companies. So neither dares to raise its prices substantially for fear of driving customers into the arms of its unloved competitor.

Even a monopoly may have little or no monopoly power if entry into its industry is cheap and easy. Such a firm knows that it can only retain its monopoly *if its behavior is not monopolistic.* If it tries to raise its price to monopoly levels for any substantial period of time, then its rivals will have an opportunity to come in and take some or all of its business away. So in industries where entry is very easy, a large firm will have no monopoly power because the perpetual threat of potential entry will keep it from misbehaving. For this reason government agencies concerned with monopoly issues explicitly avoid interfering with the actions of firms in industries where entry is cheap and easy.

The primary threat of monopoly and oligopoly to the public interest is monopoly power. This power can lead to excessive prices that exploit consumers, misallocation of resources, and inefficient and noninnovative firms. But firms that are big do not necessarily have market power.

In Part 1 of this chapter, we will begin our discussion of these issues with regulation and its history in the United States. In Part 2 of the chapter, we turn to antitrust policy.

■ PART 1: REGULATION

HOW AND WHY DID REGULATION ARISE?

Regulation of industry in the United States began when indignation over abuse of market power by the nation's railroads led to the establishment of the Interstate Commerce Commission (ICC) in 1887. There was a public outcry over the support the railroads gave to John D. Rockefeller Sr. in the battle of his Standard Oil Company against its rivals. This, along with other railroad abuses, invited government intervention. But for several decades afterward, there was little attempt to expand regulation to other industries. Then the Federal Power Commission (FPC) was established in 1920 and the Federal Communications Commission (FCC) in 1934; many of the remaining regulatory agencies were formed during the 1930s under President Franklin D. Roosevelt's New Deal.

Today, several federal regulatory agencies control prices. Until it was abolished in 1995, the ICC regulated railroads, barges, pipelines, and some categories of trucking. Its regulatory tasks are now performed by the Department of Commerce. The FCC regulates broadcasting and telecommunications. The Federal Energy Regulatory Commission (FERC) regulates interstate transmission of electric power and sales of natural gas. The Securities and Exchange Commission (SEC) regulates sales of securities (stocks and bonds). A number of agencies, led by the Federal Reserve System, control banking operations. The work of these agencies is complemented by a variety of state agencies that regulate intrastate activities.

Despite good intentions, regulation has been criticized as a cause of inefficiency and excessive costs to the consuming public. The basic fact about regulation and

Regulation of industry is a process established by law that restricts or controls some specified decisions made by the affected firms, and is designed to protect the public from exploitation by firms with monopoly power. Regulation is usually carried out by a special government agency assigned the task of administering and interpreting the law. That agency also acts as a court in enforcing the regulatory laws.

"Won't all these new rules impact adversely on the viability of small businesses with fewer than fifty employees?"

other forms of government intervention that are designed to affect the operations of markets is that *neither* markets *nor* governmental agencies always work perfectly. In an uncontrolled market, for example, monopoly power can damage the public interest, but excessive or poorly conceived regulations or antitrust decisions can also be harmful.

WHAT IS REGULATED? BY WHOM?

The regulatory agencies in the United States can be divided, roughly, into two classes: those that limit the market power of regulated firms and those devoted to consumer and worker protection and safety. In a recent count, at least 14 federal regulatory agencies dealt with restraint of market power and about 30 handled issues such as environmental protection and product safety. An example of the latter is the Food and Drug Administration (FDA), which protects the public from harmful, impure, infected, or adulterated foods, drugs, and cosmetics by preventing their sale to the public.

The federal government also regulates the safety of automobiles and mines and the use of dangerous substances such as pesticides. Such regulation affects an enormous proportion of the nation's economic activity, including the drug industry, agriculture, auto manufacturing, and the chemical and power industries. Virtually every manufacturing industry is affected by environmental regulations.

Regulations designed to limit market power, on which this chapter focuses, affect industries that together provide perhaps 10 percent of the gross domestic product (GDP) of the United States. The list includes telecommunications, railroads, electric utilities, and oil pipelines.

Puzzle: Why Do Regulators Often *Raise* Prices?

Regulation sometimes forces consumers to pay *higher* prices than they would pay in its absence. For instance, before the airline industry was deregulated, the flight between New York City and Washington, D.C. (an interstate trip that was controlled by the federal government) used to cost *more* than the longer flight between San Francisco and Los Angeles (which was not controlled by the federal government, because it's entirely within the state of California). The California trip was nearly *twice* as long as the East Coast trip, and it did not have a substantially lower cost per passenger mile. So why did regulators, whose job is to protect the public interest, deliberately price the New York–Washington hop about 25 percent higher? Later in the chapter, you will be able to answer this question.

■ SOME OBJECTIVES OF REGULATION

Economists recognize a number of reasons that may justify the regulation of an industry.

CONTROL OF MARKET POWER RESULTING FROM ECONOMIES OF SCALE AND SCOPE

As we learned at the beginning of this chapter, a main reason for regulation of industry is to prevent the use of or acquisition of market power by regulated firms. In some industries, it is far cheaper to have production carried out by one firm than by many, and the relatively large firms that result may gain market power. One cause is economies of large-scale production. Railroad tracks are a particularly good example of such *economies of scale*. The total cost of building and maintaining the tracks when 100 trains traverse them every day is not much higher than when only one train uses them. So substantial savings in average cost result when rail traffic increases. As we saw in Chapter 8, scale economies lead to an average cost curve that goes downhill as output increases (see Figure 20–1). This means that a firm with a large output can cover its costs at a price lower than a firm whose output is smaller. In the figure, point *A* represents the larger firm whose AC is $5, whereas point *B* is the smaller firm with an AC of $7.

A single, large firm may also have a cost advantage over a group of small firms when it is cheaper to produce a number of different commodities together rather than making each separately in a different firm. Savings made possible by simultaneous production of many different products by one firm are called **economies of scope.** One clear example of economies of scope is the manufacture of both cars and trucks by the same producer. The techniques employed in producing both commodities are similar, which provides a cost advantage to firms that produce both.

In industries where there are great economies of scale and scope, costs will be much higher if government intervenes to preserve a large number of small, and therefore costly, firms. Moreover, where economies of scale and scope are strong, society will not be able to preserve free competition, even if it wants to. The large, multiproduct firm will have so great a cost advantage over its rivals that the small firms simply will be unable to survive.

> Where monopoly production is cheapest, so that free competition is not sustainable, the industry is a natural monopoly. When monopoly is cheaper, society may not want to have competition; if free competition is not sustainable, it will not even have a choice in the matter.

But even if society reconciles itself to monopoly in such cases, it will generally not want to let the monopoly firm wield its market power without limits. Therefore, it will consider regulating the company's decisions on matters such as pricing.

MONOPOLY POWER AND THE PRICES OF "BOTTLENECK" FACILITIES

BOTTLENECK FACILITIES Monopoly power can arise for reasons other than economies of scale and scope. One source that is currently a center of attention in regulatory discussion is the possession by a single firm of facilities that other firms

FIGURE 20-1

Economies of Scale

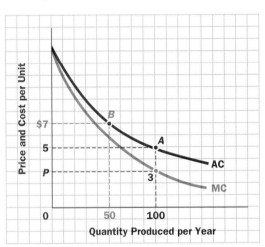

Economies of scope are savings that are obtained through simultaneous production of many different products and occur if a firm that produces many commodities can supply each good more cheaply than a firm that produces fewer commodities.

A facility or service owned by a single firm and needed for the activities of rival firms is called a **bottleneck facility** (or, simply, a **bottleneck**).

must use if they are to compete successfully with the owner of that facility. Such a facility owned by a single firm and needed for the activities of rival firms is called a **bottleneck facility.** How to price the use of these bottleneck facilities is a critical regulatory problem.

Picking up our previous railroad example, let's suppose that several competing railroads need to go over a single mountain pass, but that access to the pass is owned by one of those railroads. That pass is, then, a bottleneck facility, because no railroad can compete in that particular market without using the resource.

The same situation arises in the telecommunications and electricity industries. For instance, most long-distance telephone calls to or from points in Ohio or Illinois (whether carried by AT&T, MCI, or Sprint) must at some point get to homes or businesses via the local telephone network (called "the local loop" in regulatory parlance), which is owned by a telecommunications company called Ameritech. Now, Ameritech is hoping to get into some of the long-distance business itself. But if it does, then it, along with AT&T, MCI, and Sprint, will have to make use of its own bottleneck local loop. Here's another example: In the electric power industry, rival generators of electricity must all use the bottleneck transmission facilities (the wires, poles, and so on) owned by the utility that also generates electricity of its own.

If competition is to be maintained in both these cases, the rival firms that do not own the bottleneck facility must clearly be permitted to use the facility—after, of course, paying an appropriate price. But what price is appropriate? This issue has become central in litigation and negotiation with regulatory agencies throughout the industrial world. Clearly, if the owner of the bottleneck is able to use monopoly power in setting the price of the bottleneck facility, then that price may well end up far above the competitive price level. But if the price the owner is allowed to charge rivals for use of the bottleneck facility is too high, it can drive the competitors out of business. On the other hand, if regulators force the bottleneck owner to charge a price that is too low to cover its costs, it will be subsidizing its rivals and will find it difficult or impossible to compete with them.

What price, then, is neither too high nor too low? The answer provided by one group of economists is suggested by analogy with a simpler situation. Suppose, in our railroad example, that two railroads, A and B, need to use the bottleneck mountain

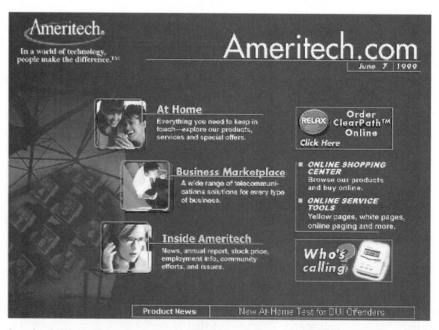

Ameritech Web site

● THE PRIVY COUNCIL APPROVES "PARITY-PRINCIPLE" ACCESS PRICING

New Zealand Telecom, the formerly monopoly telephone company of New Zealand, faced competition from an entrant called Clear Communications. Clear offers long-distance service and hopes to provide local service as well. For Clear's long-distance messages to reach their intended recipients, however, it is generally necessary to make use of NZ Telecom's local facilities (the local "loop"). After negotiations over the price for this *bottleneck* service broke down, Clear sued Telecom. Telecom offered to adopt the parity-principle price for access to its local loop, but Clear refused.

The High Court of New Zealand, with some reservations, decided that the parity-principle offer was appropriate, but this decision was overturned by the court of appeal on grounds related to special features of New Zealand law. That decision then was reviewed by the final appeals body, the Privy Council in London. In October 1994, the council issued its judgment, fully supporting the parity principle and holding that there were no difficulties in New Zealand law of the sort cited by the court of appeal. The decision of the Privy Council stated in part:

> Both the High Court and the Court of Appeal proceeded on the basis, with which their Lordships [that is, the judges of the Privy Council] agree, that if the terms Telecom was seeking to extract were no higher than those which a hypothetical firm would seek in a perfectly contestable market, Telecom was not using its

dominant position [that is, it was not behaving as a monopolist]. . . . The [parity principle] rule is a closely reasoned economic model which seeks to show how the hypothetical firm would conduct itself. . . . [T]he underlying object [of the relevant New Zealand law] will be achieved if the [parity principle] rule is applied.

SOURCE: Privy Council Appeal No. 21 of 1994, Judgment of the Lords of the Judicial Committee of the Privy Council, pp. 21 and 27.

pass, but the owner of the pass is not itself a railroad. To provide what regulators call a "level playing field" for the two rival railroads, it is necessary for the owner of the mountain pass to charge the same toll to Railroad A that it charges to Railroad B. Then, both railroads will be paying the same fee to use the pass. As a result, the railroad that has the lower *remaining* cost in carrying the traffic from origin to destination can clearly afford to charge a lower freight rate for the route and capture the traffic that goes over it.

THE PARITY-PRICING PRINCIPLE Next, suppose that the owner of the mountain pass decides to enter the rail-transport business in competition with Railroad A and Railroad B. How does that affect the proper price to charge for the use of the pass? The answer is that all three railroads should now pay the same price. This is called the *parity-pricing principle*, though it still leaves a calculation problem: that of determining exactly what price the owner of the pass really pays to *itself* for use of it. (For confirmation of the legitimacy of the parity-pricing rule by the judges of the Privy Council in London, see the accompanying box, "The Privy Council Approves 'Parity-Principle' Access Pricing.")

UNIVERSAL SERVICE AND RATE AVERAGING

A third objective of regulation of the prices and other choices of firms in a regulated industry is the desire for "universal service." By this we mean the availability of service to everyone at "reasonable prices," particularly to impoverished consumers and small communities where the limited scale of operations may make costs extremely high. In such cases regulators may encourage or require a public utility

Cross-subsidization means selling one product at a loss, which is balanced by higher profits on another product.

(such as an electric power supplier) to serve some consumers at a financial loss. But a loss on some sales is financially feasible only when the regulated firm is permitted to make up for it by obtaining higher profits on its other sales. Charging higher prices to one set of customers to finance lower prices to another customer group is called **cross-subsidization.**

But this sort of cross-subsidization is possible only if the regulated firm is protected from price competition and free entry of new competitors in its other, more profitable markets (in which it charges the higher prices that subsidize the financing of the mandated low prices). If no such protection is provided, potential competitors will sniff out these profit opportunities in the markets where service is supplied at prices well above cost. Many new firms will enter the business and drive prices down in those markets—a practice referred to as *cream skimming.* The entrants choose to enter only the profitable markets and skim away the "cream" of the profits for themselves, leaving the unprofitable markets (the skimmed milk?) to the supplier who had attempted to provide universal service. This phenomenon is one reason why regulatory rules, until recently, made it very difficult or impossible for new firms to enter when and where they saw fit.

Airlines and telecommunications are two industries in which these issues have arisen. In both cases, it was feared that without regulation of entry and rates, or special subsidies, less populous communities would effectively be isolated, losing their airline services and obtaining telephone service only at cripplingly high rates. Many economists question the validity of this argument for regulation, which, they say, calls for hidden subsidies of rural consumers by everyone else. The airline deregulation act provided for government subsidies to help small communities attract airline service. In fact, this market has since been taken over to a considerable extent by specialized "commuter" airlines flying much smaller aircraft than the major airlines, which have withdrawn from many such routes.

A similar issue affects the U.S. Postal Service, which charges the same price to deliver a letter anywhere within the United States, regardless of the distance or the special difficulties and costs of a particular route. To maintain this pricing scheme, the law must protect the Postal Service from direct competition in many of its activities—otherwise, its extreme form of uniform pricing would soon deprive it of its most profitable routes. Thus, the goal of providing universal service leads to the regulation of entry into and exit from the affected industry, and not just price control.

■ TWO KEY ISSUES THAT FACE REGULATORS

Regulators around the world face (at least) two critical issues that are of fundamental importance for economic policy. They are at the heart of recent legal battles before regulatory agencies almost everywhere.

HOW CAN REGULATORS SET PRICES THAT BEST PROTECT CONSUMERS' INTERESTS BUT ENABLE REGULATED FIRMS TO COVER THEIR COSTS?

When governments regulate prices they usually want to prevent those prices from being so high that they bring monopoly profits to the firm. But at the same time governments want to set prices at levels that are "compensatory." That is, the prices must be sufficiently high to enable the firms to cover their costs and, consequently, to survive financially. Regulators also are asked to select prices that best serve the public interest. But these goals, as we will see next, can often be at odds.

■ *Prices intended to promote the public interest may cause financial problems for firms.* We saw in Chapters 10 and 11 that the consumer's welfare is most effectively promoted by setting the price of a product equal to that product's marginal cost. But we will see presently that such a rule would condemn many regulated firms to bankruptcy. What should the regulator do in such a case?

■ *Preventing firms with monopoly power from earning excessive profits without elimi-nating all incentive for efficiency and innovation may prove difficult.* The firm's incentive and reward for the effort and expenditure needed to improve effi-ciency and to innovate is the higher profit that it expects to obtain if it suc-ceeds. But a frequent objective of regulation is to put a ceiling on profit in order to prevent monopoly earnings. How can monopoly profits be prevented without destroying incentives?

Let's now analyze these issues, which arise frequently in today's crucial regulatory policy debates.

MARGINAL VERSUS AVERAGE COST PRICING

Regulatory agencies often have the task of controlling the prices of regulated firms. Acrimonious debate over the proper levels for those prices has filled hundreds of thou-sands of pages of regulatory-hearing records and has involved literally hundreds of millions of dollars of expenditures in fees for lawyers, expert witnesses, and research. The question has been: What constitutes the proper formula to set these prices?

Where it is feasible, most economists favor setting price equal to marginal cost because, as was shown in Chapter 11, this pricing policy provides the incentive for firms to produce output quantities that serve consumers' wants most efficiently. However, a serious practical problem often prevents use of marginal-cost pricing. The problem is that, in many regulated industries, the firms would go bankrupt if all prices were set equal to marginal costs!

This seems a startling conclusion, but it follows inescapably from three simple facts:

Fact 1. In many regulated industries, there are significant economies of large-scale production. As we pointed out earlier, economies of scale are one of the main reasons why certain industries were regulated in the first place.

Fact 2. In an industry with economies of scale, the long-run average cost curve is downward sloping. This means that the long-run average cost falls as the quan-tity produced rises, as was illustrated by the AC curve in Figure 20–1. Fact 2 is something we learned back in Chapter 8. The reason, to review briefly, is that where there are economies of scale, if all input quantities are doubled, output will *more than double.* But costs will obviously only double if input quantities double. Thus, costs will rise more slowly than output and cost per unit of output must fall. That is, because average cost (AC) is simply total cost (TC) divided by quan-tity *(Q)* with economies of scale, AC = TC/*Q* must decline when all input quantities are doubled.

Fact 3. If average cost is declining, then marginal cost must be below average cost. This fact follows directly from one of the general rules relating marginal and average data that were explained in the appendix to Chapter 9. Once again, the logic is simple enough to review briefly. If, for example, your average quiz score is 90 percent but the next quiz pulls your average down to 87 percent, then the grade on this most recent test (the marginal grade) must be below both the old and the new average quiz scores. That is, it takes a marginal grade (or cost) that is below the average to pull the average down.

Putting these three facts together, we conclude that in many regulated industries, marginal cost (MC) will be below average cost, as depicted in Figure 20–1. Now suppose that regulators set the price at the level of marginal cost. Because *P* then equals MC, *P* must be below AC and the firm must lose money, so "*P* equals MC" is simply not an acceptable option. What, then, should be done? One possibility is to set price equal to marginal cost and to make up for the deficit out of public funds. However, subsidies to large regulated firms are not very popular politically and may also not be sensible.

A second option, which is quite popular among regulators, is to (try to) set price equal to average cost. But this method of pricing is neither desirable nor possible to carry out except on the basis of arbitrary decisions. The problem is that almost no firm produces only a single commodity. Almost every company produces a number of different varieties and qualities of some product, and many produce thousands of different products, each with its own price. Even General Motors, a fairly specialized firm that produces many makes and sizes of cars and trucks, also sells home mortgages and quite a few other things. In a multiproduct firm, we cannot even define AC = TC/Q, because to calculate Q (total output), we would have to add up all the apples and oranges (and all of the other different items) that the firm produces. But we know that one cannot add up apples and oranges. Because we cannot calculate AC for a multiproduct firm, it is hardly possible for the regulator to require P to equal AC for each of the firm's products, though regulators sometimes think they can do so.

THE RAMSEY PRICING RULE   Economists have been attracted to an imaginative, alternative approach to the problem of pricing in regulated industries that produce many products. This approach derives its name from its discoverer, Frank Ramsey, a brilliant English mathematician who died in 1930 at the age of 26 after making several enduring contributions to both mathematics and economics.

The **Ramsey pricing rule** is a rule for determining prices that promote consumer welfare while covering the producer's cost.

The basic idea of the **Ramsey pricing rule** can be explained in a fairly straightforward manner. We know that prices must be set above marginal costs if a firm with scale economies is to break even, but how much above? Suppose the firm makes two products, A and B, and the demand for A is much more elastic than that of B. This means that a given percentage price rise will induce consumers to cut their purchases of A much more than those of B. It then makes sense to raise price most above marginal cost for product B—the one with the less elastic demand. Why? Because a given price increase for B will interfere less with consumers' purchase decisions than a similar rise in the price of A. This insight is the essence of the Ramsey pricing rule:

> **In a multiproduct, regulated firm in which prices must exceed marginal cost in order to permit that firm to break even, other things being equal, the ratios of *P* over MC should be largest for those of the firm's products whose elasticities of demand are the smallest.**

Economists accept this pricing rule as the correct conclusion on theoretical grounds. It has even been proposed for postal and telephone pricing, and various regulatory commissions have used it as a general guide for the regulation of prices.

PREVENTING MONOPOLY PROFIT BUT KEEPING INCENTIVES FOR EFFICIENCY AND INNOVATION

Opponents of regulation claim that it seriously impairs the efficiency of American industry and reduces the benefits of free markets. One obvious source of inefficiency is the endless paperwork and complex legal proceedings that prevent the firm from responding quickly to changing market conditions.

In addition, economists believe that regulatory interference in pricing causes economic inefficiency. By forcing prices to differ from those that would prevail in a free, competitive market, regulations lead consumers to demand a quantity of the regulated product that does not maximize consumer benefits from the quantity of resources available to the economy. (This resource misallocation issue was discussed in Chapter 14.)

But there is a third source of inefficiency that may be even more important. It occurs because regulators often are required to prevent the regulated firm from earning excessive profits, while at the same time offering it financial incentives for maximum efficiency of operation and allowing it enough profit to attract the capital it needs when growing markets justify expansion. It would seem to be ideal if the regulator would permit the firm to earn just the amount of revenue that covers its costs, including the cost of its capital. Thus, if the current rate of profits in competitive markets is 10 percent, the regulated firm should recover its costs plus 10 percent on its investment and not a penny more or less. The trouble with such a rule is that it removes all profit incentive for efficiency, responsiveness to consumer demand, and innovation. It, in effect, guarantees just one standard rate of profit to the firm, no more and no less—regardless of whether its management is totally incompetent or extremely talented and hardworking.

Competitive markets do not work this way. Although under perfect competition the average firm will earn just the illustrative 10 percent, a firm with an especially ingenious and efficient management will do better, and a firm with an incompetent management is likely to go broke. It is the possibility of great rewards and harsh punishments that gives the market mechanism its power to cause firms to strive for high efficiency and productivity growth.

When firms are guaranteed fixed returns no matter how well or how poorly they perform, gross inefficiencies often result. For example, many contracts for purchases of military equipment have prices calculated on a so-called cost-plus basis, meaning that the supplier is guaranteed that its costs will be covered and that, in addition, it will receive some prespecified profit. Studies of such cost-plus arrangements have confirmed enormous supplier inefficiencies. A regulatory arrangement that in effect guarantees a regulated firm its cost plus a "fair rate of return" on its investment obviously has much in common with a cost-plus contract. Fortunately, there are also substantial differences between the two, and so regulatory profit ceilings need not always have serious effects on the firm's incentives for efficiency.

Curiously, the much-criticized delay that characterizes many regulatory procedures, known as *regulatory lag*, is perhaps the main reason that profit regulation has not eliminated all rewards for efficiency and all penalties for inefficiency. Suppose, for example, that the regulatory commission approves some prices expected to yield exactly the fair rate of return to the company, say, 10 percent. If management then successfully reduces its costs, the effective rate of return under the old prices may rise to, say, 12 percent. If it takes three years for the regulators to adjust the prices they previously approved to the new cost levels, the company will earn a 2 percent bonus as a reward for its efficiency during the three years of regulatory lag. Similarly, if management makes a series of bad decisions that reduce the company's return to 7 percent, the firm may ask the regulator for price increases to recoup its losses. If the regulator takes 18 months to act, the firm suffers a penalty for its inefficiency. But regulatory lag penalizes inefficiency and rewards superior performance very imperfectly. It still leaves provision of incentives for efficiency as one of the fundamental problems of regulation. How can one prevent regulated firms from earning excessive profits, but also permit them to earn enough to attract the capital they need and, above all, still allow rewards for superior performance and penalties for poor performance?

PRICE CAPS AS INCENTIVES FOR EFFICIENCY A regulatory innovation designed to prevent monopoly profits while offering incentives for the firm to improve its efficiency is now in use in many countries—for electricity, telephones, and airport services in Great Britain, for example, and for telephone rates in the United States and elsewhere. The basic idea is a planned extension of the incentive for efficiency provided by regulatory lag.

Under this program, the regulators assign ceilings (called *price caps*) for the *prices* (not the profits) of the regulated firms. However, the price caps (which are measured in real, inflation-adjusted terms) are reduced each year at a rate based on the rate of cost reduction (productivity growth) previously achieved by the regulated firm. Thus, if the regulated firm subsequently achieves cost savings (by innovation or other means) greater than those it obtained in the past, the firm's real costs will fall faster than its real prices, and it will be permitted to keep the resulting profits as its reward. Of course, there is a catch. If the regulated firm reduces its costs only by, say, 2 percent per year whereas in the past its costs fell 3 percent per year, the price cap will also be falling at a 3 percent rate. The firm will therefore lose profits, though consumers will continue to benefit from falling real prices.

Thus, under price-cap regulation management is constantly forced to look for ever more economical ways of doing things. This approach clearly gives up any attempt to limit the profit of the regulated firm—leaving the possibility of higher profits as an incentive for efficiency. But it protects the consumer nonetheless by controlling the firm's prices. Indeed, it makes those prices lower and lower, in real terms.

THE PROS AND CONS OF "BIGNESS"

We have described several goals for regulation, including control of monopoly power, increased availability of bottleneck facilities, and the provision of universal service. Is it desirable, in addition to these regulatory goals, to try to make big firms become smaller? In other words, are the effects of "bigness" always undesirable? We have already seen that only relatively big firms have any likelihood of possessing monopoly power. We have also seen that monopoly power can cause a number of problems, including undesirable effects on income distribution, misallocation of resources, and inhibition of efficiency and innovation.

But we have also seen that big firms at least sometimes do not possess monopoly power. More generally, there is another side of the picture. Bigness in industry can also, at least sometimes, benefit the general public. Again, this is true for a number of reasons, among them:

ECONOMIES OF LARGE SIZE

Probably the most important advantage of bigness is found in industries where technology makes small-scale operation inefficient. One can hardly imagine the costs if automobiles were produced in little workshops rather than giant factories. The notion of a small firm operating a long-distance railroad does not even make sense, and a multiplicity of firms replicating the same railroad service would clearly be incredibly wasteful.

On these grounds, most policymakers have never even considered any attempt to eliminate bigness. Of course, it does not follow that every industry in which firms happen to be big is one in which big firms are best. Some observers argue that many firms, in fact, exceed the sizes required for cost minimization.

REQUIRED SCALE FOR INNOVATION

Some economists have argued that only large firms have the resources and the motivation for really significant innovation. Many inventions are still contributed by individuals. But, because it is often an expensive, complex, and large-scale undertaking to put a new invention into commercial production, usually only large firms can afford the funds and bear the risks that such an effort demands. In addition, according to this view of the matter, only a large firm has the motivation to lay out the funds required for the innovation process because it gets to keep a considerable share of the benefits. A small company, on the other hand, will find that its innovative idea is soon likely to be followed by close imitations, which enable competitors to profit from its research outlays.

There have been many studies of the relationships among firm size, industry competitiveness, and the level of expenditure on research and development (R&D). Although the evidence is far from conclusive, it does indicate that highly competitive industries composed of very small firms tend not to spend a great deal on research. Up to a point, R&D outlays and innovation seem to increase with size of the firm and the concentration of the industry. However, some of the most significant innovations introduced in this century have been contributed by firms that started very small. Examples include the electric light, alternating current (AC) electricity, the photocopier, the electronic calculator, and the desktop computer.

The bottom line here is that bigness in business firms receives a mixed score. It can produce undesirable results, but in other cases it is necessary for efficiency and low costs and offers other benefits to the public. A rule requiring regulators to combat bigness per se, wherever it occurs, is likely to have undesirable results, and would, in any event, be unworkable.

● **THE TELECOMMUNICATIONS ACT OF 1996**

After much debate and argument by the affected firms, Congress passed the Telecommunications Act of 1996. This act was intended to increase competition among cable television suppliers and telecommunications firms. Of course, there already is vigorous price rivalry among suppliers of long-distance services, as we see in their television ads almost every evening, but other telecommunications services are often provided by monopolies.

The Telecommunications Act of 1996 was designed to permit telephone companies to enter into cable television service, thus providing competitors to the cable companies, which now rarely have rivals in a given geographic area. The act was also designed to permit and make it easy for the long-distance firms—AT&T, MCI, Sprint, and others—to carry local telephone calls, in competition with the current local phone monopolies. Finally, it permitted the local phone companies to compete in the long-distance business for the first time. However, the act provided that the largest local companies could invade the long-distance business only after entry had occurred in local service—that is, when the local monopoly was effectively ended.

A number of problems have since emerged. For one thing, entry into cable service has been slow to materialize because it turns out to be quite costly. Even though telephone equipment can be used to transmit cable programs through telephone wires into homes, those facilities have to be modified for that purpose at considerable expense. Competition from satellite and wireless service providers is also making entry by telephone companies into the cable business less profitable than had been hoped.

The entry of long-distance firms into local telephone service has involved even greater frustration. It is enormously costly for new entrants to construct new local facilities that replicate those of the monopolies already in place. Moreover, the facilities already available have plenty of excess capacity for them to carry many more calls. It has therefore been proposed that the local companies be required to rent space on these *bottleneck* facilities to firms that want to enter the market. This has led to battles over the *price* the local companies would be allowed to charge Sprint, MCI, AT&T, and the others for use of their facilities. (See the discussion of bottleneck pricing on pages 409–411.) The local companies claim that the prices offered by the long-distance firms are too low, whereas the long-distance firms maintain that the prices advocated by local firms are far too high. As it stands now, all these issues are tied up in court litigation, and some observers have concluded that the 1996 Act is a total failure. Others believe that the Act has led to *some* progress in introducing competition into the business and that, with luck, the court decisions will yet enable most of the goals of the legislation to be attained.

■ **DEREGULATION**

Because regulators have sometimes adopted rules and made decisions that were ill-advised and were demonstrably harmful to the public interest, and because the bureaucracy that is needed to enforce regulation is costly and raises business costs, there have long been demands for reduced regulation. Beginning in the mid-1970s, Congress responded to such arguments by deregulating several industries, such as airlines and trucking, eliminating most of the powers of the relevant regulatory agencies. In other industries, such as railroads and telecommunications, rule changes now give regulated firms considerably more freedom in decision making. This process is still under way. For instance, Congress engaged in a major—and highly charged—debate over telecommunications regulation in 1995, ending in a major piece of legislation in 1996 (see the accompanying box, "The Telecommunications Act of 1996").

THE EFFECTS OF DEREGULATION

One way to deal with the regulation difficulties just discussed is to shut regulation down—simply leave everything to the free market and get rid of the regulators. Many observers think that would be a good idea in a number of cases, but sometimes it would be unacceptable, as in markets that are virtually pure monopolies. Thus, the move toward deregulation has proceeded slowly, eliminating regulation in some fields, reducing it in others. Deregulation's effects in the United States are still being debated, but several conclusions seem clear:

EFFECTS ON PRICES   There seems little doubt that deregulation has generally led to lower prices. Airline fares, railroad freight rates, and telephone rates have all declined on the average (in real, inflation-adjusted terms) after total or partial deregulation. At least in the case of the airlines, however, the rate of decline slowed abruptly toward the end of the 1980s. Still, observers conclude that most of these prices are well below the levels that would have prevailed under regulation.

EFFECTS ON LOCAL SERVICES   At first it was widely feared, even by supporters of deregulation, that smaller and more isolated communities would be deprived of services because small numbers of customers would make those services unprofitable. It was feared that airlines, railroads, and telephone companies would withdraw from such communities once there was no longer any regulation to force them to stay. These worries have proved largely groundless. Although larger airlines have left smaller communities, they have usually been replaced by smaller commuter airlines that have often provided more frequent service.

EFFECTS ON ENTRY   As a result of deregulation, older airlines invaded one another's routes, several dozen new airlines sprang up, and about 10,000 new truck operators entered the market, though many of them have since dropped out, as profits and wages were driven down by competition. Almost all of the new airlines also ran into trouble and were sold to the older airlines. But since 1990, many small airlines have been launched. A battle is now shaping up over whether the small airlines need special protection from tough competition by the larger airlines.

EFFECTS ON UNIONS   Deregulation has badly hurt unions such as the Teamsters (of the trucking industry) and the Airline Pilots Association. In the new, competitive climate firms have been forced to make sharp cuts in their workforces and to resist wage increases and other costly changes in working conditions. Indeed, there has been strong pressure for retrenchment on all of these fronts. It should not be surprising, then, that unions often oppose deregulation.

EFFECTS ON CONCENTRATION AND MERGERS   Particularly in aviation and rail freight transportation, deregulation was followed by a wave of mergers in which two firms agreed to join together or in which one firm agreed to be bought out by another. As a result, the sizes of the largest companies in the affected industries have expanded. That this has happened should not be surprising because, as we saw earlier in the chapter, industries with substantial economies of scale are the most likely targets for regulation. Once freed from regulatory constraints, one could expect firms in such industries to take advantage of opportunities to achieve cost reductions through rapid expansion or by mergers.

EFFECTS ON PRODUCT QUALITY   The public has been unpleasantly surprised by another effect of deregulation. At least in the case of aviation, increased price competition has been accompanied by sharp reductions in "frills." To cut costs, airlines have made meals less elaborate (to put it mildly) and have limited the number of flights to avoid empty seats—which has increased crowding. To fill planes with more passengers, many airlines turned to "hub and spoke" systems (see Figure 20–2). Instead of running a flight directly from a low-demand airport, A, to another low-demand airport, B, the airline flies all passengers from Airport A to its "hub" at Airport H, where all passengers bound for destination Airport B are asked to reboard an airplane flying to B. This clearly saves money and gives passengers more options as the number of flights between hubs and spokes increases. But it is less convenient for passengers than a direct flight from origin to destination. Critics of deregulation have placed a good deal of emphasis on the reductions in passenger comfort. But economists argue that competition would not bring such results unless passengers as a group prefer the reduction in fares to the greater standards of luxury that preceded them.

EFFECTS ON SAFETY   Also in the case of airline deregulation (though the issue can well arise elsewhere), some observers have been concerned that cost cutting after deregulation would lead to skimping on safety measures. As Figure 20–3 shows, deregulation seems not to have produced any increase in the rate of airline accidents. Still, deregulation may require special vigilance to guard against neglect of

---

FIGURE 20-2

A "Hub and Spoke" Airline Routing Pattern

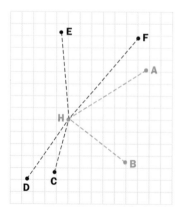

safety as a cost-cutting measure. Some observers suggest that the reduced profits that competition has caused in truck transportation has led truckers to cut corners in terms of safety.

U.S. Airline Accident Rates, 1960–1999

FIGURE 20-3

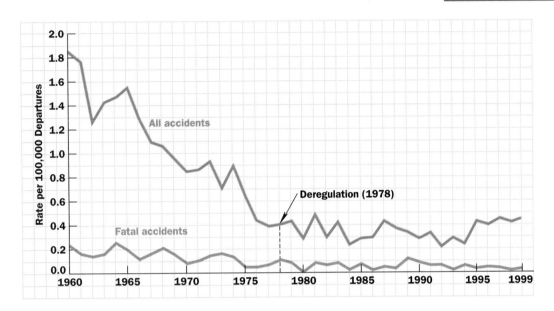

SOURCE: National Transportation Safety Board (www.ntsb.gov). Data are for all scheduled service of U.S. airlines operating under 14 CFR 121.

EFFECTS ON PROFITS AND WAGES   As the previous discussion suggested, deregulation has generally strengthened competition, and the increased power of competition has, in turn, tended to depress profits and wages. This, of course, is just the other side of reduced prices to consumers. In some cases, the profit and wage cuts were very substantial and had significant consequences. The financial problems that result for airlines and trucking firms have already been noted, and the pressures for decreases in the very high earnings of airline pilots has led to frequent confrontations with the airlines, as in the battle between American Airlines and its pilots in February 1999.

The general conclusion is that deregulation has usually worked out well, but hardly perfectly in promoting the welfare of consumers. But the battle for deregulation is far from over. Even if those who wish for a return to the good old days of regulation (and there are some) do not succeed, many areas exist in which regulation of the old-time variety still continues its grip or has been reintroduced in disguised form.

Puzzle Revisited: The Reason Why Regulators Often Push Prices Upward

We can now return to the puzzle we posed earlier: Why would regulators, who are supposed to protect the interests of the public, raise prices? As we will see now, the answer is that regulators sometimes push for higher prices when they want to prevent the demise of any existing firms in an industry. We saw earlier that strong economies of scale and economies of scope may make it impossible for a number of firms to survive. The largest firm in an industry may have such a big cost advantage over its competitors that it will be able to drive them out of the market while still operating at a profit.

Firms that are hurt by such competitive pressures often complain to regulatory commissions that the prices charged by a rival are "unfairly low." These commissions, afraid that unrestrained pricing will reduce the number of firms in the industry, then attempt to "equalize" matters by imposing price floors (below which prices cannot be set). Such price floors are designed to permit *all* the firms in the industry to operate profitably, even those that operate inefficiently and incur costs far higher than their competitors' costs.

But many economists maintain that this approach to pricing is a perversion of the idea of competition. The virtue of competition is that, where it occurs, firms force one another to supply consumers with products of high quality at low prices. Any firm that cannot do this is driven out of business by market forces. A regulatory arrangement may allow efficient and inefficient firms to coexist only by preventing them from competing with one another, but this only preserves the appearance of competition while destroying its substance, and forces consumers to pay the higher prices necessary to keep the inefficient firms alive.

■ PART 2: ANTITRUST LAWS AND POLICIES

Antitrust policy refers to programs and laws that preclude the deliberate creation of monopoly and prevent powerful firms from engaging in related "undesirable practices."

In Part 1 of this chapter we described the process of regulation, which governments use to control monopoly or oligopoly firms that are deemed to have dangerous power to control their markets. In Part 2 we will analyze the second of government's instruments for protecting competition: **antitrust policy.** Antitrust policy (often referred to, simply, as "antitrust") refers to programs that preclude the deliberate creation of monopoly and prevent powerful firms from engaging in related "undesirable practices." Firms accused of violating the U.S. antitrust laws are likely to be sued by the federal government or other private firms. Antitrust suits seek to prevent such undesirable behavior from recurring, provide compensation to the victims, and punish offenders via fines or even imprisonment.

What justifies investment of so much power in such government agencies as the Department of Justice or the Federal Trade Commission? What are the purposes of the antitrust laws? How well has antitrust policy succeeded? These are the issues that we will discuss in the remainder of the chapter.

■ THE PUBLIC IMAGE OF BUSINESS WHEN THE ANTITRUST LAWS WERE BORN

Congress was first led to interfere with freedom of business enterprise in response to widely publicized and criticized business practices during the half-century following the Civil War. No doubt, many businesses in that era were beyond reproach. But the more daring breed of entrepreneurs called "robber barons" made the headlines, and tales of their exploits competed with those of the Wild West. The story of John D. Rockefeller Sr. and his Standard Oil Company is a prime example. In 1870, about five years after entering into the oil-refining business with an investment of $4,000, Rockefeller and his partners created the Standard Oil Company. The company soon combined with or bought out a number of refineries and shippers, becoming powerful enough to force the railroads to provide discounts to members of the group and not to its competitors. It even forced the railroads to give the group "drawbacks"—that is, payments on every shipment of oil refined by a rival firm. By 1879, Standard Oil and its associated companies were producing some 90 percent of the nation's refined oil and controlled all of its pipelines.

Then, in 1882, to lock in its powers, the 40 associated firms formed the Standard Oil Trust (from which the word *antitrust* derives). The trust closed down "excessive" and inefficient refinery operations, involving more than half of its plants, in order to limit output, raise prices, and earn monopoly profits.

Other trusts soon followed in the sugar, whiskey, lead, and cottonseed and linseed oil industries. In 1892, the Supreme Court of Ohio ordered the dissolution of the Standard Oil Trust, which nevertheless survived as a cooperating set of firms, with directors of the major refining companies serving on each other's boards.

Other, more lurid tales of business practices in this period are easy to find: J. P. Morgan hired an army of toughs to engage literally in pitched battle for a contested section of railroad outside Binghamton, New York. Philip Armour and his confederates obtained control of meat processing by an understanding with their rivals that each day a different one of them would offer a low bid for the morning shipment of cattle and no one would enter a higher bid. Advocates of control measures warned the public that it faced a country "in which the citizen was born to drink the milk furnished by the milk trust, eat the beef of the beef trust, illuminate his home by grace of the oil trust and die and be carried off by the coffin trust."[1] The circumstances were clearly propitious for some legislative action.

■ THE ANTITRUST LAWS

Five acts of Congress constitute the basis of the federal government's antitrust policy. Major provisions of these acts are summarized in Table 20–1. Congress passed the Sherman Act, the first of the U.S. antitrust laws, in 1890, soon after the trust-creating activity reached its peak. The act is brief and very general, containing two main provisions: Section 1 of the act prohibits all contracts, combinations, and conspiracies in restraint of trade, and Section 2 bans monopolization in interstate and foreign trade.

Basic Antitrust Laws

TABLE 20-1

Name	Date	Major Provisions
Sherman Act	1890	Prohibits "all contracts, combinations and conspiracies in restraint of trade" (Section 1) and monopolization in interstate and foreign trade (Section 2).
Clayton Act	1914	Prohibits price discrimination, "exclusive contracts" under which sellers prevent buyers from purchasing goods from the sellers' competitors, and "tying contracts" under which a customer who wants to buy some product from a given seller is required as part of the price to agree to buy some other product or products from that same seller. Prohibits acquisition by one corporation of another's shares if these acts are likely to reduce competition or tend to create monopoly. Prohibits directors of one company from sitting on the board of a competitor's company.
Federal Trade Commission Act	1914	Established the FTC as an independent agency with authority to prosecute unfair competition and to prevent false and misleading advertising.
Robinson-Patman Act	1936	Prohibits special discounts and other discriminatory concessions to large purchasers unless based on differences in cost or "offered in good faith to meet an equally low price of a competitor."
Celler-Kefauver Antimerger Act	1950	Prohibits any corporation from acquiring the assets of another where the effect is to reduce competition substantially or to tend to create a monopoly.

[1] Matthew Josephson, *The Robber Barons, The Great American Capitalists, 1861–1901* (New York: Harcourt Brace, 1934), p. 358.

● THE SIZE AND SCOPE OF AN ANTITRUST CASE

Alleged violations of the antitrust laws are usually dealt with by bringing the accused firm to court or by threatening to sue it in hope that the accused firm will surrender and accept a compromise. Antitrust suits are frequently well-publicized affairs because the accused firms are often the giants of industry involving such names as Standard Oil, U.S. Steel, the Aluminum Company of America (Alcoa), General Electric, International Business Machines (IBM), American Telephone and Telegraph (AT&T), and Microsoft. Even some of the nation's most prestigious colleges and universities have been accused of engaging in a pricing conspiracy.

The magnitude of an antitrust suit is difficult to imagine. After the charges have been filed, it is not unusual for more than five years to elapse before the case even comes to trial. The parties spend this period laboriously preparing their cases. Dozens of lawyers, scores of witnesses, and hundreds of researchers are likely to participate in this process. The trial itself also can run for years. A major case produces literally thousands of volumes of material, and it can easily cost the defendant several hundred million dollars. In addition, if it loses, the defendant may have to pay billions of dollars in fines.

Thus, the power of the government or another firm to haul a company into court on antitrust charges is an awesome one. Win, lose, or draw, such a case is a very heavy burden on the accused firm, draining its funds, taking the time and attention of its management, and delaying business decisions until the outcome of the legal proceedings is determined.

SHERMAN ACT

"PER SE" ISSUES UNDER THE SHERMAN ACT   From the inception of the Sherman Act, Section 1 has been invoked primarily against price-fixing agreements—that is, agreements under which several ostensibly competing firms coordinate their pricing decisions. In interpreting Section 1, the courts have held that such agreements are illegal *per se;* in other words, they have held that no excuses or exonerating circumstances can make a price-fixing agreement legal.

"RULE OF REASON" ISSUES UNDER THE SHERMAN ACT   Section 2 of the Sherman Act deals with individual decision makers, rather than with groups of conspirators, focusing on attempts to create monopolies. In dealing with Section 2, the courts formulated the troublesome *rule of reason,* which held that monopolizing trade restraints are not necessarily illegal *per se.* According to this rule, a restraint is against the law only if it is "unreasonable." For example, one court ruled (and many economists agree) that size, by itself, does not constitute an offense—that a firm must commit objectionable overt acts to be guilty of violating Section 2 of the Sherman Act.

Because many people believed that the Sherman Act did not provide adequate protection to the public, in 1914 Congress passed two supplemental laws: the Clayton Act and the Federal Trade Commission Act.

CLAYTON ACT OF 1914

PRICE DISCRIMINATION IN RESTRAINT OF TRADE   The Clayton Act deals with certain specific practices thought to facilitate the encroachment of monopoly. First, it prohibits price discrimination (see Chapter 12), which it defines as the act, by a seller, of charging different prices to different buyers of the same product. This provision would, for example, have banned the railroad rebates that Rockefeller used to squeeze out his rivals.

EXCLUSIVE CONTRACTS AND TYING CONTRACTS   Second, the Clayton Act prohibits *exclusive contracts,* arrangements under which sellers prevent buyers from purchasing goods from the sellers' competitors, and *tying contracts,* arrangements under which a customer who wants to buy some product from a given seller is required as part of the price to agree to buy some other product or products from that same seller.

STOCK PURCHASES AND INDEPENDENCE   Third, the Clayton Act prohibits one firm from purchasing the stock of another if that acquisition tends to reduce competition by ending the independence of its rivals. This provision was later strengthened by the Celler-Kefauver Antimerger Act of 1950.

● PROTECTION OF COMPETITION, NOT PROTECTION OF COMPETITORS

The courts have repeatedly emphasized that the antitrust laws are not intended to make life easier for individual firms that encounter difficulties coping with competitive market pressures. The following quotation from a recent decision of the U.S. Supreme Court makes this clear:

"The purpose of the Sherman Act is not to protect businesses from the working of the market, it is to protect the public from the failure of the market."

SOURCE: *Spectrum Sports Inc.* v. *McQuillan*, US 122 L.Ed 2d 247 [1993], p. 506.

INTERLOCKING DIRECTORATES Finally, the Clayton Act prohibits interlocking directorates between competitors, under which some individuals are members of the boards of directors of two rival firms.

FTC ACT

The Federal Trade Commission Act created a commission to investigate "unfair" and "predatory" competitive practices and declared illegal all "unfair methods of competition and commerce." The Federal Trade Commission (FTC) was a rather ineffective agency during its first quarter-century. In 1938, however, it was given the task of preventing false and deceptive advertising, to which it has since devoted much of its effort.

ROBINSON-PATMAN ACT

In 1936, Congress passed the Robinson-Patman Act to protect independent sellers—both wholesalers and retailers (primarily those who sold groceries and drugs)—from the "unfair competition" of chain stores and mass distributors. The Robinson-Patman Act differed from other antitrust laws, because it sought to *restrain* competition by protecting small firms from the competition of larger ones.

■ MEASURING MARKET POWER: CONCENTRATION

In enforcing these laws, one piece of evidence that the U.S. Department of Justice and the Federal Trade Commission use to test whether a firm under investigation for antitrust violations is likely to possess monopoly power is the *concentration* of the markets in which the firm carries out its activities. A market or an industry is said to be "highly concentrated" if it contains only a few firms, most or all of which sell a large share of the industry's products. In contrast, an industry with many small firms is said to be "unconcentrated." Thus, concentration is a useful index of the relative bigness of the firms in the industry. Now, we have seen that big firms do not always have market power, though relatively small firms never (or almost never) do. Still, concentration is one useful piece of evidence in deciding whether market power exists in any case under investigation.

Concentration is measured in a number of ways. The most straightforward method is to calculate what share of the industry's output is sold by some selected number of the industry's firms. Most often a *four-firm* **concentration ratio** is used for this purpose. Thus, if the four largest firms in an industry account for, say, 58 percent of the industry's sales, we say that the four-firm concentration ratio is 0.58. Other formulas are used to measure concentration, but they are all designed to evaluate the same thing—how much of the industry's sales are carried out by its largest firms.

A **concentration ratio** is the percentage of an industry's output produced by its four largest firms. It is intended to measure the degree to which the industry is dominated by large firms.

Ultimately, we care about concentration ratios if they are a good measure of market power. The question, then, is this: If an industry becomes more concentrated, will the firms necessarily increase their ability to price their products above

---

The charming courtroom is old but recently refurbished, and the air conditioning is inadequate. It is often difficult to hear what is happening. The defendant firm has been accused of predatory pricing, that is, of charging very low prices in order to drive a competitor out of the market, and is defending itself against a judgment that could run into billions of dollars.

For the past two months, both sides have called up many witnesses—company executives, accountants, statisticians. The female lawyers are dressed in conservative outfits, the men in somewhat seedy two-piece matching suits. It would not do to appear too wealthy, for this is a jury trial, and the nine men and women wear casual attire including sneakers, jeans, and sports clothes. Although determined to see justice done, they are having a hard time staying awake under a hurricane of technical arguments and contradictory figures.

The judge follows the proceedings closely, often interrupting with questions of her own. Sometimes she jokes with the witnesses.

The lawyers call in an expert witness who is a specialist in the field—in this case an economist who has written on predatory pricing. He explains to the court and the jury the current thinking of the economics profession on the definition of predatory pricing and the standards by which one judges whether or not it has occurred. He is persuasive.

But the judge and jury have already heard from another economist, equally distinguished, representing the other side. Their analyses, which were quite technical, reached opposite conclusions. Which one are the jurors to believe, and on what basis?

competitive levels? Many economists have, in fact, concluded that although increased concentration *often* facilitates or increases market power, it does not *always* do so. Specifically, the following three conclusions are now widely accepted:

- If, after an increase in concentration, an industry still has a very low concentration ratio, then its firms are very unlikely to have any market power either before or after the rise in concentration.

- If circumstances in the industry are in other respects favorable for successful price collusion, a rise in concentration will facilitate market power. It will do so by reducing the number of firms that need to be consulted in arriving at an agreement and by decreasing the number of firms that have to be watched to make sure they do not betray the collusive agreement.

- Where entry into and exit from the industry are easy and quite inexpensive, that is, where the market is highly *contestable*, then even when concentration increases, market power will not be enhanced because an excessive price will attract new entrants who will soon force the price down.

THE EVIDENCE ON CONCENTRATION IN REALITY

Still, concentration data may be the best evidence that we have on the effectiveness of antitrust programs. Table 20–2 shows concentration ratios in a number of industries in the United States. We see that concentration varies greatly from industry to industry: automobiles, breakfast cereals, and aircraft are produced by highly concentrated industries, whereas the jewelry, clothing, and soft-drink industries show very little concentration.

Since the beginning of this century, concentration ratios in the United States have, on the average, remained remarkably constant. It has been estimated that, at the turn of the century, 32.9 percent of manufactured goods were produced by industries in which the concentration ratios were 50 percent or more (meaning that at least 50 percent of industry output was produced by the four largest firms). By 1963, the figure had risen only to 33.1 percent, and by 1992, it had actually fallen to 26.4 percent. These figures and those for other years are shown in Table 20–3. Over the course of the 20th century, concentration in individual U.S. industries has shown no tendency to increase.

Concentration Ratios for Representative Industries, 1992 — TABLE 20-2

Industry	Four-Firm Ratio	Industry	Four-Firm Ratio
Electric lamps, bulbs, and tubes	86	Bottled and canned soft drinks	37
Cereal breakfast foods	85	Motors and generators	36
Motor vehicles and car bodies	84	Dolls and stuffed toys	34
Hard surface floor coverage	83	Boat building and repairing	32
Aircraft	79	Pharmaceutical preparations	26
Rubber tires and inner tubes	70	Musical instruments	25
Primary aluminum	59	Brooms and brushes	23
Fabricated metal cans	56	Fluid milk	22
Ship building and repairing	53	Bolts, nuts, rivets, and washers	17
Fasteners, buttons, needles, and pins	41	Jewelry, precious metal	16
Prerecorded records and recorded tapes	40	Apparel: women's, misses', juniors' dresses	11
Apparel: men's and boys' suits and coats	39		

NOTE: Ratios are percent of output produced by the four largest firms in each industry.

SOURCE: U.S. Bureau of the Census, "Concentration Ratios in Manufacturing," *1992 Census of Manufactures*. Thanks to Andrew W. Hait, Special Reports Branch, U.S. Bureau of the Census.

The Trend in Concentration in Manufacturing Industries, 1901–1992 — TABLE 20-3

	Around 1901	1947	1954	1958	1963	1966	1970	1972	1982	1987	1992
Percentage of value added in industries with four-firm concentration ratios over 50 percent	32.9	24.4	29.9	30.2	33.1	28.6	26.3	29.0	25.2	27.9	26.4

SOURCES: P.W. McCracken and T.G. Moore, "Competitive and Market Concentration in the American Economy," Subcommittee on Antitrust and Monopoly, U.S. Senate, March 29, 1973; F.M. Scherer, *Industrial Market Structure and Economic Performance* (Boston: Houghton Mifflin, 1980), p. 68; F.M. Scherer and David Ross, *Industrial Market Structure and Economic Performance*, 3rd ed. (Boston: Houghton Mifflin, 1990), p. 84; Personal communication with Professor F.M. Scherer, March 10, 1993; and personal communication with Andrew W. Hait, Special Reports Branch, U.S. bureau of the census, January 18, 1996.

Such information may suggest that the antitrust laws have to some degree been effective in inhibiting whatever trend toward bigness may in fact exist. But even this very cautious conclusion has been questioned by some observers, who argue that the size of firms has been held down by market forces and technical developments (such as declining computer costs that make it easier for small firms to increase their efficiency, or the takeover of much of freight traffic from large railroads by small trucking firms). These observers argue that antitrust laws have made virtually no difference in the size and the behavior of American business.

A CRUCIAL PROBLEM FOR ANTITRUST: THE RESEMBLANCE OF MONOPOLIZATION AND VIGOROUS COMPETITION

One problem that haunts most antitrust litigation and lies at the heart of the sensational Microsoft case (discussed further in the next two pages), among many others, is that vigorous competition may look very similar to acts that *undermine* competition and support monopoly power. The resulting danger is that the courts will prohibit, or the antitrust authorities will prosecute, acts that *appear* to be anticompetitive but that really are the opposite.

The difficulty is that effective competition by a firm is always tough on its rivals. It forces rivals to charge lower prices, to improve product quality, and to spend money on innovations that will cut their costs and improve their products. Competition will legitimately force rivals out of business if they are inefficient and therefore cannot keep their prices low or provide products of acceptable quality. But when competition destroys a rival in this way it is difficult to tell whether it was, so to speak, murdered or died of natural causes. In both cases the surviving competitor bears some responsibility. But if the cause of the rival's demise is legitimate competition, consumers will benefit; if, however, the end of the rival was part of a process of monopoly creation, then the public will end up paying. This is a very real issue that constantly recurs in today's antitrust litigation.

■ ANTICOMPETITIVE PRACTICES AND ANTITRUST

A central purpose of the antitrust laws is to prevent "anticompetitive practices," actions by a powerful firm that threaten to destroy competitors, to force them to compete less vigorously, or to prevent the entry of new rivals.

PREDATORY PRICING

Predatory pricing is pricing that threatens to keep a competitor out of the market. It is a price that is so low that it will be profitable for the firm that adopts it only if a rival is driven from the market.

Typical of such accusations of anticompetitive behavior is the claim, frequent in antitrust cases, that the defendant has adopted unjustifiably low prices in order to force other firms to lose money, thereby driving competitors out of business. This practice is called **predatory pricing.** Deciding whether pricing is "predatory" is difficult, both for economists and for courts of law, because low prices generally benefit consumers. Therefore, the courts do not want to discourage firms from cutting prices by being too eager to declare that lower prices are intended to destroy a rival.

One principle widely followed by the courts holds that prices are predatory only if they are below either marginal or average variable costs. The logic of this criterion as a test for whether prices are "too low" is that even under perfect competition, prices will not, in the long run, fall below that level, but will equal marginal costs. But even in cases where prices are below marginal or average variable costs, they may be held to be predatory only under two conditions:

- If there is evidence that the low price would have been profitable *only* if it succeeded in destroying a rival or in keeping it out of the market.

- When there is a real probability that the allegedly predatory firm could raise prices to monopoly levels after the rival was driven out, thereby profiting from its venture in crime.

Many successful firms—including AT&T, American Airlines, and Microsoft—have been accused of predatory pricing. The defendants typically argue that their low prices cover both marginal and average variable costs, that the prices are low because of superior efficiency, and that the lawsuit was brought to prevent the defendants from competing effectively. The courts have generally accepted these arguments. There have been many predatory pricing cases, but few convictions.

OTHER POSSIBLY ANTICOMPETITIVE PRACTICES: ABUSE VIA BOTTLENECKS

The litigation involving Microsoft Corporation illustrates two other practices that can conceivably be anticompetitive. Microsoft is the enormously successful software supplier of computer operating systems that enable you to communicate with and control your computer; it also supplies other very popular computer programs. Microsoft's sales are huge, and it is clearly a tough and energetic competitor. The difficulty of distinguishing vigorously competitive behavior from anticompetitive acts is illustrated by the Microsoft antitrust case, in which the U.S. Department of Justice accused the firm of various anticompetitive practices. The firm has been found guilty in the lower court, but the decision has been appealed. The Microsoft case raises many issues, two of which are discussed here as illustrations.

ABUSE VIA BOTTLENECKS Microsoft *Windows*, an operating system that runs about 90 percent of all personal computers, is a prime example of a bottleneck, which we discussed earlier in this chapter. To reach any substantial proportion of personal computer customers, the producer of any word processor, spreadsheet, or graphics program must use *Windows*. And there is some likelihood that any alternative to *Windows* will soon capture a large share of customers. In part, this is because *Windows* is widely considered a good program, but even more because of the desire for *user* compatibility—computer users communicate with each other, and that is easier if all these users employ the same operating system. The bottleneck problem arises because Microsoft itself supplies not only *Windows* but also many applications (such as *Word*, a word-processing program, *Excel*, a spreadsheet program, and *Explorer*, an Internet browser software). The worry is that Microsoft will use *Windows* in a way that favors its own programs and handicaps programs that its competitors develop.

BUNDLING: LEGITIMATE AND ILLEGITIMATE Microsoft promotes its own products by providing them more cheaply to computer manufacturers if these makers buy a *bundle* of Microsoft programs, not just *Windows* alone. But this means that rival producers of word processors, spreadsheets, and Internet browsers are handicapped in selling their products to PC owners. The question is whether Microsoft's low bundle price is legitimate or if it constitutes a case of predatory pricing whose only purpose is to destroy competitors. Economists often take the position that a **bundling** discount is legitimate if it is cheaper for the firm to supply several products at once than to supply them one at a time, and if the price cut corresponds to the cost saving. However, they question the legitimacy of the bundle discount if the cost saving is considerably less than the difference between the bundled price and the sum of the prices of the included products (when bought individually).

Bundling refers to a pricing arrangement under which the supplier offers substantial discounts to customers if they buy several of the firm's products, so that the price of the bundle of products is less than the sum of the prices of the products if they were bought separately.

■ MERGERS AND COMPETITION

HORIZONTAL MERGERS **Mergers** have long been an object of suspicion by the antitrust authorities. This is particularly true when a merger is *horizontal*, meaning that the merging firms compete directly by supplying products that are identical or very similar. In these cases, it is often feared that competition will decline because there will be fewer firms in the industry.

A **merger** refers to unification of two previously independent firms, as when one purchases the other or the two simply decide to combine into a single enterprise.

The Department of Justice and the Federal Trade Commission are both concerned with mergers. They do not wish to impede mergers that seem likely to increase efficiency. But the antitrust agencies do want to prevent mergers that threaten to reduce competition.

To help firms decide whether a proposed merger will get them into trouble, and for other reasons as well, the Department of Justice and the FTC together issue guidelines indicating when they are (or are not) likely to try to block a merger. For example, they generally will not oppose mergers in industries in which concentration is low or into which entry is very easy. However, in industries that are highly concentrated and where entry is difficult, the merger of two large firms will often be opposed.

RECENT SURGES IN MERGER ACTIVITY During the early 1980s, the Justice Department issued several sets of new, more permissive guidelines. This loosening of the anti-merger rules, coupled with the Reagan administration's view that mergers were generally good for the economy, spawned a much-publicized increase in merger activity. In total, about $1.5 trillion was spent on "deal-making" activity (including mergers, acquisitions, and leveraged buyouts) during the decade of the 1980s. After a brief slowdown in the early 1990s, the merger pace picked up again. In 1998 *alone*, a record $1.6 trillion in mergers took place, with such headline-making deals as the

$77 billion takeover of Mobil Oil by Exxon, and the merger of Citibank and Travelers Group, forming the world's largest financial services company.[2]

This rash of mergers has given rise to much controversy. Some observers believe that it increases the likelihood of monopoly power, whereas others believe that it serves largely to make the merged firms more efficient. In any event, defenders argue that mergers have not historically increased the market share of big business in the United States. For example, in 1999 the share of the labor force employed by the corporations listed in the *Fortune 500* was about 17 percent, the same as its share in 1970.[3]

ARE MERGERS ANTICOMPETITIVE?   Though by no means unanimous on the subject, many economists agree that mergers sometimes reduce competition, particularly in markets that are not contestable, so that threats of entry do not prevent the merged firms from raising prices above competitive levels.[4] On the other hand, where there is reason to believe that mergers will *not* reduce competition, most economists oppose impediments to them. Many economists believe that mergers that are not undertaken to reduce competition can have only one purpose—to achieve greater efficiency. For example, the larger firm that results from the merger may enjoy substantial economies of scale not available to smaller firms. Or the two merging companies may learn special skills from one another or offset one another's risks.

DO MERGERS IMPROVE PERFORMANCE?   Mergers have sometimes proved disappointing and brought limited cost savings; a number have subsequently been dissolved. Several studies have found that more than one-third of acquisitions are eventually divested. But economists who defend freedom to merge when there is no demonstrated threat to competition pose a challenging question: Who can judge better than the firms involved whether their marriage is likely to make their activities more efficient? Indeed, a number of recent studies of merger activity during the 1980s have all reported significant productivity increases following mergers.[5]

■ USE OF ANTITRUST LAWS TO PREVENT COMPETITION

Finally, let us turn to an issue that some observers consider very serious: the *misuse* of the antitrust laws to prevent competition. Many firms that have been unable to compete effectively on their own merits have turned to the courts to seek protection from their successful competitors—and some have succeeded.

Firms that try to protect themselves in this way always claim that their rivals have not achieved success through superior ability but, rather, by means that they call "monopolization." Sometimes the evidence is clear-cut, and the courts can readily discern whether an accused firm has violated the antitrust laws or whether it has simply been too efficient and innovative for the complaining competitor's tastes. In other cases, however, the issues are complicated, and only a long and painstaking legal proceeding offers any prospect of resolving them.

Various steps have been suggested to deal with the misuse of U.S. antitrust laws. In one proposal, if the courts decide that a firm has been falsely accused by another of violating the antitrust laws, then (as is done in other countries) the *accuser* should pay the legal costs of the innocent defendant. Another proposal is to subject such

---

[2] *Economic Report of the President 1999* (Washington, D.C.: U.S. Government Printing Office, February 1999) and "The Year of the Merger," BBC News online network, December 26, 1998, http://news.bbc.co.uk/.

[3] *Fortune*, May 1971 and April 17, 2000.

[4] See Chapter 13, pages 264–266, for a definition and discussion of contestable markets.

[5] See, for example, Frank Lichtenberg, *Corporate Takeovers and Productivity* (Cambridge, Mass.: MIT Press, 1992); Paul M. Healy, Krishna G. Palepu, and Richard S. Ruback, "Does Corporate Performance Improve After Mergers?" *Journal of Financial Economics* 31 (1992): 135–175; and Robert H. McGuckin and Sang V. Nguyen, "On Productivity and Plant Ownership Change: New Evidence from the Longitudinal Research Database," *RAND Journal of Economics* 26, no. 2 (Summer 1995): 257–276.

● CAN ANTITRUST LAWS BE USED TO *PREVENT* COMPETITION?

Many observers are concerned that the antitrust laws are often used by inefficient firms to protect themselves from the competition of more efficient rivals. When they are unable to win out in the marketplace, the argument goes, firms simply file lawsuits against their competitors claiming that those rivals have achieved success by means that violate the antitrust laws.

Not only do they seek protection from the courts against what they describe as "unfair competition" or "predatory practices," but they often sue for compensation which, under the law, can sometimes be three times as large as the damages that they claim to have suffered. Moreover, even if the defendant is found innocent, it must normally pay the very high costs of the litigation itself. Aside from the enormous waste that such lawsuits entail, observers worry that this is a perversion of the antitrust laws, which were, after all, designed to promote competition, not to prevent it.

Two recent examples illustrate the nature of such litigation.* These cases also show that the courts are often wise enough to throw out such attempts to use the antitrust laws to prevent competition.

AMI VERSUS IBM

Allen-Myland Inc. (AMI) is a small firm that specialized in the upgrading of computers, an activity that had earned it handsome profits in a period of time when expanding a computer's capacity was very laborious. However, technological progress by IBM then transformed what was once a labor-intensive task requiring considerable skill into the routine installation of a small and highly reliable part. This rendered obsolete many of the services offered by AMI. So AMI sued IBM, seeking to persuade the court to impose an artificial and expensive market niche for upgrading services, with AMI permanently protected from competitive pressures. The court's decision completely rejected AMI's position (Eastern District of Pennsylvania, 1988).

SEWELL PLASTICS VERSUS COCA-COLA, SOUTHEASTERN CONTAINER, ET AL.

The Sewell Plastics Company once had a preponderant market share in the manufacture of plastic soft-drink bottles in the United States, selling 2-liter bottles for more than 30 cents each. A group of Coca-Cola bottlers in the Southeast considered the price too high and formed a cooperative firm (Southeastern Container) to manufacture their own plastic bottles.

Within five years, Southeastern had reduced its cost below 14 cents per bottle, and real retail prices of soft drinks also fell. Despite rising national sales and profits, Sewell sued Southeastern, seeking to force its owners to sell the firm to Sewell or, as a possible alternative, to force Southeastern's customers to sign exclusive purchasing contracts with Sewell. In the spring of 1989, the judge dismissed Sewell's claims, holding that there was no need for a trial (U.S. District Court, Western District, North Carolina, April 1989).

*One of the authors of this book, William Baumol, was involved as an expert witness in both cases.

suits to prescreening by a government agency, as is done in Japan. But these issues are hardly open-and-shut, for there is no such thing as a perfect legal system. Anything that restricts anticompetitive, private antitrust suits will almost certainly also inhibit legitimate attempts by individual firms to defend themselves from genuine acts of monopolization by rival enterprises (for more on this issue, see the accompanying box, "Can Antitrust Laws Be Used to *Prevent* Competition?").

■ CONCLUDING OBSERVATIONS

As we noted at the beginning of this chapter, monopoly and monopoly power are rightly judged to cause market failure—they prevent the market from serving consumer interests most effectively by providing the products the public desires at the lowest possible prices. But the alternative is government intervention, and governments, too, sometimes make imperfect decisions. Thus, before deciding whether to regulate more or deregulate, whether to toughen antitrust laws or loosen them, informed citizens should carefully weigh the prospects for market failure against the possibility of government failure in terms of the contemplated change. Monopolists have sometimes succeeded in preventing the introduction of useful new products. They have raised prices to consumers and held down product quality. But large firms have also sometimes been innovative and their service to customers has in some cases been considered of high quality. Government has also had its missteps.

It has initiated costly lawsuits, sometimes on questionable grounds. It has forced regulated firms to adopt pricing rules that were clearly not beneficial to consumers, and it has handicapped the operations of industries, for example, arguably almost destroying the nation's railroads. Yet government, too, has done useful things in influencing industry behavior, preventing various monopolistic practices, protecting consumers from impure foods and medications, and so on. Most economists believe that by the 1970s government intervention had clearly gone too far in some respects and that deregulation was, consequently, in the public interest. However, the general issue is hardly settled.

SUMMARY

1. *Regulation* has two primary purposes: to put brakes on the decisions of industries with monopoly power and to contribute to public health and safety.

2. In the United States, regulation of prices and other economic decisions is generally applied only to large firms, including railroads, telecommunications, and gas and electricity supply.

3. In recent years there has been a major push toward reduction of regulation. Among the industries that have been deregulated in whole or in part are air, truck, and rail transportation.

4. Among the major reasons given for regulation are (a) *economies of scale* and *economies of scope*, which make industries into natural monopolies, and (b) the *universal service* goal, which refers to the provision of service to poor people and isolated areas where supply is unprofitable.

5. Regulators often reject proposals by regulated firms to cut their prices, and sometimes the regulators even force firms to *raise* their prices. The purposes of such actions are to prevent "unfair competition" and to protect customers of some of the firm's products from being forced to *cross-subsidize* customers of other products. Many economists disagree

with most such actions and argue that the result is usually to stifle competition and make all customers pay more than they otherwise would pay.

6. Economists generally argue that a firm should be permitted to cut its price as long as it covers its marginal cost. However, in many regulated industries, firms would go bankrupt if all prices were set equal to marginal costs.

7. By putting ceilings on profits to prevent monopoly earnings, regulation can eliminate the firm's incentive for efficiency and innovation. *Price caps*, which put (inflation-adjusted) ceilings on prices, rather than profits, are used widely to deal with this problem.

8. To prevent the undermining of competition, the owner of a (monopoly) *bottleneck facility* must charge all users of the facility (including itself) the same price for access.

9. *Antitrust policy* refers to policies and programs designed to control the growth of monopoly and to prevent big business from engaging in "anticompetitive" practices.

10. The *Sherman Act* is the oldest U.S. antitrust law. It prohibits contracts, combinations, and conspiracies in restraint of trade, and it also prohibits monopolization.

11. Collusion among horizontal competitors to fix prices is *illegal per se* under the Sherman Act. Acts of monopolization—that is, acts that attempt to acquire monopoly power—are tested under the *rule of reason.*

12. Several other important antitrust laws exist, including the *Clayton Act*, which prohibits price discrimination that tends to reduce competition or create monopoly; the *Federal Trade Commission Act*, which created the commission as an independent antitrust agency; and the *Robinson-Patman Act*, which generally prohibits discriminatory price discounts.

13. *Predatory pricing* is pricing that is low relative to the marginal or average variable costs of the firm and so threatens to drive a competitor out of the market. There must also be a likelihood that if the prices do destroy a competitor the firm will acquire market power enabling it to charge prices well above competitive levels.

14. *Bundling* refers to a price reduction given to customers who purchase several of the firm's products simultaneously.

It is considered unobjectionable if it is cheaper for the firm to bundle its products and the price cut merely passes the savings on to customers. However, bundling can be used to destroy competitors who sell only some of the bundled products.

15. The evidence indicates that there has been no significant increase in the *concentration* of individual U.S. industries into fewer, relatively larger firms during the 20th century. Evidence as to whether antitrust laws have been effective in preventing monopoly is inconclusive, and observers disagree on the subject.

16. Unregulated monopoly is apt to distribute income unfairly, produce undesirably small quantities of output, and provide inadequate motivation for innovation.

17. However, sometimes only large firms may have funds sufficient for effective research, development, and innovation; where economies of scale are available, large firms can serve customers more cheaply than can small ones.

KEY TERMS

Economies of scale   406

Monopoly power   406

Regulation   407

Economies of scope   409

Bottleneck facilities   409

Parity-pricing principle   411

Cross-subsidization   412

Marginal versus average cost pricing   413

Ramsey pricing rule   414

Regulatory lag   415

Price cap   415

Deregulation   417

Antitrust policy   420

Rule of reason   422

Concentration of industry   423

Concentration ratios   423

Predatory pricing   426

Bundling   427

Mergers   427

QUESTIONS FOR REVIEW

1. Why is an electric company in a city often considered to be a natural monopoly? What would happen if two competing electric companies were established? How about telephone companies? How can changes in technology affect your answer?

2. Suppose that a 20 percent cut in the price of coast-to-coast telephone calls brings in so much new business that it permits a long-distance telephone company to cut its charges for service from Chicago to St. Louis, but only by 2 percent. In your opinion, is this equitable? Is it a good idea or a bad one?

3. In some regulated industries, regulatory agencies prevented prices from falling, and as a result many firms opened for business in those industries. In your opinion, is this competitive or anticompetitive? Is it a good idea or a bad one?

4. Regulators are much concerned about the prevention of "predatory pricing." The U.S. Court of Appeals has, however, noted that "the term probably does not have a well-defined meaning, but it certainly bears a sinister connotation." How might one distinguish "predatory" from "nonpredatory" pricing? What would you do about it?

5. Do you think that it is fair or unfair for rural users of telephone service to be cross-subsidized by other telephone users?

6. Suppose that a firm in a regulated industry is prohibited from earning profits higher than it is getting and it begins selling a

new product at a price above its long-run marginal cost. Explain why the prices of other company products will, very likely, have to be reduced.

7. To provide incentives for increased efficiency, several regulatory agencies have eliminated ceilings on the profits of regulated firms but instead put caps on their prices. Suppose that a regulated firm manages to cut its prices in half, but in the process, it doubles its profits. Should rational consumers consider this to be a good or a bad development? Why?

8. A shopkeeper sells his store and signs a contract that restrains him from opening another store in competition with the new owner. The courts have decided that this contract is a reasonable restraint of trade. Can you think of any other types of restraint of trade that seem reasonable? Can you think of any that seem unreasonable?

9. Which of the following industries do you expect to have high concentration ratios: automobile production, aircraft manufacture, hardware production, railroads, production of expensive jewelry? Compare your answers with the numbers in Table 20–2.

10. Why do you think the specific industries you selected in Review Question 9 are highly concentrated?

11. Do you think it is in the public interest to launch an antitrust suit that costs $1 billion? What leads you to your conclusion?

12. In Japan and a number of European countries, the antitrust laws are much less severe than those in the United States. Do you think that this helps or harms American industry in its efforts to compete with foreign producers? Why?

13. Can you think of some legal rules that can discourage the use of antitrust laws to prevent competition while at the same time not interfering with legitimate antitrust actions?

14. Do you think that the antitrust authorities should interfere more than they do now in corporate mergers? What are some pros and cons?

15. During the oil crisis in the 1970s, long lines at gas stations disappeared soon after price controls were removed and gas prices were permitted to rise. Should this be interpreted as evidence that the oil companies have monopoly power? Why or why not?

16. Some economists believe that firms rarely attempt predatory pricing because it would be a very risky act even if it were legal. Why may this be so?

17. Firm X cuts its prices and soon competing firm Y goes out of business. How would you judge whether this price cut was an act of legitimate and vigorous competition or an anticompetitive act?

18. Increasingly, the electric utility companies, which used to be the sole generators of electricity in their assigned areas, will face the competition of other electricity generators. However, electric utilities are generally the sole owners of the transmission lines needed to carry the electricity from the generating plant to the user, so that transmission lines are a bottleneck facility. If you were the regulator, how would you determine the price the utility will be allowed to charge a competitor for use of the transmission lines? Or would you leave that price to the free market? Why or why not?

CHAPTER

21

The taxing power of the government must be used to provide revenues for legitimate government purposes. It must not be used to regulate the economy or bring about social change.

Ronald Reagan

TAXATION AND RESOURCE ALLOCATION

"Nothing is certain but death and taxes," proclaims an old adage. In recent decades, however, American politics has turned this aphorism on its head. Nowadays, it seems, the surest route to political death is to raise taxes.

Tax-cutting fever came out of California in the late 1970s and swept the nation during the presidency of Ronald Reagan—who won two landslide elections. After pledging not to raise taxes, President George Bush agreed to some small tax increases in 1990—a decision that some think cost him the 1992 election. Next came President Bill Clinton, who made income-tax increases for upper-income taxpayers a major component of his deficit-reduction plan in 1993. The next year, the Democrats were annihilated at the polls by a Republican party pledging to cut taxes.

Politicians watch election returns carefully. So it was no wonder that the bipartisan balanced-budget program, which passed Congress in 1997, reduced the deficit entirely through spending cuts, not tax hikes. And one of the major issues of the 2000 presidential campaign was how much to reduce taxes—and which taxes should be cut.

Antitax sentiment is nothing new in America, where taxes have never been very popular. Indeed, our country was born, in part, out of a tax revolt. But taxes are inevitable in any modern, mixed economy, as we noted in Chapter 3. Although the vast majority of economic activities in the United States is left to the private sector, some—such as provision of national defense and highways—are reserved for the government. And any such government spending requires tax revenues to pay the bills. So do transfer programs like Social Security and unemployment insurance.

In addition, the government sometimes deliberately interferes with the workings of the market in order to promote some social goal. Often, these interferences involve levying taxes. For example, we will see in the next chapter that policymakers can use taxes to correct misallocations of resources caused by externalities.

This chapter discusses the types of taxes that are used to raise what President Reagan called "revenues for legitimate government purposes," the effects of taxes on resource allocation and income distribution, and the principles that distinguish "good" taxes from "bad" ones.

Issue: Should We Flatten the Income Tax?

In recent years, a number of economists and politicians have advocated transforming our current income tax into a "flat tax." Under this system, the same low tax rate would apply to all income above a certain threshold. At first blush, the idea seems extremely attractive. After all, with one low tax rate for everyone and essentially no deductions or tax-favored sources of income, tax considerations would play only a minor role in economic decision making, and a tax return could fit on a postcard.

But the issue is actually a good deal more complicated than that—which is why flat-tax proposals have been so controversial. In this chapter, we will learn the principles by which tax systems are judged, and then we will apply these principles to appraising the flat tax.

■ THE LEVEL AND TYPES OF TAXATION

Many Americans believe that taxes have been gobbling up an ever-increasing share of the U.S. economy. Figure 21–1, however, shows that this is not true. By charting the behavior of both federal and state and local taxes *as a percentage of gross domestic product (GDP)* since 1929, we see that the share of federal taxes in GDP has been rather steady since the early 1950s. It climbed from less than 4 percent in 1929 to 20 percent during World War II, fell back to 15 percent in the immediate postwar period, and has fluctuated in the 18 to 21 percent range ever since. (It is now about 20 percent.)

The share of GDP taken by state and local taxes climbed substantially from World War II until the early 1970s. But since then it, too, has remained remarkably stable—at about 10–11 percent. Whether these shares are too high or too low is a matter of some debate. But:

The shares of GDP taken in taxes by the federal, state, and local governments have been approximately constant for nearly 30 years.

Taxes as a Percentage of Gross Domestic Product   FIGURE 21-1

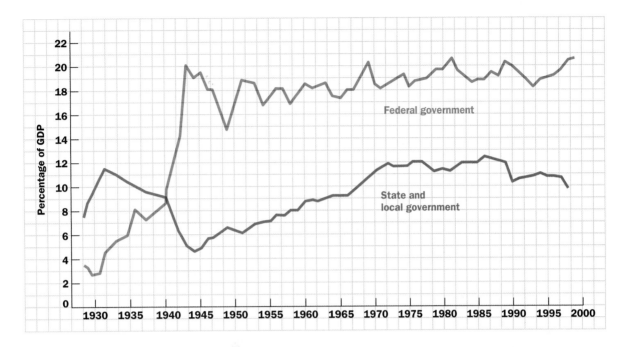

SOURCE: *Economic Report of the President, 1999* (Washington, D.C.: U.S. Government Printing Office, 1999).

As we noted in Chapter 3 (see, especially, page 48), the tax share is considerably lower in the United States than it is in most other industrial countries.

PROGRESSIVE, PROPORTIONAL, AND REGRESSIVE TAXES

Economists classify taxes as *progressive, proportional,* or *regressive.* Under a **progressive tax** like the personal income tax, the fraction of income paid in taxes *rises* as a person's income increases. Under a **proportional tax** like the payroll tax, this fraction is constant. And under a **regressive tax** like the notorious *head tax,* which charges every person the same amount, the fraction of income paid to the tax collector *declines* as income rises.[1] Because the fraction of income paid in taxes is called the **average tax rate,** we can reformulate these definitions as they appear in the margin.

Often, however, the *average* tax rate is less interesting than the **marginal tax rate,** which is the fraction of each *additional* dollar that is paid to the tax collector. The reason, as we will see, is that the *marginal* tax rate, not the *average* tax rate, most directly affects economic incentives.

DIRECT VERSUS INDIRECT TAXES

Another way to classify taxes is to classify them as either **direct taxes** or **indirect taxes.** Direct taxes are levied directly on *people:* primary examples are *income taxes* and *inheritance taxes.* In contrast, indirect taxes are levied on particular activities, such as buying gasoline, using the telephone, or owning a home.

The federal government raises revenues mainly by direct taxes, whereas states and localities rely more heavily on indirect taxes. *Sales taxes* and *property taxes* are the most important indirect taxes in the United States, although many other countries including the members of the European Union (EU) rely heavily on the *value-added tax*—or VAT, a tax that has often been discussed, but never adopted, in the United States. In fact, as a broad generalization, the U.S. government relies more heavily on direct taxes than do the governments of most other countries.

A **progressive tax** is one in which the average tax rate paid by an individual rises as income rises.

A **proportional tax** is one in which the average tax rate is the same at all income levels.

A **regressive tax** is one in which the average tax rate falls as income rises.

The **average tax rate** is the ratio of taxes to income

The **marginal tax rate** is the fraction of each *additional* dollar of income that is paid in taxes.

Direct taxes are taxes levied directly on people.

Indirect taxes are taxes levied on specific economic activities.

---

[1] In 1990, Prime Minister Margaret Thatcher caused riots in the United Kingdom by instituting a head tax.

■ THE FEDERAL TAX SYSTEM

The *personal income tax* is the biggest source of revenue to the federal government. Few people realize that the *payroll tax*—a tax levied on wages and salaries up to a certain limit and paid by employers and employees—is the next biggest source. Furthermore, payroll taxes have been growing more rapidly than income taxes for decades. In 1960, payroll tax collections were just 36 percent of personal income tax collections; today this figure is about 70 percent. In fact, most Americans pay more in payroll taxes than they do in income taxes.

The rest of the federal government's revenues come mostly from the *corporate income tax* and from various excise (sales) taxes. Figure 3–18, which is reproduced here for convenience as Figure 21–2, shows the breakdown of federal revenues for the fiscal year 1999 budget. Let us now look at these taxes in more detail.

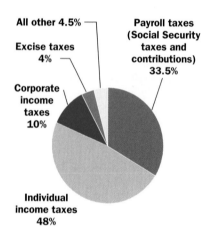

FIGURE 21-2

Sources of Federal Revenue

All other 4.5%
Excise taxes 4%
Payroll taxes (Social Security taxes and contributions) 33.5%
Corporate income taxes 10%
Individual income taxes 48%

SOURCE: *Economic Report of the President, 2000* (Washington, D.C.: U.S. Government Printing Office, 2000).

A **tax loophole** is a special provision in the tax code that reduces taxation below normal rates (perhaps to zero) if certain conditions are met.

A particular source of income is **tax exempt** if income from that source is not taxable.

A **tax deduction** is a sum of money that may be subtracted before the taxpayer computes his or her taxable income.

THE FEDERAL PERSONAL INCOME TAX

The tax on individual incomes traces its origins to the 16th Amendment to the Constitution in 1913, but it was inconsequential until the beginning of World War II. Washington then raised the tax substantially to finance the war, and it has been the major source of federal revenue ever since.

Many taxpayers have little or no additional tax to pay when the annual April 15th day of reckoning comes around because employers withhold income taxes from payrolls and forward those funds to the U.S. Treasury. In fact, many taxpayers are "over-withheld" during the year and receive refund checks from Uncle Sam. Nevertheless, most taxpayers dread the arrival of their Form 1040 because of its legendary complexity.

The personal income tax is *progressive*. That fact is evident in Table 21–1, which shows that average tax rates rise as income rises. Ignoring a few complications, the current tax law has five basic marginal rates, each of which applies within a specific tax bracket. As income rises above certain points, the marginal tax rate increases from 15 percent to 28 percent, to 31 percent, and then finally to 36 percent and 39.6 percent on very high incomes (more than $283,000 of taxable income for a married couple).

But the income tax is actually less progressive than it seems, owing to a variety of **tax loopholes.** Let us examine a few major ones.

TAX-EXEMPT STATUS OF MUNICIPAL BOND INTEREST To help state and local governments and certain public authorities raise funds, Congress has made interest on their bonds **exempt** from federal income tax. Whether or not it was Congress' intent, this provision has turned out to be one of the biggest loopholes for the very rich, who invest much of their wealth in tax-free municipal bonds. Such tax-conscious investing has long been the principal reason why some multimillionaires pay virtually no income tax.

TAX BENEFITS FOR HOMEOWNERS Among the sacred cows of our income tax system is the deductibility of payments that homeowners make for mortgage interest and property taxes. These **tax deductions** substantially reduce homeowners' tax bills and give them preferential treatment compared to renters. Clearly, Congress' intent is to encourage home ownership. However, because homeowners are, on the average, richer than renters, this loophole also erodes the progressivity of the income tax.

But why call this a "loophole" when other interest expenses and taxes (such as those paid by shopkeepers, for example) are considered legitimate deductions? The answer is that, unlike shopkeepers, homeowners do not pay taxes on the income they earn by incurring these expenses. This is because the "income" from owning a home accrues not in cash, but in the form of living without paying rent.

An example will illustrate the point. Jack and Jill are neighbors. Each earns $30,000 a year and lives in a $100,000 house. The difference is that Jack owns his home, while Jill rents. Most observers would agree that Jack and Jill *should* pay the same income tax. Will they? Suppose Jack pays $2,000 a year in local property taxes

Federal Personal Income Tax Rates in 1999 for a Married Couple Filing Jointly

TABLE 21-1

Taxable Income	Tax	Average Tax Rate	Marginal Tax Rate
$ 10,000	$ 1,500	15.0%	15.0%
25,000	3,750	15.0	15.0
50,000	8,404	16.8	28.0
100,000	22,404	22.4	28.0
150,000	37,782	25.3	31.0
250,000	73,355	29.3	36.0
1,000,000	369,161	36.9	39.6

and has an $80,000 mortgage at an 8 percent interest rate, which costs him about $6,400 a year in interest. Both property taxes and mortgage interest are tax deductible, so he gets to deduct $8,400 in housing expenses. But Jill, who may pay $8,400 a year in rent, does not. Thus, Jill's tax burden is higher than Jack's.

We could go on listing more tax loopholes, but enough has been said to illustrate the main point:

Every tax loophole encourages particular patterns of behavior and favors particular types of people. Furthermore, because most loopholes mainly benefit the rich, they erode the progressivity of the income tax.

This problem was much more serious in the United States before the major tax reform of 1986, when the tax code was thoroughly rewritten. But it has by no means disappeared. Indeed, making the tax code simpler and fairer by closing more loopholes is one of the chief arguments for adopting a flat tax.

THE PAYROLL TAX

The second most important tax in the United States is the payroll tax, whose proceeds are earmarked to be paid into various "trust funds." These funds, in turn, are used mainly to pay for Social Security, Medicare, and unemployment benefits. The payroll tax is levied at a fixed percentage rate (now about 16 percent), shared about equally between employees and employers. This means that a firm paying an employee a gross monthly wage of, say, $5,000 will deduct $400 (8 percent of $5,000) from that worker's check, add an additional $400 of its own funds, and send the $800 to the government.

On the surface, this seems like a *proportional* tax, but it is actually highly *regressive* for two reasons. First, only wages and salaries are subject to the tax; interest and dividends are not. Second, because Social Security benefits are subject to upper limits, earnings above a certain level (which changes each year) are exempted from the tax. In 2000, this level was $76,200 per year. Above this limit, the *marginal payroll tax rate* is zero.[2]

THE CORPORATE INCOME TAX

The tax on corporate profits is also considered a "direct" tax, because corporations are fictitious "people" in the eyes of the law. All large corporations currently pay a basic marginal tax rate of 35 percent. (Firms with smaller profits pay a lower rate.) Because the tax applies only to *profits*—not to income—all wages, rents, and interest paid by corporations are deducted before the tax is applied. Since World War II, corporate income-tax collections have accounted for a declining share of federal revenue—now just 12 percent.

---

[2] This is not quite true. The portion of the payroll tax that pays for Medicare is applied to all earnings, without limit.

EXCISE TAXES

An excise tax is a sales tax on the purchase of a particular good or service. Though sales taxes are mainly reserved for state and local governments in the United States, the federal government does levy excise taxes on a hodgepodge of miscellaneous goods and services, including cigarettes, alcoholic beverages, gasoline, and tires.

Although these taxes constitute a minor source of federal government revenue, raising revenue is not the only goal. Some taxes seek to discourage consumption of a good by raising its price. For example, Congress and the president engaged in pitched political battles in both 1998 and 1999 over raising the cigarette tax. The avowed purpose of the proposed sharp tax hike was not to raise revenue—it was to discourage teenage smoking.

THE PAYROLL TAX AND THE SOCIAL SECURITY SYSTEM

In government statistical documents, the payroll tax euphemistically appears as "contributions for social insurance," although these "contributions" are far from voluntary. The term signifies the fact that, unlike other taxes, the proceeds from this particular tax are set aside in "trust funds" to pay benefits to Social Security recipients and others.

But the standard notion of a trust fund does not apply. Some private pension plans *are* trust funds. You pay money into them while you are working, the trustees invest those savings for you, and you withdraw it bit by bit in your retirement years. But the Social Security system does not function that way. For most of its history, the system has simply taken the payroll tax payments of current workers and handed them over to current retirees. The benefit checks that your grandparents receive each month are not, in any real sense, dividends on the investments they made while they worked. Instead these checks are paid out of the payroll taxes that you or your parents pay each month.

For many years, this "pay as you go" system managed to give every generation of retirees more in benefits than it had contributed in payroll taxes. Social Security "contributions" were indeed a good investment! How was this miracle achieved? It relied heavily on growth: both population growth and economic growth. As long as the population grows, there will always be more and more young people to tax in order to pay the retirement benefits of senior citizens. Similarly, as long as wages keep rising, the same payroll tax *rates* permit the government to pay benefits to each generation in excess of that generation's contributions. Ten percent of today's average wage is, after all, a good deal more money than 10 percent of the wages your grandfather earned 50 years ago.

Unfortunately, the growth magic stopped working in the 1970s. First, the growth in real wages slowed dramatically, as we saw in Chapter 18. But Social Security benefits continued to grow rapidly, and in 1975 they became fully protected from inflation by *indexing*, whereas wages were not. So the burden of financing Social Security grew more onerous.

Second, population growth slowed significantly in the United States. Birthrates in this country were very high from the close of World War II until about 1960 (the postwar baby boom) and fell thereafter. As a result, the fraction of the U.S. population that is over 65 has climbed from only 7.5 percent in 1945 to 12.7 percent today, and it is certain to go much higher in the next century as baby boomers retire. Thus, there will be fewer working people to support each retired person.

Third, life expectancy keeps rising. Although this fact is undoubtedly good news for Americans, it is bad news for the financial soundness of the Social Security system. The reason is simple: as people live longer, they spend more years in retirement. When Congress set the normal Social Security retirement age at 65, many Americans did not live that long. Nowadays most do, and many live 20 years or more beyond retirement.

With the growth magic over and the long-run funding of Social Security clearly at risk, the government trimmed Social Security benefits and raised payroll taxes in 1983 to shore up the system's finances. Furthermore, and most significantly, Social

---

● **POLICY DEBATE** ▮ SAVING SOCIAL SECURITY

According to the government's long-range projections, Social Security benefits that have already been promised exceed expected future payroll tax receipts by a wide margin. So although Social Security faces no immediate financial problem, something must be done eventually to put the system on a sound financial footing.

For years, experts assumed that some combination of higher payroll taxes and lower Social Security benefits—two politically unpalatable alternatives—would be needed to do the job. But when large federal budget surpluses emerged in the late 1990s, President Bill Clinton saw an opportunity to "fix" Social Security with far less political pain. Specifically, his 1999 and 2000 State of the Union addresses proposed assigning the majority of the looming budget surpluses to the Social Security Trust Fund—an idea the Republican Congress soon adopted.

But even that vast sum (about $2.3 trillion over 10 years) was not enough to eliminate Social Securilty's financing gap. So Al Gore, while running for president in 2000, pledged to go even further and dedicate to the Trust Fund much of the interest that would be saved by paying off the national debt. Doing so, he said, would keep Social Security solvent until at least 2050.

Candidate George W. Bush objected that the Gore plan would only postpone the day of reckoning, and offered instead a bold, new idea that, he said, would end Social Security's financial woes forever. Rather than dedicate even more money to the Trust Fund, Mr. Bush proposed returning a portion of the payroll tax to workers—provided they would save it in special individually-owned accounts. Since these new private accounts would earn higher returns than the Social Security

Trust Fund (which invests only in U.S. government bonds), he argued, they would more than make up for any lost Social Security benefits.

Mr. Gore countered that the Bush plan for partial privatization of Social Security was too risky. Instead, he proposed to create a different type of individually-owned account to help people save for their retirement outside of Social Security. Under his plan, no payroll tax revenue would be diverted from Social Security. Instead, individuals would contribute their own money, and savers earning less than $50,000 per year would receive government matching funds. The match would be particularly generous for low-income people.

The American people were thus offered two quite different versions of how to save Social Security. The debate was joined.

Security abandoned its tradition of pay-as-you-go financing. Congress decided instead to start accumulating funds in advance so that the Social Security Administration (SSA) would be able to pay the baby boomers' retirement benefits.

Since then, the trust fund has taken in more money than it has paid out. The annual Social Security surplus is now running at about $150 billion. If current projections of population, real wages, and retirement behavior prove reasonably accurate, these annual surpluses will accumulate into a huge trust fund balance 10 to 12 years from now and then start to be drawn down. But the long-run funding problem has not been solved, for those same projections show the trust fund running out of money by about 2037. It is therefore clear that some combination of lower Social Security benefits and higher payroll taxes loom on the long-run horizon. (See the accompanying box, "Saving Social Security.")

■   **THE STATE AND LOCAL TAX SYSTEM**

Indirect taxes are the backbone of state and local government revenues, although most states also levy income taxes. Sales taxes are the principal source of revenue

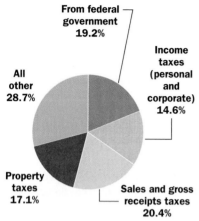

FIGURE 21-3

Sources of State and Local Revenue

From federal government 19.2%

Income taxes (personal and corporate) 14.6%

All other 28.7%

Property taxes 17.1%

Sales and gross receipts taxes 20.4%

SOURCE: *Economic Report of the President, 2000* (Washington, D.C.: U.S. Government Printing Office, 2000).

Fiscal federalism refers to the system of grants from one level of government to the next.

to the states, whereas cities and towns rely heavily on property taxes. Figure 21–3, which repeats a portion of Figure 3–18, shows the breakdown of state and local government receipts by source.

SALES AND EXCISE TAXES

These days, almost all states and many large cities levy broad-based sales taxes on purchases of goods and services, with certain specific exemptions. For example, food is exempted from sales tax in many states. Overall sales tax rates typically run in the 5 to 8 percent range. In addition, most states impose special excise taxes on such things as tobacco products, liquor, gasoline, and luxury items.

PROPERTY TAXES

Municipalities raise revenue by taxing properties, such as houses and office buildings. Educational and religious institutions are normally exempt from property tax levies. The procedure is generally to assess each taxable property based on its market value and then to place a tax rate on the community's total assessed value that yields enough revenue to cover expenditures on local services. Property taxes generally run between 1 and 3 percent of true market value.

Considerable political controversy surrounds the property tax. Because local property taxes provide the main source of financing for public schools, wealthy communities with expensive real estate are able to afford higher-quality schools than poor communities. A simple arithmetical example will clarify why. Suppose real estate holdings in Richtown average $150,000 per family, while real estate holdings in Poortown average only $50,000 per family. If both towns levy a 2 percent property tax to pay for their schools, Richtown will generate $3,000 per family in tax receipts, while Poortown will generate only $1,000.

Glaring inequalities like this have led courts in many states to declare unconstitutional the financing of public schools by local property taxes, because doing so deprives children in poorer districts of an equal opportunity to receive high-quality education. These legal decisions, in turn, have created considerable political turmoil as states scrambled to find ways to fund their schools while complying with court rulings.

FISCAL FEDERALISM

Figure 21–3 points out that federal grants provide a major source of revenue to state and local governments. In addition, grants from the states are vital to local governments. This system of transfers from one level of government to the next, which has a long history, is referred to as **fiscal federalism.**

Aid from this source has come traditionally in the form of *restricted grants*, that is, money given from one level of government to the next on the condition that it be spent for a specific purpose. For example, the U.S. government may grant funds to a state *if* that state will use the money to build highways. Or a state government may give money to a school district to spend on a specified program or facility.

The system of grants from the federal government to the states, in particular, has been in the political spotlight of late. For years, state governments complained that Congress was saddling them with "unfunded mandates"—legal obligations to provide certain services, but without the money needed to pay the bills. In 1995, Congress responded by passing legislation to end the practice of unfunded mandates.

But that was just the beginning. Acting on the belief that state governments are more attuned to local circumstances and needs, Congress made "devolution"—the transfer of powers from the federal government to the states—a major rallying cry after the 1994 election. For example, state governments have been given much more freedom to determine the rules for programs like welfare and Medicaid.

Is devolution a good idea? Supporters see state governments as more flexible and closer to the people. They also view the states as "laboratories of democracy," where creative solutions can be developed to make government more efficient. But critics argue that the history of state government gives little reason to see them as efficient providers of public services. These people worry that minimum national standards in welfare and health care might be sacrificed as states husband their limited financial resources.

■ THE CONCEPT OF EQUITY IN TAXATION

Taxes are judged on two criteria: *equity* (Is the tax fair?) and *efficiency* (Does the tax interfere unduly with the workings of the market economy?). Although economists are mostly concerned with the latter, public discussions about tax proposals focus almost exclusively on the former. Let us, therefore, begin our discussion by investigating the concept of equitable taxation.

HORIZONTAL EQUITY

There are three distinct concepts of tax equity. The first, **horizontal equity,** simply asserts that equally situated individuals should be taxed equally. Few would quarrel with that principle. But it is often difficult to apply in practice, so violations of horizontal equity can be found throughout the tax code.

> **Horizontal equity** is the notion that equally situated individuals should be taxed equally.

Consider, for example, the personal income tax. Horizontal equity calls for two families with the same income to pay the same tax. But what if one family has eight children and the other has one child? Well, you answer, we must define "equally situated" to include equal family sizes, so only families with the same number of children can be compared on grounds of horizontal equity. But what if one family has unusually high medical expenses, and the other has none? Are they still "equally situated"? By now the point should be clear: determining when two families are "equally situated" is no simple task. In fact, the U.S. tax code lists dozens of requirements that must be met before two families are construed as "equal."

VERTICAL EQUITY

The second concept of fair taxation seems to flow naturally from the first. If equals are to be treated equally, it appears that unequals should be treated unequally. This precept is known as **vertical equity.**

Just saying this, however, does not get us very far, for vertical equity is a slippery concept. Often it is translated into the **ability-to-pay principle,** according to which those most able to pay should pay the highest taxes. But this still leaves a definitional problem similar to the problem of defining "equally situated": How do we measure ability to pay? The nature of each tax often provides a straightforward answer. In income taxation, we measure ability to pay by income; in property taxation, we measure it by property value, and so on.

> **Vertical equity** refers to the notion that differently situated individuals should be taxed differently in a way that society deems to be fair.
>
> The **ability-to-pay principle** of taxation refers to the idea that people with greater ability to pay taxes should pay higher taxes.

A thornier problem arises when we try to translate the notion into concrete terms. Consider the three alternative income-tax plans listed in Table 21–2. Families with higher incomes pay higher taxes under all three plans. So they all can be said to follow the ability-to-pay principle. Yet the three plans produce radically different distributive consequences. Plan 1 is a progressive tax, like the individual income tax in

Three Alternative Income-Tax Plans

TABLE 21–2

Income	Plan 1		Plan 2		Plan 3	
	Tax	Average Tax Rate	Tax	Average Tax Rate	Tax	Average Tax Rate
$ 10,000	$ 300	3%	$ 1,000	10%	$1,000	10%
50,000	8,000	16	5,000	10	3,000	6
250,000	70,000	28	25,000	10	7,500	3

the United States: The average tax rate is higher for richer families. Plan 2 is a proportional tax: Every family pays 10 percent of its income. Plan 3 is regressive: Because tax payments rise more slowly than income, the average tax rate for richer families is lower than that for poorer families.

Which plan comes closest to the ideal notion of vertical equity? Many people find that Plan 3, the regressive tax, offends their sense of "fairness," for it makes the distribution of income *after taxes* more unequal than the distribution *before taxes*. But people agree much less over the relative merits of progressive versus proportional taxation. Often, in fact, the notion of vertical equity is taken to be synonymous with progressivity. Other things being equal, progressive taxes are seen as "good" taxes in some ethical sense, whereas regressive taxes are seen as "bad." On these grounds, advocates of greater equality of incomes support progressive income taxes and oppose sales taxes.

THE BENEFITS PRINCIPLE

Whereas the principles of horizontal and vertical equity, for all their ambiguities and practical problems, at least do not conflict with one another, the final principle of fair taxation often violates commonly accepted notions of vertical equity. According to the **benefits principle** of taxation, those who reap the benefits from government services should pay the taxes.

> The **benefits principle** of taxation holds that people who derive benefits from a service should pay the taxes that finance it.

The benefits principle is often used to justify earmarking the proceeds from certain taxes for specific public services. For example, receipts from gasoline taxes typically go to finance construction and maintenance of roads. Thus, those who use the roads pay the taxes roughly in proportion to their usage. Most people seem to find this system fair. But in other contexts—such as public schools, hospitals, and libraries—the body politic has been loath to apply the benefits principle because it clashes so dramatically with common notions of fairness. So these services are normally financed out of general tax revenues rather than by direct charges for their use.

THE CONCEPT OF EFFICIENCY IN TAXATION

Economic efficiency is among the most central concepts of economics. The economy is said to be *efficient* if it has used every available opportunity to make someone better off without making someone else worse off. In this sense, taxes almost always introduce *inefficiencies*. That is, if the tax were removed, some people could be made better off without anyone being harmed.

However, that is not a terribly pertinent comparison. The government does, after all, need revenue to pay for the services it provides. So when economists discuss the notion of "efficient" taxation, they are usually seeking taxes that cause the *least* amount of inefficiency for a given amount of tax revenue. In the more colorful words of Jean-Baptiste Colbert, treasurer to King Louis IV of France, "The art of taxation consists in so plucking the goose to obtain the largest amount of feathers, with the least possible amount of hissing."

To explain the concept of efficient taxation, we need to introduce one new term. Economists define the **burden of a tax** as the amount the taxpayer would have to be given to be just as well off in the presence of the tax as in its absence. An example will clarify this notion and also make clear why:

> The **burden of a tax** to an individual is the amount one would have to be given to be just as well off with the tax as without it.

The burden of a tax normally exceeds the revenue raised by the tax.

Suppose the government, in the interest of energy conservation, levies a high tax on the biggest gas-guzzling cars, with progressively lower taxes on smaller cars.[3] For example, a simple tax schedule might be the following:

---

[3] A tax like this has been in effect since 1984.

Car Type	Tax
Cadillac Catera	$1,000
Chrysler 300	500
Ford Escort	0

Harry has a taste for big cars and has always bought Cadillacs. (Harry is clearly no pauper.) Once the new tax takes effect, he has three options. He can still buy a Cadillac Catera and pay $1,000 in tax; he can switch to a Chrysler 300 and avoid half the tax, or he can switch to a Ford Escort and avoid the entire tax.

If Harry sticks with the Caddy, we have a case in which the burden of the tax is exactly equal to the tax he pays. Why? Because if someone gave Harry $1,000, he would be exactly as well off as he was before the tax was enacted. In general:

> When a tax induces no change in economic behavior, the burden of the tax is measured accurately by the revenue collected.

However, this is not what we normally expect to happen, and it is certainly not what the government intends by levying a tax on big cars. Normally, we expect taxes to induce some people to alter their behavior in ways that reduce or avoid tax payments. So let us look into Harry's other two options.

If Harry decides to purchase a Chrysler, he pays only $500 in tax. But $500 understates his burden because Harry is greatly chagrined by the fact that he no longer drives a Cadillac. How much money would it take to make Harry just as well off as he was before the tax? Only Harry knows for sure. But we do know that it is more than the $500 tax that he pays. Why? Because if someone gave Harry the $500 needed to pay his tax bill, he would still be less happy than he was before the tax was introduced, owing to his switch from a Cadillac to a Chrysler. Whatever the (unknown) burden of the tax is, the amount by which it exceeds the $500 tax bill is called the **excess burden** of the tax.

Harry's final option makes the importance of understanding excess burden even more clear. If he switches to an Escort, Harry will pay no tax. Are we therefore to say he has suffered no burden? Clearly not, for he longs for the Cadillac that he no longer has. The general principle is:

The **excess burden** of a tax to an individual is the amount by which the burden of the tax exceeds the tax that is paid.

> Whenever a tax induces people to change their behavior—that is, whenever it "distorts" their choices—the tax has an *excess burden*. This means that the revenue collected systematically understates the true burden of the tax.

The excess burdens that arise from tax-induced changes in economic behavior are precisely the inefficiencies we noted at the outset of this section. The basic precept of efficient taxation is to try to devise a tax system that *minimizes* these inefficiencies. In particular:

> In comparing two taxes that raise the same total revenue, the one that produces less excess burden is the more efficient.

Notice the proviso that the two taxes being compared must yield the *same* revenue. We are really interested in the *total* burden of each tax. Because:

> Total burden = Tax collections + Excess burden

we can unambiguously state that the tax with less *excess* burden is more efficient only when tax collections are equal.

Excess burdens arise when consumers and firms alter their behavior on account of taxation. So this precept of sound tax policy can be restated in a way that sounds consistent with President Reagan's statement at the beginning of this chapter:

> In devising a tax system to raise revenue, try to raise any given amount of revenue through taxes that induce the smallest changes in behavior.

● **EXCESS BURDEN AND MR. FIGG**

Humorist Russell Baker discussed the problem of excess burden in the newspaper column reproduced here. It seems that every time his mythical Mr. Figg took a step to avoid paying taxes and to satisfy the tax man, he became less and less happy.

NEW YORK—The tax man was very cross about Figg. Figg's way of life did not conform to the way of life several governments wanted Figg to pursue. Nothing inflamed the tax man more than insolent and capricious disdain for governmental desires. He summoned Figg to the temple of taxation.

"What's the idea of living in a rental apartment over a delicatessen in the city, Figg?" he inquired. Figg explained that he liked urban life. In that case, said the tax man, he was raising Figg's city sales and income taxes. "If you want them cut, you'll have to move out to the suburbs," he said.

To satisfy his local government, Figg gave up the city and rented a suburban house. The tax man summoned him back to the temple.

"Figg," he said, "you have made me sore wroth with your way of life. Therefore, I am going to soak you for more federal income taxes." And he squeezed Figg until beads of blood popped out along the seams of Figg's wallet.

"Mercy, good tax man," Figg gasped. "Tell me how to live so that I may please my government, and I shall obey."

The tax man told Figg to quit renting and buy a house. The government wanted everyone to accept large mortgage loans from bankers. If Figg complied, it would cut his taxes.

Figg bought a house, which he did not want, in a suburb where he did not want to live, and he invited his friends and relatives to attend a party celebrating his surrender to a way of life that pleased his government.

The tax man was so furious that he showed up at the party with blood-shot eyes. "I have had enough of this, Figg," he declared. "Your government doesn't want you entertaining friends and relatives. This will cost you plenty."

Figg immediately threw out all his friends and relatives, then asked the tax man what sort of people his government wished him to entertain. "Business associates," said the tax man. "Entertain plenty of business associates, and I shall cut your taxes."

To make the tax man and his government happy, Figg began entertaining people he didn't like in the house he didn't want in the suburb where he didn't want to live.

Then was the tax man enraged indeed. "Figg," he thundered, "I will not cut your taxes for entertaining straw bosses, truck drivers, and pothole fillers."

"Why not?" said Figg. "These are the people I associate with in my business."

"Which is what?" asked the tax man.

"Earning my pay by the sweat of my brow," said Figg.

"Your government is not going to bribe you for performing salaried labor," said the tax man. "Don't you know, you imbecile, that tax rates on salaried income are higher than on any other kind?"

And he taxed the sweat of Figg's brow at a rate that drew exquisite shrieks of agony from Figg and little cries of joy from Washington, which already had more sweated brows than it needed to sustain the federally approved way of life.

"Get into business, or minerals, or international oil," warned the tax man, "or I shall make your taxes as the taxes of 10."

Figg went into business, which he hated, and entertained people he didn't like in the house he didn't want in the suburb where he did not want to live.

At length the tax man summoned Figg for an angry lecture. He demanded to know why Figg had not bought a new plastic factory to replace his old metal and wooden plant. "I hate plastic," said Figg. "Your government is sick and tired of metal, wood, and everything else that smacks of the real stuff, Figg," roared the tax man, seizing Figg's purse. "Your depreciation is all used up."

There was nothing for Figg to do but go to plastic, and the tax man rewarded him with a brand new depreciation schedule plus an investment credit deduction from the bottom line.

SOURCE: Russell Baker, *International Herald Tribune*, April 13, 1977, p. 14. © 1977 by *The New York Times* Company. Reprinted by permission.

Sometimes, however, a tax is levied not primarily as a revenue raiser, but as a way to induce individuals or firms to alter their behavior—in contrast to President Reagan's dictum. For example, we mentioned earlier that President Clinton sought to use higher taxes on cigarettes to reduce teen smoking. The possibility of using taxes to change consumer behavior will be discussed in a few pages.

TAX LOOPHOLES AND EXCESS BURDEN

We noted earlier that loopholes make the income tax less progressive than it appears to be on paper. Having learned that tax-induced changes in behavior lead to excess burdens, we can now understand the second reason why tax specialists condemn tax loopholes: loopholes make the income tax less *efficient* than it could be. Why? Because most loopholes involve imposing different tax rates on different types of income. Given a choice between paying, say, a 40 percent marginal tax rate on one type of income and a 20 percent rate on another, most rational taxpayers will favor the latter. Thus:

> **When different income-earning activities are taxed at different marginal rates, economic choices are distorted by tax considerations, and this impairs economic efficiency.**

One major objective shared by tax reformers, including both contemporary advocates of a flat tax and many of their opponents, is to enhance both the equity and efficiency of the personal income tax by closing loopholes and lowering tax rates. The Tax Reform Act of 1986 represented a giant step in this direction. By roughly doubling the personal exemption, the law removed about 6 million households from

"LOOK AT THIS FEDERAL BUDGET. BILLIONS OF DOLLARS ARE BEING WASTED. I'D REALLY BE FURIOUS IF WE WERE PAYING TAXES."

the tax rolls. For most other taxpayers, progressivity—as measured by *average* tax rates—was left nearly unchanged even though *marginal* tax rates dropped sharply. This was accomplished by closing many important tax loopholes. Tax rates on different sources of income were equalized. The new code reduced or eliminated many deductions and exemptions. Abusive tax shelters such as special real estate deals were a particular target of tax reformers, though the details are best left to more advanced courses on taxation.

On balance, most observers believe we have a much better tax code today than we did in 1985. But it is far from perfect. In fact, since 1986 Congress has allowed a number of tax loopholes to reappear and has created some new ones. Proponents of a flat tax believe the time is ripe for another thorough-going reform.

SHIFTING THE TAX BURDEN: TAX INCIDENCE

The **incidence of a tax** is an allocation of the burden of the tax to specific individuals or groups.

The **flypaper theory of tax incidence** holds that the burden of a tax always sticks where the government puts it.

When economists speak of the **incidence of a tax,** they are referring to who actually bears the burden of the tax. In discussing the tax on gas-guzzling autos, we adhered to what has been called the **flypaper theory of tax incidence:** that the burden of any tax sticks where the government puts it. In this case, the burden stays on Harry, our luxury car fan. But often things do not work out this way.

Consider, for example, what will happen if the government levies a $1,000 tax on luxury cars like Cadillacs. We learned how to deal with such a tax in a supply-and-demand diagram back in Chapter 5: The supply curve shifts up by the amount of the tax, in this case, $1,000. Fig. 21–4 shows such a shift by the movement from $S_0 S_0$ to $S_1 S_1$. If the demand curve DD does not shift, the market equilibrium shifts from point A to point B. The quantity of luxury cars declines as Harrys all over America react to the higher price by buying fewer luxury cars. Notice that the price rises from $40,000 to $40,600, an increase of $600. So people who continue buying luxury cars bear a burden of only $600—less than the tax that they pay!

FIGURE 21–4

The Incidence of an Excise Tax

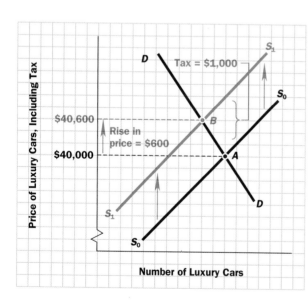

Does this mean that the tax imposes a *negative* excess burden? Certainly not. What it means is that consumers who refrain from buying the taxed commodity manage to *shift* part of the tax burden away from consumers as a whole, including those who continue to buy luxury cars. Who are the victims of this **tax shifting?** There are two main candidates. First are the automakers or, more precisely, their stockholders. To the extent that the tax reduces auto sales and profits, stockholders bear the burden. The other principal candidates are auto workers. To the extent that reduced production leads to layoffs or lower wages, the automobile workers bear part of the tax burden.

People who have never studied economics almost always believe in the flypaper theory of incidence, which holds that sales taxes are borne by consumers, property taxes are borne by homeowners, and taxes on corporations are borne by stockholders. Perhaps the most important lesson of this chapter is that:

The flypaper theory of incidence is often wrong.

Tax shifting occurs when the economic reactions to a tax cause prices and outputs in the economy to change, thereby shifting part of the burden of the tax onto others.

Failure to grasp this basic point has led to all sorts of misguided tax legislation in which members of Congress or state legislatures, *thinking* they were placing a tax burden on one group of people, inadvertently placed it squarely on another. Of course, there are cases where the flypaper theory of incidence is roughly correct. So let us consider some specific examples of tax incidence.

THE INCIDENCE OF EXCISE TAXES

Excise taxes have already been covered by our automobile example, because Figure 21–4 could represent any commodity that is taxed. Our basic finding is that *part of* the burden will fall on consumers of the taxed commodity (including those who stop buying it because of the tax), and part will be borne by the firms and workers who produce the commodity.

How is the burden shared between buyers and sellers? It all depends on the slopes of the demand and supply curves. Intuitively speaking, if consumers are very loyal to the taxed commodity, they will continue to buy almost the same quantity regardless of price. In that case, they will get stuck with most of the tax bill because they leave themselves vulnerable to it. Thus:

The more inelastic the demand for the product, the larger the share of the tax that consumers will pay.

Similarly, if suppliers are determined to supply the same amount of the product no matter how low the price, then they will wind up paying most of the tax. That is:

The more inelastic the supply curve, the larger is the share of the tax that suppliers will pay.

One extreme case arises when no one stops buying luxury cars when their prices rise. The demand curve becomes vertical, like the demand curve *DD* in Figure 21–5. Then no tax shifting can take place. When the supply curve shifts upward by the amount of the tax ($1,000), the price of a luxury car (inclusive of tax) rises by the full $1,000—from $40,000 to $41,000. So consumers bear the entire burden.

The other extreme case arises when the supply curve is totally inelastic, as depicted by the vertical line *SS* in Figure 21–6. Because the number of luxury cars supplied is the same at any price, the supply curve will not shift when a tax is imposed. Consequently, automakers must bear the full burden of any tax that is placed on their product. Figure 21–6 shows that the tax does not change the market price (including tax), which, of course, means that the price received by sellers must fall by the full amount of the tax.

Demand and supply schedules for most goods and services are not as extreme as those depicted in Figures 21–5 and 21–6, so buyers and sellers share the burden. Precisely how it is shared depends on the elasticities of the supply and demand curves.[4]

THE INCIDENCE OF THE PAYROLL TAX

We can view the payroll tax as an excise tax on the employment of labor. As we mentioned earlier, the U.S. payroll tax comes in two parts: Half is levied on employees (via payroll deductions) and half on employers. A fundamental point, which people who have never studied economics often fail to grasp, is that:

The ultimate incidence of a payroll tax is the same whether it is levied on employers or on employees.

A simple numerical example will illustrate why this must be so. Consider an employee earning $100 a day with a 16 percent payroll tax that is shared equally between the employer and the employee, as under our present law. How

FIGURE 21–5

An Extreme Case of Tax Incidence

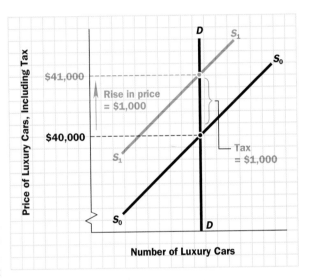

FIGURE 21–6

Another Extreme Case of Tax Incidence

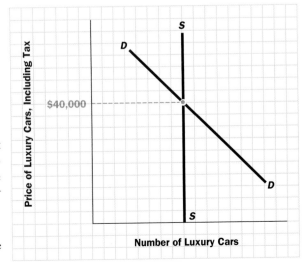

much does it cost the firm to hire this worker? It costs $100 in wages paid to the worker plus $8 in taxes paid to the government, for a total of $108 a day. How much does the worker receive? He gets $100 in wages paid by the employer less $8 deducted and sent to the government, or $92 a day. The difference between wages paid and wages received is $108 − $92 = $16, the amount of the tax.

Now suppose Congress tries to "shift" the burden of the tax entirely onto firms by raising the employer's tax to $16 while lowering the employee's tax to zero. At first, the daily wage is fixed at $100, so firms' total labor costs (including tax) rise to $116 per day and workers' net income rises to $100 per day. Congress seems to have achieved its goal.

But the achievement is fleeting, for what we have just described is not an equilibrium situation. With the daily cost of labor at $116 for firms, the quantity of labor *demanded* will be *less* than when labor cost only $108 per day. Similarly, with take-home pay up to $100 for workers, the quantity of labor *supplied* will be *more* than when the after-tax wage was only $92. Therefore, a *surplus of labor* on the market will arise (an excess of quantity supplied over quantity demanded), and this surplus will place downward pressure on wages.

How far will wages have to fall? We can easily see that an after-tax wage of $92 will restore equilibrium. If daily take-home pay is $92, the same as it was before the tax change, quantity supplied will be the same. From the firm's perspective, labor now costs $108 per day, just as it did before the tax change. So they will demand the same quantity as they did when the payroll tax was shared. Thus, in the end, the market will completely frustrate the intent of Congress.

The payroll tax is an excellent example of a case in which Congress, misled by the flypaper theory of incidence, thinks it is "taxing firms" when it raises the employer's share and "taxing workers" when it raises the employee's share. In truth, who really pays in the long run depends on the incidence of the tax. But no lasting difference results from a change in the employee's and the employer's shares.

Who, then, really bears the burden of the payroll tax? Like any excise tax, the incidence of the payroll tax depends on the elasticities of the supply and demand schedules. In the case of labor supply, a large body of empirical evidence points to the conclusion that the quantity of labor supplied is not very responsive to price for most population groups. The supply curve is almost vertical, like that shown in Figure 21–6. The result: Workers as a group can shift little of the burden of the payroll tax to employees.

But employers *can* shift it in most cases. Firms view their share of the payroll tax as an additional cost of using labor. So when payroll taxes go up, firms try to substitute cheaper factors of production (capital) for labor wherever they can. This reduces the quantity of labor demanded, lowering the wage received by workers. And this is how market forces shift part of the tax burden from firms to workers.

To the extent that the supply curve of labor has some positive slope, the quantity of labor supplied will fall when the wage goes down, and in this way workers can shift some of the burden back onto firms. But firms, in turn, can shift that burden onto consumers by raising their prices. As we know from Part III, prices in competitive markets generally rise when costs (like labor costs) increase. It is doubtful, therefore, that firms bear much of the payroll tax burden. The flypaper theory of incidence could not be further from the truth. Even though the tax is collected by the firm, it is really borne by workers and consumers.

WHEN TAXATION CAN IMPROVE EFFICIENCY

We have spent much of this chapter discussing the kinds of inefficiencies and excess burdens that arise from taxation. But, before we finish this discussion, we must point out two things.

First, economic efficiency is not society's only goal. For example, a tax on energy causes inefficiencies if it changes people's behavior patterns. But this, presumably, is exactly what the government intends. The government wants to conserve energy and is willing to tolerate some economic inefficiency to accomplish this goal. We can, of course, argue whether that is a good idea—whether the conservation achieved is worth the efficiency loss. But the general point is that:

Some taxes that introduce economic inefficiencies are nonetheless good social policy because they help achieve some other goal.

We have already mentioned the excise tax on cigarettes, which aims to change behavior. Another important example is the high tax on alcoholic beverages.

A second, and more fundamental, point is that:

Some taxes that change economic behavior may lead to efficiency gains, rather than to efficiency *losses*.

As you might guess, this can happen only when the system has an inefficiency prior to the tax. Then an appropriate tax may help set things right. One important example of this phenomenon came up in Chapter 14 and will occupy much of the next chapter. Because firms and individuals who despoil clean air and water often do so without paying any price, these precious resources are used inefficiently. A corrective tax on pollution can remedy this problem.

■ EQUITY, EFFICIENCY, AND THE OPTIMAL TAX

In a perfect world, the ideal tax would raise the revenues the government needs, reflect society's views on equity in taxation, and induce no changes in economic behavior—and so have no excess burden. Unfortunately, no one has ever been able to devise such a tax.

Sometimes, in fact, the taxes with the smallest excess burdens are the most regressive. For instance, a head tax, which charges every person the same number of dollars, is incredibly regressive. But it is also perfectly efficient. Because no change in economic behavior will enable anyone to avoid it, no one has any reason to change behavior. As we have noted, the regressive payroll tax also seems to have small excess burdens.

Fortunately, however, there is a tax that, though not ideal, still scores highly on both the equity and efficiency criteria: a comprehensive personal income tax with few loopholes.

Although it is true that income taxes can be avoided by earning less income, we have already observed that in reality the supply of labor changes little because of tax policies. People can also reduce their tax bills by investing in relatively safe assets (like government bonds) rather than riskier ones (like common stocks), because safer assets pay lower rates of return. But it is not clear that the income tax actually induces such behavior. Why? Because, although the government shares in the profits when investments turn out well, it also shares in the losses when investments turn sour. Finally, because an income tax reduces the return on saving, many economists have worried that it would discourage saving and thus retard economic growth.[5] But empirical evidence does not suggest that this happens to any great extent.

On balance, then, although unresolved questions remain and research is continuing:

Most of the studies that have been conducted to date suggest that a comprehensive personal income tax with no loopholes induces few of the behavioral reactions that would reduce consumer well-being, and thus has a rather small excess burden.

On the equity criterion, we know that personal income taxes can be made as progressive as society deems desirable, though if marginal tax rates on rich people get

---

[5] For this reason, some economists prefer a tax on consumption to a tax on income.

extremely high, some of the potential efficiency losses might get more serious than they now seem to be. On both grounds, then, many economists—including both liberals and conservatives—view a comprehensive personal income tax as one of the best ways for a government to raise revenue.

Issue Revisited: The Pros and Cons of a Flat Tax

How does the flat tax stack up against these criteria? Quite well on most, at least in its ideal form.

■ A *low* tax rate for everyone would mean that taxes would create only small tax distortions. Excess burdens would be minimal.

■ A *uniform* tax rate on all types of income would eliminate tax loopholes.

■ If the exemption is large enough, the income tax can maintain progressivity at the bottom of the income distribution. For example, some plans would exempt the first $30,000 or more of income from taxation.

■ As noted at the start of this chapter, filing your income-tax return under a flat tax would be extremely simple, thereby saving millions of taxpayer hours (and making many CPAs unhappy).

These are all notable virtues, which explains why the flat tax has attracted many adherents. But once we leave the realm of the *ideal* and confront the *real,* some serious problems arise:

■ Some flat-tax plans would tax only *earnings,* leaving all income from capital free of tax. This would not only create strong incentives to evade the tax by transforming labor income into capital income, but it would also erode progressivity.

■ It seems unlikely that Congress would eliminate *all* tax preferences. Among other things, they would have to tax the value of employer-provided fringe benefits (like health insurance) and eliminate the deductibility of home mortgage interest—two steps that would surely be politically unpopular.

"I've been thinking about the flat tax and how it would inflict hardship on the poor, and I can live with that."

- If large tax preferences like these remain, or if income from capital is tax free, a higher tax rate will be needed to raise the required revenue. Thus, under a realistic flat tax, most Americans might actually face a *higher* marginal tax rate than they do now.

- No flat tax can maintain progressivity at the top. Under the current tax code, the very rich pay taxes equal to about 40 percent of their taxable incomes. Under, say, a 22 percent flat tax, they would pay just 22 percent. Some Americans wonder why the very rich should get such a large tax break.

Where does this partial accounting of the pros and cons of the flat tax leave us? As usual in a serious public policy debate, with plenty of room for reasonable people to disagree! As we said back in Chapter 1, economics is not supposed to give you all the *answers*. It is supposed to teach you how to ask the right *questions*.

SUMMARY

1. Taxes in the United States have been quite constant as a percentage of gross domestic product since the early 1970s.

2. The federal government raises most of its revenue by *direct taxes*, such as the personal and corporate *income taxes* and the payroll tax. Of these, the payroll tax is increasing most rapidly.

3. The Social Security system relied successfully on pay-as-you-go financing for decades. In recent years, however, it has been accumulating a large trust fund to be used to pay benefits to the baby boom generation when it retires. But experts do not think that trust fund will be enough.

4. State and local governments raise most of their tax revenues by *indirect taxes*. States rely mainly on sales taxes, whereas localities depend on property taxes.

5. There is controversy over whether local property taxes are an equitable way to finance public education.

6. In our multilevel system of government, the federal government makes various sorts of grants to state and local governments, and states in turn make grants to municipalities and school districts. This system of intergovernmental transfers is called *fiscal federalism* and is highly controversial these days.

7. The three concepts of fair, or "equitable," taxation occasionally conflict. *Horizontal equity* simply calls for equals to be treated equally. *Vertical equity*, which calls for unequals to be treated unequally, has often been translated into the *ability-to-pay principle*—that people who are better able to pay taxes should be taxed more heavily. The *benefits principle* of tax equity ignores ability to pay and seeks to tax people according to the benefits they receive.

8. The *burden of a tax* is the amount of money an individual would have to be given to be as well off with the tax as without it. This burden normally exceeds the taxes that are paid, and the difference between the two is called the *excess burden* of the tax.

9. Excess burden arises whenever a tax induces some people or firms to change their behavior. Because excess burdens signal *economic inefficiencies*, the basic principle of efficient taxation is to utilize taxes that have small excess burdens.

10. When people change their behavior on account of a tax, they often shift the burden of the tax onto someone else. This is why the *"flypaper theory of incidence"*—the belief that the burden of any tax sticks where Congress puts it—is often incorrect.

11. The burden of a sales or *excise tax* normally is shared between the suppliers and the consumers. The manner in which it is shared depends on the elasticities of supply and demand.

12. The *payroll tax* is like an excise tax on labor services. Because the supply of labor is much less elastic than the demand for labor, workers bear most of the burden of the payroll tax. This includes both the employer's and the employee's share of the tax.

13. Sometimes, "inefficient" taxes—that is, taxes that cause a good deal of excess burden—are nonetheless desirable because the changes in behavior they induce further some other social goal.

14. When there are inefficiencies in the system for reasons other than the tax system (for example, externalities), taxation can conceivably improve efficiency.

KEY TERMS

Progressive, proportional, and regressive taxes   435

Average and marginal tax rates   435

Direct and indirect taxes   435

Personal income tax   436

Tax loopholes   436

Tax exempt   436

Tax deductions   436

Payroll tax   437

Corporate income tax   437

Excise tax   438

Social Security system   438

Property tax   440

Fiscal federalism   440

Horizontal and vertical equity   441

Ability-to-pay principle   441

Benefits principle of taxation   442

Economic efficiency   442

Burden of a tax   442

QUESTIONS FOR REVIEW

1. "If the federal government continues to raise taxes as it has been doing, it will ruin the country. Americans are already overtaxed." Comment.

2. Soon after taking office in 1993, President Clinton proposed a package of tax increases, including higher income tax rates for wealthy taxpayers and higher taxes on energy. Critics argued that these taxes would harm the economy. Why did they say this?

3. Using the following hypothetical income tax table, compute the marginal and average tax rates. Is the tax progressive, proportional, or regressive?

Income	Income Tax
$20,000	$2,000
30,000	2,700
40,000	3,200
50,000	3,500

4. Which concept of tax equity, if any, seems to be served by each of the following:

   a. The progressive income tax

   b. The flat income tax

   c. The excise tax on cigarettes

   d. The gasoline tax

5. Use the example of Mr. Figg (see the box, "Excess Burden and Mr. Figg" on page 444) to explain the concepts of efficient taxes and excess burden.

6. Think of some tax that you personally pay. What steps have you taken or could you take to reduce your tax payments? Is there an excess burden on you? Why or why not?

7. Suppose the supply and demand schedules for cigarettes are as follows:

Price per Carton	Quantity Demanded	Quantity Supplied
$3.00	360	160
3.25	330	180
3.50	300	200
3.75	270	220
4.00	240	240
4.25	210	260
4.50	180	280
4.75	150	300
5.00	120	320

NOTE: Quantity is in millions of cartons per year.

   a. What is the equilibrium price and equilibrium quantity?

   b. Now the government levies a $1.25 per carton excise tax on cigarettes. What is the equilibrium price paid by consumers, the price received by producers, and the quantity now?

   c. Explain why it makes no difference whether Congress levies the $1.25 tax on the consumer or the producer. (Relate your answer to the discussion of the payroll tax in the text.)

   d. Suppose the tax is levied on the producers. How much of the tax are producers able to shift onto consumers? Explain how they manage to do this.

   e. Will there be any excess burden from this tax? Why? Who bears this excess burden?

   f. By how much has cigarette consumption declined on account of the tax? Why might the government be happy about this outcome, despite the excess burden?

8. Now suppose the supply schedule is instead:

Price per Carton	Quantity Supplied
$3.00	60
3.25	105
3.50	150
3.75	195
4.00	240
4.25	285
4.50	330
4.75	375
5.00	420

NOTE: Quantity is in millions of cartons per year.

   a. What are the equilibrium price and equilibrium quantity in the absence of a tax?

   b. What are the equilibrium price and equilibrium quantity in the presence of a $1.25 per carton excise tax?

   c. Explain why your answer to part b differs from part b of the previous question, and relate this difference to the discussion of the incidence of an excise tax in this chapter.

9. The country of Taxmania produces only two commodities: rice and caviar. The poor spend all their income on rice, while the rich purchase both goods. Both demand for and supply of rice are quite inelastic. In the caviar market, both supply and demand are quite elastic. Which good would be heavily taxed if Taxmanians cared mostly about efficiency? What if they cared mostly about vertical equity?

10. Discuss President Reagan's statement on taxes quoted on the first page of the chapter. Do you agree with him?

11. Use the criteria of equity and efficiency in taxation to evaluate the idea of taxing capital gains at a lower rate than other sources of income.

> Environmental taxes are perhaps the most powerful tool societies have for forging economies that protect human and environmental health.
>
> David Malin Roodman,
> Worldwatch Institute

EXTERNALITIES, THE ENVIRONMENT, AND NATURAL RESOURCES

We learned in Chapter 14 that *externalities* (which are the incidental benefits or damages imposed on people not directly involved in an economic activity) can cause the market mechanism to malfunction. The first half of this chapter studies a particularly important application: externalities as a way to explain environmental problems. We will consider the extent to which the price mechanism bears responsibility for these problems and how that same mechanism can help remedy them. In the second half of the chapter we address a closely related subject: natural resource depletion. We will discuss fears that the world is quickly using up many of its vital resources and how, here too, the price mechanism can help.

■ PART 1: THE ECONOMICS OF ENVIRONMENTAL PROTECTION

Environmental problems are not new. What *is* new and different is the attention we now give them. Much of the increased interest stems from rising incomes, which have reduced our concerns about our most basic needs of food, clothing, and shelter and have allowed us the luxury of concentrating on the *quality* of life.

Economic thought on the subject of environmental degradation preceded the outburst of public concern by nearly half a century. In 1911, the British economist Arthur C. Pigou wrote a remarkable book called *The Economics of Welfare*, which for the first time explained these problems in terms of externalities. He also outlined an approach to environmental policy that is still favored by most economists today and gradually seems to be winning over lawmakers, bureaucrats, and even cautious environmentalists (as the opening quotation suggests). Pigou's analysis indicated that a system of *pollution charges* can be an effective means to control pollution. In this way, the price mechanism can remedy one of its own shortcomings!

EXTERNALITIES: A CRITICAL SHORTCOMING OF THE MARKET MECHANISM

Throughout this book we have sought to provide a balanced view of the private enterprise economy, carefully pointing out both its vast accomplishments and its failings. Chapter 14 listed externalities as a primary shortcoming of the market mechanism.

We also emphasized that externalities are found in many places. For example, another car's entry onto an overcrowded highway adds to delays that other travelers must endure, thereby causing those others to suffer a *detrimental* **externality.** But externalities can also be *beneficial* to third parties. In Chapter 15, on the microeconomics of innovation and growth, we emphasized that innovations usually provide beneficial externalities to persons who neither invest in an innovation nor purchase any of its products.

An activity is said to generate a beneficial or detrimental **externality** if that activity causes incidental benefits or damages to others not directly involved in the activity, and no corresponding compensation is provided to or paid by those who generate the externality.

Externalities: A Shortcoming of the Market Cured by Market Methods

EXTERNALITIES   Because those who create harmful externalities do not pay for the damage done to others, they have little incentive to desist. In this way the market tends to create an undesired *abundance* of damaging externalities. Similarly, because those who create *beneficial* externalities are not compensated for doing so, they will have little incentive to supply as large a quantity as will serve the interests of society best. Therefore, the market tends to supply an undesirably *small* amount of such beneficial externalities. In sum, economists conclude that unless something is done about it, the market will provide an overabundance of harmful externalities and an undersupply of desirable ones. Either case is far from ideal.

You may remember that externalities are one of our *Ideas for Beyond the Final Exam* because they are so important for the welfare of society and the efficient functioning of the economy. They play a crucial role in environmental deterioration, affecting the health of the population and threatening our natural resource heritage. This chapter discusses the character and magnitude of the problem and the methods that can be used to contain its harmful consequences.

In this chapter we focus on one of the most publicized externalities—pollution. Toxic fumes from a chemical plant affect not only the plant's employees and customers, but other people as well. Because the firm does not pay for this *incidental* damage, the firm's owners have no financial incentive to limit their emissions of pollution, particularly because pollution controls cost money. Instead, the owners of the polluting firm will find it profitable to continue their toxic emissions as though the fumes caused no external damage to the community.

THE FACTS: IS EVERYTHING REALLY GETTING STEADILY WORSE?

First, let's see what the facts really are. The popular press often gives the impression that environmental problems have been growing steadily worse and that *all* pollution is attributable to modern industrialization and the profit system. The problems are, indeed, serious and some of them are extremely urgent. But it is nevertheless possible to exaggerate the situation.

For one thing, pollution is nothing new. Medieval cities were pestholes; streets and rivers were littered with garbage and the air stank of rotting wastes—a level of filth that was accepted as normal. And early in the 20th century, the automobile was hailed for its major *improvement* in the cleanliness of city streets, which until then had fought a losing battle against the proliferation of horse dung.

Since World War II, there has been marked progress in solving a number of pollution problems. Air quality has improved in U.S. cities during the past two decades, and concentrations of most air pollutants are still declining. Most dramatic has been the nearly 100 percent decrease in ambient concentrations of lead since the 1970s. Figure 22–1 portrays the encouraging trends in national air pollution levels. With the exception of ozone, average concentrations are well below the national ambient air quality standards (NAAQS). Rapid declines in automobile pollution have played a large role in this improvement, along with decreases in emissions from power plants. There have also been some spectacular gains in water quality. In the Great Lakes region, where the Cuyahoga River once caught fire because of its toxic load and where Lake Erie was pronounced dead, tough pollution controls have gradually effected a recovery.

U.S. National Air Quality Trends, 1975–1998 | **FIGURE 22-1**

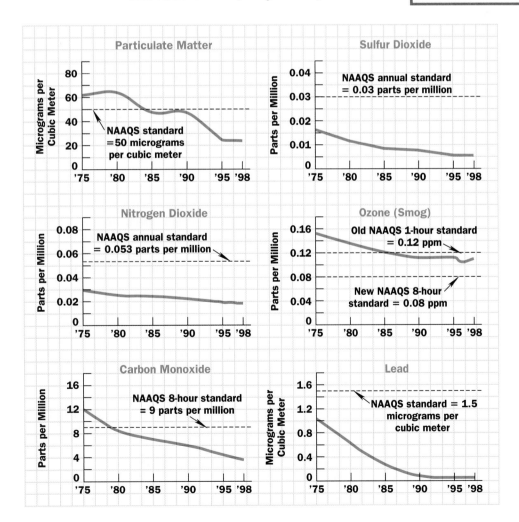

NOTE: Measures are average ambient concentrations of six pollutants. After 1987, particulate matter is measured by PM10 only, an indicator of those particles smaller than 10 micrometers.

SOURCE: Council on Environmental Quality, *Environmental Quality 1993, 24th Annual Report of the CEQ*, Washington, D.C., April 1995; and U.S. Environmental Protection Agency, *National Air Quality and Emissions Trends Report 1998*, www.epa.gov, accessed June 2000.

● CHINA OFFICIALLY LIFTS FILTER ON STAGGERING POLLUTION DATA

For the Record

No Silver Lining

China's major cities have some of the highest concentrations of air pollutants in the world, far exceeding international safety guidelines.

1995 Concentrations of air pollutants in micrograms per cubic meter; annual mean concentration

	Total suspended particles	Sulfur dioxide
	Maximum safe range under World Health Organization guidelines	
Beijing	370	94
Shanghai	246	53
Chongqing	322	338
Taiyuan	568	424
Bangkok	200	13
Los Angeles	76	8
New York	59	26
Tokyo	55	22

Sources: China's Environmental Protection Agency; World Health Organization; World Bank

SOURCE: Elisabeth Rosenthal, "China Officially Lifts Filter on Staggering Pollution Data," *The New York Times*, June 14, 1998. The article cites China's Environmental Protection Agency, the World Health Organization, and the World Bank.

The Europeans are making progress as well. For example, the infamous killing fogs of London, once the staple backdrop of British mystery fiction, are a thing of the past because of the air quality improvement since 1950. The Thames River has been cleaned up enough to allow large-scale fishing of giant conger eels to resume after a 150-year hiatus. The point is that pollution problems are not a uniquely modern phenomenon, nor is every part of the environment deteriorating relentlessly.

Free-market economies certainly have no monopoly on pollution. Though it may seem that a centrally planned economy should be able to cope much better with the environmental problems caused by externalities, such economies have in reality been the *biggest* environmental disasters. China, the last large communist society, has some of the world's worst air pollution, mainly from the burning of low-quality, high-sulfur coal and an almost complete lack of even rudimentary pollution control devices. Urban smog levels in China are far greater than those in Los Angeles, a place that Americans tend to think invented smog. (The accompanying box, "China Officially Lifts Filter on Staggering Pollution Data," compares such problems in Chinese cities with those in Los Angeles, New York, and Tokyo.)

Grave environmental problems also plague eastern Europe and the countries of the former Soviet Union. Poland, for example, is one of the most polluted industrialized countries in the world, with 11 percent of its land (on which 40 percent of its population lives) now declared "ecologically hazardous." High pollution levels contribute to severe health problems in these countries. The collapse of communism in the former Soviet Union revealed a staggering array of environmental horrors, including massive poisoning of air, ground, and water in the vicinity of industrial plants. This has resulted in widespread illness and countless premature deaths. The Soviet Union produced monumental ecological disasters. For example, the Aral Sea, once the world's fourth largest inland sea, has been reduced to less than half of its original volume.[1]

---

[1] "The Former Soviet Bloc: Environmental Crises Caused by Communist Rule," National Center for Policy Analysis, www.ncpa.org, accessed November 1998; Piotr Skubala, "Both Threats and Hopes in Upper Silesia," *The Baltic Sea Project Newsletter*, Stockholm 1997, www.skolverket.se, accessed November 1998; Murray Feshbach and Alfred Friendly, Jr., *Ecocide in the USSR: Health and Nature under Siege* (New York: Basic Books, 1992).

● **UNSCENELY**

Pardon the pun, but the future is unclear for scenic viewpoints in some national parks. . . .

National parks are reporting high ozone rankings this summer from Cape Cod National Seashore, Mass., to Indiana Dunes National Lakeshore. Air-quality experts say ozone levels at some parks actually are higher than those of nearby cities; the ozone-pollution levels over the Great Smoky Mountains are twice those of cities, such as Knoxville, Tenn., at lower elevations.

So far this summer, the Great Smoky Mountains National Park has already experienced 14 unhealthy days because of ozone problems. Acadia National Park in Maine has had seven unhealthy days, and Shenandoah National Park in Virginia has reported three.

SOURCE: Michelle Higgins, "Takeoffs & Landings," *The Wall Street Journal*, July 31, 1998, p. W4.

Yet our own environment here in the United States is hardly free from problems. Despite improvements, many U.S. urban areas still suffer many days of unhealthful air quality, particularly during summer months. According to the U.S. Environmental Protection Agency (EPA), 107 million Americans live in areas where pollution levels in 1997 still exceeded at least one national air quality standard.[2] Ozone (the presence of which 12 miles up in the stratosphere protects humans from the fiercest part of the sun's ultraviolet radiation) is the most important component of serious ground-level urban air pollution—smog. And formerly pristine wilderness areas are threatened by air pollution too (see the accompanying box, "Unscenely").

Our world is frequently subjected to new pollutants, some far more dangerous than those we have reduced, although less visible and less malodorous. Improperly dumped toxic substances—such as PCBs (polychlorinated biphenyls), chlorinated hydrocarbons, dioxins, heavy metals, and radioactive materials—can cause cancer and threaten life and health in other ways. The danger presented by some of these substances can persist for thousands of years, causing all but irreversible damage.

But even these problems pale when compared to an uncertain, but very real, environmental threat—the long-term warming of the earth's atmosphere. Many researchers (including scientists at the National Aeronautics and Space Administration) believe that the documented global warming of the past century, and especially in the past decade, is at least partly a consequence of human activities that have increased "greenhouse gases" in the atmosphere. Carbon dioxide buildup from the burning of fossil fuels such as oil, natural gas, and coal is suspected of being a significant contributor. Figure 22–2 charts the warming trend. Though sometimes disputed, forecasts of future warming range from 1.8° to 6.3° Fahrenheit by the year 2100, a dramatic change that may shift world rain patterns, disrupt agriculture, threaten coastal cities with inundation, and expand deserts.

THE FAR SIDE   By GARY LARSON

"The picture's pretty bleak, gentlemen. ... The world's climates are changing, the mammals are taking over, and we all have a brain about the size of a walnut."

Although environmental problems are neither new nor confined to capitalist, industrialized economies, we continue to inflict damage on ourselves and our surroundings.

[2] Source: U.S. Environmental Protection Agency, *National Air Quality and Emissions Trends Report 1997*, December 1998, www.epa.gov.

FIGURE 22-2   **Annual Mean Global Surface Air Temperature, 1880–2000**

SOURCE: National Aeronautics and Space Administration, Goddard Institute for Space Studies, www.giss.nasa.gov, (first 8 months only of 2000).

THE LAW OF CONSERVATION OF MATTER AND ENERGY

The physical law of conservation of matter and energy tells us that objects cannot disappear—at most they can be changed into something else. Petroleum, for instance, can be transformed into heat (and smoke) or into plastic—but it will never vanish. This means that after a raw material has been used, either it must be used again (recycled) or it becomes a waste product that requires disposal.

If it is not recycled, any input used in production must ultimately become a waste product. It may end up in some municipal dump, it may literally go up in smoke, contributing to atmospheric pollution, or it may be transformed into heat, warming up adjacent waterways and killing aquatic life. But the laws of physics tell us nothing can be done to make used inputs disappear altogether.

We create an extraordinary amount of solid waste—each American discards an average of 4.5 pounds of trash every *day*, despite our efforts to reduce this waste. Fortunately, in the face of this rising tide of garbage, recycling rates for many commonly used materials (like aluminum, paper, and glass) are rising in the United States and many other industrial countries. In the United States recycling has increased substantially—according to the EPA, Americans recycled or composted 27 percent of municipal solid waste in 1995, up from under 10 percent in 1980. Switzerland recycles more than 20 percent of its municipal solid waste, and the statistics for Japan, Sweden, the Netherlands, Germany, and Spain are all in the 15 to 20 percent range.[3]

---

[3] U.S. Environmental Protection Agency, "Characterization of Municipal Solid Waste in the United States, 1997 Update," Report No. EPA530-R-98–007, May 1998, www.epa.gov; and "International Solid Waste Practices," MSW Factbook, www.epa.gov, accessed January 1999.

  We should point out that recycling is not always as benign as it seems. The very process of preparing materials for reuse often can produce dangerous emissions. The recycling of waste oil is a clear example, because used petroleum products are often combined with toxic chemicals that can be released in the recycling process.

THE ROLE OF INDIVIDUALS AND GOVERNMENTS IN ENVIRONMENTAL DAMAGE

Many people think of industry as the primary villain in environmental damage. But:

Although business firms do their share in harming the environment, private individuals and government are also major contributors.

Individual car owners are responsible for much of the air pollution in cities; wood-burning stoves and fireplaces are a source of particulate pollution, and wastes from flush toilets and residential washing machines also cause significant harm.

Governments, too, add to the problem. Municipal treatment plant wastes are a major source of water pollution. Military aircraft create exhaust and cause noise pollution. Obsolete atomic materials and by-products associated with chemical and nuclear weapons are among the most dangerous of all wastes, and their disposal remains an unsolved problem.

Governments also construct giant dams and reservoirs that flood farmlands and destroy canyons, often causing salt to seep into the earth and render surrounding soil unusable. Swamp drainage has altered local ecology irrevocably; canal building has diverted the flow of rivers. The U.S. Army Corps of Engineers has been accused of acting on the basis of a so-called *edifice complex*. But this kind of grandiose construction reached its greatest heights in the communist states under Stalin, whose pride in enormous (but environmentally destructive) hydroelectric installations and huge canals was well publicized in the Soviet press.

ENVIRONMENTAL DAMAGE AS AN EXTERNALITY

Our very existence makes some environmental damage inevitable. In order to eat and protect ourselves from the elements, people must use up the earth's resources and generate wastes.

Environmental damage cannot be reduced to zero. As long as the human race survives, eliminating such damage completely is impossible.

Why do economists believe that though environmental damage cannot be reduced to zero, the *public interest* requires it to be reduced below its free-market level? Why do economists conclude that the market mechanism, which is so good at providing about the right number of running shoes and refrigerators, generates too much pollution? Pollution is an externality, which means that it results from a price mechanism malfunction that prevents the market from doing its usual effective job of carrying out consumers' wishes.

Here, the *failure of the pricing system* is caused by a pollution-generating firm's ability to use up some of the community's clean air or water without paying for the privilege. Just as the firm would undoubtedly use oil and electricity wastefully if they were available at no charge, the firm will use "free" air wastefully, despoiling it with chemical fumes far beyond the level justified by the public interest. The problem is that *price* has not been permitted to play its usual role here. Instead of having to pay for the pure air that it uses up, a polluting firm gets that valuable resource free of charge.

Externalities play a crucial role affecting the quality of life. They show why the market mechanism, which is so efficient in supplying consumers' goods, has a much poorer record in terms of environmental effects. The problem of pollution illustrates the importance of externalities for public policy.

SUPPLY-DEMAND ANALYSIS OF ENVIRONMENTAL EXTERNALITIES

We can use basic supply-demand analysis to explain both how externalities lead to environmental problems and how these problems can be cured. As an illustration, consider the environmental damage caused by massive garbage generation.

FIGURE 22-3

Free Dumping of Pollutants as an Inducement to Environmental Damage

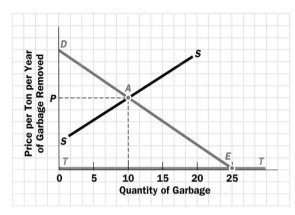

NOTE: Quantity is in millions of tons per year.

Figure 22–3 shows a hypothetical demand curve, *DE*, for garbage removal. As usual, this curve has a negative slope, meaning that if garbage removal prices rise, people will demand less removal. They may take more waste to recycling centers, repair broken items rather than throwing them out, and so on.

The graph also shows the supply curve, *SS*, of an ideal market for garbage removal. As we saw in our analysis of competitive industries (Chapter 10), the position of the market's long-run supply curve is the average cost of garbage removal. If suppliers had to pay the full costs of removal—including costs (like laundry and doctor's bills) of pollution caused when garbage is burned at the dump—the supply curve would be comparatively high (as drawn in the graph). For the community depicted in the graph, the price of garbage removal is *P* dollars per ton, and 10 million tons are generated (point *A*).

But what if the community's government decides to remove garbage "for free"? Of course, the consumer still really pays for garbage removal through taxes, but not in a way that makes each household pay for the quantity of garbage it actually produces. The supply curve is then no longer *SS*. Rather it becomes the red line *TT*, which lies along the horizontal axis, because any household can increase the garbage it throws away at no cost to itself. Now the intersection of the supply and demand curve is no longer point *A*. Rather it is point *E*, at which the price is zero, and the quantity of garbage generated is 25 million tons—a substantially greater amount.

Similar problems occur if a community offers the dissolved oxygen in its waterways and its atmosphere's purity without charge. The amount wasted and otherwise used up is likely to be enormously greater than if users had to pay for the cost of their actions to society. That is a key reason for the severity of our environmental problems.

> The magnitude of our pollution problems is largely attributable to the fact that the market lets individuals, firms, and government agencies deplete such resources as clean water and pure air without charging them any money for using up those resources.

It follows that one way of dealing with pollution problems is to charge those who emit pollution, and those who despoil the environment in other ways, a price commensurate with the costs they impose on society.

"IT'S HARD TO BELIEVE THAT HER BIGGEST PASSION IS FOR A CLEANER ENVIRONMENT."

● FOILED BY THE "SEATTLE STOMP"

If rubbish disposal is free, people will produce too much rubbish. The obvious economic solution is to make households pay the marginal cost of disposing of their waste. That will give them an incentive to throw out less and recycle more. . . . But as Don Fullerton and Thomas Kinnaman, two American economists, have found, this seemingly easy application of economic sense to an everyday problem has surprisingly intricate and sometimes disappointing results.

In the past few years several American towns and cities have started charging households for generating rubbish. The most common system is to sell stickers or tags which householders attach to rubbish bags or cans. . . . The price of a sticker or tag is, in effect, the marginal price the household pays for creating another bag of rubbish.

In a paper published last year Messrs Fullerton and Kinnaman studied the effects of one such scheme, introduced in July 1992 in Charlottesville, Virginia, a town of about 40,000. Residents were charged 80 cents for each sticker.

. . . [T]he number of bags or cans collected did fall sharply, by 37 percent between May and September 1992. But this was largely thanks to the "Seattle Stomp," a frantic dance first noticed when that city introduced rubbish pricing. Rather than buy more tags, people simply crammed more garbage—about 40 percent more—into each container. . . . The weight of rubbish collected in Charlottesville (a better indicator of disposal costs than volume) fell by a modest 14 percent. In 25 other Virginian cities where no pricing scheme was in place, and which were used as a rough-and-ready control group, it fell by 3.5 percent.

Less pleasing still, some people resorted to illegal dumping rather than pay to have their rubbish removed. [The authors guessed] that illegal dumping may account for 30–40 percent of the reduction in collected rubbish. The one bright spot in all this seems to have been a 15 percent increase in the weight of materials recycled, suggesting that people chose to recycle free rather than pay to have their refuse carted away.

SOURCE: *The Economist,* June 7, 1997, p. 80, which cites Don Fullerton and Thomas Kinnaman, "Household Responses to Pricing Garbage by the Bag," *American Economic Review,* September 1996, and "Garbage and Recycling in Communities with Curbside Recycling and Unit-Based Pricing," NBER Working Paper No. 6021, April 1997.

■ BASIC APPROACHES TO ENVIRONMENTAL POLICY

In broad terms, there are three ways to control activities that damage the environment:

■ *Voluntary efforts,* such as nonmandatory investment in pollution-control equipment by firms motivated by social responsibility, or voluntary recycling of solid wastes by consumers.

■ *Direct controls,* which either (a) impose legal ceilings on the amount any polluter is permitted to emit or (b) specify how particular activities must be carried out—for example, direct controls may prohibit backyard garbage incinerators or high-sulfur coal burning or require smokestack "scrubbers" to capture the emissions of power plants.

■ *Taxes on pollution,* or the use of other monetary incentives or penalties to make it unattractive financially for pollution emitters to continue to pollute as usual.

All of these methods have useful roles. Let's consider each of them in turn.

VOLUNTARISM Voluntarism often has proved weak and unreliable. Some well-intentioned business firms, for example, have voluntarily made sincere attempts to adopt environmentally beneficial practices. Yet competition has usually prevented them from spending more than token amounts for this purpose. No business, whatever its virtues, can long afford to spend so much on "good works" that rivals can easily underprice it. As a result, voluntary business programs sometimes have been more helpful to the companies' public relations activities than to the environment.

Yet voluntary measures do have their place. They are appropriate where surveillance and, consequently, enforcement is impractical, as in the prevention of littering by campers in isolated areas, where appeals to people's consciences are the only alternative. And in brief but serious emergencies, which do not allow for time to plan and enact a systematic program, voluntary compliance may be the only viable approach.

Several major cities have, for example, experienced episodes of temporary but dangerous concentrations of pollutants, forcing the authorities to appeal to the public for drastic emissions cuts. Public response to appeals requiring cooperation for short periods often has been enthusiastic and gratifying, particularly when civic pride was a factor. During the 1984 Summer Olympic Games, for example, Los Angeles city officials asked motorists to carpool, businesses to stagger work hours, and truckers to restrict themselves to essential deliveries and to avoid rush hours. The result was an extraordinary decrease in traffic and smog, such that the 6,000-foot San Gabriel Mountains suddenly became visible behind the city.

DIRECT CONTROLS Direct controls have been the chief instrument of environmental policy in the United States (the so-called command and control approach). The federal government, through the Environmental Protection Agency, formulates standards for air and water quality and requires state and local governments to adopt rules that will ensure achievement of those goals. For example, the standards for automobile emissions require new automobiles to pass tests showing that their emissions do not exceed specified amounts. As another example, localities sometimes prohibit industry's use of particularly "dirty" fuels or require firms to adopt processes to "clean" those fuels.

TAXES ON POLLUTION EMISSIONS Most economists agree that relying exclusively on direct controls is a mistake and that, in most cases, *financial penalties* on polluters can do the same job more dependably, effectively, and economically.

The most common suggestion is that governments permit firms to pollute all they want but be forced to pay a tax for the privilege, in order to make them *want* to pollute less. Under such a plan, the quantity of the polluter's emissions is metered just like the use of electricity. At the end of the month the government sends the polluter a bill charging a stipulated amount for each gallon (or other unit) of emissions. (The amount can also vary with the emissions' quality—a higher tax rate being imposed on emissions that are more dangerous or unpleasant.) Thus, in such a scheme, the more environmental damage done, the more the polluter pays. Emissions taxes are deliberately designed to *encourage* polluters to take advantage of the tax loophole—by polluting less, the polluter can reduce the amount of tax owed.

In terms of Figure 22–3, if the tax is used to increase the payment for waste emissions from zero (red supply line TT) and instead forces the polluter to pay its true cost to society (line SS), then emissions will automatically be reduced from 25 million to 10 million tons.

Businesses *do* respond to such taxes. One widely publicized example is the Ruhr River basin in Germany, where emissions taxes have been used for many years. Though the Ruhr is one of the world's most concentrated industrial centers, the rivers that are protected by taxes are clean enough for fishing and other recreational purposes. Firms have also found it profitable to avoid taxes by extracting pollutants from their liquid discharges and recycling them. (See the accompanying box, "Making the Polluter Pay," for another example of the response to taxes.)

EMISSIONS TAXES VERSUS DIRECT CONTROLS

It is important to see why taxes on emissions may prove more effective and reliable than direct controls. Direct controls rely on the criminal justice system for enforcement. But a polluter who violates the rules must first be caught. Then the regulatory agency must decide whether it has enough evidence to prosecute. Next, it must win its case in court.

● MAKING THE POLLUTER PAY

In the Netherlands, a set of charges originally intended only to cover the costs of wastewater treatment has produced a classic demonstration of the pollution-preventing power of charges themselves. Since 1970, gradually rising fees for emissions of organic material and heavy metals into canals, rivers, and lakes have spurred companies to cut emissions, but without dictating how. Between 1976 and 1994, emissions of cadmium, copper, lead, mercury, and zinc plummeted 86–97 percent, primarily because of the charges, according to statistical analyses. . . . And demand for pollution control equipment has spurred Dutch manufacturers to develop better models, lowering costs and turning the country into a global leader in the market. The taxes have in effect sought the path of least economic resistance—of least cost—in cleaning up the country's waters.

SOURCE: David Malin Roodman, "Getting the Signals Right: Tax Reform to Protect the Environment and the Economy," Worldwatch Paper 134, May 1997, pp. 10–12.

Industrial Discharges of Selected Heavy Metals into Surface Waters of the Netherlands, 1976–1994

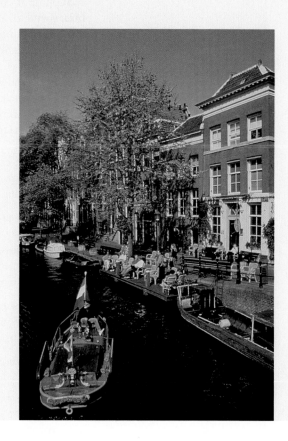

Finally, the court must impose a penalty strong enough to matter. If any *one* of these does not occur, the polluter gets away with the environmentally damaging activities.

ENFORCEMENT ISSUES Enforcement of direct controls requires vigilance and enthusiasm by the regulatory agency, which must assign the resources and persons needed to carry out enforcement. But in many cases the resources devoted to enforcement are pitifully small. The effectiveness of direct controls also depends on the speed and rigor of the court system. Yet the courts are often slow and lenient. In the notorious case of the Reserve Mining Company, more than a decade of litigation was required to stop this company from pouring its wastes (which contain asbestos-like fibers believed to cause cancer) into Lake Superior, the drinking water source for a number of communities.

Finally, direct controls work only if the legal system imposes substantial penalties on violators. Lately, judges have imposed significant penalties in several cases (for instance, in 1998 Louisiana Pacific Corporation was fined a record $37 million for violations of the Clean Air Act), and some polluters have even served prison terms for their misdeeds. But much more often large firms have been convicted of polluting and fined amounts beneath the notice of even a relatively small corporation. Even the $37 million fine just cited looks small next to the company's $2.5 billion in sales.[4]

> In contrast, pollution taxes are automatic and certain. No one need be caught, prosecuted, convicted, and punished. The tax bills are sent out automatically by the untiring tax collector. The only sure way for the polluter to avoid paying pollution charges is to pollute less.

EFFICIENCY IN CLEANUP   A second important advantage of emissions taxes is that they tend to cost less than direct controls. Statistical estimates for several pollution-control programs suggest that the cost of doing the job through direct controls can easily be twice as high as under the tax alternative. Why should there be such a difference? Under direct controls, emissions cutbacks are usually *not* apportioned among the various firms on the basis of ability to reduce pollution cheaply and efficiently.

Suppose it costs Firm A only 3 cents a gallon to reduce emissions whereas Firm B must spend 20 cents a gallon to do the same job. If each firm spews out 2,000 gallons of pollution a day, authorities can achieve a 50 percent reduction in pollution by ordering both firms to limit emissions to 1,000 gallons a day. This may or may not be fair, but it is certainly not efficient. The social cost will be 1,000 × 3 cents (or $30) to Firm A, and 1,000 × 20 cents (or $200) to Firm B, a total of $230. If the government had instead imposed a tax of 10 cents a gallon, Firm A would have done all the work at a lower cost. Why? Firm A would have eliminated its emissions altogether, paying the 3-cents-a-gallon cost to avoid the 10-cents-a-gallon tax. Firm B would have gone on polluting as before, because the tax would be cheaper than the 20-cents-a-gallon cost of controlling its pollution. In this way, under the tax, *total daily emissions would still be cut by 2,000 gallons a day.* But the total daily cost of the program would be $60 (3 cents × 2,000 gallons) as opposed to $230 under direct controls.

> The secret of a pollution tax's efficiency is straightforward. Only polluters who can reduce emissions cheaply and efficiently can afford to take advantage of the built-in loophole—the opportunity to save on taxes by reducing emissions. The tax approach therefore assigns the job to those who can do it most effectively—and rewards them by letting them escape the tax.

ADVANTAGES AND DISADVANTAGES   Given all these advantages of the tax approach, why would anyone want to use direct controls?

In three important situations, direct controls have a clear advantage:

- *Where an emission is so dangerous that it must be prohibited altogether.*

- *Where a sudden change in circumstances—for example, a dangerous air-quality crisis—calls for prompt and substantial changes in conduct, such as temporary reductions in use of cars.* Tax rule changes are difficult and time-consuming, so direct controls will usually do a better job here. The mayor of a city threatened by a dangerous air-quality crisis can, for example, forbid use of private passenger cars until the crisis passes.

- *Where effective and dependable pollution metering devices have not been invented or are prohibitively costly to install and operate.* In such cases authorities cannot operate an effective tax program because they cannot determine the emissions levels of an individual polluter and so cannot calculate the tax bill. The only effective option may be to *require* firms to use "clean" fuel or install emissions-purification equipment.

ANOTHER FINANCIAL DEVICE TO PROTECT THE ENVIRONMENT: EMISSIONS PERMITS

The basic idea underlying the emissions-tax approach to environmental protection is that financial incentives induce polluters to reduce their environmental damage. But at least one other form of financial inducement deserves our consideration:

---

[4] "$37 Million Fine Levied for Clean Air Violation," *The New York Times*, May 28, 1998, p. A22.

● FOOD FOR THOUGHT: ARE EMISSIONS PERMITS JUST "LICENSES TO POLLUTE"?

In the following excerpt from *The New York Times,* Harvard University professor Michael J. Sandel addresses the morality of emissions trading.

Despite the efficiency of international emissions trading, such a system is objectionable for three reasons.

First, it creates loopholes that could enable wealthy countries to evade their obligations. Under the Kyoto formula [for trading in greenhouse gas emissions], for example, the United States could take advantage of the fact that Russia has already reduced its emissions 30 percent since 1990, not through energy efficiencies but through economic decline. The United States could buy excess credits from Russia, and count them toward meeting our obligations under the treaty.

Second, turning pollution into a commodity to be bought and sold removes the moral stigma that is properly associated with it. If a company or a country is fined for spewing excessive pollutants into the air, the community conveys its judgment that the polluter has done something wrong. . . .

The distinction between a fine and a fee for despoiling the environment is not one we should give up too easily. Suppose there were a $100 fine for throwing a beer can into the Grand Canyon, and a wealthy hiker decided to pay $100 for the convenience. Would there be nothing wrong

in his treating the fine as if it were simply an expensive dumping charge? . . .

A third objection to emission trading among countries is that it may undermine the sense of shared responsibility that increased global cooperation requires.

SOURCE: Michael J. Sandel, "It's Immoral to Buy the Right to Pollute," *The New York Times,* December 15, 1997, p. A23.

requiring polluters to buy *emissions permits* that authorize the emission of a specified quantity of pollutant. Such permits can be offered for sale in limited quantities fixed by the government authorities at prices set by demand and supply.

Under this arrangement, the environmental agency decides what quantity of emissions per unit of time (say, per year) is tolerable and then issues a batch of permits authorizing (altogether) just that amount of pollution. The permits are sold to the highest bidders, with the price determined by demand and supply. The price will be high if the number of permits offered for sale is small and a lot of firms need permits to carry out their industrial activities. Similarly, the price of a permit will be low if authorities issue many permits but the quantity of pollution firms demand is small.

Emissions permits in many ways work like a tax—they make it too expensive for firms to continue polluting as much as before. However, the permit approach has some advantages over taxes. For example, it reduces *uncertainty* about the *quantity* of pollution that will be emitted. Under a tax, we cannot be sure about this in advance, because that depends on polluters' response to a given tax rate. In the case of permits, environmental authorities decide on an emissions ceiling in advance, then issue permits authorizing just that quantity of emissions.

Many people react indignantly to the notion of emissions permits, calling them "licenses to pollute" (as evidenced in the accompanying box, "Food for Thought: Are Emissions Permits Just 'Licenses to Pollute'?"). Yet the EPA has introduced some compromise measures that seem politically palatable and can be regarded as approximations to a market in emissions permits. The accompanying box, "Using the Market to Protect the Environment: Emissions Trading," describes the successful "acid rain" market for sulfur dioxide pollution permits, which has cut both SO_2 emissions and polluter costs.

● USING THE MARKET TO PROTECT THE ENVIRONMENT: EMISSIONS TRADING

To reduce the damage that acid rain causes to lakes, streams, buildings, and visibility throughout the eastern United States and Canada, the 1990 Clean Air Act established the largest market ever devised for trading in emissions permits. The following excerpts from an Environmental Defense Fund news release demonstrate the success of the sulfur dioxide emissions trading program and also how the economist's way of doing things has been embraced wholeheartedly by environmentalists.

> The Environmental Defense Fund today released *More Clean Air for the Buck: Lessons from the Acid Rain Emissions Trading Program,* a report detailing the unprecedented success, to date, of the Clean Air Act acid rain reduction program in cutting emissions of sulfur dioxide (SO_2), a principal cause of acid rain. Highlighting the report is the finding that the program, which caps power plant SO_2 emissions at reduced levels while permitting companies to trade any extra SO_2 reductions they make, has resulted in about 1/3 more cuts in SO_2 throughout the Eastern U.S. than mandated by law.
>
> The report also reveals that the highest-emitting plants in the Midwest have been foremost among those making the extra reductions. At the same time, the cost of those cuts appears to be dramatically lower than predicted when Congress adopted the program in 1990. While analysts and industry put costs anywhere from $350 to $1,000 per ton, the price of extra reductions being traded actually ranges from $62 to $170 per ton.

SOURCE: "Acid Rain Cuts Hold Important, Affordable Lessons for Global Warming," Environmental Defense Fund, www.edf.org, 1997.

The principal broker of SO_2 pollution permits, the private firm Cantor Fitzgerald Environmental Brokerage Services, publishes advertisements like this one on the Internet—bids to buy SO_2 permits, offers to sell nitrogen oxide (NOx) permits, and the like.
SOURCE: Cantor Fitzgerald EBS, www.cantor.com, 1998.

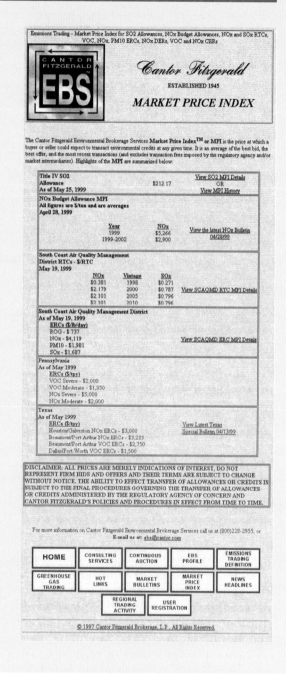

■ TWO CHEERS FOR THE MARKET

In the first part of this chapter, we have learned that environmental protection cannot be left to the free market. Because of the large externalities involved, the market will systematically allocate insufficient resources to the job. However, this market failure does not imply that we should disregard the price mechanism. On the contrary, we have seen that a legislated market solution based on pollution charges may often be the best way to protect the environment. At least in this case, the market mechanism's power can be harnessed to correct its own failings.

We turn now, in the second half of the chapter, to the issue of natural resources, where the market mechanism also plays a crucial role.

■ PART 2: THE ECONOMICS OF NATURAL RESOURCES

> Since Fuel is become so expensive, and will of course grow scarcer and dearer; any new Proposal for saving the [fuel] . . . may at least be thought worth Consideration.
>
> *Benjamin Franklin, 1744*

One of the most significant forms of environmental damage is the waste of natural resources. We saw earlier in this chapter that externalities can lead to just this sort of waste—as when governments, individuals, or business firms use up clean air and clean water without cost or penalty. There is a close analytic connection between the economics of environmental protection that we have just investigated and the economics of natural resources, to which we now turn.

Twenty-five years ago the world was rocked by a sudden "energy crisis." Oil prices shot up and consumers found themselves waiting in long lines to buy gasoline. This event had profound effects throughout the world and ended the widespread assumption that the stock of natural resources was unlimited and simply ours for the taking. Indeed, back in the late 1970s and early 1980s there was near-panic about the threatened exhaustion of many natural resources. The front page of a leading magazine even asked, "Are we running out of *everything*?"

Natural resources have always been scarce, and they have often been used wastefully. Nevertheless, we are *not* about to run out of the most vital resources. In many cases substitutes are available, and many of the shortages of the 1970s can largely be ascribed to the folly of government programs rather than the imminent exhaustion of natural resources.

Puzzle: Those Resilient Resource Supplies

It is a plain fact that the earth is endowed with only finite quantities of such vital resources as oil, copper, tin, and coal. This reality underlies many worried forecasts about the inevitable, and imminent, exhaustion of one resource or another. For instance, the accompanying box, "The Permanent Fuel Crisis," lists a number of bleak prophecies about oil production in the United States, all of which proved far off the mark.

In fact, far from running out, available supplies of many key minerals and fuels are *growing*. In recent decades, known supplies of most minerals have grown at least as fast as production, and in many cases have far outstripped it. For example, in 1995 world reserves of tin were estimated at 7 million metric tons (mmt). During 1996, 196,000 metric tons of tin were mined from the earth. Nonetheless, by 1997 world reserves of tin had *risen* to 8 mmt. For bauxite (the ore used to produce aluminum), known reserves in 1995 were 23,000 mmt and production in 1996 amounted to 120 mmt, but 1997 reserves were still estimated at 23,000 mmt. A similar odd story is true for zinc, copper, and many more.[5] How is this possible? Aren't the quantities of these resources finite? Economic principles, as we will see, help to clear up these mysteries.

■ ECONOMIC ANALYSIS: THE FREE MARKET AND PRICING OF DEPLETABLE RESOURCES

If statistics on known mineral reserves behave as peculiarly as those we have just seen, we may begin to doubt their ability to tell us whether we are running out of certain resources. Is another indicator more reliable? Most economists say there is one—*the price of the resource.*

---

[5] U.S. Geological Survey, *Minerals Yearbook*, various years, www.minerals.er.usgs.gov.

● THE PERMANENT FUEL CRISIS

Humanity has a long history of panicking about the imminent exhaustion of natural resources. In the 13th century a large part of Europe's forests was cut down, primarily for use in metalworking (much of it for armor). Wood prices rose, and there was a good deal of talk about depletion of fuel stocks. People have been doing it ever since, as the accompanying table illustrates.

SOURCE: William M. Brown, "The Outlook for Future Petroleum Supplies," in Julian L. Simon and Herman Kahn, eds., *The Resourceful Earth: A Response to Global 2000* (Oxford, England: Basil Blackwell, 1984), p. 362, who cite Presidential Energy Program, Hearings before the Subcommittee on Energy and Power of the Committee on Interstate and Foreign Commerce, House of Representatives, 1st session on the implication of the President's proposals in the Energy Independence Act of 1975, Serial No. 94–20, p. 643. February 17, 18, 20, and 21, 1975.

Past Petroleum Prophecies (and Realities)

Date	U.S. Production Rate	Prophecy	Reality
1866	0.005	Synthetics are available if oil production should end. *U.S. Revenue Commission*	In the next 82 years, the U.S. produces 37 billion barrels with no need for synthetics.
1891	0.05	Little or no chance for oil in Kansas or Texas *U.S. Geological Survey*	Production exceeds 14 billion barrels in these two states since 1891.
1914	0.27	Total future production only 5.7 billion barrels. *Official of U.S. Bureau of Mines*	More than 34 billion barrels produced since 1914, or six times the prediction.
1920	0.45	U.S. needs foreign oil and synthetics; Peak domestic production almost reached. *Director, U.S. Geological Survey*	1948 U.S. production exceeds consumption and is more than four times 1920 output.
1939	1.3	U.S. oil supplies will last only 13 years. *Radio Broadcasts by Interior Department*	New oil found since 1939 exceeds the 13 years' supply known at that time.
1947	1.9	Sufficient oil cannot be found in U.S. *Chief of Petroleum Division, State Department*	4.3 billion barrels found in 1948, the largest volume in history and twice U.S consumption.
1949	2.0	End of U.S. oil supply almost in sight *Secretary of the Interior*	Recent industry data show ability to increase U.S. production by more than 1 million barrels daily in the next five years.

NOTE: U.S. oil production rate in billions of barrels per year.

SCARCITY AND RISING PRICES

As a resource becomes scarcer, we expect its price to rise for several reasons. One is that we do not deplete a resource simply by gradually using up a homogeneous product, every unit of which is equally available. Rather, we generally use up the most accessible and highest-quality resource deposits first and then turn to less accessible supplies that are more costly to retrieve or deposits of lower purity or quality. Oil is a clear example. First, Americans relied primarily on the most easily found domestic oil. Then they turned to imports from the Middle East with their higher transport costs. At that point it was not yet profitable to embark on the dangerous and extremely costly process of bringing up oil from the floor of the North Sea. We know that the United States still possesses a tremendous amount of petroleum embedded in shale (rock), but so far this has been too difficult and, therefore, too costly to extract.

> **Increasing scarcity of a resource such as oil is not usually a matter of imminent and total disappearance. Rather, it involves exhaustion of the most accessible and cheapest sources so that new supplies become more costly.**

Growing scarcity also raises resource prices for the usual supply-demand reason. As we know, goods in short supply tend to become more expensive. To see just how this works for natural resources, imagine a mythical mineral, "economite," consistent in quality, which has negligible extraction and transportation costs. How quickly will the reserves of this mineral be used up, and what will happen to its price as time passes?

If the market for economite is perfectly competitive, we can provide remarkably concrete answers, discovered by the American economist Harold Hotelling. They tell us that as long as the supply of the mineral lasts, its price must rise at a rate equal to the prevailing interest rate. That is, if in 1999 the price of economite is $100 per ounce and the interest rate is 10 percent, then its price in 2000 must be $110.

> **Under perfect competition, the price of a depletable resource whose transportation and extraction costs are negligible must rise at the rate of interest. If the interest rate is 10 percent, the price of the resource must rise 10 percent every year.**

Why is this so? The reason is simple. People who are considering tying up money in inventories of economite must earn exactly as much per dollar of investment as they would by putting their money into, say, a government bond. Suppose instead that $100 invested in bonds would next year rise in value to $112, whereas $100 in economite would grow only to $110, and suppose the two investments were equally risky. What would happen? Investors would obviously find it unprofitable to buy the mineral and would put their money into bonds instead. But because economite lacked demand, its *current* price would then fall. The economite that would be worth $110 one year in the future would now cost less than $100. This fall in current price would continue until the return on economite equaled the return on bonds—the interest rate.

The same process, working in reverse, would apply if economite prices were rising faster than the interest rate. Investors would switch from bonds to economite, and current prices of the mineral would rise.

This fundamental principle tells us what will happen to the price of $100 worth of economite over, say, four years:

Initial Date	1 Year Later	2 Years Later	3 Years Later	4 Years Later
$100	$110	$121	$133.10	$146.41

These prices follow from the fact that $110 is 10 percent higher than $100, $121 is 10 percent higher than $110, and so on. Note that, because of compounding, the dollar price grows faster each year. Economite's price rises $10 in the first year, $11 in the second year, $12.10 in the third, $13.31 in the fourth, and so on indefinitely.

> **The basic law of pricing of a depletable resource tells us that as its stocks are used up, its price in a perfectly competitive market will rise every year by greater and greater dollar amounts.**

SUPPLY-DEMAND ANALYSIS AND CONSUMPTION

Although we can predict the price of economite without knowing anything about its supply or consumer demand for it, we do need to know something about supply and demand to determine what will happen to economite's consumption—the rate at which it will be used up.

Figure 22–4(a) is a demand curve for economite, *DD*, which shows the amount people want to use up *per year* at various price levels. On the vertical axis, we show how the price must rise from year to year in the pattern we have just calculated—from $100 per ton in the initial year to $110 in the next year and so on. Because of the demand curve's negative slope, it follows that consumption of this mineral will fall each year. That is, *if there is no shift in the demand curve, as in Panel (a)*, consumption will fall from 100,000 tons initially to 95,000 tons the next year and so on.

| FIGURE 22-4 | **Consumption over Time of a Depletable Resource** |

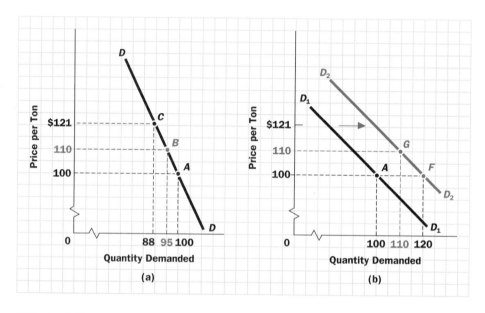

NOTE: Quantity is in thousands of tons per year.

But in reality such demand curves rarely stay still. As the economy grows and population and incomes increase, demand curves shift outward, and this has probably been true for most scarce resources. Such shifts in the demand curve will offset at least part of the reduction in quantity demanded that results from rising prices. Nevertheless, rising prices do cut consumption growth relative to what it would have been if price had remained unchanged. In Figure 22–4(b) we depict an outward shift in demand from curve D_1D_1 in the initial period to curve D_2D_2 a year later. If price had remained constant at the initial value, $100 per ton, quantity consumed per year would have risen from 100,000 tons to 120,000 tons. But because, in accord with the basic principle, price must rise to $110, quantity demanded will increase only to 110,000 tons. Thus, whether or not the demand curve shifts, we conclude:

> The ever-rising prices accompanying increasing scarcity of a depletable resource discourage consumption (encourage conservation). Even if quantity demanded grows, it will grow less rapidly than if prices were not rising.

ACTUAL RESOURCE PRICES IN THE 20TH CENTURY

How do the facts match up with this theoretical analysis? As we will see now, their correspondence is very poor indeed. Figure 22–5 shows the behavior of the prices of three critical metals—lead, zinc, and copper—since the beginning of the 20th century. This graph shows the prices of these three resources relative to other prices in the economy (in other words, the *real* prices, after adjustment for any inflation or deflation). What we find is that instead of rising steadily, as the theory leads us to expect, lead and zinc prices actually remained amazingly constant, even though they are gradually being used up. The price of copper has been all over the map but also has shown no upward trend.

Figure 22–6 shows the real price of crude oil in the United States since 1949 (again, adjusted for inflation). It gives price at the wellhead, that is, at the point of production, with no transportation cost included. Notice how constant these prices were until the first "energy crisis" in 1973, when oil prices rose precipitously. A second dramatic increase occurred in the late 1970s and early 1980s, but since then real oil prices have remained well below their "energy crisis" levels.

FIGURE 22–5

Real Prices of Copper, Zinc, and Lead, 1900–1998

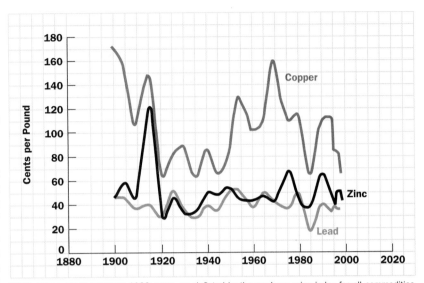

NOTE: Prices are in constant 1982 cents, as deflated by the producer price index for all commodities.

SOURCES: U.S. Bureau of the Census, *Historical Statistics of the United States, Colonial Times to 1970*, Washington, D.C.: 1975; *Statistical Abstract of the United States*, Washington, D.C., various issues; U.S. Department of Labor, Bureau of Labor Statistics, *Producer Price Index*, http://stats.bls.gov; and U.S. Geological Survey, *Minerals Yearbook*, various years, www.minerals.er.usgs.gov.

INTERFERENCES WITH PRICE PATTERNS

How does one explain this strange behavior in the prices of finite resources, which surely are being used up, even if only gradually? Although many things can interfere with the price patterns that theory leads us to expect, we will mention only three:

1. *Unexpected discoveries of reserves whose existence was previously not suspected.* If we were to stumble upon a huge and easily accessible reserve of economite, which came as a complete surprise to the market, the price of economite would obviously fall. This is illustrated in Figure 22–7, where we see that people originally believed that the S_1S_1 curve represented available supply. The discovery of the new economite reserves

FIGURE 22–6

Real Price of Domestic Oil at the Wellhead, 1949–2000

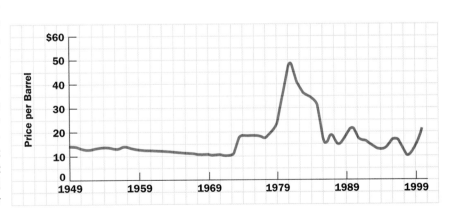

NOTE: Price is in constant 1992 dollars, as deflated with implicit GDP price deflators (first quarter only of 2000).

SOURCE: U.S. Department of Energy, Energy Information Administration, www.eia.doe.gov; and Department of Commerce, Bureau of Economic Analysis, www.bea.doc.gov.

leads them to recognize that the supply is much larger than they had thought. This causes a rightward shift of the supply curve (curve S_2S_2), because the suppliers' cost of any given quantity is reduced by the discovery, so it will pay them to supply a larger quantity at any given price. Like any outward shift in a supply curve, this can be expected to cause a price decrease (from P_1 to P_2). A clear historical example was the Spaniards' 16th-century discovery of gold and silver in Mexico and South America,

**Price Effects of a Discovery
of Additional Reserves**

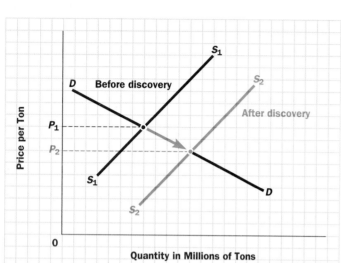

which led to substantial drops in European prices of these precious metals. The same effect can result from innovations that use the resources more efficiently. If a new invention doubles the number of miles one can travel on a gallon of gasoline, that is tantamount to doubling the supply of petroleum that still remains in the ground.

2. *The invention of new methods of mining or refining that may significantly reduce extraction costs.* This, too, can lead to a rightward shift in the supply curve as suppliers are able to deliver a larger quantity at any given price. The situation is therefore again represented by a diagram like Figure 22–7, only now a reduction in cost, not a new discovery of reserves, shifts the supply curve to the right. (See the accompanying box, "Innovation Can Increase Resources," for a real-world example.)

3. *Price controls that hold prices down or decrease them.* A legislature can pass a law prohibiting the sale of the resource at a price higher than P^* (see Figure 22–8). Sometimes this doesn't work; in many cases an illegal black market emerges, where suppliers charge very high prices more or less secretly. But when price controls do work, shortages usually follow. Because the objective is to make the legal ceiling price, P^*, lower than the market equilibrium price, P, then at price P^* quantity demanded (5 million tons in the figure) will be higher than the free-market level (4 million tons). Similarly, we may expect quantity supplied (2 million tons in the figure) to be less than its free-market level (again, 4 million tons). Thus, as always happens in these cases, quantity supplied is less than quantity demanded, and a shortage results (measured in Figure 22–8 by the length of *AB*, or 3 million tons).

**Controls on the Price
of a Resource**

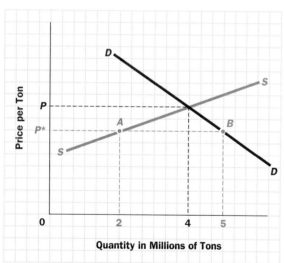

Many economists believe that this is exactly what happened after 1971 when President Nixon decided to experiment with price controls. It was then that the economy experienced a plague of shortages, and we seemed to be "running out of nearly everything." After price controls ended in 1974, most of the shortages disappeared.

We can explain each of our examples of minerals whose price did not rise by one or more of these influences. For example, copper and zinc have benefited from technological changes that lowered extraction costs. In addition, the development of direct electroplating techniques has made copper production much more efficient. In the case of lead, new mines in Missouri held abundant quantities of ore that were much easier to extract and much cheaper to refine than what had been available before. Obviously, real events are more complex than a naïve reading of theoretical models might lead us to believe.

IS PRICE INTERFERENCE JUSTIFIED?

Despite these influences, if a resource does become very scarce and costly to obtain, its price must ultimately rise unless government interferes. Moreover:

In a free market, quantity demanded can never exceed quantity supplied, even if a finite resource is undergoing rapid depletion. The reason is simple: In any free market, price will automatically adjust to eliminate any difference between quantity supplied and quantity demanded.

● INNOVATION CAN INCREASE RESOURCES

This advertisement in a British magazine illustrates technological innovation's ability to increase our natural resources.

> More than a quarter of the petrol you buy owes its existence to an idea and to late night scribbles in the notebooks of two Mobil scientists. They discovered that a synthetic catalyst (crystals the size of a speck of flour) could make crude oil yield far more petrol than ever before. Their breakthrough led to a process that is now being used in nearly every major refinery in the world. It has saved consumers billions of pounds a year and has greatly extended the Earth's precious oil reserves. It has also caused Charles Plank and Edward Rosinski, who together hold 159 U.S. patents and whose careers epitomise Mobil's commitment to science and technology, to be inducted into the U.S. National Inventors Hall of Fame.

SOURCE: "©1996 Mobil Corporation," *The Economist,* October 17, 1998.

28% of the world's petrol was discovered here.

In theory, any shortage—any excess of quantity demanded over quantity supplied—must be artificial, ascribable to a decision to prevent the price mechanism from doing its job.

To say that the cause is artificial, of course, does not settle the basic issue—whether freedom of price adjustments is desirable when resources are scarce, or whether interference with the pricing process is justified.

Many economists believe that this is a case in which the disease—shortages and their resulting economic problems—is far worse than the cure—deregulation of prices. They hold that the general public is misguided in regarding these price rises as the problem, when in fact they are part of the (admittedly rather painful) cure.

It is, of course, easy to understand why no consumer loves a price rise. It is also easy to understand why many consumers attribute any such price increase to a plot—a conspiracy by greedy suppliers who somehow deliberately arrange shortages to force prices upward. Sometimes, this view is even correct. For example, the members of the Organization of Petroleum Exporting Countries (OPEC) have openly and frankly tried to influence the flow of oil in order to increase its price. But it is important to recognize from the principles of supply and demand that when a resource grows scarce its price will tend to rise automatically, even without any conspiracies or plots.

ON THE VIRTUES OF RISING PRICES

Rising prices help to control resource depletion in three basic ways:

- They discourage consumption and waste and provide an inducement for conservation.

- They stimulate more efficient resource use by industry, providing incentives for employment of processes that are more sparing in their use of the resource or that use substitute resources.

- They encourage innovation—the discovery of other, more abundant resources that can serve the same role and of new techniques that permit these other resources to be used economically.

Growing Reserves of Exhaustible Resources: Our Puzzle Revisited

Earlier in Part 2 of this chapter we saw, strangely enough, that reserves of many mineral resources have actually been increasing, despite growing world production. This paradox has a straightforward economic explanation: rising mineral reserves are a tribute to the success of pricing and exploration activity. Minerals are not discovered by accident. Exploration and discovery entail costly work requiring geologists, engineers, and expensive machinery. Industry does not consider this money worth spending when reserves are high and mineral prices are low.

In the 20th century, every time some mineral's known reserves fell and its price tended to rise, exploration increased until the decline was offset. The law of supply and demand worked. In the 1970s, for example, the rising price of oil led to very substantial increases in oil exploration, which helped to build up reserves. Although, to protect ourselves from OPEC, it may not be wise for us to *consume* more oil from American sources, it certainly does seem prudent for us to increase our reserves through exploration. Increased profitability of exploration is perhaps the most effective way to get that done.

SUMMARY

1. Pollution is as old as human history and, contrary to popular notions, some forms of pollution were actually decreasing even before government programs were initiated to protect the environment.

2. Both planned and market economies suffer from substantial environmental problems.

3. The production of commodities *must* cause waste disposal problems unless everything is recycled, but even recycling processes cause pollution (and use up energy).

4. Industrial activity causes environmental damage, but so does the activity of private individuals (as when they drive cars that emit pollutants). Government agencies also damage the environment (as when military airplanes emit noise and exhaust or a hydroelectric project floods large areas).

5. Pollution is an *externality*—when a factory emits smoke, it dirties the air in nearby neighborhoods and may damage the health of persons who neither work for the factory nor buy its products. Hence, the public interest in pollution control is not best served by the free market. This is another of our *Ideas for Beyond the Final Exam*.

6. Pollution can be controlled by voluntary programs, *direct controls*, *emissions taxes*, or other monetary incentives for emissions reduction.

7. Most economists believe that the monetary incentives approach is the most efficient and effective way to control damaging externalities.

8. The quantity demanded of a scarce resource can exceed the quantity supplied only if something prevents the market mechanism from operating freely.

9. As a resource grows scarce on a free market, its price will rise, inducing increased conservation by consumers, increased exploration for new reserves, and increased substitution of other items that can serve the same purpose.

10. In fact, in the 20th century the relative prices of many resources have remained roughly constant, largely because of the discovery of new reserves and cost-saving innovations.

11. In the 1970s, OPEC succeeded in raising petroleum's relative price, but the price increase led to a substantial decline in world demand as well as to an increase in production in countries outside OPEC.

12. *Known reserves* of depletable scarce resources have not tended to fall with time because as the price of the resource rises with increasing scarcity, increased exploration for new reserves becomes profitable.

KEY TERMS

Externality   454

Direct controls   462

Pollution charges (taxes on emissions)   462

Emissions permits   464

Known reserves   467

Organization of Petroleum Exporting Countries (OPEC)   473

Paradox of growing reserves of finite resources   474

1. What sorts of pollution problems would you expect in a small African village? In a city in India? In communist China? In New York City?

2. Suppose you are assigned the task of drafting a law to impose a tax on smoke emission. What provisions would you put into the law?

   a. How would you decide the size of the tax?

   b. What would you do about smoke emitted by a municipal electricity plant?

   c. Would you use the same tax rate in densely and sparsely settled areas?

   What information will you need to collect before determining what you would do about each of the preceding provisions?

3. Production of Commodity X creates 10 pounds of emissions for every unit of X produced. The demand and supply curves for X are described by the following table:

Price	Quantity Demanded	Quantity Supplied
$10	80	100
9	85	95
8	90	90
7	95	85
6	100	80
5	105	75

What is the equilibrium price and quantity, and how much pollution will be emitted?

4. If the price of X to consumers is $9, and the government imposes a tax of $2 per unit, show that because suppliers get only $7, they will produce only 85 units of output, not the 95 units of output they would produce if they received the full $9 per unit.

5. With this tax, how much pollution will be emitted?

6. Compare your answers to Review Questions 3 and 5 and show how large a reduction in pollution emissions occurs because of the $2 tax on the polluting output.

7. Discuss some valid and some invalid objections to letting rising prices eliminate shortages of supplies of scarce resources.

8. Why may a rise in fuel prices lead to more conservation after several years have passed than it does in the months following the price increase? What does your answer imply about the relative size of the long-run elasticity of demand for fuel and its short-run elasticity?

CHAPTER

23

No nation was ever ruined by trade.

Benjamin Franklin

INTERNATIONAL TRADE AND COMPARATIVE ADVANTAGE

International trade is vital to the health of any nation, so it is essential to our study of economics. The world's major economies have always been linked in various ways. But dramatic improvements in transportation, telecommunications, and international relations in recent decades have drawn the industrial nations of the world ever closer together. This process, called "globalization," is often portrayed as something new. But in fact it is not, as the box, "Is Globalization Something New?" points out on page 479.

Economic events in other countries affect the United States for both macroeconomic and microeconomic reasons. This chapter takes up some of the microeconomic linkages among nations: How are patterns and prices of world trade determined? How and why do governments interfere with foreign trade? The central idea of this chapter is one we have encountered before (in Chapters 1 and 4): the law of comparative advantage.

Issue: How Can Americans Compete with "Cheap Foreign Labor"?

Why do Americans (and the citizens of many other nations) often want their government to limit or prevent import competition? One major reason is the common belief that imports take bread out of American workers' mouths. According to this view, "cheap foreign labor" steals jobs from Americans and pressures U.S. businesses to lower wages.

But actually, the facts are not consistent with this story. For one thing, wages in industrialized countries that export to the United States have risen spectacularly in recent decades. Table 23–1 shows that wages in seven leading countries rose from an average of only 46 percent of American wages in 1970 to 110 percent by 1997.

By 1997, labor costs in Sweden, the Netherlands, western Germany, and Japan exceeded our own, and costs in France were about equal. Yet American imports of Toyotas from Japan, Volkswagens from Germany, and Volvos from Sweden grew as wages in those countries rose relative to American wages.

By comparison, when European and Japanese wages were far below those in the United States in the 1950s, American industries had no trouble marketing our products abroad. In fact, the main problem then was to raise their imports up to the level of our bountiful exports. Ironically, our position in the international marketplace deteriorated as wage levels in Europe and Japan began to rise closer to our own.

Clearly, then, cheap foreign labor must not be a major obstacle to U.S. sales abroad, as a "common sense" view of the matter suggests. In this chapter we will see what is wrong with that view.

TABLE 23–1	**Labor Costs in Industrialized Countries as a Percentage of U.S. Labor Costs**

	1970	1997
France	41%	99%
United Kingdom	35	85
Italy	42	92
Japan	24	106
Netherlands	51	113
Sweden	70	122
(West) Germany	56	155

NOTE: Data are compensation estimates per hour, converted at exchange rates, and relate to production workers in the manufacturing sector.
SOURCE: U.S. Bureau of Labor Statistics.

● IS GLOBALIZATION SOMETHING NEW?

Few people realize that the industrialized world was in fact highly globalized prior to World War I, before the ravages of two world wars and the Great Depression severed many international linkages. Furthermore, as the British magazine *The Economist* points out, globalization has not gone nearly as far as many people imagine.

> Despite much loose talk about the "new" global economy, today's international economic integration is not unprecedented. The 50 years before the first world war saw large cross-border flows of goods, capital and people. That period of globalisation, like the present one, was driven by reductions in trade barriers and by sharp falls in transport costs, thanks to the development of railways and steamships. The present surge of globalisation is in a way a resumption of that previous trend. . . .
>
> Two forces have been driving [globalization]. The first is technology. With the costs of communication and computing falling rapidly, the natural barriers of time and space that separate national markets have been falling too. The cost of a three-minute telephone call between New York and London has fallen from $300 (in 1996 dollars) in 1930 to $1 today. . . .
>
> The second driving force has been liberalisation. . . . Almost all countries have lowered barriers to trade. . . . [T]he ratio of trade to output . . . has increased sharply in most countries since 1950. But by this measure Britain and France are only slightly more open to trade today than they were in 1913. . . .
>
> Product markets are still nowhere near as integrated across borders as they are within nations. Consider the example of trade between the United States and Canada, one of the least restricted trading borders in the world. On average, trade between a Canadian province and an American state is 20 times smaller than domestic trade between two Canadian provinces, after adjusting for distance and income levels.
>
> The financial markets are not yet truly integrated either. Despite the newfound popularity of international investing, capital markets were by some measures more integrated at the start of this century than they are now. . . . [And] labour is less mobile than it was in the second half of the 19th century, when some 60m people left Europe for the New World.

SOURCE: "Schools Brief: One World?" *The Economist,* October 18, 1997.

■ WHY TRADE?

The earth's resources are not equally distributed across the planet. Although the United States can produce its own coal and wheat, it depends almost *entirely* on the rest of the world for such items as rubber and coffee. Similarly, Saudi Arabia has little land that is suitable for farming but sits atop a huge pool of oil. Because of the seemingly whimsical distribution of vital resources, every nation must trade with others to acquire what it lacks.

Even if countries had all the resources they needed, other differences in natural endowments such as climate, terrain, and so on would lead them to engage in trade. Americans *could*, with great difficulty, grow their own bananas and coffee in hothouses. But these crops grow much more efficiently in Honduras and Brazil, where the climates are appropriate.

The skills of a nation's labor force also play a role. If New Zealand has a large group of efficient farmers and few workers with industrial experience, while the opposite is true in Japan, it makes sense for New Zealand to specialize in agriculture and let Japan concentrate on manufacturing.

Finally, a small country that tried to produce every product would end up with many industries too small to utilize mass-production techniques and other methods that confer cost advantages on large-scale operations. For example, some countries operate their own international airlines for reasons that can only be described as political, not economic.

To summarize, the main reason why nations trade with one another is to exploit the many advantages of **specialization,** some of which we discussed back in Chapter 4. International trade greatly enhances living standards for all parties involved because:

Specialization means that a country devotes its energies and resources to only a small proportion of the world's productive activities.

1. **Every country lacks some vital resources that it can get only by trading with others.**

2. **Each country's climate, labor force, and other endowments make it a relatively efficient producer of some goods and an inefficient producer of other goods.**

3. **Specialization permits larger outputs and can therefore offer economies of large-scale production.**

MUTUAL GAINS FROM TRADE

Many people have long believed that a nation can gain from trade only at the expense of another. After all, nothing new is produced by the mere act of trading. So if one country gains from a swap, it is argued, the other country must necessarily lose. One consequence of this mistaken belief was and continues to be a policy prescription calling for each country to try to take advantage of its trading partners on the (fallacious) grounds that one nation's gain must be another's loss.

Yet, as Adam Smith emphasized, and as we learned in Chapter 4, both parties must expect to gain something from any *voluntary exchange*. Otherwise, why would they agree to trade?

But how can mere exchange of goods leave both parties better off? The answer is that although trade does not increase the total output of goods, it does allow each party to acquire items better suited to its tastes. Suppose Scott has four cookies and nothing to drink, whereas William has two glasses of milk and nothing to eat. A trade of two of Scott's cookies for one of William's glasses of milk does not increase the total supply of either milk or cookies, but it almost certainly improves the welfare of both boys.

By exactly the same logic, both the United States and Mexico must be better off if Mexico voluntarily ships tomatoes to the United States in return for chemicals. In general, as we emphasized in Chapter 4:

Trade Is a Win-Win Situation

VOLUNTARY EXCHANGE Both parties must expect to gain from any *voluntary exchange*. Trade brings about mutual gains by redistributing products so that both parties end up holding more preferred combinations of goods than they held before. This principle, which is one of our *Ideas for Beyond the Final Exam,* applies to nations just as it does to individuals.

■ INTERNATIONAL VERSUS INTRANATIONAL TRADE

The 50 states of the United States may be the most eloquent testimony to the gains from specialization and free trade. Florida specializes in growing oranges, Iowa in growing corn, Pennsylvania makes steel, and Michigan builds cars. All these states trade freely with one another and enjoy great material prosperity. Try to imagine how much lower your standard of living would be if you could consume only items produced in your own state.

The essential logic behind international trade is no different from that underlying trade among different states; the basic reasons for trade are equally applicable within a country or among countries. Why, then, do we study international trade as a special subject? There are at least three reasons.

POLITICAL FACTORS IN INTERNATIONAL TRADE

First, domestic trade takes place under a single national government, whereas foreign trade always involves at least two governments. But a nation's government is normally much less concerned about the welfare of other countries' citizens than it is about its own. So, for example, the U.S. Constitution prohibits tariffs on trade among states, but it does not prohibit the United States from imposing tariffs on imports from abroad. One major issue in the economic analysis of international trade is the use and misuse of impediments to free international trade.

THE MANY CURRENCIES INVOLVED IN INTERNATIONAL TRADE

Second, all trade within the borders of the United States is carried out in U.S. dollars. But trade across national borders almost always involves at least two currencies. Rates of exchange between different currencies can and do change. In 1985, it took about 250 Japanese yen to buy a dollar; now it takes only about 105. Variability in exchange rates brings with it a host of complications and policy problems.

IMPEDIMENTS TO MOBILITY OF LABOR AND CAPITAL

Third, it is much easier for labor and capital to move about within a country than to move from one country to another. If jobs are plentiful in Michigan but scarce in West Virginia, workers can move freely to follow the job opportunities. Of course, personal costs like the financial burden of moving and the psychological cost of leaving friends and familiar surroundings may discourage mobility. But such relocations are not inhibited by immigration quotas, by laws restricting the employment of foreigners, or by the need to learn a new language.

There are also greater impediments to the transfer of capital across national boundaries than to its movement within a country. For example, many countries have rules limiting foreign ownership; even the United States limits foreign ownership of broadcast outlets and airlines. Foreign investment is also subject to special political risks, such as the danger of outright expropriation or nationalization after a change in government.

But even if nothing as extreme as expropriation occurs, capital invested abroad faces significant risks from exchange rate variations. An investment valued at 250 million yen will be worth $1.0 million to American investors if the dollar is worth 250 yen, but it is worth $2.5 million if the dollar is worth just 100 yen.

■ THE LAW OF COMPARATIVE ADVANTAGE

The gains from international specialization and trade are clear when one country is better at producing one item while its trading partner is better at producing another. For example, no one finds it surprising that Brazil sells coffee to the United States while the United States exports aircraft to Brazil. We know that coffee can be produced using less labor and other inputs in Brazil than in the United States. And the United States can produce airplanes at a lower resource cost than can Brazil.

We say that in such a situation Brazil has an **absolute advantage** in coffee production, and the United States has an absolute advantage in aircraft production. In such cases, it is obvious that both countries can gain by producing the item in which they have an absolute advantage and then trading with one another.

What is much less obvious, but equally true, is that these gains from international trade still exist *even if one country is more efficient than the other in producing everything.* This lesson, the principle of **comparative advantage**, is one we first learned in

One country is said to have an **absolute advantage** over another in the production of a particular good if it can produce that good using smaller quantities of resources than can the other country.

One country is said to have a **comparative advantage** over another in the production of a particular good relative to other goods if it produces that good less inefficiently as compared with the other country.

Chapter 4.[1] It is, in fact, one of the most important of our *Ideas for Beyond the Final Exam*, so we repeat it here for convenience.

> **COMPARATIVE ADVANTAGE** Even if one country is at an absolute disadvantage relative to another country in the production of every good, it is said to have a *comparative advantage* in making the good at which it is least inefficient (compared with the other country).
>
> The great classical economist David Ricardo (1772–1823) discovered almost 200 years ago that two countries can still gain from trade, even if one is more efficient than the other in every industry—that is, even if one has an absolute advantage in producing every commodity.
>
> In determining the most efficient production patterns, it is *comparative* advantage, not *absolute* advantage, that matters. Thus, a country can gain by importing a good even if that good can be produced more efficiently at home. Such imports make sense if they enable the country to specialize in producing goods at which it is even more efficient.

THE ARITHMETIC OF COMPARATIVE ADVANTAGE

Let's see precisely how this works using a hypothetical example first suggested in Chapter 4. Table 23–2 gives a somewhat exaggerated impression of the trading positions of the United States and Japan a few years ago. We imagine that labor is the only input used to produce computers and television sets in the two countries and that the United States has an absolute advantage in manufacturing both goods. In this example, a year's worth of labor can produce either 50 computers or 50 TV sets in the United States but only 10 computers or 40 televisions in Japan. So the United States is the more efficient producer of both goods. Nonetheless, as we shall now show, it pays for the United States to specialize and trade with Japan.

To demonstrate this conclusion, we begin by noting that the United States has a comparative advantage in computers, whereas Japan has a comparative advantage in producing TVs. Specifically, the numbers in Table 23–2 show that the United States can produce 50 televisions with a year's labor whereas Japan can produce only 40; so the United States is 25 percent more efficient than Japan in producing TV sets.

However, the United States is five times as efficient as Japan in producing computers: It can produce 50 per year of labor rather than 10. Because America's competitive edge is far greater in computers than in televisions, we say that the United States has a *comparative advantage* in computers.

From the Japanese perspective, these same numbers indicate that Japan is only slightly less efficient than the United States in TV production but drastically less efficient in computer production. So Japan's comparative advantage is in the television industry. According to Ricardo's law of comparative advantage, then, the two countries can gain if the United States specializes in producing computers, Japan specializes in producing TVs, and the two countries trade. Let's verify that this is true. Suppose Japan transfers 1,000 years of labor out of the computer industry and into TV manufacturing. According to the figures in Table 23–2, its computer output falls by 10,000 units while its TV output rises by 40,000 units. (See the middle column of Table 23–3.) Suppose, at the same time, the United States transfers 500 years of labor

TABLE 23-2	**Alternative Outputs from One Year of Labor Input**

	In the U.S.	In Japan
Computers	50	10
Televisions	50	40

[1] To review, see page 62.

Example of the Gains from Trade

TABLE 23-3

	U.S.	Japan	Total
Computers	+25,000	−10,000	+15,000
Televisions	−25,000	+40,000	+15,000

out of television manufacturing (thereby losing 25,000 TVs) and into computer making (thereby gaining 25,000 computers). Table 23–3 shows us that these transfers of resources between the two countries increase the world's production of both outputs. Together, the two countries now have 15,000 additional TVs and 15,000 additional computers—surely a nice outcome.

Was there some sleight of hand here? How did both the United States and Japan gain both computers and TVs? The explanation is that the process we have just described involves more than just a swap of a fixed bundle of commodities. It is also *a change in the production arrangements*, with some of Japan's inefficient computer production taken over by more efficient American makers, and with some of America's TV production taken over by Japanese television companies who are *less* inefficient at making TVs than Japanese computer manufacturers are at making computers. The underlying principle is both simple and fundamental:

When every country does what it can do best, all countries can benefit because more of every commodity can be produced without increasing the amounts of labor and other resources used.

THE GRAPHICS OF COMPARATIVE ADVANTAGE

FIGURE 23-1

Per-Capita Production Possibilities Frontiers for Two Countries

The gains from trade can also be displayed graphically, and doing so helps us understand whether such gains are large or small.

The lines *US* and *JN* in Figure 23–1 are closely related to the production possibilities frontiers of the two countries, but they differ in that they pretend that each country has the same amount of labor available. In this case, we assume that each has 1 million person-years.[2] For example, Table 23–2 tells us that for each 1 million person-years of labor, the United States can produce 50 million TVs and no computers (point *U* in Figure 23–1), 50 million computers and no TVs (point *S*), or any combination between (the line *US*). Similar reasoning leads to line *JN* for Japan.

America's actual production possibilities frontier would be even higher, relative to Japan's, than shown in Figure 23–1 because the U.S. population is larger. But Figure 23–1 is more useful because it highlights the differences in efficiency that determine both absolute and comparative advantage. Let us see how.

The fact that line *US* lies *above* line *JN* means that the United States can manufacture more televisions and more computers than Japan with the same amount of labor. This reflects our assumption that the United States has an *absolute* advantage in both commodities.

America's comparative advantage in computer production and Japan's comparative advantage in TV production are shown in a different way by the relative *slopes* of the two lines. Look back to Table 23–2, which shows

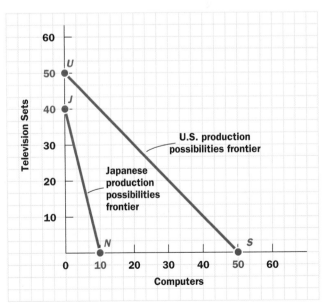

NOTE: Quantities are in millions.

---

[2] To review the concept of the production possibilities frontier, see Chapter 4.

that the United States can acquire a computer on its own by giving up one TV. Thus, the *opportunity cost* of a computer in the United States is one television set. This opportunity cost is depicted graphically by the slope of the U.S. production possibilities frontier in Figure 23–1, which is $OU/OS = 50/50 = 1$.

Table 23–2 also tells us that the opportunity cost of a computer in Japan is four TVs. This is depicted in Figure 23–1 by the slope of Japan's production possibilities frontier, which is $OJ/ON = 40/10 = 4$.

> A country's *absolute* advantage in production over another country is shown by its having a higher per-capita production possibilities frontier. The difference in the *comparative* advantages between the two countries is shown by the difference in the slopes of their frontiers.

Because opportunity costs differ in the two countries, gains are possible if the two countries specialize and trade with one another. Specifically, it is cheaper, in terms of real resources forgone, for *either* country to acquire its computers in the United States. By a similar line of reasoning, the opportunity cost of TVs is higher in the United States than in Japan, so it makes sense for both countries to acquire their televisions in Japan.[3]

Notice that if the slopes of the two production possibilities frontiers, *JN* and *US*, were equal, then opportunity costs would be the same in each country. In that case, no potential gains would arise from trade. Gains from trade arise from *differences* across countries, not from similarities. This is an important point about which people are often confused. Some argue that two very different countries, say the United States and Mexico, cannot gain much by trading with one another. In fact:

> Two very similar countries may gain little from trade. Large gains from trade are most likely when countries are very different.

How the two countries divide the gains from trade depends on the prices that emerge from world trade, which is the subject of the next section. But we already know enough to see that world trade must, in our example, leave a computer costing more than one TV and less than four. Why? Because, if a computer bought less than one TV (its opportunity cost in the United States) on the world market, the United States would produce its own TVs rather than buying them from Japan. And if a computer cost more than four TVs (its opportunity cost in Japan), Japan would prefer to produce its own computers rather than buy them from the United States.

We conclude, therefore, that if both countries are to trade, the rate of exchange between TVs and computers must be somewhere between 4 to 1 and 1 to 1. To illustrate the gains from trade in a concrete example, suppose the world price ratio settles at 2 to 1; that is, one computer costs the same as two televisions. How much, precisely, do the United States and Japan gain from world trade in this case?

Figure 23–2 is designed to help us see the answers. The blue production possibilities frontiers *US* in Panel (b) and *JN* in Panel (a) are the same as in Figure 23–1. But the United States can do better than line *US*. Specifically, with a world price ratio of 2 to 1, the United States can buy two TVs for each computer it gives up, rather than just one (which is the opportunity cost of a computer in the United States). Hence, if the United States produces only computers—point *S* in Figure 23–2(b)—and buys its TVs from Japan, America's *consumption possibilities* will be as indicated by the red line that begins at point *S* and has a slope of 2 indicating that each computer sold brings the United States two television sets. Because trade allows the United States to choose a point on *AS* rather than on *US*, trade opens up consumption possibilities that were simply not available before.

The story is similar for Japan. If the Japanese produce only television sets—point *J* in Figure 23–2(a)—they can acquire a computer from the United States for every two TVs they give up as they move along the red line *JP* (whose slope is 2). This is better than they can do on their own, because a sacrifice of two TVs in Japan

---

[3] As an exercise, provide this line of reasoning.

The Gains from Trade   FIGURE 23-2

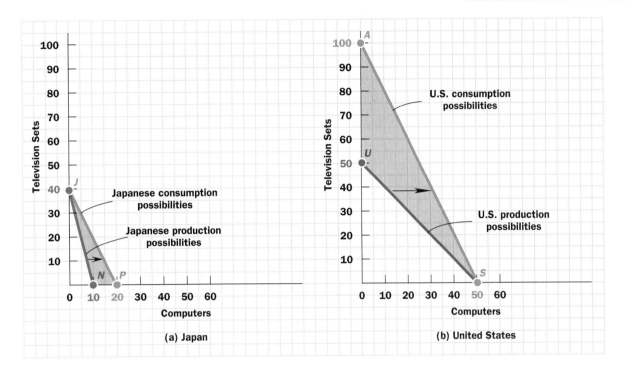

NOTE: Quantities are in millions.

yields only one-half of a computer. Hence, world trade enlarges Japan's consumption possibilities from *JN* to *JP*.

Figure 23–2 shows graphically that gains from trade arise to the extent that world prices (2 to 1 in our example) differ from domestic opportunity costs (4 to 1 and 1 to 1 in our example). So it is a matter of some importance to understand how prices in international trade are established. We shall do so shortly.

Issue Resolved: Comparative Advantage Exposes the Fallacy of "Cheap Foreign Labor"

But first let us observe that the principle of comparative advantage takes us a long way toward uncovering the fallacy in the "cheap foreign labor" argument described at the start of this chapter. Given the assumed productive efficiency of American labor, and the inefficiency of Japanese labor, we would expect wages to be much higher in the United States. Indeed, they were until recent years.

In these circumstances, one might expect American workers to be apprehensive about an agreement to permit open trade between the two countries: "How can we hope to meet the unfair competition of those underpaid Japanese workers?" And Japanese laborers might also be concerned: "How can we hope to meet the competition of those Americans, who are so efficient in producing everything?"

The principle of comparative advantage shows us that both fears are unjustified. As we have just seen, when trade is opened between Japan and the United States, *workers in both countries will be able to earn higher real wages than before* because of the increased productivity that comes about through specialization.

As Figure 23–2 shows, once trade opens, Japanese workers should end up with more TVs and more computers than they had before. So their living standards should rise, even though they have been left vulnerable to competition from "super-efficient" Americans. Workers in the United States should also end up with more TVs and with more computers, so their living standards should also rise even though they have been exposed to competition from "cheap" Japanese labor. These higher standards of living, of course, reflect the higher real wages earned by workers in both countries.

The lesson to be learned here is elementary:

Nothing helps raise living standards more than a greater abundance of goods.

■ SUPPLY-DEMAND EQUILIBRIUM AND PRICING IN WORLD TRADE

How parties share the gains from trade depends on the prices that emerge from world trade. As usual, price determination in a free market depends on supply and demand.

When applied to international trade, however, the supply-demand model runs into several new complications. First, it involves at least two demand curves: that of the exporting country and that of the importing country. Second, it may also involve two supply curves, because the importing country may produce part of its own consumption. Third, equilibrium does not take place at the intersection point of *either* pair of supply-demand curves. Why? Because if they trade at all, the exporting country must supply more than it demands, whereas the importing country demands more than it supplies.

These complications are illustrated in Figure 23–3, where we show the supply and demand curves of a country that exports wheat in Panel (a) and of a country that imports wheat in Panel (b). For simplicity, we assume that these countries do not deal in wheat with anyone else. Where will the two-country wheat market reach equilibrium?

| FIGURE 23-3 | **Supply-Demand Equilibrium in the International Wheat Trade** |

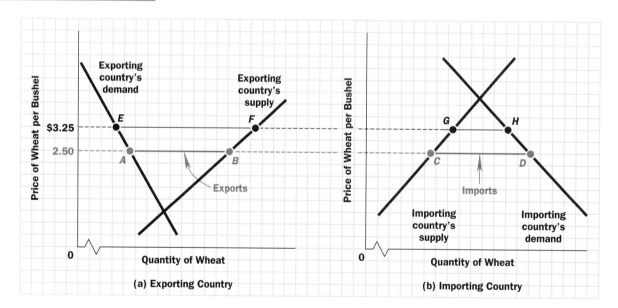

(a) Exporting Country   (b) Importing Country

If there is free trade, the equilibrium price must satisfy two requirements:

1. **The price of wheat must be the same in both countries.**

2. **The quantity of wheat exported must equal the quantity of wheat imported.**

In Figure 23–3, this happens at a price of $2.50 per bushel. At that price, the distance *AB* between what the exporting country produces and what it consumes equals the distance *CD* between what the importing country consumes and what it produces.

This means that, at a price of $2.50 per bushel, the amount the exporting country wants to sell exactly equals the amount the importing country wants to buy.

At any price above $2.50, producers in both countries will want to sell more and consumers in both countries will want to buy less. For example, if the price rises to $3.25 per bushel, the exporter's quantity supplied will rise from *B* to *F* whereas its quantity demanded falls from *A* to *E*, as shown in Figure 23–3(a). As a result, more wheat will be available for export—*EF* rather than *AB*. For exactly the same reason, the price increase will cause higher production and lower sales in the importing country, leading to a reduction in imports from *CD* to *GH* in Panel (b).

But this means that the higher price, $3.25 per bushel, cannot be sustained in a free and competitive international market. With export supply *EF* far greater than import demand *GH*, there must be downward pressure on price and a move back toward the $2.50 equilibrium price. Similar reasoning shows that prices below $2.50 also cannot be sustained. Thus:

> In international trade, the equilibrium price is the one that makes the exporting country want to export exactly the amount that the importing country wants to import. Equilibrium will thus occur at a price at which the horizontal distance *AB* in Figure 23–3(a) (the excess of the exporter's quantity supplied over its quantity demanded) is equal to the horizontal distance *CD* in Figure 23–3(b) (the excess of the importer's quantity demanded over its quantity supplied). At this price, the *world's* quantity demanded equals the *world's* quantity supplied.

■ TARIFFS, QUOTAS, AND OTHER INTERFERENCES WITH TRADE

Despite the mutual gains from international trade, nations often interfere with the operation of free international markets. In fact, until the rise of the free-trade movement about 200 years ago (with such economists as Adam Smith and David Ricardo as its vanguard), it was taken for granted that one of the essential tasks of government was to impede trade, presumably in the national interest!

Many argued then (and many still argue today) that the proper aim of government policy was to promote exports and discourage imports, for that would increase the amount foreigners owed the nation. According to this so-called **mercantilist** view, a nation's wealth consists of the amount of gold or other monies at its command.

Mercantilism is a doctrine that holds that exports are good for a country, whereas imports are harmful.

Obviously, governments can only pursue such a policy within certain limits. A country *must* import vital foodstuffs or critical raw materials that it cannot supply for itself. Moreover, it is mathematically impossible for *every* country to sell more than it buys, for one country's exports *must* be some other country's imports. If everyone competes in this game and cuts imports to the bone, then obviously exports must go the same way. The result will be that everyone is deprived of the mutual gains from trade—which is precisely what happens in a trade war.

After the protectionist 1930s, the United States moved away from mercantilist policies designed to impede imports and gradually assumed a leading role in promoting free trade. Over the past 50 years, tariffs and other trade barriers have been reduced dramatically. In recent years, the United States has led the world to complete the Uruguay Round of tariff reductions and has joined Canada and Mexico in the North American Free Trade Agreement (NAFTA). The latter caused a political firestorm in the United States in 1993 and 1994, with critic (and 1992 presidential contender) Ross Perot predicting a "giant sucking sound" as American workers lost their jobs to competition from "cheap Mexican labor." (Does that sound familiar?)

Modern governments use three main devices when seeking to control trade: tariffs, quotas, and export subsidies. A **tariff** is simply a tax on imports. An importer of wheat, for example, may be charged $1 for each bushel brought into the country. The United States is generally a low-tariff country, with only a few notable exceptions, such as the 25 percent tariff on light trucks. However, many other countries rely on heavy tariffs to protect their industries. Tariff rates of 100 percent or more are not uncommon.

A **tariff** is a tax on imports.

<table>
<tr><td>●</td><td>**HOW SWEET IT IS: THE U.S. SUGAR QUOTA**</td></tr>
</table>

The United States has restricted sugar imports since 1934. But the current program, which many economists believe is the most egregious of all our agricultural subsidies, dates only from 1990. It is called a "tariff-rate quota," which most economists view as a fancy name for grotesque protectionism.

Each year a small amount of imported sugar is allowed to enter the United States under a negligible tariff. Beyond that, however, the U.S. government posts a tariff so high that no one wants to pay it in order to import sugar. In consequence, our domestic price of sugar is far above the world price.

This high price is, of course, a great boon to American producers of sugar and sugar-substitutes like corn syrup. But it costs U.S. consumers of sugar and manufacturers of candy and soft drinks between $1 billion and $2 billion per year. And it has also led to some bizarre

attempts to evade the quota, like importing sugar as an ingredient in chocolate and powdered drinks and then removing the sugar content in the United States.

A **quota** specifies the maximum amount of a good that is permitted into the country from abroad per unit of time.

A **quota** is a legal limit on the amount of a good that may be imported. For example, the government might allow no more than 25 million bushels of wheat to be imported in a year. In some cases, governments ban the importation of certain goods outright—a quota of zero. The United States now imposes quotas on a smattering of goods, including textiles, meat, and sugar. But most imports are free of quotas.

An **export subsidy** is a payment by the government to exporters to permit them to reduce the selling prices of their goods so they can compete more effectively in foreign markets.

An **export subsidy** is government payment to an exporter. By reducing the exporter's costs, such subsidies permit exporters to lower their selling prices and to compete more effectively in world trade. Although export subsidies are minor in the United States, some foreign governments use them extensively to assist their industries—a practice that provokes bitter complaints from American manufacturers about "unfair competition." For example, years of heavy government subsidies helped the European Airbus consortium take a sizable share of the world commercial aircraft market away from American manufacturers like Boeing and McDonnell-Douglas.

HOW TARIFFS AND QUOTAS WORK

Both tariffs and quotas restrict supplies coming from abroad and drive up prices. A tariff works by raising prices, which in turn cuts the demand for imports, whereas the sequence associated with a quota is just the reverse—a restriction in supply forces prices up.

The supply and demand curves in Figure 23–4 illustrate how tariffs and quotas work. Just as in Figure 23–3, the equilibrium price of wheat under free trade is $2.50 per bushel (in both countries). At this price, the exporting country produces 125 million bushels—point *B* in Panel (a)—and consumes 80 million (point *A*). So its exports are 45 million bushels—the distance *AB*. Similarly, the importing country consumes 95 million bushels—point *D* in Panel (b)—and produces only 50 million (point *C*), so its imports are also 45 million bushels—the distance *CD*.

Now suppose the government of the importing nation imposes a quota limiting imports to 30 million bushels. The free-trade equilibrium with imports of 45 million bushels is no longer possible. Instead, the market must equilibrate at a point where both exports and imports are only 30 million bushels. As Figure 23–4 indicates, this requires different prices in the two countries.

Quotas and Tariffs in International Trade

FIGURE 23-4

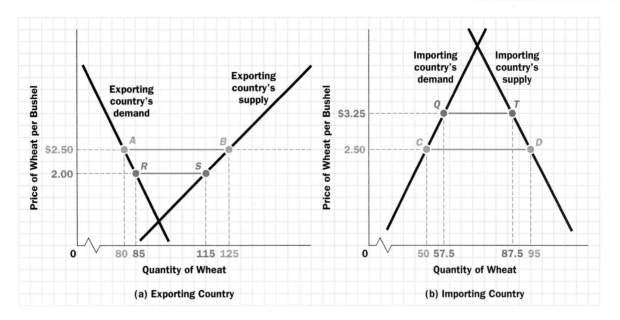

(a) Exporting Country

(b) Importing Country

NOTE: Quantities are in millions of bushels.

Imports in Panel (b) will be 30 million—the distance QT—only when the price of wheat in the importing nation is $3.25 per bushel, because only at this price will quantity demanded exceed domestic quantity supplied by 30 million bushels. Similarly, exports in Panel (a) will be 30 million bushels—the distance RS—only when the price in the exporting country is $2.00 per bushel. At this price, quantity supplied exceeds domestic quantity demanded by 30 million bushels in the exporting country. Thus, the quota *raises* the price in the importing country to $3.25 and *lowers* the price in the exporting country to $2.00. In general:

An import quota on a product normally reduces the volume of that product traded, raises the price in the importing country, and reduces the price in the exporting country.

A tariff can accomplish the same restriction of trade. In our example, a quota of 30 million bushels led to a price that was $1.25 higher in the importing country than in the exporting country ($3.25 versus $2.00). Suppose that, instead of a quota, the importing nation posts a $1.25 per bushel tariff. International trade equilibrium then must satisfy the following two requirements:

1. The price that consumers in the importing country pay for wheat must exceed the price that suppliers in the exporting country receive by $1.25 (the amount of the tariff).

2. The quantity of wheat exported must equal the quantity of wheat imported.

By consulting the graphs in Figure 23–4, you can see exactly where these two requirements are met. If the exporter produces at S and consumes at R, while the importer produces at Q and consumes at T, then exports and imports are equal (at 30 million bushels), and the two domestic prices differ by exactly $1.25. (They are $3.25 and $2.00.) What we have just discovered is a general result of international trade theory:

Any restriction of imports that is accomplished by a quota normally can also be accomplished by a tariff.

In this case, the tariff corresponding to an import quota of 30 million bushels is $1.25 per bushel.

TARIFFS VERSUS QUOTAS

But although tariffs and quotas can accomplish the same reduction in international trade and lead to the same domestic prices in the two countries, some important differences arise between the two types of restrictions.

First, under a quota, profits from the price increases in the importing country usually go into the pockets of the foreign and domestic sellers of the product. Because supplies are limited by quotas, customers in the importing country must pay more for the product. So the suppliers, whether foreign or domestic, receive more for every unit they sell. For example, estimates showed that U.S. import quotas on Japanese cars in the early 1980s raised the profits of both American and Japanese automakers by billions of dollars per year.

On the other hand, when trade is restricted by a tariff, some of the profits go instead as tax revenues to the *government* of the importing country. In effect, the government increases its tax revenues partly at its own citizens' expense and partly at the expense of foreign exporters, who must accept a reduced price because of the resulting decrease in quantity demanded in the importing country. (Domestic producers again benefit, because they are exempt from the tariff.) In this respect, a tariff is certainly a better proposition than a quota from the viewpoint of the country that enacts it.

Another important distinction between the two measures arises from their different implications for productive efficiency. Because a tariff handicaps all foreign suppliers equally, it still awards sales to those firms and nations that are most efficient and can therefore supply the goods most cheaply. A quota, on the other hand, necessarily awards its import licenses more or less capriciously—perhaps in proportion to past sales or even based on political criteria. There is not the slightest reason to expect the most efficient suppliers to get the import permits.

The U.S. quota on Japanese cars in the 1980s illustrates all of these effects. Japanese automakers responded to the limit on the number of cars by shipping bigger models equipped with more optional equipment. The "stripped-down" Japanese car became a thing of the past. And the newer, smaller Japanese automakers—like Subaru and Mitsubishi—found it difficult at first to compete in the U.S. market because their quotas were so much smaller than those of Toyota, Nissan, and Honda.

If a country must inhibit imports, two important reasons support a preference for tariffs over quotas:

1. **Some of the revenues resulting from tariffs go to the government of the importing country rather than to foreign and domestic producers.**

2. **Unlike quotas, tariffs offer special benefits to more efficient exporters.**

■ WHY INHIBIT TRADE?

To state that tariffs provide a better way to inhibit international trade than quotas leaves open a far more basic question: Why limit trade in the first place? It has been estimated that trade restrictions cost American consumers about $70 billion per year in the form of higher prices. Why should they be asked to pay these higher prices?

A number of answers are commonly given. Let's examine each in turn.

GAINING A PRICE ADVANTAGE

A tariff forces foreign exporters to sell more cheaply by restricting their market access. If they do not cut their prices, they will be left with unsold goods. Suppose, as in Figure 23–4(b), that a $1.25 tariff on wheat raises the price in the importing country from $2.50 to $3.25 per bushel. This higher price drives down imports from an amount represented by the length of the red line *CD* to the smaller amount represented by the blue line *QT*. To the exporting country, this means an equal reduction in exports, as illustrated by the change from *AB* to *RS* in Figure 23–4(a).

As a result, the price at which the exporting country can sell its wheat is driven down—from $2.50 to $2.00 in the example. Meanwhile, producers in the importing country—being exempt from the tariff—can charge $3.25 per bushel. So, in effect, the tariff amounts to government intervention to rig prices in favor of domestic producers.

Not bad, you say. However, this technique works only as long as foreigners accept tariff exploitation passively—which they rarely do. Instead, they will probably retaliate by imposing tariffs or quotas of their own on imports from the country that first began the tariff game. Such tit-for-tat behavior can easily lead to a trade war in which no one gains more favorable prices but everyone loses through the resulting reductions in trade. Something like this happened to the world economy in the 1930s and helped prolong the worldwide depression.

Tariffs or quotas can benefit particular domestic industries in a country that is able to impose them without fear of retaliation. But when every country uses them, everyone is likely to lose in the long run.

PROTECTING PARTICULAR INDUSTRIES

The second, and probably more frequent, reason why countries restrict trade is to protect particular industries from foreign competition. If foreigners can produce steel or shoes more cheaply, domestic businesses and unions in these industries are quick to demand protection, and their governments are often reluctant to deny them that support.

The "cheap foreign labor" argument is most likely to arise in this context. Protective tariffs and quotas are explicitly designed to rescue firms whose relative inefficiency does not permit them to compete with foreign exporters in an open world market. But it is precisely the harsh international competition to produce better products more efficiently that gives consumers the benefits of international specialization.

In our numerical example of comparative advantage, we can well imagine the complaints from Japanese computer makers as the opening of trade leads to increased importation of U.S. computers. At the same time, American TV manufacturers would probably express outrage over the flood of imported TVs from Japan. Yet Japanese specialization in televisions and U.S. specialization in computers is precisely what enables citizens of both countries to enjoy higher standards of living. If governments interfere with this process, consumers in both countries lose out.

Industries threatened by foreign competition often argue that some form of protection against imports is needed to prevent job losses. For example, the U.S. steel industry made exactly this argument recently when world steel prices plummeted and imports surged. (And the U.S. government delivered some protection!) But basic macroeconomics teaches us better ways to stimulate employment, such as raising aggregate demand.

A program that limits foreign competition will be more effective at preserving employment *in the particular protected industry*. But it will typically do so at a high cost to consumers and to the economy. Table 23–4 estimates some of the costs

Estimated Costs of Protectionism to Consumers

TABLE 23-4

Industry	Cost per Job Saved
Apparel	$139,000
Costume jewelry	97,000
Shipping	415,000
Sugar	600,000
Textiles	202,000
Women's footwear	102,000

SOURCE: Gary C. Hufbauer and Kimberly Ann Elliott, *Measuring the Costs of Protectionism in the United States* (Washington, D.C.: Institute for International Economics, January 1994), Table 1.3, pp. 12–13.

● HOW POPULAR IS PROTECTIONISM?

Although the world has been moving gradually toward freer trade, its citizens are not entirely persuaded that this trend is desirable. In 1998, a Canadian polling company asked almost 13,000 people in 22 countries the following question: "Which of the following two broad approaches do you think would be the best way to improve the economic and employment situation in this country—protecting our local industries by restricting imports, or removing import restrictions to increase our international trade?" By this measure, protectionism outnumbered free traders by a narrow margin— 47 percent to 42 percent, with the rest undecided. But protectionist sentiment was stronger in the United States, where the margin was 56 percent to 37 percent.

SOURCE: *The Economist*, January 2, 1999, page 59.

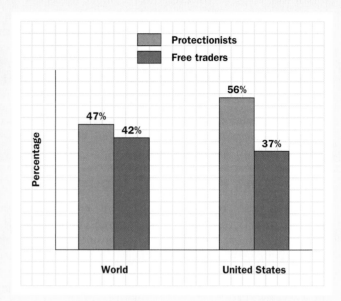

to American consumers of using tariffs and quotas to save jobs in selected industries. In every case, the costs far exceed the wages of the workers in the protected industries—ranging as high as $600,000 per job for the sugar quota.

Nevertheless, complaints over proposals to reduce tariffs or quotas are justified unless something is done to ease the cost to individual workers of switching to the product lines that trade makes profitable.

> The argument for free trade between countries cannot be considered airtight if governments provide no adequate program to assist those few citizens in each country who are harmed whenever patterns of production change drastically—as would happen, for example, if governments suddenly reduced tariff and quota barriers.

Owners of television factories in the United States and of computer factories in Japan may see heavy investments suddenly rendered unprofitable. Workers in those industries would see their special skills and training devalued in the marketplace. And displaced workers also pay some intangible costs. They may need to move to new locations as well as to new industries, uprooting their families, losing old friends and neighbors, and so on. That the *majority* of citizens undoubtedly gain from free trade is no consolation to those who are its victims.

To mitigate these problems, the United States follows two basic approaches. First, our trade laws offer temporary protection from sudden surges of imports, on the grounds that unexpected changes in trade patterns do not give businesses and workers enough time to adjust.

Trade adjustment assistance provides special unemployment benefits, loans, retraining programs, and other aid to workers and firms that are harmed by foreign competition.

Second, the government has set up **trade adjustment assistance** programs to help workers and businesses who lose their jobs or their markets because of import increases. Firms may be eligible for technical assistance, government loans or loan guarantees, and permission to delay tax payments. Workers may qualify for retraining programs, longer periods of unemployment compensation, and funds to defray moving costs. Each form of assistance is designed to ease the burden on the victims of free trade so that the rest of us can enjoy its considerable benefits.

■ OTHER ARGUMENTS FOR PROTECTION

NATIONAL DEFENSE AND OTHER NONECONOMIC CONSIDERATIONS

A third reason trade protectionists cite is the need to maintain national defense. For example, even if the United States were not the most efficient producer of aircraft, it might still be rational to produce our own military aircraft so that no foreign government could ever cut off supplies of this strategic product. The national defense argument is fine as far as it goes, but there is a clear danger: Even industries with the most peripheral relationship to defense are likely to invoke this argument on their behalf. For instance, for years the U.S. watchmaking industry argued for protection on the grounds that its skilled craftsmen would be invaluable in wartime!

Similarly, the United States has occasionally banned either exports to or imports from nations such as Cuba, Iran, and Iraq on political grounds. Such actions often have important economic effects, creating either bonanzas or disasters for particular American industries. But they are justified by politics, not by economics. Noneconomic reasons also explain quotas on importation of whaling products and on the furs of other endangered species.

THE INFANT-INDUSTRY ARGUMENT

Yet a fourth common argument for protectionism is the so-called *infant-industry argument*. Promising new industries allegedly often need breathing room to flourish and grow. If we expose these infants to the rigors of international competition too soon, the argument goes, they may never develop to the point where they can survive on their own in the international marketplace.

The argument, although valid in certain instances, is less defensible than it seems at first. Protecting an infant industry is justifiable only if the prospective future gains are sufficient to repay the up-front costs of protectionism. But if the industry is likely to be so profitable in the future, why doesn't private capital rush in to take advantage of the prospective net profits? The annals of business are full of cases in which a new product or a new firm lost money at first, but profited handsomely later.

The infant-industry argument for protection stands up to scrutiny only if private funds are unavailable for some reason, despite a industry's glowing profit prospects. Even then it may make more sense to provide a government loan than to provide trade protection.

It is hard to think of legitimate examples where the infant-industry argument applies. But even if such a case were found, we would have to be careful that the industry not remain in diapers forever. In too many cases, industries were awarded protection when young and, somehow, never matured to the point where protection could be withdrawn. We must be wary of infants that never grow up.

STRATEGIC TRADE POLICY

A stronger argument for (temporary) protection has substantially influenced U.S. trade policy. Advocates of this argument, including some top officials in the Clinton administration, agree that free trade for all is the best system. But they point out that we live in an imperfect world in which many nations refuse to play by the rules of the free-trade game. And they fear that a nation that pursues free trade in a protectionist world is likely to lose out. It therefore makes sense, they argue, to *threaten* to protect your markets unless other nations agree to open theirs.

The United States has followed this strategy in trade negotiations with several countries in recent years. One extremely prominent case arose in 1995, when the U.S. government threatened to impose 100 percent tariffs on imported Japanese luxury cars unless Japan agreed to open its domestic markets for automobiles and auto parts. A dangerous trade war was narrowly averted when the two countries struck

● CAN PROTECTIONISM SAVE FREE TRADE?

In this 1983 column, William Safire shook off his long-standing attachment to free trade and argued eloquently for retaliation against protectionist nations.

Free trade is economic motherhood. Protectionism is economic evil incarnate. . . . Never should government interfere in the efficiency of international competition.

Since childhood, these have been the tenets of my faith. If it meant that certain businesses in this country went belly-up, so be it. . . . If it meant that Americans would be thrown out of work by overseas companies paying coolie wages, that was tough. . . .

The thing to keep in mind, I was taught, was the Big Picture and the Long Run. America, the great exporter, had far more to gain than to lose from free trade; attempts to protect inefficient industries here would ultimately cost more American jobs.

While playing with my David Ricardo doll and learning nursery rhymes about comparative advantage, I was listening to another laissez-fairy tale: Government's role in the world of business should be limited to keeping business honest and competitive. In God we antitrusted. Let businesses operate in the free marketplace.

Now American businesses are no longer competing with foreign companies. They are competing with foreign governments who help their local businesses. That means the world arena no longer offers a free marketplace; instead, most other governments are pushing a policy that can be called *helpfulism.*

Helpfulism works like this: A government like Japan decides to get behind its baseball-bat industry. It pumps in capital, knocks off marginal operators, finds subtle ways to discourage imports of Louisville Sluggers, and selects target areas for export blitzes. Pretty soon, the favored Japanese companies are driving foreign competitors batty.

How do we compete with helpfulism? One way is to complain that it is unfair; that draws a horselaugh. Another way is

to demand a "Reagan Round" of trade negotiations under GATT, the Gentlemen's Agreement To Talk, which is equally laughable. Yet another way is to join the helpfuls by subsidizing our exports and permitting our companies to try monopolistic tricks abroad not permitted at home. But all that makes us feel guilty, with good reason.

The other way to deal with helpfulism is through—here comes the dreadful word—*protection.* Or, if you prefer a euphemism, *retaliation.* Or if that is still too severe, *reciprocity.* Whatever its name, it is a way of saying to the cut-throat cartelists we sweetly call our trading partners: "You have bent the rules out of shape. Change your practices to conform to the agreed-upon rules, or we will export a taste of your own medicine."

A little balance, then, from the free trade theorists. The demand for what the Pentagon used to call "protective reaction" is not demagoguery, not shortsighted, not self-defeating. On the contrary, the overseas pirates of protectionism and exemplars of helpfulism need to be taught the basic lesson in trade, which is: tit for tat.

SOURCE: William Safire, "Smoot-Hawley Lives," *The New York Times,* March 17, 1983. Copyright © 1983 by The New York Times Company. Reprinted by permission.

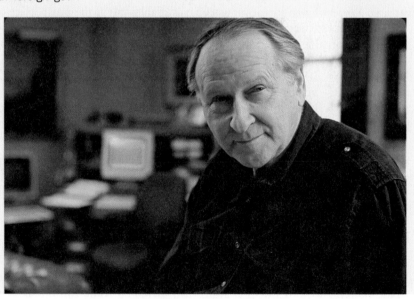

an agreement at the eleventh hour. At this writing, another such game of chicken is being played with the European Union over their restrictions on imports of hormone-treated beef.

The strategic argument for protection is a hard one for economists to deal with. Although it recognizes the superiority of free trade, it argues that threatening protectionism is the best way to achieve that end. Such a strategy might work, but it clearly involves great risks. If threats that the United States will turn protectionist induce other countries to scrap existing protectionist policies, then the gamble will have succeeded. But, if the gamble fails, protectionism increases.

● UNFAIR FOREIGN COMPETITION

Satire and ridicule are often more persuasive than logic and statistics. Exasperated by the spread of protectionism under the prevailing Mercantilist philosophy, French economist Frédéric Bastiat decided to take the protectionist argument to its illogical conclusion. The fictitious petition of the French candlemakers to the Chamber of Deputies, written in 1845 and excerpted below, has become a classic in the battle for free trade.

> We are subject to the intolerable competition of a foreign rival, who enjoys, it would seem, such superior facilities for the production of light, that he is enabled to inundate our national market at so exceedingly reduced a price, that, the moment he makes his appearance, he draws off all custom for us; and thus an important branch of French industry, with all its innumerable ramifications, is suddenly reduced to a state of complete stagnation. This rival is no other than the sun.
>
> Our petition is, that it would please your honorable body to pass a law whereby shall be directed the shutting up of all windows, dormers, skylights, shutters, curtains, in a word, all openings, holes, chinks, and fissures through which the light of the sun is used to penetrate our dwellings, to the prejudice of the profitable manufactures which we flatter ourselves we have been enabled to bestow upon the country. . . .

We foresee your objections, gentlemen; but there is not one that you can oppose to us . . . which is not equally opposed to your own practice and the principle which guides your policy. . . . Labor and nature concur in different proportions, according to country and climate, in every article of production. . . . If a Lisbon orange can be sold at half the price of a Parisian one, it is because a natural and gratuitous heat does for the one what the other only obtains from an artificial and consequently expensive one. . . .

Does it not argue the greatest inconsistency to check as you do the importation of coal, iron, cheese, and goods of foreign manufacture, merely because and even in proportion as their price approaches *zero,* while at the same time you freely admit, and without limitation, the light of the sun, whose price is during the whole day at *zero?*

SOURCE: F. Bastiat, *Economic Sophisms* (New York: G. P. Putnam's Sons, 1922).

■ CAN CHEAP IMPORTS HURT A COUNTRY?

One of the most curious—and illogical—features of the protectionist position is the fear of low import prices. Countries that subsidize their exports are accused of **dumping**—of getting rid of their goods at unjustifiably low prices. For example, Russia, Japan, and Korea have recently been accused of dumping steel on the U.S. market.

Economists find this argument strange. As a nation of consumers, we should be indignant when foreigners charge us *high* prices, not *low* ones. That commonsense rule guides every consumer's daily life. Only from the topsy-turvy viewpoint of an industry seeking protection are low prices seen as being against the public interest.

Ultimately, the best interests of any country are served when it imports as cheaply as possible. It would be ideal for the United States if the rest of the world were willing to provide us with goods at no charge. We could then live in luxury at the expense of the rest of the world.

But, of course, benefits to the United States as a whole do not necessarily inure to every single American. If quotas on, say, sugar imports were dropped, American consumers and industries that purchase sugar would gain from lower prices. But owners of sugar fields and their employees would suffer serious losses in the form of lower profits, lower wages, and lost jobs—losses they would fight hard to prevent. For this reason, politics often leads to the adoption of protectionist measures that we would likely reject on strictly economic criteria.

Dumping means selling goods in a foreign market at lower prices than those charged in the home market.

■ A LAST LOOK AT THE "CHEAP FOREIGN LABOR" ARGUMENT

The preceding discussion reveals the fundamental fallacy in the argument that American workers should fear cheap foreign labor. The average American worker's living standard must rise if other countries willingly supply their products to us more cheaply. As long as the government's monetary and fiscal policies succeed in maintaining high levels of employment at home, how can we possibly lose by getting world products at bargain prices? This is precisely what is happening to the U.S. economy as this book goes to print—imports are pouring in at low prices and U.S. unemployment is the lowest in a generation.

We must add, however, some important qualifications. First, our macroeconomic stabilization policy may not always be effective. If workers displaced by foreign competition cannot find new jobs, they will indeed suffer from international trade. But high unemployment reflects a shortcoming of the government's monetary and fiscal policies, not of its international trade policies.

Second, we have noted that an abrupt stiffening of foreign competition can hurt U.S. workers by not allowing them adequate time to adapt to the new conditions. If change occurs fairly gradually, workers can retrain and move on to the industries that now require their services. Indeed, if the change is slow enough, normal attrition may suffice. But competition that inflicts its damage overnight is certain to impose real costs on the affected workers, costs that are no less painful for being temporary. That is why our trade laws make provisions for people and industries damaged by import surges.

But these are, after all, only qualifications to an overwhelming argument. They call for intelligent monetary and fiscal policies and for transitional assistance to unemployed workers, not for abandonment of free trade. In general, the nation as a whole need not fear competition from cheap foreign labor.

> In the long run, labor will be "cheap" only where it is not very productive. Wages will be high in countries with high labor productivity, and this high productivity will enable those countries to compete effectively in international trade despite high wages. It is thus misleading to say that the United States held its own in the international marketplace until recently *despite* high wages. Rather it is much more on point to note that the higher wages of American workers were a result of higher worker productivity, which gave the United States a heavy competitive edge.

Remember, in this matter it is absolute advantage, not comparative advantage, that counts. The country that is most efficient in every output can pay its workers more in every industry.

SUMMARY

1. Countries trade because differences in their natural resources and other inputs create discrepancies in the efficiency with which they can produce different goods, and because *specialization* may offer them greater economies of large-scale production.

2. Voluntary trade will generally be advantageous to both parties in an exchange. This is one of our *Ideas for Beyond the Final Exam*.

3. International trade is more complicated than trade within a nation because of political factors, different national currencies, and impediments to the movement of labor and capital across national borders.

4. Two countries will gain from trade with one another if each exports goods in which it has a *comparative advantage*. Even a country that is inefficient across the board will benefit by exporting the goods in whose production it is *least inefficient*. This is another of the *Ideas for Beyond the Final Exam*.

5. When countries specialize and trade, each can enjoy consumption possibilities that exceed its production possibilities.

6. The prices of goods traded between countries are determined by supply and demand, but one must consider explicitly the demand curve and the supply curve of *each* country involved. Thus the equilibrium price must be where the excess of quantity supplied over quantity demanded in the exporting country is equal to the excess of quantity demanded over quantity supplied in the importing country.

7. The "cheap foreign labor" argument ignores the principle of comparative advantage, which shows that real wages

(which determine living standards) can rise in both importing and exporting countries as a result of specialization.

8. *Tariffs* and *quotas* aim to protect a country's industries from foreign competition. Such protection may sometimes be advantageous to that country, but not if foreign countries adopt tariffs and quotas of their own in retaliation.

9. Although the same trade restrictions can be accomplished by either a tariff or a quota, tariffs offer at least two advantages to the country that imposes them: some of the gains go to the government rather than to foreign producers, and they provide greater incentive for efficient production.

10. When a nation shifts from protection to free trade, some industries and their workers will lose out. Equity then demands that these people and firms be compensated in some way. The U.S. government offers protection from import surges and various forms of *trade adjustment assistance* to help those workers and industries adapt.

11. Several arguments for protectionism can, under the right circumstances, have validity. These include the national defense argument, the *infant-industry argument*, and the use of trade restrictions for *strategic* purposes. But each of these arguments is frequently abused.

12. *Dumping* will hurt certain domestic producers, but it benefits domestic consumers.

KEY TERMS

Imports 478

Exports 478

Specialization 480

Mutual gains from trade 480

Absolute advantage 481

Comparative advantage 481

"Cheap foreign labor" argument 485

Mercantilism 487

Tariff 487

Quota 488

Export subsidy 488

Trade adjustment assistance 492

Infant-industry argument 493

Strategic trade policy 493

Dumping 495

QUESTIONS FOR REVIEW

1. You have a dozen shirts and your roommate has six pairs of shoes worth roughly the same amount of money. You decide to swap six shirts for three pairs of shoes. In financial terms, neither of you gains anything. Explain why you are nevertheless both likely to be better off.

2. In the 18th century, some writers argued that one person in a trade could be made better off only by gaining at the expense of the other. Explain the fallacy in the argument.

3. Country A has a cold climate with a short growing season, but a highly skilled labor force. What sorts of products do you think it is likely to produce? What are the characteristics of the countries with which you would expect it to trade?

4. Upon removal of a quota on sugar, many U.S. sugar farms go bankrupt. Discuss the pros and cons of removing the quota in the short and long runs.

5. Country A's mercantilist government believes that it is always best to export more than it imports. As a consequence, it exports more to Country B every year than it imports from Country B. After 100 years of this arrangement, both countries are destroyed in an earthquake. What were the advantages or disadvantages of the surplus to Country A? To Country B?

6. The following table describes the number of yards of cloth and barrels of wine that can be produced with a week's worth of labor in England and Portugal. Assume that no other inputs are needed.

	In England	In Portugal
Cloth	8 yards	12 yards
Wine	2 barrels	6 barrels

a. If there is no trade, what is the price of wine in terms of cloth in England?

b. If there is no trade, what is the price of wine relative to cloth in Portugal?

c. Suppose each country has 1 million weeks of labor available per year. Draw the production possibilities frontier for each country.

d. Which country has an absolute advantage in the production of which good(s)? Which country has a comparative advantage in the production of which good(s)?

e. If the countries start trading with each other, which country will specialize and export which good?

f. What can be said about the price at which trade will take place?

7. Suppose that the United States and Mexico are the only two countries in the world and that labor is the only productive input. In the United States, a worker can produce 12 bushels of wheat *or* 2 barrels of oil in a day. In Mexico, a worker can produce 2 bushels of wheat *or* 4 barrels of oil per day.

a. What will be the price ratio between the two commodities (that is, the price of oil in terms of wheat) in each country if there is no trade?

b. If free trade is allowed and there are no transportation costs, what commodity would the United States import? What about Mexico?

c. In what range would the price ratio have to fall under free trade? Why?

d. Picking one possible post-trade price ratio, show clearly how it is possible for both countries to benefit from free trade.

8. The following table presents the demand and supply curves for microcomputers in Japan and the United States.

Price per Computer	Quantity Demanded in U.S.	Quantity Supplied in U.S.	Quantity Demanded in Japan	Quantity Supplied in Japan
1	90	30	50	50
2	80	35	40	55
3	70	40	30	60
4	60	45	20	65
5	50	50	10	70
6	40	55	0	75

NOTE: Price and quanitity are in thousands.

a. Draw the demand and supply curves for the United States on one diagram and those for Japan on another one.

b. If the United States and Japan do not trade, what are the equilibrium price and quantity in the computer market in the United States? In Japan?

c. Now suppose trade is opened up between the two countries. What will be the equilibrium price in the world market for computers? What has happened to the price of computers in the United States? In Japan?

d. Which country will export computers? How many?

e. When trade opens, what happens to the quantity of computers produced, and therefore employment, in the computer industry in the United States? In Japan? Who benefits and who loses *initially* from free trade?

9. Under current trade law, the president of the United States must report periodically to Congress on countries engaging in unfair trade practices that inhibit U.S. exports. How would you define an "unfair" trade practice? Suppose Country X exports much more to the United States than it imports, year after year. Does that constitute evidence that Country X's trade practices are unfair? What would constitute such evidence?

10. Suppose the United States finds Country X guilty of unfair trade practices and penalizes it with import quotas. So U.S. imports from Country X fall. Suppose, further, that Country X does not alter its trade practices in any way. Is the United States better or worse off? What about Country X?

Ability-to-pay principle The ability-to-pay principle of taxation refers to the idea that people with greater ability to pay taxes should pay higher taxes. (p. 441)

Absolute advantage One country is said to have an absolute advantage over another in the production of a particular good if it can produce that good using smaller quantities of resources than can the other country. (p. 481)

Abstraction Abstraction means ignoring many details in order to focus on the most important elements of a problem. (p. 11)

Affirmative action Affirmative action refers to active efforts to locate and hire members of underrepresented groups. (p. 399)

Allocation of resources Allocation of resources refers to the society's decisions on how to divide up its scarce input resources among the different outputs produced in the economy and among the different firms or other organizations that produce those outputs. (p. 60)

Antitrust policy Antitrust policy refers to programs and laws that preclude the deliberate creation of monopoly and prevent powerful firms from engaging in related "undesirable practices." (p. 420)

Applied research Applied research is research whose goal is to invent or improve particular products or processes, often for profit, though the military and health industries provide examples of not-for-profit applied research. (p. 304)

Average physical product (APP) The average physical product (APP) is the total physical product (TPP) divided by the quantity of input. Thus, $APP = TPP/X$ where $X =$ the quantity of input. (p. 143)

Average revenue (AR) The average revenue (AR) is total revenue (TR) divided by quantity. (p. 173)

Average tax rate The average tax rate is the ratio of taxes to income. (p. 435)

Basic research Basic research refers to research that seeks to provide scientific knowledge and general principles rather than coming up with any specific marketable inventions. (p. 304)

Beneficial or detrimental externality An activity is said to generate a beneficial or detrimental externality if that activity causes incidental benefits or damages to others not directly involved in the activity and no corresponding compensation is provided to or paid by those who generate the externality. (p. 272)

Benefits principle The benefits principle of taxation holds that people who derive benefits from a service should pay the taxes that finance it. (p. 442)

Bilateral monopoly A bilateral monopoly is a market situation in which there is both a monopoly on the selling side and a monopsony on the buying side. (p. 371)

Bond A bond is simply an IOU by a corporation that promises to pay the holder of the bond a fixed sum of money at the specified *maturity* date and some other fixed amount of money (the *coupon* or the *interest payment*) every year up to the date of maturity. (p. 312)

Bottleneck facility A facility or service owned by a single firm and needed for the activities of rival firms is called a bottleneck facility (or, simply, a bottleneck). (p. 409)

Bundling Bundling refers to a pricing arrangement under which the supplier offers substantial discounts to customers if they buy several of the firm's products, so that the price of the bundle of products is less than the sum of the prices of the products if they were bought separately. (p. 427)

Burden of a tax The burden of a tax to an individual is the amount one would have to be given to be just as well off with the tax as without it. (p. 442)

Capital good A capital good is an item used to produce other goods and services in the future, rather than being consumed today. Factories and machines are examples. (p. 58)

Capital Capital refers to an inventory (*a stock*) of plant, equipment, and other (generally durable) productive resources held by a business firm, an individual, or some other organization. (p. 333)

Capitalism Capitalism is an economic system in which most of the production process is controlled by private firms operating in markets with minimal government control. The investors in these firms (called "capitalists") own the firms. (p. 293)

Cartel A cartel is a group of sellers of a product who have joined together to control its production, sale, and price in the hope of obtaining the advantages of monopoly. (p. 254)

Closed economy A closed economy is one that does not trade with other nations in either goods or assets. (p. 34)

Closed shop A closed shop is an arrangement that permits only union members to be hired. (p. 369)

Closed An economy is considered relatively closed if they constitute a small share. (p. 34)

Common stock A common stock of a corporation is a piece of paper that gives the holder of the stock a share of the ownership of the company. (p. 312)

Comparative advantage One country is said to have a comparative advantage over another in the production of a particular good relative to other goods if it produces that good less inefficiently as compared with the other country. (p. 5, 61, 481)

Complements Two goods are called complements if an increase in the quantity consumed of one increases the quantity demanded of the other, all other things remaining constant. (p. 127)

Concentration ratio A concentration ratio is the percentage of an industry's output produced by its four largest firms. It is intended to measure the degree to which the industry is dominated by large firms. (p. 423)

Consumer's surplus Consumer's surplus is the difference between the value to the consumer of the quantity of Commodity X purchased and the amount that the market requires the consumer to pay for that quantity of X. (p. 103)

Consumption good A consumption good is an item that is available for immediate use by households, one that satisfies people's wants without contributing directly to the economy's future production. (p. 58)

Corporation A corporation is a firm that has the legal status of a fictional individual.

This fictional individual is owned by a number of persons, called its *stockholders*, and is run by a set of elected officers and a board of directors, whose chairman is often also in a powerful position. (p. 310)

Correlated Two variables are said to be correlated if they tend to go up or down together. But correlation need not imply causation. (p. 13)

Credible threat A credible threat is a threat that does not harm the threatener if it is carried out. (p. 263)

Cross elasticity of demand The cross elasticity of demand for Product X to a change in the price of another product, Y, is the ratio of the percentage change in quantity demanded of X to the percentage change in the price of Y that brings about the change in quantity demanded. (p. 128)

Cross licensing Cross licensing of patents occurs when each of two firms agrees to let the other use some specified set of its patents, either at a price specified in their agreement or in return for access to the other firm's patents. (p. 298)

Cross-subsidization Cross-subsidization means selling one product at a loss, which is balanced by higher profits on another product. (p. 412)

Demand curve A demand curve is a graphical depiction of a demand schedule. It shows how the quantity demanded of some product during a specified period of time will change as the price of that product changes, holding all other determinants of quantity demanded constant. (p. 71)

Demand schedule A demand schedule is a table showing how the quantity demanded of some product during a specified period of time changes as the price of that product changes, holding all other determinants of quantity demanded constant. (p. 70)

Depletable A commodity is depletable if it is used up when someone consumes it. (p. 276)

Derived demand The derived demand for an input is the demand for the input by producers as determined by the demand for the final product that the input is used to produce. (p. 332)

Direct taxes Direct taxes are taxes levied directly on people. (p. 435)

Division of labor Division of labor means breaking up a task into a number of smaller, more specialized tasks so that each worker can become more adept at a particular job. (p. 60)

Dumping Dumping means selling goods in a foreign market at lower prices than those charged in the home market. (p. 495)

Economic discrimination Economic discrimination occurs when equivalent factors of production receive different payments for equal contributions to output. (p. 389)

Economic growth Economic growth occurs when an economy is able to produce more goods and services for each consumer. (p. 58)

Economic model An economic model is a simplified, small-scale version of some aspect of the economy. Economic models are often expressed in equations, by graphs, or in words. (p. 13)

Economic profit Economic profit equals net earnings, in the accountant's sense, minus the opportunity costs of capital and of any other inputs supplied by the firm's owners. (p. 170, 203)

Economic profit Economic profit is the total revenue of a firm minus all of its costs including the interest payments and opportunity costs of the capital it obtains from its investors. (p. 345)

Economic rent Economic rent is the portion of the earnings of a factor of production that exceeds the minimum amount necessary to induce any of that factor to be supplied. (p. 338, 363)

Economies of scale Economies of scale are savings that are obtained through increases in quantities produced. Scale economies occur when an X percent increase in input use raises output by *more than* X percent, so that the more the firm produces, the lower its per-unit costs become. (p. 406)

Economies of scale Production is said to involve economies of scale, also referred to as increasing returns to scale, if, when all input quantities are doubled, the quantity of output is *more* than doubled. (p. 155)

Economies of scope Economies of scope are savings that are obtained through simultaneous production of many different products and occur if a firm that produces many commodities can supply

each good more cheaply than a firm that produces fewer commodities. (p. 409)

Efficient allocation of resources An efficient allocation of resources is one that takes advantage of every opportunity to make some individuals better off in their own estimation while not worsening the lot of anyone else. (p. 211)

Entrepreneurship Entrepreneurship is the act of starting new firms, introducing new products and technological innovations, and, in general, taking the risks that are necessary in seeking out business opportunities. (p. 330)

Equilibrium An equilibrium is a situation in which there are no inherent forces that produce change. Changes away from an equilibrium position will occur only as a result of "outside events" that disturb the status quo. (p. 78)

Excess burden The excess burden of a tax to an individual is the amount by which the burden of the tax exceeds the tax that is paid. (p. 443)

Excludable A commodity is excludable if someone who does not pay for it can be kept from enjoying it. (p. 276)

Export subsidy An export subsidy is a payment by the government to exporters to permit them to reduce the selling prices of their goods so they can compete more effectively in foreign markets. (p. 488)

Externality An activity is said to generate a beneficial or detrimental externality if that activity causes incidental benefits or damages to others not directly involved in the activity, and no corresponding compensation is provided to or paid by those who generate the externality. (p. 454)

Factors of production Factors of production are the broad categories, land, labor, capital, exhaustible natural resources, and entrepreneurship, into which we divide the economy's different productive inputs. (p. 32, 330)

Fiscal federalism Fiscal federalism refers to the system of grants from one level of government to the next. (p. 440)

Fixed cost A fixed cost is the cost of an input whose quantity does not rise when output goes up, one that the firm requires to produce any output at all. The total cost of such indivisible inputs does not change when the output changes. Any other cost of the firm's operation is called a variable cost. (p. 141)

Flypaper theory of tax incidence The flypaper theory of tax incidence holds that the burden of a tax always sticks where the government puts it. (p. 446)

45° line A 45° line is a ray through the origin with a slope of +1. It marks off points where the variables measured on each axis have equal values (assuming both variables are measured in the same units). (p. 22)

Gross domestic product (gdp) Gross domestic product (gdp) is a measure of the size of the economy or, rather, of the total amount it produces. It is, roughly speaking, the money value of all the goods and services produced in a year. (p. 32)

Horizontal equity Horizontal equity is the notion that equally situated individuals should be taxed equally. (p. 441)

Incidence of a tax The incidence of a tax is an allocation of the burden of the tax to specific individuals or groups. (p. 446)

Income elasticity of demand Income elasticity of demand is the ratio of the percentage change in quantity demanded to the percentage change in income. (p. 127)

Index fund An index fund, is a mutual fund that chooses a particular stock market index and then buys the stocks (or most of the stock) that are included in the index. The value of an investment in an index fund depends on what happens to the prices of all the stocks in that index. (p. 316)

Indirect taxes Indirect taxes are taxes levied on specific economic activities. (p. 435)

Industrial Revolution The Industrial Revolution is the stream of new technology and the resulting growth of output that began in England toward the end of the 18th century. (p. 293)

Inferior good An inferior good is a commodity whose quantity demanded falls when the purchaser's real income rises, all other things remaining equal. (p. 105)

Inflation Inflation refers to a sustained increase in the average level of prices. (p. 24)

Innovation Innovation is the process by which new products or new methods of production are introduced, including all the steps from the inventor's idea to bringing the new item to market. (p. 292, 346)

Input-output analysis Input-output analysis is a mathematical procedure that takes account of the interdependence among the economy's industries and determines the amount of output each industry must provide as inputs to the other industries in the economy. (p. 218)

Inputs or factors of production Inputs or factors of production are the labor, machinery, buildings, and natural resources used to make outputs. (p. 32, 54)

Interest Interest is the payment for the use of funds employed in the production of capital; it is measured as a percentage per year of the value of the funds tied up in the capital. (p. 333)

Invention Invention is the act of generating an idea for a new product or a new method for making an old product. (p. 346)

Investment in human capital Investment in human capital is any expenditure on an individual that increases that person's future earning power or productivity. (p. 355)

Investment Investment is the *flow* of resources into the production of new capital. It is the labor, steel, and other inputs devoted to the *construction* of factories, warehouses, railroads, and other pieces of capital during some period of time. (p. 333)

Invisible hand The invisible hand is a phrase used by Adam Smith to describe how, by pursuing their own self-interests, people in a market system are "led by an invisible hand" to promote societal well-being. (p. 68)

Labor productivity Labor productivity refers to the amount of output a worker turns out in an hour (or a week or a year) of labor. It can be measured as gross domestic product (GDP) in a given year divided by the total number of paid work hours during that year. That is, labor productivity is defined as GDP per hour of labor. (p. 292)

Labor union A labor union is an organization made up of a group of workers (usually with the same specialization, such as plumbing or costume design, or in the same industry). The unions represent the workers in negotiations with employers over issues such as wages, vacations, and sick leave. (p. 367)

Laissez faire Laissez faire refers to the practice of minimal government interference with the workings of the market system. The term means that people should be left alone in carrying out their economic affairs. (p. 215)

"Law" of demand The "law" of demand states that a lower price generally increases the amount of a commodity that people in a market are willing to buy. Therefore, for most goods, market demand curves have negative slopes. (p. 106)

"Law" of diminishing marginal utility The "law" of diminishing marginal utility asserts that additional units of a commodity are worth less and less to a consumer in money terms. As the individual's consumption increases, the marginal utility of each additional unit declines. (p. 96)

Law of supply and demand The law of supply and demand states that, in a free market, the forces of supply and demand generally push the price toward the level at which quantity supplied and quantity demanded are equal. (p. 79)

Limited liability Limited liability is a legal obligation of a firm's owners to pay back company debts only with the money they have already invested in the firm. (p. 310)

Long run The long run is a period of time long enough for all of the firm's commitments to come to an end. (p. 140)

Marginal land Marginal land is land that is just on the borderline of being used, i.e., any land the use of which would be unprofitable if the farmer had to pay even a penny of rent. (p. 339)

Marginal physical product (MPP) The marginal physical product (MPP) of an input is the increase in total output that results from a one-unit increase in the input, holding the amounts of all other inputs constant. (p. 143, 330)

Marginal profit Marginal profit is the addition to total profit resulting from one more unit of output. (p. 175)

Marginal revenue product (MRP) The marginal revenue product (MRP) of an input is the additional revenue that the producer earns from the increased sales when it uses an additional unit of the input. (p. 144, 330)

Marginal revenue Marginal revenue, often abbreviated MR, is the addition to total revenue resulting from the addition of one unit to total output. Geometrically, marginal revenue is the slope of the total revenue curve. Its formula is $MR_1 = TR_1 - TR_0$, and so on. (p. 173)

Marginal social cost (MSC) The marginal social cost (MSC) of an activity is the sum of its marginal private cost (MPC) plus the incidental cost (positive or negative) that is borne by others. (p. 273)

Marginal tax rate The marginal tax rate is the fraction of each *additional* dollar of income that is paid in taxes. (p. 435)

Marginal utility The marginal utility of a commodity to a consumer (measured in money terms) is the maximum amount of money that she or he is willing to pay *for one more unit* of that commodity. (p. 96)

Market demand curve A market demand curve shows how the total quantity of some product demanded by *all* consumers in the market during a specified period of time changes as the price of that product changes, holding all other things constant. (p. 105)

Market system A market system is a form of economic organization in which resource allocation decisions are left to individual producers and consumers acting in their own best interests without central direction. (p. 63)

Maximin criterion The maximin criterion requires you to select the strategy that yields the maximum payoff on the assumption that your opponent does as much damage to you as he or she can. (p. 261)

Mercantilism Mercantilism is a doctrine that holds that exports are good for a country, whereas imports are harmful. (p. 487)

Merger A merger refers to unification of two previously independent firms, as when one purchases the other or the two simply decide to combine into a single enterprise. (p. 427)

Mixed economy A mixed economy is one with some public influence over the workings of free markets. There may also be some public ownership mixed in with private property. (p. 49)

Monopolistic competition Monopolistic competition refers to a market in which products are heterogeneous but which is otherwise the same as a market that is perfectly competitive. (p. 190, 248)

Monopoly power Monopoly power (or market power) is the ability of a business firm to raise the prices of its products above competitive levels and to

keep those prices high for a substantial amount of time. (p. 406)

Monopsony A monopsony is a market situation in which there is only one buyer. (p. 371)

Moral hazard Moral hazard refers to the tendency of insurance to discourage policyholders from protecting themselves from risk. (p. 287)

MRP_L, the marginal revenue product of labor MRP_L, the marginal revenue product of labor, is the increase in the employer's total revenue that results when he hires an additional unit of labor. (p. 354)

Mutual fund A mutual fund, in which individual investors can buy shares, is a private investment firm that holds a portfolio of securities. Investors can choose among a large variety of different mutual funds, such as stock funds, bond funds, and so forth. (p. 315)

Nash equilibrium A Nash equilibrium results when each player adopts the strategy that gives her the highest possible payoff if her rival sticks to the strategy he has chosen. (p. 262)

Natural monopoly A natural monopoly is an industry in which advantages of large-scale production make it possible for a single firm to produce the entire output of the market at lower average cost than a number of firms each producing a smaller quantity. (p. 232)

Oligopoly An oligopoly is a market dominated by a few sellers, at least several of which are large enough relative to the total market to be able to influence the market price. (p. 190)

Open An economy is called relatively open if its exports and imports constitute a large share of its GDP. (p. 34)

Opportunity cost The opportunity cost of any decision is the value of the next best alternative that the decision forces the decision maker to forgo. (p. 4, 203, 652)

Opportunity cost The opportunity cost of some decision is the value of the next best alternative that must be given up because of that decision (for example, working instead of going to school). (p. 53)

Optimal decision An optimal decision is one which, among all the decisions that are actually possible, is best for the decision maker. For example, if profit is the sole objective of some firm, the price that

makes the firm's profit as large as possible is optimal for that company. (p. 168)

Origin The "0" point in the lower left-hand corner of a graph where the axes meet is called the origin. Both variables are equal to zero at the origin. (p. 18)

Outputs Outputs are the goods and services that consumers want to acquire. (p. 32, 54)

Partnership A partnership is a firm whose ownership is shared by a fixed number of proprietors. (p. 309)

Perfect competition Perfect competition occurs in an industry when that industry is made up of many small firms producing homogeneous products, when information is perfect, and when there is no impediment to the entry or exit of firms. (p. 192)

Perfectly contestable A market is perfectly contestable if entry and exit are costless and unimpeded. (p. 264)

Plowback Plowback (or retained earnings) is the portion of a corporation's profits that management decides to keep and invest back into the firm's operations rather than paying dividends directly to stockholders. Corporations may also buy back shares from stockholders. (p. 314)

Portfolio diversification Portfolio diversification means including a number and variety of stocks, bonds, and other such items in an individual's portfolio. If the individual owns airline stocks, for example, diversification requires the purchase of a stock or bond in a very different industry, such as a breakfast cereal producer. (p. 315)

Poverty line The poverty line is an amount of income below which a family is considered "poor." (p. 382)

Predatory pricing Predatory pricing is pricing that threatens to keep a competitor out of the market. It is a price that is so low that it will be profitable for the firm that adopts it only if a rival is driven from the market. (p. 426)

Price ceiling A price ceiling is a legal maximum on the price that may be charged for a commodity. (p. 83)

Price discrimination Price discrimination is the sale of a given product at different prices to different customers of the firm, when there is no difference in the cost of supplying different customers. Prices are also discriminatory if it costs more to supply one customer than another, but they are charged the same price. (p. 239)

(Price) elasticity of demand The (price) elasticity of demand is the ratio of the *percentage* change in quantity demanded to the *percentage* change in price that brings about the change in quantity demanded. (p. 119)

Price floor A price floor is a legal minimum on the price that may be charged for a commodity. (p. 85)

Price leadership Under price leadership, one firm sets the price for the industry and the others follow. (p. 256)

Price taker Under perfect competition, the firm is a price taker. It has no choice but to accept the price that has been determined in the market. (p. 193)

Price war In a price war, each competing firm is determined to sell at a price that is lower than the prices of its rivals, usually regardless of whether that price covers the pertinent cost. Typically, in such a price war, Firm A cuts its price below Firm B's; then B retaliates by undercutting A, and so on and so on until one or more of the firms surrender and let themselves be undersold. (p. 257)

Principle of increasing costs The principle of increasing costs states that as the production of a good expands, the opportunity cost of producing another unit generally increases. (p. 55)

Private good A private good is a commodity characterized by both excludability and depletability. (p. 276)

Process innovation A process innovation is an innovation that changes the way in which a commodity is produced. (p. 303)

Product innovation A product innovation is the introduction of a good or service that is entirely new or involves major modifications of earlier products. (p. 303)

Production function The production function indicates the *maximum* amount of product that any particular collection of inputs is capable of producing. (p. 151)

Production indifference map A production indifference map is a graph whose axes show the quantities of two inputs that are used to produce some output. A curve in the graph corresponds to some given quantity of that output, and the different points on that curve show the different quantities of the two inputs that are enough to produce the given output. (p. 23)

Production possibilities frontier A production possibilities frontier shows the different combinations of various goods that a producer can turn out, given the available resources and existing technology. (p. 54)

Productivity Productivity is the amount of output produced by a unit of input. (p. 9, 43)

Progressive tax A progressive tax is one in which the average tax rate paid by an individual rises as income rises. (p. 49)

Progressive A tax is progressive if the ratio of taxes to income rises as income rises. (p. 435)

Proportional tax A proportional tax is one in which the average tax rate is the same at all income levels. (p. 435)

Proprietorship A proprietorship is a business firm owned by a single person. (p. 309)

Public good A public good is a commodity or service whose benefits are *not depleted* by an additional user and from which it is generally difficult or *impossible to exclude* people, even if the people are unwilling to pay for the benefits. (p. 276)

Pure monopoly A pure monopoly is an industry in which there is only one supplier of a product for which there are no close substitutes and in which it is very hard or impossible for another firm to coexist. (p. 190, 230)

Quantity demanded The quantity demanded is the number of units of a good that consumers want to buy over a specified period of time. (p. 70)

Quantity supplied The quantity supplied is the number of units that sellers want to sell over a specified period of time. (p. 73)

Quota A quota specifies the maximum amount of a good that is permitted into the country from abroad per unit of time. (p. 488)

Ramsey pricing rule The Ramsey pricing rule is a rule for determining prices that promote consumer welfare while covering the producer's cost. (p. 414)

Random walk The time path of a variable such as the price of a stock is said to constitute a random walk if its magnitude in one period (say, May 2, 2000) is equal to its value in the preceding period (May 1, 2000) plus a completely random number. That is: Price on May 2, 2000 = Price on May 1, 2000 + Random number, where the random number (positive or negative) can be obtained by a roll of dice or some such procedure. (p. 313)

Ratchet A ratchet is an arrangement that permits some economic variable, such as investment or advertising, to increase, but prevents that variable from subsequently decreasing. (p. 301)

Rational decision A rational decision is one that best serves the objectives of the decision maker, whatever those objectives may be. Such objectives may include a firm's desire to maximize its profits, a government's desire to maximize the welfare of its citizens, or another government's desire to maximize its military might. The term *rational* connotes neither approval nor disapproval of the objective itself. (p. 53)

Real GDP Real GDP is the value of all the goods and services produced by an economy in a year, evaluated in dollars of constant purchasing power. Hence, inflation does not raise real GDP. (p. 24)

Recession A recession is a period of time during which the total output of the economy falls. (p. 36)

Regressive tax A regressive tax is one in which the average tax rate falls as income rises. (p. 435)

Regulation Regulation of industry is a process established by law that restricts or controls some specified decisions made by the affected firms, and is designed to protect the public from exploitation by firms with monopoly power. Regulation is usually carried out by a special government agency assigned the task of administering and interpreting the law. That agency also acts as a court in enforcing the regulatory laws. (p. 407)

Rent seeking Rent seeking refers to unproductive activity in the pursuit of economic profit—in other words, profit in excess of competitive earnings. (p. 285)

Repeated game A repeated game is one that is played over again a number of times. (p. 262)

Research and development (R&D) Research and development (R&D) is the activity of firms, universities, and government agencies that seeks to invent new products and processes and to improve those inventions so that they are ready for the market or other uses. (p. 295)

Resources Resources are the instruments provided by nature or by people that are used to create goods and services. Natural resources include minerals, the soil, water, and air. Labor is a scarce resource, partly because of time limitations (the day has only 24 hours) and partly because the number of skilled workers is limited. Factories and machines are resources made by people. These three types of resources are often referred to as *land*, *labor*, and *capital*. They are also called *inputs* or *factors of production*. (p. 52)

Shift in a demand curve A shift in a demand curve occurs when any variable other than price changes. If consumers want to buy *more* at any given price than they wanted previously, the demand curve shifts to the right (or outward). If they desire *less* at any given price, the demand curve shifts to the left (or inward). (p. 71, 129)

Short run The short run is a period of time during which some of the firm's cost commitments will *not* have ended. (p. 140)

Shortage A shortage is an excess of quantity demanded over quantity supplied. When there is a shortage, buyers cannot purchase the quantities they desire. (p. 77)

Specialization Specialization means that a country devotes its energies and resources to only a small proportion of the world's productive activities. (p. 60, 480)

Speculation Individuals who engage in speculation deliberately invest in risky assets, hoping to obtain profits from future changes in the prices of these assets. (p. 319)

Statistical discrimination Statistical discrimination is said to occur when the productivity of a particular worker is estimated to be low just because that worker belongs to a particular group (such as women). (p. 391)

Stock price index A stock price index, such as the S&P 500, is an average of the prices of a large set of stocks. These stocks are selected to represent the price movements of the entire stock market, or some specified segment of the market, and the chosen set is rarely changed. (p. 316)

Substitutes Two goods are called substitutes if an increase in the quantity consumed of one cuts the quantity demanded of the other, all other things remaining constant. (p. 128)

Supply curve A supply curve is a graphical depiction of a supply schedule. It shows how the quantity supplied of some product during a specified period of time will change as the price of that product

changes, holding all other determinants of quantity supplied constant. (p. 75)

Supply schedule A supply schedule is a table showing how the quantity supplied of some product during a specified period of time changes as the price of that product changes, holding all other determinants of quantity supplied constant. (p. 73)

Supply-demand diagram A supply-demand diagram graphs the supply and demand curves together. It depicts the equilibrium price and quantity. (p. 77)

Surplus A surplus is an excess of quantity supplied over quantity demanded. When there is a surplus, sellers cannot sell the quantities they desire to supply. (p. 77)

Takeover A takeover is the acquisition by an outside group (the raiders) of a controlling proportion of a company's stock. When the old management opposes the takeover attempt, it is called a *hostile takeover attempt*. (p. 319)

Tangent The tangent to a curve at some point, Z, on that curve is a straight line that touches point Z but does not cross the curve at that point. (p. 21)

Tariff A tariff is a tax on imports. (p. 487)

Tax deduction A tax deduction is a sum of money that may be subtracted before the taxpayer computes his or her taxable income. (p. 436)

Tax exempt A particular source of income is tax exempt if income from that source is not taxable. (p. 436)

Tax loophole A tax loophole is a special provision in the tax code that reduces taxation below normal rates (perhaps to zero) if certain conditions are met. (p. 436)

Tax shifting Tax shifting occurs when the economic reactions to a tax cause prices and outputs in the economy to change, thereby shifting part of the burden of the tax onto others. (p. 446)

Technology trading Technology trading is an arrangement in which a firm voluntarily makes its privately owned technology available to other firms either in exchange for access to the technology of the second company or for an agreed-upon fee. (p. 298)

Theory A theory is a deliberate simplification of relationships used to explain how those relationships work. (p. 12)

Time-series graph A time-series graph is a type of two-variable diagram in which time is the variable measured along the horizontal axis. It shows how some variable changed as time passed. (p. 24)

Total physical product (TPP) The firm's total physical product (TPP) is the amount of output it obtains in total from a given quantity of input. (p. 143)

Total profit The total profit of a firm is its net earnings during some period of time. It is equal to the total amount of money the firm gets from sales of its products (the firm's total revenue) minus the total amount that it spends to make and market those products (total cost). (p. 170)

Total utility The total utility of a quantity of a good to a consumer (measured in money terms) is the maximum amount of money that he or she is willing to give in exchange for it. (p. 96)

Trade adjustment assistance Trade adjustment assistance provides special unemployment benefits, loans, retraining programs, and other aid to workers and firms that are harmed by foreign competition. (p. 492)

Transfer payments Transfer payments are sums of money that certain individuals receive as outright grants from the government rather than as payments for services rendered. (p. 49)

Union shop A union shop is an arrangement under which nonunion workers may be hired, but then must join the union within a specified period of time. (p. 369)

Unlimited liability Unlimited liability is a legal obligation of a firm's owner(s) to pay back company debts with whatever resources he or she owns. (p. 309)

Variable A variable is something measured by a number; it is used to analyze what happens to other things when the size of that number changes (varies). (p. 18)

Vertical equity Vertical equity refers to the notion that differently situated individuals should be taxed differently in a way that society deems to be fair. (p. 441)

Chapter 1: p. 1 © Don Carstens/Masterfile; p. 9, "I'm a social scientist, Michael. That means I can't explain electricity . . ." © *The New Yorker* Collection, 1986, J.B. Handelsman from cartoonbank.com. All Rights Reserved. **Chapter 2:** p. 23, Topographical map of Lake Louise Area, Banff National Park, BC Canada #802. Reprinted with permission from Trails Illustrated, Evergreen, Colorado; p. 25, "Dow Jonesy enough for you?" © *The New Yorker* Collection 1998 Jack Ziegler from cartoonbank.com. All Rights Reserved. **Chapter 3:** p. 33, "Unemployment Rates In Europe" from "Economic Indicators," *The Economist*, January 23-29, 1999, p. 96 © 1999 The Economist Newspaper Group, Inc. Reprinted with permission. Further reproduction prohibited. www.economist.com; p. 33, "And may we continue to be worthy . . ." © *The New Yorker* Collection, 1992 Lee Lorenz from cartoonbank.com. All Rights Reserved; p. 38, "Essential Ingredients" From "Survey of Women and Work," from *The Economist*, July 18, 1998, p. 4. ©1998 The Economist Newspaper Group, Inc. Reprinted with permission. Further reproduction prohibited; www.economist.com; p. 43 © Caputo/Liaison Agency, Inc. **Chapter 4:** p. 57 © SuperStock. **Chapter 5:** p. 68 © Mark Harwood/Tony Stone Images; p. 69, "Price Controls at Valley Forge," Robert L. Schuettinger and Eamonn F. Butler, *Forty Centuries of Wage and Price Controls*, Washington, D.C.: Heritage Foundation, 1979, p. 41. Reprinted by permission; p. 69, Engraving: Men Gathering Wood at Valley Forge. Courtesy of The Metropolitan Museum of Art, Bequest of Charles Allen Munn, 1924 [24.90.1828(56)]; p. 74, Scatter Graph showing power prices from July to August from "A 20,000% Bounce: Now That's Volatility" by A.R. Myerson, *The New York Times*, Business Section, August 8, 1998, p. 4. Copyright ©1998 by The New York Times. Reprinted by permission; p. 74 © LM Otero/AP Wide World Photos; p. 78, ETTA HULME reprinted by permission of Newspaper Enterprise Association, Inc.; p. 84, Bill Hormell/© Corbis/Bettmann-UPI. **Chapter 6:** p. 91 © Leon Zernitsky/Masterfile; p. 94 © Didier Dorval/Masterfile; p. 94 © Larry Lefever/Grant Heilman Photography, Inc.; p. 97, "It's been fun, Dave, but I think we're entering the zone of diminishing marginal utility." © Robert Mankoff from cartoonbank.com. All Rights Reserved; p. 98 © Don Couch Photography, Austin, Texas. **Chapter 7:** p. 118 © Michael Newman/PhotoEdit; p. 126, "Why does it have to be us who prove that price elasticity really works?" SELLING SHORT, June 11, 1981, ©1981 Reprinted with permission of Universal Press Syndicate. All Rights Reserved; p. 130 © Laura Dwight/Corbis. **Chapter 8:** p. 141 © Telegraph Colour Library/FPG International; p. 151, graph excerpted from "Too many Piggies Went to Market" by David Barboza, *The New York Times*, January 7th, 1999. Copyright © 1999 by the New York Times Co. Reprinted by permission; p. 151, "Roberts, what's all this I hear about pork bellies?" © 1999 Mick Stevens from cartoonbank.com. All Rights Reserved; p. 154 © Ed Lallo/ Liaison Agency, Inc.; p. 155 © Linde Waidhofer, Western Eye 1993/Liaison Agency, Inc.; p. 155, "Input Substitution in the Forest" from "Let's Go for Growth." Reprinted from p. 60 of the March 7, 1994 issue of *Fortune* by special permission; copyright ©1994, Time, Inc.; p. 156 © Bill Aaron/PhotoEdit; p. 159 © Mark Richards/PhotoEdit. **Chapter 9:** p. 175, "Basic economics—sometimes the parts . . ." © *The New Yorker* Collection, 1993, Charles Barsotti from cartoonbank.com. All Rights Reserved; p. 179, "Please stand by. . . ." © *The New Yorker* Collection, 1990, Dana Fradon from cartoonbank.com. All Rights Reserved; p. 184, "It's true that more . . . " © *The New Yorker* Collection, 1985, Charles Saxon from cartoonbank.com. All Rights Reserved; p. 184 © PhotoDisc. **Chapter 10:** p. 189, "The Bulls and Bears in the Market," 1879 by Beard, William Holbrook (1823–1900) New York Historical Society/ The Bridgeman Art Library International, Ltd.; p. 194 © Frank Grant/International Stock; p. 205 © Michael Newman/PhotoEdit; p. 207. "So that's where it goes! Well, I'd like to . . ." © *The New Yorker* Collection, 1970, James Stevenson from cartoonbank.com. All Rights Reserved. **Chapter 11:** p. 210 © SuperStock; p. 214 © Piotr Malecki/Liaison Agency, Inc.; p. 216, "Corporate leaders gather in a field . . ." © *The New Yorker* Collection, 1992, Dana Fradon from cartoonbank.com. All Rights Reserved; p. 218 © 98 Paul Hardy/The Stock Market; p. 219 © Krododil/Sovfoto-Eastfoto; p. 225, "Singapore's Plan," *The Economist*, December 6, 1997, p. 22. © 1997 The Economist Newspaper Group, Inc. Reprinted with permission. Further reproduction prohibited. www.economist.com; p. 225, "Prices Work," from the article, "Singapore's Plan," *The Economist*, December 6, 1997, p. 22. ©1997 The Economist Newspaper Group, Inc. Reprinted with permission. Further reproduction prohibited. www.economist.com; p. 225, "Replies to a Questionnaire" adapted from Samuel Brittan, "Is There an Economic Consensus?" p. 93. Copyright Samuel Brittan, 1973. Reproduced by permission of Curtis Brown Ltd.; p. 226 © L. Mark/UPI/Bettmann/Corbis. **Chapter 12:** p. 234 Lynda Radosevich, "Top of the News: How the Software Industry Creates Monopolies," Vol. 20, *InfoWorld*, May 25, 1998. Reprinted with permission from InfoWorld; p. 234 © Amy C. Etra/PhotoEdit;p. 243 © Harry Bartlett/FPG International; p. 238, "Apex-Global-Amalgamated-Universal-Federated-United Manufacturing (Not A Monopoly)." © 2000 by Sidney Harris. **Chapter 13:** p. 247, "A Global Colossus that is Richer than Most Nations," *The New York Times*, July 26, 1998, section 4, p. 4. Copyright © 1998 by the New York Times Co. Reprinted by permission; p. 251, "Why have we come? Because only Earth . . ." © *The New Yorker* Collection, 1997, Michael Maslin from cartoonbank.com. All Rights Reserved; p. 253, excerpt from "At McDonald's, a Case of Mass BeanieMania," by Richard Gibson, *The Wall Street Journal*, June 5, 1998, p. B1&B8. Reprinted by permission of Dow Jones, Inc., via Copyright Clearance Center, Inc. © 1998 Dow Jones and Company, Inc. All Rights Reserved; p. 253 © Peter Barreras/AP Wide World Photos; p. 255, "Venezuelan Accusations against Iran Hits Oil Prices," *Financial Times*, Commodities and Agriculture, Tuesday, July 7 1998, p. 34. Reprinted by permission of Financial Times, a Pearson Company; p. 255 © Eric Vandeville/Liaison Agency, Inc.; p. 256 © Peter Christopher/Masterfile; p. 261, "Will The Internet End 'Sticky Prices'?" *The Economist*, May 16, 1998, p. 86. © 1998 The Economist Newspaper Group, Inc. Reprinted with permission, Further reproduction prohibited. www.economist.com; p. 265 © Les Stone/Sygma; **Chapter 14:** p. 280, William Gropper, "The Senate." (1935). Collection, The Museum of Modern Art, New York. Gift of A. Conger Goodyear; p. 285, "What really makes this heaven . . ." From *The Wall Street Journal*, Reprinted by permission of Cartoon Features Syndicate; p. 286 © Photopia; p. 286 © Photopia. **Chapter 15:** p. 296, Photo courtesy of Stephanie L. Kwolek; p. 297, "You'll never catch up with the new technology," © *The New Yorker* Collection, 1983, Robert Weber from cartoonbank.com. All Rights Reserved; p. 299, "Cargill and Monsanto Announce Global Feed and Processing Biotechnology Joint Venture," www.asgrow.com/corporate/cargill/html, accessed 01/11/99; p. 299 © Tony Stone Images; p. 300, FOXTROT © 1998 Bill Amend. Reprinted with permission of Universal Press Syndicate. All rights reserved. **Chapter 16:** p. 315, "To hell with a balanced portfolio. . . ." © *The New Yorker* Collection, 1957, Richard Decker from cartoonbank.com. All Rights Reserved; p. 318 © Greg Stott/Masterfile; p. 321, "Don't laugh—she's called the last five Dow Jones . . ." from *The Wall Street Journal*, August 19, 1982, Reprinted by permission of Cartoon Features Syndicate; p. 322 © PhotoDisc; p. 323, excerpt from "MARKET PLACE: 'The Continued Rise of the Market Rests in The Hands of the Superbowl Team from Green Bay,'" by Floyd Norris, *The New York Times*, January 22,1998. Copyright © 1998 by the New York Times Co. Reprinted by permission; p. 323 © Dave Martin/AP Wide World Photo; p. 324, "I've got a stock here that could really excel." by KAL © 1990 by Cartoonist and Writers Syndicate. **Chapter 17:** p. 327 © Bojan Brecelj; p. 334, Cartoon by Jeff MacNelly. © Tribune Media Services, Inc. All Rights Reserved; p. 334, "I can't sleep, I just got this incredible craving for capital." © *The New Yorker* Collection, 1995, Robert Mankoff from cartoonbank.com All Rights Reserved; p. 341 © David Lawrence/The Stock Market; p. 341, Steven K. Mayo, "Land Prices, Land Markets, and the Broader Economy," Land Lines, March 1998, Lincoln Institute of Land Policy, www.lincolninst.edu; and *The Economist*, September 12, 1998, p. 116; p. 342 © Chiasson/Liaison Agency, Inc.; p. 345, "Entrepreneurship in Poland: Survey of Business in Eastern Europe," *The Economist*, November 22, 1997, p. 10. © 1997 The Economist Newspaper Group, Inc. Reprinted with permission, Further reproduction prohibited. www.economist.com.

Selected U.S. Macroeconomic Data, 1929–1999

Year	(1) Gross Domestic Product	(2) Personal Consumption Expenditure	(3) Gross Private Domestic Investment	(4) Government Purchases	(5) Net Exports	(6) Gross Domestic Product	(7) Personal Consumption Expenditure	(8) Gross Private Domestic Investment	(9) Government Purchases	(10) Net Exports	(11) Real GDP per capita
	(in billions of dollars)					(in billions of chained 1996 dollars)[a]					(In chained 1996 dollars)
1929	103.7	77.5	16.5	9.4	0.4	822.2	625.7	93.6	110.1	−10.5	6,752.24
1933	56.4	45.9	1.7	8.7	0.1	603.3	511	17.5	118	−11	4,804.16
1939	92	67.2	9.3	14.7	0.8	903.5	689	79.6	179.7	−5.5	6,903.29
1945	223	119.8	10.8	93.2	−.9	1,693.30	851.8	69	1,041.00	−28.7	12,101.21
1950	294.3	192.7	54.1	46.9	0.7	1,686.60	1,090.90	232.5	367.4	−10.2	11,076.27
1955	415.2	259	69	86.8	0.4	2,099.50	1,310.40	262.1	580.4	−16.1	12,652.83
1960	526.6	332.2	78.8	113.2	2.4	2,262.9	1,432.6	270.5	617.2	−21.3	12,519
1965	719.1	444.3	118.0	153.0	3.9	2,881.1	1,799.1	397.2	737.6	−27.4	14,825
1970	1,039.70	648.9	152.4	237.1	1.2	3,578.00	2,317.50	436.2	931.1	−63.8	17,449.22
1971	1,128.60	702.4	178.2	251	−3.0	3,697.70	2,405.20	485.8	913.8	−74.6	17,806.45
1972	1,240.40	770.7	207.6	270.1	−8.0	3,898.40	2,550.50	543	914.9	−87.8	18,573.01
1973	1,385.50	852.5	244.5	287.9	0.6	4,123.40	2,675.90	606.5	908.3	−62	19,458.37
1974	1,501.00	932.4	249.4	322.4	−3.1	4,099.00	2,653.70	561.7	924.8	−35.6	19,167.29
1975	1,635.20	1,030.30	230.2	361.1	13.6	4,084.40	2,710.90	462.2	942.5	−7.5	18,911.61
1976	1,823.90	1,149.80	292	384.5	−2.3	4,311.70	2,868.90	555.5	943.3	−40.4	19,775.25
1977	2,031.40	1,278.40	361.3	415.3	−23.7	4,511.80	2,992.10	639.4	952.7	−65.3	20,485.89
1978	2,295.90	1,430.40	436	455.6	−26.1	4,760.60	3,124.70	713	982.2	−66.4	21,387.83
1979	2,566.40	1,596.30	490.6	503.5	−24.0	4,912.10	3,203.20	735.4	1,001.10	−45.5	21,826.17
1980	2,795.60	1,762.90	477.9	569.7	−14.9	4,900.90	3,193.00	655.3	1,020.90	10	21,568.52
1981	3,131.30	1,944.20	570.8	631.4	−15.0	5,021.00	3,236.00	715.6	1,030.00	5.2	21,881.26
1982	3,259.20	2,079.30	516.1	684.4	−20.5	4,919.30	3,275.50	615.2	1,046.00	−14.6	21,234.59
1983	3,534.90	2,286.40	564.2	735.9	−51.7	5,132.30	3,454.30	673.7	1,081.00	−63.8	21,952.42
1984	3,932.70	2,498.40	735.5	800.8	−102.0	5,505.20	3,640.60	871.5	1,118.40	−128.4	23,344.44
1985	4,213.00	2,712.60	736.3	878.3	−114.2	5,717.10	3,820.90	863.4	1,190.50	−149.1	24,029.12
1986	4,452.90	2,895.20	747.2	942.3	−131.9	5,912.40	3,981.20	857.7	1,255.20	−165.1	24,621.37
1987	4,742.50	3,105.30	781.5	997.9	−142.3	6,113.30	4,113.40	879.3	1,292.50	−156.2	25,231.45
1988	5,108.30	3,356.60	821.1	1,036.90	−106.3	6,368.40	4,279.50	902.8	1,307.50	−112.1	26,046.73
1989	5,489.10	3,596.70	872.9	1,100.20	−80.7	6,591.80	4,393.70	936.5	1,343.50	−79.4	26,707.00
1990	5,803.20	3,831.50	861.7	1,181.40	−71.4	6,707.90	4,474.50	907.3	1,387.30	−56.5	26,889.21
1991	5,986.20	3,971.20	800.2	1,235.50	−20.7	6,676.40	4,466.60	829.5	1,403.40	−15.8	26,477.57
1992	6,318.90	4,209.70	866.6	1,270.50	−27.9	6,880.00	4,594.50	899.8	1,410.00	−19.8	26,977.25
1993	6,642.30	4,454.70	955.1	1,293.00	−60.5	7,062.60	4,748.90	977.9	1,398.80	−59.1	27,397.50
1994	7,054.30	4,716.40	1,097.10	1,327.90	−87.1	7,347.70	4,928.10	1,107.00	1,400.10	−86.6	28,224.88
1995	7,400.50	4,969.00	1,143.80	1,372.00	−84.3	7,543.80	5,075.60	1,140.60	1,406.40	−78.4	28,705.12
1996	7,813.20	5,237.50	1,242.70	1,421.90	−89.0	7,813.20	5,237.50	1,242.70	1,421.90	−88.9	29,458.36
1997	8,300.80	5,524.40	1,383.70	1,481.00	−88.3	8,144.80	5,417.30	1,385.80	1,453.70	−112.1	30,415.60
1998	8,759.90	5,848.60	1,531.20	1,529.70	−149.6	8,495.70	5,681.80	1,547.40	1,478.80	−217.6	31,436.68
1999	9,256.10	6,257.30	1,622.70	1,630.10	−253.9	8,848.20	5,983.60	1,637.70	1,534.10	−323.1	32,447.74

[a] Components do not add up to GDP due to chain method of deflation.
[b] Persons 14 years and older for 1929–1945; thereafter, persons 16 years and older.
[c] Moody's Aaa rating.
[d] Trade-weighted average of broad group of U.S. trading partners.
[e] National income and product accounts basis; calendar years.